Baedeker

Austria

www.baedeker.com

Verlag Karl Baedeker

SIGHTSEEING HIGHLIGHTS ★ ★

Majestic mountain peaks, idyllic river landscapes, splendid monasteries with centuries-long histories and lively towns offering a wealth of culture and entertainment – here are Austria's highlights.

1 ★★ Klosterneuburg
The picturesque Stift Klosterneuburg houses one of the most important works of art of the Middle Ages: the famous Verdun Altar in St Leopold's Chapel.
► page 328

2 ★★ Wachau
There are no bridges here. You'll have to take the ferry across the river in this unique part of the Danube region.
► page 554

3 ★★ Vienna
Where do you start, and for that matter where do you end? Art, culture, cuisine – Vienna has it all in spades and then some. The city combines atmosphere, urban flair, and a certain cosiness. ► page 498

4 ★★ St Florian
The magnificent Augustinian abbey of St Florian – a prime example of Baroque splendour – is an appropriate setting for the final resting place of the famous musician and composer Anton Bruckner.
► page 453

Over the rooftops
Towers and domes mark the Vienna cityscape

© Baedeker

2 Wachau
1 Klosterneuburg
6 Melk
● 4 St. Florian
5 Donautal
3 Vienna
7 Salzburg ● 8 Wolfgangsee
10 Mariazell
11 Neusiedler See
9 Salzkammergut
12 Hallstätter
See
13 Admont
17 Innsbruck
14 Zeller See 15 Werfen
16 Dachstein
22 Graz
18 Krimml
Waterfalls 19 Hohe
Tauern 20 Grossglockner
High Alpine Rd.
21 Gasteiner Tal
24 Gurk
23 Millstätter S.
25 Weissensee
26 Maria Saal
27 Wörthersee

5 ✷✷ Donautal

Follow the Danube and you are following Austria's principal river and the second longest river in Europe, with any number of historical artefacts and a wealth of scenic beauty. ▸ page 213

6 ✷✷ Stift Melk

The magnificent Baroque monastery of Melk, emblem of the Wachau and UNESCO World Cultural Heritage site, is a place of superlatives. The south wing alone measures over 240m/787ft, and the library contains over 100,000 books.
▸ page 384

Night-time ambience
Grand opera before the backdrop of Salzburg's Summer Riding School

Across the river
Learn all about shipping in the medieval castle of Greinburg on the banks of the Danube

7 ✷✷ Salzburg

Mozart's birthplace is famous the world over. Every year several million visitors are welcomed into Salzburg's beautiful Old Town, not least because of the festival held here. ▸ page 426

8 ✷✷ Wolfgangsee

Wolfgangsee has always been a place of pilgrimage: from the Middle Ages until the present day pilgrims have come to the church of St Wolfgang, and since the operetta of the same name to the famous »Weisses Rössl« inn. ▸ page 579

9 ✷✷ Salzkammergut

It is the epitome of the Austrian holiday destination: the water, mountains and culture make it one of the most visited holiday regions in the country.
▸ page 452

10 ✷✷ Mariazell

The most visited pilgrimage destination in Austria with the Gnadenkapelle (Chapel of Mercy) at its centre is also a popular holiday desination and climatic spa town. ▸ page 379

Unique appeal
Visitors to Neusiedler See, Europe's largest steppe lake, have the opportunity to swim, sail or surf

11 ✶✶ Neusiedler See
The lake that is shared by Austria and Hungary is the only steppe lake of central Europe and as a national park provides a protected home to many animal species.
► page 406

12 ✶✶ Hallstätter See
2500 years ago there was a Celtic economic empire here. The site of many archaeological finds gave the name to a whole epoch.
► page 270

13 ✶✶ Admont
The Benedictine monastery of Stift Admont has one of the world's largest and most beautiful libaries, which contains precious book treasures. ► page 178

14 ✶✶ Zeller See
In summer a bathing lake and enough room in winter to go ice skating – set in charming surroundings, the Zeller See is sure to please at any time of year.
► page 585

15 ✶✶ Werfen
Along with its castle, Werfen impresses visitors with its giant Eishöhle (Ice Cave), which is one of the thirty natural wonders of the world. ► page 570

16 ✶✶ Dachstein
The beauty of this immense mountain massif, which hikers and climbers can discover on numerous wonderful tours, is indeed impressive. ► page 211

17 ✶✶ Innsbruck
With a lovely location, Innsbruck's attractions combine ideally to meet the demands of skiing and sports enthusiasts and visitors interested in culture.
► page 281

18 ✶✶ Krimml
Plunging down 380m/1250ft, the Krimml Waterfalls are the highest in central Europe and number among the most important attractions in the Eastern Alps. ► page 339

19 ✶✶ Hohe Tauern
Before the Central Alps drop away to the east, they exhibit their full magnificence one more time in this immense mountain range. ► page 274

Nightlife in Graz
Night owls are supposed to have disap-
peared for good in the »Bermudadreieck«
(Bermuda Triangle)

20 ✶✶ Grossglockner High Alpine Road
One of the most splendid and impressive roads in the high mountains, the Grossglockner-Hochalpenstrasse offers incomparable panoramas along its length of 9km/5.5mi.   ► page 254

21 ✶✶ Gasteiner Tal
The former summer resort of the rich and the beautiful is still a popular holiday destination today for hikers, skiers and those visiting the spa.   ► page 240

22 ✶✶ Graz
Graz is definitely worth the trip – the town, with its clement weather, captivates visitors with a lovely Old Town and a youthful art and culture scene and is a good starting point for trips into the scenic surroundings.   ► page 245

23 ✶✶ Millstätter See
The waters of the Millstätter See reach up to 26 °C/79 °F – the lake is a popular holiday destination for swimmers and water sports enthusiasts.   ► page 388

24 ✶✶ Gurk
The small market is home to a Romanesque treasure, the cathedral. The reliquaries kept here have attracted pilgrims for centuries.   ► page 257

25 ✶✶ Weissensee
This fjord-like lake enjoys a slightly out of the way location. The idyllic region attracts nature lovers and those seeking rest and relaxation in particular.   ► page 566

26 ✶✶ Maria Saal
Maria Saal is said to have been the place from which the country was christianized in the 8th century; the impressive pilgrimage church, which came into being from the 15th century, boasts the »Maria Saalerin«, the largest bell in Carinthia.   ► page 375

27 ✶✶ Wörther See
Carinthia's touristic centre, the Wörther See has adapted itself perfectly to travellers by means of its well developed infrastructure.   ► page 582

Rest a while...
...in the Edelweiss hut halfway along the
Grossglockner High Alpine Road – the
mountain scenery is magnificent.

BAEDEKER'S BEST TIPS

We have put the most interesting Baedeker tips in this book together for you below. Experience and enjoy Austria at its very best!

⚠ Composer's retreat
Mahler built himself a retreat on the southern shore of the Attersee. It is open to the public today. ▸ **page 187**

⚠ Cigar fans welcome
...in a walk-in humidor! Cigar smokers can indulge in their passion in a sophisticated lounge. ▸ **page 202**

⚠ The disappearing lake
It disappears almost completely in the winter; in the summer a karstic spring fills it up again, the extent depending on the amount of rainfall. But a stroll around the Grüne See is always worthwhile. ▸ **page 210**

Lake Constance
*Speciality: smoked whitefish,
a type of trout*

⚠ Fancy some fish?
Bikers, hikers and bird-watchers should not miss a stop at one of the restaurants along the banks of the Danube that specialize in fish. ▸ **page 217**

⚠ Culture for all
Be it music, dance or theatre, cabaret, film or a clown for children – the Kulturzentrum Spielboden in a refurbished factory in Dornbirn promises fun for all. ▸ **page 219**

⚠ Uhudler: a wine, not a yodel
A Uhudler isn't yodelled, it is drunk. You will have the opportunity to try it in a few communities in southern Burgenland. ▸ **page 228**

⚠ A key collection
Are you open to something unusual? If so, visit Graz, where the secrets of hundreds of objects will be unlocked. ▸ **page 250**

⚠ River trip
If you would like to enjoy the last stretch of river along the romantic Inntal valley, board the good ship *Gerda*. ▸ **page 300**

⚠ The sky at night
A fascinating perspective from Austria's highest tower ▸ **page 307**

⚠ Two-wheeled challenge
The Maiskogel is the mountain biker's equivalent of the Hahnenkamm, site of the famous downhill ski race. Those who are less daring will find plenty of gentler descents in the region. ▸ **page 312**

⚠ Wildpark Tirol
More than 200 native alpine animals live here, and visitors can observe them closely in their natural habitat. ▸ **page 319**

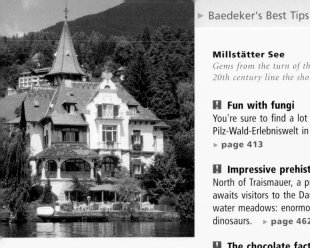

Whether cycle ways for the whole family, or demanding stretches for mountain bikers – there is a route to suit every taste
▶ **page 133**

BACKGROUND

PRACTICALITIES

*Head south on a tour of
Carinthia's best lakes*
▶ **page 171**

SIGHTS FROM A to Z

*Austria is marked by its great variety
of landscapes; here the Prebersee near
Tamsweg*
▶ **page 19**

*Traditional fishing methods
use fish traps that are easy
on fish stocks*
▶ **page 406**

Price categories

▶ **Hotels**

Luxury: from 130 Euro
Mid-range: 70–130 Euro
Budget: up to 70 Euro
per night, 2 people in a double
room

▶ **Restaurants**

Expensive: from 20 Euro
Moderate: 10–20 Euro
Inexpensive: up to 10 Euro
for a main dish

*Hikers on the Untersberg
near Salzburg*
► **page 451**

*The frescoes adorning the Salome
Alt House in Wels are certainly
worth a look*
► **page 568**

Background

IN THIS SECTION YOU WILL LEARN ALL
YOU NEED TO KNOW ABOUT THE
SMALL ALPINE REPUBLIC OF AUSTRIA:
ITS HISTORY, CLOSELY INTERWOVEN
WITH THAT OF THE REST OF EUROPE, ITS
NATURAL LANDSCAPES, ITS CULTURE,
AND WHY ITS SKIERS ARE HONOURED AS HEROES.

SERVUS AUSTRIA!

The alpine republic of Austria may be small, but it is big on attractions: replete with scenic beauty, it is an absolute highlight for all those interested in art and culture, a paradise for gourmets and an endless El Dorado for holidaymakers who are keen on sports.

The Habsburgs, who steered Austria's fate from 1273 to 1918, held with great success to their guiding principle: »Bella gerant alii, tu felix austria nube!« – »Let others make war; you, fortunate Austria, marry!« A wealth of palaces and historical gems such as those in the former royal seat of Vienna, and proud castles such as Burg Hochosterwitz bear magnificent testimony to this successful family history. Present-day Austria, too, does not stint on striking architecture, a good example of which is the gaily coloured Hundertwasser building.

Aim high
The alpine mountains offer those who conquer their peaks magnificent views and thrills to boot.

Land of Music

The country that consists of only nine provinces and its capital Vienna describes itself proudly as the »Land of Music«. Who indeed has not heard of Austria's profusion of stars of days gone by? At the very top of the tree are Wolfgang Amadeus Mozart, Joseph Haydn, Franz Schubert and the father and son Johann Strauss I and II, the »kings of the waltz«. The New Year's concert by the Vienna Philharmonic, an event that believe it or not is broadcast to more than 40 countries in the world, is a wonderful Austrian tradition. Further highlights include the festivals in Salzburg and Bregenz and performances in Vienna's venerable Staatsoper. And a certain generation will never forget Falco, the Viennese pop singer who stormed the charts in 1985 with his disco anthem *Rock Me Amadeus*.

Land of Lakes and Mountains

Well over 30 million holidaymakers come to Austria every year, and the country's magnificent landscape plays its part in attracting them. Like a rainbow in which everyone's favourite colour is represented, there is an Austrian holiday to suit every taste.

Happy hustle and bustle
The »Bischofsmütze« looks calmly down on the snow-covered pistes at its foot, where winter sports enthusiasts and the experience-hungry are busy enjoying themselves

A break for air
Fantastic surroundings and peaceful lakes framed by mountains allow visitors to find peace of mind

A stroll through the town
Museums, festivals, relaxed shopping or a bite to eat – in the town centres there is plenty to choose from

Attractions at every turn
Street entertainers amuse young audiences in front of historic façades

In grand style
Emperors, kings and spiritual leaders have left a rich inheritance in the form of majestic palaces, Baroque monasteries and churches of impressive beauty

Worth protecting
In nature parks and national parks, conservation areas and alpine gardens, the country's unique variety of species is cared for and visitors are brought closer to nature

Mountain enthusiasts are attracted to the »Dreitausender«, those Austrian peaks that exceed 3000m/9850ft, of which the 3798m/12,460ft Grossglockner in the Hohe Tauern is the highest. But the many other mountains of the main alpine ridge offer unforgettable panoramas too.

Water lovers will be drawn to the lakes of Wörthersee, Wolfgangsee and Ossiacher See, Traunsee and Mondsee, as well as numerous other inland waters, large and small. Neusiedler See (Lake Neusiedl) in Burgenland is central Europe's only steppe lake, filled with slightly salty water.

Because two thirds of Austria area is mountainous, it is no wonder that numerous winter Olympic dreams have come true here. Former skiing professionals such as Toni Sailer, Franz Klammer and Hansi Hinterseer – these days a singer of folk tunes and a television presenter who commands large audiences – once trained successfully in the country's great skiing arenas, as do skiers such as Hermann Maier, Rainer Schönfelder and Marlies Schild today.

»Island of the Blessed«

The tradition of comfort, the warm friendliness of the people and the culinary delicacies on the menu are still more reasons why holidaymakers feel at home on this wonderful patch of the Earth. Nowhere else is the country's history of racial mixing better reflected than on the menus: Wiener schnitzel, which actually comes from Milan, tafelspitz (prime boiled beef), Danube fish dishes, and dumplings stuffed with the widest variety of fillings.

Make yourself at home
An evening ended in the Buschenschänken with a glass of Heuriger, the new wine.

Some dishes are famous well beyond Austria's borders: desserts such as kaiserschmarrn (cut-up and sugared pancake with raisins) and the originally Czech palatschinken (another type of pancake), as well as millirahmstrudel (with quark – a kind of cottage cheese – and sour cream) and apfelstrudel, not forgetting the legendary Sacher torte. Eminently drinkable wines such as Grüner Veltiner, Traminer and Zweigelt come from the eastern and southern regions of Austria and are often still produced in traditional family wine presses.

Pope Paul VI once called Austria the »island of the blessed«. Those who, in the evening, perhaps with a »Glaserl« of wine, let the past day's events parade before their mind's eye can get a sense of this all-pervading blessedness, and even take the feeling home with them – perhaps the best holiday souvenir of all.

Facts

Along with Switzerland, Austria functions as the main transit country from the north across the Alps into southern Europe. Since the eastward expansion of the EU, the country once located at Europe's eastern edge is now at its centre.

Nature

Austria is predominantly a **mountainous region of moderate to high elevation**. Its 2650km/1650mi-long borders are shared with eight neighbours: an approximately 800km/500mi-long section with Germany, 430km/270mi with Italy, 550km/340mi with the Czech Republic and Slovakia, 366km/227mi with Hungary, 312km/194mi with Slovenia and about 200km/125mi with Switzerland and Liechtenstein. A 350km/220mi-long stretch of the river Danube (Donau) flows through the north of the country.

Alpine country in southeast and central Europe

Almost two thirds of the area of Austria's national territory is covered by the Eastern Alps. At least a quarter consists of lowlands and hill country, favourable for settlement, which extends as a belt of varying width along the Danube, into the region of the Viennese Basin and the Weinviertel, and southward at the eastern edge of the Alps. A tenth of the area is composed of the Austrian part of the Bohemian Massif, granite highlands that extend southward beyond the Danube in several places.

Land forms

The Austrian Alps are subdivided into three main chains, running predominantly from west to east. These are the Northern Limestone Alps, the Central Alps and the Southern Limestone Alps.

Alps

The Northern Limestone Alps (Nördliche Kalkalpen) reach from Rätikon over the Lechtal Alps – with the Parseierspitze (3038m/9967ft) as the highest peak – across the Karwendel, Kaiser and Tennen mountain ranges to Dachstein, and continue still further over the Eisenerz Alps to Schneeberg. They are not a continuous massif, instead being divided repeatedly by rivers running from north to south. Limestone plateaus and steep peaks characterize the scenery, which is especially beautiful in the Kaiser mountains or the Dachstein region. In the south, the Northern Limestone Alps are divided from the Central Alps by rivers running west to east.

◄ Northern Limestone Alps

The Central Alps extend from the Ötztal Alps via the Hohe Tauern (literally meaning »high passes«, but referring to the mountains themselves) to the Niedere Tauern (»low passes«). These huge, glacier-covered massifs of crystalline rock are separated by deep, ice-filled valleys. **The highest summit of the Central Alps and the whole of Austria is the Grossglockner (3797m/12,457ft)** in the Hohe Tauern. Valleys suitable for settlement are few and far between, and the wooded zones on the steep slopes are narrow; in contrast there are extensive areas of stony alpine pasture and wasteland.
This long mountain range, seldom falling below 3000m/9850ft, is difficult to penetrate: the most important pass is the Brenner, while the other north-south connections are either magnificent panoramic

◄ Central Alps

← *The view from Egg onto the Karawanken mountains*

routes that are closed in winter, such as the Grossglockner High Alpine Road, or tunnels underneath the main ridge like the Felbertauerntunnel or the Tauerntunnel.

Southern Limestone Alps ▶ Since 1919 Austria's border with Italy, as well as that with Slovenia, formerly with Yugoslavia, has run along the ridge of the Southern Limestone Alps (Südliche Kalkalpen), i.e. over the Karnisch Alps and the Karavanke mountains. The Drautal valley separates the Southern Limestone Alps from the Central Alps.

The highlands of the Mühlviertel and Waldviertel North of the Danube lie the elevated Mühlviertel and the Waldviertel (Wood Quarter). Their slopes (reaching up to 1380m/4500ft), part of the Bohemian Massif, are still covered with dense woodland. The raw, windy granite plateau has relatively poor soils and is thinly populated. Once a passage to Bohemia and Moravia, both regions have been far removed from the main traffic routes since the end of the Second World War.

Hill country and lowlands The upper and lower alpine country of Austria lies between the northern edge of the Alps and the Danube. Broad terraces and wooded hills drop away to the north, interrupted by rivers flowing towards the Danube.

The only extensive plains in Austria (Tullnerfeld, Marchfeld, Seewinkel etc.) extend across the Weinviertel (Wine Quarter) and northern Burgenland. Here, **Austria's granary** and its most important wine, fruit and vegetable growing areas are found. Beyond Neusiedler See, real Hungarian steppe or puszta predominates, with salt ponds or »Zick-Lacken« (from the Hungarian »szik« = salt, and the Austrian »Lacke« = puddle).

Austria Landform regions

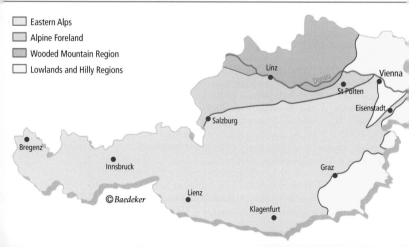

- Eastern Alps
- Alpine Foreland
- Wooded Mountain Region
- Lowlands and Hilly Regions

Linz
Donau
Vienna
St Pölten
Eisenstadt
Salzburg
Bregenz
Innsbruck
Graz
Lienz
©Baedeker
Klagenfurt

The wild Kaiser: one of the Northern Limestone Alps

In the hill country of southern Burgenland bordering Styria, the warmth of the south can already be felt. On the long, extended hills and ridges, woodland alternates with pasture, vineyards and fields, and cereals and fruit thrive in abundance.

The Alps: Natural Environment and Place of Relaxation

The United Nations declared 2002 the **International Year of Mountains** with the goal of raising consciousness about the world's mountainous regions, global considerations included. And with good reason: the mountains of the world are not only complex ecosystems with an unbelievable variety of species, they are also the store and source of about half of the earth's drinking water. Moreover, they form the living, economic and cultural environment for about a tenth of humanity. If this complex world is damaged, it is not only the nature of the region and the local population that is harmed, but also affects many other people living miles away from the area. Especially in the case of a country like Austria, an intact mountainous region is the country's most significant asset and the most important basis for tourism.

Austria is a signatory of the Convention for the Protection of the Alps (signed in 1991, in force since 1995), an agreement of the Alpine States **for the protection and sustainable development of the Alps**. This framework contract was specific content in the form of protocols on specific themes such as energy, traffic, soil protection, mountainous agriculture and tourism, which came into force in December 2002. The convention secretariat has its permanent headquarters in Innsbruck.

International Year of Mountains 2002

◄ Convention for the Protection of th Alps

Flora and Fauna

Conservation Austria has an **extraordinary variety of flora and fauna**. Since its significance not only for the cycle of nature but also for tourism has become clear, appropriate measures for nature conservancy have been taken. Programmes have been established to release the brown bear, beaver, bearded vulture and lynx into the wild in selected areas. It is necessary however to protect the habitats as well as the species, and this process is not limited to creating natural environments that are completely untouched by human activity. The protection of many animal and plant species necessitates the management of extensive areas, as in the case of litter meadow. These areas are mowed once a year and the cuttings disposed of – and the spring gentian, globe flower, common spotted orchid and the large blue butterfly are the reward for the care of this cultivated landscape.

Flora

Regional peculiarities Thanks to its variety of land forms, soil conditions and climatic influences, Austria boasts a larger variety of flora than neighbouring countries: in the north there are Baltic elements, the low mountain ranges exhibit Atlantic influences, and the east and southeast possess Pannonian and Mediterranean-Illyrian species. The Alps provide a habitat for numerous survivals and endemic plant species no longer found anywhere else.

Woodland Woodland covers more than a third of the land, making it the predominant form of vegetation. It occurs naturally in an area stretching from the floodplains of the Danube into the mountains. In the Central Alps, woodland extends to an altitude of 2000m/6500ft, in the Northern and Southern Alps to 1700m/5500ft.

Mixed woodland in hilly country and the lowlands ▶ The dominant tree species in the Mühlviertel and Waldviertel are beech, birch, spruce, fir and Scots pine. In the Pannonian regions, primarily oak-hornbeam woods (Weinviertel) and oak-beech woods (southern Burgenland, East Styria, Leitha Mountains, Wienerwald) are found. The Illyrian black pine is widespread as far north as Vienna. Along the lush floodplains of the Danube, March and Leitha, along with willow, poplar, ash and elm, alders grow in marshland similar to primeval forest.

Subalpine mixed beech-fir woodland grows in the western Wienerwald, the foothills of the Alps, the Styrian Limestone Alps of Lower Austria, in the Salzkammergut and in Bregenzerwald. The hop hornbeam tree that thrives near Graz and Innsbruck comes from the Mediterranean.

Alpine mixed woodland ▶ Moving upwards to higher elevations and further west, larch and pine become more prevalent. Above 1350m/4400ft, spruce dominates on moist slopes, while on dry slopes pine is accompanied by maple and juniper. At the edges of the woodland mostly spruce and larch are seen, and in Tauern and Tyrol the Swiss stone pine, a slow-growing, especially hardy high-altitude alpine species. Mountain pine is typical of the limestone plateaus.

The **great variety of flowers** is conspicuous. In high-altitude alpine regions the numerous brightly coloured flowers captivate hikers and climbers. The impressive colours of the predominantly short-stemmed flowers can be traced back to the high levels of ultra-violet rays in high mountainous areas. Excessive evaporation is prevented by means of thick, sometimes also hairy leaves.

Flowers and shrubs

During spring in the mountains, natural alpine pasture is a colourful sight. Another alpine formation is heathland with heather and various berries, as well as the lovely alpine rhododendron, which gives the mountain slopes a fiery red colour. As with many plant species (e.g. gentian), there is a limestone and a rock form of the alpine rhododendron: the hairy form (Rhododendron hirsutum) thrives on limestone, while the russet form (Rhododendron ferrugineum) is found in the central rocky area.

◄ Alpine pasture

> ## ? DID YOU KNOW …?
>
> - *Wulfenia carinthiaca*, a Carinthian flower with blue blossoms, is a great rarity. It is found only near Hermagor in Carinthia and on the Albania-Montenegro border.

The habitat of the flowering plant that grows at the highest altitudes in Europe, the glacier buttercup (flowers July–August), lies at elevations from 2000m/6500ft to over 4000m/13,000ft.

Rocks and crevices have their own flora: hikers and climbers can search for but not pick edelweiss and alpine auricular, which are protected species. In the rocky regions wafer-thin crustose lichens cover almost every square inch of rock in the greatest variety of colours.

◄ Rocky regions

The soil of the woodland is populated with herb paris, daphne and wood sorrel, as well as numerous orchids, even the lady's slipper, a species which has unfortunately been largely decimated.

◄ Forest soil

The Pannonian dry grassland seen in the Wachau and northern Burgenland has a completely different character. There pheasant's eye (a member of the buttercup family), pasqueflower and *Astragalus tragacanthus* grow along with various types of wild rose, blackthorn, hawthorn and dwarf medlar.

◄ Pannonian dry grassland

In the salt steppe of the Seewinkel area of Burgenland (Illmitz, Apetlon, Podersdorf), a near-desert atmosphere dominates. Only plants extremely well adapted to this environment can survive the hot, dry summer: salt cress, sea aster, saltmarsh rush, and goosefoot plants, either stem or leaf succulents (*Salicornia*), which give the ground a red appearance in autumn.

◄ Salt steppe

A great variety of grasses and shrubs thrive in the impenetrable undergrowth of the riverside woodland, along with snowdrops and arum. Yellow flag, the light blue Siberian iris, as well as marsh gladiolus, reeds and grasses grow on riverbanks. Typical plants of the

River courses, moorland

A marmot stands watch in order to warn the colony of danger

moors are cotton grass and heather, dwarf birch and the insectivorous sundew, which has mobile tentacles.

Fauna

The best-known animals are without doubt alpine species such as ibex, chamois and marmot. But in lower areas and special natural environments such as Neusiedler See there is also a wonderful animal kingdom.

Fish   Of Austria's over 80 native fish species, 60 are found in the Danube. While predominantly trout, char, grayling, tench and whitefish (a member of the salmon family) swim in alpine waters, the Danube is populated by bass, catfish, huchen (otherwise known as Danube salmon) and eel. Carp come chiefly from the ponds of the Waldviertel.

Beaver   The beaver was last hunted in 1863; in 1967 and 1985 a considerable number were released into the wild along the Danube and March rivers as well as in the Inn-Salzach valley. It was a great success: today about 1000 beavers are once again living in Austria.

Amphibians   With a little luck and some patience it is possible to observe a variety of newts, frogs and toads. Toads of the fire-bellied and lowland varieties live around lakes at lower altitudes, while yellow-bellied and mountain toads are found in and around the lakes in the low mountains. Moist deciduous and mixed coniferous forest is the preferred habitat of the fire salamander, particularly common at altitudes between 200m/650ft and 700m/2300ft.

Rarely, the **European pond turtle** is still encountered, above all in the flood meadows of the Danube. The **dice snake** is a highly threatened species that is drawn to warmth and water, while the grass snake is similarly common. Austria's longest snake, the tree-climbing **aesculapian snake** (up to 2m/6.5ft), also requires warm surroundings. The most common poisonous snake is the adder, which lives mainly on the moors and in the mountains, while the sand viper (or horned viper) prefers to inhabit piles of stones and holes in the walls in Carinthia and southern Styria.

Reptiles

The Pannonian regions provide a habitat for the singing cicada and the praying mantis. Several species are strictly protected, such as the alpine goat, stag beetle, rhinoceros beetle, swallowtail butterfly, ailanthus silk moth, death's head hawk moth, and butterfly species including the Camberwell beauty, Parnassius apollo, and the great emperor moth, Austria's largest.

Insects

The reed belt of Neusiedler See is an **internationally famous habitat for birds**, but wonderful sightings can be also made on the flood meadows of the Danube and the March: not only rare bird species, but also the more common mute swan and white stork are sure to please. The very rare and timid black stork lays its eggs in the Wienerwald and the Thayatal National Park. Pheasant and partridge are found in eastern Austria.

Birds

Foxes populate the fields and woods of alpine regions once more

Alpine fauna Animal species that are able to survive in the high Alps must be especially well adapted to the environment. The undisputed king of the air is the golden eagle, while the largest alpine bird is the bearded vulture, with a wing span of nearly 3m/10ft, which has been reintroduced into the wild. The alpine swift, raven and alpine wall creeper are characteristic of the region, while wood grouse and black grouse prefer the lower areas.

The marmot, snow mouse, snow grouse and blue hare feel at home between 1300m/4250ft and 2700m/8850ft. With a lot of luck, the pitch-black alpine salamander can be seen. The chamois, the characteristic species of antelope for alpine regions, is reproducing at increasing rates. The ibex, which had become extinct in Austria, is being reintroduced, and the same is being attempted – though so far with only limited success – with the brown bear, wolf and lynx. Moufflon (wild sheep) and fallow deer still live only in fenced-off areas, though fox and roe deer inhabit both fields and woodland. Red deer are occasionally encountered in the mountain woods.

Population · Politics · Economy

Population

Austria's **low population density** in comparison to other central European countries and the UK is explained by the large proportion of mountainous regions: approximately 60% of the total area of the country is unpopulated. Very nearly 20% of Austria's population resides in Greater Vienna. Further conurbations are found in the Donautal (Danube Valley) and the valleys of the Inn and Mur rivers. The most marked population growth is recorded in west Austrian provinces such as Salzburg, Innsbruck and Bregenz. Birth and death rates approximately balance each other out.

Foreigners and minorities About 98% of Austrian citizens speak German as a first language. The percentage of foreigners is around 9.5%, with the largest group formed by a good 340,000 individuals from the former Yugoslavia (4.2%). Turkish and German people form approx. 2.5% of the population and live in the country predominantly as immigrant workers. Members of the six recognized ethnic groups in Austria live in five federal provinces or states (Bundesländer): Burgenland and Vienna are home to Croatians and Hungarians; Austria's Slovenes live in southern Carinthia's valleys of the Gail, Rosen and Jaun rivers as well as in some places in southern Styria; and Czechs and Slovaks reside in Vienna and Lower Austria (Marchfeld and Tullnerfeld). The Roma and Sinti groups, officially recognized as ethnic groups in Austria since 1993, settle predominantly in Burgenland and Vienna.

With the exception of the province of Vorarlberg and a small part of Tyrol (Ausserfern), which are Alemannic, the Bavarian line forms the **foundation of the Austrian population**. Only Upper Austria however, which belonged to the Bavarian ancestral lands, can count as Bavarian.

◄ Bavaria

In Tyrol and Salzburg as well as in Vorarlberg the Rhaeto-Romanic population was outnumbered by the Germanic Bavarians before Carolingian times. They disappeared gradually, except in some valleys such as the Montafontal and the upper reaches of the Inntal. They still live today in the neighbouring Engadine region, to the west.

◄ Rhaeto-Romans

Predominantly in Carinthia and Styria, Bavarians spreading during the Carolingian period encountered a Slavic population. The Carinthian Slovenes, also known as the Windisch Slovenes, today represent a not insignificant minority.

◄ Slavs

Lower Austria, which just like eastern Styria and Burgenland was almost laid waste through centuries of battles with the equestrian steppe nomads from the east (lastly the Hungarians), was colonized by Germans of predominantly Bavarian origin from the 10th century on. After repeated invasions by Turks and Hungarians, Croatian refugees took up residence in the area, while in Burgenland, alongside a Croatian ethnic group of considerable size, some Hungarian border settlements have also survived from early times. Today, as defined by language, the Croatian minority numbers 19,000 people, the Slovenes in Carinthia 16,000 and the Hungarians 4000.

◄ Croatians

Extraction and origins

State and Society

Austria lies in the transitional zone between the »Atlantic« and the »Danubian« regions of central Europe. However the significance of this location has changed fundamentally several times in the course of thousands of years of history: from a position on the southeastern edge of the Occident to one at the centre of the Habsburg Empire; then back to being on a borderline in the divided Europe of the postwar period, and now at the centre of Europe and no longer ideologically separated from its eastern neighbours.

Political position

Austria originated in the funnel-shaped, narrow corridor of the Danube, where it opens into the broader Viennese Basin. The area

developed into the hub of important European traffic axes. Founded by Charlemagne as the »Ostmark« (Eastern March) to defend his empire against the Hungarians, the territory, **described originally in 996 as »Ostarrichi«**, was ruled from 976 by the Babenbergs, and soon extended over a large part of the Viennese Basin north to the Leitha-March-Thaya line (1043). Expansion to the south followed (Styria

Facts and Figures Austria

Austria

©Baedeker

Location
► from 46°20' to 49° north latitude
► from 9°30' to 17°10' west longitude

Area
► 83,871sq km/32,380sq mi

Population
► 8.3 million
► Population density 99 people per sq km/256 people per sq mi
► largest cities: Vienna (capital) population 1.68 million
  Graz population 253,000
  Linz population 190,000

Language
► Official language: German
► Regional: Croatian, Slovenian, Hungarian

Religion
► 74.1% Roman catholic
► 4.6% Protestant
► 4.3% Muslim
► 12% none

Economy
► Gross domestic product 272.7 € billion
► Gross domestic product per capita 31,800 €
► Part of GDP: industry: 28%, agriculture 2%, services 70%
► Unemployment: 4.2%
► Winter sports: about 5% of the GDP are directly or indirectly connected to winter sports

State
► Federal republic
► 9 provinces (Burgenland, Carinthia, Lower Austria, Salzburg, Styria, Tyrol, Vorarlberg, Vienna)
► Establishment of state: 1918, 2nd republic: 1945, independant from 1955
► Head of state: president, elected directly for six years (mainly representative duties)
► Head of government: chancellor
► Parlament with two chambers: National assembly with 183 members; Federal assembly (provincial representation at the federal level) with 64 delegates

Flag
► Red-white-red in horizontal fields of the same size

1192). The Habsburgs, who ruled from 1278, also pushed south (Carinthia-Carniola 1335; Duino 1335; Trieste 1382), but also west (Tyrol 1363; regions in Vorarlberg and southwest Germany in the 15th century) in order to safeguard the connection to their original territory in Switzerland and southwest Germany. From this strong position the Habsburgs eventually ascended to become a great power – through the happy conclusion of marriages and contracts of inheritance. The annexation of the Bavarian Innviertel (1779) and the episcopal principality of Salzburg (1805) came only much later.

Extent of the country today

Today's Austria is by and large the country that was left over after the handover in 1919 of large areas to opposing neighbours – Italy, Yugoslavia and Czechoslovakia. Along with large parts of Tyrol and Styria and smaller regions of Carinthia and Lower Austria, access to the Adriatic was a major loss. On the other hand Burgenland, once part of Hungary and populated predominantly by Germans, was gained. Since then the length of the country from west to east has been about 560km/350mi, while at its widest from north to south Austria measures around 280km/175mi. The western third of the country, which extends as far as Switzerland and divides Germany and Italy, is merely a narrow corridor with a width of 40–60km/25–40mi.

Settlements and highways

Naturally the **main areas of settlement are on the plains**, and as such lie at the country's periphery. Indeed, the unity of the state would be barely secured if the Eastern Alps were not comparatively well penetrated by valleys: the Arlbergtal, Inntal, Salzachtal and Ennstal in the north; the Murtal and the Mürztal, as well as the Semmering Pass, in central areas; and the Gailtal and Drautal in the south. In addition there are further long valleys running crosswise, forming a veritable grid of natural routes. Moving east, the decreasing density of the Alps – e.g. in the Klagenfurt basin – made room for the formation of independent political centres. In contrast the structure of rule in Tyrol was based on small valley areas on both sides of the Brenner and Reschen passes, namely the Burggrafenamt district in South Tyrol and the central Inntal valley.

Political structure

Since 1918 Austria has been a **democratic parliamentary federal state**. Elected by popular vote, the parliament of every state or province (Bundesland) is the »Landtag«, which then appoints the provincial government and its head or »Landeshauptmann«. In Vienna the Landtag and Landeshauptmann are at the same time the city council and mayor respectively.

Organs of state

The 183 members of the Nationalrat (National Council), Austria's legislative body, were elected by the people every four years until the snap election of 2008, when a change to the constitution extended the period to five years. The distribution of seats and the alternatives for forming coalitions among the parties represented in the Nationalrat decide the composition of the Federal Government, which appoints the Bundespräsident (Federal President) elected by the people for a period of six years and answerable to the Nationalrat. The Bundesrat (Federal Council), composed of 64 provincial delegates, functions as a States Chamber (Länderkammer) with the right to object to laws passed by the Nationalrat.

International memberships

Austria is member of the United Nations and most of the UN Specialized Agencies, as well as the Council of Europe and the OSCE (Organization for Security and Co-operation in Europe). UN Specialized Agencies including the United Nations Industrial Development Organization (UNIDO) have their headquarters in the buildings of the Vienna International Centre (generally known as UNO-City) east of Vienna's old town, as do autonomous institutions within the United Nations. The International Atomic Energy Agency (IAEA), a monitoring body for the atomic weapons non-proliferation treaty, is among the latter. Austria has been a member of the European Union since 1995.

The **red-white-red flag** has been the national flag of the Austrian republic since 1918. The origin and significance of the colours are not completely clear. It is supposed that they go back to the Babenberg family, from whom the large red shield with the silver band, the »Bindenschild«, in the centre of the federal coat of arms was adopted. The federal coat of arms (►p.28) shows an eagle deriving from imperial times. The bird wears a so-called »Stadtmauerkrone«, a crown with three city wall towers, which is a symbol for the citizens; it holds a hammer and sickle symbolizing the workforce and farming community. After the Second World War the broken chain on the eagle's legs was reintroduced as a symbol of liberation from Nazi dictatorship.

> ## ? DID YOU KNOW ...?
>
> ■ According to a legend Leopold V, Duke of Austria, wore a white cloak at the conquest of Acre during the Third Crusade. When he returned to camp after the slaughter, the cloak was soaked in blood. The cloak remained white only under the belt the duke had been wearing – and from then on the Babenberg coat of arms has featured the red-white-red pattern.

Provinces

Burgenland

Burgenland, the **easternmost Austrian province**, extends in a comparatively narrow, 160km/100mi-long strip along the Austrian-Hungarian border from the Danube in the north to the Slovenian border in the south. Constricted like the waist of a wasp to a mere 4km/2.5mi across at its centre, the province shares more of its border with other countries than with Austria itself. In the northern part, home to Europe's only steppe lake, Neusiedler See – Burgenland's emblem, in fact – the broad lowland plains of the puszta (Hungarian steppe) adjacent to the eastern slopes of the Leitha Mountains stretch beyond the border into Hungary and all the way to the Carpathian Mountains. Rich in woodland, southern Burgenland is composed of low mountains belonging to the eastern foothills of the Alps. Its landscape is characterized by pasture, fruit cultivation and viniculture.

Burgenland is not named after the numerous castles (German: Burg) found in its southern region, the former border area. The moniker has much more to do with the common component in the names of the former administrative districts of western Hungary: Ödenburg, Pressburg, Wieselburg and Eisenburg. For this reason, the name »Vierburgenland«, referring to the four districts, was originally coined when the people of Burgenland voted to join Austria in 1918 after the demise of the Austrian-Hungarian monarchy.

Carinthia

Bordering Italy and Slovenia in the south, the rectangular province of Carinthia (Kärnten) is **the sunny south of Austria**. It is especially the broad basin of Lower Carinthia, bounded by mountain ranges on all sides, which profits from the Mediterranean-type climate. The area has more than 200 lakes in the river valley of the lower Drau, which flows along almost the entire length of the province. The natural structure of the basin with its large valleys resembles a seashell, with a level floor and deep grooves, at whose edge immense mountains arch upwards: in the north the Hohe Tauern and Gurktal Alps; in the east the Saualpe and Koralpe ranges; in the south the Karavanke mountains and the Karnisch Alps; and in the west the Lienz Dolomites. Mountains are also decisive in shaping the surface of the interior, and the higher altitudes are valued as areas for winter sports. The western part of Upper Carinthia in the north is completely dominated by the Hohe Tauern, and indeed 57% of the surface area of Carinthia lies at elevations higher than 1000m/3300ft. The climate in the province, which was probably named after a Celtic tribe called the Karner, is often Mediterranean in character. This is due to its location south of the main alpine ridge, which keeps masses of cold air at bay. As a rule, areas of high pressure over Italy reach over into Carinthia, so that the number of sunny days in the province is well above the average for Austria.

Lower Austria

Lower Austria (Niederösterreich) was a valued area for settlement from prehistoric times onwards. Regarded as Austria's heartland, it is the **largest of the nine Austrian provinces**. It is also the province with the largest area of cultivable land in the republic and surrounds the federal capital, ▶Vienna, which is located in the midst of farmland. The Lower Austrian government ran its provincial politics from Vienna until St Pölten was declared provincial capital in 1986.

In the north and east, Lower Austria borders the Czech Republic and Slovakia, in the southeast Burgenland, in the south Styria and in the west Upper Austria. The Danube flows through the province from west to east for a distance of 232km/144mi, dividing Lower Austria

Republic of Austria *Provinces*

Province Borders

into two regions of similar size. North of the river lies the Waldviertel, flat at first but becoming increasingly hilly towards the Czech border, and east of this is the Weinviertel (Wine Quarter). South of the Danube the country rises gradually towards wooded hills and mountains, continues to the Wienerwald, and then ascends to the peaks of the Northern Limestone Alps. In Schneeberg and the Rax – a popular holiday area, especially for the Viennese – this high mountain region reaches elevations of more than 2000m/6600ft. Lower Austria is a landscape of great cultural riches, in which palaces, castles, monasteries and small towns with art-historical significance are found. No wonder then that tourism has represented an important source of income since the 19th century.

Upper Austria Upper Austria (Oberösterreich), which was known as »**Austria ob der Enns**« (Austria above the river Enns) until the 19th century, borders Germany to the west, the Czech Republic to the north, Lower Austria to the east, Styria to the south and the province of Salzburg to the southwest. It stretches from the Dachstein Massif to the Böhmerwald region and from the Inn to the Enns rivers. The Danube splits Upper Austria into two unequal halves. North of the Danube lies the Mühlviertel – a part of the Bohemian Massif – with its primeval mountain landscape, while south of the river lies the heart of the province, the fertile, densely populated alpine foothills with the Innviertel, Hausruckviertel and Traunviertel, which to the south merge into the high mountains of the Northern Limestone Alps. Upper Austria is extremely rich in natural sights: striking mountainous backdrops, caves and grottoes such as the famous Dachstein Caves as well as picturesque ravines and gorges like the »Gosauzwang« near Hallstatt. In addition the numerous large lakes in the Salzkammergut of Upper Austria have attracted both Austrian and foreign tourists to the region since the end of the 19th century.

Salzburg (province)

The province of Salzburg, which got its name because of its rich salt deposits, borders Germany in the north, whose district of Berchtesgadener Land reaches deep into Salzburg country. To the north and northeast Salzburg province borders Upper Austria, in the southeast Styria, in the south Carinthia, East Tyrol and Italy, in the west Tyrol. It sits between the Upper Bavarian plateau and the hilly alpine foothills in the north, the Hohe Tauern in the south and the landscape dominated by the Dachstein Massif in the east, and on both sides of the Salzachtal valley, a main artery carved deep into the landscape. The predominantly mountainous province, whose capital Salzburg is located at the entrance to the mountains, is distinguished by the variety of its landscape. Since the 19th century, in both summer and winter, the lakes of the Salzkammergut (which Salzburg province shares with Upper Austria and Styria) have fascinated visitors, as have the stretches of unspoilt nature with peaceful woods, wild and romantic gorges and idyllic mountain lakes, as well as the numerous homely villages and small towns. Salzburg province is, by the way, **the Austrians' favourite winter holiday destination**.

Styria

Styria (Steiermark) was named after the counts of Steyr in the Traungau, which today however lies in Upper Austria. It is the second largest Austrian province after Lower Austria. The **»green heart of Austria«** boasts the largest proportion of woodland in the alpine republic. It borders Upper Austria and Lower Austria to the north, Burgenland to the east, Slovenia to the southeast and south and Carinthia and Salzburg to the west. From the northern alpine massifs in the Salzkammergut via the main alpine ridge heading southeast to the foothills of the Alps, Styria features high-altitude alpine land forms with glaciated mountains, deep gorges and valleys, large areas of woodland and chains of gently rolling hills. The difference in altitude between the approximately 3000m/9900ft-high Dachstein Massif and the province's lowest point near Bad Radkersburg is around 2800m/9200ft. From the glacier ice at high elevations down to the vine-rich lowlands, an impressive range of landscapes can be seen, from the peaks of the Limestone Alps and the Tauern with their clear mountain lakes to the green pasture of the Seetal Alps as well as the Koralpe and Gleinalpe mountains, and via the pleasant wooded hills of the Fischbach Alps to the sunny and fertile hill country of east and west Styria.

Tyrol

No other Austrian province triggers so many associations as Tyrol (Tirol): immense mountains and glaciers, fascinating alpine pastures and valleys, Innsbruck with its famous Maria-Theresien-Strasse and the Goldenes Dachl (Golden Roof), the »Schuhplattler« folk dance and yodellers, leather breeches, women in flowing dirndl dresses, hearty food, fruit schnapps and, last but not least, winter sports.

The province of Tyrol, whose name is derived from the ancestral palace of the counts of Tyrol near Meran, borders Carinthia and Salzburg to the east, Italy to the south, Vorarlberg and Switzerland to the west, and Germany to the north. The North Tyrol and East Tyrol regions have been separated since 1919 by South Tyrol, which has been part of Italy since that year. For this reason, East Tyrol, completely surrounded by high mountains, has strong links in terms of both transport and tourism with the neighbouring province to the east, Carinthia. The scenery of North Tyrol is also predominantly characterized by mountains. The Inntal valley cuts a trench across the province from the Swiss border in the southwest to the German border in the northeast, and side valleys branch off from the Inntal to the right and left, while still smaller valleys emerge from these. All of them lead into a magnificent mountain landscape. Tyrol is also a land of mountain passes (Brenner Pass, Timmelsjoch, Arlberg etc.). The only access to Tyrol that does not make use of such a pass is at the point where the Inn river emerges from the mountains and enters the alpine foothills near Kufstein, which is why the most important motorway, road and rail links run into the interior of Tyrol from here.

Functioning as a connection between Germany and Italy, for centuries the Austrian province **in the heart of the Alps** was a land of transit traffic, while its high-lying valleys were hardly accessible to visitors.

Vorarlberg

Vorarlberg is Austria's **westernmost and second smallest province**: in terms of area only Vienna is smaller, and only Burgenland has a lower population. In the north Vorarlberg borders Germany, in the west and south Switzerland and the principality of Liechtenstein, in the east Tyrol. As the name suggests the principality lies, in contrast with the rest of Austria, »in front of the Arlberg mountain range«, and is only connected to other parts of the country through passes and the Arlberg Tunnel. Vorarlberg is distinct from the rest of Austria in terms of demographics, too: the people of Vorarlberg are the only Austrians who do not have their origins in Bavaria; instead they are an Alemannic people. After the withdrawal of the Romans, this Germanic tribe advanced to Lake Constance and into the Rhine Valley. The language of the people of Vorarlberg is also more related to that of the Swiss, Liechtensteinians and Swabians than to that of the Tyrolese people, whose origins lie in Bavaria.

Two thirds of the area of the province lies over 1000m/3300ft. It is a mere 70km/45mi from north to south, but this stretch provides a complete cross section through all main alpine ranges, and it is only an hour's drive from Lake Constance, at an altitude of 400m/1300ft and reminiscent of the Mediterranean, via a richly wooded area of low mountains to the glaciated 3000m/9900ft peaks of the Silvretta. Deep, steep-sloped valleys, bizarrely pointed mountain peaks, fertile fields and broad valley meadows, pretty mountain lakes, clear rivers and streams, flowery alpine pastures and idyllic sections along the banks of Lake Constance, as well as pleasant villages and small towns, give the province a unique appeal.

Vienna, the capital of the Republic of Austria, is the province with the smallest area but the **highest population density and the most industry**. It lies at the foot of the Wienerwald (Vienna Woods), the northeasternmost foothills of the Alps, and on Danube, which enters the Viennese Basin here and is up to 285m/935ft wide. In spite of its peripheral location geographically speaking, Vienna is the political, economic, spiritual and cultural centre of the country. Visitors from all over the world stream into the city the whole year round and Vienna has created an image for itself as an arena for international meetings at the highest level as well as for countless congresses and conferences.

Vienna

Economy

Austria's main exports today are, in order of worth, machines, transport equipment, electronic products (chips, integrated circuits) and

Foreign trade

Farming the alpine pasture is hard work, even if the scenery does have a calming effect

chemical products. **Austria's main trading partner is Germany** (imports 2007: 46.3%; exports 2007: 32%). Trade with Germany exceeds by some distance that with, in descending order, Italy, Switzerland, the USA, Hungary, France, the UK and the Czech Republic.

Agriculture

Agriculture and forestry in Austria between the wars was strongly biased towards a traditional farming mindset based on self-sufficiency. Under pressure caused by increasing migration away from agriculture and into jobs in industry and services, postwar production became enormously mechanized and rationalized. Many farming businesses moved away from agricultural production as the main source of income. Today, 0.8% of employed people in Austria still work in agriculture, and approximately 40% of the total area of the country is used for agricultural purposes. Despite the industry's **modest contribution to Austria's gross domestic product**, it can cover the country's demand for all important agricultural products. Economically, Austria's agriculture – predominantly composed of small and medium-sized farms – cannot compete with that in the west of Europe and elsewhere. However enough importance is attached to its value as custodian and caretaker of the alpine cultural landscape for the necessary public support to be granted. Moreover, a major rethink has been taking place over the years, seeing agriculture move in the direction of organic farming and regional marketing. Here, Austria is an absolute frontrunner: well over 10% of farms are run along organic lines.

Mountain farming ▶

The reasons for choosing a life in the mountains, often due to political, religious and nationalist persecution or because it protected the farmer against the collection of money by landowners (mountain farmers were the first »free farmers«), have to a large extent ceased to apply. Many farms are not taken on by those who inherit them: work on the steep slopes is particularly laborious and the profits are minimal. Even the contribution made from public funds is insufficient compensation. The work of mountain farmers is more lucrative in those places where tourism provides an additional way of making a living, especially in western Austria. Here, the depopulation of the mountains has been held within tight limits in comparison with the rest of the Alps. It is more difficult in the high-altitude areas of the Mühlviertel and Waldviertel, the mountains of the eastern bounding ranges and the eastern part of the Niedere Tauern, though in these areas there is increasing success exploiting the opportunities offered by low-impact tourism, the cultural wealth of the region and the sheer relaxation the mountains can provide.

Industry

The development of Austrian industry began in three different regions: thanks to the favourable traffic situation, an initial sufficiency of water power, and the proximity of the capital, the most important industrial area of today's Austria was created in the 19th century in **Vienna and the Viennese Basin**. The iron industry emerged in the

A colossal source of energy: at the end of the Maltatal valley towers Austria's highest dam, the Kölnbreinsperre

small valleys of the »Eisenwurzen« region in southwest Lower Austria, in southeast Upper Austria and in northern Styria. In demand for the construction of the railways, it shifted in the second half of the 19th century into the large **valleys and areas opened up by the main rail routes**: into the valleys of the Mur and Mürz rivers (Murtal and Mürztal), up to the edge of the alpine foothills, into the Viennese Basin and to the edge of the southeastern lowlands and hilly country. The **Rhine Valley in Vorarlberg** forms the third industrial region. Here, the 19th century saw the emergence of a centre of the textile industry, which originated in Switzerland.

The early industrial areas formed the »rich« regions within the former Austrian alpine provinces. In contrast, the barely industrialized alpine areas, scrimping a living from mountain farming, were poor – in spite of the early tourism that developed in conjunction with the construction of the railways.

One consequence of the connection of Austria with the Third Reich was a second wave of industrialization with several shifts of emphasis: Linz became the home of an important armaments industry (iron and steelworks, nitrogen works) and major industry (aluminium smelting at Ranshofen near Braunau, cellulose at Lenzing) also took root in other parts of Upper Austria. ◀ Second World War

After the Second World War industrialization continued in the western parts of Austria occupied by the Allies (Vorarlberg, Tyrol, Salzburg, Carinthia, Styria, and Upper Austria south of the Danube) – partly aided by funds from the Marshall Plan, partly by the movement of businesses out of the area occupied by Soviet forces (Lower Austria, Burgenland, Upper Austria north of the Danube) into the west. At the same time, industry in the Soviet-occupied zone suffered heavy losses due to the dismantling and seizure of a large number of companies. ◀ Postwar period

West-east divide ► Even when the occupying powers withdrew in 1955, eastern Austria recovered only slowly. In addition, the area's **location at the periphery of the »Iron Curtain«** had an effect economically. The development of the eastern part of Austria fell behind the west to the tune of almost twenty years, a lag that has not been made up to this day. This west-east divide represents a reversal of the east-west divide seen at the time of the Austrian monarchy. The fact that tourism is concentrated in western Austria only accentuates the division.

Development of economic structure ► Industrial development in the last decades has been characterized by the deterioration of primary industry and growth in the production of manufactured goods. As in most industrial states this development took place at a time when industry contributed less and less to gross domestic product and offered employment to decreasing numbers of people. Because of cheap competition from abroad, the textile industry, too, was in crisis. New growth industries (the automotive industry and its supply industry; electronics) can take up residence in the old industrial areas only to a limited extent, and this led therefore to a more even distribution of industry across Austria.

Sites of industry today ► **Vienna is Austria's largest industrial region** with the electrical and electronics industry, mechanical engineering, vehicle construction, and the food and semi-luxury food industries. The Viennese Basin has lost some of its importance. The second most important industrial site in the country is central Upper Austria (Linz, Steyr, Wels and Traun), which still boasts an important iron and steel industry as well as vehicle construction and mechanical engineering. As a location for the iron and steel industry, the Styrian »Mur-Mürz-Furche« (a valley carved out by the Mur and Mürz rivers) could not compete. In vehicle construction (Graz), the production of engines and gears is the most important part with an export ratio of over 90%. Approximately 800,000 engines are produced per annum, ending up in many well-known makes of car. In spite of the structural difficulties of the region, a significant textile industry operates in the Rhine Valley in Vorarlberg. Important companies in the cellulose and paper industry (Hallein, Lenzing, Steyrermühl, Frantschach), the iron and steel and metal processing industries (Ranshofen, Reutte, Gailitz, Radenthein), the electrical and electronics industry (Villach, Klagenfurt, Treibach-Althofen, Lebring), the optical industry (Wattens), the sports equipment industry (Ried im Innkreis, Mittersill, Altenmarkt im Pongau) and the clothing industry (Spittal an der Drau) are based outside these industrial conurbations.

Mining **»Austria is rich in poor deposits«** – this is indeed the best description of the situation in the alpine republic. Domestic mining still makes a very limited contribution to the basis of the country's industry and its energy supply. The mining of hard coal ceased a long time ago, and the extraction of lignite takes place in only two mining areas: the district of Köflach-Voitsberg west of Graz and the Wolfsegg-Traunthal area near Ampflwang in the Hausruck region of

Upper Austria. The last Austrian iron ore mining operation on the Erzberg in Styria contributes only moderately to the raw materials demanded by the country's iron and steel industry. Rock salt is extracted in the salt mines near Hallstatt, Bad Aussee and Bad Ischl. The significance of the extraction of mineral oil and natural gas in the Viennese Basin and in the alpine foothills is declining markedly. In contrast, the deposits of magnesite in Radenthein (Carinthia), Breitenau and Oberdorf (Styria) make a weightier contribution to the economy.

Energy

About two thirds of energy generation in Austria is achieved by means of the amply available **water power** – the country is number one in the European Union in this regard. With the exception of the Wachau and the flood meadows east of Vienna, hydroelectric power stations have been built almost everywhere along the Danube. Further power stations have been erected on the central Salzach, the lower Enns and the Drau. Storage power stations, for the creation of »peak current«, were created after the barrages of Kaprun, already begun in the Second World War. These power stations are located above all in the Illtal valley (Vorarlberg), in the Kaunertal valley, at the far end of the Zillertal valley (Tyrol), in the region of the Möll and in the Maltatal valley (Carinthia). The use of alternative sources of energy (sun and wind, biomass, and the natural heat of the earth) is becoming increasingly important.

The share claimed by the **services sector**, both in terms of the number of employed people and the contribution to GDP, has continually risen since the end of the Second World War. The increase has been particularly large during the last two decades. Growth in the services sector has an effect on all its sub-sectors: administration, the education system, the health service, trade, the monetary system, tourism and transport.

> **? DID YOU KNOW ...?**
>
> ■ ... that Austria does not have a single nuclear power station on its grid? Although it had been completed, the inauguration of the Zwentendorf nuclear power station in Tullnerfeld, west of Vienna, was prevented by a referendum on 5 November 1978.

Tourism

It was above all the English who, in the 19th century, distinguished themselves as alpine mountain climbers. German holidaymakers, mainly from Berlin and Sachsen, also visited the western Alps – Vorarlberg, Tyrol, Salzburg, and the Salzkammergut and Carinthian lakes to some extent – and contributed considerably to the economic progress of those areas. The eastern parts of the country played host predominantly to Viennese, Germans from the Sudetenland, Czechs and Hungarians. Quite soon after the Second World War, German visitors began to travel to the regions they had always preferred – and in larger numbers than ever before.

The region lying west of a line running from the Salzkammergut to the Carinthian lakes is clearly emphasized in Austrian tourism. East of this line, tourism is of marked importance in only a few areas, around Neusiedler See and in the Wachau. However, several regions in eastern Austria profit from visitors from the large Austrian cities Vienna, Graz and Linz on day trips and holidays for rest and relaxation. Moreover, the influx of Hungarian and Czech guests into the Alps is on the increase.

Economic significance ▶ Tourism is one of the largest employers in the country. The hotel business, the catering trade and other companies in tourism employed about 500,000 individuals in 2007 (nearly 160,000 in catering and hotels alone). Total turnover was nearly 28 billion euros in 2007. The number of visitors from the UK reached 850,000 at the end of 2007, while 60,000 Irish holidaymakers now visit Austria every year.

Transport Because of Austria's topography, its traffic network is very uneven. Flows of traffic are concentrated along the outskirts of the Alps and **Main traffic routes ▶** through the easily passable alpine passes. One of the main traffic routes is the Westbahn railway and Westautobahn motorway from Salzburg to Vienna. Once a »blind alley« of the southern German traffic network, it has now assumed the function of a central European west-east axis extending to Budapest. The southern autobahn from Vienna via Graz and the Klagenfurt Basin to northern Italy is also important. Transit traffic through Austria is served mainly by the Brenner route between Germany and Italy via the Inntal valley and the Brenner Pass, the Tauern route between southern Germany and northern Italy via Salzburg, and the routes in the direction of

Tourism is one of Austria's most important sources of income

the countries of southeastern Europe via the Tauern and Villach, as well as the Pyhrn route, running from southern Germany via Wels, the Phyrn Pass and Graz. The most important inland waterway is the Danube (Donau). Austrian air traffic is focussed around Vienna International Airport (Flughafen Wien-Schwechat), with the regional airports at Salzburg, Graz, Klagenfurt, Innsbruck and Linz also playing a role.

◄ Traffic load

The voices of those protesting over the **immense increase in heavy vehicle traffic** on Austria's roads, whether as transit traffic or vehicles entering or leaving the country itself, are ever more emphatic. »Alpine valleys have limits; they cannot stand unlimited traffic« runs the slogan against the permanent noise and exhaust fumes. The fact that lorries are becoming quieter and produce a lower level of exhaust emissions is counteracted by the enormous increase in the number of journeys. Until the expiry of the transit agreement – negotiated when Austria joined the EU – at the end of 2003, the number of journeys through the country was limited to 1.6 million. This limit now no longer applies. What remains is the system of so-called ecopoints (»Ökopunkte«), which allows different quantities of points to be calculated for each vehicle according to its emission of nitric oxide. The total number of ecopoints that can be given decreases yearly, a policy intended to persuade road haulage contractors to use lorries with low emissions. These steering measures are seen as interim rules which will apply in exceptional circumstances until the formulation of the road toll guidelines within the EU has been completed. However some traffic problems are home-made: journeys through the country involving cross-border traffic, whose number subject to restrictions until recently, were defined as trips which crossed two borders, a rule which completely excluded traffic within Austria itself and led to criticism that Austria was giving preference to domestic haulage companies.

◄ Road toll guidelines

The planned EU road toll guidelines have still not come into force. When they do, external costs such as those incurred in dealing with the consequences of accidents or environmental damage caused by commercial road transport will be added to the tolls, and is likely that this form of traffic will become around 50% more expensive.

◄ Brenner Basis Tunnel

Another possibility is transport by rail, as has been happening in Switzerland for years. However rail transport has limited capacity, and the necessary investment is high: the largest-scale planned project at this time, the 55km/34mi-long Brenner Basis Tunnel, will cost at least 6 billion euros, of which Austria and Italy will probably foot 40% each and the EU 20% of the final bill. On 30 June 2006 the symbolic groundbreaking took place, and 3 December 2007 saw the first detonation to create the exploratory tunnel in Aicha. Completion is planned for 2012.

? DID YOU KNOW ...?

■ ... that at the present time a third of freight traffic across the Alps goes via the Brenner Pass?

History

Many impressive remains attest to the long history of Austria. The details of the country's recent history, so closely intertwined with that of Germany – a fact that evokes rather mixed feelings – are even better known.

Prehistory

180,000 BC	Traces of human activity discovered
32,000 BC	»Venus of Galgenberg«
5300 BC	»Ötzi«, mummified body from the Neolithic Age
from 8000 BC	Human settlement begins.
from 2200 BC	Skill in metalworking develops.
800–400 BC	Hallstatt culture

Stone Age

Traces of human activity in the region of Austria can be traced back about 180,000 years. The oldest artefacts take the form of flint hand axes and blades, as found in the Gudenushöhle (Gudenus Cave) near Hartenstein in the Kremstal valley of Lower Austria. Furthermore, stone axes made of serpentine and chert, as well as tools fashioned from antlers, were discovered in the Drachenhöhle (Dragon's Cave) near Mixnitz in Styria. Two of the most impressive Stone Age finds are the 7cm/3in-tall **»Venus of Galgenberg«, which is approximately 32,000 years old and recognized as being the oldest sculpture of a human figure yet discovered**, and the »Venus of Willendorf«, a 11cm/4.5in-tall figure, dated to about 25,000 BC. Primitive tools found in a cave in the Osterhorn mountains of Salzburg, specifically on Mt. Schlenken near Hallein, verify that the rough, high mountains were also settled early on: the tools are estimated to be 50,000 years old. In 1991, on the Similaun glacier in the Ötztal Alps, tourists discovered an approximately 5300-year-old mummified corpse of a man from the Neolithic Age, who became known as »Ötzi« or the »ice man«. Humans began to settle as of the Middle Stone Age (8000–5500 BC), log cabins and houses on stilts (Mondsee culture, around 2300 BC) replacing simpler living quarters. Examples of band ceramics and linear ceramics (band-like decoration of earthenware vessels) have been found in Burgenland and the Weinviertel.

Bronze Age

In the Bronze Age (2200–800 BC) the art of metalworking began to develop, and tools and jewellery were made from bronze, amber and gold. The flat graves of the early Bronze Age already contain lavish burial objects, and such objects found in the tumuli of the Middle Bronze Age bear extravagant designs.

Iron Age

The **Hallstatt culture** (800–400 BC), named after the burial ground near Hallstatt in Upper Austria (►Hallstätter See), began with the Illyrians, who created great wealth through the trade in salt with neighbouring cultural areas and through iron working. In the late

← *St John lay at the centre of the battles waged by Tyrolese freedom fighters in the 19th century*

Austria   *Historical Development*

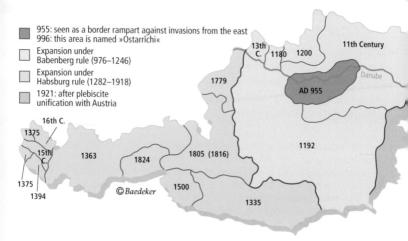

- 955: seen as a border rampart against invasions from the east
- 996: this area is named »Östarrîchi«
- Expansion under Babenberg rule (976–1246)
- Expansion under Habsburg rule (1282–1918)
- 1921: after plebiscite unification with Austria

11th Century
13th C.   1180   1200
Danube
1779
AD 955
16th C.
1375
15th C.
1375
1394
1363
1824
1805 (1816)
1192
1500
1335
©*Baedeker*

Iron Age, the La Tène period (from approx. 400 BC), Celtic tribes migrated to the area from the west and subjugated the Illyrian population. As a rule the Celts, who spread across the whole of Europe, lived in tribal groups. An exception is the Celtic kingdom of Regnum Noricum, a self-contained territory that in the 2nd century BC lay between Salzburg to the north and Burgenland to the south. While the Noric people mined the valuable Noric iron, the Celtic Taurisci tribe (the origin of the name »Tauern«), who had migrated to Carinthia, devoted themselves to gold mining.

Antiquity

150 BC	Romans establish economic relations.
15 BC	Occupation of North Tyrol and Vorarlberg (all of Noricum)
3rd century AD	Teutonic tribes force their way into the eastern Alps.

Roman times   Attracted by highly sought-after trade goods – salt, iron and gold – the Romans established economic relations with the Noric and Taurisci peoples in the mid-2nd century. In order to secure the border of the empire against constant invasion by the Teutons (in 113 BC the Romans were defeated by the Cimbri tribe near Noreia in Carinthia), Rome gradually annexed the eastern Alps. In the year 15 BC the two adopted sons of Emperor Augustus, Drusus and Tiberius, the latter of whom would later become emperor, occupied the regions of North Tyrol and Vorarlberg and brought the whole of Noricum under their control. The area occupied by today's Austria was eventually split into three provinces: Raetia (west of the Zillertal valley), Noricum (east up to the Mürz and Mur) and Pannonia (eastern edge of the Alps). To secure these provinces the new rulers built the **Upper German-Raetian Limes** (a border rampart). Civilian settlements included Brigantium (Bregenz), Aguntum near Lienz, Virunum in Zollfeld near Klagenfurt, Iuvavum (Salzburg), Carnuntum near Hainburg and Vindobona (Vienna).

Population shift

The Roman period, which lasted about 150 years, brought an enormous cultural and economic upswing. After this, from the 3rd century AD, Teutonic tribes forced their way into the eastern alpine region ever more frequently, and Rome, at the end of the day, was unable to defend itself against them. Around AD 500 the Romans finally withdrew completely from their three former provinces. Until the end of the 8th century the Austrian region remained a transit zone, a passage for streams of migrating peoples. Teutons crossed the Danube; Hunnic equestrian nomads travelled from the east all the way to France. Later on, the Avars settled in eastern Austria, and the Bavarians advanced down the Danube from southern Germany. Slavic peoples took up residence in northern Lower Austria, Carinthia and southern Styria.

For about 400 years Petronell-Carnuntum near Hainburg was an important Roman centre for the military and trade

»Of all the precious stones that the earth gives us, salt is the most precious of all.«
(Justus von Liebig)

WHITE GOLD

What would a meal be without salt? It is hardly imaginable! In spite of its unremarkable appearance, salt is of inestimable worth to humankind – partly because of the diverse uses to which it can be put.

Salt was mined from very early on in the Salzkammergut and Hallein, and the history of the mineral went through highs and lows from the very start. When in 1989 the unprofitable Dürrnberger salt mine near Hallein was closed, it marked the end of a chapter in history that had lasted around 3000 years.

Small crystals, big deal

Although its crystals are so small and unremarkable, salt once enjoyed almost the same status as gold. Cities that traded salt attained **great riches**; salt influenced the development of transport and trade, the course of highways and travel routes, and the sites of ports. As extraction, sales and consumption are easy to keep track of, the **interest of the state** was aroused at very a early period, and **salt tax** became one of its most important sources of income. The possible uses of salt (chemical formula NaCl, a compound of sodium and chlorine), which comes from seawater, saline lakes, salt mines and brine, are vast, and new uses are constantly being added to the list.

Salt is a **basic foodstuff** – for microorganisms, plants and animals. It gives foods taste and regulates the water balance in the body. Because of its hygroscopic ability (i.e. it readily takes up and retains moisture) it can help in the conservation of all kinds of foods. As it reduces the freezing point of water from 0 °C/32 °F to −18 °C/ 0 °F it can be used to combat snow and ice on roads in winter. And what is less well known: the white, crystalline material forms one of the **most important raw materials** for the chemical industry – along with mineral oil, it is the basic material used in the manufacture of almost all plastic goods.

»Good luck!« A tour of the salt mine in Hallstatt

Ups and downs

In the eastern alpine region of pre-Christian times, salt mining was limited to **Hallstatt** and the **Dürrnberg** mountain. As archaeological finds attest, Stone Age hunters were making use of the sources of salt in the Northern Limestone Alps more than 4500 years ago. Salt extraction in Hallstatt experienced its first peak from 800 to 500 BC, while salt mining on the Dürrnberg first began around the mid-6th century BC. Trade with the white mineral at this time helped the Celts, who had a large and important settlement near Hallein, to achieve considerable prosperity. From the 2nd century BC, salt from production both on the Dürrnberg and in Hallstatt. The demand for salt was now met with **sea salt**, of which the Romans had large quantities at their disposal. However from the 6th century Reichenhall once again attained economic importance and affluence and was able to maintain its monopoly in the salt market until the end of the 12th century. Then production on the Dürrnberg began again, and the centre of salt production moved once more – not least thanks to the transport route provided by the Salzach river – into the south of the bishopric of Salzburg. Now, however, a different, more economical mining method was used:

For centuries salt was a rare and highly sought-after raw material, whose value was measured in terms of gold.

Dürrnberg and Hallstatt was faced with serious market competition in the form of **Bad Reichenhall** salt, which was of better quality and easier to mine. But with the beginning of Roman rule over the Eastern Alps (15 BC) came a temporary halt in salt in dry rock salt mining, i.e. when there is a high concentration of salt in the rock, the salt is broken up in underground chambers, raised using winches and afterwards brought into boiling huts where extraction takes place in lead or iron pans over a wood

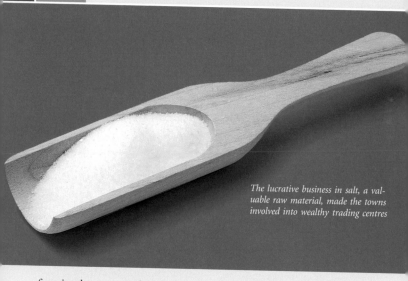

The lucrative business in salt, a valuable raw material, made the towns involved into wealthy trading centres

fire; in the new method however, artificially created spaces in the interior of the salt mine were flooded with water which, now enriched with dissolved salt, was pumped to **boiling huts**. This is known as the brine process.

A state within a state

It was not until 1311 that salt mining began again in Hallstatt. In subsequent centuries the Salzkammergut formed a »**state within a state**«. The Habsburgs allowed foreigners to enter their salt vault only with special permission: the region, which at first extended from Gmunden in the north to Hallstatt and to Ausseerland in the south, was the personal property of the emperor and under the control of the Hofkammer, which administered the ruler's income. The miners were required to settle permanently in the area. In return they received **privileges**: they did not have to join the army, were provided with medical care, were not required to pay taxes and could claim a pension. Alongside

those working for the state, there were self-employed **salt traders** (»Salzfertiger«) to whom the state entrusted the sale of salt. Many of them earned princely sums. In the course of time however, the emperor took away their privileges, so that by 1848 the sale of salt was also in state hands.

»Black Hallein«

After production of salt had ceased in the saltworks of Hallein and on the Dürrnberg, the extraction of the mineral was concentrated only in the mines in Altaussee, Bad Ischl and Hallstatt. Today the Dürrnberg salt mines are a popular alpine **tourist attraction**.

The town of Hallein, lying in the shadow of the Dürrnberg, is also worth a trip, which was not always the case: in the 1820s the town tried to emulate the spa town of Bad Ischl by opening a saline bath. The attempt failed, and the town remained run-down and dirty. A half-day stop in »black Hallein« is enough, according to the Baedeker guide of 1830.

Middle Ages

around 700	Christianization and Bavarian rule in the eastern alpine region
788	Charlemagne creates a stronghold against the Avars.
955	Otto I defeats the Magyars at the Battle of Lechfeld (Augsburg).
976	Government of Ostmark (Eastern March) is entrusted to the Babenbergs.
1278	German king Rudolf I defeats Ottokar II of Bohemia.
1438	Albrecht V is the first Habsburg to become Holy Roman Emperor.
1491	Maximilian I unites both Habsburg lines once again.

Bavaria

Austrian history really begins with the rule of the Bavarians in the Danube and alpine regions. By 750, the Bavarian dukes of the Agilolfing family had brought Upper Austria, the west of Lower Austria, Carinthia, Salzburg and Tyrol under their control. In this epoch, around 700, systematic Christianization of the eastern alpine region began through Irish and Anglo-Saxon missionaries.

Franconia

After deposing Bavaria's Duke Tassilo III, in 788 Charlemagne incorporated Bavaria – until then largely independent – and the Austrian regions belonging to it into his empire. The new ruler created the Carolingian March between the Danube and the Drau rivers as a stronghold against further advances of the Avars, who were eventually so annihilated in bloody campaigns by Frankish troops that a short time later they were to disappear from the picture for ever. In order to conclusively secure the newly won land in the east, Charlemagne established the Ostmark (Eastern March) between the Enns, Raab and Drau rivers.

Battle of Lechfeld (955)

But soon a new danger threatened from the east. From 900 the Magyars (Hungarians) invaded the German empire on an almost annual basis. The Bavarian settlers had to give up the areas they had occupied for almost a century. It was not until 955 that King Otto I, later to become emperor, managed to defeat the Magyars at the Battle of Lechfeld near Augsburg and in this way ended their invasions. As a result the Ostmark – named »Ostarrichi« for the first time in 996 – between Enns and Traisen was formed once again. Historians therefore refer to the **Battle of Lechfeld as the hour of Austria's birth**.

The Babenbergs (976–1246)

In the year 976 Emperor Otto II entrusted the government of the Ostmark to a Bavarian noble family, the Babenbergs. At this time Austria was still thinly populated. In the following centuries the Babenbergs extended their sphere of control in an extremely decisive manner, and through cleverly planned political marriages became one of the leading families in the empire. In 1156, the margravate of the Babenbergs received a large degree of independence from Emperor Friedrich Barbarossa: the Ostmark became a hereditary dukedom with the royal seat in Vienna. When the Babenberg line died out around the mid-13th century, they had significantly enlarged the area under their rule (the dukedom of Styria fell to Austria in 1192), and moreover had made a small, embattled border territory into a politically, culturally and economically powerful dukedom.

Rise of the House of Habsburg (from 1273)

After the Babenberg dynasty died out in 1246 a period of disordered political relations began for Austria. Neither emperor nor king was there to grant the two fiefdoms of Austria and Styria to a new ruler, so the Austrian nobility took matters into their own hands and turned towards King Ottokar II of Bohemia as their new ruler. But Rudolf I, who came from the southwest German Habsburg dynasty and was elected as German king in 1273, then showed interest in this region in the east of the empire. In 1278 at the **decisive Battle on the Marchfeld** between the two opposing sides, Ottokar finally lost both his life and the empire, whereupon Rudolf I presented Austria and Styria as imperial fiefdoms to his two sons Rudolf and Albrecht. This marked the beginning of the rule of the House of Habsburg over Austria, which was to last almost six and a half centuries.

Expansion of the sphere of influence ▶

The Habsburgs now began to extend their sphere of influence with determination and great skill. In 1335 the Austrian Duke Albrecht II was invested with the fiefs of Carinthia and Carniola by Emperor Ludwig IV, and in 1363 Margarethe Maultasch, the last ruler of Tyrol, had to cede her land to Austria. Between 1363 and 1523 single estates in Vorarlberg were sold to Austria; in 1382 the Habsburgs were able to add Trieste to their allodial lands. After the death of Rudolf IV (1339–65), however, his brothers split the country into two independent territories in the Treaty of Neuberg of 1379: Albrecht received the wealthy Upper and Lower Austria, while Leopold took possession of Styria, Carinthia, Tyrol, Carniola, Istria and the alpine foothills. Leopold and his descendants tried to extend their sphere of influence into Switzerland, but to no avail; meanwhile in 1438, Duke Albrecht V from the Albertinian line, who was married to the daughter of Emperor Sigismund, gained the **title of emperor for the House of Habsburg for the first time** after the death of his father-in-law.

Emperors (from 1438) ▶

From this point on the Habsburgs were the almost uninterrupted holders of the German imperial crown until 1806 (with the exception of the period 1742–45). The foundations for the great power of the Habsburgs were laid by Emperor Friedrich III (1440–93): as duke, he had already chosen a motto based on the five vowels, AEIOU, which contemporaries and future generations readily interpreted as »Austriae Est Imperare Orbi Universo« (»The whole world is subject to Austria«) or as »Austria Erit In Orbe Ultima« (»Austria will exist for ever«). In 1477 he arranged the marriage of his son, who later became **Emperor Maximilian I** (1493–1519; ►Famous People), to Mary of Burgundy and so incorporated the Netherlands and the Free County of Burgundy into the House of Habsburg. In 1491 Maximilian reunited the two Habsburg lineages, expanded Habsburg power by means of marriage and inheritance contracts – his son Philip married the sole heiress to Spain and its dominions including Naples and the new colonies in America – and secured the line of succession in Bohemia and Hungary (1515), prerequisites for the creation of the Habsburg Empire.

Early Modern Period

1519–56	Charles V, on whose empire »the sun never set«
1618–48	Habsburg and Bavaria are the most important power bases on the Catholic side.
since the 15th century	Ottomans repeatedly attempt to conquer Austria.
1701–14	War of the Spanish Succession
1740–80	Maria Theresia holds her ground against the Prussians and Bavarians.

Maximilian's grandchild Charles V went down in history as the ruler on whose empire »the sun never set«. He was Holy Roman Emperor of the German Nation (as Karl V, 1519–56) and as King of Spain (Carlos I) ruled over the Spanish possessions in America and Africa. However the **huge complex of Spanish, Austrian and Low Countries territory** could not be held together in the long term. First through the investiture of Charles` brother Ferdinand I as regent for Austria (1521–22) and conclusively after the abdication of Charles V (1556), Habsburg rule split into a Spanish and an Austrian line. The decisive step to form a great European power had been made by the Austrian House of Habsburg 30 years before: in 1526 the contract of inheritance with Bohemia and Hungary was executed, and the Bohemian and Hungarian crowns fell to the Habsburgs.

Empire

The Reformation movement triggered by Martin Luther was very well received in Austria, in particular by the rulers of the provinces. These princes also determined the religious denomination of their subjects, so that until the mid-16th century the Habsburg provinces were in large part Protestant and only a fifth of the population of Austrian still professed the Catholic faith. Of the fanatically Catholic Habsburgs, Ferdinand's son and successor Maximilian II (1564–76)

Reformation and Counter-Reformation

A painted geneaology of the House of Habsburg in Schloss Tratzburg near Schwaz in the Inntal valley

was the only one who was thought sympathetic to the Protestant faith; indeed he was even considered a secret Protestant. However after his death the Habsburg territories saw the beginning of the Counter-Reformation on a large scale, and Protestants were expelled from Styria, Carinthia and Carniola. The recatholization of the country carried out by Emperor Rudolf II (1576–1612) and his successors was so successful that today's Austria is still mainly Roman Catholic.

Thirty Years' War (1618–48)

The Thirty Years' War began as a struggle for power and religious domination between Protestants and Catholics and ended as a general conflict involving most of Europe. Along with the Bavarian-led Catholic League in Germany, the House of Habsburg was the most important power base on the Catholic side. The first years of war would have the greatest effect on Austria. In the Bohemian-Palatinate War (1618–23) the imperial troops managed to annihilate the Protestant nobility in Bohemia, whose uprising against the emperor (**»Defenestration of Prague«**) had triggered the war. Apart from that, Austria was a theatre of war only in the final phase of the greatest European conflict of the 17th century, when in 1636 the Swedes advanced almost to Vienna and later into the Rhine Valley of Vorarlberg. Though the Treaty of Westphalia of 1648 curtailed the influence of the emperor on the German princely states in the Holy Roman Empire, in Austria itself the elimination of the Protestants cleared the way for Habsburg absolutism in their hereditary territories.

Ottoman Wars 1529, 1664, 1683

The onslaught of the Turks was still more dangerous than the Thirty Years' War for the continued existence of Austria: from the 15th century on, the Ottoman Turks made repeated attempts to invade. In 1529, Vienna was besieged for the first time, though without result. In 1664 the imperial army under the command of Count Montecuccoli was able to defeat the Turks near St. Gotthard on the eastern border of Styria; during the second Turkish siege of Vienna in 1683 the imperial and Polish armies achieved victory over the Ottomans in the Battle of Vienna at Kahlenberg, and the Ottoman Empire now retreated further and further. The Habsburgs pursued them and by 1699 were able to chase the Ottomans out of Hungary, in doing so laying the foundations of the Habsburg's great power in eastern and southeastern Europe.

Great power of the Habsburgs

The Turks were not the only enemies of the Habsburg Empire. Since the reign of Maximilian I, the battle between Austria and France had been a dominant influece on European politics. After the demise of the Spanish Habsburg line the Houses of Habsburg and Bourbon quarrelled over their inheritance. In the wake of the **War of the Spanish Succession** (1701–13/14) the Austrian claim to the Spanish throne had to be abandoned, in return for which however Austria received the Netherlands (approximately today's Belgium and Luxembourg), which until that point had been united with Spain, as well as parts of Italy. With this territorial gain under Karl VI (1711–40), the »Monarchia Austriaca«, a loose construction of states composed of kingdoms, archduchies and principalities, counties and provinces, finally became a great power.

Second siege of Vienna by the Turks in 1683

Maria Theresia (1740–80)

A further endurance test for the empire came in the form of the War of the Austrian Succession (1740–48), in which Prussia and Bavaria attempted to divide the Austria territories among themselves. Maria Theresia (1740–80; ►Famous People), fighting for recognition of her right of succession, was able to hold her ground against her enemies. However, in the Silesian Wars (1740–63) that the Habsburgs lost Silesia to Frederick the Great of Prussia. On the other hand Austria reached agreement with Prussia and Russia on the partition of Poland and as part of the deal received most of Galicia and Ruthenia. Domestic politics at the end of the 18th century was characterized by reforms. Under the rule of Maria Theresia's son, Joseph II (1781–90), an advocate of enlightened absolutism, in 1781 the Edict of Tolerance was enacted, the Serfdom Patent in Bohemia toned down and German declared the sole official language (1784). Joseph also abolished all monasteries that did not work for the public good and, with the founding of humanitarian establishments such as poorhouses and hospitals, created the basis for the modern welfare state. However there was bitter resistance to these reforms, which took place over a short period of time, so that shortly before his death Joseph had to revoke many decrees.

Modern Times

1804	Franz I becomes the first »Emperor of Austria«.
1814–15	Congress of Vienna
1870–71	Creation of the German nation-state excluding Austria
1914	Assassination of the Austrian heirs apparent
1918	Austria-Hungary disintegrates; the end of Habsburg rule
1919	The Austrian Republic
1938	Annexation of Austria by Nazi Germany
1945–55	Austria is divided into four occupation zones.
1986–92	»Waldheim Affair«
1995	Austria joins the European Union

Danube Monarchy (1804–1918)

In 1805 Napoleon Bonaparte, who had emerged from the turmoil of the French Revolution as emperor of France, declared war on Austria. Following the Corsican's decisive victory at the Battle of Austerlitz in Moravia, Vienna lost Veneto to the Kingdom of Italy, and Tyrol and Vorarlberg to Bavaria. In 1806 Emperor Franz II renounced the Roman-German imperial title, and in doing so dissolved the Holy Roman Empire of the German Nation. However two years before he had assumed the title »Emperor of Austria« as Franz I, and thereby founded the Danube Monarchy.

After the victory of the coalition between Prussia, Great Britain, Russia and Austria over Napoleon, the statesmen of Europe met in Vienna in 1814–15 (**»Congress of Vienna«**) to discuss a new division of power for the continent. The driving force behind the new European order was Prince Metternich (►Famous People). Within the framework of the Holy Alliance founded by Russia, Austria and Prussia, he sought to restore the absolutist order that had swept away by the French Revolution and the Napoleonic Wars. Help came from the German Alliance (Deutscher Bund), an amalgamation of 39 states (35 principalities and 4 free cities), with Austria assuming the role of chairman. Although rigorous police-state measures, such as censorship and espionage, were taken against revolutionary and nationalist movements, Metternich, who enjoyed the unreserved trust of Franz I (1804–35) and Ferdinand I (1835–48), was unable to avert liberal demands in the long term.

Restoration

The fall of Metternich initiated the revolution of 1848, which was bloodily crushed in October and at first changed nothing in the system. After the abdication of Ferdinand I, known euphemistically as »Ferdinand the Benign« due to his lack of assertiveness and physical impairment – he suffered from epilepsy – his nephew Franz Josef (1848–1916), only 18 years old, ascended the throne and continued the to govern the country on absolutist principles until 1860. During this time the Habsburg monarchy lost international influence. In the war of 1859 with France and Piedmont-Sardinia, Austria had to cede the rich Lombardy. In 1866, in the Austro-Prussian War over supremacy in the German states, the Austrians suffered a **military defeat near Königgrätz** at the hands of the Prussians, which led to the dissolution of the German Alliance and ultimately to the creation of the German nation-state (1870–71) with the exclusion of Austria. Defeat at the Battle of Königgrätz also had political consequences at home: under pressure from the Hungarian nationalist movement, which took advantage of the weakened position of the emperor, Franz Josef I was crowned King of Hungary in 1867. This led to the creation of the so-called Dual Monarchywhereby Hungary became an independent part of the empire with its own government and parliament. This period is often referred to in Austria as the »k. & k.« monarchy (»königlich & kaiserlich«, meaning »royal and imperial«). From this time until the outbreak of the First World War, the fate of Austria-Hungary would be increasingly determined by the nationality problem in this multiracial state.

Franz Josef I (1848–1916)

In 1878 Austria made an attempt to occupy the Turkish provinces of Bosnia and Herzegovina. As a consequence of this Vienna came into conflict with Russia, which supported the independence of the Slavic peoples of the Balkans. As a precautionary measure against Russia and the Ottoman Empire, Austria and the German Empire formed an alliance, which in 1882 was joined by Italy. Then, in 1908, Austria

Development in the Balkans

really did annex Bosnia and Herzegovina. The Serbs, supported by the Russians, wanted to establish a southern Slavic state with the inclusion of the annexed regions, and offered fierce resistance.

First World War (1914–18)

The assassination of the heir to the Austrian throne and his wife by Greater Serbian nationalists in Sarajevo on 28 June 1914 was the spark that ignited the powder keg in the Balkans. The Serbs were immediately prepared to meet all the demands that the Austrian foreign minister set out in an ultimatum – after all, the assassin had not acted on the orders of the Serbian government, as the Austrians tried to claim. Nevertheless on 28 July 1914 Austria-Hungary declared war on Serbia, and the First World War began. In spite of initial successes, by 1918 the Central Powers, Germany and Austria-Hungary, had been defeated by the opposing Allies: Great Britain, France, the USA (from 1917) and Italy, which had declared war on Austria in 1915. The efforts of Emperor Franz Josef's great nephew and successor Karl I to negotiate a peace settlement, intended to preserve the multiracial state, came to nothing.

Fall of the Habsburg Empire

With this defeat Austria-Hungary dissolved, and the 600-year rule of the Habsburgs came to an end. On 3 November 1918 the armistice between Austria-Hungary and the Allies began, on 11 November Emperor Karl I relinquished all part in government, and a day later a

The heir to the throne, Franz Ferdinand, and his wife Sophie were shot dead in Sarajevo on 28 June 1914 in this very car (Heeresgeschichtliches Museum, Vienna)

republic was proclaimed. In accordance with the Treaty of Saint-Germain-en-Laye signed on 10 September 1919, Austria had to cede South Tyrol, Istria, Trieste, some parts of Dalmatia, Carinthia and Carniola to Italy, and recognize the now independent states Czechoslovakia, Poland, Hungary and Yugoslavia with the appropriate cession of territory. The remains, reduced to the German-speaking regions of today's Austria, represented only 12% of the area of the old monarchy. While Karl I had renounced participation in state affairs, he had not abdicated the throne. For him, the rule of the House of Habsburg was not yet over, and he attempted to restore the monarchy in Hungary. However he was exiled by the Allies to the Portuguese island of Madeira, where he died in 1922.

The new state, »German Austria«, was proclaimed as early as 12 November 1918. The first chancellor was Karl Renner. The republic of German Austria was seen as part of an pan-German republic and doubt was cast on the viability of this »rump state«. As set out in the Treaty of Saint-Germain, however, the Allies did not allow amalgamation, in order to limit the power of Germany. Even the name »German Austria« was forbidden. With the ratification of the treaty on **21 October 1919** the name was changed to the **»Republic of Austria«**.

◄ First Republic

As in Germany, Austrian politics was from the very beginning characterized by radical and polarizing positions, with parties and associations on the extreme right and the extreme left gaining strength. In particular, paramilitary units of the Social Democrats' Republikanischer Schutzbund (Republican Protection Militia) and the Christian Socialists' Heimwehr (Home Guard) fought it out on the ideological battlefield. From 1918 to 1934 hundreds of people lost their lives in street fighting.

Political polarization

To safeguard the independence of Austria against the increasing power of the National Socialists, who were influenced were their German counterparts and supported the annexation of Austria, in March 1933 the diminutive chancellor **Engelbert Dollfuss** (known as »Mini-Metternich«) implemented a coup, stripped the parliamentary constitution of its power and installed an authoritarian corporate state (»Austrofascism«). All political parties were banned apart from the Vaterländischer Front (Fatherland Front), which he had founded. However the National Socialists remained the greatest internal political problem. The Nazi attempt at a coup (the »July Putsch«) against the chancellor in 1934, in which Dollfuss was murdered, may have ended a failure, but his successor Kurt Schuschnigg's struggle to preserve the independence of Austria was in vain. In 1936 his cabinet sealed a friendship agreement with Hitler, in the hope of preserving Austrian independence. While this agreement normalized German-Austrian relations, it also supplied the German dictator with a pretext to interfere hugely in the internal affairs of his smaller neigh-

Austrofascism and annexation

bour. Under pressure from Germany Schuschnigg had to grant an amnesty to Austrian National Socialists and approve their admission into the government. In March 1938 Hitler forced the Austrian chancellor to resign, ordering his troops to march into Austria to carry out its annexation – referred to as the »Anschluss« – to the Nazi German Reich, a move that was welcomed by many Austrians.

The German Reich and the Second World War

After annexation on 10 April 1938, which was approved by popular vote, the name Austria disappeared from the map, replaced by »Ostmark« and later by »Donau- and Alpengaue« (Danube and Alpine provinces). For seven years Austria shared the fate of the German Reich. The Nazi system was transferred to the annexed land, and Jews there became victims of the Holocaust. In the Second World War Austrians fought in the German Wehrmacht in all theatres of battle. Cities suffered destruction, firstly due to air raids and later in attacks by Allied ground forces, and Austrian Nazis played their part in the war crimes of the Hitler regime.

Occupation (1945–55)

As in Germany, after the end of the war the victorious powers divided Austria **into four occupation zones**: the Soviet zone consisted of Lower Austria and Upper Austria north of the Danube, as well as Burgenland; the American zone took in Upper Austria south of the Danube and Salzburg; the British zone covered Styria, Carinthia and East Tyrol; and the French zone consisted of North Tyrol and Vorarlberg. The Allies also divided the capital Vienna into four sectors.

Second Republic ▶

Ten years after the end of the war, in the Austrian State Treaty of 1955, the occupying powers and the Austrian government (the first election for the Nationalrat took place as early as November 1945) agreed on the unity of the state and the withdrawal of all occupying forces, and Austria was a sovereign nation once more. However it had to commit itself to **»everlasting neutrality«**, and was forbidden to enter into any alliance with Germany, whether political or economic. In the same year the alpine republic became a member of UNO.

International integration

This neutral and economically strong Austria, which like Germany had undergone a postwar economic miracle thanks to the Marshall Plan, took on a new international role as mediator between East and West. Important international conferences took place on Austrian soil. Kurt Waldheim, the incumbent federal president in the period 1986–92, was diplomatically isolated however as, in spite of the facts, he claimed never to have been a member of the Nazi Students' Union or the SA (the Sturmabteilung, a paramilitary organization of the Nazi Party). The »Waldheim Affair« brought Austria's role in the Nazi period back into the realms of public debate.

Geopolitical change

With the end of Eastern bloc communism, Austria's entry into the European Union (EU) in 1995, and the planned EU expansion eastward, the geopolitical position of the republic has shifted and Austria can now be considered a Central European country. This has been accompanied by a gradual dismantling of the political neutrality that once defined Austria's identity.

Austria in the 21st century

After the Nationalrat elections in October 1999, the right-wing Freedom Party (FPÖ) emerged as the party with the second largest number of votes after the centrist Social Democratic Party (SPÖ). Austria caused an international sensation when the conservative People's Party (ÖVP) and the Freedom Party, led by the populist head of government of the province of Carinthia, Jörg Haider, agreed to form a coalition. This met with strong disapproval both at home and abroad and even resulted in a temporary freeze of bilateral relations with Austria by the other EU member states.

In the 2002 Nationalrat elections, held earlier than planned, the People's Party came out on top while the Freedom Party's share of the vote dropped to 10%. Nevertheless the result was a new version of the old coalition. In April 2005 the members of the government and parliamentarians of the Freedom Party split from the coalition and joined the newly founded Alliance for the Future of Austria (BZÖ) under the leadership of Jörg Haider.

In the Nationalrat elections held on 1 October 2006 the Social Democrats were the strongest party and in January 2007 formed a grand coalition with the People's Party. Alfred Gusenbauer of the SPÖ became chancellor, while Wilhelm Molterer of the ÖVP accepted the posts of vice-chancellor and finance minister. After only 18 months the grand coalition collapsed, partly because of the differing policies of the two main parties regarding Europe. New elections were called for September 2008.

2008 elections

Austria introduced another change to the constitution for the elections of September 2008: the age limit for voting was lowered to 16. Perhaps aided by the lower voting age, two far-right parties, the Freedom Party and the Alliance for the Future of Austria, took 30% of the vote. Both ran campaigns focussing on anti-immigrant and anti-European Union policies. Meanwhile, the Social Democrats and the People's Party faced the worst election results in their history. It fell to the Social Democrats, the marginal winners of the election with less than 30% of the vote, to form a government. Talks resumed with the objective of forming yet another grand coalition. The death the leader of the Alliance for the Future of Austria, Jörg Haider, in a car crash in October 2008 was a further twist in the complex tale of Austrian politics.

Euro 2008

The other major event in 2008 was that Austria – together with Switzerland – hosted the UEFA European Football Championship. The venues for the event were Vienna, Graz, Innsbruck and Salzburg.

Arts and Culture

Arts and sciences enjoy a high status in Austria and are keenly observed from far beyond the country's borders. From the Stone Age to today's avant-garde – the small alpine republic has produced many great artists of international renown.

History of Art

Note

In essence the following outline is concerned with the region representing today's Austria. In general, external artistic influences come to fruition in Austria with a certain initial delay, a time lag which in some cases can amount to one and a half centuries. As a consequence the accepted time frames of the Romanesque, Gothic and Baroque periods are considerably later in Austria than in Germany, France and Italy.

Prehistoric Times

First finds

The **first find with relevance for the history of art** to be discovered on Austrian soil is the »Venus of Galgenberg«, excavated in 1988 in the vicinity of the Lower Austrian town of Krems (copy in Weinstadtmuseum Krems, original in Naturhistorisches Museum Wien – Natural History Museum Vienna). The excavator who dug up the approximately 7cm/3in-high and 32,000-year-old figure up named it »Fanny – the dancing Venus of Galgenberg«, a homage to the famous Austrian dancer Fanny Elssler. The 27,000-year-old, approximately 11cm/4.5in-high »Venus of Willendorf« (Naturhistorisches Museum Wien) dates from the Palaeolithic Age. The cult statuette of a woman was named after the place in Lower Austria where it was found.

The next batch of interesting finds attests to a considerably later period, namely the **Hallstatt period** (800–400 BC), named after Hallstatt in Upper Austria where the majority of the finds were made. The treasures of this time include burial objects from the over 2000 tombs that were discovered, among them richly decorated bronze utensils, which indicate the use of sophisticated decorative techniques. Important finds from this epoch, the early Iron Age, are predominantly to be seen in the Prähistorisches Museum (Prehistoric Museum) in Hallstatt and the Naturhistorisches Museum in Vienna.

Venus of Willendorf

The Keltenmuseum (Celtic Museum) in Hallein in the province of Salzburg provides a comprehensive insight into the Celtic culture that shaped the **later Iron Age**.

Roman Times and the Early Middle Ages

Roman times

When Raetia and Noricum were annexed as provinces to the Roman Empire in 15 BC, Austria became Roman territory. One piece of evidence is the »Jüngling vom Magdalensberg« (Magdalensberg Boy),

← *Rococo in pastel: Stift Wilhering*

the life-size Roman copy of a Greek statue found in 1502 near Sankt Veit an der Glan in Carinthia. Interesting finds are to be seen in the open air museum at Petronell and Museum Carnuntum near Hainburg, in Teurnia near St Peter im Holz and in Aguntum near Lienz.

Mass migration After the withdrawal of the Romans (around AD 400), Teutons, Huns, Avars, Slavs and finally Bavarians moved in turn through Austria during the Migration Period, some settling in the country. Though hardly a well-documented period in history, some artistic highlights are nevertheless to be discovered: at the end of the 7th century Stift St Peter (St Peter's Archabbey) and Stift Nonnberg, a nunnery, were founded in Salzburg, while the Benedictine abbey of Stift Mondsee came into being in 748.

Carolingian period Named after Charlemagne, Carolingian art attempted to bring about a synthesis of ancient and Christian use of forms, i.e. classical traditions were combined with the skills of craftsmanship possessed by the Christianized inhabitants of Austria. Monumental stone buildings represented a new type of architecture that was based on the ancient basilica as well as the hall church, and made use of Roman building forms such as columns and round arches. The Tassilo Chalice, kept in Stift Kremsmünster (Kremsmünster Abbey) and donated by Duke Tassilo III on the occasion of its founding in 777, is a masterpiece of goldsmith work. Carolingian art, which found further expression in highly embellished book illumination (e.g. the Vienna Coronation Gospels), continued to exert an influence into 10th century until it was superseded by Romanesque style.

Romanesque Period

Church commissions Like all the art of the Middle Ages, Romanesque art, the first unified occidental style since antiquity, was created in Austria almost entirely in response to commissions by the church. With the founding and renovation of their abbeys, Benedictines, Cistercians and Augustinians contributed to the continuous development of art in Austria from the 12th century. Only in the city of Salzburg were there signs – evident since Ottonian times – of an unfolding art movement bearing its own stamp, art that found expression in particular in the illuminated manuscripts of the 11th century.

Painting Monumental painting developed in a similar way to the art of the book. Remains of wonderful Romanesque frescoes have been preserved in the collegiate church on Salzburg's Nonnberg hill, in St John's Chapel in Pürgg in the Ennstal valley and in the Benedictine abbey of Lambach. The **Verdun Altar** in Stift Klosterneuburg (an Augustinian abbey) is a unique work from this epoch. Created in 1180 by Nicholas of Verdun, the enamel panels with scenes from the Old and New Testaments were put together to form a winged altar in 1331.

The architecture of the 12th century was shaped in western Austria **Architecture**
principally through the Benedictines (the abbeys of St Peter, Nonnberg, Mondsee, Lambach, Kremsmünster), and in the east of the
country mainly through the Cistercians, who from 1135 built a series
of abbeys (Heiligenkreuz, Zwettl, Lilienfeld). The nave of the collegiate church of Heiligenkreuz in the Wienerwald and the chapter
house of Stift Zwettl are evidence of this early phase of construction.
But it is the **Dom zu Gurk** (Gurk Cathedral, Carinthia) that is considered the most magnificent Romanesque building in Austria. A colossal pillar basilica consecrated in 1174, the cathedral has a crypt supported by one hundred marble columns and a remarkable late-
Romanesque cycle of frescoes (around 1260) on the west gallery.

It was also the Cistercians who first took up Gothic influences: in the **Transitional**
richly decorated cloisters of Zwettl, Heiligenkreuz and Lilienfeld, **period**
which were built from the beginning of the 13th century, Gothic elements are already visible; the collegiate church of Lilienfeld, a pillar
basilica with a choir ambulatory, was completed in 1263 and em-
bodies Burgundian early Gothic style. Even though the local master
builders were motivated to take some new ideas on board, the squat
and massive design of most buildings of the late Babenberg period,
such as the charnel houses of Tulln and
Mödling, and the nave of the Franciscan
church in Salzburg, still place them very
definitely in the realm of Romanesque
architecture.

Gothic Period

Gothic style was able to gain a foothold in
Austria only around the end of the 13th
century. The Gothic art of the 14th century was closely associated with the **House
of Habsburg**, which had come to power in
1278 with Rudolf I. Because of the lively
connections that existed between the Viennese and the Prague court – the residence
of the emperor at times – French, Italian
and German influences reached Vienna
and Austria by way of Bohemia.

Important works of Gothic **sculpture** include the figures on the Singertor portal of
the Stephansdom (St Stephen's Cathedral)
in Vienna and the Virgin Mary sculptural
group in Stift Klosterneuburg. The stained
glass in the choir of the parish church in
Viktring in Carinthia is especially beauti-

The Fountain House of Stift Lilienfeld is one of the most beautiful Gothic buildings in Austria.

ful. The main emphasis of **painting** during the Gothic period however lay in the art of panel painting. A picture of Rudolf IV, created in 1365, was **Austria's first portrait**. In the late Gothic period, painting and sculpture enjoyed a heyday. Local schools with a pronounced creative will arose in Vienna and Salzburg. Along with stone sculpture (partly realistic, partly in the rounded »soft style«), framed wood carvings were also made including accomplished winged altars (Kefermarkt, around 1500; St Wolfgang, Michael Pacher, 1481). Important painters of altarpieces include the Master of the Albrecht Altar (Stift Klosterneuburg); the Viennese Master of the Scots (Monastery of the Scots, Vienna), on whose *Flight into Egypt* of 1469 the first view of the city of Vienna is to be seen; Conrad Laib (Museum Carolino Augusteum, Salzburg; Cathedral of Graz; Unteres Belvedere, Vienna); and Rueland Frueauf the Elder (Unteres Belvedere, Vienna). In Innsbruck, Jörg Kölderer painted the frescoes on the Goldenes Dachl, where the balance of proportions already points to a new age.

Danube School The painting style of the so-called Danube School developed around the turn of the 15th into the 16th century. It did not start with one artist in particular, instead unifying a wealth of work from various studios and artists. Its characteristic feature is the close connection of the content of the depicted scenes with nature, the expressive landscape in which the story of the picture is embedded. With this come glowing colours and an occasionally unconventional line. Its main representatives include Rueland Frueauf the Younger (Stift Klosterneuburg), Lucas Cranach the Elder (Stift St Florian), Albrecht Altdorfer (Stift St Florian) and Wolf Huber (Feldkirch parish church), who came from Vorarlberg. The stylistic phase of the Danube School was gradually displaced by the Renaissance in the mid-16th century.

Architecture Furthermore, in Lower Austria a flourishing artistic life developed in the Cistercian order: the choir and the pump room of Stift Heiligenkreuz are pure Gothic works. In addition, the Leechkirche in Graz and the Augustinerkirche (St Augustine's Church) in Vienna also number among the milestones of Gothic building in the 14th century. The 15th century heralded a golden age of late-Gothic architecture. The Viennese Cathedral Construction Guild of St Stephen achieved great importance, and the most imposing evidence for its capabilities is the Stephansdom (St Stephen's Cathedral) with its immense south tower (known as »Steffl«), built in only 25 years. In contrast to the slender Viennese late Gothic style of St Stephen's, as well as the Kirche Maria am Gestade (Church of St Mary on the Strand) with its charming openwork spire and the »Spinnerin am Kreuz«, a stone pillar on top of the Wienerberg, the spacious hall church was preferred in the rest of Austria. The choir of the Salzburg Franziskanerkirche (Church of St Francis) is an example of this. One feature of Austrian late Gothic style is rich reticulated and star-

A real gem at the parish church of St Wolfgang: the Pacher Altar

ribbed vaulting, the most unconventional example of which is in the Gailtaler Dom in Kötschach-Mauthen. The Kornmesserhaus, built around 1500 in Bruck an der Mur in Styria, is considered the most beautiful Gothic town house in Austria.

Renaissance

Not least because of the discoveries of Christopher Columbus, the medieval conception of the world changed. With the emergence and growing importance of money transactions, the structure of the economy also changed. Renaissance thought, which also originated in Italy, spread across Europe. In conscious opposition to the withdrawal from worldly considerations and concentration on the hereafter seen in the Middle Ages, this **»rebirth of antiquity«** placed the human being at the centre of attention. In Austria this period of transition was embodied by the figure of Emperor Maximilian I (▶ Famous People): although he was named »the last knight« as an allusion to his attachment to the past, he was in fact receptive to anything new, attracted forward-looking artists to his court and fostered both crafts and sciences. The monument commissioned by the emperor himself that was erected in the court church of Innsbruck numbers among the most interesting works of art of this transitional epoch: the 28 larger than life-size bronze statues were executed in part according to plans by Albrecht Dürer and Peter Vischer.

Fundamental changes

The fact that Renaissance art is much less represented in Austria than that of the Gothic or Baroque periods can be traced back to Austria's violent clashes with the Ottoman Empire. For two centuries, from the time of Maximilian onward, fighting took place – mostly in the Balkans but also often on Austrian soil. In the years 1529 and 1683

Make war not art

the Turks laid siege to Vienna; though the siege was in vain, they ravaged the surrounding countryside and repeatedly attacked Carinthia and Styria. With every ounce of strength devoted to these wars, there was little energy and funding left to maintain the arts.

Castles The line of defence against the Turks was strengthened: fortresses were built in Klagenfurt, Graz and Vienna. In Graz in 1557–65 the fortress builder Domenico d'Allio also built the main section of the Landhaus with its beautiful arcaded courtyard, while in Vienna the Amalia Wing of the Hofburg (imperial palace), with the Schweizertor (Swiss Gate), was created. Further examples of this building work include the magnificent Burg Hochosterwitz in Carinthia, Schloss Riegersburg in Styria and the fortresses of Burgenland. Schloss Porcia in Spittal an der Drau (Carinthia) and Schloss Schallaburg in Lower Austria, whose splendid courtyard is decorated with terracotta, are among the most beautiful buildings of this period. Most buildings are the work of Italian fortress builders, and they characterize Austrian architecture of the Renaissance and Early Baroque period.

Mannerism It was under the rule of Emperor Rudolf II, who resided in the Prague court, that the ideas of Mannerism, an independent style of art between Renaissance and Baroque, found their way into artistic work. Typical for the style is the rejection of classical forms in favour of distorted, asymmetrical, sometimes bizarre portrayals in bright colours. Examples include the imperial crown of 1602 in the Schatzkammer (Treasury) of the Hofburg in Vienna, as well as the great works of Mannerist painting by Giuseppe Arcimboldo in Vienna's Kunsthistorisches Museum (Museum of Art History, known as the KHM for short). In Salzburg buildings were designed in a pure Italian, Mannerist-early Baroque style, as in the new cathedral (1624–28) by Santino Solari, who also built the summer residence of Schloss Hellbrunn.

Baroque

Development Only after the dangers of the Ottoman wars had been eliminated could Austrian and Habsburg concepts of government be carried through. This also heralded the breakthrough of the Baroque style, which made its mark on the **outstanding epoch in Austrian art**. As absolutist ideas took hold, the Catholic Church, which had been shaken by the Reformation, also regained strength and scored a conclusive victory in Catholic countries through the Counter-Reformation. The consequence was a tremendous upswing in building activity that led to the construction of numerous churches, monasteries (immense palatial abbeys) and palaces. In sculpture and painting, too, great works were created. Many old buildings were given a new Baroque appearance; the characteristic onion domes on slender Gothic church steeples originated in this period.

Italian architects ushered in the Baroque epoch, among them Donato Felice d'Allio (Stift Klosterneuburg) and Giovanni Pietro de Pomis (Mausoleum of Ferdinand II, Graz). After this preparatory phase, architecture culminated in the ceremonious splendour of the High Baroque. The magnificent buildings of this epoch were commissioned by the ruling dynasty, the aristocracy and the church. Vienna enjoyed a glittering period on its way to becoming the »imperial city«. Castles and palaces were built in large number, above all in the suburbs, which were coming to life again after the devastation of the past.

Architecture

The most outstanding artistic figures of this time in the field of architecture were Lucas von Hildebrandt (Schloss Belvedere, Vienna; reconstruction of Schloss Mirabell, Salzburg; Church of the Piarist Order, Vienna; the courtyard of Schloss Halbturn east of Neusiedler See), Johann Bernhard Fischer von Erlach and his son Joseph Emanuel (St. Charles's Church, National Library, Bohemian Court Chancellery, Winter Palace of Prince Eugene and the plague column on Graben, all in Vienna; the Collegiate Church in Salzburg), Jakob Prandtauer (Stift Melk) Joseph Munggenast (Stiftskirche Dürnstein – the abbey church) and Carlo Antonio Carlone (St Florian; fish ponds of Stift Kremsmünster).

Baroque architects

The building activity of the Baroque period was accompanied by a flowering sculpture and painting. Among the most remarkable sculptors were Matthias Steinl or Steindl, Meinrad Guggenbichler,

Painting and sculpture

Impressions of Schloss Halbturn: charming groups of flowers in the »Triumph of Light«, a ceiling fresco by Franz Anton Maulpertsch

Balthasar Permoser (*The Apotheosis of Prince Eugene*, Baroque Museum in the Unteres Belvedere, Vienna), Balthasar Moll (Sarcophagus of Maria Theresia and Franz I in the imperial crypt, Vienna), Georg Raphael Donner (fountain at Neuer Markt, Vienna; *Pietà*, Cathedral of Gurk) and Franz Xaver Messerschmidt (grotesque sculptures in the Historical Museum of Vienna). The most important Baroque painters, who created above all altar wings and large fresco cycles, were Johann Michael Rottmayr, Daniel Gran, Bartolomeo Altomonte, Paul Troger, Martin Johann Schmidt (called »Kremser Schmidt«) and Franz Anton Maulpertsch. Some of these artists worked during the second half of the 18th century, a time viewed in art history as already belonging to the Rococo period.

Rococo   Since the dynamism of the high and late Baroque period persisted beyond the mid-18th century in Austria, only to come to a somewhat sudden end, the Rococo period was less developed here. Examples of the style are the Cistercian monastery of Stift Wilhering; the Trappist monastery in Engelhartszell; Wilten basilica, Tyrol; and the interior decoration of Schloss Schönbrunn, Vienna.

Transitional period   The Napoleonic Wars that followed on from the French Revolution meant a new shift of energy and considerable sums of money towards the upkeep of armies, so that it was only after the Congress of Vienna (1814–15) that more attention was once again paid to the arts. To protect the imperial regalia from advancing French troops, Franz II had taken the precaution of transferring them from Nuremberg to Vienna, where they are to be seen in the Schatzkammer (Treasury) of the Hofburg today.

Classicism and Biedermeier

Painting   While Heinrich Friedrich Füger and Johann Peter Krafft painted in the classical style, East Prussian artists Ludwig Ferdinand Schnorr von Carolsfeld and Joseph von Führich, who worked in Vienna and whose pictures reveal the influence of the Nazarenes, were associated with Romanticism. Like Führich, Moritz von Schwind and Leopold Kupelwieser introduced Romantic characteristics into the later Historicism of Vienna's so-called Ringstrassen era. However the actual painting of the Biedermeier era was, in terms of its themes, determined by the milieu of the middle class. Worthy of note here are Moritz Michael Daffinger, Friedrich von Amerling and Peter Fendi. Ferdinand Waldmüller is an exception: his portraits and landscapes can hardly be assigned to any specific art genre.

Architecture   International-style classicism is represented only sparsely in Austria. The principal works are the Gloriette in the park of Schloss Schönbrunn by Ferdinand von Hohenberg (1775), the tomb of Archduchess Marie Christine in the Augustinerkirche (St. Augustine's

Church) in Vienna by Antonio Canova (1805) and the Äussere Burgtor (outer castle tower) in Vienna by Peter von Nobile (1824). The genre was soon replaced by the Austrian Biedermeier style, which focussed more on the private sphere. The most important architect of this period was Josef Kornhäusel (Stadtensemble, Baden bei Wien; Husarentempel in Föhrenberge Nature Park, Mödling).

Historicism

Historicism, which denotes a movement in which historical styles were again taken up, carried a negative connotation for a long time. **Development**

The representatives of the Neo-Romanesque, Neo-Gothic and Neo-Baroque styles were criticized as being incapable of creating new, original work. According to newer findings, however, recourse to past eras is not just a phenomenon of the second half of the 19th century but was already being practised earlier, although not with the same intensity.

The outstanding **painters** of Historicism included Emil Jacob Schindler, August von Pettenkofen and Hans Makart, who developed his Neo-Baroque »Makart style«. Anton Romako, in whose works naturalistic and expressionistic elements are discernible, was already committed to a new era.

With the expansion of the city of Vienna, begun in 1859, the construction of Ringstrasse offered a unique opportunity to give permanence to the idea of Historicism in the form of

Magnificent entry into the Burgtheater beneath the frescoes of Klimt and Matsch

a generously proportioned overall design. The leading **Ringstrasse architects** were Theophil von Hansen (Academy of Fine Arts, parliament, stock exchange), Heinrich von Ferstel (Museum of Applied Art, Votivkirche, university), Friedrich Schmidt (city hall), August Siccard von Siccardsburg and Eduard van der Nüll (opera house), Gottfried Semper and Carl von Hasenauer (Burgtheater, Neue Hofburg, museums on Maria-Theresien-Platz).

Late 19th Century and 20th Century

The turning point of art at the beginning of the 20th century became evident in the paintings and designs for frescoes by the artist Gustav **Vienna Secession**

Hrdlickas monument against war and fascism in Vienna

Klimt (► Famous People), who succeeded in making a connection between the Romantic affinity to nature and symbolic abstract ornamentation. In 1897 the »Vienna Secession«, committed to Art Nouveau, was founded; alongside **Klimt, its principal representative**, the painter and craftsman Koloman Moser, the architect Joseph Maria Olbrich (Secession Building in Vienna, 1897–98) and the set designer Alfred Roller were prominent members of this association of artists. Linked to Art Nouveau, craftwork also developed vigorously, which was manifested in the founding of the Wiener Werkstätte by architect Josef Hoffmann. From 1903 well-known artists worked here with craftsmen on the manufacture of craft products (glass, porcelain, leather, jewellery and textiles). In 1910 the Secession caused a sensation with the exhibition *The Art of the Woman*, which for the first time offered an overview of the artistic creations of women from the 16th to the beginning of the 20th century with works of famous woman artists such as Tina Blau, Marie Egner, Angelika Kauffmann, Olga Wiesinger-Florian, Käthe Kollwitz and Berthe Morisot. The exhibition was organized by the Austrian Association of Women Artists, founded in 1910. Well-known architects of this period, alongside Olbrich and Hoffmann, were Adolf Loos, whose epoch-making building on Vienna's Michaelerplatz caused a scandal in 1910, and Otto Wagner, founder of the »Vienna School«, who was responsible for Vienna's Stadtbahn train stations and built the Post Office Savings Bank building in 1904–06.

Expressionism Outside the Secession the Tyrolese Albin Egger-Lienz, an Expressionist of monumental and severe vitality, became well known. Egon Schiele, with his intense portrayals of people and delicate depictions of nature, was a leading representative of early Expressionism. Along with Oskar Kokoschka, Alfred Kubin, a master of gloomy dream worlds, should also be mentioned.

Between the wars During the interwar period only a few important fine artists are to be found, among them the painters Ingeborg Spann-Cramer and Herbert Boeckl, the sculptors Anton Hanak and Fritz Wotruba, who with his archaic use of forms became a classic artist of modern sculpture, as well as the architects Clemens Holzmeister, Karl Ehn and Lois Welzenbacher.

The so-called Nötsch Circle (Nötscher Kreis) is worthy of mention. **Nötsch Circle**
Bound to no particular agenda, the group of artists centred around
Anton Kolig, Sebastian Isepp, Franz Wiegele and Anton Mahringer
formed a connection between Austrian Expressionism and Viennese
Symbolism and the French artists' group »Les Nabis« and Cézanne.

Soon after the Second World War the painter and writer Albert Paris **Vienna School of**
Gütersloh inspired the »Wiener Schule des phantastischen Realis- **Fantastic Realism**
mus« with lasting effect. This **specifically Austrian art movement** is
close to Surrealism. Its most important representatives were Erich
(Arik) Brauer, Rudolf Hausner, Wolfgang Hutter, Anton Lehmden
and Ernst Fuchs.

Praised and criticized in equal measure, Austrian artist **Friedensreich** **Modern**
Hundertwasser (► Baedeker Special p.535), who died in 2000, is **architecture**
hardly categorizable. He became known not only for his pictures but
also for his highly original style of architecture. It is easy to recognize
the works of the architect and town planner Boris Podrecca, who
drew attention to himself through both his life-enhancing design
work on inner city squares and his contributions to Vienna's Millennium Tower. In addition, the Coop Himmelb(l)au company (Gasometer B, Vienna), Gustav Peichl, Rudolf Weber (Millennium Tower,
Vienna), Hans Hollein (Haas-Haus, Vienna) and Wilhelm Holzbauer
(Studienhaus St Virgil, Salzburg-Aigen) are among the Austrian architects best known internationally.

The painters Arnulf Rainer and Maria Lassnig, the sculptor and **Contemporary**
graphic artist Alfred Hrdlicka, the sculptors Annemarie and Joannis **art**
Avramidis and Rudolf Hoflehner were important artists in Austria
and beyond after 1950. Artists such as Hermann Nitsch, Günter Brus
and Walter Pichler number among the circle of Viennese Actionism,
while Friedrich Achleitner, Gerhard Rühm, H. C. Artmann and Konrad Bayer belong to the Vienna Group. More recent ideas are represented by Valie Export, Peter Kubelka and Peter Weibel. Marie Luise
Lebschik, Siegfried Anzinger, Martha Jungwirth, Gunther Damisch,
Otto Zitko, Lore Heuermann, Birgit Jürgenssen, Herbert Brandl and
Friederike Pezold also enjoy international renown. Ines Doujak and
Branko Lenart stand for photo art, while Elke Krystufek and Walter
Obholzer, along with many others, produce installations, performances and object art.
The contemporary Austrian art scene is not only extraordinarily
lively and diverse; it also owes its international reputation to the way
in which the means of artistic expression that have been handed
down from previous generations are expanded upon with vigour and
esprit. The Gelatin group's extensive multimedia installation in the
Austrian Pavilion at the Venice Biennale in 2002 provided an example of this.

Famous People

The great and the good of Austria are found in every area of public life. It is not only the heroes of winter sports who bring home international accolades – Austria's lasting fame all over the world as a cultural nation is also justified by its intellectual, political and social greats.

Prince Eugene (1663–1736)

Prussian ruler Frederick the Great wrote this about Prince Eugene: »... he governed not only the Austrian territories, but also the empire. Actually he was emperor ...«. Because of Prince Eugene of Savoy-Carignan's diminutive stature and his plain appearance, Louis XIV refused him admission to the French army. The Sun King advised Eugene, who had grown up in his court, to enter the clergy. Eugene however preferred to go to Vienna to the imperial court, where he joined the Habsburg army and soon had the opportunity to distinguish himself in battle against the Turks, who had laid siege to Vienna. He rapidly built a career in Austria. In the service of three Habsburg emperors – Leopold I and his sons Joseph I and Karl VI – Eugene rose from a simple officer to the rank of field marshal, eventually being named President of the Imperial War Council and imperial marshal. He is reported to have once said about the three monarchs: »Emperor Leopold was my father, Joseph my brother, Karl my lord.« Eugene sealed his reputation as field marshal with his **decisive victory over the Turks** near Zenta in 1697, which brought Austria the whole of Hungary, Transylvania, Croatia and Slovenia. His successes against the Turks, crowned in 1717 with the conquest of Belgrade, ensured that he would live on in folk songs as »Prince Eugene, the noble knight«. Eugene was however not only the greatest military genius of his time, but also the leading statesman of the Habsburg Empire, taking a decisive role in almost all the peace negotiations of the time. In addition he was a great supporter and patron of the arts and sciences, and Vienna owes many exquisite buildings to him.

Military commander and statesman

Empress Elisabeth (1837–98)

▶Baedeker Special p.301

Sigmund Freud (1856–1939)

Though many of his theories are now considered out-dated or have meanwhile been proven wrong, modern psychology is unimaginable without Sigmund Freud. The Viennese neurologist and lecturer in neuropathology is considered to be the discoverer of the unconscious and the **founder of psychoanalysis**. Freud saw psychological events as being steered by drives and desires: these urges, especially the sex drive, work at the unconscious level to seek gratification. Psychological disorders are rooted in suppressed traumatic experiences, above

Doctor and psychologist

← *Anyone who is anyone in the aristocracy is here: one of the many balls at the Wiener Hofburg*

all the suppression of events in early childhood, and the resulting faulty interaction of the three types of psychological energy that determine human experience: the »id« (unconscious) and the »ego«, the conscious part of the psyche that mediates between the demands of the id and those of the outside world, the »super-ego«. In order to

expose such pathogenic experiences he developed the process known as psychoanalysis, which made use of the interpretation of dreams and, more rarely, hypnosis. A number of terms in common use today, such as Oedipus complex, pleasure gain and death wish, were first coined by Freud.

Freud, who because of his Jewish descent had to emigrate to London in 1938, once voiced his opinion about psychoanalysis and Vienna. The accusation was being forcefully made that psychoanalysis, and especially the theory that neuroses could be traced back to sexual disorders, only could have arisen in such a sensuous and immoral city as Vienna, and reflected particularly Viennese attitudes. After dismissing this theory as nonsensical, Freud wrote: »The city of Vienna has however also done everything it can to disown its contribution to the development of psychoanalysis. In no other place is the hostile indifference of learned and erudite circles to the analyst so clearly perceptible as in Vienna.«

Heinrich Harrer (1912–2006)

Explorer The Carinthian Heinrich Harrer became famous as a sporting great in the Austrian skiing team during the 1936 Winter Olympic Games. But he created real headlines in his native country when in 1938 he and three colleagues were successful in their ascent of the dreaded **North Face of the Eiger**, the first time this had been achieved. Mountaineering was Harrer's great passion, and his most fervent wish was to take part in an expedition to the Himalayas. The Nazi propaganda machine was now happy to come to the aid of citizens of the »Greater German Reich«: in 1939 Harrer was surprisingly summoned to take part in the expedition to Nanga Parbat, one of the highest mountains in the Himalayas – he was only given four days to pack. With no consideration for his heavily pregnant wife he accepted the offer; he would only get to know his child twelve years later. Taken by surprise at the outbreak of the war, the members of the expedition were interned by the British in Kashmir. In 1944 Harrer, together with his mountaineering colleague and fellow countryman Peter Aufschnaiter, was able to escape from the camp over the Himalayan mountains into the mysterious forbidden city of Lhasa in Tibet, where a friendship grew between the Austrian refugee and the young ruler, the Dalai Lama. The young regent was hungry for knowledge: Harrer tutored him in English and geography and explained Western culture to him. But he was also schooled by his pupil, and learnt to see the world through the young Dalai Lama's eyes. After his return in 1951, the Carinthian explorer undertook expeditions to endangered peoples in the Amazon region, in the jungles of Suriname, central Africa, Borneo, and New Guinea, in the Andaman Islands and northern Canada. His book **Seven Years in Tibet** became the subject of a film in 1997, with Brad Pitt taking on the leading role. Harrer, however, was not able to attend the film premiere when the US authorities refused him entry after surprising revelations emerged that he had been a member of the SS – a fact until then concealed by Harrer. The famous mountaineer died at the age of 93 on 7 January 2006 in Friesach in Carinthia.

Andreas Hofer (1767–1810)

No other great freedom fighter of the Tyrolese rebellion against Napoleon and his Bavarian allies comes close to the **legendary Andreas Hofer**. By far the most famous figure in the history of the province, on the scale of fame even Emperor Maximilian I is relegated to second place by Hofer as far as the Tyrolese population is concerned.

Freedom fighter

The keeper of the Sandwirt inn from St Leonhard in the Passeiertal valley in South Tyrol led the Tyrolese in revolt against their Bavarian rulers, who wanted to wipe Tyrol off the map. In the Battle of Austerlitz of 1805 Napoleon had annihilated Austria, and in the subsequent peace treaty Tyrol was transferred from the Austrian crown to the new kingdom of Bavaria. The Bavarians raised taxes, deleted the name »Tyrol« from the map and embarked on a harsh anticlerical course – for the devout Tyrolese the worst thing of all – which along with the dissolution of monasteries and the transfer of priests even stipulated that Midnight Mass should be forbidden. In 1809 the Tyrolean people began the fight against the Bavarian occupying power. Four times Hofer led his warriors on the Bergisel against the French and the Bavarians in battle, three times emerging victorious. On 15 August 1809 Hofer, acclaimed by the people as the saviour of Tyrol, marched into the provincial capital Innsbruck and for two months was imperial high commander of Tyrol. When in the Treaty of Schönbrunn of 14 October Austria once again relinquished its western territory and Napoleon ordered the

Memorial to Andreas Hofer beneath the Bergisel Schanze near Innsbruck

return of Tyrol to Bavaria, Hofer's freedom fighters rebelled a fourth time against the usurpers. On 3 November 1809 they were defeated by Napoleon's soldiers on the Bergisel. Hofer managed to flee over the Brenner Pass, but was betrayed to the French by a former companion in arms and brought to Mantua in chains. Napoleon wanted Hofer's head at any price. Even Viceroy Beauharnais, Napoleon's stepson, came out in support of the rebel leader, and the citizens of Mantua collected 5000 silver thalers in ransom money for him, but to no avail. On 20 February 1810 the freedom fighter faced a firing squad. The French sergeant in charge of the shooting was so emotional that he could not give the command to fire, and it was Hofer himself who gave the order. His myth will probably inspire Tyrol for all time.

Friedensreich Hundertwasser (1928–2000)

▶Baedeker Special p.535

Elfriede Jelinek (born 1946)

Controversial writer Elfriede Jelinek, born in Mürzzuschlag in Styria, began to study organ, recorder and, later, composition at the Vienna Conservatory while still a schoolgirl in 1960. Before 1945 her father, Friedrich Jelinek, worked as a chemist in a field that contributed to the war effort and in this way to some extent avoided anti-Semitic persecution. Friedrich's mental illness became apparent in the early fifties. In 1964 Elfriede Jelinek began the study of art history and theatre studies at Vienna University, but after some semesters gave up the courses due to her critical mental state. She spent 1968 in absolute isolation, for a whole year never leaving her parents' house, and it was during this time that she began to write her first poems. Her father died in 1969 in a psychiatric clinic. After 1969 Elfriede Jelinek became involved in the student movement and in the literary discussions in the magazine *manuskripte*. In 1971 she was »very successful« in her final examinations as an organ player at the Vienna Conservatory, and wrote her first radio plays. Since 1974 she has been married to Gottfried Hüngsberg, who was associated with Rainer Werner Fassbinder's circle in the sixties. In 1974 Jelinek joined the Communist Party of Austria. More radio plays and translations followed. In 1982 the screenplay *Die Ausgesperrten* (based on the 1980 novel whose English title is *Wonderful, Wonderful Times*) was made into a film. The first big scandal around Jelinek was caused in 1983 by the premiere of *Burgtheater*, a drama that tackles the inadequacy of the process of coming to terms with Austria's Nazi past. Essays on poetry and further translations followed, then a collaboration with the composer Patricia Jünger (*The Piano Player*, 1988). In 1990 Jelinek wrote the screenplay *Malina* with Werner Schroeter, based on a novel by Ingeborg Bachmann. In 1991 she withdrew from the Communist

Party (KPÖ) together with the two party leaders Susanne Sohn and Walter Silbermayer. **In 2004 she was awarded the Nobel Prize for Literature** for her »musical flow of voices and counter-voices in novels and plays that, with extraordinary linguistic zeal, reveal the absurdity of society's clichés and their subjugating power«.

Elfriede Jelinek, whose work attacks against abuses in the public, political and the private life of Austrian society, employs a sarcastic, provocative style. For years controversy has raged between those who, because of her writings and her publicly proclaimed political views, are provoked into vituperative and aggressivie responses, and those who celebrate her as a true artist of the written word.

Gustav Klimt (1862–1918)

Painter

»I can paint and draw. I have never painted a self-portrait. I am less interested in myself as a subject for a painting than I am in other people, above all women. But other subjects interest me even more. I am convinced that I am not particularly interesting as a person. There is nothing special about me. I am a painter who paints day after day from morning until night. Figures and landscapes, portraits less often.« These words are attributed to painter and graphic artist Gustav Klimt, the **pioneer of modern painting in Austria and main representative of Viennese Art Nouveau**, when he was in the second phase of his work as an artist. In his early creative years Klimt was still strongly committed to the academic classical tradition. He gradually moved away from this traditional approach and in 1897, with painters Joseph Maria Olbrich and Josef Hoffmann, he founded the **Vienna Secession**, which consciously turned away from the paintings of Historicism. Shortly afterwards Klimt developed his own typical style. Elongated bodies, growing out of mosaic-like two-dimensional geometric patterns that cover the whole picture, now dominated his paintings. The masterful drawings and softly coloured paintings, whose decorative effect was often enhanced by the use of gold paint, showed multiple nudes and portraits of women. Women were now the focus of Klimt's art, and his portraits of women ranged from historical images to allegorical and mythological figures and on to erotic and classical subjects (*Judith I*, 1910; *Portrait of Adele Bloch-Bauer I*, 1907; *The Kiss*, 1907–08). There is much speculation about the rela-

tionship Klimt, who became one of the most sought-after portraitists of ladies of distinguished Vienna society, may have had with the women he painted. While his family attempted to preserve the image of a family man, in the meantime it is recognized that the painter acted with less restraint than that image suggests. An intimate friendship with the well-known Viennese fashion designer Emilie Flöge lasted until his death – and according to some sources the famous painting *The Kiss* portrays Klimt and Emilie. He had various affairs with ladies of high society, at least three illegitimate children, and preferred black- or red-haired women. Be that as it may, he paid his models a handsome fee.

Franz Lehár (1870–1948)

Composer Two great men gave him the most important advice of his life: when, during violin lessons at the Prague Conservatory, Franz Lehár composed one sonatina in D minor and one in F major, Anton Dvořák and Johannes Brahms advised him to devote himself to composing. The musician from Komorn in Hungary was happy to take this good advice. He achieved his breakthrough with the operetta ***The Merry Widow*** (1905), which became an international success and allowed Lehár access to high society. The fact that as of 1906 he liked to spend the summer in Bad Ischl, where Emperor Franz Josef I and Austria's nobility enjoyed their annual summer holidays, is sure to have contributed to his integration into these circles. With melancholy »Slavic« melodies, simple dance tunes, and operettas such as *Paganini* (1925) and *The Land of Smiles* (1930) the composer conquered not only the stages of the world but also the hearts of many an audience. However he faced a problematic situation when Austria was annexed to Nazi-Germany in 1938: although Adolf Hitler was one of his declared admirers, Lehár's wife was of Jewish descent. Lehár declined all offers from abroad and categorically refused to give up his comfortable accommodation in Vienna and Bad Ischl. Thanks to his prominence, he felt sufficiently safe. Indeed he was lucky, and his family were spared the horrors of the Holocaust. Shortly before his death in 1948 Lehár bequeathed his villa in Bad Ischl to the municipal authorities on the condition that it be remodelled as a museum dedicated to himself.

Maria Theresia (1717–80)

Sovereign When Emperor Karl VI died in 1740, the Habsburg Empire was plunged into a deep crisis. Because the emperor had several daughters but no sons, no male successor was available to ascend the throne. Instead, his oldest daughter Maria Theresia became ruler, as determined by the so-called Pragmatic Sanction. Only a few European powers recognized this succession law. The Prussian King Friedrich II wasn't alone in wanting to make short work of the »skirt on the Viennese throne«; almost all the Habsburgs' neighbours scented a chance to attack the young ruler, who took office at the age of 23. However, she taught the greedy powers lesson, governing the empire with a steady hand and soon earning the respect of her enemies, who joked that the ruler in Vienna was the only man that the House of Habsburg had ever produced. Thanks to her, the Habsburg Empire, which stretched from the coast of the English Channel to the Carpathian mountains, emerged from the prolonged War of the Austrian Succession (1740–48) without suffering great loss of territory. Only Silesia was ceded to Friedrich II of Prussia in the two Silesian Wars.

Maria Theresia also performed remarkably well at home. She introduced **comprehensive state reform**, whose measures included the formulation of a new penal code, the regulation of the educational system, the abolition of torture and the alleviation of serfdom. The Austrian people love their ruler, and Maria Theresia went down in history as »Kaiserin« or empress, an office she in fact never held. Actually she was only Archduchess of Austria, as well as Queen of Hungary and Bohemia. She owed her honorary title of empress to her husband, Holy Roman Emperor Franz I, who she loved very much – rather the exception in the dynasties of the time – and with whom, in spite of his numerous extra-marital affairs, she had 16 children (»One cannot have enough of them«, she was in the habit of saying). When she died in 1780, Friedrich II wrote: »I regretted to hear of the death of the empress-queen: she did credit to her throne and her lineage. I may have fought wars against her, but I was never her enemy.«

Maximilian I (1459–1519)

Emperor

Emperor Maximilian I went down in history as **»the last knight«**. He was the last emperor to lead his troops onto the battlefield; he was shot off his horse in the tumult of battle. He loved old-style jousting tournaments with all his heart. But Maximilian also had an eye for new developments, and was in many ways more modern than some of his contemporary rulers. His special liking for tournaments originated from his period in Burgundy (1477–82), when he was married to Europe's most sought-after heiress, Mary of Burgundy. Burgundian knightly tales also had a great influence on him, which was given expression in the autobiographical novels *Theuerdank* (*The Knight of Adventurous Thoughts*), *Freydal* (*Free Spirit*) and *Weisskunig* (*White King*) which he commissioned. However Maximilian, »the last knight«, recognized that in his time there was no longer a place for romantic knighthood, and other means would be necessary to hold his own. As a consequence he called for modern techniques of warfare, namely the new but very powerful infantry of lansquenet mercenaries and artillery to support the soldiers, who were armed with rifles and long spears. The necessary funding for his campaigns and his diplomatic manoeuvres came from the large silver and copper mines of the province of Tyrol, of which he had been elected prince in 1490. He surrounded himself with painters, poets and musicians, erected buildings of high artistic merit and supported the sciences, which in humanist circles earned him a reputation as a **Renaissance prince**. Moreover Maximilian, who was very popular with the Tyrolese people thanks to his passion for hunting and his affable nature, understood very well how to gain excellent publicity: he made use of the new art of printing and distributed leaflets to the people announcing victories or ridiculing enemies. When Maximilian wanted to claim the imperial crown, but hostile Venice blocked the way to Rome and the Pope, he without further ado proclaimed himself emperor in 1508 in the Cathedral of Trent – an event that put an end to imperial coronations in Rome for ever. He set new trends by broadening the sphere in which Habsburg politics operated, entering into alliances with England and the Spanish realms against France, with whom he feuded over Italy for years. After his death, Maximilian left behind a dynasty that governed a huge empire (Austria, Spain, Burgundy), aspired to inherit Bohemia and Hungary, and had risen to be a great European power.

Prince Metternich (1773–1859)

Statesman

He was the very image of a late 18th-century aristocrat: good-looking, elegant, skilled in rhetoric, self-confident and immensely vain. Intellectually, too, Klemens Lothar Wenzel Metternich was still very attached to the 18th century. He believed firmly in the monarchical and aristocratic order – the French Revolution, parliamentarianism and equal rights for citizens were an abomination to him, especially after his family, which was descended from Rhenish nobility, was driven out of his birthplace, Koblenz, by French troops. In Vienna, his new home, his unstoppable rise to becoming a statesman began. First he was imperial ambassador in Dresden, Berlin and Paris, then in 1809 he took over the Austrian foreign office, and in 1813 he was made a prince. The high point of his career as a statesman was the **Congress of Vienna** of 1814–15, which under his leadership was charged with untangling the chaos in Europe after the fall of Napoleon. In so doing Metternich was able to restore the pre-revolutionary political order in Europe and became the central figure of the European restoration. With regard to foreign affairs he attempted to create a balance of the great powers, while at home he established a restoration-style absolutist government, founded on police-state methods. At this time he was truly the lord and master of events in Europe, and no-one – least of all the prince himself – harboured doubts that his political system would remain in place for a long time to come. However in March 1848 revolution broke out in Vienna. A hated representative of reactionary thinking, Metternich was forced to flee from Austria. After spending some years in Great Britain and Belgium, in 1851 at the age of 78 he returned to Vienna, where he remained until his death in 1859.

Wolfgang Amadeus Mozart (1756–91)

▶Baedeker Special, p.430

Max Reinhardt (1873–1943)

Max Reinhardt is one of the **most important figures in the entire**   Theatre director
history of the theatre. Born Max Goldmann in Baden bei Wien to a Jewish family, he changed his name to Reinhardt in 1904, not least because of the pervading anti-Semitism of the time. He began his career on the stage. In 1893 he was an actor in Salzburg, and from 1894 to 1903 performed in the Deutsches Theater in Berlin. In 1905 he made his triumphant breakthrough as director with his first production of Shakespeare's *A Midsummer Night's Dream*. In the same year he took charge of the Deutsches Theater, which with short breaks he headed in the role of director until 1933. Together with Hugo von Hofmannsthal and Richard Strauss he initiated the **Salzburg Festival** of 1920, which he led until 1937. In 1929 he founded the Max Reinhardt Seminar in Vienna, a directing and drama school. In 1933 the Nazis offered him the so-called »Ehrenarierschaft«, an »honorary membership« of the Aryan race that disregarded Jewish descent. Outraged, Reinhardt declined. Instead he emigrated to Austria, and finally in 1937 to the USA. He died on 31 October 1943 in New York after a stroke.

Max Reinhardt is considered the founder of the modern director's theatre. He made use of what at that time was the latest stage technology (revolving stage, cyclorama, lighting techniques). He attempted to provide every play with its own location and constantly looked for new stage sets and environments for performances (gardens, palaces, churches). Intensive collaboration with the actors was extraordinarily important to him, and he paid particular attention to teaching the up-and-coming generation. Besides putting on contemporary pieces, Reinhardt also focussed on the reworking of classic dramas. The highest principle for him was to follow to the greatest possible extent the literary model provided by the author. His productions served one purpose only – aesthetic enjoyment; he conscientiously avoided imparting any ideological, social or literary message. Literature and acting, painting and technology, music and dance were components of equal worth to be united – this was Reinhardt's idea of theatre as an event to be celebrated.

Romy Schneider (1938–82)

Actress The actress Romy Schneider, born in Vienna, was one of the few stars to emerge from the German-speaking countries after the Second World War who enjoyed international recognition, even if her German-Austrian fan base had a different image of her than did her admirers in France. For the majority of Germans and Austrians she would remain »Sissi« till her dying day, a woman who moved to Paris to become a vamp and was severely punished by life for her folly. They were not willing to forgive the actress who had conquered many a heart in three films about Austria's Empress Elisabeth (»Sissi«, ▶ Baedeker Special p.301) for leaving the country of her birth to rid herself of her »sweet girl« image. In France on the other hand she was seen as a woman who was emancipated and yet could still love a man. Romy Schneider herself suffered in her lifetime from

the »Sissi image« (»the sweet pudding that people stuck on me«). The second and third Sissi films were made under protest due to pressure from her mother, who also played the role of the mother in the Sissi films, and her stepfather. When a fourth part was planned, she finally categorically refused. This did not harm her career in the slightest. On the contrary, in about 60 films, including *The Trial* (*Der Prozess*) and *The Assassination of Trotsky* (*Das Mädchen and der Mörder*), the pretty Austrian actress often had great success, especially in France, her new home. In her private life however she experienced one catastrophe after the other. Her »pretty mummy« and her »smart daddy«, as Romy lovingly called her parents, actress Magda Schneider and actor Wolf Albach-Retty, had had no time for their little girl and were divorced when Romy was seven years old. Schneider's engagement to the French film star Alain Delon did not last long, and her marriage to the actor and director Harry Meyen was just as short lived – Meyen committed suicide after the divorce. A marriage to Daniel Biasini broke up after a short time. But the hardest thing of all for Schneider to bear was the loss of her 14-year-old son, who was killed in a tragic accident in 1981. »Romy Schneider has killed herself«, read the headlines of the tabloid press on 29 May 1982 – though heart failure was on the death certificate. All her life, Romy was hounded by inferiority complexes and deep depressions; fasting cures, pills and alcohol had taken their toll. When she died at the age of 43 in Paris, she was completely destitute. »In a certain sense«, said biographer Curt Riess, »Romy really did commit suicide. She didn't want to go on.«

Arnold Schoenberg (1874–1951)

Composer

He smoked 60 cigarettes a day and drank three litres of black coffee, with plenty of liqueur on the side. Plagued by fears of not earning enough to support his family, the Viennese composer Arnold Schoenberg nevertheless wilfully trod new, original paths. It was extremely difficult for him to gain recognition for **atonal twelve tone music**, the technique of composition he developed that made use of a set of twelve tones related only to each other. Nevertheless, such pupils as Anton von Webern and Alban Berg gathered around the great master, who due to his Jewish descent had to give up his teaching post at the Academy of the Arts in Berlin in 1933 and emigrate to the USA. Arnold Schoenberg also came to the fore as a painter. His portraits and pictures earned praise from Oskar Kokoschka and Vassily Kandinsky, but the works were too unusual for most. »Only a very small number of people believe in these pictures«, said one critic. »Most instinctively hate them at first sight.« Schoenberg made a name for himself solely in the field of music: with his oeuvre including the opera *Moses and Aaron* and the oratorio *A Survivor from Warsaw*, he is considered to be the boldest and most versatile composer of his time. Nevertheless in his seventies he frankly confessed: »I am aware of the fact that full understanding of my works cannot be expected for some decades to come.«

Johann Strauss II (1825–99)

Composer

While it is true that Johann Strauss senior (1804–49), the composer of waltzes and the founder of the Strauss dynasty, named his oldest son Johann, he was absolutely determined the boy would not become a musician. Did the old master fear competition from his own family, had he perhaps instinctively caught on to the musical talent of his oldest child? At any rate the boy caused surprise by composing a waltz at the age of six. As his father wished, Strauss the Younger completed his grammar school education and began training as a bank clerk, but behind his father's back – with support from his mother – he took violin lessons and composed. In 1844 he founded his own orchestra, performing with them for the first time in the same year and playing pieces by his father alongside his own works. The conflict between father and son did not remain hidden from the people of Vienna, and it was rumoured that Strauss the Elder bribed landlords and restaurant proprietors not to allow his son to play concerts. In any case the first concert by Johann Strauss II was a magnificent success – Strauss senior no longer reigned supreme in the world of the Vienna waltz. After the death of his father Johann Strauss undertook long concert tours, which also led to Russia. In 1863 he was appointed conductor of the Vienna Court Ball. He is said to have had great fear of illness, one newspaper once describing him as a hypochondriac, and he was also afraid of failure, poverty and death. Perhaps it was the fear of becoming poor again, along with the mercilessly demanding Viennese music industry, that pushed him to work constantly: day and night, as the story goes. His life's work amounts to almost 300 works, among them 169 waltzes and 16 operettas. His masterpieces *Die Fledermaus* (*The Bat*; 1874) and *Der Zigeunerbaron* (*The Gypsy Baron*; 1885), with which the classic form of Viennese operetta was founded, enjoyed the greatest popularity. The waltz **The Blue Danube** (*An der schönen blauen Donau*; 1867) brought not only world fame but also the envy of Johannes Brahms: »Unfortunately, not by Johannes Brahms«, he is said to have written on a fan offered to him for an autograph by Strauss's wife. In 1890, when Strauss was 65 years old, a survey stated that he was one of the three most popular people in the world, after Queen Victoria and Bismarck. While it is true that the father is still today considered the inventor of the Vienna waltz, the Viennese view the son as their true **»king of the waltz«**.

Bertha von Suttner (1843–1914)

Pacificist She was the daughter of a lieutenant, hated war and fought hard against it. For her courageous advocacy for peace and international understanding and because of her intrepid struggle against the militarization of politics, the lunacy of the arms policies of the great powers, warlike governments and arms lobbyists, Bertha von Suttner was derisively referred to as »Friedensbertha« (»peace Bertha«), »Friedensfurie« (»the peace harridan«), or »Rote Bertha« (»red Bertha«). Her weapon of choice was the written word, having inherited a talent for writing probably from her mother, who had been born into the family of German poet and soldier Theodor Körner. She send out her rousing writings in support of the preservation of world peace from Schloss Harmannsdorf in Lower Austria, where she lived with her husband, the writer and baron Arthur Gundaccar von Suttner. It was in the palace too that she wrote *Die Waffen nieder!* (*Lay Down Your Arms*), her most famous and successful novel. Only one thousand copies were initially printed by a hesitant publisher in 1889, but within 15 years more than 30 new editions had been brought out. In order to gain publicity for the idea of peace and active participation, she founded the »Verein der Friedensfreunde« in Vienna in 1891. This peace society undertook lecture tours and made contact with many prominent writers and politicians, including August Bebel and Wilhelm Liebknecht. She also contacted the Swedish industrialist and inventor of dynamite Alfred Nobel and inspired him to set up and fund the **Nobel Peace Prize, which Bertha herself received in 1905**. However Europe did not disarm. On the contrary in spite of the growing popularity of pacifist movements the sabre-rattling only increased. In the end Bertha von Suttner was even abandoned by the Social Democrats, on whose desire for peace she had counted, but who in 1914 endorsed militaristic government policy.

When she died on 21 June 1914, she was at least spared what would have been the most dreadful disappointment of her life, namely the mass slaughter that she had always feared in war-torn Europe. A week after her death came the fateful shots in Sarajevo that were to trigger the First World War.

Stefan Zweig (1881–1942)

Stefan Zweig, son of an industrialist, was never seriously threatened **Author** by material want and supported some of his writer colleagues. But not all of his fellow authors liked him. Hugo von Hofmannsthal, also not exactly from a poor family background, avoided his Viennese professional colleague and best-selling author and mocked him for his wealth. During the First World War Stefan Zweig worked in the

Austrian military press headquarters, and in 1917 moved to Switzerland, where he denounced the killing. Afterwards he lived mostly in Salzburg, where he spent the most productive literary years of his life. He worked on his biographical principal work *Die Baumeister der Welt* (translated as *Master Builders*), wrote the novel *Ungeduld des Herzens* (*Beware of Pity*), numerous novellas mostly about emotional entanglements and underlying passions (collected in the volume *Verwirrung der Gefühle* (*Confusion of Feelings*), as well as dramas, stories and essays. Stefan Zweig, a Jew, left Austria in 1934 due to the spread of anti-Semitic tendencies in the country (»better a year too early than a day too late!«). In Petrópolis in Brazil, his final land of exile, suffering from depression or, as is often claimed, in despair over the destruction of his spiritual home of Europe, he and his second wife Lotte took their own lives on 23 February 1942.

A special feature of Zweig's style of telling a story is the psychological characterization of his protagonists. In biographical essays on Balzac, Kleist and Hölderlin, and biographical novels on Mary, Queen of Scots and Marie Antoinette, he painted psychological portraits and interpreted decisive historical events. His autobiographical work *Die Welt von gestern* (*The World of Yesterday*; 1942), written in a highly pressured situation and bearing the subtitle *Memoirs of a European*, imparts an impression of spiritual life in the first half of the 20th century. »It is actually not so much my own fate that I relate,« wrote Zweig in the preface to his memoirs, »but that of a generation.«

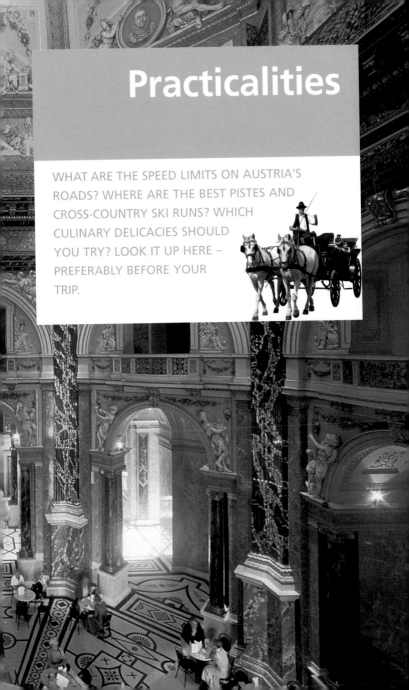

Practicalities

WHAT ARE THE SPEED LIMITS ON AUSTRIA'S ROADS? WHERE ARE THE BEST PISTES AND CROSS-COUNTRY SKI RUNS? WHICH CULINARY DELICACIES SHOULD YOU TRY? LOOK IT UP HERE – PREFERABLY BEFORE YOUR TRIP.

Accommodation

Camping and Caravanning

Nice camp sites Camping is very widespread in Austria. The country boasts numerous, often very well-located camp sites, not only in the mountains, especially in the high valleys rich in alpine meadowland and on the tops of the passes, but also along the shores of the warm lakes of Carinthia and the Salzkammergut as well as on the banks of the Danube and in other regions. As a rule the sites are equipped with **every modern convenience**. Members of camping clubs frequently receive a discount.

Wild camping Camp sites aside, it is permitted to spend one night only at motorway rest areas, but gaining permission to stay in other public spaces is rare. Wild camping is forbidden in Vienna, Tyrol and all conservation areas, especially in the vicinity of lakes.

Road closed Drivers should be aware that some sections of road are closed to vehicles towing caravans. For more information on this subject contact an automobile club (▶Emergency).

Camping in winter Winter camping has been gaining importance rapidly in Austria. As the demand for suitably equipped camp sites by far exceeds supply, book a pitch for your tent early.

On farm holidays children can see the animals up close

Holidays on the Farm

Farm holidays are very popular in Austria. Guests have about 29,000 farms with 300,000 beds to choose from. The range includes especially child-friendly farms, organic farms, holiday farms and still others offering horse-riding or cycling. The addresses of landlords are available from town and regional tourist offices (►Information). »Urlaub am Bauernhof« (Farm Holidays) is an association of 3000 family farms spread throughout Austria; for further details see their website, www.farmholidays.com.

Hotels

Hotels in the larger Austrian towns and cities and in Austria's tourist centres offer comparable standards of comfort to those seen internationally. In the inns of medium-sized and smaller towns, too, visitors can in the main expect a good standard of accommodation and catering. The numerous guesthouses and private rooms available constitute an alternative source of comfortable accommodation offering quite good value for money.

International standards

During the summer months, the winter sports season and on national holidays, booking a room well in advance is highly recommended. Hotels and guesthouses in areas devoted to winter sports are often closed in summer.

> ### i Price categories
>
> - Luxury: from €130
> - Mid-range: €70–€130
> - Budget: up to €70
>   for double occupancy per night
>   without breakfast
> - Hotels and guesthouses ►Sights from A to Z

There are groupings of Austrian hotels that concentrate on special target groups, publishing their own catalogues and running websites. For details see Urlaub am Bauernhof (these pages), the Wellness section (►Sport and Outdoors) and the entry on Kinderhotels (►Children in Austria).

The Romantik Hotels & Restaurants Association aims to provide accommodation with an unmistakable historical ambience (Romantik Hotels & Restaurants International, Hahnstrasse 70, D-60528 Frankfurt/Main, tel. 0 69/66 12 34-0, fax 66 12 34-56, www.romantik hotels.com).

◄ »Romantik hotels«

Those who fancy a holiday in palatial surroundings and are willing to pay the price have plenty of opportunity to do so in the land of the former Dual Monarchy (Schlosshotels und Herrenhäuser, Moosstrasse 60, A-5020 Salzburg, tel. 06 62/83 06 81 41, fax 83 06 81 61, www.schlosshotels.co.at).

◄ Schloss hotels

Hotel registers for individual towns and holiday destinations are available from Österreich Werbung (►Information) or from each respective tourist office.

Note

IMPORTANT ADDRESSES

CAMPING · CARAVANNING

▶ **The Camping and Caravanning Club**
Greenfields House
Westwood Way
Coventry CV4 8JH
Tel. 0845 130 7701 (Carefree international booking service)
www.campingandcaravanning-club.co.uk

▶ **Österreichischer Campingclub (ÖCC)**
Schubertring 1–3
A-1010 Wien
Tel. 01/713 61 51
Fax 7 11 99 27 54

▶ **Camping- und Caravaning-Club Austria (CCA)**
Mariahilfer Strasse 180
A-1150 Wien
Tel. 01/89 12 12 22
Fax 89 12 12 74
www.cca-camping.at

FARM HOLIDAYS

▶ **Bundesverband Urlaub am Bauernhof (Farm Holidays)**
Gabelsbergerstrasse 19
A-5020 Salzburg
Tel. 06 62/88 02 02
Fax 88 02 02-3

▶ **www.farmholidays.com**
Comprehensive database with holiday farms and rural accommodation across the whole of Europe.

YOUTH HOSTEL ASSOCIATIONS

▶ **International Youth Hostel Federation (IYHF)**
Trevelyan House
Dimple Road, Matlock
Derbyshire, DE4 3YH
Tel. 0 16 29 / 59 26 00
Fax 59 27 02
www.yha.org.uk

▶ **Öst. Jugendherbergsverband**
Gonzagagasse 22
A-1010 Wien
Tel. 01/5 33 53 53
Fax 5 35 08 61
www.oejhv.or.at

▶ **Öst. Jugendherbergswerk**
Helferstorfer Strasse 4
A-1010 Wien
Tel. 01/5 33 18 33, fax 5 33 18 33 85
www.oejhw.or.at

▶ **Jugend- & Familiengästehäuser**
Idlhofgasse 74, A-8020 Graz
Tel. 03 16/70 83, fax 70 83-88
www.jgh.at

Youth Hostels

For young people in particular, but also for families, youth hostels (»Jugendherbergen« or »Jugendgästehäuser«) offer inexpensive overnight accommodation. Often located **in areas of scenic beauty**, they are open to anyone who is a member of the Youth Hostels Association. The maximum length of stay normally depends on occupancy. In the high season booking in advance is recommended.

Arrival · Before the Journey

How to Get There

By rail

Although there are good rail connections between the UK and Austria, the trip by train is a long one. The most direct routes are via either Brussels or Paris. For the former, take an afternoon Eurostar to Brussels and a high-speed connecting train on to Cologne, then the City Night Line overnight sleeper to Linz or Vienna, arriving the following morning. There is also a morning train from Cologne to Vienna (journey time 13 hours). Alternatively, board a Eurostar to Paris, and take one of the two daily trains from Gare de l'Est to Vienna (journey time 14 hours 45 minutes) or the City Night Line sleeper train from Paris to Munich with connections the next morning to Innsbruck, Salzburg, Graz, Klagenfurt and Vienna.

The direct high-speed trains from London (St Pancras International) to Paris (Gare du Nord) and to Brussels (Midi/Zuid) are operated by Eurostar and Rail Europe.

By car

Those willing to spend up to 24 hours behind the wheel may elect to drive from the UK to Austria. The quickest way across the English Channel is via the Channel Tunnel: passengers drive their cars onto the train, *Le Shuttle*, which covers the distance from Folkestone to Coquelles near Calais in 35 minutes. At peak times there are four trains every hour (tel.: 0870 535 3535; www.eurotunnel.com). Taking the ferry is sometimes cheaper; it takes 1 hour 30 minutes to make the crossing from Dover to Calais. It is 1310km/820mi from Calais to Vienna. Head towards Brussels, then continue via Cologne, Frankfurt and Nuremberg. Alternatively, take the A1 autobahn, one of the busiest roads between Germany and Austria, via Munich (466km/291mi from Vienna), Salzburg and Linz. While use of Belgian and German motorways is free, in Austria a toll is payable: a vignette may be purchased at border crossings and petrol stations (►Transport).

> ## *i* Distances
>
> - London – Salzburg 1029km/639mi
> - London – Vienna 1237km/769mi
> - London – Graz 1226km/762mi
> - Salzburg – Vienna 299km/186mi
> - Innsbruck – Vienna 482km/300mi

By bus or coach

Eurolines run coaches daily (departing at 8am) from London Victoria to Vienna. The journey time is 23 hours 15 minutes.

By air

Austrian airports are served by a wide variety of airlines. Vienna Schwechat (VIE) is the main hub for air traffic, but international flights also touch down in Graz, Innsbruck, Klagenfurt, Linz and Salzburg (►Transport). Carriers offering direct flights from London

IMPORTANT ADDRESSES

RAIL

► **Austrian Railways (ÖBB)**
Wagramer Strasse 17–19
A-1220 Wien
Tel. +43 1 93000-0, www.oebb.at

► **Eurostar**
St Pancras International
Pancras Road, London NW1 2QP
Tel. 08705 186 186
www.eurostar.com

► **Rail Europe Travel Centre**
178 Piccadilly
London W1V 0BA
Tel. 0870 8 37 13 71
www.raileurope.co.uk

MOTORAIL

► **Railsavers**
Tel. 01253 595555
www.railsavers.com

BUS

► **Blaguss-Reisen**
R.-Strauss-Str., A-321230 Wien
Tel. 00 43 (0)1/6 10 90
Fax 50 18 01 99, www.blaguss.at

► **Eurolines**
52 Grosvenor Gardens
Victoria, London SW1
Bookings online and in UK
through National Express
Tel. 0870 514 3219

www.eurolines.com and
www.nationalexpress.com

AIRLINES

► **Aer Lingus**
Tel. (IRL) 0818 365000
Tel. (UK) 0870 8765000
www.aerlingus.com

► **Austrian Airlines**
Tel. 020 7766 0300, www.aua.com

► **bmi**
Tel. 0870 6070 555
www.flybmi.com

► **British Airways**
Tel. 0844 493 0787
www.britishairways.com

► **Easyjet**
Tel. 0871 244 2366
www.easyjet.com

► **Flybe**
Tel. 0871 700 0535
www.flybe.com

► **Lufthansa**
Tel. 0871 945 9747
www.lufthansa.com

► **Swiss**
Tel. 0845 601 0956
www.swiss.com

Heathrow to Austria include Austrian Airlines, British Airways and bmi, while Swiss flies from London City Airport via Zurich or Basel, and Lufthansa from Heathrow to Vienna and other Austrian airports via Frankfurt, Stuttgart or Munich. Germanwings flies from London Stansted to Vienna via Cologne, and Air Berlin operates a service from Stansted to Vienna via either Düsseldorf or Berlin. Easyjet offers flights direct to the Austrian capital from London Luton. Flybe run a service to Salzburg from the airports in Exeter and Southampton, with flights every few days. Austrian Airlines and Aer Lingus both fly direct from Dublin to Vienna. Flights to Austria from the USA include the direct Austrian Airlines connections to Vienna from Washington DC and New York. Those flying from Canada usually have to change planes in the USA or one of the major European airports, though Austrian Airlines does provide a direct service to Vienna from both Montreal and Toronto. Austrian Airlines also offers direct flights to Vienna from Australia, with a daily service from Sydney and flights three times weekly from Melbourne.

Ships navigate the Danube from May to September, following a route steeped in imperial tradition: from Passau in Germany via Linz, Melk and Krems to Vienna (►Transport). *By boat*

Immigration and Customs Regulations

The identity cards and passports of EU citizens are often no longer checked. However, since random inspections are carried out at the border and identification is required at airports, all visitors must be able to show their **passports** when they enter the country. Children under 16 years of age must carry a children's passport or be entered in the parent's passport. *Travel documents*

Always carry your driving licence, the motor vehicle registration and the international green insurance card when driving in Austria. Motor vehicles must have the oval sticker showing nationality unless they have a Euro licence plate. *Car documents*

Those who wish to bring pets (dogs, cats, ferrets) to Austria require a **pet pass**, which replaced the documentation required by the individual European states in October 2004. Among other things, it contains an official veterinary statement of health (no more than 30 days old), a rabies vaccination certificate at least 20 days and no more than eleven months old, and a passport photo. In addition, the animal must be fitted with a microchip (transponder) or have an identifying tattoo. Those travelling with dogs should take a muzzle, the use of which may be insisted upon. Contact the Austrian embassy for the latest information. *Pets and travel*

The European Union member states (including Austria) form a common economic area within which the movement of goods for private purposes is largely duty-free. There are certain maximum quantities which apply: 800 cigarettes or 400 cigarillos or 200 cigars or 1000g tobacco; 10 litres of spirits with more than 22% alcohol content or 20 litres with less than 22%; 90 litres of wine; and 110 litres of beer per person. During random inspections customs officers must be convinced that the wares are actually intended for private use. *Customs regulations for EU citizens*

Customs regulations for non-EU citizens For travellers from outside the EU, the following duty-free quantities apply: 200 cigarettes or 100 cigarillos or 50 cigars or 250g of tobacco; 2 litres of wine and 2 litres of sparkling wine or 1 litre of spirits with an alcohol content of more than 22% vol.; 500g of coffee or 200g of coffee extracts; 100g of tea or 40g of tea extract; 50ml of perfume or 0.25 litres of eau de toilette. Gifts up to a value of €175 are also duty-free.

Casinos

Austria boasts at present **twelve gambling casinos**, which work together with the Austrian tourist centres: in Baden bei Wien, Bad Gastein, Bregenz, Graz, Innsbruck, Kitzbühel, Kleinwalsertal (Riezlern), Linz, Schloss Klessheim bei Salzburg, Seefeld, Velden and Vienna.

French roulette, American roulette, black jack, baccarat, poker, red dog, sic bo, European seven eleven, punto banco, wheel of fortune are all on offer, as well as fruit machines. Casinos are normally open daily from 3pm or 7pm. Admission is not permitted for minors.

i **Casinos Austria AG**

▪ Dr.-Karl-Lueger-Ring 14
A-1015 Wien
Tel. 01/507 77 50
www.casinos.at

Children in Austria

Kinderhotels Austria's family-friendly Kinderhotels are specialized to meet the needs of families with small children. These hotels, often with daycare facilities, swimming pools, farm animals and other attractions, promise recreation for children and relaxation for parents.

Numerous museums and cultural monuments **offer something special for the little ones,** from guided theme tours suitable for children to hands-on experiments. Museums exhibiting teddy bears, dolls or toys can constitute near-magical attractions, and leisure parks, mountain railways, vintage railways, boat trips on rivers and lakes, caves, mines open to the public, old castles and the like are sure to get an enthusiastic response. Austria boasts Europe's longest summer toboggan run and has the largest number of skate parks in Europe.

i **Kinderhotels**

▪ Kinderhotels Europa
Seeblickstr. 49a
A-9580 Villach-Drobollach
Tel. 0 42 54/42 54, fax 45 55
www.kinderhotels.com

▶ THE BEST LEISURE PARKS

► **Archäologischer Park Carnuntum**
Carnuntum Archaeological Park brings together three museums: the Freilichtmuseum (Open Air Museum) Petronell, the Amphitheater Bad Deutsch Altenburg and the Archäologisches Museum Carnuntinum.
►Hainburg, Surroundings

► **Böhmischer Prater**
Tivoli-Center
Laaer Wald 30 C, A-1100 Wien
Tel. 01/6 89 91 91, fax 6 89 91 91 12
www.tivoli.at
May–Sept
With ferris wheel, child-friendly rides, merry-go-round and crazy golf, this amusement park is something for all the family.

► **Erlebnispark Strasswalchen**
Märchenweg 1
A-5204 Strasswalchen (KÄ)
Tel. 0 62 15/81 81, fax 81 82
www.erlebnispark.at
19 April–end Oct 10am–6pm
This theme park goes from a fairytale forest and Dracula's haunted castle via the Wild West to Africa, land of adventure, finishing up in the 3D cinema. A wide range of entertainment indeed.

► **Erlebnisausstellung Hubhof**
The wonderful world of optical illusions and phenomena
► Wachau, Maria Laach

► **Erlebniswelt Holzknechtland**
►Maria Zell, Surroundings

► **Familienparadies Reichenhauser**
Reauz 3
A-9074 Keutschach-See
Tel. 0 42 73/23 25, fax 23 25-8
www.familienparadies-reichen-hauser.at
May–end Oct 10am–7pm
An adventure playground, a magic wood and a land of Red Indians make children's eyes light up.

► **Fun-Spielpark Leutasch**
Weidach 381 e
A-6105 Leutasch (TI)
Tel. 0 52 14/67 85, fax 67 85 37
May–Oct 9am–6pm
All who love to play are welcome here – for children from four to 94.

► **1. Kärntner Erlebnispark**
►Gailtal

► **Märchenpark Neusiedler See**
►Neusiedler See, St. Margarethen

► **Märchenwald Steiermark**
►Judenburg, Surroundings

► **Minimundus**
► Klagenfurt

► **Laziland**
Bahnhof 150
A-3352 St. Peter i. d. Au
Tel. and fax 0 74 77/4 27 88
www.laziland.at
All year round 9am–6pm
Nature trail, rural culture, playgrounds, fixed rope route – Laziland in the Mostviertel combines acquiring knowledge with a lot of fun.

► **No Name City**
Westernstrasse 1
A-2752 Wöllersdorf
Tel. 0 26 22/4 34 00, fax 4 34 00-10
www.nonamecity.at

April, May, Sept and Oct
Thu–Sun and holidays
10am–7pm,
June–Aug daily 10am–7pm
The Western town for fans of the
Western from eight to 88

▶ **Saurierpark Traismauer**
▶St. Pölten, Surroundings

▶ **Styrassic Park**
Dinoplatz 1
8344 Bad Gleichenberg
Tel. 0 31 59/2 87 50
www.styrassicpark.at
1 March–14 March Sat and Sun
9am–4pm, 15 March–Sept daily
until 5pm, Oct until 4pm, Nov Sat
and Sun 10am–3pm

Expeditions through the world of
dinosaurs, mammoths, sabre-
toothed tigers and cave bears.

▶ **Swarovski Kristallwelten**
▶Hall in Tirol, Surroundings

▶ **Wurstelprater**
▶ Vienna, Prater

▶ **Zwergenpark Gurktal**
A-9324 Gurk
Tel. 0 42 66/80 77, fax 80 77-4
www.zwergenpark.com
Mid-May–mid-Sept 10am–4pm,
July/Aug until 6pm
A Lilliputian train chuffs through
the colourful world of garden
gnomes.

Electricity

Austria's mains supply is 220 volts AC. An adapter is required for de-
vices with British or other non-European plugs.

Emergency

Breakdown

Note When being towed in Austria, do not turn on the hazard warning
lights. The tow vehicle must have its headlights on, both day and
night. The maximum speed when towing is 25mph/40kmh. Vehicles
that have broken down on the autobahn can be towed to the next exit only.

▶ IMPORTANT NUMBERS

EMERGENCY NUMBERS IN AUSTRIA

▶ **Ambulance**
Tel. 144

▶ **Fire**
Tel. 122

▶ **Police**
Tel. 133

▶ **Breakdown assitance**
  ▶Automobile Clubs

AUTOMOBILE CLUBS

▶ **Österreichischer Automobil-, Motorrad- und Touring Club (ÖAMTC)**
  Schubertring 1–3, A-1010 Wien
  Tel. 01/71 19 90
  www.oeamtc.at
  Breakdown service: Tel. 120
  (ÖAMTC)

▶ **Auto-, Motor- und Radfahrer-bund Österreichs (ARBÖ)**
  Mariahilfer Strasse 180
  A-1150 Wien
  Tel. 01/8 91 21, fax 8 91 21-2 36
  www.arboe.or.at
  Travel emergency number:
  Tel. 01/8 95 60 60
  Breakdown service:
  Tel. 123 (ARBÖ)

▶ **ADAC Wien**
  Tel. 01/9 85 69 66
  (all year round; 24 hours)

BREAKDOWN SERVICES IN UK

▶ **RAC**
  Tel. 08705 722 722
  (customer services)
  Tel. 0800 82 82 82
  (breakdown assistance)

▶ **AA**
  Tel. 0800 88 77 66
  (emergency breakdown)
  Tel. +44 161 495 8945
  (international enquiries)

INTERNATIONAL AIR AMBULANCE SERVICES

▶ **Cega Air Ambulance (world-wide service)**
  Tel. +44(0)1243 621097
  Fax +44(0)1243 773169
  www.cega-aviation.co.uk

▶ **US Air Ambulance**
  Tel. 800/948-1214 (US; toll-free)
  Tel. 001-941-926-2490
  (international; collect)
  www.usairambulance.net

Etiquette and Customs

»**The Austrian is distinguished from the German by a common language**«, explained Karl Kraus, the sharp-tongued Austrian writer and critic. He has a point. Though Austria shares much with its out-sized neighbour, there are certain differences in fine tuning, as it were. Where Germans are straightforward to the point of bluntness, Austrians have a more baroque way of expressing themselves, especially those from Vienna. Perhaps in this regard the Anglophone visitor will be on common ground with his Austrian host, but mind your p's and q's: Austrians, especially the older generation, value politeness highly.

German language, Austrian style

The Viennese in particular are known for their »**Schmäh**«, a certain brand of humour that they deliver with a wink of an eye. They are a complex bunch, marked by a curious combination of inferiority complex and defiant self-satisfaction, which historians well-versed in psychology explain is the result of having lived for centuries at the focal point of an empire only to find themselves, at a stroke, reduced to a tiny state that lay at the outer edge of Europe.

Dos and don'ts   A few **basic rules**: don't forget to **tip** bar staff, taxi drivers, hairdressers, petrol pump attendants and lavatory attendants, as they depend on this supplement to their income to make ends meet; don't simply order a »Kaffee« in a Traditionscafé – please read our coffee lexicon on p.108.

If you are tempted to pick flowers, it is recommended that you check with the appropriate authority first, as many of Austria's plant species are strictly protected. Those who fancy a spot of **mushroom picking** should be aware that strict rules apply: it is permitted to collect a maximum of 1kg/2.2lbs per person from 7am to 7pm only on days when the date is an even number.

One needs to know the etiquette here

Festivals · Holidays · Events

▶ HOLIDAYS AND FESTIVALS

NATIONAL HOLIDAYS

1 January: New Year's Day
6 January: Epiphany
Easter Sunday/Easter Monday
1 May: Labour Day
Ascension Day
Whit Monday
Corpus Christi
15 August: Assumption of the Virgin
26 October: national holiday
1 November: All Saints' Day
8 December: Immaculate Conception
25/26 December: Christmas

JANUARY

▶ **New Year's Concerts**
Concerts by the Vienna Philharmonic, the Vienna Symphonic and the Vienna Hofburg orchestras.

▶ **Vierschanzentournee**
First week of January: the third and fourth rounds of the ski-jumping tournament in Innsbruck and Bischofshofen.

▶ **Epiphany**
In many places on 6 January there are processions to celebrate the Three Magi (Three Kings) – in Gmunden the Three Wise Men sail in a boat on the Traunsee.

▶ **Aperschnalzen**
In many communities near Salzburg winter is driven away with loud cracks of the whip between Epiphany and Ash Wednesday.

▶ **Hahnenkamm-Rennen**
Downhill ski race in Kitzbühel.

▶ **Mozartwoche**
Internationally renowned artists can be heard during Salzburg's Mozart Week.

FEBRUARY/MARCH

▶ **Tiroler Fasnacht**
In many communities in Tyrol, such as Imst, Nassereith and Telfs, masked processions at carnival time mark the end of winter and herald the new spring.

▶ **Funkensonntag**
The first Sunday after Ash Wednesday: pieces of firewood (»Funken«), onto whose ends a life-size rag doll, the »Funkenhexe« (firewood witch) is attached, are ceremonially burned. When the flames reach the witch, she explodes due to the gunpowder in her belly.

▶ **Diagonale**
Festival of Austrian film at which an annual retrospective of cinema and TV films of the past year of production is shown, along with an overview of current film work.

MARCH/APRIL

▶ **Salzburger Osterfestspiele**
Sir Simon Rattle's Berlin Philharmonic Orchestra is always a highlight at the Salzburg Easter Festival, which was founded in 1967 by Herbert von Karajan.

MAY

▸ **Maibaum**
In many places a maypole is erected.

▸ **Schubertiade**
Concerts in honour of and featuring works by Franz Schubert, but also by Wolf, Brahms, Schumann and others, in Schwarzenberg in the Bregenzerwald (Bregenz Forest) in the second half of May (again at the end of August/beginning of September).

▸ **Ausseerland Narzissenfest**
In Altaussee, Bad Aussee and Grundsee elaborate figures are artfully formed from flowers and presented in a parade of cars or boats.

Boat procession at the Narzissenfest in Bad Ausee

MAY TO SEPTEMBER

▸ **Graz erzählt**
Festival of the art of story-telling held in Graz at Whitsun.

▸ **Linzer Kultursommer**
The Linz Culture Summer offers concerts featuring the widest variety of music genres, theatre performances and open-air events.

▸ **Urfahraner Markt**
Twice a year, at the end of April/ beginning of May and at the end of September/beginning of October, Austria's oldest and largest funfair take place in Linz, with festival tents and a colourful programme of entertainment.

JUNE

▸ **Donauinselfest**
Europe's largest party for young people, with hundreds of rock and pop musicians on 18 stages, takes place in Vienna (admission free).

▸ **Donaufestival Niederösterreich**
A festival featuring various types of entertainment (music, dance, theatre) in Lower Austria's Krems, St Pölten, Tulln, Melk, Weissenkirchen and Göttweig.

▸ **Glocknerwallfahrt**
A pilgrimage at the end of June from Ferleiten over the Hochtor to Heiligenblut.

▸ **KlangBogen Wien**
Performances of compositions from the Baroque era to the present take place between June and September in the Neues Rathaus (New Town Hall, Vienna), at Schloss Schönbrunn, on the Rathausplatz (Town Hall Square)

and in Viennese concert halls, churches and parks.

JUNE/JULY

► Jazz Fest Wien

At Vienna's jazz festival in June/ July international jazz artists perform in the Staatsoper, the Volkstheater and at open-air-concerts.

► Innsbrucker Tanzsommer

Innsbruck's dance festival welcomes the world's most famous dance companies: from classical ballet to the most diverse forms of modern dance, jazz dance and modern expressive dance.

► styriarte

Styrian music festival in Graz, from early to Romantic music, with the conductor Nikolaus Harnoncourt.

JUNE TO SEPTEMBER

► Festival at the Burgarena Finkenstein

Operettas, concerts, musicals, cabaret in the remnants of a 12th-century castle.

JULY/AUGUST

► Salzburger Festspiele

The Salzburg Festival is one of the most important music and theatre

The natural arena created by the Finkenstein castle ruins is the venue for important cultural events.

festivals in the world with classical and contemporary operas, concerts and plays.

▸ **Bregenzer Festspiele**
The Bregenz Festival offers music theatre on the world's largest open-air floating stage.

▸ **Seefestspiele Mörbisch**
Held just outside Vienna, the Mörbisch Festival on the Lake has established itself as a centre of classical operetta. It takes place on one of the largest open-air stages in Europe.

In addition many small places host summer cultural events with music, dance and readings.

JULY TO SEPTEMBER

▸ **Carinthischer Sommer**
The Carinthian Summer Music Festival, an internationally renowned event featuring classical and modern music, takes place in Ossiach and Villach.

▸ **Bad Ischl Operetta Festival**
The festival in Bad Ischl goes back to an idea of Franz Lehár's. Every year there are two operettas, one by Lehár. In addition there are concerts by orchestras, cabaret and readings.

AUGUST

▸ **International Folk Festival**
Austria's largest folk festival takes place in Hallein and features the best folk groups in the world.

▸ **Seebühne Wörthersee**
Musicals in Klagenfurt on the Wörthersee's floating stage.

SEPTEMBER

▸ **Internationale Haydntage**
The festival in Eisenstadt's Schloss Esterházy is dedicated to Haydn.

▸ **Musikfest Brahms**
Classical concerts in Mürzzuschlag, where Brahms spent a fair few summers and where he composed his fourth symphony.

▸ **Festlicher Almabtrieb**
At the end of September the cattle on the summer alpine pastures are adorned with festive decorations and driven down into the stalls of the valley communities.

OCTOBER

▸ **Viennale**
The large urban film festival in Vienna featuring the highlights of Austrian and international filmmaking.

OCTOBER/NOVEMBER

▸ **steirischer herbst**
Avantgarde festival in Graz with contemporary opera and theatre performances, concerts and readings.

▸ **Salzburger Jazz-Herbst**
Top international and Austrian jazz stars give of their best for ten days in November.

DECEMBER

▸ **Christkindlmärkte**
Magical Christmas markets are found in all large towns.

Food and Drink

Restaurants

Austrian restaurants and pubs generally have a well-run kitchen. Lunch is served between 12 noon and 2pm in larger restaurants, often earlier in smaller ones. Afternoon coffee, known like every other between-meal snack as »Jause«, is taken between 4pm and 5pm. Dinner is served from 6pm.

On the Menu

Austrian cuisine is extremely diverse and the recipes of this once multiracial state reveal southern German, Bohemian, Hungarian, Croatian, Slovenian and Italian influences. Schnitzel comes from Milan, Mehlspeise desserts from Bohemia and goulash from Hungary. The menu is generously peppered with dialect expressions. Meat dishes and desserts are singled out for special praise in Austrian cuisine, which incidentally can be called neither light nor low in calories. The selection of freshwater fish is wonderful too, as is the quality of game.

Austrian cuisine

Price categories

- Expensive: from €20
- Moderate: from €10
- Inexpensive: up to €10
- Restaurants ►Sights from A to Z

»Fischbeuschlsuppe« is a soup with roe and some vegetables, and beef broth is often supplemented with dumplings such as Markknödel or Griessnockerl, or with pasta of various types. Other additions to soups include »Gerstl«, made of pasta dough; small baked balls of choux pastry known as »Backerbsen«; »Schöberl« made of cut-up sponge dough; and pancakes cut into strips for the famous »Frittatensuppe«. Soups are served with bread rolls, known in Vienna as »Semmel« or »Weckerl«.

Soups

Wiener schnitzel, a veal cutlet coated with breadcrumbs, is known the world over. The recipe actually originated in Milan. Rindfleisch (preceded by »garniertes« or »feines«) is boiled beef with accompanying vegetables; Lungenbraten and Tafelspitz are among the cuts of beef tenderloin, the latter mostly being served with Apfelkren (horseradish with apple). Beinfleisch, Tellerfleisch and Kruschpelspitz, beef with fat running through it, is often eaten with a chive sauce. Wiener Esterházyrostbraten is a rib of beef served with seasoned root vegetables. Generous amounts of pepper and paprika characterize goulash and the similarly prepared Paprikahuhn (paprika chicken), introduced from Hungary. Roast pork tenderloin with caraway seeds is called Jungfernbraten, while Krenfleisch is meat from a sucking pig on a spit served with horseradish. Kaiserfleisch is roast rib of pork,

Meat

Stelze is boiled knuckle of pork, Geräuchertes is salted, smoked meat, mince is known as Faschiertes, Schöpsernes is mutton. Braised Wiener Beuschl or Lüngerl is prepared by pickling calf lung and heart. Popular poultry dishes include stuffed goose breast, capon in anchovy sauce, pheasant wrapped in bacon and roast snipe. Backhendl is chicken in breadcrumbs, panierte Hähnchen, while basted Kalbsvogerln are small veal roulades. Rissoles are called Fleischlaberl, while Wiener sausages, oddly, are called Frankfurters in Austria. Notable game dishes are wild pig in cream sauce with Serviettenknödel (dumplings cooked in a napkin), venison ragout with bacon, saddle of venison in a sauce with pickled root vegetables, and saddle of hare in wine sauce.

? DID YOU KNOW ...?

■ ... that »gekochte Fledermaus« (»cooked bat«) is not the nocturnal winged mammal served up on a plate? In fact it is the name for a juicy, tender cut of beef, about the size of the palm of the hand. It is served with beef soup seasoned with saffron and boiled with horseradish, and accompanied by bread rolls and sometimes also roast potatoes.

Fish dishes

Typical fish dishes in addition to Fischbeuschlsuppe include Wurzelkarpfen (carp cooked with carrots, celeriac and turnip) with garlic butter, Fogoschfilet (pike-perch) fried in bacon or with a pepper sauce, steamed catfish and common bleak.

Vegetables

»Heurige Erdäpfel« are new potatoes, and fried potatoes, chopped small, are known as »geröstete (roast) Erdäpfel«. Fisolen are green beans, Karfiol is cauliflower, Paradeiser are tomatoes, Sprossenkohl are Brussels sprouts, Kukuruz is sweet corn, Kren is horseradish, Häuptesalat is lettuce, Vogerlsalat is lamb's lettuce, Risipisi is rice with green peas and Schwammerln are mushrooms.

Mehlspeise desserts

The world-famous Salzburger Nockerln consist mostly of air – with a shell made of sugar, eggs and flour. Strudel made of thinly rolled pasta or butter dough with fruit, quark, poppy seeds or other fillings is considered to be Austria's most popular dessert; the most sought-after variations include Millirahmstrudel with vanilla sauce and Apfelstrudel, which is garnished with Schlag or Obers (whipped cream). Palatschinken or Topfenpalatschinken is a sweet pancake made with eggs and filled with quark, while the much prized Kaiserschmarrn is a thick pancake with raisins which is baked, fried in sugar and butter and torn apart in the pan with two forks. Topfenknödel (quark dumplings) are often served with Zwetschgenröster, a traditional plum compote; Powidl are yeast dough dumplings filled with thickened plum jam, which has little or no added sugar, and sprinkled with poppy seeds. In addition don't miss trying apricot dumplings or Powidltaschkerln as well as the delicious Buchteln or Wuchteln, which are stuffed sweet yeast dumplings cooked in milk and sugar. Dobostorte, a sponge cake filled with chocolate cream is also deli-

A piece of Sacher torte with your coffee – irresistible!

SWEET TEMPTATIONS

What would Austrian cuisine be without Mehlspeisen, the country's famous desserts? Though »Mehl« means flour, this is actually not the major ingredient in these delicacies, which Napoleon helped to make popular. Not all Mehlspeisen originated in the alpine republic either. But the fact that the Austrians take their tempting sweets very seriously is proven by a famous controversy over Sacher torte.

As the Viennese *Appetit-Lexikon* of 1894 puts it: »Mehlspeisen are the pinnacles of Viennese cuisine, each one ever more surprising, dazzling and deserving of praise than the last. These compositions of enchanting richness and sweetness, these gastronomical ghazals (an Oriental form of poetry), are constructed in such a wonderful, intricate way that the layman can only stop and gape in astonishment.«

The great variety of Mehlspeisen in Austrian cuisine, such as strudel, dumplings (Knödel), bakes (Aufläufe), puddings, chopped up pancakes (Schmarren), sweet yeast dumplings (Dampfnudel), egg pancakes (Eierkuchen), deep-fried pastries (Schmalzgebäcke), gâteaux and so on do indeed leave the beholder in raptures, even if they also lead to terrible worries about the figure. Because the essential element – which we reduce in our diets as much as possible by using every trick in the book – is not flour but, much worse, sugar!

Napoleon takes some of the blame

It was partly thanks to Emperor Napoleon that warm Mehlspeisen, which basically developed from Lenten food (Fastenspeisen), came into fashion around 1800. Napoleon's Continental System of 1806, forbidding his allies and conquered territories to trade with the British, meant that hardly any sugar, already an expensive

Delicious, but unfortunately not particularly healthy: Mehlspeise desserts such as the Kaiserschmarrn

commodity, could be imported. This forced the cultivation of a cheap alternative, sugar beet. Sugar produced in this way quickly became a »foodstuff of the people«, and the Mehlspeise desserts prepared with this sugar became an essential item on the menu both in restaurants and at home.

From foreign climes

Many Mehlspeisen are so typical of Austria that it is easy to believe they originated from here. However quite a number of specialities have been adopted from other countries and cultures. Strudel for example, whose name incidentally comes from its round, eddy-like form, is of Middle Eastern origin. Mehlspeise was first mentioned in Austria in 1715 in the *Frauenzimmer-Lexikon*, and how much it is at home here, in all its innumerable variations (Apfelstrudel, Topfenstrudel, Tiroler Strudel etc.), is demonstrated by certain Austrian turns of phrase such as »sich abstrudeln«, which means »to slave away«. Alongside roast chicken (Backhendl) and schnitzel, Wiener Faschingskrapfen (carnival doughnuts) are a characteristic dish in Austrian cuisine. Like Wiener schnitzel, they were not invented in Vienna at all, even if local historians do claim that a Viennese woman by the name of Krapf created them. Stuffed doughnuts were being consumed back in the times of the Greeks and the Romans, who baked them at spring Bacchanalia. Palatschinken is clear evidence of foreign influence. The name comes from the Latin word »placenta«, meaning cake, which led to the Romanian »placinta« and the Hungarian »palacsinta«. The Austrians eventually took both the name and the dish from the Czech »palacinka«, stuffed egg-pancakes. The Palatschinken dough plays only a secondary role; it is intended merely to surround the filling, for example jam.

Genuinely Austrian foods

»A bake (Auflauf) should rise, and a firm, open crust should form, which should jut out on one side with grace,« as an old Austrian cookery book says. The absolute »Queen of the Auflauf« is the Salzburger Nockerl,

allegedly first served to the Archbishop of Salzburg, Wolf Dietrich von Raitenau (1559–1617).

Schmarren is another speciality created by Austrians. In contrast to strudel with its fine pastry shell, Schmarren, made in the pan, was originally a rural dish from the alpine region, and only became accepted in polite society quite late on. The word Schmarren, which comes from »Schmer«, meaning lard, first appeared in a wedding sermon in 1563. Probably the best-known Schmarren was made for Empress Elisabeth by Viennese chefs in 1854. However Sisi (Baedeker Special p.301), always concerned for her figure, enjoyed the delicacy rather less than her husband Franz Joseph I, which is why Kaiserschmarren is named after the emperor rather than the empress.

It is often said that Linzer Torte was invented in 1822 by Bavarian confectioner Johann Konrad Vogl, who had come to Linz that same year. However the name appears in Anna Margarita Sagramosa's cookery book of 1653. Vogl's contribution is to have made the Linz delicacy famous far beyond the town's borders.

The *Appetit-Lexikon* of 1894 writes the following of Sacher torte, which had become acceptable at court in 1836: »Sacher torte is a chocolate gâteau of the finest type, which stands out from its peers in that under its dress of chocolate it wears a shirt of apricot jam.« In the 1950s a controversy raged over this gâteau in Vienna, and one that is surely only possible in Austria: Haus Sacher and the confectioner Demel argued over the right to make the original Sacher torte.

The argument was resolved with Solomonic wisdom: Sacher made the original Sacher torte, Demel manufactured the one with the Eduard Sacher seal. But whether from Sacher or Demel, Sacher torte is one of the few Mehlspeisen with a long shelf-life and one that makes an easily transportable souvenir.

cious. As the crowning glory, treat yourself to a piece of the most legendary chocolate tart of all: the apricot jam-filled Sachertorte.

Language lesson Eierspeise: scrambled egg; Ribisl: blackcurrants; Ringlotten: greengage; Kipferl: croissant; Obers: cream; Schlagobers: whipped cream.

Beer The well-known beer brands are Schwechater, Gösser, Puntigamer, Stiegl and Zipfer. »Märzen« beer has nothing in common with the stronger Bavarian »Märzenbier«; instead it is comparable to a lager. The bitter, hoppier beers of the pilsner type are also popular, but darker beers are less common. A Krügel mug holds 0.5 litres, a Seidel 0.35 litres.

Viennese Coffee Specialities

Basic knowledge The basis of Vienna's coffee specialities is always the mocha coffee bean. If the uninitiated order a »Kaffee«, as a rule they are served a »Braunen« or »brown«. In Viennese coffee houses a cup of coffee is always accompanied by a glass of water, which is refilled on request (several times if desired). As ordering coffee is something of an art in itself, here is a brief compilation of the vocabulary:

A CONCISE COFFEE LEXICON

Brauner (kleiner, grosser)	small or large cup of mocha coffee with a little milk
Dunkel	with even less milk
Einspänner	hot mocha and whipped cream in a glass
Eiskaffee	cold mocha, vanilla ice cream, whipped cream and wafer, served in a glass
Espresso (Es)	mocha from the espresso machine
Fiaker	»grosser Schwarzer« in a glass
Gestreckt	with added water
Gold	golden brown »Melange«
Kaffee ohne Kaffee	decaffeinated coffee
Kaffee verkehrt	a little mocha and a lot of milk
Kaisermelange	»Schwarzer« with egg yolk
Kapuziner	dark brown »Melange«
Konsul	»Schwarzer« with a shot of cream
Kurz	especially strong
Licht	light in colour, with a lot of milk
Mazagran	a glass of cold mocha with Maraschino liqueur, ice cubes and a straw

Melange	medium-dark milky coffee
Mokka (Mocca)	strong black Viennese coffee
Mokka gespritzt	mocha with a shot of cognac
Nussschwarzer	mocha
Obers	cream
Obers gespritzt	cream with a dash of mocha
Portion Kaffee	mocha with milk to add yourself
Schale	cup
Schlag(obers)	whipped cream
Schwarzer (kleiner, grosser)	mocha, small or large
Schwarzer gespritzt	mocha with a shot of rum
Teeschale	a cup of milk
Teeschale Obers gespritzt	a cup of cream with some mocha
Türkischer	mocha Turkish-style, with the coffee grounds and, if desired, sugar boiled and served in a copper pot
Weisser	decaffeinated coffee

Wine

Wine growing has a **long tradition** in Austria. Widespread as early as Roman times, there is evidence of viniculture from the 5th century onward. The first viniculture school was opened in Klosterneuburg bei Wien in 1860.

Austria has an area of about 44,500ha/110,000ac of cultivable land for wine growing. Of total production, about 85% are white wines and 15% red wines. Lower Austria, with the Weinviertel and the Wachau, claims the largest share of wine production, but there are considerably sized wine-growing areas in Burgenland, Styria and the province of Vienna.

Viniculture

The white grapes of the Grüne Veltliner yield a fruity, sparkling white wine, Welschriesling and Rheinriesling produce finely aromatic, lively white wines, with Rheinriesling considered the finer type of grape. Wines that are mild, fruity and tend towards sweetness are produced from Müller-Thurgau, Muskat-Ottonel and Traminer grapes; Weissburgunder and Zierfandler grapes yield strong wines with a rich bouquet.

White wine

Blaufränkisch and Blauburgunder grapes produce ruby-red, fruity wines, while the Blaue Wildbacher grape yields Schilcher, a rosé wine. Dark, strong red wines come from the Blaue Portugieser and the St Laurent grape varieties, as well as the Blaue Zweigelt, a cross between the former two.

Red and rosé wines

Wine-growing regions	The wine-growing regions of Lower Austria lie around Krems (Wachau), in the Weinviertel, Wagram (Klosterneuburg) and south of Vienna on the »Thermenlinie«, a geological fault line with thermal springs between the Northern Limestone Alps and the Vienna Basin (Bad Vöslau–Baden–Mödling). Along with white wines (Grüner Veltliner, Weissburgunder, Rheinriesling, Welschriesling), red wines (Blaufränkisch, Blauer Portugieser, Blauer Zweigelt) are also cultivated in Wagram near Gumpoldskirchen and around Baden bei Wien and Bad Vöslau.

Lower Austria ▶ The wine-growing regions of Lower Austria lie around Krems (Wachau), in the Weinviertel, Wagram (Klosterneuburg) and south of Vienna on the »Thermenlinie«, a geological fault line with thermal springs between the Northern Limestone Alps and the Vienna Basin (Bad Vöslau–Baden–Mödling). Along with white wines (Grüner Veltliner, Weissburgunder, Rheinriesling, Welschriesling), red wines (Blaufränkisch, Blauer Portugieser, Blauer Zweigelt) are also cultivated in Wagram near Gumpoldskirchen and around Baden bei Wien and Bad Vöslau.

Burgenland ▶ Burgenland is known for its full-bodied white and red wines. The main areas for viniculture lie around the Neusiedler See. The wine-growing region near Rust produces Spätlese (»late harvest«) wines of high quality. The predominant grape varieties in Burgenland are Welschriesling, Muscat, Traminer and Weissburgunder as well as Blauburgunder and Blaufränkisch.

Styria ▶ Styrian vines grow on steep south-facing slopes with an almost Tuscan atmosphere. Along with sparkling whites, a fruity, light red wine called »Schilcher« is created here.

Vienna ▶ The vineyards of Vienna, extending right into the municipal area, produce well-known white wines. Both Vienna locals and visitors enjoy taking day trips to the suburbs of Sievering, Grinzing or Nussdorf to sample the new wine, known as »Heuriger«, in the Heurigenlokale and Buschenschenken. These often privately run local bars can be identified by a broom or a bunch of flowers placed in front of or hanging over the door.

Language of the wine label A little help in understanding what is in the bottle: »Naturwein« is unsweetened wine; »reinsortig« are wines made from just one type of grape; the »Ried« is the location from which the wine originates. The **Austrian Quality Wine Seal** is the stamp of quality for the country's wines. The designation »Wein aus Österreich« identifies a controlled Austrian table wine, usually of a simple type.

As a consequence of the wine scandal in the mid-1980s, when it emerged that wines had been contaminated with diethylene glycol, strict **wine laws** now apply in Austria. They provide for a completely truthful description of a wine's origin, variety and year. Furthermore the producer, level of quality, alcohol and sugar content must be provided. The requirement for precise recording and reporting as well as regulations on checking and controlling, from the grape on the vine to the sale of the end product, provide protection against dishonesty.

Homely atmosphere – Haas Beisl in Vienna-Margarethen

For Tafelwein (table wine), Landwein (»country wine«, or what the French call »vin ordinaire«), and Qualitätswein (wine of certified quality), improvement of the must by the addition of sugar is only permitted within narrow limits (generally up to 3.5%; for Tafelwein up to 4.5%). A designation of origin only applies to wines made from grapes exclusively from the stated region.

Tafelwein (table wine) is a wine made from Austrian grapes with a minimum specific gravity of the must of 13 ° KMW (Klosterneuburger Mostwaage).

Tafelwein

Landwein, commonly referred to as »country wine«, is like Tafelwein, and contains a maximum of 11.5% alcohol by volume and a maximum of 6g/0.2oz of residual sugar per litre. Only grapes from a single wine-growing region can be used.
Tafelwein and Landwein (with the exception of the light red Schilcher) is sold in bottles of at least 1l/33 fl. oz.

Landwein

A Qualitätswein is a wine made from a registered grape variety; the grapes are permitted to come from only one wine-growing region. The wine must be state-certified, and the label must bear the corresponding number.

Qualitätswein

A Kabinettwein is a high-quality wine with a specific gravity of the must of at least 17 ° but not more than 19 °KMW. The must may not be improved and the wine should not contain more than 9g/0.3oz residual sugar.

Kabinettwein

A Prädikatswein is a Qualitätswein of special maturity and vintage that is not permitted to be improved by adding sugar and whose residual sweetness is achieved only through interrupting the fermentation process. The wine's vintage must be stated. Such wines as Spätlese, Auslese, Eiswein, Beerenauslese, Ausbruch and Trockenbeerenauslese fall into this category.

Prädikatswein

Sturm is the name for the drink made from fermented grape must with more than 1% alcohol content, as long as it is in a state of fermentation. Sturm can sold only from 1 August until 31 December of the harvest year.

Sturm

Health

The provision of medical care in doctors' practices and hospitals, as well as help in emergencies, is in principle a given in Austria. For UK residents, the European Health Insurance Card (EHIC) entitles the

Health insurance

holder to free or reduced cost state-provided medical treatment while visiting any country in the European Economic Area (EEA). The EHIC replaced the old E111 form in January 2006. It is available from post offices. Comprehensive health insurance is advised for travellers from outside the EU. Treatment on location normally has to be paid by the patient and a detailed invoice will be required by the insurer before reimbursing any costs. Generally it is advisable to take out additional insurance that will cover costs should transport to the home country be necessary.

Pharmacies As a rule the opening hours of pharmacies are Mon–Fri 8am–noon and 2pm–6pm, Sat 8am–noon. If closed, a sign in the window indicates the nearest open pharmacy in the vicinity.

Information

● IMPORTANT ADDRESSES

INFORMATION IN THE UK

► **Austrian National Tourist Board**
Tel. (GB) 0845 101 18 18
Fax 0845 101 1819
Tel. (Ireland) 189 093 01 18
Fax 189 093 01 19
www.austria.info

INFORMATION IN AUSTRIA

► **Österreich Werbung**
Margaretenstrasse 1
A-1040 Wien
Tel. 01/58 86 63 50 and
Tel. 0180/210 18 18
Fax 586 79 20
abcn@austria.info
www.austria.info

INFORMATION IN THE FEDERAL PROVINCES

► **Burgenland Tourismus**
Schloss Esterházy
A-7000 Eisenstadt
Tel. 0 26 82/6 33 84-0, fax 6 33 84 20
www.burgenland.info

► **Kärnten Werbung (Carinthia)**
Casinoplatz 1
A-9220 Velden
Tel. 0 42 74/5 21 00-0
Fax 5 21 00 50
www.kaernten.at

► **Niederösterreich Information (Lower Austria)**
Im Palais Niederösterreich
Herrengasse 13
A-1014 Wien
Tel. 01/53 61 00
Fax 53 61 01 98 58
www.noe.co.at

► **Landesverband für Tourismus in Oberösterreich (Upper Austria)**
Freistädter Str. 119, A-4010 Linz
Tel. 07 32/727 71 00
Fax 727 71 30
www.oberoesterreich-tourismus.at

► **Osttirol Werbung (East Tyrol)**
Albin-Egger-Strasse 17

A-9900 Lienz
Tel. 0 48 52/653 33, fax 65 33 32
www.osttirol.com

► **Salzburger Land Tourismus**
Wiener Bundesstr. 23
A-5300 Hallwang bei Salzburg
Tel. 06 62/66 88-0, fax 66 88 66
www.salzburgerland.com

► **Steirische Tourismus GmbH (Styria)**
St. Peter Hauptstrasse 243
A-8042 Graz
Tel. 03 16/4 00 30, fax 40 03 10
www.steiermark.com

► **Tirol Info (Tyrol)**
Maria-Theresia-Strasse 55
A-6010 Innsbruck
Tel. 05 12/72 72-0, fax 7 27 27
www.tourismus-tirol.com

► **Vorarlberg-Tourismus**
Bahnhofstrasse 14
A-6901 Bregenz
Tel. 0 55 74/42 52 50, fax 42 52 55
www.vorarlberg-tourism.at

AUSTRIAN EMBASSIES AND
CONSULATES

► **Australia**
12 Talbot St
Forrest, Canberra ACT 2603
Tel. 02 6295 1376
www.austriaemb.org.au

► **Canada**
445 Wilbrod St
Ottawa, Ontario K1N 6M7
Tel. 613 789 1444
www.austro.org

► **Republic of Ireland**
15 Ailesbury Court Apartments
93 Ailesbury Road, Dublin 4
Tel. 01 269 4577 / 269 1451
dublin-ob@bmaa.gv.at

► **New Zealand (consulate only)**
Level 2, Willbank House
57 Willis St, Wellington
Tel. 04 499 6393
diessl@ihug.co.nz

► **UK**
18 Belgrave Mews West
London SW1X 8HU
Tel. 020 7235 3731
www.austria.org.uk

► **USA**
3524 International Court NW
Washington, DC 20008
Tel. 020 7235 3731
washington-ob@bmaa.gv.at

EMBASSIES AND
CONSULATES IN AUSTRIA

All embassies listed are in Vienna.

► **American Embassy**
4th floor, Hotel Marriot
Gartenpromenade 2–4
Tel. 319 39
www.usembassy.at

► **Australian Embassy**
Mattiellistrasse 2
Tel. 506 74 0
www.australian-embassy.at

► **British Embassy**
Jaurèsgasse 12
Tel. 716 13 0
www.britishembassy.at

► **Canadian Embassy**
Laurenzerberg 2
Tel. 531 38 3000
www.kanada.at

► **Embassy of the Republic of Ireland**
5th floor, Rotenturmstrasse 16–18
Tel. 715 42 46
vienna@iveagh.irlgov.ie

► **New Zealand**
(honorary consulate)
Karl-Tornay-Gasse 34
Tel. 318 85 08
www.nzembassy.com

INTERNET

► **www.austria-tourism.at**
The official site for holidays in
Austria excels at providing useful
information and relevant links.

► **www.austria.gv.at**
The website of the Austrian government with information on the
country's current politics.

► **www.kulturleben.at**
Tips for special cultural events or
initiatives including an up-to-date
listing of exhibitions in Austria's
museums.

► **www.tiscover.at**
A very comprehensive website on
the country and its people offering
the possibility to book accommodation online and giving current
travel offers, weather forecasts,
information on infrastructure and
sights as well as numerous addresses and links.

Language

Austria's official language is German, albeit with some salient differences in vocabulary. There are quite a number of regional dialects in
the small country, some of which are closer to Swiss German than
High German. »The Austrian is distinguished from the German by a
common language,« as Karl Kraus once amusingly put it. The grammar is the same: three genders, masculine, feminine and neuter; the
nominative, accusative, dative and genitive cases and the complex
way they affect articles and nouns; the word order, and so on. But
Austrian German contains many expressions peculiar to the alpine
republic. *Servus* is a greeting or a farewell. *Grüss dich* or *Griassdi* is
another way of saying hello, and the standard phrase for goodbye is
Auf Wiederschauen. Austrian menus feature a variety of country-spe-
cific terms: potatoes, for example, are *Erdäpfel* – »earth apples«; *Lungenbraten*, »roast lungs«, is actually a porterhouse steak.

Pronunciation   Many of the sounds in German can be found in English. If two vowels appear together, pronounce the second one, so that **ie** is the ee in
»beef« and **ei** is the i in kite. The umlaut changes the sound: for
example **o** is like the o in »dot«, but **ö** is like the er in »her«. The **r**
consonant sound is a little difficult to master: it is pronounced further back in the throat than in English. The **ch** sound is tricky too: it
is similar to the ch in »loch«, or sometimes (after the vowels e and i)
a simpler »sh« sound. Practice makes perfect, as the phrase has it –
however your Austrian hosts will not expect perfection, and though
many speak good English they are sure to appreciate any effort to
communicate in »Österreichisch«!

SOME AUSTRIAN TERMS

Adabei	pompous ass
Anrainer	local resident
Backhendl	deep-fried chicken in breadcrumbs
Beuschel	boiled lungs
Blunzen	black pudding
10 Deka(gramm)	100 grammes
Doppler	two-litre bottle of wine
Eierschwammerl	chanterelle mushrooms
Eitrige	cheesecake
Erdäpfel	potatoes
Faschiertes	minced meat
Fisolen	green beans
Frankfurter	Frankfurters, Wiener sausages
Frittaten	strips of pancake
G'spritzter	wine with soda water
Karfiol	cauliflower
Kasten	cupboard
Kracherl	lemonade
Kren	horseradish
Krügerl	0.5l glass of beer
leiwand	good, great
Lungenbraten	porterhouse steak
Marillen	apricots
Melanzani	aubergines
Obers	whipped cream
Paradeiser	tomato
Ribisl	blackcurrant
Sackerl	bag
Schanigarten	pavement café or restaurant
Seidel	0.33l glass of beer
Semmel	bread roll
Sessel	chair (also not upholstered)
Topfen	quark
Trafik	tobacconist and newsagent
Verhackerts	spread for bread made from smoked pork
Vogerlsalat	lamb's lettuce
Weichsel	sour cherry
Zwetschkenröster	stewed plums

GERMAN

General

Yes / No	Ja / Nein

Perhaps. / Maybe.	Vielleicht.
Please.	Bitte.
Thank you. / Thank you very much.	Danke. / Vielen Dank!
You're welcome.	Gern geschehen.
Excuse me!	Entschuldigung!
Pardon?	Wie bitte?
I don't understand.	Ich verstehe Sie / Dich nicht.
I only speak a bit of ...	Ich spreche nur wenig ...
Can you help me, please?	Können Sie mir bitte helfen?
I'd like ...	Ich möchte ...
I (don't) like this.	Das gefällt mir (nicht).
Do you have ...?	Haben Sie ...?
How much is this?	Wieviel kostet es?
What time is it?	Wieviel Uhr ist es?
What is this called?	Wie heißt dies hier?

Getting acquainted

Good morning! / Good afternoon!	Guten Morgen! / Guten Tag!
Good evening!	Guten Abend!
Hello! / Hi!	Hallo! / Grüß Dich!
My name is ...	Mein Name ist ...
What's your name?	Wie ist Ihr / Dein Name?
How are you?	Wie geht es Ihnen / Dir?
Fine thanks. And you?	Danke. Und Ihnen / Dir?
Goodbye! / Bye-bye! /See you! / Bye!	Auf Wiedersehen! / Tschüss!
Good night!	Gute Nacht!

Travelling

left / right	links / rechts
straight ahead	geradeaus
near / far	nah / weit
Excuse me, where's ..., please?	Bitte, wo ist ...?
... the train station	... der Bahnhof
... the bus stop	... die Bushaltestelle
... the harbour	... der Hafen
... the airport	... der Flughafen
How far is it?	Wie weit ist das?
I'd like to rent a car.	Ich möchte ein Auto mieten.
How long?	Wie lange?

Traffic

My car's broken down.	Ich habe eine Panne.

Is there a service station nearby?	Gibt es hier in der Nähe eine Werkstatt?
Where's the nearest gas station?	Wo ist die nächste Tankstelle?
I want	Ich möchte ...
... liters / gallons of ...	Liter / Gallonen (3,8 l) ...
... regular/premium.	.... Normalbenzin/Super.
... diesel.	... Diesel.
... unleaded.	... bleifrei.
Full, please.	Volltanken, bitte.
Help!	Hilfe!
Attention!/Look out!	Achtung!/Vorsicht!
Please call ...	Rufen Sie bitte ...
... an ambulance.	... einen Krankenwagen.
... the police.	... die Polizei.
It was my fault.	Es war meine Schuld.
It was your fault.	Es war Ihre Schuld.
Please give me your name and address.	Geben Sie mir bitte Namen und Anschrift.
Beware of ...	Vorsicht vor ...
Bypass (with road number)	Ortsumgehung (mit Straßennummer)
Bypass (Byp)	Umgehungsstraße
Causeway	Brücke, Pontonbrücke
Construction	Bauarbeiten
Crossing (Xing)	Kreuzung, Überweg
Dead End	Sackgasse
Detour	Umleitung
Divided Highway	Straße mit Mittelstreifen
Do not enter	Einfahrt verboten
Exit	Ausfahrt
Hill	Steigung / Gefälle/unübersichtlich (Überholverbot)
Handicapped Parking	Behindertenparkplatz
Junction (Jct)	Kreuzung, Abzweigung, Einmündung
Keep off ...	Abstand halten ...
Loading Zone	Ladezone
Merge (Merging Traffic)	Einmündender Verkehr
Narrow Bridge	Schmale Brücke
No Parking	Parken verboten
No Passing	Überholen verboten
No Turn on Red	Rechtsabbiegen bei Rot verboten
U Turn	Wenden erlaubt
No U Turn	Wenden verboten
One Way	Einbahnstraße
Passenger Loading Zone	Ein- und Aussteigen erlaubt
Ped Xing	Fußgängerüberweg
Restricted Parking Zone	Zeitlich begrenztes Parken erlaubt

Right of Way	Vorfahrt
Road Construction	Straßenbauarbeiten
Slippery when wet	Schleudergefahr bei Nässe
Slow	Langsam fahren
Soft Shoulders	Straßenbankette nicht befestigt
Speed Limit	Geschwindigkeitsbegrenzung
Toll	Benutzungsgebühr, Maut
Tow away Zone	Absolutes Parkverbot, Abschleppzone
Xing (Crossing)	Kreuzung, Überweg
Yield	Vorfahrt beachten

Shopping

Where can I find a ...?	Wo finde ich ... eine / ein ..?
... pharmacy	... Apotheke
... bakery	... Bäckerei
... department store	... Kaufhaus
... food store	... Lebensmittelgeschäft
... supermarket	... Supermarkt

Accommodation

Could you recommend ... ?	Können Sie mir ... empfehlen?
... a hotel / motel	... ein Hotel / Motel
... a bed & breakfast	... eine Frühstückspension
Do you have ...?	Haben Sie noch ...?
... a room for one	... ein Einzelzimmer
... a room for two	... ein Doppelzimmer
... with a shower / bath	... mit Dusche / Bad
... for one night / ... for a week	... für eine Nacht / ... für eine Woche
I've reserved a room.	Ich habe ein Zimmer reserviert.
How much is the room	Was kostet das Zimmer
... with breakfast?	... mit Frühstück?

Doctor

Can you recommend a good doctor?	Können Sie mir einen guten Arzt empfehlen?
I need a dentist.	Ich brauche einen Zahnarzt.
I feel some pain here.	Ich habe hier Schmerzen.
I've got a temperature.	Ich habe Fieber.
Prescription	Rezept
Injection / shot	Spritze

Bank / Post

Where's the nearest bank?	Wo ist hier bitte eine Bank?
ATM (Automated Teller Machine)	Geldautomat
I'd like to change dollars/pounds into euros.	Ich möchte Dollars/Pfund in Euro wechseln.
How much is ...	Was kostet ...
... a letter ...	... ein Brief ...
... a postcard ...	... eine Postkarte ...
to Europe?	nach Europa?

Numbers

1	eins	2	zwei
3	drei	4	vier
5	fünf	6	sechs
7	sieben	8	acht
9	neun	10	zehn
11	elf	12	zwölf
13	dreizehn	14	vierzehn
15	fünfzehn	16	sechzehn
17	siebzehn	18	achtzehn
19	neunzehn	20	zwanzig
21	einundzwanzig	30	dreißig
40	vierzig	50	fünfzig
60	sechzig	70	siebzig
80	achtzig	90	neunzig
100	(ein-)hundert	1000	(ein-)tausend
1/2	ein Halb	1/3	ein Drittel
1/4	ein Viertel		

Restaurant

Is there a good restaurant here?	Gibt es hier ein gutes Restaurant?
Would you reserve us a table for this evening, please?	Reservieren Sie uns bitte für heute Abend einen Tisch!
The menu please!	Die Speisekarte bitte!
Cheers!	Auf Ihr Wohl!
Could I have the check, please?	Bezahlen, bitte.
Where is the restroom, please?	Wo ist bitte die Toilette?

Frühstück / Breakfast

Kaffee (mit Sahne / Milch)	coffee (with cream / milk)
koffeinfreier Kaffee	decaffeinated coffee

heiße Schokolade	hot chocolate
Tee (mit Milch / Zitrone)	tea (with milk / lemon)
Rühreier	scrambled eggs
pochierte Eier	poached eggs
Eier mit Speck	bacon and eggs
Spiegeleier	eggs sunny side up
harte / weiche Eier	hard-boiled / soft-boiled eggs
(Käse- / Champignon-)Omelett	(cheese / mushroom) omelette
Pfannkuchen	pancake
Brot / Brötchen / Toast	bread / rolls / toast
Butter	butter
Zucker	sugar
Honig	honey
Marmelade / Orangenmarmelade	jam / marmelade
Joghurt	yoghurt
Obst	fruit

Vorspeisen und Suppen / Starters and Soups

Fleischbrühe	broth / consommé
Hühnercremesuppe	cream of chicken soup
Tomatensuppe	cream of tomato soup
gemischter Salat	mixed salad
grüner Salat	green salad
frittierte Zwiebelringe	onion rings
Meeresfrüchtesalat	seafood salad
Garnelen- / Krabbencocktail	shrimp / prawn cocktail
Räucherlachs	smoked salmon
Gemüsesuppe	vegetable soup

Fisch und Meeresfrüchte / Fish and Seafood

Kabeljau	cod
Krebs	crab
Aal	eel
Schellfisch	haddock
Hering	herring
Hummer	lobster
Muscheln	mussels
Austern	oysters
Barsch	perch
Scholle	plaice
Lachs	salmon
Jakobsmuscheln	scallops
Seezunge	sole
Tintenfisch	squid

Forelle	trout
Tunfisch	tuna

Fleisch und Geflügel / Meat and Poultry

gegrillte Schweinerippchen	barbecued spare ribs
Rindfleisch	beef
Hähnchen	chicken
Geflügel	poultry
Kotelett	chop / cutlet
Filetsteak	fillet
(junge) Ente	duck(ling)
Schinkensteak	gammon
Fleischsoße	gravy
Hackfleisch vom Rind	ground beef
gekochter Schinken	ham
Nieren	kidneys
Lamm	lamb
Leber	liver
Schweinefleisch	pork
Würstchen	sausages
Lendenstück vom Rind, Steak	sirloin steak
Truthahn	turkey
Kalbfleisch	veal
Reh oder Hirsch	venison

Nachspeise und Käse / Dessert and Cheese

gedeckter Apfelkuchen	apple pie	Schokoladen-plätzchen	brownies
Hüttenkäse	cottage cheese	Sahne	cream
Vanillesoße	custard	Obstsalat	fruit salad
Ziegenkäse	goat's cheese	Eiscreme	icecream
Gebäck	pastries		

Gemüse und Salat / Vegetables and Salad

gebackene Kartoffeln in der Schale	baked potatoes
Pommes frites	french fries
Bratkartoffeln	hash browns
Kartoffelpüree	mashed potatoes
gebackene Bohnen in Tomatensoße	baked beans
Kohl	cabbage
Karotten	carrots
Blumenkohl	cauliflower

Tomaten	tomatoes
Gurke	cucumber
Knoblauch	garlic
Lauch	leek
Kopfsalat	lettuce
Pilze	mushrooms
Zwiebeln	onions
Erbsen	peas
Paprika	peppers
Kürbis	pumpkin
Spinat	spinach
Mais	sweet corn
Maiskolben	corn-on-the-cob

Obst / Fruit

Äpfel	apples	Birnen	pears
Aprikosen	apricots	Orange	orange
Brombeeren	blackberries	Pfirsiche	peaches
Kirschen	cherries	Ananas	pineapple
Weintrauben	grapes	Pflaumen	plums
Grapefruit	grapefruit	Himbeeren	raspberries
Zitrone	lemon	Erdbeeren	strawberries
Preiselbeeren	cranberries		

Getränke / Beverages

Bier (vom Fass)	beer (on tap)
Apfelwein	cider
Rotwein / Weißwein	red wine / white wine
trocken / lieblich	dry / sweet
Sekt, Schaumwein	sparkling wine
alkoholfreie Getränke	soft drinks
Fruchtsaft	fruit juice
gesüßter Zitronensaft	lemonade
Milch	milk
Mineralwasser	mineral water / spring water

Literature

Novels, stories, prose

Altenberg, Peter, *Telegrams of the Soul: Selected Prose of Peter Altenberg*. Archipelago Books (2005) – Born into a well-to-do Viennese Jewish family, Peter Altenberg (actually: Richard Engländer,

1859–1919) was an eccentric who favoured loose-fitting clothes and the company of prostitutes. These prose poems feature Viennese shopkeepers and pretty women alongside more famous figures from the city such as Egon Schiele, Gustav Mahler, Arnold Schoenberg and Ludwig Wittgenstein.

Roth, Joseph, *The Radetzky March*. Overlook TP (2002). – Masterful swan song to the Dual Monarchy.

Segel, Harold B., *The Vienna Coffeehouse Wits, 1890–1938*. Purdue University Press (1993). – Segel's anthology of writings evokes the cultural life of fin-de-siecle Vienna through the work of Peter Altenberg, Karl Kraus and other Austrian authors.

Torberg, Friedrich, *Tante Jolesch or The Decline of the West in Anecdotes*. Ariadne Press (2008). – This often melancholy description of the largely Jewish coffeehouse world in wartime and postwar Vienna is now a classic.

Beller, Steven, *A Concise History of Austria*. Cambridge University Press (2007). Austria's history in a single volume. Good introductory reading.

History, politics, philosophy

Beller, Steven, *Vienna and the Jews, 1867–1938: A Cultural History*. Cambridge University Press (1991). – A solidly researched, well-argued treatise on the importance of Jews in Vienna's cultural life.

Janik, Allan, and Toulmin, Stephen Edelson, *Wittgenstein's Vienna*. Ivan R. Dee, Publisher (1996). – The critics loved this book about the most important and original philosopher of our age, the demise of the Austro-Hungarian Empire, and fin-de-siecle Vienna.

Morton, Frederic *Thunder at Twilight: Vienna 1913/1914*. Da Capo Press (2001). – Such figures as Hitler, Trotsky, Stalin and Freud are brought to life in this energetic account of the events and personalities in Vienna surrounding the assassination of Franz Ferdinand, the deed that precipitated the First World War.

Havlicek, Alfred, Mayer, Horst F., *Austria, Through the Eyes of the Eagle*. Styria (2001). – This unique illustrated book contains exclusively aerial pictures: 170 photos, shot from a helicopter.

Illustrated books

Siepmann, Martin, Voigt, Marion, *Austria*. Sturtz (2004). – More than 230 pictures show all the facets of the alpine republic.

Davies, Cecil, *Mountain Walking in Austria*. Cicerone Press; 2nd edition (2001). – A revised edition of Cecil Davies' classic, this guide to 25 mountain groups in the Eastern Alps describes 98 walks.

Walking and cycling

Higginson John, *The Danube Cycle Way.* Cicerone Press (2003). – A guide to the most popular holiday cycling route in mainland Europe.

Money

Currency Austria's monetary unit is the **euro (€)**. There are bank notes to the value of 5, 10, 20, 50, 100 and 500 euros and coins to the value of 1 cent (reverse: gentian), 2 cents (edelweiss), 5 cents (alpine primrose), 10 cents (Stephansdom), 20 cents (Belvedere) and 50 cents (Secession) as well as 1 euro (W. A. Mozart) and 2 euro (Bertha von Suttner) pieces. 1 pound sterling is currently worth 1.35 euros; 1 dollar is 73 eurocents.

Cash can be obtained using credit cards and bank cards from Austrian **ATM machines** using a PIN. Most banks, hotels and almost all petrol stations accept credit cards, as do restaurants and large shops – nevertheless it is a good idea to check beforehand. Mastercard, Visa and Eurocard are more widely accepted than American Express and Diners Club. Loss of a card must be reported immediately.

▶ CONTACT DETAILS FOR CREDIT CARDS

In the event of lost bank or credit cards you can contact the following numbers in UK and USA (phone numbers when dialling from Austria):

▶ **Eurocard/MasterCard**
Tel. 001 / 636 7227 111

▶ **Visa**
Tel. 001 / 410 581 336

▶ **American Express UK**
Tel. 0044 / 1273 696 933

▶ **American Express USA**
Tel. 001 / 800 528 4800

▶ **Diners Club UK**
Tel. 0044 / 1252 513 500

▶ **Diners Club USA**
Tel. 001 / 303 799 9000
Have the bank sort code, account number and card number as well as the expiry date ready.
The following numbers of UK banks (dialling from Austria) can be used to report and stop lost or stolen bank and credit cards issued by those banks:

▶ **HSBC**
Tel. 0044 / 1442 422 929

▶ **Barclaycard**
Tel. 0044 / 1604 230 230

▶ **NatWest**
Tel. 0044 / 142 370 0545

▶ **Lloyds TSB**
Tel. 0044 / 1702 278 270

National Parks

Numerous institutions in Austria exist to protect the country's flora: national parks and nature parks, alpine gardens and conservation areas. The at present **seven national parks** play a particularly important role. Hohe Tauern National Park is shared by three provinces. Two national parks cross borders with neighbouring countries, making it clear that the notion of protecting the natural environment is important enough to transcend national barriers: Neusiedler See-Seewinkel National Park (shared with Hungary) with its salt lakes, marshes and broad reed beds on Europe's westernmost steppe lake, and Thayatal National Park (shared with the Czech Republic) with the wonderful transverse valley of the river Thaya. One of Europe's last pasture landscapes between Vienna and the Slovakian border is protected by the Donauauen National Park. The Nockberge, Kalkalpen and Gesäuse national parks have fantastic mountain landscapes and unique flora.

Environmental empathy in Austria

Under the motto »Experience nature – understand nature« the **approximately 40 nature parks** (»Naturparke«) in Austria aim to bring their visitors closer to the country's scenic beauty and diversity. With various events, nature trails, themed walks and guided tours, young visitors in particular should be able to experience the individual characteristics of each nature park in a playful way. The landscapes range from high alpine regions to hilly country, dry steppe regions, heathland, moorland, woods, wine-growing areas, and river valleys. Most national parks lie in Lower Austria, Styria and Burgenland. Detailed information on all of Austria's nature parks is provided in English at www.naturparke.at. Those who speak some German can learn about projects aimed at protecting individual species at www.wwf.at.

Nature parks

The alpine gardens or »Alpengärten« offer a nature-friendly way of examining the fascinating world of alpine flora. Here, diverse species with the ability to survive in adverse environmental conditions are brought together in the smallest of areas for visitors to admire.

Alpine gardens

> NATIONAL PARKS AND ALPINE GARDENS

NATIONAL PARKS

► **Donau-Auen**
(Vienna, Lower Austria; ►p.218)
Area: 93 sq km/36 sq mi
www.donauauen.at

► **Gesäuse**
(Styria; ►p.180)
area: 124 sq km/48 sq mi
www.nationalpark.co.at

► **Hohe Tauern**
(Carinthia, Southern Burgenland,

Adorning the banks of natural river courses – the Siberian iris

Tyrol; ►p.276)
Area: 1788 sq km/690 sq mi
www.hohetauern.at

► **Nockberge**
(Carinthia; ►p.244), area: 184 sq km/71 sq mi
www.nationalparknockberge.at

► **Neusiedler See-Seewinkel**
(Burgenland, Hungary; ►p.407)
Area in Austria: 95 sq km/37 sq mi
www.nationalpark-neusiedlersee-seewinkel.at

► **Kalkalpen**
(Upper Austria; ►p.484)
Area: 181 sq km/70 sq mi
www.kalkalpen.at

► **Thayatal**
(Lower Austria; ►p.561)

Area in Austria: 13 sq km/5 sq mi
www.np-thayatal.at

**ALPINE GARDENS
(Selection)**

► **Bad Aussee**
2km/1.2mi northwest of the town

► **Graz**
Botanischer Garten

► **Graz-St. Veit**
Alpengarten Rannach

► **Innsbruck**
Botanischer Garten der Universität on the Patscherkofel mountain at an elevation of 1900m/6234ft

► **Klagenfurt**
Botanischer Garten

► **Kühtai**
near the Dortmunder Hütte

► **Linz**
Botanischer Garten

► **Rax**
near the Ottohaus

► **Reutte**
on the Hahnenkamm mountain

► **Schruns**
near the Lindauer Hütte

► **Villacher Alpengarten**
Villacher Alpe

► **Wachau**
Schönbühel

► **Vienna**
Botanischer Garten, Belvedere
Botanischer Garten, Universität

Post and Communications

Post office counters are usually open Mon–Fri 8am–noon and 2pm–6pm. Some main post offices in large towns are open around the clock. **Postage stamp machines** stand in front of most post offices.
Stamps can be purchased in both post offices and tobacconists (»Trafiken«). It costs €0.55 to send postcards and standard letters (up to 20g/0.7oz) within the EU; a €1.25 stamp is required for letters to the rest of the world.

Post offices

It is possible to make international calls from all public telephones. These normally take either **coins** or **phonecards**, which are available from either post offices or tobacconists. After dialling the country code, the zero that precedes the subsequent local area code is omitted.
Long-distance calls both within Austria and to other countries are cheaper Mon–Fri 8pm–6am and at the weekend.

Telephone

UK travellers can use their mobile in Austria using the A-1 network. Check on roaming tariffs, which can be pricey, before you leave. The other major networks are One and T-Mobile, and there are smaller operators such as Telering. It is possible to buy prepaid SIM cards – refills are available from tobacconists or supermarkets.

◀ *Mobile phones*

DIRECTORY ENQUIRIES AND DIALLING CODES

▶ **Dialling codes to Austria**
from the UK and Republic of Ireland:
Tel. 00 43 (to Vienna: 00 43 1)
from the USA, Canada and Australia: tel. 00 11 43

▶ **Dialling codes from Austria**
to the UK: tel. 00 44
to the Republic of Ireland:

Tel. 00 353
to the USA and Canada:
Tel. 00 1
to Australia: tel. 00 61

▶ **Directory enquiries in Austria**
National and international:
Tel. 11 88 77
(€1.35/min)

Prices and Discounts

Ask about price reductions in tourist information offices: for example, the Salzburgcard and the Kärntencard provide free or discounted admission to museums and other institutions.

Discounts

WHAT DOES IT COST?

Three-course meal
from €20

Simple meal
from €7

Cup of coffee
from €2.50

Rental car
from €50
per day

Petrol
€1.35

Single room
from €30

Tipping   It is usual in Austria to give a tip of 10% to bar staff and taxi drivers. Room service should receive €1 per day, and porters €1 per piece of baggage.

Shopping

Opening Hours

Shops   Generally speaking, shops are open Mon–Fri 9am–6pm and Sat 9am–noon. Every first Saturday in the month shops in towns are permitted to stay open until 5pm. Shops in smaller places are often closed between noon and 2pm or 3pm. Grocery stores often open before 8am and close around 6.30pm. In addition there are shops in stations and airports whose opening hours reflect the times of day when people are on the move (sometimes until 11pm).
In tourist resorts and town centres special rules sometimes apply at weekends.

Banks   Most Austrian banks are open Mon–Fri 8am–12.30pm and 1.30pm–3pm (Thu until 5pm).

Souvenirs

Arts and crafts   A whole range of **typical products of the local craft industry** is still available in Austria today. The most popular souvenirs are ceramics, textiles, fine wrought-iron work and wood carvings. Wood carvings, embroidery, glassware and ceramics are the principal items on offer in Vorarlberg and Tyrol; in Salzburg, Styria and Carinthia it is fine

A popular souvenir: Gmund ceramics with typical rustic patterns have been made by hand for centuries

wrought-iron work, locally-produced costume and the associated jewellery, pewter and ceramic goods; in Lower Austria wrought-iron work. Burgenland has retained a tradition for pottery and ceramics production that goes back to Roman times, and is also considered a centre for basket-making. Carinthia is also known for its leather goods and furs. Fans of porcelain, antiques and craftwork are most likely to find what they are looking for in Vienna and Salzburg, where annual antique trade fairs take place.

The finest sweets, cakes, pastries and confectionery, as well as cheese **Tasty treats** products and other specialities such as pumpkin seed oil, are always a welcome gift for the folks back home. Red and white wines as well as liqueurs and schnapps specialities are among the most popular souvenirs for those who enjoy a dram or two.

Sport and Outdoors

Angling

Austria offers anglers a wealth of opportunities to enjoy **coarse fish-** **Sport and leisure** **ing, spin fishing and fly fishing**. Strict government regulations regarding sewage disposal ensure that the levels of harmful substances in fishing waters are very low. In the country's lakes, anglers can fish

▶ ADDRESSES FOR SPORTING HOLIDAYS

ANGLING

▶ **Fischwasser Österreich**
Ossiacher-See-Süduferstr. 59
A-9523 Landskron/Villach
Tel. 0 42 42/442 00 30

MOUNTAINEERING

▶ **Verband
Alpiner Vereine Österreichs**
Bäckerstr. 16
A-1010 Wien
Tel. 01/5 12 54 88
www.vavoe.at

▶ **Österreichischer Alpenverein
(ÖAV)**
Olympiastr. 37
A-6020 Innsbruck
Tel. 05 12/5 95 47
Fax 57 55 28
www.alpenverein.at

▶ **British Mountain Guides**
Siabod Cottage

Capel Curig, Conwy
North Wales, LL24 0ET
Tel. 01286 871763
www.bmg.org.uk

GOLF

▶ **Österreichischer Golf-Verband**
Marxergasse 25
A-1030 Wien
Tel. 01/5 05 32 45 16
Fax 5 05 49 62
www.golf.at

▶ **Golf in Austria**
Glockengasse 4D
A-5020 Salzburg
Tel. 06 62/64 51 53
www.golfinfo.at

AVIATION

▶ **Österreichischer Aero-Club
(Austrian Aeroclub)**
Prinz-Eugen-Strasse 12
A-1040 Wien

The Inntal Cycle Way runs along the river, on well-made paths well away from the roads: a family-friendly cycling experience without too much effort

Tel. 01/5 05 10 28
Fax 5 05 79 23
www.aeroclub.at

▶ **Austro-Control (Austrian Civil Aviation Administration)**
Schnirchgasse 11
A-1030 Wien
Tel. 5 17 03-0
www.austrocontrol.at

CYCLING

▶ **Argus – cycling lobby**
Frankenberggasse 11
A-1040 Wien
Tel. 01/505 09 07
www.argus.or.at

▶ **Radtouren in Österreich**
c/o Landesverband für Tourismus
in Oberösterreich
Freistädter Strasse 119
A-4041 Linz
Tel. 07 32 / 22 10 22
Fax 727 77 01
www.radtouren.at
Organizes cycling tours, gives information on cycle ways and offers accommodation booking in bike hotels.

▶ **Bike-Hotels e.V.**
Marketing Tourismus Synergie
Austria GmbH
Saalfeldnerstrasse 14
5751 Maishofen
Tel. 06542 / 804 80-22 (23)
Fax 06542 / 804 80-4
www.bike-holidays.com

WATER SPORTS

▶ **Österreichischer Segelverband**
Seestr. 17b
A-7100 Neusiedl am See
Tel. 02167/ 402 430
Fax 40 375
www.segelverband.at

Only the fearless plunge from Krippenstein into the wide blue yonder

▶ **Surf- und Segelwetter**
Tel. 04 50/19 91 15 66 11

▶ **Österreichischer Kanu-Verband**
Giessereistrasse 8
A-5280 Braunau
Tel. 077 22/8 16 00
Fax 8 26 00
www.kanuverband.at

▶ **Rafting**
Information from tourist office in
▶Hallein and at www.montee.com

HIKING

▶ **Österreichs Wanderdörfer e.V.**
Unterwollaniger Strasse 53
A-9500 Villach
Tel. 0 42 42/25 75 31
Fax 21 66 30
www.wandern-in-oesterreich.at

for lake trout, lake char, pike and sheatfish, as well as catfish and pike-perch, while rainbow trout and brown trout are found in the mountain lakes. Anglers must hold an **official fishing licence**, issued by the provincial administrative authority and valid for the whole province. In addition, a fishing permit from the owner or leaseholder of the inshore fishing water in question is required. The statutory close seasons vary from district to district. As many angling districts issue only a limited number of guest licences, it is advisable to obtain a permit for your chosen holiday destination in good time.

Annual licence ▶ An alternative that offers good value for money is the annual fishing license. Information on membership and prices is provided by »Fischwasser Österreich« (address p.130).

Mountaineering

An El Dorado for mountain climbers ▶ Austria is a **classic mountaineering country** and there is an almost inexhaustible choice of mountaineering tours and climbing trips of all levels of difficulty on offer. Alpine dangers such as sudden changes in the weather and rock falls should not be underestimated. For this reason climbers should never set out alone into high-altitude regions. Only when accompanied by expert guides and having – without fail – informed a third party (e.g. hotel staff or the hut landlord) of the itinerary should the trip commence. Guides can be arranged in all mountain towns; in many places it is possible to take part in mountaineering courses.

Those who get into **difficulties while climbing** should preferably use the alpine distress signal, recognized throughout the whole alpine region, to call for help. The signal involves repeating an action intended to draw the attention of other climbers (blowing a whistle, waving a brightly coloured garment) six times in a minute, followed by a minute's pause. This pattern is repeated until help arrives.

Österreichischer Alpenverein ▶ The Austrian Alpine Association (ÖAV), founded in 1862, provides both members and non-members with numerous huts for shelter on the mountains.

Golf

Above par ▶ Golf is of increasing significance in Austria. There are **numerous golf courses** – in major holiday resorts as well as in rural regions. Visiting players are welcome on Austrian golf courses, as long as they are members of a golf club at home or can produce confirmation of the so-called »Platzreife«, documentation from Austria or Germany regarded as proof that the player knows the rules and etiquette of the game and has been allocated a (not necessarily low) handicap. The brochure *Golf in Austria*, produced by the Österreichischer Golf-Verband, is an excellent compilation of all the necessary information. It is possible to download brochures in English at www.austria.info.

Furthermore, there are golf hotels (exclusively four and five-star establishments) in Austria, which put their own course at guests' disposal or are located in the vicinity of a golf course.

Aviation

Before using private airfields a permit must be obtained from the airfield management. Thanks to the JAR-FCL regulations, a UK-issued **European Pilot Licence** is recognized in Austria. An American FAA licence must be converted to make it valid in Europe – this necessitates additional skill tests, and pilots must have 100 hours of flight time under their belt. Flight permits issued for sporting purposes to pilots without European-issued licences are valid for a limited period only.

Requirements

There are numerous gliding schools in Austria. Both sport airfields and commercial airports can be used for engine-powered flights. Aircraft can be hired at most airfields. Information is available from the appropriate departments of the Austrian Aeroclub (address p.130).

Gliding and engine-powered flight

In 1973, Sepp Himberger of Tyrol founded the world's first hang-gliding club together with a flying school in Kössen at the foot of the Wilden Kaiser mountains. In the meantime the number of such clubs has increased markedly: a series of »**Zivilluftfahrtschulen für Hängegleiter**« provide training for glider and paraglider pilots. Information can be obtained from the appropriate department of the Austrian Aeroclub (address p.130).

Hang-gliding, paragliding

Balloon rides enjoy great popularity in Austria. A colourful spectacle at dizzy heights is offered by the **Hot Air Balloon Week in Filzmoos in January**. More information is available at www.filzmoos.at.

Hot air ballooning

Cycling

Along with the popular Danube Cycle Way (Donau-Radweg) there is also the Inntal-Radweg, Tauern-Radweg (along the Salzach and Saalach rivers), Salzkammergut-Radweg (a round trip), Grenzland-Radweg (through the Mühlviertel), Neusiedler-See-Radweg (in Burgenland; partly in Hungary), Mur-Radweg and Drau-Radweg. The routes are **very well signposted**, lead along cycle ways free of traffic or quiet side roads and often follow rivers or the shores of lakes. The brochure *Cycling Holidays in Austria*, available from Österreich Werbung or the Austrian National Tourist Board (► Information), provides detailed information. It is possible to download brochures in English at www.austria.info.

Wonderful cycle ways

Approximately 100 Austrian hotels that which lie on the routes of cycle ways and are specially equipped to meet the needs of cyclists (»Radhotels«) are listed in the brochure.

◄ Bike hotels

Cycle hire ▶ It is possible to rent a bike at many Austrian railway stations. The specific locations are listed in the brochure.

Mountain biking ▶ The sport of mountain biking is growing in popularity in Austria. Routes of varying degrees of difficulty are designated and there are Austrian hotels specializing in guided mountain bike tours. Moreover, the mountain bike world championships are organized here. See www.bike-holidays.com for more details.

Water Sports

Broad range There are many possibilities to take part in water sports on almost all of Austria's rivers and lakes. Visitors will find bathing beaches, boat hire, and sailing and windsurfing schools. There is also the opportunity to go waterskiing.

Motor boats ▶ On the Danube (Donau) and Lake Constance (Bodensee), the international regulations that every good skipper must know apply. Private traffic is sometimes limited to certain times of day and not infrequently completely prohibited on other Austrian inland waters. The Austrian federal police force (Gendarmerie) will provide information.

Sailing ▶ With the exception of Lake Constance, no special approval is necessary for sailing on Austrian inland waters. On Lake Constance sailing boats of more than 12 sq m/129 sq ft require the »Schein D« permit. Knowledge and observance of **generally applicable rules** are required everywhere, and the customary life-saving equipment must be brought along (yellow or red life jacket). There are sailing clubs and boat hire companies at most lakes.

Some like it wet: rafting on the Inn river

Because the great majority of sailing areas lie in Upper Austria, Carinthia and Salzburg Province, **alpine influences** are of prime importance: reckon on rapid shifts in wind speed and direction and sudden changes in the weather.

The scale ranges from more sedate river trips or »**Flusswandern**« on the Danube, Drau, Inn, Mur and Salzach all the way to the **most difficult stretches of white water** on mountain rivers such as the Salza, Steyr, Möll, Lieser, Ziller and Lech. The Möll river is the scene of the annual international Wildwasserwoche (White Water Week).

Rowing, canoeing

The Inn and its tributaries are considered to constitute **one of Europe's best rafting areas**, i.e. for white water rafting trips in large rubber dinghies carrying up to 30 people. Rafting is also possible however on the Salzach river and its left-hand tributary, the Saalach. Points of departure for these trips are Salzburg, Hallein and Abtenau.

Rafting

Hiking

Idyllic valleys, deep gorges, thundering waterfalls, clear mountain streams, blooming alpine pasture, imposing glaciers – Austria has a great deal to offer the hiking enthusiast. With countless footpaths, theme routes, and hill and mountain trails, there is **something to suit the taste of every walker**. Approximately 50,000km/30,000mi of signposted footpaths and a total of 13,500 mountain accommodations are at the disposal of visitors who wish to explore the country by shank's pony. Less practised hikers should take into consideration that the body must first adapt to the altered environmental conditions before its normal capacity is attained. Suitable clothing and stout, well worn-in footwear, waterproofs and headgear are all important and contribute to the unfettered enjoyment of the magnificent landscape.

Good infrastructure

A brochure is available from Österreich Werbung or the Austrian National Tourist Board (►Information) with details of hiking villages and regions, tips on walking trips with children, information on hiking in the mountains and tackling the peaks as well as lists of hiking package deals, hiking specialists, theme routes and hiking hotels (Wanderhotels). It is possible to download brochures in English at www.austria.info.

Spas and Wellness

With its numerous medicinal and mineral springs, its moorland, mud deposits, and favourable climate, Austria is a country of spas and baths par excellence. Over and above this, for some years now the number of people who simply treat themselves to a little time off

Land of spas and baths

▶ ADDRESSES FOR SPAS AND WELLNESS

▶ **Öst. Heilbäder- und Kurorteverband**
Josefsplatz 6, A-1010 Wien
Tel. 01/5 12 19 04, fax 5 12 86 93

▶ **Österreichischer Kneippbund**
Kunigundenweg 10
A-8700 Leoben
Tel. 0 38 42/2 17 18, fax 2 17 19
www.kneippbund.at

▶ **schlank und schön in Austria**
Ossiacher-See-Süduferstr. 59
A-9523 Landskron/Villach
www.schlankundschoen.at

▶ **Best Wellness Hotels Austria**
Brixnerstr. 3/3
A-6020 Innsbruck
Tel. 05 12/36 02 61
www.wellnesshotel.com

in Austria in order to relax and allow themselves to be spoiled – for the good of their health – has been on the increase. Alongside the **health resorts**, which offer holidays under medical supervision to guests who wish to take preventative measures or who are already struggling with health complaints, there is also an increasing number of **wellness resorts**, which offer their guests a variety of opportunities to enjoy sporting activities along with the appropriate care and relaxation.

Zoos and Animal Parks

Alpine animals
Animal lovers, too, get their money's worth in Austria: in zoos and animal parks, enclosures and compounds, visitors can observe the wonders of the alpine animal kingdom in particular.

▶ THE BEST ZOOS AND ANIMAL PARKS

▶ **Wildpark Altenfelden**
▶Mühlviertel

▶ **Wildpark Aurach**
Wildparkweg 5, A-6370 Aurach
Tel. 053 56 / 652 51
www.wildpark-tirol.at
South of Kitzbühel: red deer and fallow deer, yak, lynx
Opening times: mid-May–mid-Nov daily 9am–5pm, Christmas–mid-May Wed–Sun 10am–5pm

▶ **Wildpark Feld am See**
A-9544 Feld am See
Tel. 042 46 / 27 76
www.alpen-wildpark.com
Located east of Millstätter See, this 11ha/27ac outdoor enclosure has more than 100 native game animals, a »Streichelzoo« where animals can be stroked and fed, and a »fish museum«. Opening times: May–Sept daily 9am–6pm, Oct until 5pm

► Fieberbrunn, Kleintierpark Grosslehen

Lehen 21 A-6391 Fieberbrunn
Tel. 053 54 / 564 55
South of St. Johann in Tirol with moufflons, apes, lamas and kangaroos. Opening times: mid-May–Oct daily 10am–7pm; feeding: 4.30pm (closed Tue during off season)

► Fusch, Wildpark Ferleiten

►Grossglockner-Hochalpen-strasse

► Tierpark Diana

►Gmünd, Surroundings

► Grünau, Cumberland-Wildpark

►Traunsee

► Tierpark Haag

Salaberg, A-3350 Haag
Tel. 074 34/45 40 81
www.tierparkstadthaag.at
The Schloss Salaberg park north of Steyr is home to about 80 native and exotic animal species. Opening times: April–Sept 8.30am–5.30am).

► Tier- und Naturpark Schloss Herberstein

Buchberg 50
A-8223 Stubenberg am See
Tel. 031 76 / 80 77 70
Located a good 40km/25mi north of Graz. Approximately 100 animal species from all over the world. Opening times: May–Sept daily 9am–5pm, Oct daily, Nov and Dec Sat and Sun 10am–4pm).

► Wildpark Hochkreut

►Traunsee

► Reptilienzoo Happ

►Klagenfurt

► Alpenzoo Innsbruck

►Innsbruck

► Linzer Tiergarten

►Linz

Alpine lama on a trekking tour

► Wildpark Wildbichl

Gränzring 30
A-6342 Niederndorferberg
Tel. 053 73 / 622 33
www.wildbichl.com
This park a few miles northeast of Kufstein is home to ibex, chamois, moufflon and lynx. Open all year round (Nov–March 10am–4.30pm)

► Pamhagen, Steppentierpark

►Neusiedler See

► Wildpark Rosegg

A-9232 Schloss Rosegg 1
Tel. 042 74 / 523 57
www.rosegg.at/tierpark.htm
Located south of Velden on the Wörthersee Carinthia's largest animal park is home to about 400 animals of 35 different species. Opening times: mid-March–Oct daily 9am–6pm

▶ **Zoo Salzburg**
  ▶Salzburg, Surroundings

▶ **Vogelpark Turnersee**
  ▶Völkermarkt, Klopeiner See

▶ **Tierpark Wels**
  ▶Wels

▶ **Zoologischer Garten Schmiding**
  ▶Wels, Surroundings

▶ **Tiergarten Schönbrunn**
  ▶Wien, Schönbrunner Park

▶ **Vienna, Lainzer Tiergarten**
  Located on the western edge of the city, red deer, roe deer and mouflons can be seen here. Opening times: mid-Feb–mid-Nov until dusk, otherwise 9am–5pm

Time

An hour ahead

Austria is in the central European time zone (CET), one hour ahead of Greenwich Mean Time. For the summer months from the beginning of April to the end of October European summer time is used (CEST = CET+1 hour).

Transport

By Car

Road network

The very **dense Austrian road network** consists of autobahns, »Schnellstrassen« (expressway system), »Bundesstrassen« (main routes bearing blue and yellow numbered signposts), »Landesstrassen« (country roads) and »Gemeindestrassen« (secondary communal/city roads).

Alpine roads

The **condition of Austria's roads is good in every respect**. Minor alpine roads, in particular, can be quite narrow with numerous twists and turns. In any given situation, the driver for whom it is easier should always give way to the other vehicle. In summer special care should be taken on alpine roads due to the heavy traffic at this time of year. Vehicles travelling downhill should always give way to those heading uphill. From October to May, depending on the weather, drivers can expect mountain passes to be closed. Automobile clubs will provide information (▶Emergency).

Autobahn tolls, the »vignette«

A toll is payable on Austrian autobahns and expressways in the form of a vignette (windscreen sticker). For cars (up to 3.5 tons) and motorcycles there are vignettes for one year, two months and ten days.

The one-year vignette (valid from one calendar year including the December of the previous year and the January of the next) costs €73.80 (€29.50 for motorcycles). The two-month vignette costs €22.20 (€11.10 for motorcycles) and the ten-day vignette €7.70 (€4.40 for motorcycles). Those without a vignette are liable to a fine of up to €4000. It is not necessary to buy a separate vignette for caravans. The vignette is available from tobacconists, post offices and automobile clubs in Austria, and automobile clubs can supply them in other countries. They are also sold at petrol stations near the Austrian border.

◄ Where to buy a vignette

A **toll is payable on some sections of road** in spite of the vignette. These are as follows: Arlbergtunnel, Brennerautobahn, Felbertauernstrasse, Felbertauerntunnel, Gerlosstrasse, Grossglockner-Hochalpenstrasse, Karawankentunnel, Pyhrnautobahn (Bosrucktunnel, Gleinalmtunnel), Silvretta-Hochalpenstrasse, Timmelsjoch-Hochalpenstrasse and the car shuttle service known as the Tauernschleuse (Böckstein–Mallnitz). Tolls may also be payable on small mountain roads.

◄ Other toll roads

Austrians drive on the right-hand side of the road. In other ways, too, the Austrian highway code and regulations correspond to those in other European countries.

Road signs

Unlike in the UK, traffic joining a roundabout has right of way, unless otherwise indicated. The rule »right before left« applies.

◄ Roundabouts

The following speed limits apply for motorcycles and cars: on autobahns 80mph/130kmh, on other roads 62mph/100kmh, in built-up areas 31mph/50kmh. From 10pm to 5am the speed limit on autobahns, with the exception of the A 1 Salzburg–Vienna and the A 2 Vienna–Villach, is 68mph/110kmh.

Traffic regulations

For cars towing trailers or caravans up to 3.5 tonnes (US: 3.8 short tons) in weight the speed limit outside towns and on autobahns is 62mph/100kmh; the maximum speed for cars towing more than 3.5 tonnes as well as mobile homes up to 7.5 tonnes (US: 8.2 short tons) in weight is 43mph/70kmh outside towns and 50mph/80kmh on autobahns.

The driver and all passengers must wear seat belts. In case of a crash, insurance benefits are reduced if the injured parties were not wearing seat belts. The law also stipulates that an advance warning triangle and a reflecting warning vest be carried in the vehicle.

The **blood alcohol limit** when driving is **0.5g/l**. Severe fines are imposed on those discovered at the wheel with higher levels, and the offending party may lose his driving licence.

All those involved in accidents, whether or not they are deemed responsible, will be tested for the consumption of alcohol or drugs; refusal to comply with these tests is understood as an admission of guilt. Mobile phones may only be used with a hands-free kit while driving.

Accident

⏵ CAR RENTAL

IN THE UK

▶ **Avis**
Tel. 0844 581 0147, www.avis.com

▶ **Budget**
Tel. 0844 581 9998
www.budget.co.uk

▶ **Europcar**
Tel. 0845 758 5375
www.europcar.com

▶ **Hertz**
Tel. 08708 44 88 44
www.hertz.com

IN AUSTRIA

▶ **Avis**
Tel. 0 26/8 22 05 65 39

▶ **Europcar**
Tel. 01/8 66 16 33

▶ **Hertz**
Tel. 01/7 95 32

▶ **Sixt/Budget**
Tel. 08 00/24 10 70
and 0 08 00/11 11 74 98

Children	Children under twelve years of age may not travel in the front passenger seat of a car. Child car seats with seat belts are recommended. Car drivers are expected to always allow children to cross the highway. It is not permitted to overtake school buses when the yellow-red warning lights are illuminated.
Parking	Yellow zigzag lines indicate that parking or stopping is strictly prohibited. In many towns there are short-term parking zones, sometimes free of charge, but for which a parking disc is required. New laws giving foreign authorities the right to obtain information from the Driver and Vehicle Licensing Agency (DVLA) mean that **Austrian parking (and speeding) fines will be sent to the registered owner of the vehicle in their home country**.
Winter tyres and snow chains	In snowy conditions winter tyres are highly recommended (and sometimes stipulated by law). Snow chains are necessary on various mountain roads and passes. The Austrian automobile associations, ÖAMTC and ARBÖ (▶Emergency), have set up offices from which snow chains can be hired out.
Motorcyclists	Motorbike and moped riders must wear a helmet, use dipped headlights during the day and carry a first-aid box. The minimum age for child passengers on motorcycles is ten years.
Traffic accidents	The police must be called out to accidents in which people have been injured; if not, only call the police if the identity of the parties involved cannot be established.

Lead-free »Normalbenzin« (91 Octane), »Euro-Super« (lead-free, 95 Octane), »Super Plus« (lead-free, 98 Octane), diesel and liquid gas are available in Austria.

Petrol

▶Emergency

Breakdown service

By Rail and Bus

With the exception of a few local railway lines that are only important to the tourism industry, **the railways in Austria are state-owned** (ÖBB – Austrian Federal Railways). The network for Intercity and Eurocity trains is well developed. The Eurocity connection from Bregenz to Vienna runs through German territory in the corridor between Wörgl (Tyrol) and Salzburg.

Österreichische Bundesbahnen (ÖBB)

On all of Austria's important main lines, a networked timetable of departures at regular one and two-hour intervals makes it possible to change trains quickly. The high-speed connections on the Westbahn and Südbahn operate at hourly intervals; on all other lines mostly at two-hourly intervals. The ÖBB has information centres in the larger towns and cities. Travel agents offering train tickets will also provide information.

◀ *Information*

Tickets for distances up to and including 100km/62mi are valid for one day, from 101km/63mi single tickets are valid for three days and return tickets for one month. The use of high-speed trains incurs a surcharge (»Zuschlag«), as does travel in Eurocity and Intercity trains and other trains offering a higher level of comfort. **Children** less than seven years old travel free when accompanied by an adult (a maximum of two children per adult), and those under 16 enjoy a 50% price reduction. Various groups – families, old age pensioners and others – receive **considerable discounts** on ÖBB lines. Ask when you buy your ticket.

◀ *Tickets*

Motorail services within Austria run between Vienna and Villach, Salzburg, Bischofshofen, Innsbruck, Feldkirch and Lienz as well as between Feldkirch and Linz, Graz and Villach.

◀ *Motorail trains*

Bicycles can be hired at approximately 50 Austrian railway stations from April to October. They can be **returned to any participating station**. Booking in advance is recommended, especially during the high season and at weekends. Those with an ÖBB train ticket pay less. Official photographic proof of identity is required.

◀ *Cycle hire at the station*

In most European countries, standard-gauge train track has a width of 1435mm/56.5in. Steam trains of bygone days often ran on narrow gauge track. Some of Austria's narrow-gauge railways, mountain railways and tram systems included, have been »saved« in recent times and their nostalgic charms attract train fans.

Narrow-gauge railways

Bus lines are a **very important means of transport in Austria**, particularly in alpine regions. There are two different bus lines: Postbus and

Transport by bus

▶ IMPORTANT ADDRESSES

FEDERAL RAILWAYS

▶ **Österreichische Bundesbahnen**
Wienerbergstr. 11
A-1100 Wien
Tel. 01/93 00 00
Fax 93 00 02 50 01
www.oebb.at

▶ **Zentrale Zugauskunft Wien**
Tel. 01/17 17 (charged as a local call from the whole of Austria)

▶ **Train and bus enquiries (including Postbus services)**
Tel. 01/7 11 01

NARROW-GAUGE RAILWAYS

▶ **Bregenzer Waldbahn**
Bezau–Schwarzenberg-Bersbuch
Route length: 6.1km/3.8mi
Gauge: 760mm/30in
Steam operated; in summer at weekends

▶ **Stubaitalbahn**
Innsbruck–Fulpmes
Route length: 18.2km/11.3mi
Gauge: 1000mm/39.4in
Electrically operated; all year round

▶ **Strassen- und Mittelgebirgsbahn**
Innsbruck–Igls
Route length: 8km/5mi
Gauge: 1000mm/39.4in
Electrically operated; all year round

▶ **Achenseebahn**
Jenbach–Achensee
Route length: 6.8km/4.2mi
Gauge: 1000mm/39.4in
Steam-operated rack railway; May–Sept

▶ **Zillertalbahn**
Jenbach–Zell a. Ziller–Mayrhofen
Route length: 31.7km/19.7mi
Gauge: 760mm/29.9in
Steam and diesel operated; all year round

For more than 100 years the rack railway trains have been chuffing up the Schneeberg

► **Pinzgauer Lokalbahn**
Zell am See–Krimml
Route length: 52.7km/32.7mi
Gauge: 760mm/29.9in
Electrically and (rarely)
steam operated; all year round

► **Reisseck-Höhenbahn**
Berghotel Reisseck–Reisseck
Route length: 3.3km/2.1mi
Gauge: 600mm/23.6in
Diesel operated; May–Oct

► **Taurachbahn**
Mauterndorf–Mariapfarr–
St. Andrä
Route length: 11km/6.8mi
Gauge: 760mm/29.9in
Diesel and steam operated; in
summer at weekends

► **Murtalbahn**
Unzmark–Murau–Tamsweg
Route length: 65.5km/40.7mi
Gauge: 760mm/29.9in
Diesel and steam operated; all year
round; special steam trains and
amateur locomotive trips by arrangement with the management
in Murau

► **Museumstramway
Klagenfurt/See**
Lendkanal–terminus »Im Moos«
Route length: 800m/875yd
Horse-drawn trams; in July and
August at weekends

► **Schafbergbahn**
St. Wolfgang–Schafberg
Route length: 5.9km/3.7mi
Gauge: 1000mm/39.4in
Steam and diesel operated; April–
Oct

► **Attergaubahn**
Vöcklamarkt–St. Georgen–
Attersee

Route length: 13.3km/8.3mi
Gauge: 1000mm/39.4in
Electrically operated; all year
round

► **Strassenbahn Gmunden**
Connects with all ÖBB trains at
Gmunden main station
Route length: 2.4km/1.5mi
Gauge: 1000mm/39.4in
Electrically operated

► **Traunseebahn**
Gmunden–Vorchdorf
Route length: 14.6km/9.1mi
Gauge: 1000mm/39.4in
Electrically operated; all year
round

► **Museumsbahn St. Florian**
St. Florian–Pichling
Route length: 6km/3.7mi
Gauge: 900mm/35.4in
Electrically operated; in summer
on Sundays and national holidays

► **Linzer Pöstling-Bergbahn**
Route length: 2.9km/1.8mi
Gauge: 1000mm/39.4in
Electrically operated; all year
round

► **Waldviertler
Schmalspurbahn**
Gmünd–Litschau and
Heidenreichstein
Route length: 38.3km/23.8mi
Gauge: 760mm/29.9in
Steam operated; in summer at
weekends

► **Steyrtalbahn**
Steyr–Grünburg
Route length: 17km/10.6mi
Gauge: 760mm/29.9in
Steam operated; in summer on
Sundays

▶ **Ybbstalbahn**
Waidhofen–Lunz–Ybbsitz
Route length: 76.7km/47.7mi
Gauge: 760mm/29.9in
Steam operated

▶ **Gurktalbahn**
Pöckstein–Zwischenwässern
Route length: 3.3km/2.1mi
Gauge: 760mm/29.9in
Steam operated; in summer at
weekends

▶ **Stainzer Bahn**
Preding–Stainz
Route length: 10.6km/6.6mi
Gauge: 760mm/29.9in
Steam operated; in summer
several times weekly

▶ **Feistritztalbahn**
Weiz–Birkfeld
Route length: 23.9km/14.9mi
Gauge: 760mm/29.9in
Steam operated; in summer twice
weekly

▶ **Die Krumpen Bahn**
Ober–Grafendorf–Wieselburg
Route length: 62.3km/38.7mi
Gauge: 760mm/29.9in
Electrically operated; in summer
special steam trains

▶ **Mariazellerbahn**
St. Pölten–Mariazell
Route length: 91.3km/56.7mi
Gauge: 760mm/29.9in
Electrically operated; special steam
trains

▶ **Höllentalbahn**
Payerbach–Reichenau–
Hirschwang
Route length: 5.2km/3.2mi
Gauge: 760mm/29.9in
Electrically, steam and diesel
operated

▶ **Schneebergbahn**
Puchberg–Hochschneeberg
Route length: 9.7km/6.0mi
Gauge: 1000mm/39.4in
Steam-operated rack railway; end
of April–end of Oct

BY AIR

▶ **Central flight information**
Vienna Airport
Tel. 01/70 07-22 31 and -22 32
Austrian Airlines
Tel. 00 43 (0) 5/17 66 10 00

BY SHIP

▶ **DDSG Blue Danube**
Schiffahrt GmbH
Handelskai 265, A-1020 Wien
Tel. 01/588 80 00, fax 58 88 04 40
www.ddsg-blue-danube.at

▶ **Donauschiffahrt Wurm + Köck**
Untere Donaulände 1
A-4020 Linz
Tel. 07 32/78 36 07, fax 7 71 09 09
www.donauschiffahrt.at

▶ **Donauschiffahrt Ardagger**
A-3321 Ardagger 155
Tel. 0 74 79/6 46 40, fax 64 65 10
www.tiscover.at/donauschiffahrt

▶ **International marketing**
organization »Die Donau«
Floragasse 7/701, A-1040 Wien
Tel. 01/23 00 01 31 07
Fax 23 00 01 35 50
www.danube-river.org

▶ **Viking River Cruises**
UK Limited
Nelsons House
83 Wimbledon Park Side
London SW19 5LP
Tel. 020 8780 7900
Fax 020 8780 7930
www.vikingrivercruises.co.uk

Bahnbus (ÖBB). Public transport by bus in Austria consists of more than 2000 scheduled routes, and almost all destinations relevant to tourists can be reached by bus.

By Air

Domestic services operated by the Austrian Airlines Group connect the airports Vienna-Schwechat, Graz, Innsbruck, Klagenfurt, Linz and Salzburg, which also offer international connections.

By Ship

With a fleet of 11 ships, Wurm + Köck is the largest excursion shipping company in the area offering Danube cruises from Passau to Linz or Vienna. The firm DDSG Blue Danube Schiffahrt GmbH sails between Melk and Krems and offers day trips from Vienna into the Wachau, various theme excursions in Vienna and – on a hydrofoil – trips to Bratislava and Budapest. With its home port in Ardagger in the Strudengau, as the narrow valley of the Danube east of Linz is called, Donauschiffahrt Ardagger organizes tours of the Strudengau and charter tours. Alongside pleasure cruises on the Danube within Austria, members of the international marketing organization Die Donau offer **cruises along the whole length of the Danube**. Viking River Cruises runs tours along the Rhine, Main and Danube rivers.

Danube

In summer **boat tours and pleasure cruises** take place on the larger Austrian lakes. Besides the cruises on Lake Constance (Vorarlberg), ships ply the waters of the following lakes: Plansee (Tyrol), Achensee (Tyrol), Zeller See (Salzburg Province), Mondsee (Upper Austria), Wolfgangsee (Upper Austria), Attersee (Upper Austria), Traunsee (Upper Austria), Hallstätter See (Upper Austria), Grundlsee (Styria), Ossiacher See (Carinthia), Wörthersee (Carinthia).

Lakes

Travellers with Disabilities

IMPORTANT ADDRESSES

AUSTRIA

▶ **Verband aller Körper-
behinderten Österreichs**
Lützowgasse 24–28
A-1014 Wien
Tel. 01/9 11 32 25 and 9 14 55 62
Fax 9 11 32 25

UNITED KINGDOM

▶ **Tourism for All**
c/o Vitalise
Shap Road
Kendal LA9 6NZ
Tel. (020) 72 50 32 22
www.tourismforall.org.uk

USA

► **SATH (Society for the Advancement of Travel for the Handicapped)**
347 5th Ave., no. 610

New York, NY 10016:
Tel. (21) 4 47 72 84
www.sath.org

When to Go

Climate ► Austria has a **cool, temperate climate influenced by the Alps**, corresponding to its location at the southeastern edge of central Europe and the mountainous nature of the country. Moving east the climate acquires increasingly continental characteristics.

Northern edge of the Alps ► The northern edge of the Alps has a particularly damp climate. The predominating westerly and northwesterly winds of central Europe bring over damp Atlantic air masses, which rise and cool when they reach the mountainous barrier. The consequence of this is strong cloud formation and precipitation: in areas between 1000m/3280ft and 1500m/4920ft, precipitation is double that seen in valley regions. Areas where such weather patterns occur are normally associated with a distinct stream of cold air that can lead to snow even at relatively low elevations.

The alpine climate is less damp than on the northern edge of the Alps, but is still very rainy or snowy and has short, cool summers. During fine weather, the intense solar radiation ameliorates the perceived chilliness that is due to the low air temperatures.

> *i* **Winds of change**
>
> ■ The foehn, a warm, dry wind that occurs on the leeward slopes of a ridge of mountains, is a special feature of the alpine climate that is seen predominantly in the western half of Austria. It occurs mainly in the spring and autumn, when a low pressure system north of the Alps pulls in air from an anticyclone south of the mountain range. As regards your travel plans, take heed: they say that rain follows the foehn!

Inner Alps ► There are distinct differences in the landscape between the sunny south-facing slopes and the north-facing slopes, which are in shade. In autumn and winter the mountain and peak areas are blessed with significantly more sunshine and clear air (good views!) than are the valleys. There is often a sudden and extreme change in the weather. It is not only hikers and climbers who should take heed of this phenomenon; car drivers and motorcyclists using the passes during autumn or spring must also be prepared.

Northern and eastern alpine foreland ► From the mid-Danube region moving eastwards, the central European climate changes into one of a more pronounced continental character. The daily and annual fluctuations in temperature become larger, and precipitation decreases, especially in the Wachau and the Weinviertel. In Vienna for example precipitation is half that in Salz-

Austria Climate Stations

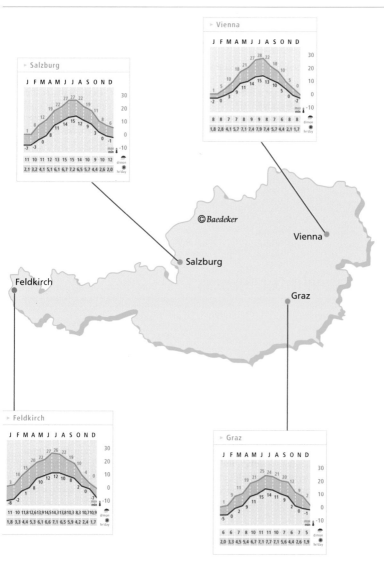

— Highest daytime temp.   — Lowest night-time temp.
☔ Rainy days   ☀ Hours of sunshine / day

burg; in particular, the heavy summer downpours are absent. The eastern alpine foreland bears the distinct characteristics of a **continental steppe climate** – with a short spring, a hot summer, a fine dry autumn, and a cold winter.

Best times to travel

The best time to go to the foothills of the Alps is mid-May–early July; for the high mountains, along with July and August, September, which brings predominantly settled weather and clear views, is the most favourable time to visit. May, June and September are preferable for hiking in the low mountains. The time of year when the trees are in blossom and the autumn have special appeal in wine-growing regions (Wachau, Burgenland).

The larger holiday resorts are often crowded in high summer – and correspondingly expensive. Those planning a **wine-tasting holiday** should consider late spring, early summer and autumn.

In **winter** Austria is a veritable El Dorado for winter sports enthusiasts and in the popular holiday centres there are quite likely to be queues at the ski lifts. Fortunately, stunning views across snowy peaks in sparkling sunshine provide some compensation for the long wait.

Winter Sports

Ideal holiday destination

Austria is a **paradise for winter sports enthusiasts**. There is often deep snow for months on end in Austria's medium and high-altitude mountain regions and in some regions skiers can even indulge themselves in summer. In many places there are pistes to suit the less able ski enthusiast as well as the absolute expert. There is plenty of opportunity, too, for cross-country skiing.

Ski resorts ▶

In the meantime tourist centres and whole ski areas have joined together, so that one ski pass allows use of all ski lifts in winter sports regions with several ski resorts. This is the case for example in the »Sportwelt Amadé« (Salzburger Sportwelt, Schladming-Dachstein Tauern, Gasteiner Tal, Hochkönig and Grossarltal resorts). Sometimes season tickets for several ski areas are available.

Information ▶

Österreich Werbung and the Austrian National Tourist Board (▶Information) provide more detailed information on winter sports areas and the towns within them.

 IMPORTANT ADDRESSES AND SKI AREAS

SNOW REPORTS

www.bergfex.at
www.schneehoehen.de
www.ski-online.de

www.snowreporter.com
www.wetteronline.de/ski.htm

see map p.149

WINTER SPORTS CENTRES

► 1. Bodensee/Rheintal
Locations: Bregenz, Buch, Dornbirn, Eichenberg, Hohenems
Ski lifts: up to 1100m/3600ft ASL
Cross-country ski runs: approx. 40km/25mi

► 2. Vorarlberger Oberland
Locations: Feldkirch, Frastanz/Bazora, Laterns, Zwischenwasser/Furx
Ski lifts: up to 1800m/5900ft ASL
Cross-country ski runs: approx. 35km/22mi

► 3. Brandnertal–Bludenz
Locations: Bludenz, Brand, Bürs, Bürserberg
Ski lifts: up to 1920m/6300ft ASL
Cross-country ski runs: approx. 30km/20mi

► 4. Montafon
Locations: Gargellen, Gaschurn, Gortipohl, Partenen, St. Gallenkirch, Schruns, Silbertal, Tschagguns, Vandans
Ski lifts: up to 2380m/7800ft ASL
Cross-country ski runs: approx. 40km/25mi

► 5. Grosswalsertal
Locations: Fontanella/Faschina, Raggal/Marul, Sonntag
Ski lifts: up to 2000m/6600ft ASL
Cross-country ski runs: approx. 25km/16mi

► 6. Bregenzer Wald
Locations: Alberschwende, Andelsbuch, Au, Bezau, Bizau, Damüls, Egg, Hittisau, Mellau, Schoppernau, Schröcken, Schwarzenberg, Sibratsgfäll, Sulzberg, Warth
Ski lifts: up to 2050m/6730ft ASL
Cross-country ski runs: approx. 320km/200mi

► 7. Kleinwalsertal
Locations: Hirschegg, Mittelberg, Riezlern
Ski lifts: up to 2200m/7200ft ASL
Cross-country ski runs: approx. 50km/30mi

► 8. Klostertal
Locations: Braz, Dalaas, Klösterle/Langen, Wald
Ski lifts: up to 2300m/7550ft ASL
Cross-country ski runs: approx. 25km/16mi

○ Winter sports centres
◑ Summer ski resorts

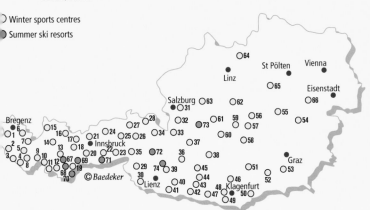

© Baedeker

If you want to be a skiing ace, start early

▶ 9. Arlberg
Locations: Lech, St. Anton,
St. Christoph, Stuben, Zürs
Ski lifts: up to 2810m/9220ft ASL
Cross-country ski runs: approx.
100km/60mi

▶ 10. Paznauntal
Locations: Galtür, Ischgl, Kappl,
Pians
Ski lifts: up to 2870m/9420ft ASL
Cross-country ski runs: approx.
100km/60mi

▶ 11. Oberstes Inntal
Locations: Fiss, Ladis, Nauders,
Pfunds, Ried im Oberinntal,
Serfaus, Tösens
Ski lifts: up to 2750m/9000ft ASL
Cross-country ski runs: approx.
170km/105mi

▶ 12. Kaunertal–Landeck
Locations: Feichten, Fliess, Grins,
Imsterberg, Kauns, Landeck,
Mils, Prutz-Faggen-Fendels,
Schönwies, Zams
Ski lifts: up to 3200m/10,500ft ASL
Cross-country ski runs: approx.
90km/55mi

▶ 13. Pitztal–Imst
Locations: Arzl-Wald, Haiming,
Imst, Innerpitztal, Jerzens, Nas-
sereith, Roppen, Tarrenz, Wenns-
Piller
Ski lifts: up to 3200m/10,500ft ASL
Cross-country ski runs: approx.
210km/130mi

▶ 14. Lechtal
Locations: Bach, Boden-Bschlabs,
Elbigenalp, Forchach, Häselgehr,
Hinterhornbach, Holzgau, Stan-
zach, Steeg, Vorderhornbach,
Weissenbach
Ski lifts: up to 1800m/5900ft ASL
Cross-country ski runs: approx.
130km/80mi

▶ 15. Tannheimer Tal
Locations: Grän-Haldensee,

Jungholz, Nesselwängle, Schatt-
wald, Tannheim, Zöblen
Ski lifts: up to 1900m/6230ft ASL
Cross-country ski runs: approx.
50km/31mi

► 16. Zwischentoren–Reutte
Locations: Berwang, Biberwier,
Bichlbach, Ehrwald, Heiterwang,
Höfen, Lähn-Wengle, Lechaschau,
Lermoos, Reutte
Ski lifts: up to 2950m/9680ft ASL
Cross-country ski runs: approx.
220km/140mi

► 17. Seefelder and Mieminger Plateau
Locations: Leutasch, Mieming,
Mösern, Obsteig, Reith bei See-
feld, Scharnitz, Seefeld, Telfs, Wil-
dermieming
Ski lifts: up to 2100m/6890ft ASL
Cross-country ski runs: approx.
370km/230mi

► 18. Inntal and Sellrain
Locations: Gries im Sellraintal,
Hatting, Inzing, Kematen, Kühtai,
Mötz, Oberperfuss, Rietz, St. Sig-
mund-Praxmar, Sellrain, Silz,
Stams, Zirl
Ski lifts: up to 2500m/8200ft ASL
Cross-country ski runs: approx.
130km/80mi

► 19. Ötztal
Locations: Gries im Ötztal,
Längenfeld-Huben, Niederthai,
Obergurgl/Hochgurgl, Ötz, Sau-
tens, Sölden/Hochsölden, Um-
hausen, Vent, Zwieselstein
Ski lifts: up to 3250m/10,660ft ASL
Cross-country ski runs: approx.
160km/100mi

► 20. Wipptal and Stubaital
Locations: Fulpmes, Gries am
Brenner, Gschnitz, Matrei am

Brenner, Mieders, Navis, Neustift,
Obernberg, St. Jodok-Schmirn,
Schönberg, Steinach am Brenner,
Telfes, Trins
Ski lifts: up to 3250m/10,660ft ASL
Cross-country ski runs: approx.
460km/285mi

► 21. Innsbruck and surrounding areas
Locations: Aldrans, Axams, Bir-
gitz, Götzens, Grinzens, Inns-
bruck-Igls, Lans, Mutters, Natters,
Patsch, Sistrans
Ski lifts: up to 2340m/7680ft ASL
Cross-country ski runs: approx.
170km/105mi

► 22. Östlich von Innsbruck
Locations: Absam, Ampass,
Baumkirchen, Fritzen, Gnaden-
wald, Hall in Tirol, Mils bei Hall,
Rinn, Rum, Tulfes, Volders, Wat-
tens
Elevation: 550m/1800ft–920m/
3020ft ASL
Ski lifts: up to 2200m/7220ft ASL
Cross-country ski runs: approx.
100km/62mi

► 23. Zillertal
Locations: Dornauberg-Ginzling,
Finkenberg, Fügen, Gerlos, Hart,
Hippach, Kaltenbach, Mayrhofen,
Ried, Schlitters, Strass, Stumm-
Stummerberg, Tuxertal, Uderns,
Zell a. Ziller
Ski lifts: up to 3260m/10700ft ASL
Cross-country ski runs: approx.
240km/150mi

► 24. Achental-Schwaz and surrounding areas
Locations: Achenkirch, Jenbach,
Maurach-Eben, Münster, Pertisau,
Schwaz-Pill, Stans, Steinberg am
Rofan, Vomp, Weerberg, Weer-
Kolsass-Kolsassberg, Wiesing

Ski lifts: up to 2000m/6560ft ASL
Cross-country ski runs: approx.
220km/140mi

▶ 25. Inntal–Wildschönau–Alpbachtal

Locations: Alpbach, Angerberg,
Brandenberg, Breitenbach am Inn,
Brixlegg, Kramsach, Kundl, Lang-
kampfen, Mariastein, Rattenberg-
Radfeld, Reith im Alpbachtal,
Wildschönau (Oberau, Niederau,
Auffach), Wörgl
Ski lifts: up to 2000m/6560ft ASL
Cross-country ski runs: approx.
280km/175mi

▶ 26. Kitzbüheler Alpen

Locations: Aurach, Brixen im
Thale, Ellmau, Hopfgarten im
Brixental, Itter, Jochberg, Kelch-
sau, Kirchberg, Kitzbühel, Obern-
dorf, Reith bei Kitzbühel, Söll,
Westendorf
Ski lifts: up to 2000m/6560ft ASL
Cross-country ski runs: approx.
250km/155mi

▶ 27. Kufstein and surrounding areas

Locations: Angath, Bad Häring,
Ebbs, Erl, Hinterthiersee, Kirchbichl, Kufstein, Landl, Niedern-
dorf, Scheffau, Schwoich, Thiersee
Ski lifts: up to 1700m/5580ft ASL
Cross-country ski runs: approx.
240km/150mi

▶ 28. Kaiserwinkel

Locations: Erpfendorf, Fieber-
brunn, Going, Hochfilzen, Kirch-
dorf, Kössen, St. Jakob i.H.,
St. Johann in Tirol, St. Ulrich am
Pillersee, Schwendt, Waidring,
Walchsee
Ski lifts: up to 1870m/6140ft ASL
Cross-country ski runs: approx.
470km/290mi

▶ 29. Osttirol nördlich von Lienz

Locations: Hopfgarten im Defereggental, Huben, Kals am Grossglockner, Matrei in Osttirol,
Prägraten, St. Jakob im Defereggental, St. Veit im Defereggental,
Virgen
Ski lifts: up to 2500m/8200ft ASL
Cross-country ski runs: approx.
130km/80mi

▶ 30. Pustertal and Lienzer Dolomiten

Locations: Abfaltersbach, Ainet,
Amlach, Anras, Ausservillgraten,
Dölsach, Heinfels, Innervillgraten,
Iselsberg-Stronach, Kartitsch,
Lavant, Lienz, Nikolsdorf, Ober-
lienz, Obertilliach, Sillian,
Strassen, Thal-Assling, Tristach
Ski lifts: up to 2400m/7870ft ASL
Cross-country ski runs: approx.
220km/135mi

▶ 31. Salzburg and surrounding areas

Locations: Anif, Salzburg
Ski lifts: up to 1100m/3610ft ASL
Cross-country ski runs: approx.
20km/12mi

▶ 32. Tennengau, Salzburger Salzkammergut

Locations: Abtenau, Annaberg,
Bad Dürrnberg, Faistenau, Hin-
tersee, Krispl-Gaissau, Kuchl,
Lungötz, Russbach, St. Gilgen,
St. Martin am Tennengebirge,
Strobl
Ski lifts: up to 1600m/5250ft ASL
Cross-country ski runs: approx.
250km/155mi

▶ 33. Hochkönig, Tennengebirge

Locations: Bischofshofen,
Mühlbach am Hochkönig, Pfarr-
werfen, Werfen, Werfenweng
Ski lifts: up to 1900m/6230ft ASL

Cross-country ski runs: approx.
80km/50mi

34. Pinzgauer Saalachtal
Locations: Leogang, Lofer, Maishofen, Maria Alm, Saalbach-Hinterglemm, Saalfelden, Unken
Ski lifts: up to 2000m/6560ft ASL
Cross-country ski runs: approx.
260km/160mi

35. Unterpinzgau, Europa-Sportregion, Oberpinzgau
Locations: Bruck am Grossglock-
ner, Fusch an der Grossglocknerstrasse, Kaprun, Königsleiten,
Krimml, Mittersill, Neukirchen
am Grossvenediger, Rauris, Utten-
dorf/Weissensee, Zell am See
Ski lifts: up to 3000m/9840ft ASL
Cross-country ski runs: approx.
220km/137mi

36. Gasteinertal and Grossarltal
Locations: Bad Gastein, Bad Hof-
gastein, Dorfgastein, Grossarl,
Hüttschlag
Ski lifts: up to 2700m/8860ft ASL
Cross-country ski runs: approx.
120km/75mi

37. Radstädter Tauern, Sonnenterrasse
Locations: Altenmarkt-Zauchen-
see, Eben im Pongau, Filzmoos,
Flachau, Goldegg, Kleinarl, Ober-
tauern/Untertauern, Radstadt,
St. Johann/Alpendorf, Wagrain
Ski lifts: up to 2300m/7550ft ASL
Cross-country ski runs: approx.
180km/110mi

38. Lungau
Locations: Mariapfarr, Mautern-
dorf, Obertauern/Tweng,
St. Margarethen, St. Michael,
Tamsweg, Thomatal-Schönfeld

Ski lifts: up to 2400m/7870ft ASL
Cross-country ski runs: approx.
250km/155mi

39. National park region, Goldberge and Mölltal
Locations: Flattach, Grosskirch-
heim-Döllach, Heiligenblut, Kolb-
nitz-Reisseck, Lurnfeld/
Möllbrücke, Mallnitz, Obervellach, Rangersdorf, Stall, Winklern
Ski lifts: up to 2700m/8860ft ASL
Cross-country ski runs: approx.
160km/100mi

40. Upper Drautal
Locations: Berg im Drautal, Del-
lach im Drautal, Greifenburg,
Irschen, Klebach-Lind, Oberdrau-
burg, Steinfeld, Weissensee-
Techendorf
Ski lifts: up to 2200m/7220ft ASL
Cross-country ski runs: approx.
100km/60mi

41. Karnische Skiregion
Locations: Dellach im Gailtal,
Hermagor-Nassfeld, Kirchbach
im Gailtal, Kötschach-Mauthen,
Lesachtal, St. Stefan im Gailtal,
Weissbriach/Gitschtal
Ski lifts: up to 2000m/6560ft ASL
Cross-country ski runs: approx.
250km/155mi

42. Mid-Drautal region
Locations: Paternion, Stockenboi,
Weissenstein
Ski lifts: up to 2100m/6890ft ASL
Cross-country ski runs: approx.
80km/50mi

43. Millstätter See
Locations: Baldramsdorf, Feld am
See, Ferndorf, Fresach, Lendorf,
Millstatt, Radenthein-Döbriach,
Seeboden, Spittal an der Drau
Ski lifts: up to 2100m/6890ft ASL

Austria offers great skiing conditions

Cross-country ski runs: approx. 230km/145mi

▶ **44. Bad Kleinkirchheim**
Location: Bad Kleinkirchheim
Ski lifts: up to 2000m/6560ft ASL
Cross-country ski runs: approx. 20km/12mi

▶ **45. Liesertal and Maltatal**
Locations: Gmünd, Krems in Kärnten, Malta, Rennweg-Katschberg
Ski lifts: up to 2200m/7220ft ASL
Cross-country ski runs: approx. 50km/30mi

▶ **46. Turrach region, Hochrindl, Simonhöhe**
Locations: Albeck/Sirnitz, Ebene Reichenau–Turracher Höhe, Feldkirchen, Glanegg, Gnesau, Himmelberg, St. Urban am Urbansee, Steuerberg
Ski lifts: up to 2300m/7550ft ASL

Cross-country ski runs: approx. 210km/130mi

▶ **47. Wintersportregion Villach**
Locations: Arnoldstein, Arriach, Bad Bleiberg, Faaker See–Finkenstein, Hohenthurn, Nötsch im Gailtal, Ossiach, St. Jakob, Steindorf, Treffen/Sattendorf, Villach, Warmbad Villach
Ski lifts: up to 1900m/6230ft ASL
Cross-country ski runs: approx. 250km/155mi

▶ **48. Wörthersee region**
Locations: Klagenfurt, Moosburg, Velden am Wörthersee
Ski lifts: up to 600m/ft ASL
Cross-country ski runs: approx. 260km/160mi

▶ **49. Rosental region**
Locations: Feistritz, Ferlach, Ludmannsdorf, Zell
Ski lifts: up to 1100m/3610ft ASL

Cross-country ski runs: approx.
70km/44mi

50. Völkermarkt region
Locations: Bleiburg, Diex, Eisen-
kappel-Vellach, Griffen, Neuhaus,
Sittersdorf, Völkermarkt
Ski lifts: up to 2000m/6560ft ASL
Cross-country ski runs: approx.
220km/135mi

51. St Veit an der Glan region
Locations: Metnitz, St Veit an der
Glan, Weitensfeld-Flattnitz
Ski lifts: up to 1900m/6230ft ASL
Cross-country ski runs: approx.
70km/45mi

52. Lavanttal region
Locations: Bad St Leonhard, Lav-
amünd, Preitenegg, Reichenfels,
St. Andrä i. Lavanttal, St Paul i.
Lavanttal, Wolfsberg
Ski lifts: up to 2200m/7220ft ASL
Cross-country ski runs: approx.
90km/55mi

53. Weststeiermark
Locations: Bad Gams, Modriach,
Pack, Salla, St Oswald ob Eibis-
wald, Schwanberg, Soboth,
Trahütten
Ski lifts: up to 1800m/5900ft ASL
Cross-country ski runs: approx.
80km/50mi

54. Mürztal, Roseggers Wald-
heimat, Steirischer Semmering,
Mürzer Oberland, Oberes Feis-
tritztal
Locations: Falkenstein, Fischbach,
Kapellen an der Mürz, Kindberg,
Krieglach/Alpl, Langenwang,
Mürzsteg, Mürzzuschlag, Neuberg
an der Mürz, Ratten, Rettenegg,
St. Kathrein am Hauenstein, Spi-
tal/Steinhaus am Semmering
Funicular railways: up to 1400m/

4590ft ASL
Cross-country ski runs: approx.
200km/125mi

55. Alpenregion Hochschwab
Locations: Aflenz-Kurort,
Breitenau bei Mixnitz, Etmissl,
Gusswerk, Halltal, Mariazell,
St. Sebastian, Seewiesen, Tragöss,
Turnau
Ski lifts: up to 1800m/5900ft ASL
Cross-country ski runs: approx.
110km/mi

56. Alpenregion Gesäuse
Locations: Admont, Altenmarkt/
St. Gallen, Ardning, Hieflau,
Johnsbach, St. Gallen, Weng bei
Admont
Ski lifts: up to 1500m/4920ft ASL
Cross-country ski runs: approx.
120km/75mi

57. Alpenregion Liesingtal
Locations: Gai, Kalwang, Kam-
mern, Mautern, Traboch, Wald am
Schoberpass
Ski lifts: up to 1200m/3940ft ASL
Cross-country ski runs: approx.
40km/25mi

58. Upper Murtal
Locations: Judenburg, Krakaudorf,
Murau, Obdach/St. Wolfgang
am Zirbitz, Oberwölz, Oberzei-
ring, Predlitz-Turrach, St. Geor-
gen–St. Lorenzen, St. Johann am
Tauern, St. Lambrecht
Ski lifts: up to 2300m/7550ft ASL
Cross-country ski runs: approx.
260km/160mi

59. Heimat am Grimming
Locations: Aigen am Putterersee,
Donnersbach-Planneralm, Don-
nersbachwald-Riesneralm, Ird-
ning, Liezen-Lassing, Pürgg-

Trautenfels/Wörschachwald,
St. Martin am Grimming, Weis-
senbach bei Liezen
Ski lifts: up to 1600m/5250ft ASL
Cross-country ski runs: approx.
120km/75mi

▶ 60. Dachstein-Tauern region

Locations: Aich-Assach, Gössen-
berg, Gröbming, Haus im Ennstal,
Mitterberg, Öblarn, Pruggern,
Ramsau am Dachstein, Rohr-
moos-Untertal, Schladming
Ski lifts: up to 2700m/8860ft ASL
Cross-country ski runs: approx.
250km/155mi

▶ 61. Steirisches Salzkammergut

Locations: Altaussee, Bad Aussee,
Bad Mitterndorf, Grundlsee,
Pichl/Kainisch, Tauplitz/
Tauplitzalm
Ski lifts: up to 2000m/6560ft ASL
Cross-country ski runs: approx.
100km/62mi

▶ 62. Pyhrn-Eisenwurzen

Locations: Gaflenz-Forsteralm,
Hinterstoder, Klaus, Spital/Pyhrn,
Ternberg, Vorderstoder,
Windischgarsten
Ski lifts: up to 1900m/6230ft ASL
Cross-country ski runs: approx.
200km/125mi

▶ 63. Oberösterreichisches Salzkammergut

Locations: Altmünster, Bad Goi-
sern, Bad Ischl, Ebensee, Gmun-
den, Gosau, Grünau im Almtal,
Hallstatt, Mondsee, Obertraun,
St. Wolfgang, Scharnstein,
Weyregg am Attersee
Ski lifts: up to 2100m/6890ft ASL
Cross-country ski runs: approx.
140km/85mi

▶ 64. Mühlviertel

Locations: Bad Leonfelden, Freis-
tadt, Haslach, Hellmonsödt,
Klaffer, Sandl, St. Johann am
Wimberg, Schwarzenberg,
Ulrichsberg
Ski lifts: up to 1400m/4590ft ASL
Cross-country ski runs: approx.
780km/485mi

▶ 65. Niederösterreichisches Voralpenland

Locations: Annaberg, Gaming,
Göstling a. d. Ybbs, Hollenstein
a. d. Ybbs, Lackenhof am Ötscher,
Lilienfeld, Lunz am See, Mitter-
bach am Erlaufsee, Puchenstuben,
St. Aegyd am Neuwalde, Türnitz,
Waidhofen a. d. Ybbs, Ybbsitz
Ski lifts: up to 1800m/5900ft ASL
Cross-country ski runs: approx.
150km/95mi

▶ 66. Niederösterreich alpin

Locations: Aspangberg-St. Peter,
Grünbach am Schneeberg,
Mönichkirchen, Puchberg am
Schneeberg, Reichenau an der
Rax, Rohr im Gebirge, St. Corona
am Wechsel, Semmering
Ski lifts: up to 1600m/5250ft ASL
Cross-country ski runs: approx.
100km/60mi

SUMMER SKI AREAS

▶ 67. Mittelbergferner

Glacier region at 2730m/
8960ft–3240m/10,630ft
Place of departure: St Leonhard-
Mittelberg im Pitztal

▶ 68. Rettenbachferner and Tiefenbachferner

Glacier region at 2700m/
8860ft–3300m/10,830ft
Place of departure: Sölden im
Ötztal

▶ **69. Stubaier Gletscher
and Daunkogelferner**
Glacier region at 2600m/
8530ft–3200m/10,500ft
Place of departure: Ranalt im
Stubaital

▶ **70. Weissseeferner**
Glacier region at 2750m/
9020ft–3160m/10,370ft
Place of departure: Feichten im
Kaunertal

▶ **71. Hintertuxer Ferner**
Glacier region at 2660m/
8730ft–3270m/10,730ft
Place of departure: Hintertux

▶ **72. Kitzsteinhorn**
Glacier region at 2450m/
8040ft–3030m/9940ft
Place of departure: Kaprun

▶ **73. Dachstein**
Glacier region at 2520m/
8270ft–2700m/8860ft
Place of departure: Ramsau

▶ **74. Mölltaler Gletscher**
Glacier region at 2200m/
7220ft–3122m/10,243ft
Place of departure: Flattach (Gletscherexpress)

Tours

THE MAJESTY OF THE
MOUNTAINS OR THE
CULTURE OF THE CITY?
A DIP IN A WARM LAKE OR A HIKE THROUGH
WILD GORGES? IN THE CAR, ON FOOT OR BY BIKE?
WE REVEAL WHERE AND HOW YOU CAN BEST DIS-
COVER AUSTRIA.

TOURS THROUGH AUSTRIA

There is much to discover in Austria. Whether remarkable landscapes, lovely recreation areas or the numerous possibilities for a holiday with a cultural slant – we will show you the most beautiful routes through the country.

TOUR 1   **Discover Austria**
Have you got time for a long holiday? Then this tour with its mixture of valleys and mountains, cities and countryside, expanses of water and plentiful culture is just right for you.   ▶ **page 164**

TOUR 2   **From Lake Constance into the High Mountains**
Over the course of two or three days, follow a beautiful route from the Mediterranean flair of Lake Constance into the high mountains and back through Bregenz Forest.   ▶ **page 168**

TOUR 3   **Salzkammergut – Lakeland**
On this three-day tour the Salzkammergut will fascinate visitors with its captivating lakeland scenery, cultural highlights and the immense beauty of the Dachstein Massif.   ▶ **page 169**

TOUR 4   **Heading South**
Warm bathing lakes with picturesque mountain backdrops and a host of historic and cultural sights are on the itinerary of this tour. Depending on how fast you want to go, it will take at least two days.   ▶ **page 171**

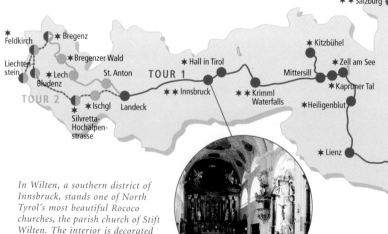

In Wilten, a southern district of Innsbruck, stands one of North Tyrol's most beautiful Rococo churches, the parish church of Stift Wilten. The interior is decorated in black, white and gold.

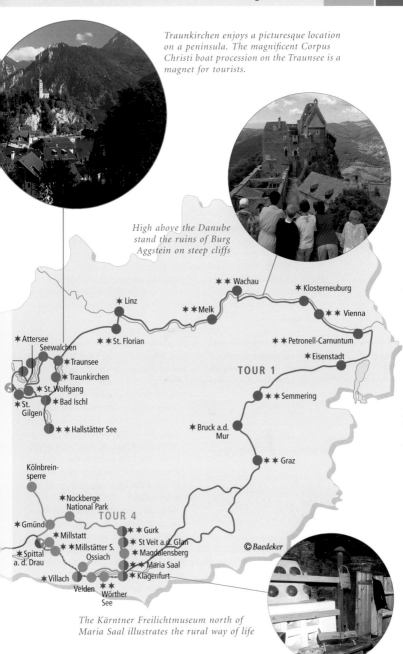

Traunkirchen enjoys a picturesque location on a peninsula. The magnificent Corpus Christi boat procession on the Traunsee is a magnet for tourists.

High above the Danube stand the ruins of Burg Aggstein on steep cliffs

The Kärntner Freilichtmuseum north of Maria Saal illustrates the rural way of life

Map labels:

* Attersee
Seewalchen
* Traunsee
* Traunkirchen
* St. Wolfgang
* St. Gilgen
* Bad Ischl
* * Hallstätter See

* Linz
* * St. Florian
* * Wachau
* * Melk
* Klosterneuburg
* * Vienna
* * Petronell-Carnuntum
* Eisenstadt

TOUR 1

* * Semmering
* Bruck a.d. Mur
* * Graz

Kölnbrein-sperre
* Nockberge National Park
TOUR 4
* Gmünd
* Millstatt
* * Millstätter S.
Ossiach
* Spittal a. d. Drau
* Villach
Velden
* * Wörther See

* * Gurk
* St Veit a.d. Glan
* Magdalensberg
* * Maria Saal
* Klagenfurt

©Baedeker

Travelling in Austria

A varied holiday For those in the know Austria has long since shed its image as a somewhat fuddy-duddy alpine republic. It is not only the customary culture vultures, hiking fans and skiing enthusiasts who turn up here; in the meantime Austria, with its many opportunities for sport and leisure, has become an interesting holiday destination for young people too. Visitors here get everything that makes a holiday great: relaxation, wellness, nature, sport and culture – and the best of it all at that. Even tireless sun-worshippers can get their money's worth on the Carinthian lakes.

On the water or overland There are several ways for visitors to discover Austria without a car. For those who like to get moving there are attractive and well-signposted cycle ways, which come in various levels of difficulty (► p.133). An appealing alternative is to cruise down the Danube (Donau) river, from which you can observe the country in complete peace and quiet from a rather different perspective. The train too, whether along a main line, a historical stretch or at higher elevations, is a wonderful way to travel. One thing is certain: a means of transport exists to suit every tempo.

Culinary treats On a tour through Austria, on no account miss out on the many regional culinary specialities on offer. After all, good food is part of a successful holiday! Whether a fan of the grape or the grain, both lovers of a nice drop of wine and those who prefer to quench their thirst with a good gulp of beer have a rich selection to choose from in Austria. In the southeast and east of the country in particular, wine drinkers find wonderful, cosy »Buschenschänken« serving hearty home cooking and a nice drop of the local produce along the wine roads.

Austrian coffee-house culture, more pronounced in the cities, offers coffee for every occasion in every variation. Alongside the mocha bean, Austrian Mehlspeise desserts are also typical for the country. Those with a sweet tooth will do well to forget the calorie count for once. The influences on Austrian cuisine are diverse; hardly surprising given its past as a multiracial state. But it is good solid fare that prevails here.

✓ DON'T MISS

- the Weinviertel in Lower Austria
- the Schilcher-Weinstrasse (Schilcher Wine Road) in western Styria
- the Südsteirische Weinstrasse (South Styrian Wine Road) – here two 2.5km/1.6mi-long sections of road form (probably uniquely) the border with Slovenia.

The legendary Drachenwand towers above the Mondsee →

Tour 1 Discover Austria

Distance: approx. 1700km/1050mi   **Duration:** at least 3 weeks

It takes at least three weeks to gain a deeper insight into Austria's diversity and beauty. Without having to keep up a hectic pace, those with plenty of time on their hands can view the most important sights and enjoy a variety of landscapes, from the high mountains to the puszta plain.

From the Baroque city of ❶ ✳ ✳ **Salzburg**, whose attractions and sights draw millions of visitors every year, especially at festival times, the tour continues into the Salzkammergut via the **Wolfgangsee** to

The massive Schloss Tratzberg stands high above the Inntal valley. The castle served as a hunting lodge for both Emperor Maximilian and the Fugger family.

✳ Bregenz

✳ Feldkirch — 35

38 km/23,6 mi

11 km 6,8 mi — 33

22 km/13,7 mi

✳ Hall in Tirol

90 km 55,9 mi

✳ Kitzbühel 8 km 5 mi

✳ Zell am See

34 — 32 Bludenz

65 km 40,4 mi

Landeck

79 km 49 mi — 28

29 km 18 mi — 26 — 24 km 14,9 mi

Mittersill — 25 — 24 — 23

59 km 36,6 mi

Liechten-stein — 31

31 km 19,3 mi

30

29 — 10 km 6,2 mi — 27

26 km 16,1 mi — ✳ Kapruner Tal — 22

✳ ✳ Innsbruck

✳ ✳ Krimml Waterfalls

✳ Heiligenblut

38 km 23,6 mi

✳ Silvretta-Hochalpenstrasse

✳ Lienz — 21

The Grossglockner Road winds through magnificent mountain scenery, providing access to the Hohe Tauern National Park.

❷ ✳ **Bad Ischl**. Head southward here and make a detour to the
❸ ✳ ✳ **Hallstätter See** and **Dachstein**. The main tour route leads further north on the western shore of the **Traunsee** and along the river
Traun via **Lambach** and **Wels** to the Danube (Donau) and the Upper
Austrian capital ❹ ✳ **Linz**. A side trip to
❺ ✳ ✳ **St Florian** is a must for Bruckner
fans.

Downriver on the Danube follow the river
sections Strudengau and Nibelungengau
with the **Maria Taferl** pilgrimage church,
eventually reaching ❻ ✳ ✳ **Stift Melk**, a
Benedictine abbey. Continuing further in
the direction of Vienna, the route reaches
the famous ❼ ✳ ✳ **Wachau**, which has

*A display of many colours –
the Hundertwasser building in*

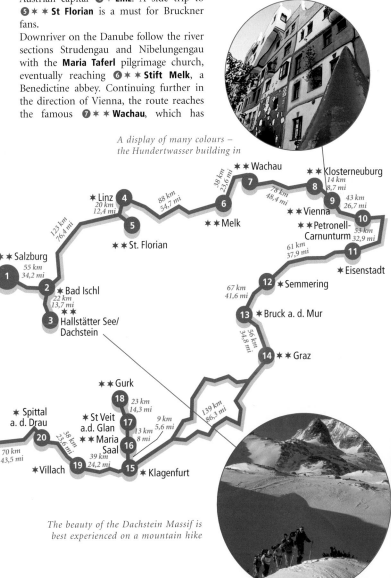

*The beauty of the Dachstein Massif is
best experienced on a mountain hike*

been on the World Heritage list on the basis of both its natural and its cultural importance since 2000. Heading through ❽ **Klosterneuburg**, whose abbey of Augustinian canons houses the precious Verdun Altar, the tour eventually arrives in the federal capital, ❾ ✳ ✳ **Vienna**.

From Vienna follow the Danube east through the **Nationalpark Donau-Auen**, one of Europe's last intact water-meadow landscapes, in order to take a trip into the Roman past in the archaeological park of ❿ ✳ ✳ **Petronell Carnuntum**. Further south, in the midst of the puzsta landscape, lies **Neusiedler See** (Lake Neusiedl). The provincial capital of Burgenland, ⓫ ✳ **Eisenstadt** recalls Joseph Haydn, who worked in the service of the princely Esterházy family here for 30 years. Via **Wiener Neustadt**, head westward to ⓬ **Semmering** with its **Semmeringbahn** railway, a brilliant technical achievement of the 19th century that in the meantime has also made the World Heritage list. Following the Mürz downstream, the tour reaches ⓭ ✳ **Bruck an der Mur** and continues along the river Mur, via **Frohnleiten** with its flower park and medieval town square to ⓮ ✳ ✳ **Graz**, whose Old Town has been a UNESCO World Heritage site since 1999. A worthwhile side trip leads east to the spa region of **Thermenland Styria** and the **Südsteirische Weinstrasse (South Styrian Wine Road)**.

Take either the A 2 autobahn to ⓯ ✳ **Klagenfurt** or the 20km/12mi-longer but extremely picturesque stretch along the Schilcherstrasse (Schilcher Wine Road) to **Eibiswald**, turning west to Klagenfurt

Nature and culture in unique harmony – the mark of the Wachau. Here, Schloss Schönbühel stands above the shores of the Danube

there. From Klagenfurt a side trip to the north is recommended: to the pilgrimage church in ⓰ ✳ **Maria Saal**, the mighty **Burg Hochosterwitz** in ⓱ ✳ **St. Veit an der Glan** and ⓲ ✳ **Gurk** Cathedral.

Rejoining the route, head from Klagenfurt along the beautiful southern shore of the **Wörther See**. Shortly before reaching ⓳ ✳ **Villach**, the impressive **Landskron ruins** are seen, from which a short detour to the **Ossiacher See** can be made. Beyond Villach the road follows the Drautal valley to ⓴ ✳ **Spittal an der Drau**. From there it is only a few miles to the western shore of the **Millstätter See**. Continuing up the valley the route reaches ㉑ ✳ **Lienz** in East Tyrol, located at the foot of the rugged, deeply fissured Lienz Dolomites. Some distance east the road branches off to the north to the Grossglockner, at 3798m/12,460ft Austria's highest mountain. The almost 50km/30mi-long **Grossglockner-Hochalpenstrasse** (Grossglockner High Alpine Road) begins in ㉒ ✳ **Heiligenblut** and offers splendid views of the fantastic mountain scenery of the Hohe Tauern, in particular at the turn-off to the Franz-Josefs-Höhe at the foot of the Grossglockner.

The route continues from the northern end of the Grossglockner-Hochalpenstrasse to ㉓ ✳ **Zell am See**, where, at the **Schmittenhöhe**, one of Austria's loveliest high-altitude walks, the **Pinzgauer Spaziergang**, begins. It is only a few miles to the ㉔ ✳ **Kapruner Tal**, a valley with a summer ski area on the Kitzsteinhorn Glacier. Continue further along the Salzach river, taking a detour north at ㉕**Mittersill** to ㉖ ✳ **Kitzbühel**. West of Mittersill are the ㉗ ✳ ✳ **Krimml Waterfalls**, at which the water cascades downwards for a total of 380m/1250ft in three stages – an impressive natural spectacle. Near Zell am Ziller the road turns northward and leads through the lower Zillertal valley into the Inntal valley. Continue west via ㉘ ✳ **Hall in Tirol** to the Tyrolese provincial capital, ㉙ ✳ ✳ **Innsbruck**, which attracts visitors with its charming Old Town, the Goldenes Dachl and the Hofkirche with the tomb of Emperor Maximilian I.

Heading up the Inntal valley, beyond ㉚**Landeck** is the turning into the **Paznauntal** valley, where snow is assured. At the valley's far end the ㉛ ✳ **Silvretta-Hochalpenstrasse** (Silvretta High Alpine Road) offers fantastic views of the Silvretta mountain range to the south and the Verwallgruppe range to the north. The **Bielerhöhe** marks the border of Vorarlberg, Austria's westernmost province. From the high-lying valley of **Montafon**, where Ernest Hemingway whistled down the slopes on skis, through the lovely **Rätikon** mountains, the route leads into the former silver-mining town of ㉜ ✳ **Bludenz** and to the border town of ㉝ ✳ **Feldkirch**, which has a medieval feel. From there it is worth taking a side trip into the ㉞**Principality of Liechtenstein**, which boasts not only an appealing mountain landscape but also an important art museum. This tour of Austria ends a few miles north in the festival town ㉟ ✳ **Bregenz**, whose location on Lake Constance (Bodensee) is a point where the borders of three countries meet.

Tour 2 From Lake Constance into the Mountains

Distance: approx. 290km/180mi

Duration: approx. 3 days

Holidaymakers bound for Bregenz who want to see a little more than Lake Constance will find this two-day tour worthwhile. Taking in interesting towns in the Rhine Valley, the spectacular high mountains of western Austria and the gently rolling hills of the Bregenz Forest, there is a wealth of glorious countryside to be enjoyed on this route.

The tour begins in ❶ ✶ **Bregenz** on Lake Constance (Bodensee). Head south through the Rhine Valley past Dornbirn to the border town of ❷ ✶ **Feldkirch**, which has a medieval atmosphere.

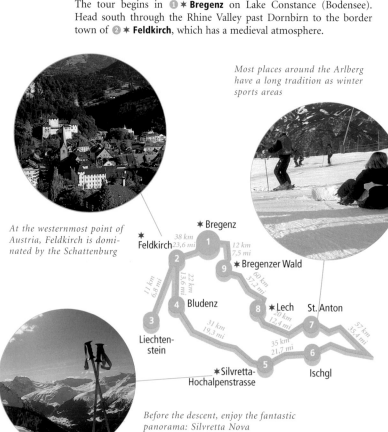

Most places around the Arlberg have a long tradition as winter sports areas

At the westernmost point of Austria, Feldkirch is dominated by the Schattenburg

✶ Bregenz
✶ Feldkirch
38 km / 23,6 mi
12 km / 7,5 mi
✶ Bregenzer Wald
11 km / 6,8 mi
22 km / 13,6 mi
60 km / 37,2 mi
Bludenz
✶ Lech
St. Anton
Liechten-stein
31 km / 19,3 mi
20 km / 12,4 mi
57 km / 35,4 mi
✶ Silvretta-Hochalpenstrasse
35 km / 21,7 mi
Ischgl

Before the descent, enjoy the fantastic panorama: Silvretta Nova

From here it is worth taking a side trip into the ❸ **Principality of Liechtenstein**, known to most simply as a tax haven. Yet fans of a leisurely holiday will find pleasant footpaths in the tiny state, which has something to offer culturally too. Stamp collectors in particular head directly to the museum in **Vaduz**, and art lovers are strongly attracted to the new Kunstmuseum with exhibits from the royal collection.

The expressway leads from Feldkirch to the former silver-mining town of ❹ ✳ **Bludenz** and its appealing Old Town. Southeast of Bludenz, follow the road for about 40km/25mi through the **Montafon** valley, between the Rätikon mountains to the west and the Verwallgruppe range to the east.

The rugged, deeply fissured mountains along this high-lying valley, through which the Ill river flows, attracts visitors in both summer and winter. At the end of the Montafon lies the ❺ ✳ **Silvretta-Hochalpenstrasse** (Silvretta High Alpine Road), which winds upwards in sharp bends to Europe's highest-lying reservoir, the **Silvretta-Stausee** at the foot of the Piz Buin, and to the Bielerhöhe, which forms the border between Vorarlberg and Tyrol. From here the route continues steeply uphill into the **Paznauntal**. Snow is assured in this valley, whose main town is ❻ **Ischgl**. Head towards **Landeck**, shortly before which the route turns west in the direction of ❼ **St Anton** on the **Arlberg** mountain range and then follows the road north via Zürs to ❽ ✳ **Lech**, a well-known and popular winter sports area, home to many skiers who have achieved Olympic or World Championship glory. In **Warth** continue northwest to the Hochtannbergpass, then along the Bregenzer Ache, a tributary of Lake Constance, through ❾ ✳ **Bregenzerwald** (Bregenz Forest). By way of **Alberschwende** the route returns to ❶ ✳ **Bregenz**.

Tour 3 Salzkammergut – Lakeland

Distance: approx. 230km/140mi   **Duration:** approx. 3 days

Lakeland scenery, mountains and culture all feature in this tour, for which about three days is required. Delightful landscapes and diverse cultural monuments are in store, not to mention a few stubbornly persistent legends.

Set out eastwards from ❶ ✳✳ **Salzburg** on the A1 autobahn and leave the motorway by taking the exit to the warmest lake of the Salzkammergut, the ❷ ✳ **Mondsee**. Some of the oldest traces of human settlement in the alpine region are preserved in the Pfahlbaumuseum in the town of Mondsee. The route continues along the

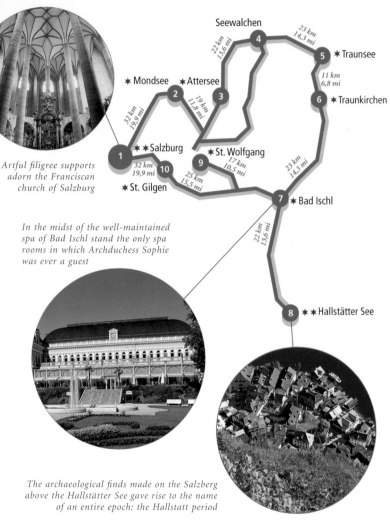

Artful filigree supports adorn the Franciscan church of Salzburg

Seewalchen

Mondsee ✳ ✳ Attersee

✳ ✳ Salzburg

St. Wolfgang

✳ St. Gilgen

✳ Traunsee

✳ Traunkirchen

✳ Bad Ischl

✳ ✳ Hallstätter See

32 km / 19,9 mi
22 km / 13,6 mi
23 km / 14,3 mi
19 km / 11,8 mi
11 km / 6,8 mi
17 km / 10,5 mi
25 km / 15,5 mi
23 km / 14,3 mi
22 km / 13,6 mi
32 km / 19,9 mi

In the midst of the well-maintained spa of Bad Ischl stand the only spa rooms in which Archduchess Sophie was ever a guest

The archaeological finds made on the Salzberg above the Hallstätter See gave rise to the name of an entire epoch: the Hallstatt period

northern shore of the Mondsee with a view of the **Drachenwand** (Dragon Wall) opposite. It is not far to the southern end of the ❸ ✳ **Attersee**. Here, choose between the western or the eastern shore – where music lovers can take a look inside the composer's retreat in which Gustav Mahler worked – and continue to ❹ **Seewalchen** at the lake's nothern end, with a view of Schloss Kammer. From Stein-bach, a mountain road rich in views leads east to the ❺ ✳ **Traunsee**. The prettily situated town of **Gmunden** on the lake's northern shore is famous for its ceramics, one of the most popular souvenirs for holidaymakers in Austria. The 17th-century palace Seeschloss Ort has an idyllic location on an islet in the lake. Following the Österreichische Romantikstrasse (Austrian Romantic Road), head south along the western shore of the Traunsee via picturesque ❻✳ **Traunkirchen** to Ebensee and continue further to ❼✳ **Bad Ischl**, where Emperor Franz Joseph I and Elisabeth, the famous Sisi, were engaged to be married. The Kaiservilla and Lehár-Villa nostalgically attest to the time of the Dual Monarchy.

Bad Ischl is the starting point of the extremely worthwhile side trip south to the ❽✳✳ **Hallstätter See** and **Hallstatt**, a UNESCO World Cultural and Natural Heritage site located at the northern foot of the colossal **Dachstein Massif**. Whether for the view over picturesque Hallstatt, for the journey into the salt mine, a guided tour through the fantastic Dachsteinhöhlen (Dachstein Caves), or simply for the view of the Dachstein Massif itself – every individual attraction on its own would be reason enough for this trip.

From Bad Ischl the route leads west to the **Wolfgangsee**, on whose northern shore ❾ **St Wolfgang**, its magnificent pilgrimage church and the **Weisses Rössl**, known from Benatzky's merry waltz-filled operetta *The White Horse Inn*, are worth a detour. Those who wish to view a considerable part of the tour from above should take the Schafberg funicular. With views to the Schafberg, the route continues along the southern shore to ❿ **St Gilgen**, once the home town of Mozart's mother and later of his sister Nannerl, and from there, after a brief nod at the Fuschlsee, back to ❶✳✳ **Salzburg**.

Tour 4 Heading South

Distance: approx. 270km/170mi   **Duration:** approx. 2 days

For those who haven't yet decided where to go next for a swimming and sunbathing holiday, this tour through Carinthia could provide some useful ideas. It runs through a series of pretty and warm bathing lakes with picturesque mountain backdrops, also calling in on interesting towns such as Klagenfurt and Villach. At least two days are required, but travellers with plenty of time could extend that to two weeks or more.

Starting in ❶✳ **Spittal an der Drau**, with the delightful Renaissance Schloss Porcia, the tour follows the Liesertal valley, parallel to the autobahn, to ❷✳ **Gmünd**, where the impressive **Porschemuseum** attracts automobile fans.

The picturesque **Maltatal** valley branches off to the northwest in Gmünd and comes to an end, after waterfalls and a game park, at the ❸**Kölnbrein-Sperre**, one of Austria's mightiest dams.

The main route leads from Gmünd further north, and after Krems turns east onto the winding, 35km/22mi-long Nockalmstrasse (toll payable), which traverses the ❹ ✳ **Nationalpark Nockberge**. After a

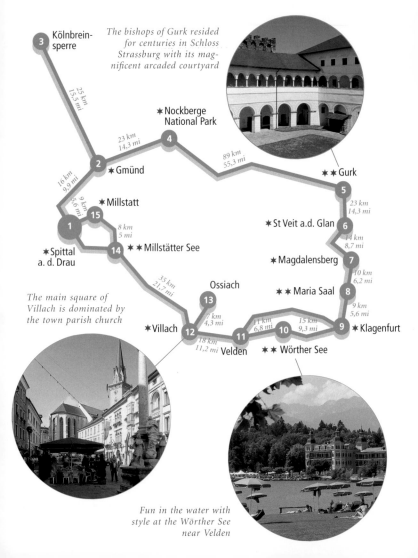

The bishops of Gurk resided for centuries in Schloss Strassburg with its magnificent arcaded courtyard

Kölnbrein-sperre ③

25 km
15,5 mi

✳ Nockberge
National Park

23 km
14,3 mi

②

89 km
55,3 mi

✳ Gmünd

16 km
9,9 mi

✳ ✳ Gurk

✳ Millstatt

⑤

9 km
5,6 mi

23 km
14,3 mi

① ⑮

✳ St Veit a.d. Glan ⑥

8 km
5 mi

14 km
8,7 mi

✳ Spittal
a. d. Drau

⑭ ✳ ✳ Millstätter See

✳ Magdalensberg ⑦

10 km
6,2 mi

35 km
21,7 mi

Ossiach

✳ ✳ Maria Saal ⑧

The main square of Villach is dominated by the town parish church

⑬

9 km
5,6 mi

7 km
4,3 mi

11 km
6,8 mi

15 km
9,3 mi

✳ Villach ⑫

⑪ ⑩ ⑨ ✳ Klagenfurt

18 km
11,2 mi

Velden ✳ ✳ Wörther See

Fun in the water with style at the Wörther See near Velden

short section along the small Gurk river, turn to the east in the Ebene Reichenau region and head in the direction of Deutsch-Griffen and **Gurk**. ❺ ✳ ✳ **Gurk Cathedral** numbers among the most important Romanesque churches in Austria. In Gurk the route continues south once more and leads to ❻ ✳ **St. Veit an der Glan**.

The main attraction in St. Veit an der Glan is **Burg Hochosterwitz**, located some miles east. The road providing access to the mighty castle is secured by 14 gateways. On the way south, turn left in Willersdorf – a few miles further on is the ❼ ✳ **Magdalensberg**, one of the most important Celtic-Roman settlements in Austria, today an extensive excavation site. The next item on the itinerary, just before the town of Maria Saal, is the »**Kärntner Herzogstuhl**«, the »Carinthian Duke's Throne« situated at the side of the road. The Kärntner Freilichtmuseum Maria Saal (an open-air museum) illustrates the way of life in centuries gone by. In **Maria Saal** it is worth paying a visit to the splendid ❽ ✳ ✳ **pilgrimage church**. It is only a few miles now to ❾ ✳ **Klagenfurt**, the Carinthian provincial capital.

Continue west to the much-visited ❿ ✳ ✳ **Wörther See**. On its southern shore lies **Maria Wörth**, whose picturesque old town centre on a peninsula in the lake is one of the most popular destinations on the Wörther See. The route can now follow the lake's **southern shore** to the elegant spa town of ⓫**Velden**, a favourite haunt of the jetset. A stroll along the promenade is obligatory. A few miles south lies the small Faaker See, one of Carinthia's most famous bathing lakes. From here the road leads to Warmbad Villach, where you can treat yourself to a break in the well-maintained thermal baths, and on to ⓬ ✳ **Villach**.

A nice alternative is to travel along the lively **northern shore** of the Wörther See via Moosburg and Feldkirchen to the Ossiacher See. This lake attracts not only water sports enthusiasts but also music fans who congregate there for the **Carinthischer Sommer** festival in the main town of ⓭**Ossiach** on the southern shore. On the northern shore, after 12km/7mi of winding road there is a wonderful view from the Gerlitzen mountain down onto the lake and over to the Karawanken mountain range to the south.

The B 100, parallel to the autobahn, leads northwest from Villach. In Feistritz the route turns north to the ⓮ ✳ ✳ **Millstätter See**. This delightful lake, lying between the Seerücken hills in the south and the Nockbergen mountains in the north, is not known as »Carinthia's sunny region« for nothing and is one of the most popular bathing lakes in the area. ⓯**Millstatt** on the northern shore, which was settled as early as Roman times, boasts an abbey church that is worth taking a look at. From here it is only a few miles to the starting point of this Carinthian tour, ❶ ✳ **Spittal an der Drau**.

Sights from A to Z

IMPRESSIVE MOUNTAIN LANDSCAPES, LOVELY ALPINE PASTURES, CRYSTAL CLEAR LAKES AND TOWNS WITH BOTH CULTURE AND CHARM: AUSTRIA HAS LONG BEEN AN ATTRACTIVE AND MULTIFACETED HOLIDAY DESTINATION – AND NOT JUST IN WINTER!

✳ Achensee

Province: Tyrol   **Elevation:** 929m/3048ft

Lake Achen, with its light green waters, is reminiscent of a Norwegian fjord. It is located northeast of Innsbruck and surrounded by dark evergreen forests. With a length of 9km/5.5mi, a width of 1km/0.6mi and a depth of 133m/436ft, the Achensee is Tyrol's largest and most beautiful lake.

Mountain air and recreational paradise

The peaks of the Karwendel mountains rise to the west and south, while the Rofan or Sonnwend mountains extend to the east. The Jenbach hydroelectric power plant takes advantage of the 380m/1247ft height difference from the Achensee to the Inntal valley. The lake offers countless recreational activities, particularly for those who enjoy sailing or surfing. Yet swimmers must be quite resilient in order to brave the Achensee's chilly waters, which even in the summer reach a maximum temperature of only 18 °C/64 °F. Two excursion cruise lines run services from mid-May to mid-October. Extra tours can be arranged with the *St Josef* propeller steamer, built in 1897 and the first steamboat to offer tours on the Achensee. A round trip lasts approximately 2 hours. Train fans will enjoy a ride from Jenbach to the Achensee with Europe's oldest steam-powered rack railway. The over 100-year-old Achenseebahn climbs 440m/1444ft over the 6.7km/4.1mi-long route. The Achensee is also a good area for mountain hiking; winter sports enthusiasts are drawn to Maurach-Eben, Pertisau and Achenkirch.

»St Benedikt«, one of the Achensee fleet, whose home harbour is in Pertisau

VISITING ACHENSEE

INFORMATION

Tourismusverband Achensee
A-6215 Achenkirch
Rathaus 387
Tel. 0 52 46/53 00, fax 53 33
www.achensee.com

WHERE TO STAY

► **Luxury**
Sporthotel Alpenrose
A-6212 Maurach am Achensee
Tel. 0 52 43/5 29 30, fax 54 66
www.alpenrose.at
This popular hotel on the Achensee offers a number of recreational activities including indoor and outdoor swimming pools, a beauty farm, and a so-called »Vitality Temple« that features a Roman, Turkish and Finnish sauna. There are some fine wines in the cellar.

Hotel Fürstenhaus
A-6213 Pertisau am Achensee
Tel. 0 52 43/54 42, fax 61 68
www.fuerstenhaus.at
The large fresco in the stairwell depicts a hunting scene: the Achensee and the surrounding forests are a fishing and hunting paradise. It was here that Emperor Maximilian I's legendary »Fischerhaus« (Fisherman's House) once stood.

Around the Achensee

The road winds upward from the Inn valley, offering some fabulous views. It then reaches the town of Maurach (960m/3150ft; pop. 1600), located at the southern end of the Achensee. Somewhat outside Eben, the administrative centre of the community, stands the **Baroque parish and pilgrimage church of St Notburga** (15th–18th century). St Notburga, a pious maiden from Rattenberg and Tyrol's only female saint (1265–1313), is regarded as the patron saint of servants. A glass reliquary in the high altar contains her skeleton, which is kept in a standing position. Beautiful stucco work adorns the nave's ceiling frescoes, which display episodes from the life of the saint such as the miracle of the floating sickle: when Notburga's master, a farmer, commanded her to keep working in the field even after hearing the Angelus bells and prevented her from going to her evening devotions, she threw her sickle in the air, saying: »Let my sickle be judge between me and you«. The sickle remained suspended in the air, hanging as if from a ray of sunlight.

From the township of Maurach, the Rofan cable car travels 2km/1.2mi to reach the 1834m/6017ft-high Erfurter Hütte (mountain lodge; food and drink available) on the peak of the Mauritzköpfl. Aside from the magnificent panoramic views, there are also worthwhile walks from here to neighbouring summits.

Around 5km/3mi northwest of Maurach-Eben, on the west bank of the lake, lies the holiday resort town of Pertisau (950m/3117ft; pop.

Maurach-Eben

◄ *Pilgrimage church*

◄ *Mauritzköpfl*

Pertisau

460). From here, take a slight detour to the **Mineral Oil Demonstration Mine** on the Seeberg mountain. A precious healing mineral oil was mined here for medical use until 1917.

Achenkirch The Achenseestrasse is an impressive stretch of country road that passes through tunnels and offers views of the water from the east bank of the lake up to the north. On the opposite bank, the 2053m/6736ft-high Seekarspitze takes a steep plunge into the water. Achenkirch (930m/3051ft; pop. 1900) is a long, narrow village on the northern end of the lake. Aside from its marvellous old farmhouses, it is worth visiting the parish church of 1748 and the local museum (Heimatmuseum) in Sixenhof, which features original artefacts from rural life of days gone by. A summer toboggan run is one of the many recreational activities on offer here. The Austrian-German border runs around 9km/5.5mi to the north, just before the Achen Pass (941m/3087ft).

✦ ✦ Admont

M 4

Province: Styria   **Elevation:** 639m/2096ft
Population: 2900

Admont, situated in the centre of a broad basin of the river Enns, offers a unique attraction: its monastic library, which is probably the largest and most beautiful in the world. Yet not only culture is found in this small town – the »Gesäuse«, Austria's newest national park, also begins near Admont.

✦ Stift Admont

Funded by the legacy of St Hemma of Gurk, the Benedictine abbey of Admont was founded by Archbishop Gebhard of Salzburg in 1074. With the exception of its prized library, the abbey was almost completely destroyed by fire in 1865, and then rebuilt in subsequent years. Its former courtyards have now been converted into a park. Stift Admont is the **oldest existing monastery in Styria**, and continues to serve as a spiritual, cultural and economic centre of the region today (opening times: mid-March–early Nov daily 10am–5pm). Its operations (forestry, building and cultural departments, gardening, etc.) employ around 1000 secular workers.

! *Baedeker* TIP

Virtual visit

A good source of information on the magnificent Benedictine abbey is the website at www.stift admont.at. Among other things it has an events listing, tips for exhibitions and an interesting set of photos.

The library of the Benedictine abbey of Admont numbers among the most beautiful monastery libraries in the world

The **church** is dominated by two 70m/230ft-high towers. Its interior consists of a central nave and two side aisles. Its furnishings include a portrait of Maria the Immaculate by Martin Altomonte and a carved Christmas manger (1755). The high altar is surrounded by embroidered tapestries; in front of it is a copy of the *Admonter Maria* (*Virgin of Admont*, 1310; original in the Landesmuseum Joanneum in Graz).

Abbey church

In terms of art history, the Baroque library (72m/237ft long, 14m/46ft wide) in the east wing of the abbey is the most important part of the entire complex. Altomonte's ceiling frescoes, with depictions of the »four last things« (heaven, hell, death and judgement), and the larger than life-size statues of the prophets Moses and Elijah as well as the apostles Peter and Paul are its most noteworthy features. The library contains well over 100,000 volumes, including 1100 manuscripts and 900 incunabula (books printed before 1501).

✷ ✷
Library

In addition to a comprehensive collection of minerals, insects, birds and mammals, the abbey's Naturhistorisches Museum (Museum of Natural History) displays a highly valuable collection of historic art as well as modern art exhibits (library and collections opening times: mid-March–early Nov daily 10am–5pm, otherwise by appointment with 20 persons or more; tel. 0 36 13/23 12-0).

Collections

Around Admont

The Ennstal Alps consist of a densely wooded, steep-sloped chain of mountains belonging to the Northern Limestone Alps near Admont. The mountains here are characterized by picturesque rock formations, and their highest peak is the Hochtor (2372m/7783ft). Seasoned climbers and mountaineers will find dozens of worthwhile routes in this region.

Ennstal Alps

▶ VISITING ADMONT

INFORMATION

Tourismus Verband
Alpenregion
Nationalpark Gesäuse
Hauptstrasse 35,
A-8911 Admont
Tel. 0 36 13/211 60 10
Fax 211 60 40
www.alpenregion.cc

WHERE TO EAT

▶ **Moderate**
Zur Ennsbrücke
Hall 300, A-8911 Admont
Tel. 0 36 13/22 91
Located directly at the entrance to the town, this cosy restaurant prepares its meals using seasonal products from the region.

Nationalpark Gesäuse

✴ The »Gesäuse« is a high-lying alpine gorge between Admont and the town of Hieflau to the east. Its name is intended to convey the noise that the River Enns makes as it passes between the towering cliffs. In 2002, this impressive section of the Ennstal Alps was promoted to the status of a national park. Between Admont and Hieflau the waters of the thunderous River Enns have carved their way through 16km/10mi of an immense massif of the Limestone Alps; the Gesäuse is therefore named **»a symphony of rock and water«**. Regardless of how visitors take in this magnificent landscape – by car or by train, on a hike, a mountain climb, or by bike – it remains an unforgettable experience.

Schloss Röthelstein

Schloss Röthelstein (817m/2681ft; 17th century), a two-storey castle with a courtyard and a Baroque chapel, lies in an area of forest 3km/2mi south of the market town of Admont. The castle's collection of over 300 paintings, which was severely damaged during the Second World War, is displayed in the chapter house and the museum. Anyone can afford to stay overnight in the Schloss Röthelstein nowadays, by the way: it has been converted to a youth hostel.

Wallfahrtskirche Frauenberg

Originally a late Gothic church, the Frauenberg pilgrimage church, 6km/3.5mi west of Admont, was converted to its present Baroque style in the 17th century. The interior features frescoes depicting the life of the Virgin Mary and a beautiful cross altar by J. T. Stammel.

Liezen

The main town of Styria's Ennstal valley is Liezen (659m/2162ft; pop. 7000), 20km/12.5mi west of Admont. Its parish church contains noteworthy paintings by Kremser Schmidt.

Spital am Pyhrn

The 945m/3101ft-high Pyhrn Pass leads to the town of Spital am Pyhrn (647m/2123ft; pop. 2200), 16km/10mi to the northeast. In addition to offering various spa activities, Spital boasts a Baroque church and a petroglyph museum.

✴ Altenburg

`P 2`

Province: Lower Austria   **Elevation:** 387m/1270ft
Population: 850

The small village of Altenburg, located around 30km/19mi north of Krems an der Donau in the ►Waldviertel, owes its fame to its Benedictine abbey, also known as the »Baroque jewel« of the Waldviertel.

✴ Stift Altenburg

The abbey building's opulent architecture and its vast, over 200m/657ft-long east façade serve as a unique contrast to the area's austere landscape. Plundering and destruction during the Thirty Years' War almost completely destroyed the monastery, which had been founded as early as 1144. The abbey buildings re-emerged in their current form during reconstruction, with splendid Baroque and Rococo stucco décor in the interior. A library, imperial wing, and marble hall were added to the original structure.

The magnificently colourful monastery library is especially worth seeing; it is one of the most superb and elaborate in all of Austria. The main hall is three storeys high and 48m/158ft long; the ceiling frescoes (the Judgment of Solomon, the Wisdom of God, the Light of Faith, and others) were done by Paul Troger. Underneath the library, a crypt has interesting frescoes, especially grotesque scenes depicting the Dance of Death.

✴ *Beautiful library*

The **abbey church**, an oval-shaped structure with a dome, was renovated by Josef Munggenast in 1730–33. The dome's fresco is one of the most monumental works by Paul Troger. The high altar features a depiction of the Assumption of Mary and, above it, the Holy Trinity.

During the past years, excavations have uncovered the **»monastery beneath the monastery«**: a refectory, chapter house, the monks' working and living quarters, a cloister, and the Romanesque and

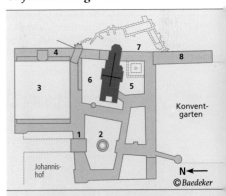

Stift Altenburg *Plan*

Konvent-garten

Johannis-hof

N ← ©Baedeker

1 Gateway / Monastery Shop   5 Fountain Garden
2 Prelates Court   6 Churchyard
3 Great Abbey Court   7 Terrace
4 Imperial Apartments   8 Crypt

► ALTENBURG

INFORMATION

Gemeinde Altenburg
Zwettlerstrasse 16
A-3591 Altenburg
Tel. 0 29 82/27 65 or 34 51 14
Fax 27 65 16
www.altenburg.at

Gothic Veitskapelle or St Vitus Chapel (opening times: Palm Sunday to 1 Nov daily 10am–5pm, mid-June–early Sept until 6pm. Guided tour available for groups all year round by arrangement; tel. 0 29 82/34 51; www.stift-altenburg.at).

Concerts by the **Altenburger Sängerknaben** (Altenburg Boys' Choir) are a real treat. When they are not on tour they often enrich church services with their singing.

Around Altenburg

Schloss Greillenstein

The imposing **Renaissance castle** of Greillenstein (16th–17th century) stands proudly approximately 7km/4mi west of Stift Altenburg. For those interested in history or law, it is a real treat: following the tour, visitors can watch a re-enactment of a historic court case from the Middle Ages, complete with old costumes. The execution of the draconian punishments typical of those times is however not to be expected (opening times: April–Oct daily 9.30am–5pm, Nov–March by arrangement for groups of five or more; tel. 0 29 89/808 00).

Rosenburg

Rosenburg Castle lies on a picturesque slope above the Kamp river southeast of Altenburg. The elaborate buildings (14th–17th century), restored and made accessible to the public as early as the 19th century, include magnificent tournament grounds. Its library is especially impressive, with a richly carved coffered ceiling and the Vogerlzimmer (Bird Room), in which the walls are adorned with depictions of birds. Rosenburg Castle is a **worthy setting for summer concerts and theatrical festivals**. A fairytale land (»Märchenwelt«) entertains young visitors, although the most popular attraction is the **falcon house**. Eagles, falcons, owls, and vultures show off their fascinating flying skills. Visitors also receive information on the protection of these species as well as the history and development of falconry. An old Lower Austrian tradition is also brought back to life: »Falknerei zu Pferde«, or hunting with a falcon (opening times: April and Oct Tue–Sun 9.30am–4.30pm, May–Sept daily until 5pm, July and Aug until 6.30pm; bird of prey shows daily 11am and 3pm; »Falknerei zu Pferd« shows in historical costumes see www.rosenburg.at).

The falconer on the Rosenberg knows his eagles, too

South of Rosenburg Castle is the town of Gars (244m/801ft; pop. **Gars**
3500), whose romantic fortress ruins are a relic of the Babenberg period and the setting of an annual summer opera festival. Music seems
to have been in the air here for quite some time: Franz von Suppé
was a summer visitor in Gars for almost 20 years and wrote his
operetta *Boccaccio* here (a Franz von Suppé memorial can be found
at Kremser Strasse 40).

The town of Horn (309m/1014ft, pop. 8000), 6km/3.5mi northeast **Horn**
of Altenburg, features not only numerous Renaissance and Baroque
buildings but also two museums that are certainly worth a visit. The
Höbarth Museum, with collections on local prehistory and history, is
included amongst the museums of the **»Kulturpark Kamptal«**, which
present geological peculiarities along with the prehistoric and early
history of the Kamptal valley. The Mader Museum displays agricultural equipment and rural household items (Wiener Str. 4; opening ⏲
times: Palm Sunday to 2 Nov daily 9am–5pm).

✶ Arlberg

D 5

Provinces: Tyrol and Vorarlberg

**Hardly any other region has produced as many Olympic and world
champions in winter sports as the Arlberg mountains. The entire
massif is covered with numerous mountain railways and hundreds
of ski lifts, which also serve hikers in the summer months.**

At an elevation of 1793m/5883ft, the Arlberg, a mountain range on **Paradise**
the border between Vorarlberg and Tyrol, is the **highest massif of** **for winter sports**
the ►Lechtal Alps. It forms not only a watershed between the Rhine
and the Danube but also a climatic divide. The result is dependably
large amounts of snow, which has led to the growth of well-known
winter sports resorts (St Anton, Lech, Zürs and Stuben) surrounding
the Arlberg massif and the Valluga mountain (2811m/9223ft), which
towers over the rest.

The Arlbergstrasse (Arlberg Road) leads from the Rhine valley **Arlbergstrasse**
through the Klostertal valley, which begins near ►Bludenz, and east
to the Inntal valley. It reaches an elevation of approximately 1800m/
590ft at the Arlberg Pass.

Heading toward the north just east of Stuben, the Flexenstrasse **Flexenstrasse**
branches off from the main road and leads to the Lechtal valley over
the 1784m/5853ft-high Flexen Pass. Constructed in 1895–1900, the
road traverses a very impressive landscape and offers magnificent
views of the mountains of the Verwallgruppe. Numerous avalanche

▶ VISITING ARLBERG

INFORMATION

Tourismusverband St Anton
Dorfstr. 8, A-6580 St Anton
Tel. 0 54 46/2 26 90, fax 25 32,
www.stantonamarlberg.com

Lech Zürs Tourismus
Dorf 2, A-6764 Lech am Arlberg
Tel. 0 55 83/2 16 10, fax 31 55
www.lech-zuers.at/lech

Lech Zürs Tourismus
Büro Zürs, A-6763 Zürs
Tel. 0 55 83/22 45, fax 29 82
www.lech-zuers.at

WHERE TO EAT

▶ Expensive
Goldener Berg
Oberlech 117
A-6764 Lech am Arlberg
Tel. 0 55 83/2 20 50
This restaurant with its panoramic
views caters to skiers in the afternoon.
The evening menu features fish and
lamb dishes.

▶ Moderate
Arlberg
Dorf 187
A-6764 Lech am Arlberg
Tel. 0 55 83/21 34

Light meals and traditional Austrian
dishes – such as Tafelspitz – are served
with an international touch in the cosy
dining rooms.

WHERE TO STAY

▶ Luxury
St Antoner Hof
A-6580 St Anton am Arlberg
Tel. 0 54 46/29 10
Fax 35 51
www.antonerhof.at
This elegant Tyrolese hotel is located
only five minutes' walk from the area's
lifts and mountain railways. Aside
from exquisite cuisine, an extensive
programme of wellness and entertainment activities awaits visitors.

Baedeker recommendation

Walch's Rote Wand
A-6764 Lech-Zug am Arlberg
Tel. 0 55 83/3 43 50
Fax 34 35 40
www.rotewand.com
Open: December – April
Walch's Rote Wand numbers among the best
accommodation on the Arlberg – with a
sauna, steam bath, beauty farm, indoor golf,
and outstanding cuisine.

screens protect the road, which runs alongside the jagged cliffs of the
Stubenbachschlucht (Stubenbach gorge). Northern access is often
closed in the winter between Warth and Lech.

Along the Arlberg

St Anton am Arlberg St Anton am Arlberg (1284m/4213ft) has a long tradition as a winter
sports resort. This was where Hannes Schneider developed his down-
hill skiing technique – the Arlberg technique – and Stefan Krucken-
hauser invented Wedeln, a style of skiing in which skiers rhythmi-

cally swing the rear of their skis from side to side as they descend. A tunnel means that the town is hardly troubled by traffic, and a very attractive pedestrian zone has emerged. The traditional skiing and local history museum, also a restaurant, tells the history of Arlberg, alpine skiing and the development of Arlberg's towns (opening times: in summer Wed–Sun noon–6pm, in winter daily 3pm–6pm; restaurant from 6pm).

◄ Ski- und Heimatmuseum

? DID YOU KNOW …?

■ … that Luis Trenker filmed his drama *Berge in Flammen* (*Mountains in Flames*) in Stuben in 1931? The film, a simple paean to alpinism and goodwill between peoples, earned him his international breakthrough.

Lech am Arlberg (1450m/4758ft; pop. 1400), the principal town of the Tannberg region, is located north of the Arlberg where the Lech river meets the Zürser Bach, a stream. A hundred years ago, the town was one of the poorest and most secluded villages in all of the Vorarlberg and was threatened with depopulation. It was saved by the rising popularity of ski tourism, which discovered the old Walser settlement. Today, Lech is Austria's highest-class winter sports resort. Its parish church was constructed by the Walser people (originally from the Wallis region) in the Gothic style in 1390 and renovated in Rococo style in 1791. The 15th and 16th-century frescoes in the choir loft and nave are particularly noteworthy, along with the two enormous bells: they had to be cast in 1746 on the church square because they were too large to be transported on the mule trails. Between 1563 and 1806, the so-called Walser Court – a group consisting of twelve jurors and a freely appointed leader – convened in the Weisses Haus (White House, no. 17), which is first mentioned in documents dating back to 1516.

✳
Lecham Arlberg

Zürs (1730m/5676ft; pop. 130) is connected to Lech by a network of pistes and has also established itself as a world-famous winter sports resort. Plentiful snow in the winter – the first ski instruction to ever be held in Austria took place here as early as 1906 – and marvellous opportunities for hikes or excursions in the summer months attract visitors who are seeking a healthy holiday.

Zürs am Arlberg

Also popular amongst winter sports enthusiasts, Stuben am Arlberg (1407m/4617ft) is a convivial village on the western slope of the Arlberg that was given the name »Stuben« (German for »parlour«) after a medieval calefactory that had once been used there by the Knights Hospitaller of the Order of St John from Feldkirch.

Stuben am Arlberg

Around the Arlberg

The **Verwallgruppe** (also referred to as the »Ferwallgruppe«) is a range north of the Silvretta between the Klostertal, Stanzer, ►Montafon and Paznauntal valleys that consists of several groups of mountains separated by deep valleys. In the north, the Arlberg Pass connects it to the Lechtal Alps and the Arlberg ski region. The range is known for its bold peaks flanked by glaciers, steep cliffs, and hollows with tiny lakes (Valschavielsee, Versailsee, Blankaseen).

Mountain hikes ▶ Although good paths connect each of the mountain huts, ascending the higher mountains of the Verwallgruppe – with its principal peak, the five-pointed Kuchenspitze (3170m/10,401ft), and the imposing, 3059m/10,037ft-high Patteriol – requires quite a bit of climbing experience. One of the Verwall's loveliest ski routes begins at Stuben am Arlberg, stops at the Kaltenberg-Hütte (Kaltenberg Lodge; 2100m/6890ft), and continues on to the Kalter Berg (2900m/9515ft). The Heilbronner Hütte (2320m/7612ft) is located in the southern Verwallgruppe mountains and is accessible by way of St Anton. It is an important stop-off point on the popular tour that runs through the Verwall range to the Silvretta.

✴ Attersee

Province: Upper Austria   **Elevation:** 465m/1526ft

Gustav Klimt captured the shimmering reflection of the water and the beauty of the towns along the Attersee in some of his paintings. With a depth of 171m/562ft, a length of 20km/12mi and a breadth of 2–3km/1.2–1.9mi, the Attersee is the largest lake of the Salzkammergut and the Austrian Alps.

Holiday out of doors The lake offers a variety of water sports, such as surfing, diving (with visibility of up to 30m/98ft!), sailing and waterskiing, but also fea-

A view to dream about: the Attersee as seen from Seewalchen

▶ VISITING ATTERSEE

INFORMATION

Tourismusverband
Ferienregion Attersee
Nussdorferstr. 15
A-4864 Attersee
Tel. 0 76 66/77 19
Fax 79 19 19
www.attersee.at

WHERE TO EAT

▶ **Moderate**

Oberndorfer
Hauptstrasse 18, A-4864 Attersee
Tel. 0 76 66/7 86 40
Enjoy wonderfully fresh fish straight out of the Attersee accompanied by a beautiful view of the lake at a restaurant that has been family-owned and run for over 100 years.

tures tennis, miniature golf, horseback riding, hiking, kite flying and paragliding.

Around the Attersee

Attersee (pop. 1500) was an imperial residence in the 9th century; the Archbishop of Salzburg had a castle built there in the 13th century. The present-day parish and pilgrimage church of **Maria Attersee** originated in the chapel of the former castle; it was converted to Baroque style from the original Gothic by Jakob Pawanger between 1722 and 1728. The high altar was the work of Josef Matthias Götz of Passau. The late Gothic Laurentiuskirche (Church of St Lawrence) in the township of Abtsdorf is also worth seeing – its high altar, side altars and pulpit were created *c*1700 by sculptor Meinrad Guggenbichler of ▶Mondsee.

Attersee (Town)

! *Baedeker* TIP

Composer's retreat

To be able to work in peace, in 1894 Gustav Mahler built himself a tiny abode on the southeast bank of the Attersee, near the Gasthof Föttinger inn in Steinbach. Today, the house is a small memorial site featuring pictures and documentation of the time Mahler spent on the Attersee (accessible all year round, bookings at the inn; tel. 0 76 63/81 00).

Beginning in 1900, Viennese painter Gustav Klimt spent countless summer retreats in the town of **Seewalchen** am Attersee (pop. 4800). He was also a guest in Villa Paulick, which is now a small hotel, through his connection to the Flöge family – the Viennese fashion designer Emilie Flöge was one of his favourite models.

Located on a picturesque headland in Schörfling, **Schloss Kammer** was immortalized by Gustav Klimt in many of his paintings. The castle is private property, but opens its gates for summer concerts.

Schörfling

✶ Bad Aussee

L 4

Province: Styria
Population: 5080

Elevation: 650–1000m/2133–3281ft

Bad Aussee is the economical and cultural centre of the Styrian part of the Salzkammergut and also the geographical centre of Austria. The idyllic town lies deep in the Traun valley between the Totes Gebirge mountains and the Dachstein Massif.

Rich in tradition

The climatic spa of Bad Aussee owes its growth to rich salt deposits, but today the town profits from its well-developed skiing areas. The region is truly captivating in the late spring, when the daffodils are in full bloom. The town became famous in the 19th century, when Archduke Johann fell in love with the daughter of the town's post-master, Anna Plochl (1804–85), much to the initial dismay of the Viennese Court. He married her in 1829 after receiving his brother's imperial permission. By the middle of the 19th century, the Aussee region had developed into a highly favoured summer retreat for members of the literary avant-garde, and the present-day »Ausseer Kultursommer« (Aussee Summer Festival) serves as a continuation of this tradition.

What to See in Bad Aussee

Kammerhof

For centuries the region profited from its rich salt deposits. Because the salt mines required considerable administration, the noteworthy Salzamt (Salt Bureau) was constructed around 1400 on Chlumecky-

▶ VISITING BAD AUSSEE

INFORMATION

Tourismusverband Ausseerland
Bahnhofstr. 132
A-8990 Bad Aussee
Tel. 0 36 22/54 04 00
www.ausseerland.at

HIKING

The approximately 12km/7.5mi-long »Via Artis« walking trail takes in former and present-day domiciles of various artists, beginning and ending in the »Künstlerwinkel« (Artists' Corner) in the centre of the town. An exhibit documents all those inspired by the muses who have lived and worked here over the years.

WHERE TO STAY

▶ **Mid-range**
Hubertushof
Puchen 86, A-8992 Altaussee
Tel. 0 36 22/7 12 80
Fax 7 12 80 80
www.herrenhaus-hubertushof.at
This elegant hotel, once the hunting lodge of the princes of the House of Hohenlohe-Schillingsfürst, is situated in peaceful surroundings amongst the trees with a view of the Altausseer See.

A boatful of day trippers cross the legendary Toplitzsee

TREASURE IN THE TOPLITZSEE

The small Toplitzsee, surrounded by steep rocky cliffs, has been the subject of wild speculation since the end of the war. It is alleged that in 1945 the Nazis sent fabulous gold treasure and confidential documents into the lake's depths. After costly diving expeditions the real secret of this mountain lake has finally seen the light of day.

In the night of 28–29 April 1945 two lorries drove to the Toplitzsee from the nearby Ebensee concentration camp. SS men jumped down, unloaded boxes into fishing boats, and rowed out onto the lake. When they returned to the shore, their boats were empty. Numerous **rumours and legends** sprang up: did the boxes contain gold and confidential papers? In 1959, Germany's *Stern* magazine tried to clear the matter up: a diving team was commissioned to recover a total of seven boxes from the bed of the lake. But the boxes contained only thick bundles of British pound notes – **counterfeit money** with which the UK financial markets were to have been flooded during the war. In another dive in 1963, once again only dud notes were salvaged. In further expeditions only German naval equipment and bombs from the last days of the war were found.

The seventh big dive in June 2000 brought up, in addition to more fake banknotes, a **tin box**, in which large quantities of beer bottle tops bearing the inscription »Leider nicht!« (»Un-fortunately not!«) were found. A group of merry regulars at a bar in Bad Aussee is said to have thrown the box into the lake one night in 1984 in an attempt to fool **marine biologist Dr Fricke**. But Fricke wasn't after Nazi treasure; instead he was exploring the uncharted depths of the Toplitzsee.

Biological sensation

He discovered that the water temperature just above the lake bed was almost 6 °C/43 °F, whereas the average temperature of alpine lakes is about 4 °C/39 °F. What's more, from a depth of about 20m/65ft downwards, there is a lack of oxygen in the 103m-deep lake. In this 80m/260ft-deep layer of water, which is increasingly saline, Fricke found some thus far unknown bacteria and worms that can live without oxygen. The fish always swim on the upper layers of this lake, and logs lying criss-cross on the lake bed do not decompose due to the lack of oxygen. This explains why the pound notes and other finds from the mountain lake's murky depths are still relatively well preserved.

platz. Now known as the Kammerhof, it houses the local history museum. It combines late Gothic and Renaissance elements and is recognized as the oldest secular building in Styria (opening times: mid–May–mid-June Tue–Sat 4pm–6pm, mid-June–mid Sept daily 10am–noon and 2pm–5pm).

Around Bad Aussee

★
Altausseer See

Just a few miles to the north, at the foot of the Totes Gebirge, lies the charming Altausseer See (Lake Altausseer). The lake can be walked around in only 2 hours, or explored comfortably by rowing boat. The best place to start is the pretty spa town of Altaussee (pop. 1900).

Salt mine

The old salt mine is located on the way to the lake;it formed the foundation of the region's economy from the 12th century and during the Second World War served as a shell-proof storage facility for countless works of art, including the *Ghent Altar* (guided tours: April daily 10am, 12pm and 2pm, May–Oct daily 10am–4pm on the hour, Nov–March Thu 2pm). From the Altaussee, the winding **panoramic road** on the Loser mountain travels upwards to an elevation of 1600m/5250ft, where visitors will find a mountain restaurant as well as a splendid view of the peaks of the Totes Gebirge and the Dachstein Massif.

Loser mountain ►

Lakes

The **Grundlsee** (709m/2327ft) is located northeast of Bad Aussee in a valley of meadows surrounded by thick forest, with the legendary **Toplitzsee** (►Baedeker Special, p.189) beyond. Although the lake is shrouded in legend, various diving expeditions have yet to discover anything to confirm the stories. The picturesque **Kammersee**, situated behind it, is only accessible on foot.

★
Totes Gebirge

The Totes Gebirge (»Dead Mountains«), the second of the Salzkammergut's main mountain ranges, features the most extensive plateau of the Northern Limestone Alps and offers one of the most beautiful panoramic views of the mountains. Its western and southern borders are formed by the Trauntal valley, while its highest and most prominent peaks, the Grosser Priel (2514m/8249ft) and the 2446m/8025ft-high Spitzmauer, stretch far to the east. In contrast to the monumentality of the high plateau and the northern face, the southern part of the range presents more cheerful, open scenery with the Altaussee and Grundlsee lakes.

Bad Mitterndorf

The climatic health spa town of Bad Mitterndorf (809m/2655ft; pop. 3200) is a popular holiday destination. With boat excursions on the 5km/3mi Salza reservoir, mountain bike tours around the area, well-kept pistes, and the Kulm, the largest ski jumping site in the world, this region excites all true fans of winter sports.

The Tauplitzalm (1650m/5414ft) has established itself as a ski region **Tauplitzalm** with a rich network of lifts that offers a wide variety of accommodation. The scenic Steirer See (Lake Steirer; 1457m/4781ft) is located a few minutes east of the upper terminus; a chair lift to the west takes visitors to the 1964m/6444ft-high Lawinenstein mountain in comfort.

A true gem of art can be found near Pürgg (786m/2579ft), just before reaching the majestic heights of the Grimming mountain: the Romanesque Johanneskapelle (Chapel of St John). It contains what are presumed to be the oldest frescoes (from around 1200) in the northern Alps. **Pürgg**

It is worth seeing Schloss Trautenfels, which with its imposing bastions and turrets was built as a fortification in the 13th century at the junction with the Ennstal valley. Its Landschaftsmuseum (Regional Museum) relates interesting facets of the region's cultural and natural history (opening times: Palm Sunday–Oct, daily 10am–5pm). **Schloss Trautenfels** ⊙

✶ Baden bei Wien

Q 3

Province: Lower Austria
Population: 28,000
Elevation: 220m/722ft

This charming small town, known for its Biedermeier architecture and its villas, was the gathering place of Viennese society between 1803 and 1834. Located just 30km/20mi south of Vienna on the eastern edge of the Wienerwald, its popularity was due to the regular presence of the Habsburg court in summer.

Baden seemed to be particularly well-liked by musicians: in addition to Mozart, Schubert, Carl Maria von Weber and Beethoven, who wrote sections of his Ninth Symphony and *Missa Solemnis* here, composers of operettas and waltzes, such as the elder and younger Strauss, Josef Lanner and Carl Millöcker were attracted by its light-hearted, lively atmosphere. **Resort with villas and spa**

Even as early as Roman times, Baden bei Wien was a prized spa town that is said to be Austria's most noteworthy sulphurous spa (Aquae Pannoniae). The sulphurous springs reach temperatures of up to 36 °C/97 °F and release over 4 million litres of water per day. The spring waters are used to treat rheumatic pain and vascular illness. ◄ **Sulphurous springs**

What to See in Baden bei Wien

On the Hauptplatz stands not only a Baroque column to the Holy Trinity and the classical Rathaus (town hall) by Joseph Kornhäusel, **Old Town**

▶ VISITING BADEN BEI WIEN

INFORMATION

Tourist Information Baden
Brusattiplatz 3
A-2500 Baden bei Wien
Tel. 0 22 52/22 60 06 00, fax 8 07 33
www.baden.at

BADENER ROSENTAGE

For fans of roses, the Doblhoffpark holds a fragrant attraction: around 25,000 rose trees and shrubs, more than 600 species, thrive and bloom in the park's Rosarium. For two weeks every June, when the roses are in full bloom, everything revolves around the »queen of flowers« during the Badener Rosentage festival. The events range from a sweet-scented stroll to the Rose Ball. The entire programme is available at www.baden.at or from the tourist information centre.

WHERE TO EAT

▶ Moderate
① *Krainerhütte*
Im Helenental
A-2500 Baden bei Wien
Tel. 0 22 25/4 45 11

A mere half-hour's drive from Vienna, this restaurant is located in the lovely Helenental valley. Its specialities: traditional Viennese cuisine and fish.

WHERE TO STAY

▶ Luxury
① *Grand Hotel Sauerhof*
Weilburgstrasse 11–13
A-2500 Baden bei Wien
Tel. 0 22 52/41 25 10, fax 4 36 26
www.sauerhof.at
The grand Biedermeier-style palais in the heart of the spa town has welcomed many illustrious guests, including the poets Franz Grillparzer and Friedrich Schlegel.

② *Hotel Schloss Weikersdorf*
Schlossgasse 9–11
A-2500 Baden bei Wien
Tel. 0 22 52/48 30 10; fax 48 30 11 50
www.hotelschlossweikersdorf.at
Elegant hotel in the Doblhoffpark. Its gourmet restaurant treats guests to Austrian specialities, and wine tastings with regional wines are held in its historical Schlosskeller.

but also the Kaiserhaus (Imperial House, 1792), a comparatively modest structure that Emperor Franz I used as his summer residence from 1813 to 1834. The Stadttheater (1909) on the Hauptplatz is especially dedicated to operettas. A plaque in the parish church, the 15th-century Pfarrkirche St Stephan, serves as a reminder that Mozart composed his *Ave Verum* here for the church's choirmaster.

On several occasions, Ludwig van Beethoven took up residence at Rathausgasse 10, where he wrote sections of his Ninth Symphony (opening times: Tue–Fri 4pm–6pm, Sat and Sun 10am–noon and 4pm–6pm).

Spa architecture — Countless beautiful baths were built during the **Biedermeier period** in particular. These days they are used for other things: for example

Baden bei Wien Map

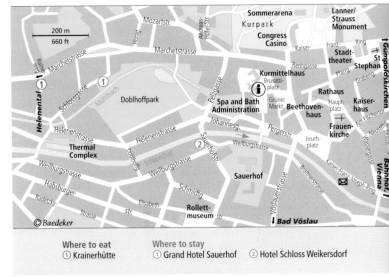

200 m
660 ft

Where to eat
① Krainerhütte

Where to stay
① Grand Hotel Sauerhof   ② Hotel Schloss Weikersdorf

the Frauenbad (Josefsplatz 5) is an exhibition centre for modern art; the Johannesbad (Johannesgasse 12–14) is the Theater on the Pier; and the Leopoldsbad (Brusattiplatz 3) now houses the tourist information centre as well as the local administrative offices for the spa and resort.

Yet the new spas are also praiseworthy: the Thermalstrandbad (thermal lido, Helenenstrasse 17–19), built in the most beautiful art nouveau style, offers not only a wide variety of playing and sporting facilities but also a huge sandy beach. The Biedermeier Römertherme (Roman baths, Brusattiplatz 4) are covered by a modern glass roof. Hotel Sauerhof (Weilburgstrasse 11–13) has had the privilege of welcoming Grillparzer and Beethoven as guests – even though it did not offer its wide selection of treatments back then.

Kurpark

Located directly at the entrance of the Kurpark (spa park) is the beautifully designed **Baden Casino**. In the park, memorials such as the Beethoven Temple (1926), the bust of Grillparzer (1899), and the bronze statue of composers Joseph Lanner and Johann Strauss (1912) commemorate influential guests. The Sommerarena (summer arena), an art nouveau structure with a moveable glass roof (1906), provides a nostalgic setting for operetta performances.

Rollettmuseum

The Rollettmuseum has extensive collections of prehistoric and Roman artefacts on display. Its most bizarre exhibit is a collection of skulls by anatomist Josef Gall (1758–1828), whose highly questionable theory of »cranioscopy« claimed that a person's character could be determined by analyzing the shape of their skull (Weikersdorfer Platz 1; opening times: Wed–Mon 3pm–6pm).

Bludenz

C 5

Province: Vorarlberg
Population: 14,000

Elevation: 588m/1831ft

Bludenz, the district capital of Vorarlberg, is situated in beautiful mountainous surroundings. It has developed from a former centre of silver mining to its current status as the economic hub of the Vorarlberger Oberland region.

Vorarlberg's economic hub
Bludenz extends along the Ill river, some 60km/35mi south of Bregenz, where five valleys intersect: ▶Montafon, Brandner Tal, Klostertal, Walgau and Grosses Walsertal. The town's economic success began with the construction of the Arlberg Railway in 1884; today it is known for trade and commerce and for the textile, chocolate and brewing industries. Bludenz is also a convenient starting-point for trips into the area's most popular skiing regions: Brandnertal, Montafon, Klostertal and Arlberg.

What to See in and around Bludenz

Bludenz was first mentioned in records dating back to 830. The city features a **quaint, tightly built Old Town** complete with the medieval city fortifications, two preserved city gates, and Baroque townhouses. Its arcades, reminiscent of those in southern Europe, are an inviting place for a stroll. For a great view of the city and its surroundings from above, take a ride over the city on the cable car to the »Sonnenbalkon« (»Sun Balcony«) or Muttersberg mountain (1412m/4633ft) to the north.

The emblem of the city is the parish church, Pfarrkirche **St Laurentius** (1491–1514), with a 50m/164ft-high tower and onion dome. The interior church features a ribbed stellar vault in the choir and two noteworthy paintings depicting the Visitation and the Marriage of the Virgin.

▶ BLUDENZ

INFORMATION

Bludenz Tourismus
Werdenbergerstrasse 42
A-6700 Bludenz
Tel. 0 55 52/6 21 70, fax 6 75 97
www.bludenz.at

WHERE TO EAT

▶ **Inexpensive**
Gasthof Sonne
Jagdbergstr. 29, tel. 0 55 50/24 19
The magnificent view of the mountainous landscape of Gross Walsertal alone merits a visit to this simply furnished inn.

The valley named Brandner Tal extends southwest of the town of Bludenz for a distance of approximately 12km/7.5mi. The mountain village of Brand (1037m/3403ft; pop. 650), a health and winter sporting resort, is considered the tourist centre of the ► Rätikon mountains.

! **Baedeker TIP**

»Köstliche Kiste«

Culinary specialities from farms within the biosphere reserve, packed in a wooden crate and marked with the catchy name »Köstliche Kiste« (»delicious box«) – who wouldn't want to dig right in? The box is available in various sizes in the shop located at the demonstration dairy (Erlebnissennerei) in Sonntag-Boden (opening times: daily 8am–12.30pm and 3.30pm–6pm, tel. 0 55 54/41 03).

The road leads uphill through 6.5km/4mi of beautiful scenery, via the Innertal valley and the Schattenlagant-Alpe to the valley station of the Lünerseebahn (Lünersee Railway, 1565m/5135ft). The upper station is located near the Neue Douglass-Hütte (New Douglass Lodge, 1979m/6493ft) on the 1.5km/1mi-long **Lüner See**, which serves as a reservoir for the Ill power plant. Starting here, it is a three-hour climb to the top of the **Schesaplana** (2965m/9728ft), the highest peak of the Rätikon range.

The Grosses Walsertal, north of Bludenz, is one of Austria's most beautiful high-lying mountain valleys. The sparsely populated valley has been recognized by UNESCO as a biosphere reserve since November 2000.

✱ Grosses Walsertal

Braunau am Inn

K 3

Province: Upper Austria
Population: 17,350

Elevation: 352m/1155ft

Even today, Braunau still suffers from the fact that it is the birthplace of Adolf Hitler. Yet the old trading town, with its long history and picturesque old centre, takes a pro-active approach to this difficult heritage: it has become a place of dialogue and reconciliation.

Braunau, on the right bank of the Inn river, is connected by a bridge to the Bavarian city of Simbach on the opposite side. First mentioned in documents dated 1220 and receiving its municipal rights in 1260, it has had various commercial privileges throughout its history. Braunau's citizens achieved a level of prosperity, which becomes evident when looking at its **beautiful Old Town**.

 **BRAUNAU**

INFORMATION

Tourismus Braunau
Stadtplatz 2
A-5280 Braunau am Inn
Tel. 0 77 22/6 26 44, fax 6 26 44 14
www.braunau.at

What to See in Braunau

Beautiful townhouses of the 16th and 17th centuries as well as the remains of the town's medieval fortifications attest to the Braunau's former importance as a commercial centre. On the Stadtplatz stands the old Salzburger Torturm (Salzburg Gate Tower) with a glockenspiel; the Stadtturm is located to the east and dates back to the town's formative years.

St Stephan

The massive, 96m/315ft-high tower of the parish church, Pfarrkirche St Stephan (1439–66), is the **third-highest church tower in all of Austria** and the landmark of Braunau. Stephan Krumenauer is credited as the main builder of this Gothic church. The pulpit is especially noteworthy, as is the 16th-century »Bäckeraltar« (Bakers' Altar) in the fifth chapel to the left of the choir. The exterior walls contain numerous gravestones, including a memorial to the former town commissioner Hans Staininger, who was famous for having a beard that was nearly 2m/6ft 6in long. The claim that he forgot to roll up its magnificent tresses when a fire broke out in the town, causing him to trip on the beard and break his neck, has never been proven.

Bezirksmuseum

The Bezirksmuseum (District Museum) is home to the beard, the patent of nobility, and charter of the coat of arms. It also has a local history room representing the Danube Swabians, a fisherman's room, a bakery, local collections, and a bell-casting workshop. The last-named was actually proven to exist here as early as 1385 (Johann-Fischer-Gasse 18–20; opening times: July–Aug Tue–Sat 10am–noon and 1pm–5pm, Sun 2pm–4pm, Sept–June Tue–Sat 1pm–5pm). The other section of the municipal museum is located nearby at Altstadt 10.

Palmpark

The adjacent Palmpark was given its name in honour of Nuremberg bookseller Johannes Palm (born 1766; bronze statue), who was sentenced to death and shot by a French military court in Braunau in 1806. He had been found guilty of writing and distributing a patriotic article. A memorial plaque commemorates the execution at Salzburger Strasse 19.

Memorial outside Hitler's birthplace

Outside Hitler's birthplace at Salzburger Vorstadt 219 stands a memorial carved out of Mauthausen rock. It is dedicated to the victims of the Nazi regime.

Around Braunau

Ranshofen

Ranshofen, located 4km/2.5mi to the south, was made an imperial residence by no less a figure than Charlemagne himself. Emperor Arnulf established a chapel, the St-Pankraz-Kapelle, in 898. The Augustinian abbey that was founded here in 1125 and closed in 1811 constructed a minster, which was lavishly remodelled in the Baroque style at the end of the 17th century.

Europareservat Unterer Inn

Stretching for a length of approximately 55km/35mi along the river north of Braunau, the unique Lower Inn European Nature Reserve is a stopover for tremendous numbers of migrating birds in the spring and the autumn, and a refuge for a large number of rare butterflies, Aesculapian snakes, and beavers. The Bavarian-Austrian »Europareservat Unterer Inn« information centre across the German border offers guided tours (opening times: mid-March–Oct Tue–Sat 10am–noon and 2pm–5pm, Sun 1pm–5pm; group guided tours by arrangement tel. 085 73 / 13 60).

✶ Bregenz

C 4/5

Province: Vorarlberg
Population: 29,000

Elevation: 395m/1296ft

Bregenz captivates visitors with its breathtaking location. Opening onto Lake Constance and surrounded by impressive mountains, the city is a tourist magnet – not forgetting its importance to fans of classical music. Every summer, they flock to the Bregenz Festival to enjoy performances on the floating stage.

City on Lake Constance

The capital and second-largest city of the state of Vorarlberg lies on a terraced plateau sloping down toward the lake at the foot of the

One of the most impressive stages at the Bregenz Festival was created for the opera »A Masked Ball« by Guiseppe Verdi

Pfänder mountain. Ever since 15 BC, when the Romans conquered the Celtic settlement of Brigantium and thereafter established a commercial metropolis and important traffic junction, Bregenz has been an **important port** for shipping on Lake Constance. The timber trade established a certain degree of prosperity here in the Middle Ages, and after its decline was followed by the grain trade. The city experienced a new economic upswing in 1884 with the introduction of the Arlberg Railway, the beginning of Austrian steamboat transport on Lake Constance, and systematic industrialization. Seat of the provincial parliament of Vorarlberg since 1860, the city on Lake Constance finally became the provincial capital in 1923. Located at the point where the borders of Germany, Austria, and Switzerland meet, Bregenz is an important traffic hub.

VISITING BREGENZ

INFORMATION
Bregenz Tourismus
Rathausstr. 35A, A-6900 Bregenz
Tel. 0 55 74/4 95 90, fax 49 59 59,
www.bregenz.at

CULTURE IN SUMMER
The Bregenzer Festspiele (Bregenz Festival) has been an integral part of the international world of opera since 1946, attracting hundreds of thousands from Austria and all over the world every July and August. Tickets and information are available at: www.bregenzerfestspiele.com

WHERE TO EAT
▶ Moderate
① *Burgrestaurant Gebhardsberg*
Gebhardsberg 1, A-6900 Bregenz
Tel. 0 55 74/4 25 15
The castle commands a panoramic view over the Gebhardsberg. The kitchen offers guests good regional dishes: turkey from the Bregenz Forest and fish from Lake Constance.

▶ Inexpensive
② *Gasthaus Maurachbund*
Maurachgasse 11, A-6900 Bregenz
Tel. 0 55 74/4 40 20

This rustic yet elegant restaurant makes a good impression with its friendly service and excellent dishes. Its specialities: Lake Constance whitefish fillet and »Maurachgässer Pfanne«.

WHERE TO STAY
▶ Luxury
① *Deuringschlössle*
Ehreguta-Platz 4, A-6900 Bregenz
Tel. 0 55 74/4 78 00, fax 4 78 00 80
www.deuring-schloessle.at
This hotel is located in the Upper Town (Oberstadt) of Bregenz. Those taking their breakfast on the terrace will just be able to catch a glimpse of the famous floating stage, the Bregenzer Seebühne. The head chef is one of the finest exponents of modern Austrian cuisine.

▶ Budget
② *Hotel Deutschmann*
Rheinstrasse 83 a, A-6900 Bregenz
Tel. 0 55 74/6 77 40, fax 67 74 12
www.deutschmann-bregenz.at
This comfortable, dignified hotel close to the city centre also provides special programmes for groups and gatherings.

Bregenz is where past and present meet: the Unterstadt (Lower Town), with its scattered white high-rises, is dominated by its modern festival theatre (Festspiel and Kongresshaus) on the lake as well as its Kunsthaus (exhibition centre for contemporary art) in the city centre. The peaceful, romantic Oberstadt (Upper Town), with its historic Old Town, its three narrow streets, and handsome half-timbered architecture is an absolute contrast: hidden behind treetops, the onion dome of the Martinsturm (St Martin's Tower) is the only landmark that can be seen from a distance. The lakeside with its wonderful view of the water is a place for visitors to stroll, cycle and go rollerblading; boats excursions operate on Lake Constance. The town

Old and new

Bregenz Map

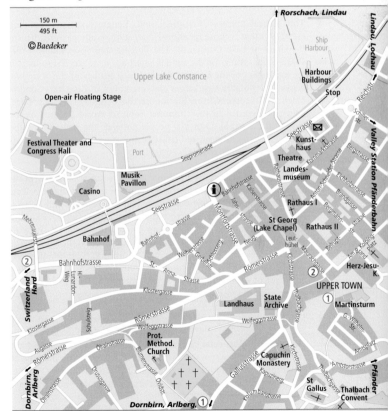

Where to eat
① Burgrestaurant Gebhardsberg
② Gasthaus Maurachbund

Where to stay
① Deuringschlössle
② Hotel Deutschmann

centre, with its shopping area, market squares, and some shopping streets with reduced traffic have real southern European atmosphere.

What to See in Bregenz

Lakeshore and promenade

Extensive parks along the shore of Lake Constance were created as early as 1888; they are separated from the centre of the Lower Town by train tracks and a main arterial road. The harbour in the east is a starting point for excursions and scheduled boat services on the lake. On the western side there are boats for hire and on occasion promenade concerts outside the music pavilion. A casino and well-equipped sporting and recreational area, with an indoor swimming pool and a marina for pleasure craft and motorboats, is located somewhat further up the shoreline.

✳ **Festival theatre with floating stage**

The festival theatre (Festspiel- und Kongresshaus), a building (1992–97) that is more functional than aesthetically pleasing, lies on the shore of Lake Constance. The floating stage (»Seebühne«) offshore is the setting for the annual »Spiel auf dem See« (»Production on the Lake«) of the **Bregenz Festival**. The history of the Seebühne began in 1946 atop two barges carrying gravel in Bregenz's Gondelhafen. 200 supports from the foundation of today's floating stage, which is recorded in the Guinness Book of World Records as the largest in the world. Over 400 people populate the stage during the opera, operetta, musical, and ballet performances; the stands accommodate an audience of nearly 7000.

Unterstadt

The centre of activity in the more modern Lower Town is **Kornmarktplatz**, which was formerly the centre of the grain trade. A fruit and vegetable market now takes place here on Tuesdays and Fridays. Between the Kornmarkt theatre and the post office (1895), exhibiting the style of the Dual Monarchy and painted in the classic shade of »Schönbrunn yellow«, stands the Kunsthaus Bregenz; the Vorarlberger Landesmuseum, with exhibits on local history, is on the northern side of the square. The Rococo-style round chapel (1757), located northeast of Kornmarktstrasse, is dedicated to St John of Nepomuk, patron saint of those in peril at sea.

✳ **Kunsthaus Bregenz**

The Kunsthaus Bregenz (KUB), designed by Swiss architect Peter Zumthor, opened in 1997. When viewed from the outside, its takes the form of a **glass cube** that seems able to absorb the changing light of the sky and the water and then reflect it depending on the time of day, atmospheric conditions, and angle of vision. Temporary exhibits ⏱ are dedicated to modern art, with an emphasis on the visual arts, architecture, and design (opening times: Tue–Sun 10am–6pm).

✳ **Vorarlberger Landesmuseum**

The Vorarlberg Provincial Museum shows its cultural and art collections with exhibits from early times through to the present. It contains artefacts from the Stone, Bronze, and Iron Ages, Roman finds from Brigantium (1st–4th century), musical instruments, goldsmith work, tapestries, and artistic works from the Carolingian, Romanesque, Gothic, and Renaissance periods (opening times: mid-June–Aug daily 10am–8pm, otherwise Tue–Sun 10am–6pm, Thu until 8pm). ⊙

Leutbühel

Rathausstrasse, on which the Rathaus stands (it was built to store grain in 1686, and has been used as the town hall since 1810), eventually leads to Leutbühel, which already served as a market square and a central traffic junction in earlier times. The Alte Rathaus (Old Town Hall, 1662) in the Upper Town is now a residential building.

★ Oberstadt

Maurachgasse, a cobblestone street, leads to the lower, crest-adorned city gate of the once fortified Upper Town (Oberstadt), which is Bregenz's Old Town. This was the earlier location of a Celtic town, later the fortified Roman town of Brigantium. The **Martinsturm** (St Martin's Tower, 1599–1602) is the emblem of the town. Its Baroque onion dome, covered in wooden shingles, is the highest in central Europe and offers a magnificent view of the city and Lake Constance. An exhibition on military history is housed on the upper floor of the tower.

Ehregutaplatz

Directly next door is, named after the legendary saviour of the city. When Bregenz was besieged by the Swiss in 1407 during the Appenzell Wars (1403–08), a beggar named Guta is said to have eavesdropped on the besiegers and heard of their plans to launch an attack. She was able to warn the people of Bregenz in good time and thus save the town. Even well into the 1920s, the keeper of the town would cry »Ehret die Guta« (»Honour Guta«) from the Martinsturm every evening at 7pm to ensure protection of Bregenz.

Capuchin monastery

To the southwest, past the Thalbach, stands thewith the Capuchin church of 1636 and Josephskapelle (Chapel of St Joseph), which was added in the 18th century.

Pfarrkirche St Gallus

The parish church is a simple Gothic building (14th–15th century; extended c1740) with a late Baroque interior in the style of the Vorarlberg school. It is considered to be an especially beautiful example of Lake Constance Baroque architecture. In the altarpiece *Adoration of the Magi*, one of the shepherdesses bears a resemblance to Austria's Archduchess Maria Theresia.

Around Bregenz

Kloster Mehrerau

The Cistercian monastery of Mehrerau, founded in 1094 and destroyed many times throughout its history, stands on a beautiful spot near Lake Constance. It has a neo-Romanesque church, renovated in 1961–64. The site is still owned by the Cistercian order and is home to a boarding school, a sanatorium, a farm, and the Klosterkeller restaurant.

Gebhardsberg Some 3km/2mi south of Bregenz is the towering Gebhardsberg, 600m/1969ft high. The ruins of Burg Hohenbregenz, which was destroyed by the Swedes in 1647, and an 18th-century pilgrimage chapel with frescoes from around 1900 are both located here. The terrace of the castle restaurant offers a splendid view of Bregenz, Lake Constance, and the Rhine Valley. A southward descent on the Ferdinand-Kinz-Weg is highly recommended.

✱ Pfänder For the best view of Bregenz, Lake Constance, and the mountainous landscape both near and far, try the 1064m/3491ft-high Pfänder, **Bregenz's landmark mountain** and the highest peak on Lake Constance. Cars on the suspension cableway transport visitors up the mountain in a matter of minutes. Its lower station, which features a lovingly designed Pfänderbahn Museum, is accessible via the town bus no. 1 (stop at Pfänderbahn), simple to reach, and a good 5 minutes' walking distance from the harbour or 15 minutes from the railway station. A narrow road also runs up the mountain from Lochau by way of Haggen. At the upper station for the cableway (1022m/3354ft) the Berghaus Pfänder holds a restaurant, an eagle observatory featuring flying demonstrations with birds of prey, and an **alpine wildlife park**. From here it is a five-minute climb to the summit. The circular hiking route, featuring an educational forest trail, can be completed in 30 minutes. Hikers can observe wild animals native to the alpine region, including alpine ibex, red deer, moufflon, and marmots. The descent is either a 45-minute drive to Lochau by way of Haggen, or an approximately 3-hour walk from the Pfänder mountain station down to Lake Constance.

> **! Baedeker TIP**
>
> **Cigar fans welcome**
>
> Lochau's traditional Messmer Inn (Landstrasse 3, A-6911 Lochau; excellent cooking, terrific wine selection) has a walk-in humidor that holds fine cigars. Cigar smokers can indulge in their passion in a sophisticated lounge.

✱ Bregenzer Wald

C/D 4/5

Province: Vorarlberg	**Elevation:** 398–2090m/1306–6857ft

Bregenz Forest covers roughly a quarter of Vorarlberg's total area. Yet the name is rather misleading, as all too many of the trees have been cleared – no more than a quarter of the region's total area is still forested today.

Sunny terraces and high mountains Bregenz Forest (Bregenzer Wald or Bregenzerwald) makes up the northern part of the Vorarlberg Alps and climbs from Lake Constance to the ▶ Arlberg. Its northern section, which reaches from Pfänderstock near Bregenz to the Hochälpele near Bezau, is slightly hilly with widely scattered settlements on its sunny terraces. Its southern section, on the other hand, has the character of a high mountain region with steep cliffs and broad meadows in between, reaching from Bezau to Schoppernau. The Bregenzer Ache valley carves a deep gash through the forest from the Hochtannberg to Lake Constance at ► Bregenz. The valley provides access to idyllic farming villages and numerous hiking areas.

Because it is open toward the north, Bregenzerwald is exposed to oceanic climatic effects and as a consequence has some of the highest precipitation levels in all of Austria. The area receives a reasonable amount of snowfall in the winter, but because of its relatively low altitude (500–2000m/1641–6562ft), the snow disappears quickly.

◄ Damp climate

Resorts and Destinations in Bregenzerwald

Alberschwende (pop. 2500) is the so-called **»Gateway to Bregenz Forest«**. This is the birthplace of Hermann Gmeiner, founder of SOS Children's Villages, an organization that now has a worldwide presence. The town's emblem is its almost 1000-year-old linden tree near the Catholic parish church.

Alberschwende

Some 4km/2.5mi east of Alberschwende lies Lingenau (pop. 1400), the floral village of Bregenzerwald and an ideal summer and winter resort with a spa and health centre. The St-Anna-Kapelle (1722; renovated 1968) was constructed of tuff in an especially pure Baroque style. The chapel has lovely stained glass windows with depictions of various saints.

Lingenau

Just over half a mile further on, the road branches off over the 88m/289ft-high Lingenau bridge into the neighbouring valley of Hittisau. Its still-functioning dairy has been turned into an interesting museum that is worth a visit (viewing by arrangement, tel. 0 55 13/62 09-50).

Hittisau

In July 2000, **Austria's first Women's Museum** opened in the new fire station. The initiator and museum director, Elisabeth Stöckler, justified its opening in Bregenzerwald – which has a reputation for being conservative – by explaining that the »strong women of Bregenz Forest« were left to handle the hard work on the farm by themselves when the men left the area in the summer to find seasonal work. The museum features temporary exhibits on social and cultural history with an emphasis both on the region and on Austria in general (opening times: 30 May to 31 Oct Thu 6pm–8pm, Fri/Sat 3pm–5pm, Sun 2pm–6pm and by arrangement; tel. 0 55 13/62 09-50).

◄ Frauenmuseum

 BREGENZER WALD

INFORMATION

Bregenzerwald Tourismus
Gerbe 1135
A-6863 Egg
Tel. 0 55 12/23 65
www.bregenzerwald.at

This mountain near Schoppernau in Bregenz Forest is reminiscent of a huge wave of stone

Egg

The next town up the valley is (pop. 3500), the economic centre of the region and a **starting point for lovely hikes**. The Heimatmuseum in the former school is the oldest in the state of Vorarlberg and features many items dealing with local culture, customs, tradition, and home décor. Its presentation of the Bregenzwald traditional costume is particularly comprehensive (opening times: June–July Wed, Sat and Sun 3pm–5pm, Aug–Oct Wed and Sat 3pm–5pm).

Schwarzenberg

Schwarzenberg lies 4km/2.5mi southwest of Egg (pop. 1700), one of the most beautiful of the forest's villages with its picturesque old quarter and 250-year-old houses. Its Baroque parish church is well-visited: the paintings of the apostles and the high altar picture were done by **Angelika Kauffmann** (1741–1807), whom the prince of poets, Goethe, declared to have »unbelievable talent«. The Heimatmuseum is dedicated to the famous Schwarzenberg painter as well, who was »possibly the most cultivated woman in all of Europe« (Herder). In reality, she only spent a few weeks in Schwarzenberg on two occasions and lived for the rest of the time in London and Rome. Yet she felt a connection to her home throughout her life. Thanks to the Schubertiade, an annual music programme focusing on Franz Schubert, the town has made a name for itself far beyond its village borders.

Bezau

Bezau (pop. 2000), the principal town of Bregenzerwald, was home to the Thumb family of master builders – Michael († 1690) and his sons Christian († 1726) and Peter (1681–1766) – who built the pilgrimage church in Birnau. From 1902 to 1980, the local railway station was the terminus of the »Wälderbähnle« (Forest Railway) that ran to Bregenz; today it is used as a museum railway that runs between Bezau and Bersbuch.

The largest attraction for the »sporting and recreation community« in Bizau (pop. 1000), located southeast of Bezau, is its **summer toboggan run**, which is the longest in the world: 1650m/5414ft long with 70 bends. Another point of interest is the 1.5km/1mi-long »Schneckenlochhöhle«, the largest and most famous karst cave in the Vorarlberg region. It features stalactites, stalagmites, a subterraneous lake, bats, etc. (visits only by guided tour in July and Aug; tel. 0 55 14/21 29).

Bizau

The birthplace and home of Vorarlberg's most prominent 19th-century poet, Franz Michael Felder (1839–69), is just up the valley. He made a name for himself as a critical contemporary and social revolutionary. Letters and documents on his life and works are on display in the municipal office   (opening times: Mon–Fri 9am–noon and 2pm–5pm). Schoppernau (860–2080m/2822–6825ft) is a starting point for mountain climbing tours and beautiful hikes as far as the Kleine Walsertal valley.

Schoppernau

Brenner

F/G 5/6

Province: Tyrol

The Brenner Pass is a major traffic artery between Germany and Italy. At an elevation of only 1374m/4508ft, it is the lowest alpine pass in western Austria and can be used all year round.

The pass road runs from the Inn Valley through the Wipptal valley over the Adriatic/Black Sea watershed into the South Tyrolese Etschtal valley. Since 1919 the Brenner has run along the Austrian-Italian border, but a road has existed along the eastern slopes of the valley over the pass since Roman times. The road, and later the autobahn, was only moved to the other side of the valley in the 19th century.

Important alpine pass

Shortly after the Second World War it became clear that the Brenner road was of very limited capacity. A new road was planned and construction began in 1959. The Brenner autobahn, which was completed in 1974, runs south from Innsbruck and then below the Patscherkofel mountain. The steep Wipptal valley was spanned by the 795m/2608ft-long and 190m/623ft-high **Europa Bridge**. When it was completed in 1963 it was the highest pier bridge in Europe. The Brennerbahn railway was opened as early as 1867. It connects the Tyrolese capital Innsbruck with Bolzano (Bozen) in South Tyrol. The route is not steep but has many curves, so the trains run slowly. In 1994 the Inntal railway tunnel was opened to bypass Innsbruck. Construction of the Brenner Basis Tunnel, which will make the Brennerbahn more efficient, should take place in the next few years. On 30 June 2006 the symbolic first cut of the spade took place.

◄ Brenner autobahn

◄ Brennerbahn

Air pollution The transit route via the autobahn and national road has been an enormous problem for the local communities along the Brenner Pass because of traffic noise and exhaust fumes. Within four decades the number of vehicles crossing the Brenner increased from 500,000 to more than 12.5 million! Four times as much freight is transported over the pass by road (in 2007 approx. 31 million tonnes) as by rail. People who live along the Brenner Pass have blockaded it several times to draw attention to the environmental damage.

What to See around the Brenner Pass

Matrei am Brenner Matrei on the Brenner (pop. 3000) is the oldest settlement in the Wipptal valley. In 1916 a fire all but destroyed the town and in 1945 damage was caused in a bombing raid. But thanks to **exemplary restoration work**, the old quarter boasts houses from around 1500 with beautifully painted façades, old gables and Gothic doors, as well as restaurants with wrought iron signs. Note the Pfarrkirche Maria Himmelfahrt (parish church of the Assumption of the Virgin), a late Gothic building (around 1310) with a Baroque interior. The ceiling frescoes, created around 1755 to designs by Josef Adam Mölk, and the painting of *Our Lord in Misery* on the Rococo high altar are especially impressive.

Maria Waldrast **Tyrol's highest pilgrimage site**, the former Maria Waldrast monastery, is located west of Matrei at 1636m/5367ft. The ceiling fresco in the late Gothic choir depicts the discovery of the Waldrast figure of the Virgin (around 1666). The 2718m/8917ft-high Serles mountain, towering over the monastery, can easily be climbed in three hours. The mountain is popularly known as the »high altar of Tyrol«: according to legend hard-hearted King Serles and his two sons turned to stone here.

Steinach am Brenner Steinach am Brenner (pop. 3200) is located about 5km/3mi away where the Gschnitztal valley meets the Wipptal valley. The town was first documented in 1286 and is a popular winter sports destination. There is a natural mineral spring here. The neo-Romanesque parish church of Steinach is not typical of Tyrol; it was built in the 19th century to replace a Baroque church that had burned down. The high altar is from the old Baroque church. The picture was painted by Martin Knoller, who was born in Steinach in 1725.

The art in the Alfons Graber Kunstmuseum is worth taking a look at (Brennerstrasse 28; opening times: Tue and Thu 4pm–6pm). It displays oil paintings and graphics by the artist who began his career as an Expressionist and later created abstract works (1901–90).

Gschnitztal The road to Trins runs through the Gschnitztal valley, which meets the Silltal valley at Steinach. From Trins, with a Baroque-style church and Schloss Schneeburg (18th century), the road continues to

Gschnitz with its old farmhouses with painted façades, decorated gables and interesting inscriptions. On the southern valley slopes of the Gschnitztal is the pilgrimage chapel of St Magdalena auf dem Bergl (on the mountain), which was constructed on the site of a sacred spring from pre-Christian times. There are Romanesque frescoes inside depicting Adam and Eve in Paradise and the Flight to Egypt.

Gries am Brenner

Gries (pop. 1200) is located just before the top of the pass, at the foot of the Padauner Kogel mountain (2068m/6785ft). It is a popular holiday destination in both summer and winter. The parish church, Pfarrkirche Maria Heimsuchung, which was documented as a chapel around 1530 and reconstructed in the 19th century, has a remarkable ceiling painting as well as two panel pictures of the fourteen auxiliary saints from the dismantled Holy Helper Chapel.

From the valley station in Gries take the chairlift up to the Sattelalm (1652m/5420ft), where visitors can get a bite to eat and a drink. From the Sattelalm the hike up to the 2113m/6932ft-high Sattelberg mountain takes about one and a half hours; there is a wonderful view as far as South Tyrol.

Brennersee and Brenner

About 5km/3mi beyond the Brennersee is the Brenner (Italian: Brennero) Pass and with it the border between Austria and Italy. The border divides the town of Brenner (pop. 1000) into a smaller Austrian and a larger Italian part.

✳ Bruck an der Mur

Province: Styria
Population: 13,500

Elevation: 498–1630m/1634–5348ft

Bruck an der Mur was founded precisely at the point where the Mürz and the Mur rivers meet. Documented as far back as 860, the town was important in past centuries because of its location on the salt and iron trade routes.

Old trading town

The town got its name from the bridges (derived from the variations »prukka«, »prukke« and »prukkha«; German »Brücke«, meaning »bridge«). Bruck is still an **important trans-regional hub for road and rail traffic**, as well as a business and trading town. The most important industries are wire and paper production. The town also has the only school of forestry in Austria.

History

King Ottokar II re-established the former Roman settlement of Poedicum in 1263 and it received municipal rights from Rudolf of Habsburg in 1277. In the Middle Ages Bruck was the main staple town for trade with Venice and it had extensive brewing and trading privi-

Bruck an der Mur Map

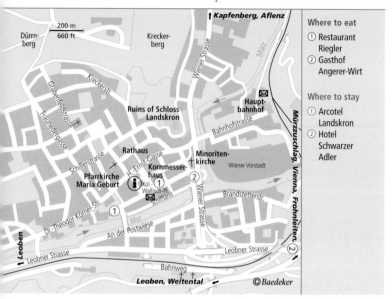

Where to eat
① Restaurant Riegler
② Gasthof Angerer-Wirt

Where to stay
① Arcotel Landskron
② Hotel Schwarzer Adler

leges; in the 16th century it was the seat of the state parliament. Today's town was built after a major fire in 1792. Bruck's greatest period of prosperity was after 1844 when the railway line Mürzzuschlag–Bruck–Graz was opened; 24 years later the Bruck–Leoben line was added.

Around Mur and Mürz
The town's houses are on both sides of the Mur and Mürz rivers; the old town centre is north of the Mur. The town wall, castle gate and tower of the fortifications have been preserved. The best shopping is to be found in Mittergasse and Burggasse; the pedestrian zone has developed into a restaurant area. Hohenlimburg bridge is a zone for pedestrians and bicycles only and connects the old town centre with the suburbs.

What to See in Bruck an der Mur

Koloman-Wallisch-Platz
The Eiserne Brunnen (Iron Fountain) is located on Koloman-Wallisch Square, one of the largest central squares of any town in Styria. This Renaissance fountain from 1626, with a fine wrought-iron cover, once supplied the town with water. In 1710 the citizenry had the plague column erected to keep the plague away from the town.

★
Kornmesserhaus
The iron dealer Pankraz Kornmess had a magnificent house built in 1499–1505 on the Hauptplatz (main square). It was clearly influ-

VISITING BRUCK AN DER MUR

INFORMATION

Stadtmarketing Bruck an der Mur
Koloman-Wallisch-Platz 1
A-8600 Bruck an der Mur
Tel. 0 38 62/89 01 21, fax 89 01 02
www.bruckmur.at

WHERE TO EAT

► **Moderate**

① *Restaurant Riegler Schmankerlwirtshaus*
Hauptplatz 11
A-8600 Bruck an der Mur
Tel. 0 38 62/549 04
This restaurant serves Styrian dishes and specializes in game. Diners enjoy Styrian, Lower Austrian and Burgenland vintage wines with the food.

► **Inexpensive**

② *Gasthof Angerer-Wirt*
Frauenberg 3
A-8600 Bruck an der Mur
Tel. 0 38 64/4 28 42
The terrace has a view of the Mürztal valley and the Hochschwab mountain. The restaurant also has plentiful, partially covered outdoor seating with room for 100 guests. There is a playground and petting zoo for young guests. In the winter skaters can experience the joys of the natural skating rink.

WHERE TO STAY

Baedeker recommendation

► **Mid-range**

① *Arcotel Landskron*
Am Schiffertor 3
A-8600 Bruck an der Mur
Tel. 0 38 62/58 45 80, fax 58 45 86
www.arcotel.co.at/landskron.htm
Along with conference rooms the hotel has a restaurant, sauna/steam bath, and a spacious terrace with a view of the countryside. Free internet access is provided to guests.

► **Budget**

② *Hotel Schwarzer Adler*
Minoritenplatz 8
A-8600 Bruck an der Mur
Tel. 0 38 62/5 67 68, fax 0 38 61/41 41
www.tiscover.at/minoriten
Small hotel in the centre of town, ideal for businesspeople, those wishing to stroll around town or cyclists. All of the rooms have satellite TV, telephone and internet access.

enced by Venetian style and is one of the most beautiful late Gothic secular buildings in Austria. The ground floor has an arcade and a beautiful loggia decorates the façade. The **arcaded courtyards** of the Apothekerhaus (pharmacy, 1520–30), the Fabriziushaus, one of the oldest patrician houses in the city, and the Rathaus (town hall, 1530) are all worth seeing. The latter has been carefully restored and the courtyard has been given a glass roof.

The 15th-century Gothic parish church towers above Koloman-Wallisch-Platz. The elaborate cross-ribbed vaulting and the sacristy door (1500), a beautiful oak and wrought-iron Austrian Gothic-style   **Stadtpfarrkirche Maria Geburt** work, are noteworthy. In the 17th century the interior was remodelled in Baroque style; the 19th-century altar picture was painted by Matthias Schiffer.

Minoritenkirche Maria im Walde Mittergasse leads eastwards to the 13th-century Minorite church. It belonged to a monastery that was disbanded in 1782 and is considered to be **one of the oldest and most important hall churches in Austria**. The 14th-century wall paintings and an early Gothic cloister are worth seeing.

Landskron ruins From Minoritenplatz, ascend the steps (5 minutes) to the castle ruins of Burg Landskron with its clock tower. The climb is well worth it.

Around Bruck an der Mur

Weitental There is an expansive recreational area just a few minutes' walk south of the town centre. It includes centuries-old trees, nature trails, hiking paths, mountain bike routes, a nature centre with a collection station for endangered species, a petting zoo and a forest playground that was designed by children(!). The hike up the **Hochanger** (1312m/4304ft; food and drink served) is one of the most beautiful routes in the area. The road near Tragöss-Oberort about 25km/15mi northwest of Bruck ends at the foot of the Hochschwabgruppe mountains, which are equally suitable for hikers or climbers.

> **! *Baedeker* TIP**
>
> **The disappearing lake**
> The Grüne See (757m/2484ft) lies northwest of Tragöss. It disappears almost completely in the winter; in the summer a karst spring fills it up again, the extent depending on the amount of rainfall. It is a pleasant half-hour walk from the car park to the lake, and it takes about an hour to walk around it. Two inns serve refreshments.

Northeast of Bruck lies the town of Kapfenberg, with the 14th-century **Burg Oberkapfenberg** towering above it. The castle bar, knight's hall and falcon house are also popular destinations for an excursion (falcon shows: May–Oct Tue–Sun 11am and 3pm; tel. 038 62 / 273 09).

Bärenschütz-klamm Mixnitz, 12km/7mi southeast of Bruck, is the starting point for a hike through the romantic Bärenschützklamm, **one of the most beautiful rock gorges in Austria**. It is about 1300m/4200ft long and covers a difference in elevation of 350m/1148ft.

Frohnleiten Frohnleiten (pop. 7400), 26km/15mi south of Bruck, is considered to be the »**Styrian Rothenburg ob der Tauber**« and is a good example of a medieval market town that stretches along one street. Burg Rabenstein nearby is a charming venue for exhibitions and concerts.

Hikes bring out the full beauty of the Dachstein region

★ Dachstein

Provinces: Salzburg, Upper Austria and Styria

Highest elevation: Hoher Dachstein (2995m/9826ft)

At 2995m/9826ft, Hohe Dachstein is the highest peak in the massif of the same name. It is an ideal skiing region: the glacier makes it possible to ski all year round.

The Dachstein is an immense, strongly karstified mountain massif in the Northern Limestone Alps with wide, high plateaus, located where the borders of Upper Austria, Salzburg and Styria meet. The giant massif, which inclines toward the north, has a series of peaks with stark profiles at heights from 2000m/6600ft to almost 3000m/10,000ft. Impressive glaciers lie between the peaks, including the Grosse Gosau and the Hallstätter glaciers. The northern wall of the Dachstein mountains embraces the pretty Gosauseen lakes and ► Lake Hallstatt. Since 1997 the historic cultural landscape of the Hallstatt-Dachstein region, along with its rare flora and fauna and its important archaeological excavations, have been on the **UNESCO list of World Cultural and Natural Heritage**.

Immense mountain massif

The Dachstein, on the whole, is an ideal area for challenging climbs – beginners should take care. Anyone who has mastered the relatively simple route to the top of the glacier can attempt the steep ridges (for example the Torstein at 2948m/9672ft, and the Grosser Koppenkarstein at 2865m/9400ft).

Climbing area

Hoher Dachstein ►

✳ Good trails lead to the major mountain cabins in the glacier area: from the Simony cabin (2206m/7238ft) near the Hallstatt glacier or the Adamek cabin (2196m/7200ft) on the Gosau glacier the climb to the top of the Hohe Dachstein takes about 3 hours.

Gosaukamm ►

✳ The magnificent Gosaukamm to the northwest, a wild, zigzag-shaped mountain range high above the Gosautal valley, is also popular. The Hofpürgl cabin (1703m/5587ft) southeast of Bischofsmütze (2459m/8068ft) is accessible from the Adamek cabin via the Linzer Steig. Below the Gosaukamm, the trail leads to the Gablonzer Haus (1550m/5085ft) on the Zwieselalm, one of the most beautiful alpine pastures in the Salzkammergut. From here it takes about two hours to climb Grosse Donnerkogel (2054m/6739ft).

Immediately to the east of the Dachstein massif is the waterless, sinkhole-covered high plateau »Auf dem Stein« (on the stone). In its northern wall, facing the Hallstätter See and the Trauntal valley are two immense caves, the **Dachsteinhöhlen** (► Hallstätter See).

! Baedeker TIP

Skywalk

Those who wish to have that special alpine feeling without the effort of the climb should pluck up the courage to try the Dachstein-Skywalk. The viewing platform with a glass floor, directly next to the upper station of the Dachstein funicular, is perched above the steep face of Hunerkogel, which plunges over 250m/820ft. The views are magnificent (opening times: mid-May–Nov 8am–5pm).

Skiing and hiking area

There are three large skiing areas here: Dachstein West on the Gosaukamm, Ramsau on the Dachstein with the glacier skiing areas, and Dachstein-Krippenstein south of Obertraun.

Hikers get their money's worth, too. The Vorderen Gosausee (933m/3061ft) is surrounded by steep mountain walls; a footpath leads around it and offers a wonderful view to the Dachstein with the Gosau glacier. From here a hiking trail leads to the Holzmeisteralm (973m/3192ft), Gosaulacke and the beautifully situated Hintere Gosausee (1154m/3876ft); the hike takes about two hours.

▶ **DACHSTEIN**

INFORMATION

Schladming-Dachstein Tourismus
Ramsauerstr. 756, A-8970 Schladming
Tel. 0 36 87/233 10, fax 232 32
www.schladming-dachstein.at

The walk across the plateau is rewarding for fitter hikers in both summer and winter: either head east from the Hohe Dachstein to the Guttenberg-Haus at the southern edge (2145m/7037ft), or further east to the Kemet mountains and the Brünner Hütte (1747m/5732ft) at **Stoderzinken** with its panoramic view.

The **Grimming** mountains (2351m/7713ft) are the eastern foothills of the Dachstein and the Salzatal valley separates them from the Kemet mountains; they are the landmarks of the middle Ennstal valley and form the most impressive mountain range in Styria.

★ Danube Valley (Donautal)

A–S 1–4

Provinces: Upper Austria and Lower Austria

Austria and the Danube – rarely is the name of a river so closely tied to the name of a country, even though the river only runs through Austria for about 350km/210mi of its length.

The Danube is the second longest river in Europe after the Volga, and the main river in Austria. From its source rivers the Brigach and the Breg in southern Germany to its mouth in the Black Sea in Romania, the Danube is 2900km/1800mi long.

Austria's main river

As the **only European waterway that runs from west to east**, the Danube has played an important role in the history of the nations of Europe for thousands of years. It marked the route of the great military road from the Rhine to the Black Sea, the Romans built fortified camps on its banks (Vindobona, Carnuntum) and the Nibelungen, the royal family of the Burgundians who settled at Worms, followed the river to their destiny. The Franks under Charlemagne, the crusaders under Emperor Friedrich Barbarossa and Napoleon I took this route too.

Historical significance

Viewing point at the bend in the Danube river near Schlögen

DANUBE VALLEY

INFORMATION

Donautal Oberösterreich
Lindengasse 9
A-4041 Linz
Tel. 07 32/727 78 00, fax 727 78 04
www.danube.at

Donautal Niederösterreich
Schlossgasse 3
A-3620 Spitz
Tel. 0 27 13/300 60 60, fax 300 60 30
www.donau.com

Attila led the Huns in the opposite direction, upriver to France; the Avars and Hungarians also advanced into the west this way. Bloody battles that decided the fate of Europe were fought on the Danube's banks. Twice the Occident withstood the onslaught of the Turks at Vienna (1529, 1683), and the military and political decline of Napoleon I began with the battle of Aspern in 1809.

For many decades the Danube and its banks were polluted by sewage and waste products, and by the effects of power plants. In the mean-

Nature conservation　time efforts are being made to reduce this burden. The Wachau, on the World Cultural and Natural Heritage list, and the stretch of river between Vienna and Hainburg are the last remaining free-flowing sections of the Danube in Austria (Nationalpark Donau-Auen, p.218).

From Passau to Bratislava　Between the German-Austrian border at Passau and the Upper Austrian capital Linz, the Danube runs in large loops through the forested valley between the Mühlviertel in the north and the Innviertel in the south. Beyond Linz comes the Strudengau, a forested, narrow valley between Ardagger and Ybbs, then the Nibelungengau valley as far as Melk.

The Wachau with its old towns between Melk and Krems is the most famous region, and then the river flows through the Tulln basin to Vienna. The Danube lowlands east of Vienna towards the Slovakian capital of Bratislava already show signs of the transition to the Hungarian puszta landscape.

Road and rail ▶　Roads and railway lines follow the river. Sometimes they take short cuts but always find their way back to the water, especially in the most beautiful sections. Biking tours along the Danube are popular:

Danube Cycle Way ▶　the sections between Passau and Vienna or Hainburg are among the most beautiful cycle ways in all of Europe. The **Donau Radwanderweg (Danube Cycle Way) runs all the way from Donaueschingen to Budapest** (1260km/750mi).

Sections with charming and diverse landscape such as the Schlögener Schlinge (Schlögen Bend), the Wachau vineyards or a variety of river meadows alternate with those passing attractive castles, collegiate churches and towns. Many of the inns along the routes accommodate cyclists, have safe places for parking bikes as well as drying rooms, and provide information on distances, alternative routes or Danube ferries. The entire cycle way has been well developed and signposted. It is flat, almost completely paved and hardly ever comes into contact with cars; it is therefore especially suitable for families with children of eight years and older.

It is possible to experience the Danube from the water, not only for the entire Austrian section but also far beyond its borders. Dates, times and prices are available at the offices of the various companies (addresses ►p.144).

◄ Passenger ships

✴ Through the Danube Valley

The river leaves Passau, which has an almost Mediterranean feel, where the Inn and Ilz converge with the Danube. It then flows through a winding, wooded valley to Obernzell, the last town in Bavaria.

From Passau to Linz

The first castle on the banks of the Upper Austrian section of the river is **Krempelstein**, the legendary »Schneiderschlössl« (tailor's castle). High up on a hill on the right bank stands Schloss Vichtenstein. Then comes the Jochenstein power plant and on the left bank – right on the Danube Cycle Way – the Haus am Strom (house on the river), an environmental station with an educational exhibition about water (closed Nov–Mar). Soon after Engelhartszell, where the **only Trappist monastery in Austria** is located, the Danube Valley gets narrower and two castles, Schloss Rannariedl and Schloss Marsbach, appear on the left.

◄ Schneiderschlössl
◄ Jochenstein, Haus am Strom

Around the immense bend of the Schlögener Schlinge, with beautiful vantage points, the picture changes: the banks are now lined with friendly holiday resorts like Obermühl and Neuhaus – whose castle can be seen from far and wide. Near **Aschach**, one of the oldest market towns along the Danube with beautiful 16th–18th-century gabled houses, the hills come back and there is a spectacular view of the Alps. A short distance south of the Danube lies the town of **Eferding**, which was mentioned in the Song of the Nibelungen. A visit to the late Gothic parish church and Schloss Starhemberg (13th century, remodelled several times) with its classical front, is worthwhile.

✴
◄ Schlögener Schlinge

? DID YOU KNOW …?

■ … that a tailor who lived in the »Schneiderschlössl« (tailor's castle) wanted to put his sick goat out of its misery by throwing it from the castle walls? Unfortunately he got caught in the goat's horns, was dragged over the wall and drowned in the castle moat – according to legend.

Opposite privately owned Schloss Ottensheim is the extensive complex of Stift Wilhering (► Linz, Surroundings). The interior of the outwardly unadorned collegiate churchis one of the most accomplished Rococo works in Austria. Kürnberger Wald (Kürnberg Forest) lies along the southern banks of the Danube and has traces of Stone Age settlements.

◄ Stift Wilhering

In Linz, the view from the landing stage gives an impression of the city's beautiful location.

◄ Linz

Mauthausen Plan

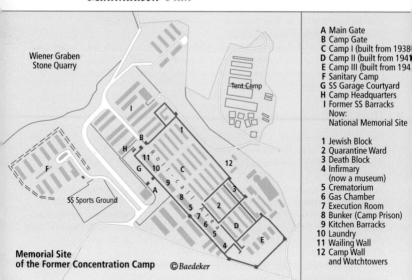

A Main Gate
B Camp Gate
C Camp I (built from 1938)
D Camp II (built from 1941)
E Camp III (built from 194...)
F Sanitary Camp
G SS Garage Courtyard
H Camp Headquarters
I Former SS Barracks
  Now:
  National Memorial Site

1 Jewish Block
2 Quarantine Ward
3 Death Block
4 Infirmary
  (now a museum)
5 Crematorium
6 Gas Chamber
7 Execution Room
8 Bunker (Camp Prison)
9 Kitchen Barracks
10 Laundry
11 Wailing Wall
12 Camp Wall
   and Watchtowers

Wiener Graben
Stone Quarry

Tent Camp

SS Sports Ground

Memorial Site
of the Former Concentration Camp   ©*Baedeker*

| From Linz to Melk | From Linz, take a side trip 15km/9mi southeast to the famous ▶ St Florian Monastery of Augustinian canons and continue 2km/1.2mi further east to the open-air museum at Sumerauerhof. |

From Linz to Melk

From Linz, take a side trip 15km/9mi southeast to the famous ▶ St Florian Monastery of Augustinian canons and continue 2km/1.2mi further east to the open-air museum at Sumerauerhof.

Mauthausen ▶

Opposite the confluence of the Enns River is the old Mauthausen customs house and Schloss Pragstein (15th century). The Romanesque chapel of St Barbara of the parish church has 14th-century murals. A salt storehouse (Salzstadel) at the edge of the town recalls the major role that the salt trade played in the Middle Ages. Mauthausen has Austria's largest granite quarries. From 1938 to 1945 prisoners in the notorious concentration camp about 3km/2mi northwest of the town were forced to work there. In the camp – including the 49 outer camps – more than 200,000 people were imprisoned; over half of them died because of the inhuman conditions. The Austrian government has converted one building into a museum and maintains the rest of the camp as a memorial. Various monuments indicate from which countries the prisoners came.

Former concentration camp (memorial) ▶

Enns ▶

The **oldest town in Austria**, Enns, about 4km/2.5mi up the Enns river, was built on the remains of the Roman camp of »Lauriacum«. Under the Gothic basilica St Laurenz (13th century) the foundations of the Roman capitol, an early Christian basilica as well as a Carolingian church complex have been excavated. In the medieval old quarter a 60m/200ft-high tower, the Stadtturm (1564–68), and the Lauriacum Roman museum are worth taking a look at (opening times: April–Oct daily except Mon 10am–noon and 2pm–4pm, in winter only Sun and holidays).

East of Mauthausen stands the Habsburg castle Schloss Wallsee with a striking 14th-century tower. Ardagger Markt marks the beginning of the Strudengau, a narrow, romantic river valley. The Bauernmuseum (Farming Museum) on national road 119 has several thousand objects from the rural life of the past; the Wehrmachtsmuseum (Armed Forces Museum) nearby exhibits weapons, uniforms and vehicles from 1918 to 1945.

Strudengau

About 2.5km/1.5mi southeast is the hamlet of Ardagger Stift with the former collegiate church (1049–1784) of the same name. The late Romanesque columned basilica has late Gothic, Baroque and classical-style furnishings, and the impressive St Margaret's Window (around 1240) in the east choir. The Mostgalerie (Must Gallery) explains the history and production of this popular drink (opening times: Tue–Sun 10am–6pm).

◀ Ardagger Stift

The picturesque shipping town of Grein is next on the left bank of the Danube. Its mighty castle houses the Oberösterreichische Schifffahrtsmuseum (Upper Austrian Shipping Museum; opening times: May and Oct daily except Mon 10am–noon and 1pm–5pm, June–Sept daily except Mon 10am–6pm). The **Greinburg** is also known for its charming 17th-century arcaded courtyard. On the town square stands one of Austria's oldest Rococo theatres, still in use in the summer.

◀ Grein

The town of Persenbeug is dominated by Schloss Persenbeug, where the last Austrian emperor Karl I (1887–1922) was born. A bridge connects Persenbeug to Ybbs. Along the historic culture trail, the Gothic parish church and the town centre with old houses

> ! **Baedeker TIP**
>
> **Fancy some fish?**
> Bikers, hikers and bird-watchers should not miss a stop at one of the restaurants along the banks of the Danube that specialize in fish. The Uferhaus in Orth, one of the most traditional restaurants on the river, also offers a perfect view. Enjoy carp with a glass of elderberry lemonade and watch the huge cruise ships chug upriver (www.uferhaus.at).

and a Renaissance fountain are worth seeing. The **Nibelungengau** begins here; it got its name from the Song of the Nibelungen, which originated in early medieval Bavaria and Austria, and in which the region plays an important role.

The Ybbs river flows into the Danube from the right and after a few miles the Baroque pilgrimage church of ▶ Maria Taferl (443m/ 1453ft) appears high on a mountain on the left. On the right after this is the old town of Pöchlarn (▶Maria Taferl, Surroundings).

▶see Wachau

Wachau

Krems is an important traffic hub and the starting point for excursions into the ▶ Wachau, the ▶ Waldviertel and the Dunkelsteiner Wald (Dunkelstein Forest) on the other side of the Danube. From here on, the Danube Valley widens and the Tullner Feld lowlands

From Krems to Vienna

Storks find food in abundance on the Danube river meadows

stretch along the riverbank. Islets appear in the river. On the northern banks lies the town of Altenwörth, where Charlemagne defeated the Avars in 791. Zwentendorf became famous for a nuclear power plant that was not put into operation after a referendum in 1978.

Tulln ▶ Just beyond Zwentendorf on the right bank comes Tulln (▶Klosterneuburg, Surroundings). King Etzel came here to meet his bride Kriemhild, and the Romans built the settlement »Comegena« here even earlier. Art lovers should stop off at the **Egon Schiele Museum**. Near Höflein the Danube flows past the last foothills of the Wienerwald (Vienna Woods), turns toward the southwest and passes Korneuburg (▶Weinviertel) and Klosterneuburg with its famous Augustinian abbey.

From Vienna to Hainburg

✳

Nationalpark Donau-Auen ▶

The significance of the Danube lowlands as a floodplain was witnessed in the floods of August 2002: the damage was not nearly as bad here as it was further upriver in the Wachau and Kamptal valley. The Donau-Auen National Park begins shortly outside Vienna and extends to the confluence with the March near ▶Hainburg about 38km/23mi away. **One of the last intact river floodplain landscapes in Europe**, with its unique flora and fauna, is under nature protection here. Along with the successful settlement of beavers, it is now planned to bring sea eagles back to the Danube floodplains. The best way to see the park is to take one of the guided tours conducted by park employees (information: www.donauauen.at).

Other destinations ▶ ▶Hainburg, Petronell-Carnuntum

Dornbirn

C 5

Province: Vorarlberg
Population: 42,000

Elevation: 436m/1430ft

Dornbirn, the largest town in the province of Vorarlberg, is only a few miles south of Bregenz. It is the economic centre of the region and an international trade fair venue.

The residents affectionately call it the »**garden city in the country**« and it is the second youngest city in the province after Hohenems: five smaller communities merged to form the largest village in the Danube monarchy, which in 1901 was granted its municipal charter. After the First World War, in 1919 70% of the population voted in a plebiscite for annexation to Switzerland. But the subject was not even mentioned in the negotiations of Saint-Germain. Today many famous textile and metal manufacturers are located here, and sports fans flock to the trade fair grounds (autobahn exit Dornbirn-Süd), which has developed in recent years into a multi-sports centre (tennis, climbing, track and field, ice skating etc.). The city centre is a pedestrian zone around the marketplace, which is especially busy on Wednesdays and Saturdays during markets. Dornbirn has a good reputation in the region as a shopping city.

From village to popular city

 ! *Baedeker* **TIP**

Culture for all
Be it music, dance or theatre, cabaret, film or a clown for children – the Kulturzentrum Spielboden in Dornbirn, a culture centre housed in an beautifully refurbished factory at Färbergasse 15, promises fun for all. Programme information and reservations at tel. 0 55 72/ 2 19 33 or www.spielboden.at.

What to See in Dornbirn

The mighty classical façade on the church of St Martin on the marketplace is striking. Its massive, temple-like columned vestibule (1840) with a painted gable and the classical parsonage are grouped around the free-standing Gothic bell tower from 1493.

St Martin

The Rote Haus (Red House), built in 1639 by the well-known Vorarlberg family of Rhomberg, is a typical wooden house of the Rhine Valley with an outer stairway, bull's-eye window panes and pointed gables. It was painted red to imitate a Strasbourg half-timbered brick house – at that time the colour was made from ox-blood. Today the building houses a restaurant serving excellent food.

Rotes Haus

The municipal museum is in the Lorenz Rhomberg Haus, a 200-year-old patrician house on the marketplace (opening times: Tue–Sun 10am–noon and 2pm–5pm).

Stadtmuseum
⏲

Dornbirn Map

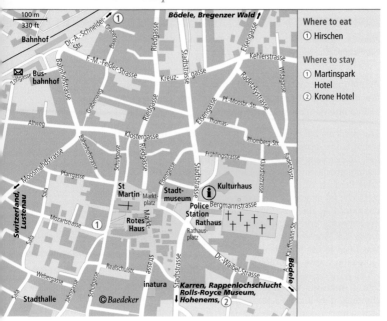

Where to eat
① Hirschen

Where to stay
① Martinspark Hotel
② Krone Hotel

©Baedeker

inatura On Marktstrasse to the south is the »inatura Erlebnis Naturschau Dornbirn«, a museum on Vorarlberg's flora and fauna, geology and mineralogy. The lifelike dioramas on various aspects of nature in Vorarlberg, including extinct animal species, are especially impressive (opening times: daily 10am–6pm).

Around Dornbirn

Karren The Karren mountain (975m/3199ft) with its unusually-designed panorama restaurant, is located about 2.5km/1.5mi south of the city. The peak can be reached comfortably in a cable car.

Rolls-Royce Museum The Rolls-Royce Museum, with Franz Vonier's collection, was opened in a 150-year-old former spinning works just outside the entry into Rappenloch Gorge in Gütle in 1999. It mainly contains cars from the »Golden Years« (1923–38) once owned by famous figures such as King George V and John Lennon (opening times: April–Oct daily 10am–6pm, Nov–March daily until 5pm).

Krippenmuseum In the immediate vicinity of the Rolls-Royce Museum, the Krippenmuseum exhibits 120 cribs from all over the world (Gütle 11c; opening times: May to 6 Jan Tue–Sun 10am–5pm).

▶ VISITING DORNBIRN

INFORMATION

Dornbirn Tourismus
Rathausplatz 1, A-6850 Dornbirn
Tel. 0 55 72/221 88, fax 312 33,
www.dornbirn.info

WHERE TO EAT

▶ Moderate

① *Hirschen*
Haselstauderstrasse 31
A-6850 Dornbirn, tel. 0 55 72/2 63 63
Regional dishes and international
specialities. The »Leberle mit Rösti
vom Ländle-Kalb« (calf's liver with
fried potatoes) is delicious.

WHERE TO STAY

▶ Luxury

① *Martinspark Hotel*
Mozartstrasse 2, A-6850 Dornbirn
Tel. 0 55 72/37 60, fax 3 76 03 76

www.martinspark.at
Austria's first design hotel was conceived down to the last detail by the
architect duo Carlo Baumschlager &
Dietmar Eberle. The hotel also has
conference rooms.

▶ Mid-range

② *Krone Hotel*
Hatlerstrasse 2, A-6850 Dornbirn
Tel. 0 55 72/2 27 20, fax 2 27 20 73
www.kronehotel.at
Centrally located, rooms with all the
amenities, conference rooms and spa.
The new wing is fully accessible for
those with disabilities.
The restaurant was given a »Grüne
Haube«, an award for Austria's best
organic and environmentally friendly
cooking, and serves select seasonal
dishes made from local products.

The Gasthof Gütle inn is the starting point for exploring the wild,   **Rappenloch-**
romantic Rappenloch Gorge, with the Ache River roaring through it.   **schlucht**
The walk along secured paths, walkways and over bridges to the
Staufensee takes about 30 minutes; from there continue on to the
picturesque Alploch with its 120m/393ft-high waterfall.

About 10km/6mi to the east above Dornbirn lies Bödele (1148m/   **Bödele**
3766ft), a charming spot with fields, a moor lake and pine forests. It
is valued both as a recreational area in the summer and a skiing region where snow is assured with about 23km/13mi of pistes; it was
once the training site for Austria's ski troops. The wonderful view
extends from Säntis mountain to the west across the Lake Constance
region and up to the Allgäu Alps and the Braunarlspitze (2649m/
8691ft), the highest peak in Bregenzerwald.

6km/4mi southwest of Dornbirn is the former Rhine Valley res-   **Hohenems**
idence of Hohenems (433m/1421ft; pop. 14,000). Despite medieval
municipal rights the community was only elevated to the status of a
town in 1983, which makes it the newest town in Vorarlberg. On the
Schlossberg, which can be climbed in about 40 minutes, stand the
ruins of Alt-Ems (713m/2339ft; 12th century) and Burg Neu-Ems

(or Schloss Glopper; 14th century), built as a second castle. In the town stands the parish church, Pfarrkirche St Karl Borromäus, which is decorated with frescoes by Andreas Brugger and boasts a Renaissance high altar.

Nibelungen manuscripts ►

Right next to it is an extraordinary example of the Italian Renaissance, the **palace of the counts of Waldburg-Zeil** (1562). Manuscripts C and A of the Song of the Nibelungen were found in its archives in 1755 and 1779.

Jüdisches Museum ►
⊙

Built in 1864, Villa Heimann-Rosenthal was converted into a Jewish museum in 1991. It provides remarkable documentation of the life of the Hohenems Jews and their role in the region (Schweizer Strasse 5, www.jm-hohenems.at; opening times: Tue–Sun 10am–5pm).

✴ Eisenerz

N 4

Province: Styria	**Elevation:** 745m/2444ft
Population: 6200	

The old mining town of Eisenerz is situated at the foot of Styria's mighty Erzberg in the midst of magnificent mountain ranges. The mines on the Erzberg – also called the »Styrian loaf« – still supply a considerable part of Austria's iron requirements.

Old Town

Some of the historic Radmeisterhöfe – as the smelters or blast furnaces were once called – can still be seen in the town. Especially around Bergmannplatz, several 16th–18th-century buildings are to be seen in Eisenerz. The fortified Gothic parish church, Pfarrkirche St Oswald (1470–1518), bears various mining motifs. The shift tower a short distance to the west, whose bell was cast from Turkish cannons in 1581, was once used to ring in the new shift in the mines.

▶ EISENERZ

INFORMATION

Informationsbüro Eisenerz
Körnerplatz 1, A-8790 Eisenerz
Tel. 0 38 48/37 00, fax 21 00
www.eisenerz.at

Stadtmuseum

The municipal museum in the **Kammerhof** has exhibits on the history and techniques of local mining as well as on the crafts associated with iron working (Schulstrasse 1; opening times: May–Oct Mon–Fri 10am–noon and 2pm–5pm).

✴
Steirischer Erzberg

Siderite with an iron content of about 33% is mined at the Steirische Erzberg (1465m/4806ft; »Styrian Iron Mountain«). Once mined in shafts and open pits, in the last 200 years only stepped strips have been used. The Romans are said to have mined iron ore here, but the first visible evidence of mining activity dates from the 12th century. The shift tower, the vantage point at the Krumpental railway station, and the Polster mountain (►Surroundings) all offer a good overview of the site.

A show mine has been built in the last active shaft, which was closed in 1986. A ride around the site in Hauly, an 860-horsepower truck, is quite an experience (www.abendteuer-erzberg.at; tel. 0 38 48 / 32 00; guided tours: May–Oct daily 10am–3pm).

Show mine

Nostalgic train fans will enjoy a ride on the Erzbergbahn from 1891, which was used to transport iron from Eisenerz to Vordernberg. This is the **steepest normal-gauge railway in Austria** and it is run in the summer as a museum train with railed buses.

Around Eisenerz

From **Polster** mountain (1910m/ 6266ft), 10km/6mi east of Eisenerz, there is a unique view of the stepped pyramid of the Erzberg and the chain of peaks of the Eisenerz and Ennstal Alps.

Northeast of the town of Eisenerz is the **Frauenmauerhöhle** cave, only accessible on foot. Its west entrance (1435m/4708ft) can be reached in about 3 hours via Gsoll. The winding, approximately 640m/2100ft-long chamber (Eiskammer) runs diagonally through the mountain. A guided tour and warm clothing are highly recommended (tours June–Sept Sat, Sun and holidays from the west entrance at 9am, 11am and 1pm, from the east entrance at 10am, noon and 2pm).

A ride on the Hauly is fun for young and old alike

The east entrance (1560m/5118ft) can be reached via Polster mountain in two hours; from the mountain there is a wonderful view of the Hochschwabgruppe mountain range. The Naturpark Eisenwurzen with its dense forests, green mountain pastures and rugged peaks offers recreation away from the tourist crowds.

✴ Eisenstadt

R 4

Province: Burgenland   **Elevation:** 182m/597ft
Population: 13,300

Eisenstadt, the capital of Burgenland, has retained its charm as the residence of the ducal family of Esterházy up to the present day. It is attractively located between Vienna (50km/30mi) and the Neusiedler See (15km/9mi), at the edge of a seemingly endless plain stretching eastwards.

Ducal residence

Peaches, apricots, even almonds flourish here – along with an excellent wine. Eisenstadt and classical music are inseparable: Duke Nikolas Esterházy was the patron of the composer and court conductor Joseph Haydn (1732–1809), who lived in Eisenstadt for 30 years.

Eisenstadt was mentioned in a historical chronicle as early as 1118, in another document in 1264, and it was granted its municipal charter in 1373. It belonged to the Habsburgs from 1445 to 1648; in 1648 it became a royal Hungarian free city and residence of the dukes of Esterházy. In 1921 it was returned to Austria and it has been the capital of Burgenland since 1925.

What to See in Eisenstadt

Schloss Esterházy

The palace of the dukes of Esterházy dominates the town. The medieval castle was originally built with four corner towers and an inner courtyard (1388–92), and was later remodelled from 1663 by the

Eisenstadt Map

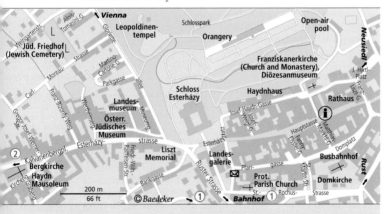

Where to eat
① Reisner

Where to stay
① Gasthof Ohr
② Hotel Burg Bernstein

The magnificent decorations and acoustics in the Haydn Hall impress concert-goers

Italian Baroque architect Carlone. In the late 18th century the Frenchman Moreau modernized it and gave it its present form. Its centrepiece is the three-storey-high Haydn Room with its beautiful frescos; it was here that the composer premiered many of his works. Today the renowned acoustics can be experienced first-hand during the Haydn Festival, which is held every year in September. The permanent Esterházy exhibition, which gives an impression of the life of the ducal family, can only be viewed on a guided tour (guided tours: mid-March–mid-Nov daily 8.30am–6pm, mid-Nov–mid-March Mon–Thu 9am–5pm, Fri until 3pm).

◀ **Haydnsaal**

The Wine Museum, housed in the historical cellar vault of the palace, provides an overview of the tradition of viniculture in Burgenland (opening times: Mon–Fri 10am–6pm; May–Oct also Sat and Sun).

◀ **Weinmuseum**

Opposite the palace the former stables are used by Burgenland's Provincial Gallery for its exhibitions (opening times: Tue–Sat 9am–5pm, Sun from 10am).

◀ **Landesgalerie**

Behind the palace lies a wonderful park in the style of an English garden.

◀ **Schlosspark**

For historical reasons the old quarter east of Esterházy Square is also called the »Freistadt« (»free town«): in 1648 the citizens of Eisenstadt bought their freedom from Duke Esterházy for the princely sum of 16,000 guilders and 3000 pails of wine (about 159,000 litres or 34,980 imperial gallons, worth about 9,000 guilders).

Altstadt

The cathedral in Pfarrgasse, a 15th-century Gothic hall church, is dedicated to the patron saint of Burgenland, St Martin.

◀ **Domkirche**

Music lovers are drawn to the Haydn-Haus at Haydngasse 21, once the composer's residence. Original instruments, portraits, manuscripts and so on are on display (opening times: mid-March–mid-Nov daily 9am–5pm).

Haydn-Haus

Jüdisches Museum When the Jews were expelled from Vienna by Emperor Leopold I, an enclosed Jewish quarter developed in the 17th century in the lower part of Eisenstadt, northwest of the palace. It remained in existence until the 20th century. The Jewish cemetery is also found here. The Austrian Jewish Museum is located in the house of the Hungarian Rabbi Wertheimer, which was built in 1694. Wertheimer's private synagogue is especially beautiful (Unterbergstrasse 6; opening times: May–Oct Tue–Sun 10am–5pm, Nov–April Mon–Thu 9am–4pm, Fri until 1pm).

Burgenländisches Landesmuseum Nearby, the Burgenländisches Landesmuseum (Burgenland Provincial Museum), located in the former home of the Jewish Wolf family, has exhibits on the history, ethnography and natural history of Burgenland, including the great variety of birds at the Neusiedler See (Museumgasse; opening times: Tue–Sat 9am–5pm, Sun from 10am).

Kalvarienberg The artificially constructed Kalvarienberg (1701–05) rises to the west with its very impressive **way of the cross**. There are more than 300 wooden or stone figures along the 24 stations. The massive Berg-

Bergkirche ▸ kirche stands at the top; it has a round ground plan and short towers.

Haydn-Mausoleum ▸ Joseph Haydn's ostentatious mausoleum under the north tower was donated on the occasion of his 200th birthday by Duke Paul Esterházy. Haydn was buried in Vienna and only later were his remains moved to Eisenstadt.

▶ VISITING EISENSTADT

INFORMATION

Eisenstadt Tourismus
Rathaus
Hauptstr. 35
A-7000 Eisenstadt
Tel. 026 82/6 73 90, fax 6 73 91,
www.eisenstadt.at

WHERE TO EAT

▸ Expensive

① *Reisner*
Hauptstrasse 141
A-7212 Forchtenstein
Tel. 0 26 26/6 31 39
Rustic restaurant at the foot of romantic Burg Forchtenstein in Burgenland. The influence of the cooking in nearby Hungary is noticeable here.

WHERE TO STAY

▸ Mid-range

① *Gasthof Ohr*
Rusterstrasse 51, A-7000 Eisenstadt
Tel. 0 26 82/6 24 60, fax 62 46 09
www.hotelohr.at
The three-star restaurant in this centrally located but quiet family-run hotel is recommended.

② *Hotel Burg Bernstein*
A-7434 Bernstein
Tel. 06 64/2 10 02 37
Fax 0 33 54/65 20
www.burgbernstein.at
Burg Bernstein's quiet location is a good starting point for trips into central Burgenland or the hilly Bucklige Welt region.

Around Eisenstadt

The Baroque pilgrimage church of Loretto, 10km/6mi north of Eisenstadt, hosts more than 200,000 pilgrims every year. The Gnadenkapelle (Chapel of Mercy) adjoins the way of the cross towards the
courtyard. The *Black Madonna* statue can be seen behind a grille.

Wallfahrtskirche Loretto

One of the most important relics of the Neolithic Age (5500–2200
BC) – a piece of a container with the figure of a woman etched into
it – was found in Drassburg (234m/767ft; pop. 1100) to the south. It
became famous as the **»Venus of Drassburg«** and is on display in the
Burgenländisches Landesmuseum in Eisenstadt.

Drassburg

Near Mattersburg, about 16km/10mi southwest of Eisenstadt, the
imposing, early 14th-century Burg Forchtenstein stands on a high
promontory. It was fortified with doors and courts in 1635–52 by
the Esterházys as a measure against the Turkish threat. Its martial
character is reflected inside in the generous collections of weapons
and the armoury. The magnificent **treasury**, a testimony to the Esterházys' passion for collecting, offers a more cheerful atmosphere. It
contains some very exotic objects, such as an ornate silver table from
Augsburg, chests of drawers from China and a birdcage made of porcelain from Meissen (opening times: April–Oct daily 10am–6pm; in
July there are special programmes for children at weekends; tel.
0 26 26/8 12 12; www.burg-forchtenstein.at).

★ Burg Forchtenstein

The armoury in Burg Forchtenstein shows old spoils of war

Southern Burgenland

The **Naturpark Landseer Berge** nature preserve is partly in Burgenland, partly in Lower Austria. It was opened in 2001 and has several interesting sights. Near Schwarzenbach (Lower Austria) are the largest Celtic ramparts in Austria; the Keltenmuseum there documents the former Celtic princely residence. **One of the largest castle ruins in central Europe** is Burg Landsee (13th/15th–17th century), which was destroyed in 1772. It has four encircling walls and a keep that is now a viewing platform. There is a stage here for the festival held in the summer.

Ruins of Landsee Castle ►

The hamlet of Raiding (253m/830ft, pop. 800) about 20km/12mi east of Landsee is the birthplace of the celebrated piano virtuoso and composer Franz Liszt (1811–86). The house was converted into a museum as early as 1911 and is open to the public. Documents, musical scores and photographs are on display (opening times: Easter–Oct daily 9am–noon and 1pm–5pm; tel. 026 19 / 510 47).

✱ **Burg Lockenhaus**

Burg Lockenhaus (13th century) stands majestically on a mountain spur above Markt Lockenhaus, near the Hungarian border towards Köszeg. It is considered to be the last authentic knight's castle in Burgenland and is part of the transnational Naturpark Geschriebenstein. The knight's hall, a double-aisled hall with Gothic cross-ribbed vaulting, is worth seeing, as is the castle chapel with its original frescoes.

Since 1982 a **chamber music festival** has been held here every year, which was initiated by Pastor Herowitsch of Lockenhaus and the violinist Gidon Kremer, who was born in Riga. There is a birds of prey centre (opening times: April–Oct Tue–Sun 1pm–6pm, May–Sept Sat, Sun and holidays, bird shows at 2pm–4pm).

Stadtschlaining, about 25km/15mi southwest of Lockenhaus, still has remnants of its town wall and the commanding 13th-century Burg Schlaing. The castle houses the **Europäische Museum für Frieden** (European Museum for Peace), which is dedicated to the subjects of violence, conflict, the environment and the development of peace (www.friedensmuseum.at; opening times: April–Oct Tue–Sun 9am–5pm).

> ! **Baedeker TIP**
>
> **Uhudler: a wine, not a yodel**
> Uhudler is not for yodelling but for drinking. It is the collective word for various red and white wines that are only produced in a few communities in southern Burgenland. After phylloxera destroyed many European vineyards from 1860 on, American varieties were grafted with European vines. Some of the American varieties survived without being grafted and can be found today in the Uhudler wines. Taste them in the Uhudler Vinotheque at the end of the Uhudler wine trail at Hochkogel hill near Eltendorf (opening times: Fri and Sun 2pm–9pm).

East of Güssing lies the Naturpark in der Weinidylle – a lovely area with extensive lowland forests and flood-meadows, charming vineyards and romantic wine cellar quarters. The Weinidylle is **Burgenland's smallest wine-growing region**, where Blaufränkisch and Welschriesling grapes are grown. The Weinmuseum in Moschendorf has more information.

Naturpark in der Weinidylle

West of Güssing in the hamlet of Gerersdorf there is a very attractive open-air museum. The »village within a village« consists of about 30 farmhouses from Burgenland of the 18th and 19th centuries (opening times: April–Oct Mon–Fri 9am–5pm, Sat, Sun and holidays 10am–6pm). The village shop sells regional products such as fruit, honey and wine.

Freilichtmuseum Ensemble Gerersdorf ⏱

✱ Faaker See

L 6

Province: Carinthia   **Elevation:** 560m/1837ft

The picturesque Faaker See is Austria's southernmost recreational lake – and also one of the most popular. It is surrounded by broad fields and narrow strips of woodland, and towards the south the striking peak of Mittagskogel (2143m/7031ft) rises above the Karawanke mountains.

The small Lake Faak, located about 5km/3mi southeast of Villach, offers a complete range of tourist facilities and almost every kind of

Wayside shrine with the Karavanke massif and the Faaker See in the background

water sport (except motor boats). No wonder: the water temperature gets up to 27 °C/80 °F. But this holiday paradise also has something for cyclists, mountain climbers and lovers of culture. The 12km/7mi-long Faaker Radwanderweg cycle way is manageable for families with small children, and the Drauradweg and Karnischer Radweg are also nearby. The Karawanke mountains and the Villacher Alps are only a stone's throw away. Villach – a centre of carnival festivities and, along with Ossiach, the venue for the Carinthia Summer Festival – is only a few minutes' drive distant, as are Velden with its casino and the Wörther See.

Ruins of Burg Finkenstein The picturesque ruins of Finkenstein Castle can be found in the mountains south of the Faaker See; there is a castle restaurant too. In summer nearly 1200 guests enjoy concerts from classical to pop music in the Burgarena (programme information and tickets can be obtained at tel. 0 42 54/51 05 11 or www.burgarena.at).

▶ VISITING FAAKER SEE

INFORMATION

Tourismusinformation
Faak am See
Dietrichsteinerstrasse 2
A-9583 Faak am See
Tel. 0 42 54/21 10
Fax 21 10 21
www.faakersee.at

EUROPEAN BIKE WEEK

Things get pretty loud for five days in early September every year at the Faaker See, when thousands of Harley-Davidson owners meet here. Along with that Harley roar there is also live music.

WHERE TO EAT

▶ Inexpensive
Gasthof Löwen
A-6863 Egg
Tel. 0 55 12/22 07
Fax 22 07 35
One speciality of this rustic eatery – family-owned since 1856 – are the hearty Bregenzerwald cheese dishes such as noodles with cheese sauce, raclette and cheese fondue.

WHERE TO STAY

▶ Luxury
Karnerhof (Silencehotel)
A-9580 Egg
Tel. 0 42 54/21 88, fax 36 50
www.karnerhof.com
This spa hotel is an accomplished combination of luxury and taste.

▶ Mid-range
Inselhotel Faakersee
A-9583 Faak am See
Tel. 0 42 54/21-45, fax 21-36 77
www.inselhotel.at
Restful, luxurious hotel away from the rest of the world on an island in the Faaker See. Comprehensive sports and recreational programme.

▶ Budget
Finkensteiner Hof
Mallestiger Platz 1
A-9584 Finkenstein
Tel. 0 42 54/21 76, fax 21 76 80
www.finkensteinerhof.at
Centrally located hotel with a private beach and a swimming pool; bikes lent out at no charge.

✳ Feldkirch

C 5

Province: Vorarlberg
Population: 25,000

Elevation: 459m/1506ft

Feldkirch, the westernmost town in Austria, is the birthplace of renowned scientists and artists. During the Second World War many people came here because of its proximity to Switzerland and the Principality of Liechtenstein.

The town, with one of the best preserved medieval centres in Vorarlberg, is located about 35km/21mi south of Bregenz where the Ill River emerges from the Walgau and flows onto the plains of the Rhine. Feldkirch is an international rail and road traffic hub.

Westernmost border town

Many refugees from the Nazis nervously remained here at the time when the swastika flew in Austria. It was the last stop before leaving Austria for the safety of Switzerland. The Irish writer James Joyce (1882–1941), author of *Ulysses*, was forced into an extended stay in Feldkirch during the First World War in 1915.

Feldkirch is the birthplace of the physician and geographer Hieronymus Münzer (1437–1508), the painter Wolf Huber (c1480–1539), a major master of the »Danube School«, as well as the humanist, mathematician and astronomer Georg Joachim Rheticus (1514–76), a student of Nicholas Copernicus.

Founded in 1200 by Count Hugo I of Montfort, the town's name first appeared as »ad Veltkirichun« (near the field church) in 842. In the Middle Ages Feldkirch was an important centre for storage and defence. The town centre has retained much of its medieval appearance. Some of the walls, two gates and four towers of the town's for-

Townscape

Feldkirch Map

Where to eat
① Wirtschaft zum Schützenhaus
② Schlosswirtschaft Schattenburg

Where to stay
① Hotel Alpenrose
② Hotel Montfort
③ Hotel Büchel

Medieval Feldkirch lies at the foot of the old Schatten Castle

tifications are still extant. Narrow, winding lanes, arcades, half-timbered houses and richly decorated façades characterize the romantic **»Studierstädtle«** (studying town; named after its many schools). The vineyards on the Ardetzenberg hill bear witness to the fact that wine was a major source of income for centuries. When Archduke Johann visited Vorarlberg in 1839, he praised Feldkirch wine and even spoke of a typical »Feldkirch taste«.

What to See in Feldkirch

Marketplace The marketplace is the bustling centre of the Old Town (Altstadt) with its beautiful old arcades and patrician homes. The Johanneskirche on the east side was built in 1218 by Count Hugo of Montfort for the Order of St John.

Palais Liechtenstein Follow Kreuzgasse with its late Gothic houses northeast from the marketplace to the elegant Palais Liechtenstein (1697), today the town's library and archive.

Domkirche Take Herrengasse to Domplatz (cathedral square) and the Domkirche St Nikolaus with its colourful modern stained glass windows (1966). The cathedral was reconstructed in late Gothic style in 1478 after a fire in the town. The plain exterior of the most important Gothic church in Vorarlberg hides an **interior of great artistic value**: on the right-hand side altar there is a *Pieta* and in the predella *Veronica's Veil*, two paintings by Wolf Huber, and a wrought-iron tabernacle from 1540 that was converted into a pulpit.

VISITING FELDKIRCH

INFORMATION

Feldkirch Tourismus
Palais Liechtenstein
Schlossergasse 8, A-6800 Feldkirch
Tel. 0 55 22/7 34 67
www.feldkirch.at

WHERE TO EAT

▶ Moderate

① *Wirtschaft zum Schützenhaus*
Göfiser Strasse 2
A-6800 Feldkirch
Tel. 0 55 22/8 52 90, fax 85 29 04
Above the roofs of the old town,
commanding a view of Schloss
Schattenburg and the Swiss moun-
tains, stands the romantic Schützen-
haus (»marksmen's house«). The local
dishes served here are made predom-
inantly of regional products (closed
Tue and Wed).

② *Schlosswirtschaft Schattenburg*
Burggasse 1
A-6800 Feldkirch
Tel. 0 55 22/7 24 44
The restaurant in the Schattenburg is
paradise for schnitzel fans: it serves
the largest Wiener schnitzel around.

WHERE TO STAY

▶ Luxury

① *Hotel Alpenrose*
Rosengasse 4-6, A-6800 Feldkirch
Tel. 0 55 22/7 21 75, fax 72 17 55
www.hotel-alpenrose.net
Located in the centre of the Old Town.
The hotel combines the charm of an
old 16th-century patrician house with
the comfort of a modern hotel.
Tasteful Biedermeier-style rooms.

▶ Mid-range

② *Hotel Montfort*
Galuragasse 7, A-6800 Feldkirch
Tel. 0 55 22/7 21 89, fax 7 47 99 11
www.bbn.at/montfort
A quiet art hotel with bright, friendly
rooms that can be accessed freely by
those with disabilities.

▶ Budget

③ *Hotel Büchel*
Sägerstrasse 20, A-6800 Feldkirch
Tel. 0 552 2/7 33 06, fax 7 33 06 33
www.hotel-buechel.at
Family-run hotel, with a sauna and
indoor pool. The restaurant serves
Austrian and regional specialities.

Kapuzinerkloster
The Capuchin monastery (1605) is located a short distance outside
the town walls; it has the relics and cell of St Fidelis, the city's patron
saint, who was murdered in 1622 and canonized in 1746. During the
great famine of 1817 the Capuchins fed up to 2000 people every day.

Katzenturm
The cannon tower, built around 1500, attests impressively to the
town's fortifications. Today there is a bell weighing 7.5 tonnes in its
top storey. The Churertor (Chur Gate), also called the Salztor (Salt
◀ Churertor Gate), is a little further to the southwest. Its six-storey gate tower
was renovated in the late 14th century.

Illbrücke, Illkai
Next comes the Illbrücke, the bridge across the Ill. In the Middle
Ages the river Ill was easy to cross here, so additional fortifications

were built, like the massive Wasserturm (the Water Tower to the east), which was documented as early as 1482, and the Diebesturm (the Thieves' Tower to the west). On the left embankment of the Ill, the Illkai, the walk along Graf Rudolf rampart leads upriver to the armoury, the powder tower and the Mühletor (mill gate). The Illpark shopping centre and the municipal hall (Montforthaus) are located a short distance to the east.

✱
Schattenburg

Schloss Schattenburg is the largest and best preserved castle in Vorarlberg; it was built around 1260 and is accessible via Schlosssteig or Burggasse. Its name comes from Middle High German »schade« (= protector, reeve). The counts of Montfort had their residence here from the mid-13th century until 1390. The castle has a pretty courtyard with a wooden balcony, attractive rooms and a restaurant. The exhibits in the Heimatmuseum include an interesting collection of weapons (opening times: Jan–March Mon–Fri 1.30pm–4pm, Sat and Sun from 11am, April–Oct Mon–Fri 9am–noon and 1.30pm–6pm, Sat and Sun 9am–6pm).

Around Feldkirch

Rankweil

About 6km/4mi northeast of Feldkirch at the beginning of the Laternser Tal valley lies the little town of Rankweil (470m/1542ft; pop. 10,000). In the centre of town is the Liebfrauenberg (515m/1690ft; Lady Mountain) with the castle remains of Burg Hörnlingen (14th century) and a pilgrimage church, **Wallfahrtskirche Mariä Heimsuchung**, which was built into it in the 15th and 17th centuries. The church has several precious works of art, including a 15th-century statue of the Mother of God and a Romanesque wooden crucifix (late 12th century), which was covered with silver in 1728 and which is considered to work miracles. Pilgrimage has flourished here since the 13th century.

Laternser Tal

East of Rankweil the winding Laternser Tal begins with several small and pretty villages: Batschuns (570m/1870ft; pop. 1200) with its Bergkirche (mountain church; 1923), Schloss Weissenberg (1400) and a large retreat house of 1964; Innerlaterns, Bad Laterns and of course Laterns (998m/3274ft; pop. 600) itself, which can also be reached on foot from Rankweil in about two hours via the »Üble Schlucht« (»Bad Gorge«).

Alpe Furx

From Laterns, head north to Alpe Furx (1100m/3609ft), popular for winter sports and as a climatic resort. A hike via Alpwegkopf (1430m/4692ft) and Saluveralm (1609m/5279ft) to the Freschenhaus (1846m/6056ft) with the Freschenkapelle »Zum heiligen Bernhard«, a chapel built in 1952, and an alpine garden takes about 3 hours. The peak of the Hoher Freschen (2006m/6581ft) takes another 30 minutes to reach.

Friesach

M 6

Province: Carinthia
Population: 5800

Elevation: 636m/2087ft

A visit to Friesach with its medieval Old Town is just right for history buffs. Friesach played an important role in the Middle Ages because it lay on the trade route between Vienna and Venice.

Friesach's **medieval atmosphere** is unmatched in Carinthia. Austria's largest medieval festival takes place here on the last weekend in July every year – with acrobats, jousting, alchemists and actors.

Living Middle Ages

Located about 30km/18mi north of ►Klagenfurt, it was able to benefit financially from its strategic advantages. Coins were minted here from 1125 to 1300, and the Friesacher Pfennig (penny) was used for over two centuries as legal tender as far away as Hungary. The Teutonic Knights arrived in the 13th century, the Virgilienberg chapter and the Dominicans followed. Until 1803 Friesach belonged to the archbishops of Salzburg and was one of their wealthiest cities. It was besieged, plundered and destroyed several times – and always rebuilt.

In Friesach the Middle Ages come back to life every year in August at an opulent knight's feast

▶ VISITING FRIESACH

INFORMATION

Tourismusinformation Friesach
Fürstenhofplatz 1, A-9360 Friesach
Tel. 0 42 68/43 00, fax 42 80.
www.friesach.at

WHERE TO EAT

▶ **Inexpensive**

① *Schenke »zum Krebsen«*
Neumarkter Strasse 19
A-9360 Friesach
Tel. 042 68 / 23 36
The house was first documented in
1846 and has been family-owned since
1926; it serves down-to-earth Carin-
thian cooking.

WHERE TO STAY

▶ **Budget**

① *Der Metnitztaler Hof*
Hauptplatz 11
A-9360 Friesach
Tel. 0 42 68/2 51 00
Fax 25 10 54
www.metnitztalerhof.at
This hotel on Friesach's medieval main
square dates from as far back as the
16th century; indeed the wine cellar is
from the 13th century. The comfortable rooms are furnished in local
country style; there is also a spa and a
restaurant.

What to See in Friesach

Old Town

Of the massive fortifications around the Old Town the town wall,
which was completed in 1131, three defensive gate towers and the
800m/2625ft-long moat have been preserved.

Hauptplatz

The elongated Hauptplatz (main square) is the town's focal point; it
is bordered by beautiful old houses and the 16th-century Altes Rathaus (Old Town Hall), and has a Renaissance fountain with scenes
from Greek mythology.

St Bartholomäus

On Wiener Strasse north of the Hauptplatz stands the town parish
church, Stadtpfarrkirche St Bartolomäus, which was originally Romanesque. It is the **largest church in Carinthia**. The 12th-century
baptismal font, the choir window (13th–14th century), the Baroque
high altar from 1679 and the 18th-century Rococo chairs with figures of the apostles are all worth seeing.

Granary

The monumental 14th-century granary is now the site of an unusual
artistic installation: »Die Spur des Einhorns« (The Trail of the Uni-
corn) is a virtual mythological world as conceived by Hans Hoffer
(opening times: May–Oct daily 10am–6pm).

**Dominikaner-
kloster**

The Dominican monastery has stood here since 1251 and is the oldest in German-speaking Europe. The church was built in 1255–1320
and has the longest nave in Carinthia. Instead of an extravagant tow-

er it has only a small ridge turret – as befitting a mendicant order. It has two early Gothic treasures: a branch crucifix (14th century) and a sandstone Madonna (around 1300).

The **Heiligblutkirche** (Church of the Holy Blood) southwest of the Hauptplatz (main square) is said to have been the setting for a blood miracle during a mass in 1238.

The **Rotturmanlage** (Rotturm ruins) was originally part of the town's fortifications and had four towers, of which two have been preserved.

It takes about 10 minutes to walk from the Hauptplatz to the Romanesque castle church, Burgkirchlein **St Peter** on the Petersberg, which offers the best view of Friesach and its surroundings.

Above it are the remains of the romantic **Burg Petersberg**, the fortified castle of the archbishops of Salzburg (before 1077). The present castle inn was once the home of the castle's overseer. The castle festival is held every summer in the upper courtyard. Those who are not put off by the steps should visit the extensive Stadtmuseum in the six-storey castle keep.

Friesach Map

Where to eat
① Schenke »zum Krebsen«

Where to stay
① Der Metnitztaler Hof

Around Friesach

Only a few miles to the north of Friesach the Metnitztal valley runs westwards with its forests, mountain pastures and gently curving hills. It is a popular and **quiet place for holidays in both summer and winter**. Near the hamlet of Grades is the former castle of the bishops of ▶Gurk. The pilgrimage church, Wallfahrtskirche St Wolfgang, has a beautiful interior.

◀ Metnitztal
◀ Grades

About 4km/2.5mi to the west lies Markt Metnitz, which has been settled since the 9th century. Its impressive early Gothic fortified church has elaborate Baroque furnishings; on the outer wall of the octagonal charnel house is a copy of the **largest Dance of Death in Austria**.

◀ Metnitz

Gailtal

J/K 6

Province: Carinthia

The diverse mountain landscape and the beautiful valley are easily accessible by means of hiking trails and cabins. Since mass tourism has not yet reached the area, the Gailtal valley is a good place for a relaxing and restful holiday.

Relaxing holiday destination
It runs between the Gailtal Alps to the north and the Karnisch Alps to the south – along with the Lienz Dolomites they form the Southern Alps – and ends where the Gail and the Drau rivers converge near ▶Villach.

Lesachtal
The Lesachtal valley runs along the river Gail west of Kötschach-Mauthen. The quiet, high-lying valley is distinguished by rustic villages with impressive farms, expansive mountain pastures and impressive rock formations.

Kötschach-Mauthen
Kötschach-Mauthen (710m/2329ft, pop. 3600) is the principle town of the upper Gailtal. The late Gothic hall church dedicated to Unsere Liebe Frau (Our Dear Lady; 1518–27), also known as the **»Gailtaler Dom«**, with a uniquely decorated vaulted ceiling is worth visiting: the Gothic cross-ribbed vault was further developed into a highly imaginative loop vault. The fresco in the choir with scenes from the life of Mary and the picture on the high altar are also beautiful.

▶ VISITING GAILTAL

INFORMATION
Kärntens Naturarena
Hauptstr. 14
A-9620 Hermagor
Tel. 0 42 82/31 31
Fax 31 31 31
www.naturarena.com

1. KÄRNTNER ERLEBNISPARK

Don't look for a aerospace centre when you hear the names »Luna Loop« and »Nautic Jet«: they can both be found at the 1. Kärntner Erlebnispark (First Carinthian Amusement Park) at the Pressegger See. Those who do not want to go swimming can test their skills on the wobbly wheels or take the astronaut test. There is also an area for small children (www.erlebnispark.cc; opening times: May–Sept daily 9am–6pm).

WHERE TO EAT
▶ Expensive
Landhaus Kellerwand
Mauthen 24
A-9640 Kötschach-Mauthen
Tel. 0 47 15/2 69
www.sissy-sonnleitner.at
More and more gourmets are finding their way to Sissy Sonnleitner's culinary paradise. Those who want to dabble in the kitchen themselves can book a cookery class.

Long hikes in the Karnisch Alps often end at Lake Wolay

Kötschach-Mauthen has ratherunusual museums: in the town hall the »Museum 1915–1918 – From the Ortler to the Adriatic« shows, using numerous examples, the horror and absurdity of a war by relating the fate of simple soldiers and the civilian population on both sides of the conflict (opening times: mid-May–mid-Oct Mon–Fri 10am–1pm and 3pm–6pm, Sat, Sun and holidays 2pm–6pm). The open-air museum at the Plöckenpass and at Monte Piano are part of it too: they show the military positions on the alpine front lines and include historic structures and objects. The goal is to make a case for harmony and peace among nations.

Museum 1915–1918

🕐

To the east of the Plöckenpass are many imposing mountains that can be climbed relatively quickly from Gailtal, for example Gailtaler Polinik (2331m/7648ft) near Mauthen, the massive Trogkofel (2279m/7477ft) and the jagged Gartnerkofel (2195m/7201ft), where the extremely rare and strictly protected blue-coloured **»Wulfenia carinthiaca«** (▶p.23) grows. Both mountains can be reached from the Sonnenalpe Nassfeld via the Nassfeld Lodge (1513m/4964ft).

East of the Plöckenpass

Hermagor (600m/1969ft; pop. 7400) is situated in the heart of Gailtal and is the centre of about 30 communities and hamlets as well as the starting point for hikes and tours. The late Gothic parish church (15th century) was rebuilt after the wars against the Turks. 14th-century frescoes have been exposed in the choir. About 5km/3mi to the east is the 1km/0.6mi-long Pressegger See (560m/1837ft), also called the »bathtub of Gailtal« because its waters reach temperatures of up to 28°C/82°F.

Hermagor

Poludnig,
Garnitzenklamm

Garnitzenklamm ▶

In the vicinity of Möderndorf a 10km/6mi-long road begins and runs through very pleasant countryside right up the Karnisch Alps. To the southeast on the border is Poludnig mountain (2000m/ 6562ft). This road also leads to Garnitzenklamm, whose geo-trail, with panels that explain its origins, is only for those with a good head for heights and sure feet.

✶✶ Gasteiner Tal

K 5

Province: Salzburg
Elevation: 830–1137m/2723–3730ft

The façades of the Belle Epoque hotels have faded and famous guests have become rare. But with a little imagination it is easy to imagine the upper-class society that used to enjoy the elegant accommodation and beautiful panoramas of the Gastein valley.

Meeting place of the upper crust

When, in the 19th century, the nobility and wealthy middle class began to take summer holidays in the Alps, the Gasteiner Tal developed into a posh resort area. A respectable series of famous guests such as Schubert, Schopenhauer, Bismarck, Sir Arthur Conan Doyle and even royalty including Indian maharajas and Germany's Kaiser Wilhelm I appeared, above all in Bad Gastein.

Waterfall in the middle of town: the Gasteiner Ache river on its way through Bad Gastein

The 40km/24mi-long Gasteiner Tal valley still numbers among the **popular holiday regions in Austria**. From the Salzachtal valley, the romantic gorge named Gasteiner Klamm branches off south to the ▶ Hohe Tauern and gradually begins to climb. The Tauernbahn railway runs through the valley, then enters a 8.5km/5mi-long tunnel through the Tauernhauptkamm (cars are put on trains between Böckstein in the north and Mallnitz in the south). Until the Felbertauerntunnel was built, this was the only route across the Eastern Alps that was open all year round.

Visitors from all over the world appreciate the hot springs and the **hiking trails** in an unbeatable location, and in particular the three completely different **skiing regions**: the interconnected ski area Stubnerkogel – Schlossalm (with Bad Hofgastein); the region of Graukogel; and the high alpine slopes in Sportgastein where snow is assured (information: www.gastein.com).

With temperatures between 44 and 47 °C (110 and 115 °F) the thermal water in Bad Gastein comes from a total of 18 springs and was used as early as Roman times. Paracelsus also praised these springs, whose waters are prized less for their minerals than for their radon. Whether by bathing or inhaling, chronic ailments such as rheumatism and asthma, circulatory conditions or problems with the autonomic nervous system are clearly relieved.

Radon hot springs

> ## ❗ *Baedeker* TIP
>
> ### Therapy for rheumatism
> Suffering from rheumatism? A visit to the Gastein therapeutic shaft could help. Gold was mined until 1944 near Böckstein at the southern end of the valley. When some of the miners were cured of their rheumatism, doctors began to take notice. Since 1952 the mine shaft has been used for therapies that are effective because of the high concentration of radon in the air, the high temperatures (up to 42 °C/107 °F) and the high humidity.

What to See in the Gasteiner Tal

The bypass road goes around the Gasteiner Klamm at the northern end of the valley through a tunnel. The walk along a nature trail that runs from the Klammstein car park to the »Entrische Kirche«, a **natural cave**, takes about 45 minutes. From the 16th century on it was used by Protestants for secret meetings; today it serves as winter shelter for several species of bats. One part of the cave, which has beautiful stalactites and sinters, is open to the public (guided tours only, duration approx. 50 minutes, Palm Sunday to beginning of Oct Tue–Sun 11am, noon, 2pm and 3pm, July and Aug daily 10am–5pm every hour).

»Entrische Kirche«

🕑

Dorfgastein (840m/2756ft; pop. 1500) lies south of the Klamm. There are wonderful hiking trails in the surrounding mountains; Fulseck (2033m/6670ft) is a popular skiing region (interconnected region Dorfgastein-Grossarl). The town still appears to be quite rural but combines mountain atmosphere with a comprehensive range of sports such as mountain biking, paragliding, snowboarding and ice climbing.

Dorfgastein

Bad Hofgastein (860m/2822ft; pop. 6300), the old regional centre, is located in the broadest part of the valley. As a **spa, it is rich in tradition**, and it also attracts many winter sports fans, not least because of its cross-country ski runs and the well-maintained pistes on Schlossalm (2050m/6726ft), which are also suitable for beginners. In the 16th century gold mining made it the wealthiest town after Salzburg, a fact attested to by the magnificent late Gothic parish church. The sanatoriums and spa facilities get their water piped in from the radon springs in Bad Gastein, from where a walk to Bad Hofgastein takes three hours.

★
Bad Hofgastein

A wonderful location with a magnificent high mountain panorama gives this spa town (1083m/3553ft; pop. 5600) its charm. It was

★
Bad Gastein

▶ VISITING GASTEINER TAL

INFORMATION

Gasteinertal Tourismus GmbH
Tauernplatz 1
A-5630 Bad Hofgastein
Tel. 0 64 32/339 30
Fax 33 93 120, www.gastein.com

WHERE TO EAT

▶ Expensive
Zum Stern
Weitmoserstrasse 33
A-5630 Bad Hofgastein
Tel. 0 64 32/8 45 00
The view of the mountains alone is
worth the visit. Family atmosphere
and a menu with a regional bias.

▶ Moderate
Villa Hiss
Erzherzog-Johann-Promenade 1
A-5640 Bad Gastein
Tel. 0 64 34/3 82 80
Exquisite menus and delicious des-
serts.

Unterbergerwirt
Unterberg 7
A-5632 Dorfgastein
Tel. 0 64 33/70 77
The chef won the »Salzburger Nockerl
Olympics« – but he can make other
delicious dishes as well.

WHERE TO STAY

▶ Luxury
Salzburger Hof
Grillparzerstrasse 1
A-5640 Bad Gastein
Tel. 0 64 34/2 03 70
Fax 38 67
www.salzburgerhof.com
The stylish house is tastefully fur-
nished and offers good service; it is the
ideal starting point for walks and
hikes.

▶ Mid-range
Österreichischer Hof
Kurgartenstrasse 6
A-5630 Bad Hofgastein
Tel. 0 64 32/6 21 60
Fax 62 16 51
www.oehof.at
Austrian hospitality is combined here
with a personal atmosphere. There is a
restaurant for hotel guests.

Landhotel Römerhof
A-5632 Dorfgastein 22
Tel. 0 64 33/77 77
www.roemerhof.com
The oldest part of this refined hotel is
a tower dating from Roman times.
Along with comfortable rooms and
spacious apartments there is a swimming pool with a whirlpool, steam
bath and sauna.

*Bad Gastein, with its Belle Époque
palatial hotels, was once Austria's most
elegant resort*

known as early as the Middle Ages and despite the modern spa and entertainment facilities, such as a mountain pool and a casino, some of the flair of the Belle Epoque still lingers. The Gasteiner Museum shows which illustrious guests once enjoyed the landscape and the waters here. It is also informative on local mining and the spa (Haus Austria; opening times: daily 10.30am–noon and 3.30pm–6pm).

The mountains – Stubnerkogel (2246m/7369ft) to the west, Graukogel (2492m/8176ft) to the east and Kreuzkogel (2686m/8812ft) to the south – are accessible via cable cars and are a paradise for mountain climbers and skiers.

Böckstein

The old village of Böckstein is at the southern end of the Gastein valley. The historic mining community Altböckstein with its production, administrative and residential buildings forms a picturesque ensemble. The Montanmuseum Böckstein (Mining Museum) is located in the former Salzstadel (salt store; opening times: June–Oct Tue–Sun 10.30am–noon and 3.30pm – 6pm; tel. 064 34 / 22 98). ☉

✳ Gmünd

L 6

Province: Carinthia
Population: 2700

Elevation: 749m/2457ft

Looking back on a varied history, this lively town is now proud of its many art studios, galleries and exhibitions. Add to that a medieval ambience, and Gmünd becomes quite a successful mix.

Gmünd is located at the confluence of the Lieser and Malta rivers, at the beginning of the picturesque Maltatal valley. Because of its strategic location on the trade route from Salzburg to Venice, the castle from 1250 was reinforced. Gmünd was ruled from 1639 to 1932 by the counts of Lodron from South Tyrol.

Strategic location

What to See in Gmünd

The massive **Altes Schloss**, largely in ruins now, dates from the 13th to 17th centuries and was carefully restored after several fires. It is

▶ **GMÜND**

INFORMATION

Stadtgemeinde Gmünd
Hauptplatz 20, A-9853 Gmünd
Tel. 047 32/22 15 14, fax 22 15 35
www.stadt-gmuend.at

The very first Porsche coupés are on display at the Porsche Museum in Gmünd

now used for special events. The Old Town (Altstadt) is surrounded by a mighty wall with four 16th-century gates. The medieval pillory stands at the Obere Stadttor (Upper City Gate). The comparatively simple Stadtschloss (town palace) of the Lodrons was built in 1651–54 on Gmünd's Hauptplatz (main square). Its Baroque stone lions are a gift from the Mirabellgarten in Salzburg – the lion is the heraldic animal of the counts of Lodron.

> ## ! *Baedeker* TIP
>
> ### The poisoner's tale
>
> For some she was an sinister poisoner, for others a tragic victim of justice: Eva Faschauner, who was accused of having poisoned her husband with arsenic, was beheaded in 1773. She had been imprisoned and tortured for three years. The case, which caused a sensation at the time, is documented in detail in the Heimatmuseum (Kirchgasse 38; opening times: June–Sept Sat and Sun 10.30am–12.30pm, 2pm–5pm).

Even those who are not usually interested in cars might have a weak moment here: the cradle of the legendary Porsche 356 – the first car bearing the name Porsche – was in Gmünd. Ferdinand Porsche (1875–1951) had the Porsche works moved to Gmünd from 1944 to 1950: in that time 44 coupés and 8 convertibles were built by 300 employees. There is a monument to commemorate the famous engineer. In 1982 Porsche fan Helmut Pfeifhofer initiated the construction of the excellent private Porsche museum (opening times: mid-May–mid-Oct 9am–6pm, otherwise 10am–4pm).

Porsche Automuseum

Around Gmünd

Nationalpark Nockberge

The Nationalpark Nockberge, which consists of two parts, is located east of Gmünd. Its gently rounded, up to 2300m/7546ft-high peaks, broad mountain pastures, quiet lakes and moors, dark mountain forests and unique flora and fauna inspire hikers. The Nockalmstrasse is a 35km/21mi long toll road; it begins near Innerkrems and meanders southeast to the Reichenau plain. Various huts and stations along the way provide information about the national park.

★
Maltatal

The Maltatal, one of the most magnificent valleys in Austria, is about 30km/18mi long and located between the Reisseckgruppe mountain range to the southwest, the Ankogelgruppe to the west and the Haffnergruppe to the north. The **Tierpark Diana** near Feistritz has lions and tigers along with local wild animals.

The **»valley of falling waters«**, as the section of the valley that begins behind Feistritz is called, has several waterfalls including the almost 200m/660ft-high Fallbach Waterfall. From the Falleralm the road becomes the Malta-Hochalmstrasse (toll road) and winds through magnificent twists and turns over nine bridges and through six tunnels up to the Kölnbreinsperre, one of the largest and, with its 200m/660ft-high wall, the **highest dam in Austria**. There is a spectacular view from here.

◄ Kölnbreinsperre

★ ★ Graz

0 5

Province: Styria
Population: 253,000

Elevation: 368m/1207ft

Graz was the glorious royal seat of the Habsburgs during the Middle Ages and the Renaissance. From this period the city has inherited one of the best preserved old towns in central Europe and has been on the UNESCO World Heritage list since 1999.

Renaissance and modern

The times when the rest of Austria looked down on Graz as a »Pensionopolis« are over. But who would hold it against Austria's pensioners for choosing to retire to a city that combines southern European charm with a mild climate – and is much cheaper than the national capital Vienna? In the past decades the old aristocracy and down-to-earth, traditional middle class have been joined by a lively art scene, which has put Graz on the European map with its avantgarde festivals »styriarte« and »Steirischer Herbst«. As **European capital of culture in 2003** the city put on its best and created a landmark of modern architecture in its new Kunsthaus (Graz Art Museum). That mixture of traditional and avant-garde, Renaissance and modern, of retaining the tried and tested while remaining open to the new is what gives the city its charm.

Second largest city in Austria

The Schlossberg, visible from far and wide, towers over Graz. The capital of Styria and seat of the Styrian provincial government lies on

A bird's-eye view of medieval walls and roofs

the Mur river, which exits a narrow gorge here for the fertile Graz Basin. Graz has made a name for itself not only as a centre of business and trade, but also with its modern architecture. The city's three universities have attracted a total of about 50,000 students.

History		
1128	Graz documented for the first time
1379–1619	Residence of the Leopoldine line of the Habsburgs
1619	Ferdinand II made Holy Roman Emperor – Graz no longer a centre of power.
19th century	Archduke Johann promotes economy and technology – Graz has remained a successful base for industry to the present day.
2003	Graz made European capital of culture.

Excavations have shown that there was settlement here as early as AD 800, but Graz was mentioned in documents for the first time only in 1128. The name comes from the Slavic »Gradec« (»little castle«). Graz became more and more important as a centre of trade. In 1281 the Habsburg King Rudolf I gave the city special privileges; from 1379 to 1619 it was the residence of the Leopoldine line of the Habsburgs. The Old Town (Altstadt) originated mainly during this period and is one of the most beautiful and best preserved in Europe.

Graz was fortified from the 15th to the 17th centuries against the peoples advancing from the south and east – the Turks besieged the city several times but without success. Ferdinand I was elected Holy Roman Emperor in 1619 and united all the Austrian principalities. He moved his court to Vienna and put an end to Graz's role as a centre of power. In the 19th century Archbishop Johann, a popular leader close to the common people, promoted the economic and

Highlights Graz

Old Town
A stroll through the atmospheric Altstadt of Graz shows why it was placed on the World Heritage list.
▶ page 247

Landhaus
One of the most important Renaissance structures in Austria is the seat of the provincial parliament.
▶ page 249

Zeughaus
A treat for those interested in history and old weapons.
▶ page 249

Landesmuseum Joanneum
Well worth seeing with its Alte Galerie (Old Gallery) and other departments.
▶ page 250

Cathedral and mausoleum
The cathedral and mausoleum opposite the castle are among the magnificent buildings in the upper Old Town.
▶ page 251

Uhrturm
Graz's emblem is the clock tower halfway up the Schlossberg.
▶ page 251

Kunsthaus
Opinions are divided on the new art museum – nevertheless it remains a daring, unusual building by the American architect and designer Vito Acconci in an exciting setting.
▶ page 252

technical development of the city and the region. Until today motor and drive unit technology are among the most important economic bases in Graz.

What to See in Graz

The Altstadt with its colourful façades and many charming court-yards has a proud boast: it is the **largest area of Renaissance build-ings in German-speaking Europe!**

** **
Old Town

The tour begins at the Hauptplatz (main square), which has a foun-tain sculpture of Archduke Johann in the centre. The Rathaus (town hall, 1887–93) dominates the southern side of the square. To the north at the turning into Sporgasse note the fascinating Luegg House with an arcade and stucco façade (17th century) – the name comes from »um die Ecke luegen« (»looking around the corner«).

Hauptplatz

The bustling Sackstrasse runs to the northwest; it used to be a cul-de-sac (Sackgasse) and has several beautiful palaces. The Krebsenkel-ler (no. 12) has a beautiful Renaissance courtyard; Palais Herberstein (no. 16) houses the Neue Galerie am Landesmuseum Joanneum in its magnificent Rococo rooms, with 19th and 20th-century paintings (www.neuegalerie.at; opening times: Tue–Sun 10am–6pm).

Sackstrasse

*
◀ Neue Galerie
🕐

Landesmuseum Joanneum ► The Joanneum Provincial Museum of Styria was established by the archduke in 1811 and is Austria's oldest existing museum. The heir to the throne, Franz Ferdinand, was born in 1863 in Palais Khuenburg (no. 18), today the Stadtmuseum. Franz Ferdinand was famously murdered in 1914 in Sarajevo. Palais Attems (no. 17), the city's major Baroque building, stands opposite.

Sporgasse On Sporgasse there are also two beautiful palaces to admire: the Deutschritterordenshaus (House of the Teutonic Knights, no. 22) and Palais Saurau (no. 25), whose gable is decorated with the figure of a sabre-swinging Turk.

Schauspielhaus From Sporgasse, turn right onto Freiheitsplatz (Liberty Square) with the Schauspielhaus (playhouse), built in 1825. Attending a performance is definitely worthwhile, if only to see the theatre's beautiful interior!

Herrengasse Herrengasse is a pedestrian zone and runs southeast from the Hauptplatz; there are many imposing buildings along it, including the »Ge-

Graz Map

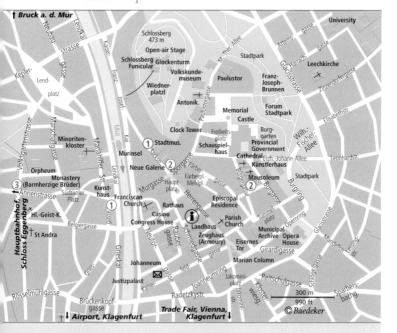

Where to eat
① Café König
② Stainzerbauer

Where to stay
① Grand Hotel Wiesler   ③ Drei Raben
② Erzherzog Johann

maltes Haus« (no. 3), with frescoes from 1742, and the house at no. 13 where Napoleon once stayed.

One of the most important Renaissance buildings in Austria by the Italian master fortress-builder Domenico dell'Allio is the Landhaus (Herrengasse no. 16; 1557–65). It was the seat of the Styrian assembly for centuries and is today the seat of the Styrian provincial parliament. Windows with round arches and a loggia define the façade that faces the Herrengasse. The pretty arcaded courtyard is bordered on two sides by splendid three-storey arcades and is a popular venue for cultural events in the summer.

★ ◄ Landhaus

Next to the Landhaus is the Zeughaus (armoury), which was built in 1642–44, with the world's largest and unique existing collection of weapons from the 16th to 19th centuries, including pieces from the time of the Ottoman wars: harnesses, helmets and dress weapons for 28,000 men! It was an impressive army even by modern standards.

★ ★ ◄ Zeughaus

VISITING GRAZ

INFORMATION
Grazer Tourismus GmbH
Herrengasse 16, A-8010 Graz
Tel. 03 16/8 07 50, fax 80 75 15
www.graztourismus.at

WHERE TO EAT
► **Moderate**
① *Café König*
Sackstrasse 14, A-8010 Graz
Tel. 03 16/83 03 26
The sweet temptations served in the refined atmosphere here are hard to resist.

② *Stainzerbauer*
Bürgergasse 4, A-8010 Graz
Tel. 03 16/8 21 10 60
One of the most popular restaurants in the centre of Graz, Stainzerbauer treats its guests to down-to-earth Styrian cooking.

WHERE TO STAY
► **Luxury**
① *Grand-Hotel Wiesler*
Grieskai 4-8, A-8020 Graz
Tel. 03 16/7 06 60, fax 70 66 76
www.hotelwiesler.com

Luxury hotel rooms with marble baths; comfort and service that leave nothing to be desired. The Art nouveau mosaic in the café is a special attraction.

Baedeker recommendation

② *Erzherzog Johann*
Sackstrasse 3 (Hauptplatz)
A-8010 Graz
Tel. 03 16/81 16 16, fax 81 15 15
www.erzherzog-johann.com
This beautiful old palace in the city centre with spa facilities stands out thanks to its arcades, which have been remodelled in the style of a winter garden.

► **Budget**
③ *Drei Raben*
Annenstrasse 43
A-8020 Graz
Tel. 03 16/71 26 86, fax 7 15 95 96
www.bestwestern.at
A comfortable city hotel with modern furnishings near the city centre, with a tram stop right in front of it.

Stadtpfarrkirche ► The city's Gothic parish church (1519) with a Baroque façade and bell tower has an art-historical treasure: *The Assumption of the Virgin* on the Johann Nepomuk Altar is ascribed to Jacopo Tintoretto. The stained glass window (1953) in the choir depicts the Passion of Christ – Hitler and Mussolini can be seen among those beating Jesus. Diagonally opposite the church is the alleyway named after the Baroque architect Johann Bernhard Fischer von Erlach (1656–1723); his birthplace is located there.

✱
Alte Galerie
Landesmuseum
Joanneum

The major works of art in the Alte Galerie (Old Gallery) of the Landesmuseum Joanneum include the Admont Madonna (around 1310) and the *Judgement of Paris* (around 1515) by Lucas Cranach the Elder (Neutorgasse 45; opening times: April–Oct Tue–Sun 10am–6pm, Nov–March Tue–Sun 10am–5pm). The botany, zoology, mineralogy and geology/palaeontology departments of the Landesmuseum Joanneum are at Raubergasse 10 (opening times: see Alte Galerie).

Stadtpark The Stadtpark (city park) lies behind the neo-Baroque opera house (1898–99); it was created in the late 19th century as an English park on the razed fortifications. In the middle stands the ornate Kaiser Franz Joseph fountain that was created for the world exhibition in Vienna in 1873.

One of the roots of the rich cultural life of Graz, the legendary **Forum Stadtpark**, can be found in the Stadtpark. It is as significant now as it was in the 1960s – artists such as Peter Handke, Barbara Frischmuth, Gerhard Roth and Wolfgang Bauer began their careers here.

On the other side of Glacisstrasse, at the eastern edge of the Stadtpark, stands the oldest church dedicated to the Virgin in Graz (1275–93). The **Leechkirche**, which was remodelled in Gothic style, has a Gothic Madonna in the tympanum over the western door; Graz's oldest painting of (14th century) is in the choir.

> ❗ *Baedeker* TIP
>
> **A key collection**
> Anyone who is open to the unusual should go to Wienerstrasse 10 in the northwest part of Graz, the Museum für Sperrmechanismen (Lock Museum) – a world of locks, keys, boxes and strongboxes. The Hanns Schell Collection unlocks the secrets of hundreds of objects (opening times: Mon–Fri 8am–4pm, Sun 9am–noon).

Castle and
cathedral

The Styrian provincial government now occupies the 15th-century castle, the former residence of Friedrich III and once an extensive site. The original double winding staircase from 1499, a fine architectural feat, has been preserved; it can be seen next to the right-hand passageway to the back courtyard. On Freiheitsplatz the statue of the last Holy Roman Emperor of the German Nation, Franz II, recalls the imperial glory of the past.

✱
Dom ►

South of the castle is the late Gothic cathedral, which was completed in 1462. The main entrance is decorated with a coat of arms in honour of the builder of the cathedral, Emperor Friedrich III. The so-called Landplagenbild (plague picture, 1480) on its south side shows Graz threatened by Turks, the plague and locusts. In the Baroque interior a small triumphal arch separates the wide hall from the choir. There are precious reliquaries (1477) on both sides of the triumphal arch. Of the original Gothic furnishings only the St Christopher fresco near the Kreuzkapelle (Chapel of the Cross) remains.

The Mannerist-Baroque mausoleum (1614–33), built for Emperor Ferdinand II, stands opposite the cathedral. It was designed by Italian architect Pietro de Pomis; J. B. Fischer von Erlach worked on the interior. It consists of the domed Katharinenkapelle (Chapel of St Catherine), and the adjoining mausoleum with the final resting places of Maria of Bavaria, the emperor's mother, and of Ferdinand II himself.

✱
◄ Mausoleum

On Glockenspielplatz two figures, each a hundred years old, dance in traditional costumes out of the gable windows of a large house at 11am, 3pm and 6pm.

Glockenspiel

The small Robert Stolz Museum on Mehlplatz attracts operetta lovers to the birthplace of the composer (entrance Färberplatz 1; closed at present).

◄ Robert-Stolz-Museum

The Schlossberg is more than 120m/390ft high and towers over the Old Town. The ascent by funicular (departs from Kaiser Franz Josef Kai) takes only three minutes; the walk up takes a somewhat strenuous 20–25 minutes.

Schlossberg

Bridging the riverbanks: the shell-shaped Mur Island (see p.252)

Uhrturm ▶

★ ★ The 28m/92ft-high clock tower (1561) halfway up the hill can be seen from great distances. Graz's beloved emblem, along with the Glockenturm it is all that is left of the once mighty fortifications, which were blown up in 1809 just after the Treaty of Vienna between Austria and France. Oddly, the hour hand is longer than the minute hand.

The Glockenturm stands on top of the hill (1588; 35m/115ft high); its bell is affectionately called »Liesl«. In the 19th century the former fortifications were converted into a beautiful park.

Kunsthaus

★ Along with all the many temporary activities, events and buildings created in Graz for its role as **European capital of culture in 2003**, there are at least two that are permanent. Fournier and Cook, the English architects of the futuristic looking Kunsthaus, which stands in exciting contrast to its surroundings on the left bank of the Mur, themselves call it the »friendly alien«. The structure consists of a large bubble that rests on the foundation; the bubble is partly transparent, partly opaque »skin« made of acrylic plates and is in symbiosis with the earliest Austrian wrought-iron construction, the Eisernes Haus (Iron House). Multicultural purposes – readings, theatre, café – are served by the Murinsel, a shell-shaped, floating, steel construction that is connected to the Mur promenades by two arched footbridges and was designed by the New York architect and designer Vito Acconci (▶photo p.251).

Murinsel ▶

Around Graz

Schloss Eggenberg

About 3km/2mi west of Graz stands Schloss Eggenberg (1625–35), a square structure that was influenced by the Spanish Escorial and designed by Pietro de Pomis (▶ Mausoleum). The castle is unique in that it **allegorizes time and the universe**: it has 365 windows, 24 halls with 52 windows and four corner towers that symbolize the four points of the compass. The early Baroque Planet Hall with paintings by the court painter H. A. Weissenkircher is the focal point. Eggenberg Castle is also one of the sites of the collection of the Landesmuseum Joanneum, which is scattered over many locations (guided tours of the castle: early May–late Oct daily at 10am, 11am, noon, 2pm, 3pm and 4pm).

The Schlosspark is a popular place to go for a stroll and has been restored to its original appearance, that of a landscape garden (opening times: daily 8am–7pm).

Luftfahrt-museum

At Graz-Thalerhof Airport the Luftfahrtmuseum (Austrian Aviation Museum) awaits fans of aeroplanes and flying technology (opening times: April–late Oct Sun 10am–6pm).

Schöckl

St Radegund (714m/2356ft; pop. 2100), about 18km/11mi northeast of Graz, is a popular excursion destination with an interesting Kalvarienberg (Calvary monument). From here a cable car goes to the top of **Graz's favourite mountain**, the Schöckl (1445m/4741ft). The famous mathematician and astronomer Johannes Kepler, who taught mathematics in Graz between 1594 and 1600, would visit the mountain to observe nature.

Lurgrotte

25km/15mi north of Graz between Semriach and Peggau lies Lurgrotte. The **largest and most beautiful stalactite cave in Austria**, it is only accessible on a guided tour from the Peggau entrance (temperature is always 9 °C/48 °F, warm clothing recommended; duration of tour approx. 1 hour; opening times: April–Oct 9am–4pm; guided tours: 10am–3pm on the hour; Nov–March by arrangement at tel. 031 27/25 80).

★
Österreichisches Freilichtmuseum

The Österreichisches Freilichtmuseum (Austrian Open-Air Museum) was built in Stübing on the right bank of the Mur in 1970. It is well worth a visit and includes more than 90 different old farmhouses, farmyards, stables, granaries, mills and special buildings such as drying, smoking and charcoal-making huts. The buildings were assembled here from all states in Austria. A tour, for which two to three hours are necessary, gives an excellent impression of the variety of farm crafts in the past. Numerous demonstrations give a practical impression of special skills including making ointments or carving plaques (opening times: mid-March– Oct Tue–Sun 9am–5pm).

Visitors to the open-air museum in Stübing can immerse themselves in farm life

About 40km/24mi west of Graz lies the village of Bärnbach (427m/1401ft; pop. 5000). In 1979 it was decided to remodel the church of St Barbara, which was only built in 1948–52. No less an artist than **Friedensreich Hundertwasser** was commissioned, who adorned the church in 1984–87 with his famous stylistic elements such as golden onion domes and bright colours (www.baernbach.at; opening times: daily 8am–6pm except during church services, guided tours by arrangement at tel. 0 31 42/6 25 81).

◄ Glasmuseum

Behind its prize-winning glass façade the museum in the Stölzle Glas-Center exhibits contemporary art objects and utensils as well as rarities. Many valuable objects document the art of glass-making over the course of time (opening times: April–mid-Dec Mon–Fri 9am–5pm, Sat until 1pm).

Gestüt Piber | At birth **Lipizzaner horses** do not yet have their famous white colouring – they are born with a grey or brown coat. The horses originally came from Spain and have been bred near the town of Lipica (Slovenia) since 1580. The Piber Stud, west of Bärnbach, offers the chance to see the horses up close (tours: mid-March–early Nov Tue–Sun 9am–noon and 1pm–5.30pm).

> ! *Baedeker* TIP
>
> **Dark gold**
>
> The colour takes some getting used to, but the taste is phenomenal! Anyone who wants to buy Styrian pumpkin seed oil should look for »g.g.A.« on the label: »geschützte geografische Angabe« – trademark protection developed by the European Union for typical regional products. Information and addresses from: Verein für Schilcherland-Spezialitäten, Schulgasse 28, A-8530 Deutschlandsberg, www.schilcherland.at.

Schilcher, pressed from the »Blauen-Wildbacher« grape and usually a rosé wine, is one of Styria's culinary emblems. The 50km/30mi-long **»Schilcher route«** runs from Ligist in the north via Stainz and Deutschlandsberg to Eibiswald near the Slovenian border. The high-quality wines can be sampled in local »Buschenschänken« (privately-run local bars). Deutschlandsberg (372m/1220ft; pop. 7600), **the centre for the production of Schilcher wine**, is also the starting point for tours into the Koralpe (Grosser Speik-Kogel, 2141m/7024ft) to the west, a popular hiking and skiing region.

Kitzeck | Around 22km/13mi east of Deutschlandsberg lies Kitzeck (562m/1844ft; pop. 1200), the wine village with the highest elevation in Austria; have a look in the Weinbaumuseum there (opening times: April–Nov Sat and Sun 10am–noon and 2pm–5pm).

★ ★ Grossglockner Road

J 5

Provinces: Salzburg and Carinthia

The Grossglockner Road is one of the greatest and most impressive high mountain roads in Europe. It crosses the Hohe Tauern, Austria's highest mountain massif, and despite more recent north-south routes it still fascinates many drivers and cyclists.

Twists, turns and views | From Bruck im Pinzgau to Heiligenblut at the foot of the Grossglockner, the road not only runs up to the pass and down the other side, it also offers an **unparalleled panoramic view** at elevations of over 2000m/6600ft for over 9km/5mi. Despite the completion of the Felbertauernstrasse and the Tauernautobahn (both open in the winter thanks to tunnels), the Grossglockner Road is still often used. There are many information points and nature trails with informa-

The view of the mountains and the Grossglockner Road is reward in itself

tion on the flora, fauna, geology and much more: on this road you will experience all climatic and vegetation zones from central European Austria to the Arctic!

The Romans had already made use of this alpine pass over the Hochtor, but a road was only laid during the High Middle Ages. Pack horses transported wine, citrus fruits, glass, silk and spices to the north; salt, furs and precious metals to the south. The advent of the car spurred the construction of a panoramic road. A toll road already existed in the north as far as Ferleiten; from the south there was a private road that belonged to the Alpine Association and ran from Heiligenblut to the Glocknerhaus, a guesthouse owned by said association. On 30 August 1930 the first dynamite charges were laid; the road was opened to traffic as soon as 3 August 1935.

◄ Age-old alpine pass

A toll is charged for the 48km/29mi-long road with a maximum gradient of 12%. It is generally open from May to October. For reasons of environmental protection the road is closed from 10pm to 5am. The »Glocknerbus« runs several times a day from Zell am See and Lienz to the Kaiser-Franz-Josefs-Hütte, an alpine shelter.

◄ Tolls, traffic restrictions

✴ ✴ Panoramic Alpine Road

From Bruck, drive about 14km/8mi south to the Wildpark Ferleiten. Among the large animals to be found here are red deer, fallow deer, Sitka deer, moufflon, chamois, ibex, wolf and lynx (opening times: May–Nov daily 8am until dark).

Wildpark Ferleiten ⏱

Just beyond the game park is the tollhouse, and about 5km/3mi further is the Piffkar car park (nature trail) at 1620m/5315ft elevation. The Hochmais car park, (1850m/6070ft) another 2.5km/1.5mi further on, is above the tree line; it offers an unusual view of the eastern flanks of Wiesbachhorn mountain (3564m/11,690ft). Near the slopes

Spectacular views

of Hexenküche (2058m/6752ft) 1.5km/1mi to the south, there are chains that were once used for convicted criminals (17th century) who were forced to walk across the Hochtor to Venice to serve their sentences on galleys. After 3km/2mi comes the Museum Alpine Naturschau with a botanic nature trail (opening times: 9am–5pm).

Side trip to Edelweissspitze
Just south of the museum a 2km/1mi-long side road (gradient up to 14%) leads up to the Edelweissspitze. The car park with a viewing platform (2571m/8435ft) is **the highest point on the Grossglockner Road**. In fair weather there is an unbelievable panoramic view of 37 peaks that are more than 3000m/10,000ft high.

Hochtortunnel
The 311m/1020ft-long Hochtortunnel marks the border between the provinces of Salzburg and Carinthia. When the road was built a small statue of Hercules – the Roman »saint of the pass« – was found. At Tauerneck (2099m/6886ft) the Grossglockner and Zamitzkehren fit on one photograph.

Side trip on Gletscherstrasse
After about 3km/2mi a turning leads along the 9km/5mi-long Gletscherstrasse. At the end of the road, at the Kaiser-Franz-Josefs-Hütte, there is a magnificent view of the highest mountain in Austria, the Grossglockner (3798m/12,460ft), as well as of the Schwerteck, Leiterköpfe, Glocknerwand, Teufelskamp, Romariswandkopf, the three belays of the Burgstall and – behind them – the Firnpyramide on the Johannisberg. Below the viewing platform and accessible via either a steep track or the funicular is the 9km/5mi-long and 1.5km/1mi-wide **Pasterze**, the largest glacier in the Eastern Alps.

● VISITING GROSSGLOCKNER ROAD

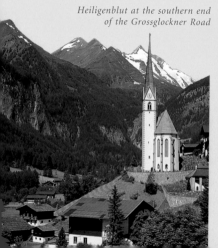

Heiligenblut at the southern end of the Grossglockner Road

INFORMATION

Tourismusverband Heiligenblut
Hof 4, A-9844 Heiligenblut
Tel. 0 48 24/20 01 21, fax 20 01 43
www.heiligenblut.at

WHERE TO STAY

▶ **Mid-range**
Senger
Hof 23, A-9844 Heiligenblut
Tel. 0 48 24/22 15, fax 2 21 59
www.romantic.at
In a beautiful location with a magnificent view of the Grossglockner. Rustic charm with lots of »old« wood in a former farmhouse.

On the Kaiser-Franz-Josefs-Höhe, which was named after its famous visitor, stands the Wilhelm Swarovski Beobachtungswarte (observation station) and a visitor centre. The 2.5km/1.5mi-long Gamsgrubenlehrweg, a nature trail providing insight into the origins and movements of glaciers and information on alpine animals, begins at the Freiwandeck car park (►Hohe Tauern).

Back on the Grossglocknerstrasse, continue 2km/1.2mi after the Guttal turn-off to the Kasereck rest stop and car park (1930m/6332ft). Remains of the original Roman trail can be seen on the mountainside.

Heiligenblut (1301m/4268ft; pop. 1200) is a popular summer recreational and winter sports resort on the steep slopes of the Mölltal valley. The 15th-century Gothic pilgrimage church of St Vinzenz is one of the most popular photo motifs on the Grossglockner Road.

★ Heiligenblut

★ ★ Gurk

M 6

Province: Carinthia   **Elevation:** 662m/2172ft
Population: 1400

Gurk Cathedral of is one of Austria's major Romanesque churches and the goal of many pilgrimages. The church and monastery were founded by Countess Hemma, who after the death of her husband and sons became one of the richest women of her time.

In 1043, Hemma founded the Marienkirche (Church of St Mary) and a convent in the hamlet of Markt Gurk, about 30km/18mi northwest of ►Klagenfurt. In 1072 the archbishop of Salzburg made it an associated diocese. Over the course of some centuries this developed into the present independent diocese of Gurk. In 1788 the cathedral chapter moved to Klagenfurt; the 51 bishops of Gurk had already been living in the Strassburg (►Around Gurk) since the 12th century. The Salvatorian order have used the 17th-century convent building since 1932.

Romanesque gem

★ Cathedral

The cathedral, a columned basilica with a transept and three apses, was built between 1140 and 1220.

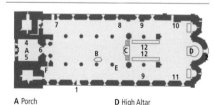

Domkirche Gurk Plan

A Porch
B Pulpit
C Cross Altar
D High Altar
E To Crypt
F To Episcopal Chapel

1 South Doorway, with figure of Christ in tympanum (1150)
2 Lion and Basilisk (1 180)
3 Gothic Wall (1340)
4 Old Testament Scenes (1340)
5 New Testament Scenes (1340)
6 Romanesque Doorway (1200)
7 St Hemma Reliquary (1955)
8 Samson in Tympanum (1200)
9 Reliefs of St Hemma (1500)
10 Fresco of St Christopher (1250)
11 Frescoes of Apocalypse (1380)
12 Choir Stalls (1680)

A modest exterior, but inside one of the most interesting churches in Austria: Gurk Cathedral

In the 12th century the relics of St Hemma were transferred into the crypt under the choir (guided tours: daily 10.30am, 1.30pm and 3pm).

The 41m/134ft-high towers on the west façade of the unadorned cathedral have had onion domes since 1682. The outer vestibule is decorated with wall frescoes and stained glass windows (around 1340); the doorway dates from 1200. The murals on the north wall depict scenes from the Old Testament; the scenes on the south wall are from the New Testament.

The styles of various centuries characterize the building interior. The nave and transept are covered by a net-vaulted ceiling, the choir by stellar vaulting. The **Samson Door** in the left wall is from 1200. The **crossing altar** is a Rococo creation by Georg Raphael Donner (1741), the Baroque **pulpit** a magnificent example of Counter-Reformation endeavour. Six colourfully painted **wooden reliefs** depict the legend of the founder St Hemma. The Saxon master Michael Hönel created the Baroque **high altar** (1626–32); it completely gilded and richly decorated with carved figures (82 angel heads and 72 statues). During Lent it is covered with the largest and oldest Lenten cloth in Carinthia (1458), with 99 scenes. At other times it can only be viewed as part of a guided tour.

✳ Bischofskapelle ▶ The **Bishop's Chapel** is also only open to tours. The room has unique late Romanesque frescoes (around 1220) in the »Zackenstil« (»jagged style«, the transition between Romanesque and Gothic).

✳ Crypt ▶ The famous **crypt** (Hemmagruft) underneath the choir, borne by one hundred columns, is the resting place of the founder Hemma († 1045). It is open to guided tours. She was not canonized until 1938, but pilgrims have visited her resting place since the 12th century.

⏵ GURK

INFORMATION
Gurk-Info
Domplatz 11, A-9342 Gurk
Tel. 0 42 66/81 25, fax 8 12 55,
www.gurk.at

Around Gurk

A few miles east of Gurk, at the foot of the castle, built in 1147 and extended repeatedly, lies the town of Strassburg (650m/2133ft; pop. 2400).

The castle was left in ruins for a long time, but then restored with a wonderful arcaded courtyard and serves as a beautiful setting for cultural events. It houses folklore exhibits as well as a **hunting museum** ⏲ (opening times: May–late Oct daily 10am–5pm).

Hainburg

R 3

Province: Lower Austria   **Elevation:** 161m/528ft
Population: 5650

One of the most important trade routes from the Baltic to the Mediterranean, the Amber Route, ran through Hainburg. Its location in the east of Austria, near the Slovak border, has made Hainburg a historically interesting town from ancient times to the present day.

In the Middle Ages the town on the Danube became a fortification on the eastern border of the Holy Roman Empire. The settlement began below a castle and was given its municipal charter in 1244. It was here in 1252 that Duchess Margarethe of Austria, the last Babenberg, married Margrave Ottokar of Moravia, later the king of Bohemia. Hainburg suffered several destructive raids by the Magyars and the Turks; in 1683 almost all of the town's 8000 residents were killed. The town's fortifications were reinforced in an attempt to meet the challenges created by its dangerous location.

History

Old masters in a dignified setting: the painting collection at Schloss Harrach

▶ VISITING HAINBURG AND CARNUNTUM

INFORMATION

Stadtamt Hainburg
Hauptplatz 23
A-2410 Hainburg
Tel. 0 21 65/6 21 11
Fax 6 24 10, www.hainburg.at

Archäologischer Park Carnuntum
(Freilichtmuseum Petronell,

Amphitheater Bad Deutsch-Alten-
burg, Archäologisches Museum
Carnuntinum)
Hauptstrasse 3
A-2404 Petronell-Carnuntum
Tel. 0 21 63/33 77-0, fax 33 77-5
www.carnuntum.co.at

What to See in Hainburg

Old Town

Hainburg has about 2.5km/1.5mi of well-preserved defensive walls with three gates and 15 towers, which run from the castle to the Danube.

✳

Wiener Tor ▶

More than 20m/66ft high, the 13th-century Wiener Tor (Vienna Gate) at the western entrance to the town is the **largest medieval town gate in Europe**. The lower part consists of 22 layers of rusticated stone, while the bay-like upper part has a pointed-arch structure. The figures on the inner sides of the gate are called Etzel and Krimhilde, who according to the Song of the Nibelungen are supposed to have stayed here. The gate houses several museums, including the city museum. A colony of mouse-eared bats use the underside of the roof in spring to bear their young.

Hainburg's oldest town gate is the massive Ungartor (Hungarian Gate; around 1230) in the east. The Fischertor (Fisherman's Gate) was the site of a Turkish raid in 1683, during which almost the whole population of the town was killed. For this reason the street leading to the Hauptplatz (main square) is called Blutgasse (Blood Alley).

Mariensäule ▶

On the Hauptplatz, take a look at the Marian column (1749), one of the most beautiful Rococo columns in Austria, and the Baroque-style Stadtkirche (town church).

Around Hainburg

Braunsberg

Braunsberg mountain northeast of Hainburg was the site of a Celtic hill fort from the 2nd century BC. A hiking trail leads along the still recognizable earthworks to a reconstructed wood fort with a tower and palisades. The hill fort was intended to protect the Danube crossing on the Amber Route.

15km/9mi to the southwest near Rohrau the **largest private collection of paintings in Austria** can be seen in Schloss Harrach. It includes more than 400 works by Spanish and Italian masters of the 17th and 18th centuries (opening times: Easter to 1 Nov Tue–Sun 10am–5pm).

The small town of Rohrau has set up a museum in the **birthplace of Joseph Haydn** to commemorate the famous composer and his brother Michael (opening times: daily except Mon 10am–4pm).

Rohrau

Northwest of Hainburg lies the Marchfeld, once the site of bitter border battles and today the »granary of Austria«. The Marchfeld castles Schloss Marchegg (hunting museum, Africa museum), Schloss Ort (fishing museum) and Schloss Niederweiden are worth visiting.

Marchfeld

✴ ✴ Petronell-Carnuntum

The towns of Bad Deutsch-Altenburg and Petronell-Carnuntum are about 5km/3mi upriver from Hainburg. More than 8km/5mi of extensive excavations mark one of the area's largest and most strategic Roman settlements of the 1st century AD.

Roman settlement

Carnuntum was mentioned as an important city in the kingdom of Noricum as early as AD 6. Emperor Tiberius's notorious Legion XV Apollinaris built a large military base here between AD 35 and 40. At the junction of the Amber Route and the Limes Route, the base and the civilian settlement developed into the capital of the province of Upper Pannonia with up to 50,000 inhabitants who were Roman citizens.

History

View of the amphitheatre of the old Roman town of Carnuntum

Petronell Carnuntum Archaeological Park

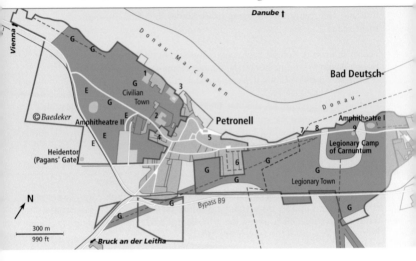

1 Great Bath (»Palace ruins«)
2 Living Quarters of Civilian Town (open-air museum)
3 Schloss Petronell
4 Petronell Round Church
5 Petronell Parish Church
6 Petronell Auxiliary Camp (Fort)
7 Governor's Palace (?)
8 Epona Shrine (?)
9 Porta principalis dextra
10 Site of Baths
11 Temple of Oriental Deities
12 Canabae in Muhlacker
13 Schloss Deutsch-Altenburg
14 Carnuntinum Museum
15 Deutsch Altenburg Parish Church and Ossuary
16 Deutsch Altenburg (Kirchenberg) Tumulus

Ancient settlement area (red: historical monuments and open excavation sites)

Ancient agriculture (planned site)

Built-up area

Protected areas of natural beauty

Roman rulers visited the town regularly. From AD 171 to 173 Carnuntum was the headquarters of Marcus Aurelius; in AD 193 Septimius Severus was declared the new Roman emperor here. Under pressure from the Goths and Huns, the Romans began to withdraw from Carnuntum around AD 400.

Freilichtmuseum Petronell

Extensive remains of the civilian settlement have been excavated at the Petronell Open-Air Museum. The foundations of homes, thermal baths and canals give an impression of what civilian life was like in Carnuntum. It is possible to watch the archaeologists at work on the excavation site. In the reconstructed Temple of Diana, finds on the themes of trade and transport are on display. A Roman building crane and a Roman road have also been reconstructed. The observation tower offers a good view (opening times: late March–mid-Nov daily 9am–5pm, tours Sat, Sun and holidays 10am, 11.30am, 2pm, 3.30pm).

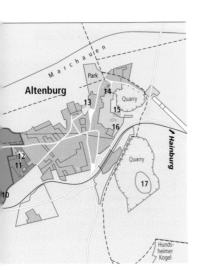

Altenburg

17 Temple of Jupiter Optimus Maximus
Carnuntinus on the Pfaffenburg
(today destroyed)

E Foundations of Main Buildings

G Graves

· — · — · — Ancient Roads

— — — — District Boundaries

About 500m/1650ft from the outdoor museum and easily reached on foot is the large thermal bath, sometimes erroneously referred to as the palace ruins. Floor heating, canals, baths and swimming pools have been exposed.

Large thermal bath

The civilian amphitheatre (Amphitheatre II) lies about 700m/2300ft away and was built in the 2nd century AD with seats for 13,000 spectators. The arena measured 68 x 51m/223 x 167ft. It is used today for theatre productions as part of the **ART Carnuntum summer festival**.

Amphitheatre II

The Heidentor (Pagan Gate) was neither a gate nor was it pagan. According to the latest evidence it was a double triumphal arch built for Emperor Constantius II in 354–361. Two mighty pillars that are connected by an arch have been preserved.

Heidentor

An amphitheatre for 8000 spectators was once in the military base of Carnuntum is in today's Bad Deutsch-Altenburg. The new Emperor Septimius Severus was presumably proclaimed here.
The Spartan life of the strictly organized Roman military legion can be seen in the reconstruction of a field camp (Marschlager, opening times: late March–mid-Nov daily 9am–5pm). There are annual summer camps for children on the theme of »life with the Romans«.

Military city
◄ **Amphitheatre I**

◄ **Field camp**
🕐

More than 3000 objects, only a small proportion of the excavated finds, can be seen in the Museum Carnuntinum, which was built in the style of a Roman country villa and opened in 1904 by Emperor Franz Joseph. Tools, weapons, jewellery, artworks and sacred objects, in particular from the Mithras cult, paint an impressive picture of the population of Carnuntinum (Hauptstrasse 3, www.carnuntum.co.at; opening times: April–mid-Nov daily 10am–5pm).

Museum Carnuntinum

🕐

★ Hall in Tirol

G 5

Province: Tyrol
Population: 13,000

Elevation: 574m/1883ft

Hall in Tirol is one of the most completely preserved medieval towns in Austria. It owes its name and its significance to salt mining, which took place here from the 13th century right up to the 1960s.

Medieval salt town

The salt town of Hall (hall = salt in the Celtic language) lies 10km/6mi east of Innsbruck at the foot of the steep mountains of the Bettelwurfkette (2725m/8941ft). The former spa rooms, which once housed saline baths, now serve as an events centre. The vibrant little town has two large idyllic squares, a wealth of nooks and crannies, picturesque alleys, and beautiful examples of Gothic and Baroque architecture, as well as over 300 historic town houses, many of which line the medieval town square.

What to See in Hall in Tirol

Unterstadt (Lower Town)

The obvious emblem of town is Burg Hasegg (around 1280) with its tower, the twelve-cornered Münzerturm, located to the south of the

 VISITING HALL IN TIROL

INFORMATION

Tourismusverband
Region Hall-Wattens
Wallpachgasse 5
A-6060 Hall in Tirol
Tel. 052 23/455 44
Fax 455 44 20
www.regionhall.at

WHERE TO EAT

▶ **Moderate**

① *Heiligkreuz*
Reimmichlstrasse 18
A-6060 Hall
Tel. 0 52 23/5 71 14
Classy restaurant on the edge of town that serves Austrian home cooking, fish dishes and Tyrolese delicacies such as spinach dumplings.

WHERE TO STAY

▶ **Luxury**

① *Parkhotel Hall*
Thurnfeldgasse 1, A-6060 Hall
Tel. 0 52 23/5 37 69
www.parkhotel-hall.at
All the rooms of this award-winning hotel in a glass tower have either panoramic views or a balcony looking out over the medieval town and the Inntal valley.

▶ **Mid-range**

② *Gartenhotel Maria Theresia*
Reimmichlstrasse 25, A-6060 Hall
Tel. 052 23/563 13,
www.gartenhotel.at
The rooms have modern furnishings and terrific views of the Tyrolese mountains.

Hall in Tirol Map

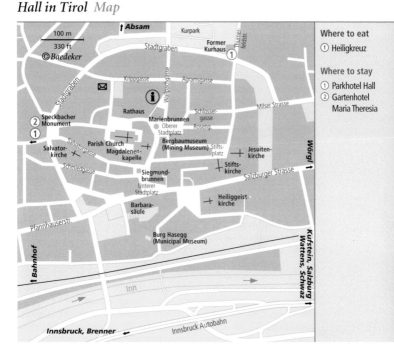

Where to eat
① Heiligkreuz

Where to stay
① Parkhotel Hall
② Gartenhotel Maria Theresia

Unterer Stadtplatz (Lower Town Square) and reached via the Münzertor gate. Coins were minted at the castle from 1486 until 1809, and the newly constructed technical museum, Museum Münze Hall, exhibits minting machines from past centuries. Also situated within the castle grounds is the Stadtmuseum, which documents Hall's cultural and economic life of recent centuries (opening times: April–Oct Tue–Sun 10am–5pm, Nov–March Tue–Sat 10am–5pm).

On the way to the historic centre from the castle, visitors pass the St Barbara Column embellished with reliefs and dedicated to their patron saint by the Brotherhood of Miners in 1486.

Barbara-Säule

The Mining Museum on Fürstengasse, just a short distance below the Oberer Stadtplatz (Upper Town Square), illustrates historic salt-mining techniques in an authentic replica mine from the Halltal valley (guided tours: daily 11.30am; tel. 052 23 / 45 54 40).

Bergbaumuseum

The heart of the elevated and picturesque centre of the Old Town is the Oberer Stadtplatz (Upper Town Square), lined by lovingly restored old houses. This is also where the medieval Rathaus (town hall) stands, in which the main hall with beams dating back to 1451

Oberer Stadtplatz

The magical realm of the Swarovki Kristallwelten glitters and sparkles fabulously

and the mayor's parlour (panelled in 1660) can be viewed. The late Gothic parish church, Pfarrkirche St Nikolaus, stands on its own terrace; it was remodelled in Rococo style in 1752. A chapel in the left front section, the Waldlaufkapelle, contains an interesting collection of relics gathered together by the knight Florian von Waldlauf.

Stiftsplatz The Jesuit Church and the Jesuit College (disbanded in 1773), which is now the regional court, stand on the small Stiftsplatz. Thanks to a faithful restoration the former Jesuit College boasts one of Tyrol's most beautiful Baroque courtyards. The abbey church (Stiftskirche), also known as the Herz Jesu Basilica, with a noteworthy doorway and an arcaded Renaissance courtyard belongs to the nunnery built by the Grand Duchess Magdalena in 1567–69. The nunnery has been closed at various times in its history but has been in service again since 1912.

Speckbacher Memorial A memorial to the Tyrolese freedom fighter Josef Speckbacher (1767–1820), who came from the hamlet of St Martin, stands by the town moat.

Around Hall in Tirol

Absam The old village of Absam (632m/2074ft) lies around 2km/1mi north of Hall and contains a much-visited pilgrimage church. It is also considered Austria's prettiest village for Nativity scenes: between Christmas and Epiphany around 250 cribs are on display here.

Wattens

★ ✳

Swarovski Kristallwelten ▶

Wattens (567m/1860ft; pop. 8300) lies on the southern shore of the Inn river, and has long been a place where glass diamonds and optical instruments have been produced. On the occasion of its company centenary in 1995, the firm Swarovski commissioned the artist **André Heller** to create Kristallwelten (Crystal Worlds) according to his own designs. Together with other artists, Heller came up with a surprising, interesting and spiritual creation on the theme of crystal. He created rooms designed to »amaze and amuse« underneath a grass-covered hill in the shape of an alpine giant's head, set next to a small lake. From the main hall, the exhibition path leads through seven extraordinary chambers, past works in crystal by renowned artists. In the park there is a maze in the shape of a hand. Swarovski Kristall-welten now numbers among Austria's most popular attractions (opening times: Nov–March Mon–Sat 8am–6pm, Sun until 5pm; April, May, Sept and Oct Mon–Sat 8am–6.30pm, Sun until 6pm; June–Aug Mon–Sat 8am–7.30pm, Sun until 7pm; www.kristall welten-swarovski.com).

Schwaz

Situated 11km/7mi further down the Inn river, Schwaz (535m/1755ft; pop. 13,000) owes its importance to silver and copper mining. Around 1500, Schwaz had 20,000 inhabitants, which made it Austria's most populous town after Vienna. The old houses around the market still date from the golden age of mining (1450–1550). Near the bridge by the Stadtplatz (Town Square), the Gothic Fugger-haus with its turrets and courtyard recalls the fact that the Fugger family once owned the most important mining and precious-metal business in Schwaz. The 15th-century parish church is the largest Gothic hall church in Tyrol, and its roof is covered by the so-called Bergsegen

> ! **Baedeker TIP**
>
> **Final frontier**
> From a mineshaft to outer space – no problem in Schwaz: Right next to the show mine a planetarium brings cosmic events close to visitors (Alte Landstraße 15; tel. 05242/72129; www.planetarium.at).

(Mountain Blessing), consisting of 15,000 nailed copper plates. Once upon a time, the northern section of this Baroque church was reserved for the town's citizens while the southern section was for miners. Pay a visit, too, to the Haus der Völker, a museum for art and ethnography on the edge of the town (opening times: daily 9.30am–6pm).

◄ Burg Freundsberg

To the southeast stands Freundsberg Castle (707m/2320ft). The seat of the Freundsberg family was first documented as early as 1100. Jörg von Freundsberg (1473–1528) was one of Emperor Maximilian I's generals, and also the »father of the landsknecht mercenaries«. The castle houses the Heimatmuseum, which focuses on mining and folk art (opening times: mid-April–mid-Oct daily except Thu 10am–5pm). Less than a mile east of Schwaz, the former Sigmund-Erb-Stollen silver mine has been set up as a show mine. On the exciting 90-minute guided tour visitors travel into the mine on the pit railway, passing sinter and dripstone formations (opening times: May–Sept daily 9am–5pm, Oct–April daily 10am–4pm).

◄ Show mine

Kellerjoch

Kellerjoch mountain (2344m/7691ft) rises to the southeast of Schwaz. A cable car reaches as far as Arbeser (1880m/6168ft), after which there is a one-hour ascent to Kellerjoch.

Vomp Schloss Sigmundslust (15th century) is located opposite Schwaz, in Vomp. Tyrol's first printing press was installed here in 1521, and the first Catholic hymn book in the German language was printed here.

★
Schloss Tratzberg Downriver on the Inn, east of Stans, the four-winged Schloss Tratzberg stands on a hillside. It once served as hunting lodge for Emperor Maximilian and also for the Fugger family. A late Gothic construction that was enlarged during the Renaissance, it has an opulent interior and is Tyrol's only palace still containing its original furnishings. A 46m/151ft-long fresco portraying 148 Habsburgs is interesting (guided tours: mid-March–early Nov daily 10am–4pm; there is a special tour for children with the castle ghost).

★ Hallein

K 4

Province: Salzburg   **Elevation:** 460m/1509ft
Population: 20,000

For thousands of years, »white gold« was mined in the ancient Celtic salt town of Hallein. The mining of salt – begun by the Celts on the Dürrnberg in around 700 BC – ensured great wealth for the town.

Hallein is located around 15km/9mi south of Salzburg, where the river Salzach leaves the mountains for the alpine foreland. During the height of the Middle Ages, salt mining established Hallein as the economic powerhouse of the Eastern Alps. Thanks to its location at one of the major north-south trade routes, and also due to the sponsorship of the Salzburg archbishops, the town gained great wealth, still in

▶ VISITING HALLEIN

INFORMATION

Tourismusverband Hallein
Mauttorpromenade
Pernerinsel
A-5400 Hallein
Tel. 062 45/853 94
Fax 853 94 29;
www.hallein.com

Oinochoe, around 400 BC, Keltenmuseum

WHERE TO EAT

▶ **Moderate**
Gasthof Hohlwegwirt
Salzburgerstrasse 84,
A-5400 Hallein-Taxach
Tel. 062 45/82 41 50
This inn is has lots of tradition and serves classic Austrian cuisine. The delicious desserts and extensive wine list are especially recommended (closed Mondays).

evidence today in the beautiful centre of the Old Town. Salt mining, which had taken place for millennia, only came to an end in 1989 with the closure of the Hallein salt works. Today Hallein is the regional capital of Tennengau and an important industrial centre for, among other things, paper, chemical works and machine construction.

What to See in Hallein

Old Town

The pretty alleyways and streets of Hallein's picturesque Old Town (Altstadt) invite visitors to take leisurely strolls past colourful Baroque and Rococo houses, arches and statues. Of the medieval parish church, only the Gothic choir has been preserved. The high altar (1799), with its altar painting by the Andreas Nesselthaler, and the late Gothic baptismal font are worth taking at look at.

At the north side of the parish church lies the grave of the organist and composer Franz Xaver Gruber (1787–1863), who wrote *Silent Night*, the most famous German Christmas carol. His former home, opposite the church, contains the »Stille Nacht« Museum (opening times: Advent Sunday to 6 January daily 11am–5pm, otherwise 3pm–5pm).

✷ Keltenmuseum

The marvellous Keltenmuseum (Celtic Museum), housed in the former offices of the saltworks, vividly illustrates how salt is mined. It contains a unique collection of guild tools, folklore items and numerous excavated finds from local settlements and graves dating back to the Hallstatt and Latène eras (750–15 BC) (Pflegerplatz 5; opening times: daily 9am-5pm; www.keltenmuseum.at).

Around Hallein

Salzwelten Salzburg (Salt World Salzburg) in Bad Dürrnberg is the **world's oldest show mine**. The journey on the pit train, the long miners' slides and the underground rafting trip across the large saltwater lake – actually on German territory – is a memorable ex-

A ride on the underground saltwater lake in the Bad Dürrnberg mine is a special experience

perience for both adults and children. Passing caverns and a glittering rockface, narrow shafts lead to the lake. An atmospheric show of light and sound accompanies the rafting trip (guided tours: mid-March–Oct daily 9am–5pm, Nov–mid-March 10am–3pm). The price includes the tour through the salt mine and admission to the Celtic village and the Celtic Museum in Hallein.

✷ Salzwelten Salzburg

Keltendorf The Celtic Village transports visitors back to an earlier age: a homestead and a knight's grave have been recreated on the site of a former Celtic settlement where Celtic life about 2500 years ago is demonstrated (opening times: as Salzwelten, see p.269).

Adnet marble Although the beauty of Adnet marble was already appreciated by the Romans, it was not seriously mined before the late Gothic period, around 1500. It was used all over the world, from Vienna's Stephansdom to St Peter's in Salzburg, from the plague column on Munich's Marienplatz to the Church of the Holy Sepulchre in Jerusalem. The wonderful red shimmering stone comes from the marble pits near Adnet to the east of Hallein. A marble educational trail, a ball mill and the Marmormuseum (Marble Museum) offer insights into this valuable stone (opening times: March–mid-Sept Tue 9.30am–10am; bookings for groups tel. 062 45/741 49).

Golling waterfall About 12km/8mi south of Hallein lies Golling (480m/1575ft; pop. 3900) and its picturesque waterfall. It cascades down around 75m/246ft in two stages (access subject to entry fee; May–Oct).

Lammeröfen Halfway between Golling and Abtenau to the east, a footpath branches off towards the jagged Lammeröfen, a roughly 1km/0.6mi long, winding gorge that is accessible between May and October.

✶✶ Hallstätter See

L 4

Province: Upper Austria   **Elevation:** 508m/1667ft

Thanks to a wealth of prehistoric sites and a unique natural environment, the region of Hallstatt-Dachstein, with the idyllic Lake Hallstatt, was declared a UNESCO World Cultural and Natural Heritage site in 1997.

Hallstatt era The Hallstätter See, at the northern foot of the mighty Dachstein Massif, is about 9km/6mi long, up to 2km/1mi wide, and around 125m/400ft deep. Enclosed by steep forested mountainsides, its narrow shores are some of the earliest areas of human settlement in Austria.

In around 1846 almost 1000 Celtic graves with valuable funerary gifts were discovered near the Rudolfsturm on the Salzberg mountain. Extensive excavations and numerous archaeological finds have since proven that between 800 and 450 BC the Celts had an economy based on salt

► **HALLSTÄTTER SEE**

INFORMATION
Tourismusbüro Hallstatt
Seestrasse 169 (Kongresszentrum)
A-4830 Hallstatt, tel. 0 61 34/82 08
Fax 83 52; www.hallstatt.net

From the Rudolfsturm on the Salzberg there is a fantastic view of Hallstatt and the lake

mining here. It was also here that archaeologists found the first objects made of iron. This **Celtic golden age**, which also marks the beginning of the Iron Age, has since been named the Hallstatt era after the richest of the excavation sites.

What to See at the Hallstätter See

✳ ✳
Hallstatt

Alexander von Humboldt called Hallstatt **»the most beautiful lakeside spot in the world«** and, with its enchanting houses clinging to the steep hillside like so many swallow's nests, it is easy to agree with him. The most beautiful views are from the lake itself. The salt mining that took place here from prehistoric times gave Hallstatt its name (hall = salt in the Celtic language). In spite of the mines, Hallstatt only been accessible since 1890 by means of a road along the shore of the lake. The car park is at the southern exit of the bypass tunnel.

St Michaels-kapelle

The Gothic parish church is particularly notable for the strange pagoda-like roof of its spire. Inside, the two winged altars (1450, 1515) are worth taking a look at, along with the late Gothic frescoes. The crypt contains ancient skulls, many of them painted, complete with names and dates. Due to lack of space in the tiny cemetery, existing graves were quickly re-used and the bones of »predecessors« were stored in the ossuary.

Museum Hallstatt

The Museum Hallstatt is dedicated to the cultural and historical development of the region, beginning with the grave mounds on the Salzberg and ending with inclusion on the UNESCO World Heritage list (Seestrasse 56; opening times: Jan–March daily except Tue 11am–3pm, April daily 10am–4pm, May–Oct daily 9am-6pm, Nov/Dec Wed–Sun 11am–3pm).

Salzberg From the centre of Hallstatt, the Salzberg (»salt mountain«) is reached either comfortably by cable car or, with more effort, on foot via the track along the saltwater channel. At the funicular's upper station stands a tower, the Rudolfsturm, which has a pleasant viewing terrace and alpine inn. A short footpath leads visitors past the Hallstatt grave mounds to **the world's oldest salt mine** (guided tours: late April–mid-Sept 9.30am–4.30pm, mid–late Sept until 3.30pm, Oct until 3pm; minimum age 4).

Salzwelten Hallstatt ▶ ☾

✳ ✳ Dachstein Caves

Koppenbrüller-höhle Named after the Höhlenbach river that roars out of the Koppenberg, the Koppenbrüller cave is really a giant spring in the mountain. A short distance east of the Hallstätter See and Obertraun, the cave is reached via a short footpath from the edge of Obertraun, passing the Gasthaus Koppenrast (guided tours: May–early Oct 10am–4pm; stout shoes and warm clothing required).

Rare natural spectacle: the Rieseneishöhle

The **Rieseneishöhle and Mammuteishöhle** (»Giant« and »Mammoth« ice caves) both lie at the northern edge of the Dachstein plateau. The cable car south of Obertraun carries visitors to the station halfway up the slope (1350m/4429ft) on the Schönbergalm in just a few minutes. From there, it is a good 15-minute walk to either the Rieseneishöhle or Mammuteishöhle which, aside from the Eisriesenwelt near ▶ Werfen, are the most magnificent caves of the Eastern Alps. Good footwear and warm clothing are essential for any visit, as temperatures hover between 0 °C/32 °F and 3 °C/38 °F (information: tel. 0 61 34/84 00-18 30; www.dachsteinregion.at).

In the Rieseneishöhle, which is one of the largest ice caves in the world, a difference in elevation of 120m/394ft is experienced over a distance of around 800m/875yd, but the sight of the dripstone cave with its frozen waterfalls, ice palaces and ice caverns formed by frozen meltwater that has seeped into the cave is compensation for any hardships endured (guided tours: May 10.15am–2.30pm, June–Aug 9.15am–3pm, Sept–early Nov 10.15am–2.30pm).

☾ The Mammoth cave got its name due to its immense size, being over 50km/30mi long. Tourists have access to about 1km/0.6mi of its length in the form of the **»Cave of the Speleologists«**, where they can learn about the work carried out by cave scientists during research trips that often last several days.

The cable car goes from the station halfway up the mountain to the summit station (2079m/6821ft; Berghaus Krippenstein), from where the Hohen Krippenstein (2109m/6920ft) summit can be reached – a paradise for paragliders. Another cable car takes visitors down to the Gjaidalm (1795m/5889ft), which can also be reached directly from Obertraun.

★ Hoher Krippenstein

★ Hochkönig

K 5

Province: Salzburg

To the southeast, the Steinernes Meer (Sea of Stone) is adjoined by one of the most beautiful mountain chains in the Northern Alps: the Hochkönig. This mighty alpine massif with its rough rock faces is also referred to, more poetically, as the »Mountains of Eternal Snow«.

Popular hiking destination

Crowned by an arched ice field, only a small part of the Hochkönig (2941m/9649ft) summit is visible. Thanks to the open terrain around the mountain, the views from its summit are spectacular and the mountain is a popular holiday destination, even during winter, when its winter wonderland becomes part of the Amadé ski area (► St Johann im Pongau). The Hochkönig can be ascended without great difficulty to the south by setting off from the Arthur-Haus (1503m/4931ft) near Mühlbach, or from ► Werfen via the Ostpreussen hut (1630m/5348ft). The ascent from Hinterthal requires more experi-

VISITING HOCHKÖNIG

INFORMATION

Tourismusverband Maria Alm
Am Gemeinde-Platz 7,
A-5761 Maria Alm
Tel. 0 65 84/78 16, fax 76 00;
www.hochkoenig.at

WANDERBUS

During the summer months, the Wanderbus (hikers' bus) brings hikers to suitable departure points in the mornings and returns to collect tired conquerors of the summits in the afternoons. It travels between Maria Alm, Hintermoos, Hinterthal, Filzensattel, Dienten, Dientner Sattel, Mühlbach and Arthurhaus; the timetable is available from the tourist office in Dienten (tel. 0 64 61/2 63).

WHERE TO STAY

► Budget

Hotel Hochkönig
Dorf 17, A-5652 Dienten
Tel. 0 64 61/2 16, fax 21 68
www.hotel-hochkoenig.at
This friendly, family-run hotel is generous with hiking tips and can arrange for mountain guides. The hotel pool is a good place for guests to recover from their mountaineering escapades.

The foot of Hochkönig near Mühlbach is also great hiking country

ence, passing the mighty Hochseiler (2793m/9164ft). The most difficult climbing route, only suitable for experienced mountaineers, is the »Königsjodler« via the Teufelshörner.

Around Hochkönig

Complete with numerous ski lifts, **Maria Alm** (800m/2625ft; pop. 2200) to the west of the Hochkönig Massif is one of the three settlements that make up the area known as the »Hochkönigs Bergreich«. The slim 84m/276ft spire of its pilgrimage church (1480) is one of Austria's highest church towers and a clear landmark in the countryside.

Dienten The cosy and traditional mountain village of Dienten (1071m/3514ft; pop. 800) is popular with visitors for its exuberant flower displays.

Mühlbach The Bergbaumuseum (Mining Museum) and the former copper mining shaft in Mühlbach (854m/2802ft; pop. 1600) are testimony to the region's mining history that goes back thousands of years (opening times: May–Oct Thu–Sun 2pm–5pm; guided tours of the mine shaft Thu–Sun 4pm). A memorial in the village recalls local Sepp Bradl, who, in the Slovenian resort of Planica in 1936, became the world's first ski jumper to better the magic distance of 100m/109yd.

✶ ✶ Hohe Tauern

H/J/K 5

Provinces: Salzburg, Tyrol (East Tyrol) and Carinthia	**Highest elevations:** Grossglockner (3798m/12,461ft) and Grossvenediger (3674m/12,054ft)

The immense Hohe Tauern mountain range forms a natural border to the south of the province of Salzburg with East Tyrol and Carinthia. The Central Alps display all their glory here once last time before diminishing towards the east.

Fascinating mountain world The main ridge of the Hohe Tauern chain, reaching from Birluckn in the west all the way to Murtörl, offers a magnificent picture of broad snow fields and jagged hanging glaciers, steep, ice-covered crags and dazzling white snow overhangs.

Valleys on the northern slopes ► The short, deep northern valleys, plunging downwards in sheer drops, open into the Salzach valley, which runs parallel to the mountain chain. Wildly foaming glacial rivers (»Achen«) cascade down the valley ledges in **mighty waterfalls** (Krimmler falls, Kesselfall, Gasteiner Fall) or cut deep clefts and gorges (Siegmund-Thun-Klamm, Kitzlochklamm, Liechtensteinklamm).

Relatively long supplementary ridges descend towards the south from the main ridge, towards the Drautal valley and its side valleys: the East Tyrolese Iseltal valley and the Mölltal valley in Carinthia. Unlike most of the barren yet magnificent valleys on the northern side of Salzburg, these valleys are densely populated and well equipped for tourism.

◄ Ridges and valleys on the southern slopes

The western peaks of the Hohe Tauern – the Venedigergruppe – are the largest area covered by glaciers in the Austrian Alps, after the mountains of the Ötztal valley. The main summit is Grossvenediger (3674m/12,054ft), which despite its massive frozen peak surrounded by ice on all sides is not particularly difficult for experienced glacier hikers. The region is a popular destination for numerous mountaineers, and skiers appreciate the wonderful descent via the large Obersulzbachkees glacier.

Venedigergruppe ✳

◄ Grossvenediger

The barely glaciated ridge of the Granatspitzgruppe connects the Venedigergruppe to the Glocknergruppe. The highest peak in this mountain chain is not Granatspitze (3086m/10,125ft), after which the region is named, but Grosse Muntanitz (3232m/10,604ft) to the south.

Granatspitzgruppe

Around 40 glaciers, also known as »Kees« or »Winkel« in Austria, are spread around the different ridges of the Glocknergruppe. The heart of this magnificent mountain area is formed by the approximately 9km/6mi-long **Pasterze, the largest glacier of the Eastern Alps**, and the mighty Grossglockner (3798m/12,461ft), which is easily reached in summer via the ►Grossglockner Road.

The court cartographer Wolfgang Lazius already included the »Glocknerer« as the sole peak in his atlas as early as 1561. The first

Glocknergruppe

✳ ✳

◄ Grossglockner
◄ First ascent

▶ VISITING HOHE TAUERN

NATIONAL PARK ADMINISTRATION

Hohe Tauern/Carinthia
Döllach 1, A-9843 Grosskirchheim
Tel. 048 25/200 49
www.hohetauern.at

Nationalparkzentrum BIOS
A-9822 Mallnitz 36
Tel. 047 84 / 701
www.hohetauern.at

Hohe Tauern/Salzburg
Gerlosstr. 18,
A-5730 Mittersill
Tel. 065 62/408 49 32
www.hohetauern.at

Hohe Tauern/Tyrol
Kirchplatz 2, A-9971 Matrei i. O.
Tel. 048 75/51 12 35
www.hohetauern.at

Station Glocknerblick: hiking with a view of Austria's highest mountain

attempt at an ascent of the Grossglockner in August 1799 was only partially successful due to inclement weather conditions. The expedition ascended the summit of the Kleinglockner – 28m/92ft lower – which, from down in the valley, had appeared to be the higher peak. A year later, on 28 July 1800, the summit of the Grossglockner was conquered, and then by several mountaineers at once.

✳ ✳ Nationalpark Hohe Tauern

Creation of the national park The Hohe Tauern National Park extends into the provinces of Salzburg, Carinthia and Tyrol and, with an area of 1800 sq km/695 sq mi, is one of Europe's largest nature reserves.

The idea of creating a national park in the Eastern Alps is over 80 years old. With the goal of protecting flora and fauna, in 1909 the Munich nature preservation society (Münchner Verein Naturschutzpark) purchased 12 sq km/5 sq mi of mountain pasture and forest on the northern side of the Hohe Tauern, in the Felbertal and Stubachtal valleys. Over the following fifty years, parts of the Glocknergruppe mountains in East Tyrol were added, as well as areas on the Hohen Sonnenblick. The ambition to create a large-scale protected area was not realized for a long time. Only environmental protection legislation of 1970 provided the political impetus that resulted in a contractual agreement between the provinces of Salzburg, Carinthia and Tyrol in 1971. Carinthia declared a 200 sq km/77 sq mi area in the Schobergruppe and Glocknergruppe mountains a national park in 1983. Salzburg followed suit in 1984 by protecting sections of the Pinzgau on the northern slopes of the Hohe Tauern. The national park achieved its present extent in 1991, after the passing of the law on Tyrol national parks.

The protected areas are administered by state and regional authorities and divided into three sections: **secondary areas** (alpine huts and cultivated areas), **central areas** (high mountains and unspoilt natural landscapes) and **areas under special protection**. The construction of new ski lifts, roads and power installations is now forbidden in the entire area covered by the national park. Furthermore, any changes in the natural landscape in the central and specially protected areas is prohibited. The protected region encompasses an area from an elevation of around 1000m/3300ft up to the high alpine regions.

In the high mountains, the growing period for plants is short and they are often exposed to extreme weather conditions. Only dwarf heathers, cushion plants, various lichen and the glacier buttercup can be seen at the highest elevations. Another plant well adapted to this environment is the cembra pine, a slow-growing and hardy variety. Among other animals, chamois, marmot and ermine can be encountered here, as well as black grouse, snow grouse, eagles and bearded vultures.

Flora and fauna

The national parks administration is primarily concerned with introducing the wonderful mountain landscape to visitors in an environmentally friendly manner, and to impart information on the delicate ecosystem of the high Alps. 17 different visitor centres (including Bios-Erlebniswelt Mallnitz, ►Mölltal; WasserWunderWelt, ►Krimml, Waterfalls) provide information on hiking tours, mountain huts, museums and much more. During summer, guided wildlife-watching tours, hikes and trekking tours at all levels of difficulty are offered, and brochures assist those who wish to explore the high mountains independently. To relieve the region of car traffic, bus services are in operation and there are also »national park taxis« operating in the valleys closed to private vehicles.

Objectives of the national park

★ Höllental

P 4

Province: Lower Austria

The romantic gorge along the Schwarza river, around 20km/13mi southwest of Wiener Neustadt, stretches between Vienna's local mountain ranges of Rax and Schneeberg.

The cliffs along the roughly 14km/9mi route are often so close together that there is hardly room for settlements or for the road that must constantly switch between the riverbanks.

Romantic gorge

Vienna water supplies ▶ **Vienna's first alpine spring water pipe** runs parallel to the road. More details can be discovered on the relevant hiking path and at the Wasserleitungsmuseum Kaiserbrunn in Reichenau an der Rax, where the provision of drinking water and Vienna's water requirements are documented (opening times: May–Oct Sun and holidays 10am–5pm and for ten people or more by arrangement at tel. 0 26 66/525 48).

Around the Höllental

Wiener Hausberge ✳ Schneeberg ▶ The Schneeberg, forming the northeastern end of the Höllental, is Lower Austria's highest mountain and the nearest one to Vienna. During summer, it is a popular hiking region, a stone's throw from the capital. In winter it is a favoured snow and skiing paradise. From Puchberg, it is just a few minutes by double chairlift to the mountain station, at a height of 1248m/4094ft, and a network of extensive hiking routes. Fans of narrow gauge railways can take the old-time Schneebergbahn, which brings visitors to the mountain station of Hochschneeberg (1796m/5893ft) in a leisurely trip taking an hour and a half. A mildly challenging footpath leads to the summit of Klosterwappen (2075m/6808ft). On clear days the views from nearby Kaiserstein (2061m/6762ft) extend all the way to Vienna and the Neusiedler See.

Raxalpe ▶ At Hirschwang by the entrance to the Höllental, the Raxseilbahn (opened back in 1926) provides year-round transport to the Raxalpe cable car station at an elevation of 1545m/5069ft. A good network of hiking routes and mountain huts can be found in the over 30 sq km/12 sq mi area of alpine pasture at elevations ranging between 1500m/4921ft and 2000m/6562ft. Near the Otto Haus, an alpine garden displays 200 of the native plant species that grow here. The highest summit of this mountain plateau, which is also suitable for winter sports, is Heukuppe (2007m/6585ft) on its western edge.

▶ VISITING HÖLLENTAL

INFORMATION
Tourismusbüro Reichenau/Rax
Schlossplatz 9, A-2651 Reichenau
Tel. 0 26 66/5 28 65
www.tiscover.at/reichenau.noe

WHERE TO STAY
▶ **Mid-range**
Seminar-Park-Hotel Hirschwang
Hirschwang 11,
A-2651 Reichenau/Rax
Tel. 0 26 66/5 81 10, fax 5 81 10 77
www.seminarparkhotel.at

Bright, welcoming rooms, as well as restaurants, spa facilities and a gym.

▶ **Budget**
Gasthof Flackl
Hinterleiten 12,
A-2651 Reichenau/Rax
Tel. 0 26 66/5 22 91, www.flackl.at
This hotel not only offers friendly accommodation, but also exhibits over 700 pictures by local and international artists.

Imst

E 5

Province: Tyrol
Population: 8500

Elevation: 828m/2717ft

The old town of Imst lies at the beginning of the Gurgltal on a terrace overlooking the river Inn. It is also located at a major road junction between Innsbruck and Landeck and is a departure point for tours into the Ötztal and Pitztal valleys.

Imst was first documented as »Oppidum Humiste« (= bubbling spring) in 763, and was once famous for its bird traders who travelled throughout Europe with their cages and canaries. The village also became famous in 1949, when the social educationalist Hermann Gmeiner founded the first SOS Children's Village, according to his theory »Small steps, great hope«.

First SOS Children's Village

What to See in Imst

Along with its mansions, churches and chapels, Imst is noteworthy for its numerous fountains. The newly opened Museum im Ballhaus is in a 16th-century building that was once used as a store for textiles. Today, the newly adapted rooms exhibit art and objects that are relevant to local history. Special exhibitions are presented on the top floor (opening times: Tue, Thu and Fri 2pm–6pm, Sat 9am–noon). Also of interest here is the »Schemenlauf«, an alpine carnival procession that is held every three years. The late Gothic parish church, Pfarrkirche Mariä Himmelfahrt, boasts the highest church spire in Tyrol (86m/282ft) – it is the fourth-highest in Austria. Remains of frescoes from around 1500 have survived on the exterior wall, including a depiction of St Christopher.

Baroque splendour in the Stams abbey church

Around Imst

A chairlift to the west of Imst travels up to the attractive Untermarkter Alm (food and drink available) and continues up the Alpjoch (2050m/6726ft). The region offers good opportunities for ski-

Rosengartenschlucht

ing, cross-country skiing, and tobogganing. A hike through the romantic Rosengartenschlucht (Rose Garden Gorge), which contains a wealth of rocks and minerals, is also highly recommended.

Nassereith   Around 13km/8mi northeast of Imst lies Nassereith (843m/2766ft; pop. 2200), which is popular as a summer and winter sports area and a resort for recreation and relaxation. Here, too, a colourful masked procession known as the »Schellerlaufen« is held every three years on the last Sunday before Carnival Sunday (Faschingssonntag). To the north, the Fernpass (1209m/3,967ft) leads to Ehrwald, from where the road continues on to Garmisch.

Telfs   To the east, a relatively well-maintained panoramic route traverses the Mieminger Plateau towards Telfs (630m/2067ft); pop. 14,300), which is renowned for another carnival tradition, the »Schleicherlaufen«, held every five years.

Stams   Stams (671m/2201ft; pop. 1300) lies around 25km/16mi downriver on the Inn, on slightly elevated ground on the southern river bank. Stift Stams, the large Cistercian abbey, is among the most beautiful Baroque buildings in Austria. Its foundation was sponsored by Elisabeth von Bayern in 1273, in memory of her son. She was the mother of the last Hohenstaufen, Konradin, who was executed in Naples in 1268. Originally from the 13th century, and remodelled in the 17th and 18th century, the abbey church with its striking spires is the **largest Baroque church in Tyrol**, and it also contains the family vault for the Tyrolese princes. The princes' vault was sunk into the floor in 1670 and is adorned by twelve gold-leaf wooden statues of the princes and princesses laid to rest here; it is definitely worth viewing, as are the high altar of 1613, a masterpiece of Baroque carving with its 84 figures, the chancel from around 1740, and the 18th-century cast iron choir screen. The Heiligblutkapelle (Chapel of the Holy Blood; 1716) adjoining to the south contains a fine filigree rose screen.
Skigymnasium ▶   Stams is also known for its famous ski college (built in 1977–82), which has produced many famous Austrian stars.

▶ VISITING IMST

INFORMATION
Tourismusverband Imst – Gurgltal
Joannesplatz 4
A-6460 Imst
Tel. 0 54 12/69 100, fax 69 108;
www.imst.at

WHERE TO EAT
▶ **Inexpensive**
Gasthof Sonne
Johannesplatz 4, A-6460 Imst
Tel. 0 54 12/6 61 29
This inn has a beer garden and serves typical Tyrolese meals in the cosy restaurant.

✶ Innsbruck

F 5

Province: Tyrol
Population: 119,000

Elevation: 575m/1885ft

Innsbruck's particular charm lies in the juxtaposition of natural and cultural attractions: on the one hand, the city offers the pleasures of urban culture in an alpine setting; on the other hand, the Tyrolese capital serves as a good base for sporting activities, such as mountaineering, hiking and skiing.

Tyrol's capital, Innsbruck lies in »a wonderful wide and fertile valley, between high cliffs and mountains« (Goethe). The long, broad valley of the Inn is also at a crossroads of major transport routes from Germany to Italy and from Vienna to Switzerland. Views towards the mountains, which rise beyond the graceful central highland terraces, can be enjoyed all over the city: to the north lie the summits of the Karwendel chain; to the south, beyond the forested ridges of the Bergisel, are Mount Saile (2403m/7884ft) and the peaks around Mount Serles (2718m/8918ft); and to the southeast, beyond the peaks of the Lanser Köpfen, lies the rounded summit of the popular ski area around Mount Patscherkofel (2247m/7372ft). The historic city centre enchants visitors with the nooks and crannies of its narrow medieval alleys and tall, late Gothic houses that frequently display beautiful turrets and doorways. In contrast, the outer areas, especially to the east and north, are modern suburbs. The sports facili-

City in the mountains

◄ *Multifaceted city*

It is not merely the lovely location on the Inn at the foot of the Karwendel, it is also the cityscape and a lively cultural scene that make Innsbruck so attractive

Stately town houses in Rococo style line Herzog-Friedrich-Strasse

ties constructed on the occasions of the **Winter Olympic Games of 1964 and 1976** are still used as venues for national and international championships. Innsbruck is a university town and a bishopric, as well as an industrial centre where regular trade fairs are held. Thanks to a location that protects it from the north winds, the city enjoys a relatively mild climate. The regional capital is the most important tourist centre in Tyrol.

History

15 BC	Roman fort of Veldidena is built
1180	Innsbruck is founded
1239	Innsbruck granted municipal rights
1420–1665	Habsburg royal seat
1669	University founded by Emperor Leopold I
1806	Tyrol falls to Bavaria.
1814–15	Congress of Vienna transfers Innsbruck back to Austria

Bronze Age finds indicate the existence of an early settlement, and the Illyrians and Romans also left traces. Shortly after the birth of Christ, the small Roman fort of Veldidena was founded, the origin of the name of the present-day district of Wilten. The foundations of the fort are now covered by a 12th-century Premonstratensian monastery. The foundation of a market by the bridge (»Innspruke«) occurred in 1180, instigated by the counts of Andechs, who were from the Bavarian Ammersee region. Innsbruck was officially granted municipal status in 1239, and enclosed by a wall and bastions. The town fell to a minor branch of the Habsburg family in 1363, and served as their royal seat from 1420 to 1665.

The city became an administrative centre and thus a focus for art and culture under Emperor Maximilian I (1490–1519; ▶ Famous People). For a time, **Maximilian's favourite city** was the main royal seat of the German kings. The Tyrolese branch of the Habsburg fam-

Highlights Innsbruck

Goldenes Dachl
The city's most popular sight consists of almost 3000 gilded copper plates. The alcove balcony was once a lofty royal box.
▶ page 285

Dom
The early 18th-century cathedral was not restored until 1950. The interior contains many treasures, from altars to ceiling frescoes.
▶ page 287

Hofkirche
There are impressive tombs in the Court Church: in addition to the one for the freedom fighter Andreas Hofer, the nave contains the important (though empty) tomb of Maximilian I.
▶ page 289

Tiroler Volkskunstmuseum
Model Tyrolese farmsteads complete with interiors and a Christmas crib collection can be seen in the Tyrolese Folk Art Museum.
▶ page 291

Tiroler Landesmuseum Ferdinandeum
Exhibits include collections on the history and art of Tyrol, a gallery of Dutch and Flemish masters, as well as original sculptures from the Goldenes Dachl.
▶ page 291

Tiroler Landeskundliches Museum
Exhibits in the Regional Museum illustrate the region's economy, craftwork and landscapes, as well as the history of the struggle for Tyrolese liberation.
▶ page 291

Bergisel
Superb sports facilities, of which the ski jump is a particular highlight. Only for those a good head for heights.
▶ page 292

Wiltener Pfarrkirche
Wilten parish church is one of the most beautiful Rococo churches of northern Tyrol, with ceiling frescoes and stucco work.
▶ page 294

ily died out in 1665, which also signified the end of Innsbruck's status as royal residence. Emperor Leopold I founded the university four years later. In 1703, Bavarian attempts to capture Innsbruck and the whole of Tyrol were unsuccessful; however, thanks to pressure from Napoleon, Tyrol came under Bavarian control in 1806. Despite a successful liberation war and victorious battles on the Bergisel in 1809 led by Andreas Hofer, Tyrol was returned to Bavaria once more. It was only the Congress of Vienna of 1814–15 that passed Tyrol back to Austria. Innsbruck became the capital of Tyrol in the place of Merano in 1849 and, after the completion of the Brenner Pass railway route in 1867, Innsbruck's era of industrialization began.

What to See in Innsbruck

Innsbruck's Old Town (Altstadt) **is among the best preserved medieval city centres in Austria**. A key example of secular architecture is   ✶ ✶

Old Town

the Inn-Salzach-Stadthaus, whose elongated foundations support an air well between the front house and the back house, and whose narrow, four to five-storey façades have beautiful doorways and cornices. The contoured roofs have their origin in a fire regulation de-

Innsbruck Map

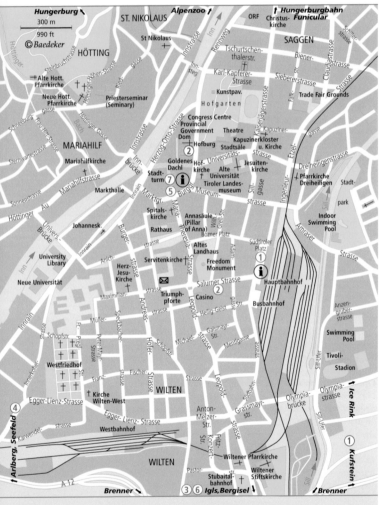

creed by Maximilian I. Notable features are the single-storey arcades that run along both sides of Herzog-Friedrich-Strasse. Innsbruck's former significance as a royal seat can be seen in its wealth of Renaissance, Baroque and Rococo buildings.

The city's most popular sight, the famous **Goldenes Dachl**, is reached from the south via Herzog-Friedrich-Strasse, which is lined by imposing town houses. In honour of Emperor Maximilian I's wedding with Bianca Maria Sforza, the late Gothic alcove balcony was covered by a roof made of 2657 gilded copper plates between 1494 and 1496, and served the royal court as a lofty royal box during folk festivals on the Hauptplatz (main square). It was built onto the Fürstenburg, which was created by the 1420 amalgamation of two town houses to make a royal residence. Originally, the balcony made up the entire top half of the building. The upper storey was only added

The famous Goldenes Dachl

in the 19th century. Coats of arms decorate the lower sections of the balcony and figural sculpture embellishes the upper storey, which was given an open platform. The Goldenes Dachl is intended to be symbolic of Maximilian I's vision that he was leading his empire into a »Golden Age«.

The Museum Goldenes Dachl (formerly the Maximilianeum), a monument to Emperor Maximilian I, has been set up in the house. The exhibits include a document bearing Maximilian's signature, a portrait of the emperor from 1507–08 by court painter Bernhard Strigel, a suit of armour and a cast iron stove plate with hunting scenes (opening times: May–Sept daily 10am–5pm, Oct and Dec–April Tue–Sun 10am–5pm).

◄ Museum Goldenes Dachl

🕐

Opposite the Goldenes Dachl, the beautiful Helbinghaus catches the eye. The building was remodelled in Baroque style in 1730, having originally been a late Gothic construction. The stucco façade with angels, acanthus leaves and additional decorative ornaments is noteworthy.

Helblinghaus

At the western end of Herzog-Friedrich-Strasse, the so-called **Ottoburg** stands on the banks of the Inn. The **residential tower** from 1495 has four oriels, and the tavern inside has a long history. In front of the building stands a bronze sculpture, made in 1909 by Christian Platter, depicting the Tyrolese freedom fighters and bearing the inscription »Anno 1809«.

Ottoburg

▶ VISITING INNSBRUCK

INFORMATION

Innsbruck Tourismus
Burggraben 3, A-6021 Innsbruck
Tel. 05 12/5 98 50, Fax 59 85 07;
www.innsbruck.info

INNSBRUCK CARD

Available from the tourism association, the Innsbruck Card (valid 24 hours, 48 hours or 72 hours) entitles holders to reduced-price admission to museums and free public transport.

SHOPPING

The area around the city hall, as well as Maria-Theresien-Strasse, Museumstrasse, Marktgraben, Burggraben and Bozener Platz all make for pleasant strolling.

WHERE TO EAT

▶ Expensive
① *Gasthof Kapeller*
Philippine-Welser-Strasse 96
A-6020 Innsbruck (Ambras)
Tel. 05 12/34 31 01
The good location and friendly service, quality cooking and a fine wine list attract diners.

▶ Moderate
② *Stiftskeller*
Burggraben 31
A-6020 Innsbruck
Tel. 05 12/58 34 90
This restaurant, housed in the Hofburg, serves tasty, plain cooking in an old-world atmosphere.

WHERE TO STAY

▶ Luxury
① *Grand Hotel Europa*
Südtiroler Platz 2, A-6020 Innsbruck
Tel. 05 12/59 31
www.grandhoteleuropa.at
Innsbruck's top hotel is opposite the

railway station and was once a regular haunt of the aristocracy. Today, it is the stronghold of both local tourism and Innsbruck society.

② *Hilton Innsbruck*
Salurner Strasse 15
A-6020 Innsbruck
Tel. 05 12/5 93 50, fax 5 93 52 20
www.hilton.de/innsbruck
This luxurious modern hotel, just a few steps from the Old Town and the Congress Centre, also houses a casino.

③ *Schlosshotel*
Viller Steig 2
A-6080 Igls
Tel. 05 12/37 72 17, fax 3 77 21 71 98
www.schlosshotel-igls.com
Every room contains antique furniture, pictures and art objects. The restaurant serves top-class cuisine.

④ *Jagdschloss Kühtai*
A-6183 Kühtai/Tirol
Tel. 0 52 39/52 01, fax 52 81
www.jagdschloss.at
The Kühtai hunting lodge with its stylishly furnished rooms and romantic medieval atmosphere is closed during summer.

Baedeker recommendation

▶ Mid-range
⑤ *Goldener Adler*
Herzog-Friedrich-Strasse 6
A-6020 Innsbruck
Tel. 05 12/57 11 11, fax 58 44 09
www.bestwestern.at
This hotel has been serving guests for over 600 years. Both Goethe and Mozart stayed the night. The stylish restaurant serves, among other things, Tyrolese specialities.

▶ Budget

⑥ Hotel Sonnenhof
Fernkreuzweg 16, A-6080 Igls
Tel. 05 12/37 73 79
Fax 377 37 95
www.sonnenhof-igls.at
This friendly, family-run hotel on the edge of town offers comfortable rooms with balconies, a gym, a solarium and a sauna.

⑦ Weisses Kreuz
Herzog-Friedrich-Strasse 31
A-6020 Innsbruck
Tel. 05 12/59 47 90, fax 5 94 79 90
www.weisseskreuz.at
The 13-year-old Mozart lived in this historic inn in the centre of the Old Town during his first journey to Italy. The restaurant serves alpine specialities.

The 57m/187ft-high **Stadtturm**, originally built in the 14th century as a watchtower along with the adjacent Alte Rathaus (Old City Hall), stands on the east side of Herzog-Friedrich-Strasse. It was later remodelled. At a height of 33m/108ft, the tower's walkway offers panoramic views.

Kohleggerhaus

The arcades of the Kohleggerhaus at Herzog-Friedrich-Strasse 35 (entrance by McDonalds) – once the home of the city judge Walter Zeller the Elder – have a heraldic vault fresco from 1495–96 decorated with the Quaternion Eagle. It bears the emblems of the ranks and countries of the Holy Roman Empire. This is the oldest public representation of the old imperial symbol.

Dom

The new Baroque cathedral, as we know it today, was originally built in 1717–24 and was reconstructed only in 1950 after heavy damage during the Second World War. Johann Jakob Herkomer (†1717) designed the original, but was replaced during the building phase by Johann Georg Fischer, Herkomer's son-in-law and pupil. In 1904, the former parish church of St James was raised to the status of a deanery and, in 1964, to a cathedral church. The exterior is characterized by an imposing dual tower frontage and the high dome of the choir. The interior impresses with its ceiling fresco (*Apotheosis of St James*), as well as with stucco work by the brothers Cosmas Damian Asam and Egid Quirin Asam. The Baroque marble altars were constructed in 1726–1732. The church's greatest treasure is

Innsbruck *Dom*

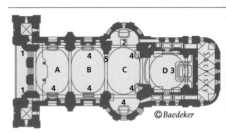

©Baedeker

A St James interceding for the church, empire, country and city
B St James begging for suffering humanity
C St James's recommendation of the adoration of the Madonna
D St James leading the Spanish against the Saracens

1 Patron Saint of Brixen Diocese
2 Monument of Archduke Maximilian III
3 High Altar
4 Side Altars
5 Pulpit

next to the high altar: the ***Maria hilf*** miraculous painting, created by Lucas Cranach the Elder (around 1530). The richly sculpted pulpit dates from 1725. The northern aisle contains an opulent tomb for Archduke Maximilian III (1558–1618), who was Grand Master of the Teutonic Knights. His tomb, designed by Hubert Gerhart, is a masterpiece of bronze sculpture produced during the German late Renaissance.

Maria-Theresien-Strasse

✱ Imposing old houses can be seen along Maria-Theresien-Strasse. The view of the 2300m/7546ft-high ridge of the northern mountain chain beyond is a great photo opportunity. The northern section of the street has been opened up into a square.

Annasäule ▶ One of Innsbruck's emblems, the St Anne's Column, stands in front of the Neues Rathaus (New City Hall). It was commissioned in 1706 to celebrate the withdrawal of Bavarian troops on St Anne's Day (26 July) in 1703. The Virgin Mary occupies the top of the column, while St Anne stands at the base alongside other saints including St George, Tyrol's patron saint.

Altes Landhaus ▶ The Altes Landhaus on the corner of Meraner Strasse was built by Georg Anton Gumpp in 1725–28. The monumental Baroque structure with an elaborate façade and intricate carved doors today serves as the home of the provincial government. The assembly hall is decorated with frescoes by Cosmas Damian Asam. The square courtyard is adjoined by the Landhaus chapel, whose façade gable is embellished by a coat of arms bearing the Tyrolese eagle and carried by angels. Diagonally opposite the Altes Landhaus stands the **Servitenkirche** (Servite Church), built in 1615 and later remodelled. The Holy Trinity fresco in the niche along the outside wall is noteworthy, and there are also sumptuously carved 17th-century benches in the interior.

? DID YOU KNOW …?

■ … that Duke Siegmund had the Burgriesenhaus (Castle Giant's House) at Hofgasse 12 built for his enormous bodyguard Niklas Haidl, who stood 2.22m/7ft 3in tall!

Triumphpforte ▶ The southern end of Maria-Theresien-Strasse is completed by the Triumphpforte (Triumphal Gate). Maria Theresia (▶Famous People) had it constructed in 1765, at what was the edge of the town, on the occasion of the marriage of her son Leopold, later Emperor Leopold II, to the Spanish Infanta Maria Ludovica. The stone blocks used came from the demolished Georgtor. The marble reliefs on the south side added in 1774 depict the wedding, while the north side shows the unexpected death of Emperor Franz I – the groom's father – during the festivities.

Hofburg Originally built in the 15th and 16th centuries, the former Hofburg (Imperial Palace) was remodelled in Baroque and Rococo style according to instructions by Maria Theresia in the 18th century, and now displays the style of late Viennese Rococo. On view are ceremonial rooms with stucco work and ceiling frescoes. The Riesensaal (Giant Hall), a festival hall clad in polished marble and white gold, with portraits of the imperial family and three large ceiling frescoes (1775) created by Franz Anton Maulpertsch, is especially worth seeing. Occupying about twelve rooms in the Hofburg, an exhibition by the Alpenverein-Museum (Alpine Association Museum) illustrates the history of mountaineering. The museum owns the world's oldest mountain relief, commissioned by Emperor Maximilian I around 1500, and portraying the Wetterstein mountain range (opening times for Hofburg and Alpenverein-Museum: daily 9am–5pm, admission until 4.30pm).

On the ground floor a branch of Vienna's famous Hotel Sacher is an inviting place to stop.

The Hofkirche (Imperial Church) was built in late Gothic style in 1553–63. The tomb of Andreas Hofer (►Famous People), who was buried here in 1823, is by the main entrance. Next to him lie his comrades in arms, Josef Speckbacher (1767–1820) and Joachim Haspinger (1776–1858).

✳ Hofkirche

The empty tomb of Emperor Maximilian I († 1519, buried in Wiener Neustadt), the most outstanding example of German Renaissance sculpture, is located in the nave of the church. The concept for this

✳ ✳ ◄ Tomb of Maximilian I

Innsbruck's loveliest view: the Anna Column with the Karwendel as backdrop

The Schwarzen Mander guard the empty tomb of Maximilian

work was that it should represent the status of the Holy Roman Empire. The main focus is the black marble sarcophagus with a bronze figure of the emperor (1584; Alexander Colin). The cast iron railing is the work of the Prague craftsman G. Schmiedhammer (1573). The sides of the tomb are panelled with 24 marble reliefs that illustrate events from the emperor's life. Gathered around the sarcophagus are 28 larger than lifesize bronze statues (1508–50) – the deceased's ancestors and contemporaries. The famous statues known as the »Schwarze Mander« (black men) represent 20 men and eight women whom the emperor considered worthy of accompanying him in death. Created in the Nuremberg workshop of Peter Vischer the Elder in around 1513, they include for example statues of the legendary King Arthur and the Visigoth King Theoderic, both of which were based on drawings by Albrecht Dürer. The sculpture of Elisabeth of Austria is ascribed to Veit Stoss and Hans Leinberger. In the northern gallery of the church stand 23 bronze statuettes that belong to the emperor's tomb: they are of saints from the Habsburg family. In addition, there are 20 bronze busts of Roman emperors.

The Ebert Organ (1555–61) is the largest surviving Renaissance organ in an almost intact state in Austria, and is the oldest example of its kind north of the Alps.

Silberne Kapelle Above the Franziskanerbogen (Franciscan Arch) that crosses the moat from Rennweg stands the Silver Chapel, built in 1578–87 as a funerary chapel for Archduke Ferdinand II (access via the Hofkirche). It takes its name from the silver Madonna and related reliefs around the altar. The wall niches contain the tombs for the archduke († 1595) and his wife Philippine Welser († 1580), which were both created by Alexander Colin.

Hofgarten The Stadtsäle (city halls) with the Landestheater (the regional theatre, built in 1846) lie on the eastern side of Rennweg. To the north lie the Court Gardens with their art and concert pavilions. The park, created in around 1400, was originally used as an orchard and vegetable garden for the court. East of the Hofgarten lies the exhibition centre, the venue for the Innsbruck autumn trade fair (Innsbrucker Herbstmesse).

At nos. 3-4, on the western side of the Rennweg, stands the congress centre, Tiroler Kongresszentrum Innsbruck. The millennium memorial bridge (Jahrtausendbrücke – Weg der Zeiten) was built at the entrance in 2000. The historical core of this building is the Dogana, a 13m/43ft-high 16th-century columned hall with an area of 2000 sq m/21,528 sq ft. Connected to the Hofburg by a passage towards the end of the Middle Ages, it once served as the Habsburgs' venue for balls, theatre performances and horse riding.

Kongresszentrum

The Jesuit College built in 1562 and restored in 1673, which became the Old University, and the Alte Universitätsbibliothek (Old University Library), remodelled in 1722, are both on Universitätsstrasse. In between the two stands the Jesuit Church, with its cruciform central building and 60m/197ft-high dome (1627–40). Opposite stands the city's most modern university building, which was built for the faculty of social and economic sciences in 1999, and won an architectural prize that same year.

Alte Universität

The Capuchin monastery founded in 1593 stands on Kaiserjägerstrasse. The most important sight, a picture of the Virgin Mary by Lucas Cranach the Elder (1528), is found in a chapel to the left.

Kapuzinerkloster

The Tyrolese Folk Art Museum at Universitätsstrasse 2 houses over 20 model Tyrolese farmsteads, including stone houses with oriels from the Upper Inntal valley and wooden houses from the Zillertal valley; also on view are folk costumes, rural furniture and tools from various regions of Tyrol, as well as glass, ceramics, weaving stools, textiles and cast iron craftwork. An exhibition of Christmas cribs dating from the 18th century to the modern day can also be seen.
As the museum is being remodelled at the present time, with plans for a new entry area with a café and a museum shop, it will remain closed until summer 2009.

✷
Tiroler Volkskunstmuseum

Pay a visit, too, to the Ferdinandeum on Museumsstrasse, with its collections on the history and art of Tyrol as well as a gallery of Dutch and Flemish masters. The original sculptures from the Goldenes Dachl are also exhibited here (opening times: Tue–Sun 9am–6pm).

✷
Tiroler Landesmuseum Ferdinandeum

A museum for regional studies lies at the eastern edge of the city centre, by the Sill river, housed in the old armoury (Zeughaus). The collections include fossils up to 240 million years old, exhibits on mineralogy, mining, cartography, hunting and technology, as well as on flood and avalanche prevention. There are collections of coins,

✷
Museum im Zeughaus

BERGISEL SKI JUMP

✳ ✳ Situated at the southern edge of Innsbruck, the Bergisel is historic ground: during the Tyrolean wars of liberation of 1809, with Andreas Hofer leading the freedom fighters, the hotly contested front ran along here. The first ski jump took place on the Bergisel hill in 1927. Even the pope himself paid the Bergisel a visit in 1988, giving a Mass in the stadium. In 2001 the renowned architect Zaha Hadid was commissioned to redesign the stadium and the ski jump. Today the »Innsbruck Lighthouse« is a modern emblem of the city.

🕐 Opening times:
June–Oct 9am–6pm, admission until 5.30pm
Nov–May daily 10am–5pm, admission until 4.30pm
www.bergisel.info

Technical data
Height of tower: 50m/164ft, top of tower is 791m/2595ft ASL
Highest point: approx. 250m/820ft above Innsbruck
Lowest point out-run: 650m/2133ft ASL
Height difference: approach run–out run 128m/420ft
Spectator capacity: 28,000
Ski-jump record: 136m/446ft (Adam Malysz, 2004)

① Ascent
Those fit enough can tackle the 455 steps from the east stadium entrance to the ski-jump tower on foot, but it is faster and more comfortable to use the new inclined lift. This can transport up to 350 people per hour and covers the 250m/275yd between entrance and tower in approx. 2 minutes. From there, an elevator brings visitors to the café and the viewing platform in the tower head.

② Tower
A 16m/52ft x 20m/66ft foundation plate bears the shaft of the tower. The mechanics, storerooms and staff areas are on the lower floors.

③ Tower head
On top of the concrete shaft of the tower sits a three-floor steel hut with a restaurant, viewing platform and safety area. The overhanging levels protrude up to 12m/39ft from the tower shaft.

④ Approach run ramp
The original design foresaw a four-fielded continuous beam with three pillars. However the steep approach run was then executed without pillars using a so-called fish-belly construction, a 68.5m/225ft steel trough with truss support at an inclination of up to 35 degrees.

⑤ Panoramic restaurant »Café im Turm«
Along with their meal, diners can enjoy the unique view across the Inntal valley through room-high glass windows. Like the stadium, the café is open daily and has room for 120 people either seated or standing at high tables or the bar.

A ski jumper soars over the roofs of Innsbruck

*glass façade of
xtends onto the
ovides protec-
wind and is a
against falling.*

*The tower head with its successful combina-
tion of sheet concrete, steel and glass in
harmonious lines bears the distinctive stamp
of star-architect Zaha Hadid.*

*Every year in January the
Bergisel plays host to the
Vierschanzen Tournee (Four
Hills Tournament). In sum-
mer the ski jump is covered
with rubber matting for the
Summer Grand Prix jumping
event.*

*Presentation
ceremony in
the arena*

🕐 clocks, and musical instruments, and an exhibition on the history of the Tyrolese struggle for liberation (opening times: Tue–Sun 9am–6pm).

Haus der Architektur

The new Tyrolese House of Architecture has been installed in the former brewhouse of the Adam Brewery, near the railway station. The upper storeys contain the archive of the Innsbruck architecture faculty, while the lower third of the building houses the former Architekturforum, now on the theme »Austrian Architecture and Tyrol« (closed at weekends).

✻ Wiltener Pfarrkirche

The southern Innsbruck district of Wilten is home to the twin-spired Wilten parish church (1751–55), **one of northern Tyrol's most beautiful Rococo churches**. The interior is decorated with ceiling frescoes by Matthäus Günther and stucco work by Franz Xaver Feichtmayr. The high altar is adorned with a 14th-century sandstone sculpture known as Maria unter den vier Säulen (Mary under the Four Columns).

Stift Wilten

Opposite the church stand the extensive buildings of Stift Wilten, a Premonstratensian abbey (1138). The complex was remodelled in Baroque style in 1670–95. The porch of the abbey church (1651–65) displays a large Gothic wooden figure (878) that apparently represents the giant Haymon, who is said to have played a role in the foundation of the abbey. Steps flanked by lions lead from of the high altar to the »Throne of Solomon« in the pediment.

✻ Alpenzoo

🕐 Downriver, northeast of the district of Hötting, Europe's highest zoo can be found at an elevation of 727m/2385ft. With a beautiful location in the midst of the mountains, the zoo introduces the entire alpine animal kingdom (opening times: daily 9am–6pm, during winter until 5pm).

✻ Bergisel

Sports facilities on the hill

A mere 15-minute walk away from Wilten, the Bergisel (750m/2460ft) rises to the south of the city. A tunnel for the Brenner autobahn and the Brenner Pass railway run through it. There are various sports facilities up on the hill.

The Bergisel is famous for the battles that took place here in 1809, when Tyrolese farmers under the leadership of Andreas Ho-

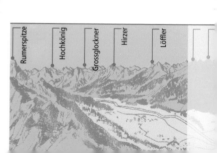

Rumerspitze | Hochkönig | Grossglockner | Hirzer | Löffler

The imposi[ng] ...
the café tha[t] ...
roof terrace ...
tion from t[he] ...
safety meas[ures] ...

From the judge's tower next to the ski jump, the jury has a clear view of the competitive events. Opposite, a similar building provides space for reporters and trainers.

In the new arena at the foot of the jump, 28,000 spectators can watch the action.

© Baedeker

fer (►Famous People) successfully liberated their capital from the Bavarians and the French no less than three times. A memorial for all Tyrolese freedom fighters – with the Andreas Hofer Memorial at its centre – was installed underneath the ski jump in 1893. There is also a memorial chapel (1909) with an honorary tomb for the Tyrolese imperial court huntsmen. The former hunting lodge houses the Regimentsmuseum with exhibits on the various battles for independence and on the history of the imperial huntsmen up to the First World War.

✳ Hafelekar and Hungerburg

North of Innsbruck, on a central mountain terrace at an elevation of around 900m/2953ft, lies the country house district of Hungerburg. It can either be reached via the Hungerburgbahn cable car that departs near the congress centre, or by road on the Höttinger Höhenstrasse. From there, the Hafelekar mountain (2334m/7658ft) and its wonderful views can be reached on the Nordkettenbahn cable car that travels a distance of 3500m/3829yd, passing the intermediate stop at Seegrube (1905m/6250ft) on the way.

Wonderful views

At the base station for the Hungerburgbahn, a circular building exhibits the famous *Bergisel-Panorama*: a giant 19th-century circular painting of 1000 sq m/10,764 sq ft that depicts the battle of 1809 during which the Tyrolese fought to repel the French under the leadership of Andreas Hofer.

Bergisel-Panorama

Around Innsbruck

To the southeast of Innsbruck, beyond the Inntal valley autobahn, stands Schloss Ambras, a fairy-tale Renaissance castle. Archduke Ferdinand II (1563–95) had it built as a summer residence for his wife Philippine Welser, a commoner from Augsburg whom he married in defiance of protocol. The name comes from the Latin phrase »ad umbras« (»in the shade«). Halls in the lower castle contain weaponry; on the first floor of the Kornschütt building is the precious Kunstkammer with sculptures and artworks. The upper castle, with

✳ Schloss Ambras

Panorama from Hafelekar

Glungezer · Olperer · Patscherkofel · Wilde Kreuzspitze · Brenner · Europabrücke · Serles · Tribulaun · Kirschbachspitze · Habicht · Kalkkögel · Schrankogel · Grubenwand · Strahlkogel · Brandjoch · Kaminspitze

a pretty courtyard, contains Philippine Welser's bathroom, and paintings and sculptures are also exhibited on the first and second floors. The **Spanische Saal** (Spanish Hall) is one of the earliest examples of a German Renaissance interior (1570–71), and is one of the most important unsupported hall structures of that era. It has a beautiful coffered ceiling and its walls bear 27 portraits of the Tyrolese Princes. The castle is surrounded by a very attractive park, with ancient woodland. On the southern side of the Spanische Saal is a »Keuchengarten«, which is typical of the Renaissance, a period when gardens had both utilitarian and decorative functions. A restaurant and garden café provide refreshment (www.khm.at/ambras; opening times: daily 10am–5pm, Aug until 7pm).

Igls   5km/3mi south of Innsbruck lies the climatic health spa and winter sports resort of Igls (870m/2854ft), known locally as **»Innsbruck's sun terrace«**. A 3700m/4048yd-long funicular ascends Patscherkofel (2247m/7,372ft), whose summit can be reached either on foot in around one hour from the summit station at 1951m/6398ft, or via a chairlift. The mountain offers good skiing and, during summer, there are attractive hiking routes to explore.

Zirbenweg ▶   The Zirbenweg is a 7km/4mi long nature trail that leads through the Eastern Alps' largest remaining forest of cembra pines. It can be reached via the summit of Patscherkofel and the path is also lined by many varieties of alpine roses. The footpath ends at the Tulfeinalm, where a chairlift descends to Tulfes.

Renaissance Schloss Ambras in front of the gates of Innsbruck

The beautiful Sellraintal valley begins near Kematen about 10km/6mi **Sellraintal** to the west of Innsbruck. Rewarding mountain walks start from the main settlement of Sellrain (909m/2982ft).

A road leads south from Gries (1238m/4062ft) into the Lüsenstal val- ◄ **Lüsenstal** ley. Continuing on the Sellraintal road heading west, the road reaches **Alm Kühtai** Kühtaisattel (Kühtai Saddle) at 2016m/6614ft, followed by Kühtai Alm (1967m/6454ft). There are numerous alpine lakes in the surrounding area. The climatic spa and winter sports resort has cable cars and ski lifts and is a veritable El Dorado for mountaineers and climbers.

Above Axams (878m/2881ft), 18km/11mi southwest of Innsbruck, **Axams** are the Olympic ski runs of the Axamer Lizum winter sports region (Lizum-Alpe, 1633m/5358ft). Cable cars and lifts provide access, including the cable car and chairlift up Hoadl (2340m/7677ft) and the chairlift up Birgitzköpfl (mountain station at 2044m/6706ft).

Not far to the east of Axams lies Götzens (868m/2848ft) which is noteworthy for its church. The parish church, Pfarrkirche zu den Aposteln Peter and Paul, was built by Franz Singer in the 18th century and is among the **most beautiful Rococo religious buildings in the German-speaking world**. The interior is a magnificent collection of altars, stucco work and frescoes. The vault frescoes are by Matthäus Günther and portray scenes form the lives of the apostles Peter and Paul. The high altar painting is by Franz Anton Maulpertsch.

> **? DID YOU KNOW ...?**
>
> ■ ... that Tyrol's oldest cookery book, with 245 recipes, was written by Philippine Welser, who was the wife of Archduke Ferdinand II?

✴ Innviertel

K/L 3

Province: Upper Austria

The Innviertel, a district characterized by villages, hamlets, farms and churches, welcomes visitors to experience its pleasant rural scenery, traditions and nature – as well as a sense of peace and tranquillity.

Until 1779, and between 1809 and 1814, the Innviertel belonged to Bavaria. The region is demarcated by the Danube to the north, the Inn and Salzach rivers to the west, the forested highlands of the Hausruck in the south, and the Innbach to the east. Local inhabitants are good at cooperating with regions beyond their own lovely hill landscape, a fact attested to by the **trans-national associations and institutions** that exist here: for example, the Römer Radweg cycle way from Bavarian Passau to the Austrian Attersee; the European

Nature Reserve of the Lower Inn near Braunau; and the Upper Austrian-Bavarian »Bierregion«, an association of breweries.

In addition to cycling, golf, horse-riding and hiking, health spas play a significant role in tourism here. Aspach, Gainberg, Gallspach and Bad Schallerbach all have various spa and thermal bath facilities on offer.

What to See in the Innviertel

Ried im Innkreis Sculptural art received a major impulse in Ried im Innkreis (429m/ 1407ft; pop. 11,400), the centrally located principal town of the Innviertel. For it was here that, from the middle of the 17th century onwards, one of sculpture's most important dynasties lived for almost two centuries. The Schwanthaler family, who lived at Schwanthalergasse 11, produced 21 sculptors. Several examples of their works are found in the parish church as well as in churches throughout the region.

Museum Innviertler Volkskundehaus ► The Museum Innviertler Volkskundehaus contains Schwanthaler sculptures, folklore collections including important exhibits on religious folk art, and the Galerie der Stadt, which is significant beyond the local region (Kirchenplatz 13; opening times: Tue–Fri 9am–noon and 2pm–5pm, Sat 2pm–5pm).

✳ Schärding A good 40km/25mi north of Ried, high above the river Inn, lies the charming little Baroque town of Schärding (313m/1026ft; pop. 5000). It still has remains of the old town wall, gates and bastions, and the elongated town square is bordered by the façades of Baroque buildings. The Silberzeile on the Oberer Stadtplatz (Upper Town Square) is a particularly impressive street of enchanting houses that were once inhabited by rich salt and wood merchants. Their wealth of silver coins presumably inspired the name of the street.

Following the Inn upriver, **Obernberg** is reached after 20km/13mi (365m/1197ft; pop. 1800). Gabled houses with beautiful Rococo façades characterize this attractive settlement that was mentioned as a market as early as 1250. The wonderful stucco façades of the Wörndle, Apotheker and Schiffsmeister houses were made by Johann Baptist Modler.

During the Middle Ages, Obernberg served as a storage town, in particular for salt transported on the Inn river. The Heimatmuseum in the Gurtental at Marktplatz 22 documents the history of rafting and shipping on the Inn (opening times: May–Oct Fri–Sun, 2pm–4pm; tel. 077 58 / 29 02).

▶ THE INNVIERTEL

INFORMATION

Tourismusverband der Stadt Ried
Kirchenplatz 13
A-4910 Ried im Innkreis
Tel. 077 52/851 80
Fax 851 80 20
www.ried.at

On the Bavarian side, northwest of Obernberg, lies the popular spa of Bad Füssing, and not far south lies its Austrian equivalent, collectively known as the »Kur- und Thermenregion Innviertel«. The slogan for the thermal baths at Geinberg, for example, is »Experience health as pleasure« – the water from the thermal spring there is some of the warmest (97 °C/207 °F) found in Austria. It is particularly recommended for those with skin complaints and rheumatism.

A region of spas and thermal springs

► Braunau

Braunau

The Benedictine abbey of Michaelbeuern lies around 5km/3mi to the southeast of Moosdorf, in the province of Salzburg. It looks back on a thousand-year history. Between the end of March and the end of October a monastery tour is offered on Sundays at 2pm. Highlights are the Baroque monastic library with its Walther Bible – a priceless work of Romanesque manuscript illumination dating from 1140 – and the abbey hall with its Rococo interior by Franz Nikolaus Streicher. The high altar in the abbey church was designed in 1691 by Meinrad Guggenbichler from Mondsee and Johann Michael Rottmayr.

Michaelbeuern

Frankenburg (519m/1702ft); pop. 5300) lies around 20km/13mi south of Ried, and every two years in July and August it serves as the open-air venue for the **»Frankenburger Würfelspiel«**, a game of dice to commemorate a gruesome historic event. A new priest was supposed to take up his post in May 1625, but his arrival was opposed by the citizens and farmers. The Bavarian overlord assured mercy to

Frankenburg

Swim to musical accompaniment in the Geinberg baths

! *Baedeker* TIP

River trip
Those who would like to enjoy the last stretch of river along the romantic Inntal valley, between Schärding und Passau, can do so from the water between April and the end of October when the ship *Gerda* plies this route (Tue–Sun 2pm and 4pm; for information tel. 0 77 12/73 50).

the locals if they were to stop their rebellion, but it turned out to be a terrible kind of mercy. 36 people were forced to pair up to play games of dice for their lives – in each case, the loser was hanged. This macabre game was one of the triggers of the Upper Austrian Farmers' Revolt in 1626. Since 1925 around 400 Frankenberger amateur performers have re-enacted the terrible game every two years (2009, 2011 etc.) for thousands of spectators as a warning against intolerance and fanaticism.

Ampflwang Horse riding fans may have heard of the riding village of Ampflwang (560m/1837ft; pop. 3800) a few miles east of Frankenburg. It has **one of Europe's largest studs for Icelandic horses and ponies in Europe**, 300km/187mi of riding and carriage tour routes, and numerous stables.

✴ **Bad Ischl**

L 4

Province: Upper Austria	**Elevation:** 469m/1539ft
Population: 14,100	

Famous as the town where Sisi – later the Empress of Austria – got engaged and a favoured meeting place for the wealthy, Bad Ischl lies in the heart of the Salzkammergut region surrounded by forested hills.

Royal airs The significance of this charming resort as a place for »taking the air« developed after Dr Wirer of Vienna advised the childless Archduchess Sophie, who had failed to conceive during the first six years of her marriage, to undertake a cure in Bad Ischl. The pleasing result: four boys, who were jokingly referred to as the salt princes. Her oldest son, Emperor Franz Joseph I, spent every summer in Bad Ischl for 60 years, and the beautiful villas and manicured parks are still testament to the village's former status. Famous musicians, such as Anton Bruckner, Johann Strauss (►Famous People) and Franz Lehár spent time here, as did poets such as Nikolaus Lenau and Johann Nestroy.

What to See in Bad Ischl

Kaiservilla **Franz Joseph I's summer residence**, the Kaiservilla, stands on the northern shore of the Ischl river. It was given to him and his wife

Elisabeth in a ball gown in a painting by Franz Xaver Winterhalter in the Hofburg

SELF-DRAMATIZATION AND DENIAL

The real Empress Elisabeth has almost nothing in common with the schmaltzy »Sissi« films made in the 1950s. Sisi never felt at home at court in Vienna, and refused her role as monarch. She created a fictional character for herself that consisted of nothing but aesthetics.

It began like a fairy tale. Actually it was Helene, the daughter of the Bavarian Duke Maximilian of the House of Wittelsbacher, who had been selected to marry Austria's Emperor Franz Joseph I. But when the **15-year-old Elisabeth** accompanied her sister to Bad Ischl for the betrothal, the young ruler fell head over heels in love with her. A short time later, the emperor's intended travelled on a paddle steamer adorned with roses down the Danube to Vienna, cheered on by masses of people lining the banks of the river. The **dream wedding** of the century, on 24 April 1854, was not to be outdone with regard to pomp and ceremony.

The unhappy empress

However after the honeymoon in Luxembourg the fairy tale had already come to an end. **Everyday imperial life** was exceedingly regimented. With a very firm hand the court attempted to make an empress out of the »Bavarian country girl«. Above all Sophie – truly a wicked mother-in-law – made sure, Argus-eyed, that Sisi, as Elisabeth was now called (the »Sissi« spelling first arose with the Romy Schneider films), complied with the stiff ceremonies at court.

Sisi loathed the empty, formal life at court, and hated Vienna and her mother-in-law. Though she was loved by her husband, government business

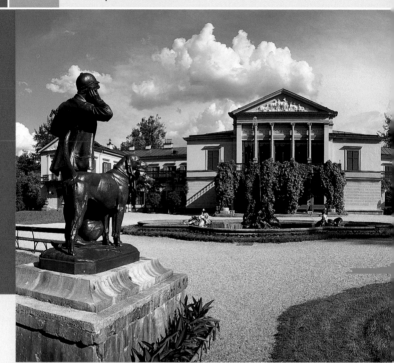

meant that Franz Joseph had little time for her and, moreover, he was under his mother's thumb. Sophie took over the **education of the children** (three daughters and a son). At first the young empress attempted to rebel against this, but eventually she capitulated. On top of all this, rumours of the emperor's amorous escapades were rife.

She even once had to listen while her own mother explained to her that a princess must learn to bear **boredom with grace**. Instead Sisi tried to step out of her role – with self-dramatization and denial.

Vain, clever and restless

For years Sisi was said to be »the most beautiful monarch in the world«. **Beauty was the main focus** of her life. By plaiting her floor-length hair, she created a hairstyle that adorned her head like a natural crown. She fasted excessively; the 1.72m/5ft 7in-tall empress never had a waist measuring more than 50cm/20in. She would appear in public only with a **flawless** appearance. She didn't smile, because she didn't like her teeth, and she normally hid her hands, as the digits of the French Empress Eugénie were finer. Later, she refused to be photographed or painted: the radiant face of her youth was not to be replaced by that of an ageing woman. In public she concealed herself behind fans and umbrellas. Sisi was a dogged **sportswoman**. She could ride for hours and went on hikes, keeping up an incredible pace for hours. She wasn't just a pretty face either: the intelligent em-

*A suitable wedding
present: the Kaiservilla
in Bad Ischl*

*Pictures of the empress
in the Kaiservilla*

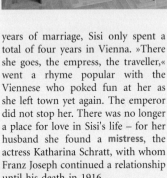

press mastered eleven languages including Hungarian, read the works of Homer in the original Greek as well as those of Heine, Byron and Shakespeare, cultivated **liberal, antimonarchical** ideas and approved – to the horror of the court – reform of the ailing Dual Monarchy. She deposited her money in the republican country of Switzerland, where she considered it safer.

Later, the empress, who today's experts believe suffered from a **manicdepressive illness**, turned her back on Vienna, the Habsburg Empire and her husband ever more frequently. She visited Greece, Spain, the Near East and England, had a palace built on the island of Corfu and an anchor tattooed on her shoulder as a sign of her desire for freedom, which shocked the doctors who carried out the post-mortem on her corpse: such a thing belonged only on the bodies of common criminals! During her 44

years of marriage, Sisi only spent a total of four years in Vienna. »There she goes, the empress, the traveller,« went a rhyme popular with the Viennese who poked fun at her as she left town yet again. The emperor did not stop her. There was no longer a place for love in Sisi's life – for her husband she found a **mistress**, the actress Katharina Schratt, with whom Franz Joseph continued a relationship until his death in 1916.

Sisi finds her murderer

After the **tragic suicide** of her son Rudolf at Schloss Mayering in 1889, Sisi lost the will to live. On **10 September 1898** in Geneva, the Italian anarchist Luigi Lucheni stabbed her – in an attack not intended for her – with a file. »She has found her murderer,« Sisi's favourite daughter Marie Válerie is said to have wailed.

Elisabeth as a wedding present by his imperial mother (guide tours: Jan–March Wed, April daily, Dec Sat and Sun 10am–4pm, May–Oct daily 9.30am–4.45pm). The Marmorschlössl (little marble castle), built for Empress Elisabeth, is hidden among trees in the beautiful Kaiserpark. Today, it houses the Upper Austrian Museum of Photography (opening times: April–Oct daily 9.30am–5pm).

◄ **Photomuseum**

Haenel Pancera-Museum

It is worth making a detour to the Haenel Pancera Museum on the way to the spa gardens. It exhibits artefacts and furniture from various epochs collected during extensive travels undertaken during the first third of the 20th century by the couple Haenel and Pancera: he was an engineer and she was a concert pianist (Concordiastrasse 3; opening times: May–Sept daily 10am–noon and 2pm–5pm; guided tours on the hour).

Kurpark

The former spa rooms (Kurhaus) stand in the carefully tended park, today used as a congress and theatre venue and providing an elegant setting for lectures, concerts, ballet, opera and operetta performances.

Stadtmuseum

The Stadtmuseum on the local history and folklore of the Salzkammergut region and Bad Ischl is housed in the former Hotel Austria. In addition an East Asian collection, the Sarsteiner-Sammlung, is on

Bad Ischl Map

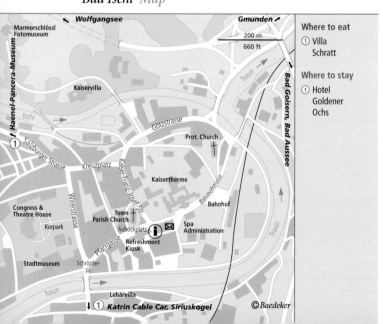

display (Esplanade 10; opening times: April–Oct daily 10am–5pm, Wed 2pm–7pm; Jan–March Fri–Sun 10am–5pm).

The villa in which Franz Lehár (►Famous People) lived from 1912 until his death in 1948 stands beyond the Traun river. The **master of Viennese operetta** donated his home on condition that the Lehár Museum would be founded in it (Lehár-Kai 8; opening times: May–Sept daily 9am–noon and 2pm–5pm).

Lehár-Villa

Around Bad Ischl

The Siriuskogel (598m/1962ft) rises directly south of Bad Ischl. Its summit can be reached by chairlift, but also easily in a 45-minute walk. A cable car continues a little further to Katrinalm (1480m/4855ft) with a beautiful view of the Dachstein glacier.

★ **Siriuskogel**

About halfway between Bad Ischl and Bad Goisern, the Technology Museum on national road 145 has exhibitions on vehicles, technology and aviation. It also displays vintage cars, a giant lamp from 1942, military motorbikes and ancient tractors – a veritable paradise for fans of nostalgia (opening times: April–Oct daily 9am–6pm).

Technisches Museum

 VISITING BAD ISCHL

INFORMATION
Tourismusverband Bad Ischl
Auböckplatz 5 (refreshment kiosk)
A-4820 Bad Ischl
Tel. 0 61 32/277 57
www.badischl.at

WHERE TO EAT
► **Expensive**
① *Villa Schratt*
Steinbruch 43
A-4820 Bad Ischl
Tel. 0 61 32/2 76 47
This stylishly restored villa has an idyllic garden. Specialities include lamb and fish, such as salmon and char. Good wines.

WHERE TO STAY
► **Mid-range**
① *Hotel Goldener Ochs*
Grazer Str. 4
A-4820 Bad Ischl

Tel. 0 61 32/23 52 90
www.goldenerochs.at
The operetta composer Franz Lehár was a regular at this hotel, founded in 1791. Comfortable rooms, most with balcony or gazebo providing romantic views across the Traun river. The hotel's own restaurant, the Lehár-Stuben, serves excellent Austrian cuisine.

Baedeker recommendation

Sweet temptation
The Zauner patisserie at Stammhaus Pfarrgasse 7 was founded in 1832. It attracts guests not only with such classics as the original Zaunerstollen but also with an enchanting art nouveau salon (opening times: daily 8.30am–6pm; esplanade: Wed–Sun 10am–8pm; art nouveau salon when required, closed in Jan).

Bad Goisern   Bad Goisern is a popular spa whose iodine spring waters are renowned for helping those with skin trouble and rheumatism. The Konrad-Deubler Museum has exhibits on the life of a farmer and philosopher (1814–84) who was incarcerated for many years and finally exiled in 1862 for his republican ideas. »Goiserer«, traditional iron-studded alpine boots still made according to the old techniques, are a famous local product.

✴ **Judenburg**

N 5

Province: Styria
Population: 10,500

Elevation: 737m/2419ft

Judenburg was an important city in Roman and medieval times due to its location at the point where several important trade routes intersected. Accordingly, in the 14th century the small town became the first in the alpine region to mint its own gold coins, the Judenburg guilder.

Old centre   Judenburg is located approximately 45km/28mi north of Klagenfurt,
of trade   set in the mountains above the right bank of the Mur. The Strettweg cult chariot (*c*600 BC) attests to the settlement of the area during the Hallstatt period. A copy of the chariot can be seen in the Stadtmuseum; the original is located in the Landesmuseum Joanneum in Graz.

Judenburg lost much of its importance due to relocation of the trade routes and to various fires within the town. It was first able to slowly regain momentum through the construction of the railway.

Trading requires money, and in order to gain access to such a scarcely available resource, quite a number of local rulers resettled some of the Jewish population in their territory and allowed themselves to be paid for this »act of generosity« in hard cash. Beginning in the late Middle Ages, the Jewish bankers were joined by Christian moneylenders who rid themselves of their Jewish competition in Austria in 1496: by convincing the emperor to force the Jews into exile, they benefited financially.

▶ **JUDENBURG**

INFORMATION

Tourismusverband Judenburg
Burggasse 5/1, A-8750 Judenburg
Tel. 0 35 72/4 71 27, fax 4 71 27-4,
www.judenburg-tourism.at

WHERE TO STAY

▶ **Luxury**

Hotel Schloss Gabelhofen
Schlossgasse 54, A-8753 Fohnsdorf
Tel. 0 35 73/5 55 50, fax 5 55 56
www.gabelhofen.at
Located 5km/3mi from Judenburg, this hotel is known for its exclusive location in the heart of the surrounding countryside; once a farmhouse, it became a castle in 1450 and was converted into a first-class hotel in 1994.

What to See in Judenburg

Old Town

Despite the number of fires that damaged the town, Styria's oldest commercial centre still has some buildings from its period of prosperity in the High Middle Ages. The town's symbol is its 75m/246ft-high tower, the Stadtturm (1449–1509), the top storey of which was added with a surrounding gallery after a fire in 1840. The Rathaus (town hall), with its Wilhelminian façade, and old town houses with lovely arcaded courtyards are grouped around the Hauptplatz (main square). The remains of the medieval castle can be found on the shores of the Mur. In the town's church, Kirche St Nikolaus, a limestone *Virgin Mother with Child* (c1420) and statues of the apostles from the workshop of Judenburg's Baroque artist Balthasar Prandstätter are particularly worth taking a look at. The Magdalenenkirche (Church of Mary Magdalene) features valuable medieval glass windows and frescoes (1370–1420).

> **! Baedeker TIP**
>
> ### The sun – from a brand new perspective
>
> The Planetarium Judenburg in the Stadtturm, Austria's highest tower, is the world's highest planetarium. Thanks to the latest technology and a 3D show, amateur astronomers can get a completely new perspective on countless heavenly bodies here (Kirchplatz 1; information at tel. 035 72 / 440 88 and www.sternenturm.at)

Burg Liechtenstein

Towering above the town are the ruins of Liechtenstein Castle (12th century), once the ancestral seat of the minstrel Ulrich von Liechtenstein (c1200–75). He was primarily known for *Frauendienst*, a collection of important minnelieds.

A view over the town from Judenburg's Stadtturm

Around Judenburg

Märchenwald Steiermark
🕐

The Märchenwald (fairy-tale forest) takes visitors back to the time when wishes came true. Situated in St Georgen ob Judenburg, the forest not only enchants visitors with over 100 fairy-tale characters but also offers a puppet theatre, a Viking ship, camps with knights and Indians, and other attractions (opening times: Easter–end of October, daily 8.30am–dusk).

Zirbitzkogel

The highest point of the Seetal Alps in the southwest is the Zirbitzkogel (2396m/7863ft), which can be reached either via the town of Neumarkt in the west or the town of Obdach in the east. The Sabathyhütte mountain lodge (1616m/5300ft) offers food and drink.

Zeltweg

Those who have always wanted to test their driving abilities on a race track can experience the real thing at the **A 1-Ring** (formerly known as the Österreich-Ring) near Zeltweg. When the racers are not there, drivers can take their own set of wheels on the skid control course (information at tel. 0 35 77/255 10 and www.a1ring.at).

Benediktiner-abtei Seckau

Around 10km/16mi north by way of Knittelfeld the road leads to the Benedictine abbey of Seckau. The abbey, completely enclosed by walls, was founded in 1140 by Augustinian canons, dissolved in 1782 and then resettled by Benedictines from Beuron in 1883. Today, the monastery runs a goldsmith's workshop, an artistic carpentry shop and a distillery, the produce of which will please both the eye and the palate (information at www.abtei-seckau.at).

Dom ▶

The originally Romanesque cathedral was dedicated in 1164 and features Gothic vaulted ceilings (1480–1510). The fresco cycle depicting the life of John the Baptist (13th century), in the left-hand aisle of the Renaissance mausoleum of Archduke Karl II, and the modern frescoes of the *Seckauer Apokalypse* (1952–60; H. Böckl) are especially noteworthy.

✳ **Kaisergebirge**

H 4

Province: Tyrol **Highest elevation:** Ellmauer Halt (2344m/7690ft)

Dark gorges separate the mighty towering peaks of the Kaisergebirge, a mountain range of incomparable might and beauty. This wild and rugged massif is a paradise for mountaineers and climbers.

Noblesse oblige

The steep, mighty mountainsides and peaks of the Kaisergebirge, also known simply as the »Kaiser«, rise directly out of the extensive foreland region of forests and fields located north of the Kitzbühel Alps and east of the Inn river. The touristic centre of the region is the charmingly situated town of Hinterbärenbad (831m/2727ft). The deep Kaisertal valley leads into the Inntal valley at Kufstein and then continues eastward as the Kaiserbachtal. It separates the northern part of the mountain range, the **Zahmer Kaiser** (»tame emperor«), with the Vordere Kesselschneid mountain and the beautiful Pyramidenspitze (1997m/6554ft), from the Wilder Kaiser (»wild emperor«) in the south.

The **famous Fohlenhof Ebbs**, first documented in 788 as »ad Episas« (= horse trough or horse brook), is home to Tyrolese Haflinger studs. The Haflingers, known for their tenacity, are a cross between a native Tyrolese mare and an Arabian stallion. They can be marvelled at from afar, but also at closer quarters: they pull horse-drawn carriages and sleighs on excursions for tourists.

Ebbs

The highest peak of the Wilder Kaiser (»Vorderer Kaiser«) can be reached via the trident-shaped Ellmauer Halt (2344m/7692ft), as well as from the Anton-Karg-Haus near Hinterbärenbad in the Kaisertal valley (approximately 5 hours), and additionally the Grutten-Hütte (1620m/5316ft) to the south near Ellmau.

Wilder Kaiser

The Walchsee is located north of the Kaisergebirge amongst open forests and fields next to the town of the same name (660m/2165ft; pop. 1700). With a surface area of 1 sq km/247ac, it numbers among Tyrol's larger lakes. The town of Walchsee is a popular destination for winter sports and offers a diverse selection of sports activities on the water.

Walchsee

Located southwest of the mountain range, the Hintersteiner See is smaller than the Walchsee yet unusually beautiful. A road southeast of Kufstein leads into the Weissache valley, extending from the foot

Hintersteiner See

 VISITING KAISERGEBIRGE

of the Wilder Kaiser to St Johann in Tyrol (►Kitzbühel, Surroundings). A marked footpath strays from the road, continuing over the Steinerne Stiege (1 hour) to the Hintersteiner See (892m/2926ft). The lake is, however, also accessible via a 4km/2.5mi-long back road starting at Scheffau near the Wilder Kaiser. The crystal clear water of the Hintersteiner See reflects the peaks of the Scheffauer mountain (2113m/6932ft).

✷ Kapruner Tal

J 5

Province: Salzburg   **Elevation:** 757m/2483ft

A morning of summer skiing on Austria's first glacier ski run, the Kitzsteinhorn, and a dip in the Zeller See in the afternoon – this successful combination is enjoyed by many a visitor to the Kaprun valley.

Glacier skiing and waterpower

Those who simply cannot go without snow and ice during the warmest time of the year must head for high-lying regions such as the Kaprun valley in the ►Hohen Tauern. Together with Zell am See, (►Zeller See) it forms the so-called **Europasportregion**.

The technically impressive hydroelectric power stations of the Kaprun valley supply Austria with a large portion of its electricity. Plans for the use of hydroelectricity were being developed as early as the beginning of the 20th century. Construction began following Austria's annexation (known as the »Anschluss«) to the Third Reich in

Glockner-Kaprun Power Station Group

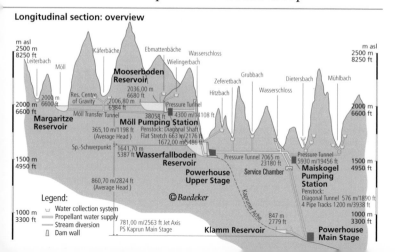

Longitudinal section: overview

Legend:
⌣ Water collection system
═ Propellant water supply
── Stream diversion
⏢ Dam wall

©Baedeker

1938, and was continued throughout the war, partly with the use of forced labour. The Kaprun valley was the largest construction site in the country after the war and received considerable financial support through the Marshall Plan. The **»Myth of Kaprun«** that arose had two aspects: first of all, the construction was highly publicized as the struggle and eventual victory of technology over the forces of nature; on the other hand, the project was a national symbol for Austria's will to rebuild after the devastation of the war, and stood for the transition from an agricultural economy into the industrial age.

Sunny resting place with excellent views of the back end of Kaprun Valley

Kaprun

A hundred years ago, Kaprun was still a minor hamlet. The construction of the power plants began its powerful rise to become the place it is today, a town completely attuned to tourism and sports. The towering castle, Burg Kaprun, first documented in 1280, has provided a dignified setting for cultural events since its restoration. Fans of vintage cars will get their money's worth at the Vötters Fahrzeugmuseum, where around 150 vehicles from the 1950s to the 1970s are sure to please (Schlossstrasse 474/621; opening times: Sun–Fri 11pm–6pm).

Kaprun also gained tragic fame on 11 November 2000 when 155 people died in a devastating funicular tunnel fire. The funicular was never reopened and was replaced by gondola lifts, Gletscherjet 1 and 2.

Hauptstufe power station

The informational centre located in the Hauptstufe power station on the southeastern edge of Kaprun presents information on the development of the power plant and the technology involved in its operation (opening times: late Jan–mid-Dec daily 8am–6pm). The Sigmund-Thun-Klamm nature trail begins near the information centre (accessible: late May–early Oct daily 9am–5pm).

★ Kitzsteinhorn

Approximately 6km/3.5mi south of Kaprun at Kaprun-Thörl, visitors find a large car park and the valley's gondola station (928m/3044ft). The »panoramic railway« and the Gletscherjet 1 take visitors to an elevation of 1978m/6488ft, where they then have access to more cable lifts, gondolas, and chairlifts into the glacial skiing area or up to the summit station, which offers a terrace with a panoramic view and the Glocknerkanzel (3029m/9937ft). The Alpincenter, at 2450m/8038ft, provides its guests with food and drink.

Tauern Kraftwerk Glockner-Kaprun

The valley road continues south, climbing to the Limberstollen car park and finally reaching the Kesselfall-Alpenhaus (1068m/3503ft), the end of the line for private vehicles. Only transit buses are permitted on the Lärchwandstrasse, which take those visiting the Glockner-Kaprun Tauern Power Station to the valley station of the Lärchwand-Schrägaufzug – claimed to be the largest electrically powered inclined elevator in Europe (mid-May–mid-Oct).

From the mountain station at 1640m/5379ft, buses follow the Limbergsperre dam and the Wasserfallboden reservoir and then continue further to the Mooserboden reservoir. Both reservoirs have the capacity to hold enormous volumes of water – well over 80 million cubic m/2.8 billion cubic ft. The visitor centre, **»Erlebniswelt Strom und Eis«**, provides information on the history of the hydroelectric power station in Museum Tauernstrom, while the »Erlebniswelt Gletschereis« presents information on that unique phenomenon of nature, the glacier. Tours through the interior of the dam are also on offer.

! **Baedeker TIP**

Two-wheeled challenge

The Maiskogel, located in the western part of Kaprun, is the mountain biker's equivalent of the Hahnenkamm, site of the famous downhill ski race. Those who are less daring will find plenty of gentler descents in the Europasportregion. Details available at www.europasportregion.info or in the tourist offices in Kaprun and Zell am See.

Experienced hikers can undertake mountain tours on well-developed trails to the huts and peaks of the surrounding Tauern mountains, e.g. a five-hour hike to the Grosse Wiesbachhorn mountain (3564m/ 11,690ft) with a stopover at the Heinrich-Schwaiger-Haus (2802m/ 9190.5ft; accommodation).

Grosses Wiesbachhorn

Others may prefer to simply enjoy the panoramic view of the glaciers at the rear of the Kaprun valley on the terrace of the Heidnische Kirche restaurant, where Protestants held secret meetings during the Counterreformation.

 VISITING KAPRUNER TAL

INFORMATION

Fremdenverkehrsband Kaprun
Salzburger Platz 601
A-5710 Kaprun
Tel. 0 65 47/8 64 30
www.kaprun.at

WHERE TO EAT

▶ **Moderate**
Hilberger's Beisl
Wilhelm-Fazokas-Strasse 149
A-5710 Kaprun, Tel. 0 65 47/7 24 61

Tasty Styrian delicacies and a large selection of high-quality local and international wines.

WHERE TO STAY

▶ **Budget**
Gasthof zur Mühle
A-5710 Kaprun 38
Tel. 065 47 / 82 54
web.kaprun.at/muehle
This hotel offers comfortable rooms and sauna facilities.

✴ Karwendel

Province: Tyrol

The Karwendelgebirge, a mountain range located between Seefeld in Tirol, Innsbruck and the Achensee, is a part of the Northern Limestone Alps. The mountains' most striking features are their mighty, steep walls and high-lying cirques.

The first nature protection acts for this region were passed as early as 1928. Today, the Karwendelgebirge is a nature preserve divided into different protected zones under the name Alpenpark Karwendel (approximately 920 sq km/355 sq mi; 730 sq km/282 sq mi in Austria, and 190 sq km/73 sq mi in Germany). The Karwendel's highest elevation is the Birkkarspitze (2749m/9017ft); the only permanently inhabited town is Weiler Hinterriss, only accessible from the north (Bavaria). The range is grouped into four parallel chains of limestone mountains, each featuring deep valleys running both longitudinally and laterally. The area is just as attractive for beginners as it is for advanced climbers: numerous summits are easily accessible via footpaths, while others can only be reached by challenging ascents.

Alpenpark Karwendel

The Eng-Alm at the Große Ahornboden in the Karwendel mountains is only reachable from Bavaria

The southernmost chain, the **Solsteinkette**, rises directly above the Inntal valley, and looks right into the streets and alleyways of Tyrol's capital city as the »Innsbrucker Nordkette«. Visitors to Innsbruck recognize the famous view of the snow-capped mountains from Maria-Theresien-Strasse that gives the city its characteristic backdrop. The Innsbruck Nordkettenbahn (funicular) runs to the 2334m/7656ft-high Hafelekar via Seegrube at 1905m/6248ft (►Panorama from Hafelekar p.294/95).

The most attractive destination in the second chain to the north, the Bettelwurfkette – otherwise known as the Gleirschkette – is the peak of the Grosse Bettelwurf mountain (2725m/8938ft), **one of the most beautiful vantage points in Tyrol**. Yet the Hoher Gleirsch (2492m/8174ft), the Speckkarspitze (2621m/8597ft) and the Grosser Lafatscher (2696m/8843ft) are also interesting for mountain enthusiasts.

Bettelwurfkette

Jutting above the Karwendelhaus (1790m/5871ft; food and drink available) in the third chain, the Hintere Karwendelkette (also

Hintere Karwendelkette

KARWENDEL

INFORMATION

Österreichischer Alpenverein
Olympiastr. 37
A-6020 Innsbruck
Tel. 05 12 / 595 74, fax 57 55 28
www.alpenverein.at

known as the Birkkarkette), is the symmetrical pyramid-shaped Birkkarspitze (2749m/9017ft). This popular climbing destination does, however, require a good level of fitness as well as surefootedness.

The northernmost chain is the **Vordere Karwendelkette**, technically part of the Karwendelgebirge, which forms the German-Austrian border. Its main summits are the Östliche Karwendelspitze (2539m/ 8328ft) and the Westliche Karwendelspitze (2385m/7823ft), which present little or no trouble to seasoned climbers.

Hiking trail Approximately 5 hours are necessary to cover one of the most spectacular hiking routes: it begins from the border town of Scharnitz underneath the Scharniz Pass, and follows the Wanderweg 201 hiking route along the Karwendelbach to the **Karwendelhaus** (1765m/ 5789ft) at the foot of the Birkkarspitze. From here, hikers can either take a tour of the Birkkarspitze or continue for an additional 5 hours – past the imposing escarpments of the Laliderer – to the **Grosser Ahornboden** (1216m/3988ft) at the very back of the Riss Valley. The walk from the Grosse Ahornboden, with its ancient maple trees, to the Achensee takes 5–6 hours.

Kaunertal

E 5/6

Province: Tyrol

Kaunertal is a 28km/17mi-long valley on the right bank of the upper Inn and is traversed by the Faggenbach. A valley road begins at Prutz and leads to the Gepatsch reservoir, reaching a maximum gradient of 14%.

Prutz Prutz (866m/2840ft; pop. 1600) is a quaint holiday resort that lies at the point where the Kaunertal valley opens into the upper Inn river. »The good Lord lets it rain down on both the righteous and the unrighteous – just not on the people of Prutz«, as the local saying about this **area of low precipitation** goes. A power station is located near the town that receives its water supply from the Gepatsch reservoir via a 14.8km/9mi-long pressure tunnel.

KAUNERTAL

INFORMATION

Tourismusbüro Kaunertal
Feichten 134, A-6524 Kaunertal
Tel. 0 54 75/29 20, fax 29 29
www.kaunertal.com

Lying west of Prutz on a terrace above the Inn are the spa and winter sports resorts of Obladis (1386m/4547ft) and Ladis (1190m/3903ft), whose old farmhouses feature painted façades from the 15th–16th centuries. Both towns have sulphurous springs; Obladis has an acidulous spring that was certainly known as far back as the 15th century, possibly earlier.

Ladis and Obladis

Around 8km/5mi beyond the village of Feichten (1289m/4228ft), the road reaches the 630m/2066ft-long and 130m/426ft-high dam of the Gepatsch reservoir, which is fed by the waters of the Gepatsch-Ferner glacier. It forms a 6km/3.7mi reservoir with an approximate capacity of 140 million cubic m/5 billion cubic ft. A narrow road extends along the lake until it reaches the end of the valley near the Gepatsch-Alm (2000m/3280ft). This is also the location of the Gepatsch-Haus, the first refuge run by a section of the German Alpine Association on Austrian soil.

Gepatsch reservoir

The Kaunertal Panoramic Glacier Road reaches a height of 2750m/9025ft (glacier restaurant); a chairlift then takes visitors to an elevation of 3010m/9880ft. It takes an additional 25 minutes to reach a spot near the Karlesspitze (3160m/10365ft) that offers an impressive view of Austria, Italy and Switzerland.

Panoramic Glacier Road

Stretching to the south of the Gepatsch reservoir is the approximately 8km/5mi-long Gepatsch-Ferner, the **second-largest glacier in the Eastern Alps after the Pasterze**. The glacier feeds the Faggenbach.

Gepatsch-Ferner

The Gepatsch-Stausee is Tyrol's biggest reservoir

✶ Kitzbühel

H 5

Province: Tyrol   **Elevation:** 800–2000m/2625–6562ft
Population: 8600

The sophisticated winter sports paradise of Kitzbühel was prosperous as early as the 16th and 17th centuries thanks to its copper and silver mines. Today, the town is known throughout the world for the famous Hahnenkamm downhill ski race.

From mining to tourism
Its popularity as a preferred winter holiday destination can be attributed to the beneficial curiosity of the self-appointed Kitzbühel citizen Franz Reisch: after reading the book *The First Crossing of Greenland* by Norwegian polar explorer Fridtjof Nansen at the end of the 19th century, Reisch wanted to know what exactly was so special about these strange shoes called skis. He arranged for a pair to be shipped to him from Norway, undertook his first trial runs in 1892–93, and organized **the first-ever ski race** in Kitzbühel with his friends as early as 1895. Kitzbühel made it into the top ten of high-class locations when the then Prince of Wales named it his favourite winter holiday destination in 1935. »Kitz« has adapted to its clientele of international holidaymakers; the jet set and those who like to see and be seen enjoy assembling here in the casino, the nightclubs, and on the golf courses.

✶ Sporting region
The optimally developed infrastructure of the region attracts ski enthusiasts in particular. Now there is even a spectacular connection between the Hahnenkamm/Pengelstein and the Jochberg/Resterhöhe ski areas: without needing to take the ski bus in the middle, a three-cable, continuous loop gondola lift, a technological innovation, has been in place since January of 2005 and transports skiers from one station to another at dizzy heights across the Saukasergraben valley.
Summer sports enthusiasts, too, can get their money's worth here, with tennis, golf, mountain climbing and mountain biking on offer. Countless spectators attend the sporting events in Kitzbühel and the surrounding area; the international Hahnenkamm Ski Race in January and the Generali Open ATP Championship Series in the summer attracts stars from all over the world.

What to See in Kitzbühel

✶✶ Picturesque farmhouse style
This idyllic, medieval town lies on an extensive hill. Two streets run through the centre of the town, the wide »Vorderstadt« and the somewhat narrower »Hinterstadt«. Lovely buildings, mine-owners' houses (»Gewerkenhäuser«), and broad, squat buildings constructed in the traditional style of the Lower Inntal valley characterize the town's appearance. In contrast to the towns of Inn-Salzach, the

The beautiful townscape with glorious mountains in the background make Kitzbühel one of the most popular holiday towns in Austria

buildings are not built flush against one another but are rather separated by narrow gaps, following the Bavarian model. This fact allowed the townspeople of Kitzbühel to avoid the strict fire codes of Emperor Maximilian (► Famous People) that would have forced them to enclose the roofs, and at the same time preserved the traditional farmhouse character of the townscape, with gabled roofs extending far beyond the exterior walls.

The simple Gothic church, the Katharinenkirche, is located across from the casino and features a modern St Christopher fresco from 1950 on its exterior wall. A winged altar, with painted outer wings, and a Madonna enthroned on a crescent (late 15th century) in the interior merit a closer look. Not far from the church is the medieval Jochberger Tor, the only city gate in Kitzbühel that has been preserved through to the present day, and which also marks the assumed location of the city's former castle.

Old Town

The Museum Kitzbühel is housed in the two most interesting buildings in the town: the former granary and the 700-year-old Südwestturm, the fortification tower that is the oldest preserved building in the town. The museum displays exhibits depicting the political, economical, and cultural history of the town and the region (opening times: 21 Dec to 8 March daily 10am–5pm, 9 March to 11 April Wed–Fri 2pm–5pm, Sat from 10am, 21 June to 14 Sept daily 10am–5pm, 16 Sept–Oct Tue–Sat 10am–1pm, Nov to 20 Dec Wed–Fri 2pm–5pm, Sat from 10am).

◄ Museum Kitzbühel

North of the Old Town (Altstadt) stands the parish church, Pfarrkirche St Andreas, which was built from 1435–1506 and later renovated in Baroque style. From the outside, the church is a massive structure; its low steeple is topped with a Baroque dome. Its interior fea-

Outside the Old Town

tures beautiful stucco work and painted ceilings. The choir is adorned with frescoes from the 15th century and is connected to the Rosaka-pelle (Chapel of St Rose), which features tracery windows and a ceiling painting of St Rose (c1750). The black and gold high altar (17th century), a work by the Kitzbühel sculptor Simon Benedikt Faisten-berger, is also of note. The lower church of the small, two-storeyed Liebfrauenkirche (Church of Our Lady) was built in 1373. The painted ceilings depict the Coronation of Our Lady (1739); the upper church was created by Simon Benedikt Faistenberger. The Rococo latticework (1781) and the organ are also worth a look. The pride of the city is the immense fortified tower with a 6332kg/13,960lbs bell, which is claimed to have the most beautiful ring in the entire country.

◀ Liebfrauenkirche

Around Kitzbühel

Bauernhaus-
museum
Hinterobernau

The Hinterobernau Farmhouse Museum outside Kitzbühel is definitely worth a visit. An almost 450-year-old farm in the Salzburg-Tyrolese single-residence style has been furnished and decorated as it would have been 100 years ago. The property includes a smoke room, a parlour and bedchambers, a stall and a barn, all outfitted with the appropriate objects, equipment and tools, as well as a small chapel and a farmhouse garden (opening times: June–Sept Mon–Sat 1pm–5pm).

 ▶ VISITING KITZBÜHEL

INFORMATION

Kitzbühel Tourismus
Hinterstadt 18, A-6370 Kitzbühel
Tel. 0 53 56/777, fax 777 77
www.kitzbuehel.com

WHERE TO EAT

▶ Expensive
Tennerhof
Griesenauweg 26, A-6370 Kitzbühel
Tel. 0 53 56/6 31 81
The harmonious creations of the Tennerhof's kitchen number among the true highlights of Tyrolese cuisine.

▶ Moderate
Gasthof Eggerwirt
Gänsbachgasse 12, A-6370 Kitzbühel
Tel. 0 53 56/6 24 55
A cosy atmosphere and traditional meals make this family-run local restaurant popular.

▶ Inexpensive
Gasthof Mauth
Hauptplatz 7
A-6380 St Johann in Tirol
Tel. 0 53 52/6 22 42
This inn offers hearty, down-to-earth meals.

WHERE TO STAY

▶ Luxury
Hotel Schloss Lebenberg
Lebenbergstrasse 17
A-6370 Kitzbühel
Tel. 0 53 56/69 01, fax 6 44 05
www.schloss-lebenberg.at
Schloss Lebenberg, located on a hill at the edge of the town, features an indoor swimming pool, a fitness studio, a spa section and its own kindergarden.

The Hahnenkamm (1655m/5428ft; cable car and chairlift) is used as a high-lying spa resort, for hiking, and for its ideal skiing terrain during the winter. The Bergbahnmuseum in the mountain station of the Hahnenkammbahn (cable car) exhibits the development of competitive skiing (opening times: daily 10am–4pm), while the skiing simulator gives visitors a deceivingly realistic glimpse of the wild ride down the notorious »Streif« ski run. A guided hike down the Streif in the summertime helps make it clear what a downhill run here really means. Thankfully it is not compulsory to tackle the world-famous Hahnenkamm race course (3.5km/2.1mi long) on real skis – there is also the more harmless »Familienstreif«, which, as the name implies, is suitable for the entire family.

✶ Hahnenkamm

Towering upwards northeast of Kitzbühel is the Kitzbüheler Horn mountain (1998m/6553ft) with its own lodge, chapel, restaurant, and broadcasting tower. In 1877, Austrian columnist Daniel Spitzer described the mountain, »the peaks of which, when viewed from the city, form two round hills that pretty closely resemble a woman's bosoms«, as he perceptively noted. The Horn, which can be easily reached by a gondola extending over the 1273m/4175ft-high Pletzeralm (ascent from Kitzbühel approximately 4–5 hours), offers a fabulous view: from the Radstädter Tauern in the south to the Ötztaler Alps, the nearby Kaisergebirge mountain range in the north, the Lechtal Alps in the far west, and the Hochkönig in the east. A garden featuring alpine flowers has been installed near the lodge (20,000 sq metres/5ac).

✶ Kitzbüheler Horn

> ## ❗ *Baedeker* TIP
>
> ### Wildpark Tirol
>
> A popular destination for a day trip is the Wildpark Tirol, which is located 8km/5mi from Kitzbühel in the town of Oberaurach. More than 200 native alpine animals live in an area of 40ha/99ac, and visitors can observe them closely in their natural habitat (opening times: Christmas–mid-Nov, Tue–Sun 9am–5pm, feeding time 2.30pm).

Located approximately 10km/6mi north of Kitzbühel is **St Johann in Tyrol** (660m/2165ft; pop. 7800). The town, located at an important traffic junction, is well-visited in both the summer and the winter thanks to its picturesque farmhouses. The twin-steepled parish church, Pfarrkirche Mariä Himmelfahrt (1723–28), which is the emblem of the town, features beautiful stucco work and an attractive ceiling painting by Simon Benedikt Faistenberger; the Antoniuskapelle (Chapel of St Anthony; 1671–74), an eight-sided, early Baroque building on a central ground plan, has a dome fresco by Josef Schöpf (1803). The »Spitalkirche in der Weitau«, located in the western part of the town, has a Rococo interior from 1740 and the only Gothic stained glass window in Tyrol – which also numbers among the largest and most significant medieval glass paintings in the entire province – consisting of ten stained glass panels with images of saints and benefactors (c1480) on a double-panelled lancet window behind the high altar.

Kitzbühel Alps The Kitzbühel Alps adjoin the Zillertal valley in the east and are bordered by the Salzachtal valley and the Pinzgau in the south. As the **longest stretch of slate Alps in Austria**, their widely ramified, gentle ridges extend for approximately 100km/62mi. Its alpine pastures are naturally void of trees and extend from the heights of the mountain ridges to the floor of countless longitudinal and lateral valleys, which certainly aided the development of the Kitzbühel Alps into one of the most comprehensive and most popular ski regions in all of Austria, even in all of Europe.

Kreuzjoch, Grosser Galtenberg, Salzachgeier ▶ Grosser Rettenstein ▶ The western section of the Kitzbühel Alps features the highest, most distinctive peaks of the entire range, from the Kreuzjoch (2558m/8390ft) to the Torhelm (2495m/8184ft) and then north over several peaks to the Grosser Galtenberg (2425m/7954ft) near Alpbach, as well as the Salzachgeier (2470m/8102ft). The most striking peak of the Kitzbühel Alps is the Grosser Rettenstein (2363m/7751ft), which is located southwest of Kitzbühel and can be reached via the Oberland-Hütte (1041m/8414ft) near Aschau.

✳ Klagenfurt

M 6

Province: Carinthia
Population: 92,000

Elevation: 445m/1460ft

Klagenfurt is a lively industrial and commercial city, yet it possesses a southern European flair with its attractive alleyways and enchanting arcades and courtyards. The city has received several awards honouring its dedication to preserving its idyllic Old Town.

Rose of the Wörther See The southernmost Austrian provincial capital, located on the eastern shore of Lake Worth, is known as the »rose of the Wörther See«. It is bordered by the wooded hills of the Sattnitz in the south, with the Karawanken mountains rising up in the background.

Literary tradition Klagenfurt is the birthplace of Robert Musil (1880–1942), who became famous through his novel *The Man Without Qualities* (1930–33). Also born here was Ingeborg Bachmann (1926–73), who mainly created a name for herself with her lyric poetry (*Borrowed Time*, 1953; *Invocation of the Great Bear*, 1956). The annual literary prize in her name is awarded during the »Tage der deutschsprachigen Literatur« (German-language Literature Festival) and numbers among the most coveted prizes for literature in the world.

History The small market town was established on a ford over the Glan River during the mid-12th century. According to recent research, the name refers to the popular superstition at the time that sinister water demons plagued the marshy area around the ford and claimed human

The Alte Platz with Trinity Column, town model and beautiful town houses

victims. This is also the origin of the legend of the Lindwurm, a dragon who lived in the marshes and preyed on local farm animals until he was killed by a brave Carinthian who was thereafter named Hercules. **Lindwurm and Hercules** are still present today – set in stone on Neuer Platz.

The city was destroyed by fire in 1514. At the time, the Carinthian Estates were looking for their own town and asked Emperor Maximilian I (► Famous People), to give them the poverty-stricken city. In 1518, he granted their request. Klagenfurt rose to become the provincial capital (formerly St Veit an der Glan) and continued to expand. The Lend Canal was built from 1527 to 1558, supplying the moat surrounding the city with water – it connects Klagenfurt and the Wörther See to this day.

What to See in Klagenfurt

Neuer Platz
◄ Lindwurm-Fountain

The central element of the **picturesque Old Town** is the spacious Neuer Platz with the Lindwurm Fountain, Klagenfurt's city emblem. The model for the head of the stone sculpture, created in 1590, was the skull of an ice-age woolly rhinoceros that was discovered in the area around the city and is now on display in the Landesmuseum. At the time, the skull was thought to be that of a dragon. The Hercules figure, crafted by Michael Hönel, who also created the high altar in the Gurker Dom, and the iron lattice work was added in 1636.

Scores of beautiful historical buildings surround Neuer Platz. The former Palais Rosenberg, built around 1650 on the western side of Neuer Platz, has served as the Rathaus (city hall) since 1918. The tourist information centre is also located here. House no. 4, no. 7, and no. 10 feature lovely arcaded courtyards; no. 9 (pharmacy) on the east side has an interior of delightful Rococo stucco work. The oldest preserved statue of the Empress Maria Theresia (► Famous People), created in 1764, stands on the eastern side of the square. The old hard-lead statue was replaced by the current bronze figure in 1873.

Kramergasse

Kramergasse is the oldest pedestrian zone in Austria (since 1961) and **one of the oldest streets in the entire city**, with buildings constructed in the Wilhelmanian and art nouveau periods. *Wörther-See-Mandls* (1965), a small sculpture by Heinz Goll, stands here (►Wörther See).

Alter Platz The centre of the oldest district of the city is the elongated Alter Platz, on which stands the Dreifaltigkeitssäule (Trinity Column; 1689). The square is framed by Baroque buildings with arcaded courtyards, including the Altes Rathaus (Old City Hall; 17th century) with its picturesque three-storey arcaded courtyard, and the Haus zur Goldenen Gans (House of the Golden Goose; no. 31; c1500), which once accommodated the emperor. He relinquished his for-

Klagenfurt *Map*

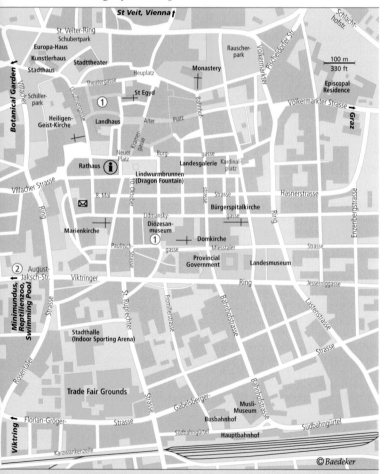

Where to eat
① Augustin

Where to stay
① Hotel Goldener Brunnen
② Schlosshotel Wörther See

Those with the patience can count the 665 coats of arms decorating the Heraldic Hall of the Landhaus

tress, which was later razed to the ground, to the Estates in exchange for the construction of the Landhaus.

To the north of Alter Platz stands the city parish church, Stadtpfarr-kirche St Egyd, an imposing yet somewhat gloomy structure from the 17th–18th centuries, with numerous coats of arms on the stone slabs and gravestones.

Stadtpfarrkirche St Egyd

Standing between Alter Platz and Heilig-Geist-Platz to the west is the most prestigious secular building of the city, the Landhaus. Built in 1574–94 on the site of a former ducal moated castle, its exterior is marked by two onion-domed stair towers and a two-storey arcaded courtyard. The Grosse Wappensaal, a grand hall featuring hundreds of coats of arms, was built in 1739–40 after a fire. 665 coats of arms from the Carinthian Estates cover the walls. A painting by Carinthian Baroque painter Joseph Fromiller from 1728, the Estates' tribute to Charles VI, adorns the ceiling (opening times: April–Oct Mon–Sat 9am–1pm and 2pm–5pm).

★ Landhaus

Northwest of the Landhaus stands the art nouveau building (1908–10) which has now become the expanded municipal theatre.

◀ Stadttheater

Ursulinengasse and then Wiesbadener Strasse lead back to Neuer Platz. Proceeding further, Karfreitstrasse heads south to the cathedral, which was built by the Protestant Estates in 1578–91. It was given to Jesuits in 1604, and has been the cathedral of the Prince-Bishop of the Gurk diocese since 1787, who resides in Klagenfurt. The interior of the **oldest pilaster church in Austria**, whose spacious feel is a result of the surrounding galleries, is adorned with stucco work and paintings from the 18th century. The lavish pulpit is most likely a work by Christoph Rudolph (1726), while the painting on the high altar was created by Daniel Gran (1752). Colourful marble décor can be seen in the side chapels.

Domkirche

Diözesanmuseum The Diocesan Museum, located on the Domplatz, exhibits religious garments, sacred art, folk art, and glass painting. Experts consider the »Magdalenenscheibe« (1170) to be Austria's oldest glass painting (opening times: June–mid-Sept Mon–Sat 10am–noon, early–mid-June also 3pm–5pm).

Landesmuseum Opposite the cathedral stands the splendid building of the provincial government. Next to it, to the east, is the Carinthian Landesmuseum, constructed in 1879–84. It holds comprehensive collections pertaining to the natural and cultural history of Carinthia, with exhibits on the Klagenfurt's history including the woolly rhinoceros skull that was the »model« for the Lindwurm Fountain. Reliefs of the Grossglockner, the Villach Alps, and the Eastern Karawanken range depict the Carinthian mountain landscape. The museum's park features Roman memorials, gravestones, and altars of stone, some of which were found in Virunum on the Zollfeld north of Klagenfurt (Museumsgasse 2; opening times: Tue–Fri 10am–6pm, Thu until 8pm, Sat and Sun until 5pm).

Robert-Musil-Literaturmuseum Located in the Bahnhofstrasse 50, the birthplace of Robert Musil is now the Robert Musil Museum of Literature. It documents the life

 VISITING KLAGENFURT

INFORMATION

Klagenfurt Tourismus
Neuer Platz 1, A-9010 Klagenfurt
Tel. 04 63/5 37 22 23, fax 5 37 62 18,
www.info.klagenfurt.at

WHERE TO EAT

▶ **Moderate**
① **Augustin**
Pfarrhofgasse 2, A-9020 Klagenfurt
Tel. 04 63/51 39 92
The beer in this Augustine inn originates in Puntigam (Graz), and the cuisine is quite down-to-earth. Speciality of the house: »Bieraufstrichbrot«, bread topped with a beer-based spread.

WHERE TO STAY

▶ **Mid-range**
① **Hotel Goldener Brunnen**
Karfreitstrasse 14, A-9020 Klagenfurt
Tel. 04 63/5 73 80; fax 51 65 20
www.goldener-brunnen.at
Guests have a view of the decoratively planted inner courtyard, with cafés and boutiques, through the glass arcades; rooms facing the street offer a view of the square in front of the cathedral.

Baedeker recommendation

▶ **Budget**
② **Schlosshotel Wörther See**
Villacher Strasse 338
A-9020 Klagenfurt
Tel. 04 63/21 15 80
Fax 21 15 88
www.schloss-hotel.at
Located near to the lakeshore, this hotel offers 35 well furnished rooms and has its own beach, conference rooms, and a rustic restaurant with international cuisine on the menu.

and works of the writers **Ingeborg Bachmann** and **Christine Lavant** ☉
(opening times: Mon–Fri 10am–5pm, Sat 10am–2pm).

West of the city centre, on the shore of the Wörther See, is the gigan- ✱
tic municipal swimming complex and the marina. Along with the **Minimundus**
Europapark, the charming Minimun-
dus certainly deserves a more extended
visit: the »little world on the Wörther
See« displays **replicas of famous structures** from all over the world on a scale
of 1:25, a dock with model ships, and
a model railroad (opening times: April
and Oct 9am–6pm, May, June and Sept
until 7pm, July and Aug until 8pm).

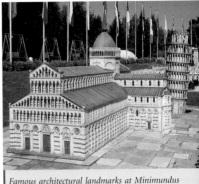

Right next to the Minimundus and also
worth a look are the planetarium and
the **Happ Reptile Zoo**, with snakes,
crocodiles, spiders, and insects from all
over the world (opening times: in winter daily 10am–5pm; in summer 8am–
6pm). This also happens to be the loca-

Famous architectural landmarks at Minimundus

tion where native endangered snake species are taken to breed before
new animals are released into the wild.

The Klagenfurt Botanical Garden is situated at the foot of the Kreuz- **Botanischer**
berg on an old quarry site northwest of the Old Town. Spices, useful **Garten**
plants and medicinal plants, in addition to endemic species, are on
display on the rocky shelves and terraces. Those who were not lucky
enough to find a *Wulfenia carinthiaca* in the wild will be more successful here (opening times: May–Sept 9am–6pm, Oct–April Mon– ☉
Thu 9am–4pm). The Botanical Garden also provides an entrance to ◄ **Bergbaumuseum**
the Mining Museum, housed in Klagenfurt's only air-raid tunnel.
The rich mining history of the country is illustrated with beautiful
mineral finds (opening times: May–Sept daily 9am–6pm; don't forget ☉
to wear warm clothes!).

Around Klagenfurt

►Maria Saal **Maria Saal**

Southwest of Klagenfurt lies Viktring, now incorporated into the city **Viktring**
and known for its former Cistercian abbey (founded in 1142 and
dissolved in 1786), **one of the most significant monastery sites in
all of Carinthia**. Today, the buildings are home to a secondary school
with an emphasis on music. During the summer months, the Musik-
forum Viktring offers master classes and concerts ranging from contemporary music to jazz. The former abbey church is the only 12-

century Cistercian church in any German-speaking country that is still intact today. The choir has valuable glass paintings from around 1400.

Karawanken South of Klagenfurt lies the jagged chain of Karawanken mountains, ranging from 20km/12mi to 40km/25mi in width and approximately 120km/74mi in length. As a part of the Southern Limestone Alps, the range continues the line of the Carnic Alps toward the east to form the border. Its long ridge extends between the valleys of the Drau and the Save. Most of its peaks are relatively easy to reach; the top offers a nice view of the Carinthian lake basin. Several hiking trails enable climbers to reach several different peaks successively without losing too much height. The highest peak of the Karawanken is the Hochstuhl (2238m/7341ft). The Karawanken range also has several alpine passes, including the Loiblpass and the Klagenfurt–Ljubljana highway.

Kleinwalsertal

D 5

Province: Vorarlberg

The Kleinwalsertal valley lies southwest of Oberstdorf near the German-Austrian border. The Grosse Walsertal extends south of Bregenz Forest and north of ►Bludenz.

Between Germany and Austria Although the 15km/9.3mi-long Kleinwalsertal is technically a part of the Austrian province of Vorarlberg, it became a part of German customs territory in 1891 – it is separated from Austria by towering mountains (Widderstein, Untschenspitze, Hoher Ifen) and therefore has no road or train connections to the rest of Vorarlberg. The town

▶ VISITING KLEINWALSERTAL

INFORMATION

Kleinwalsertal
Tourismus
Im Walserhaus
A-6992/D-87568 Hirschegg

From Austria:
Tel. 0 55 17/511 40, fax 511 44 19
www.kleinwalsertal.com

WALSERBUS

Public transport in the Kleinwalsertal

valley is well established. The Walserbus offers a service in short, regular intervals: every 15 minutes in the summer, every 8 minutes in the winter, and every hour during the off-season.
Line 1 runs between Oberstdorf and Baad, line 2 between Riezlern and Schwende and/or Egg, line 3 between Hirschegg and Wäldele, line 4 between Mittelberg and Höfle, and line 5 between Ifen and Hirschegg.

The Walserhaus is characteristic of the Kleine Walsertal valley

uses Austrian postage stamps and the cars have Austrian licence plates (duty-free zone). Yet until quite recently, anyone arrested in the Kleinwalsertal could not be transported to Austria by way of Germany, and was therefore forced to undertake a several-hour march over numerous ridges and passes to Austria accompanied by an experienced mountain guide. In the 14th century, criminals in the Kleinwalsertal could expect a different punishment: serious offenders were sentenced to single-handedly chisel three crosses, so-called »Sühnekreuze«, out of stone and to erect them at the crime scene. Today, the crosses stand in Mittelberg beneath Pfarrkirche St Jodok, the parish church next to the Walmendinger Horn funicular station.

The Kleinwalsertal is a wide valley through which the Breitach river flows surrounded by wooded slopes and rugged limestone cliffs. It is **one of Austria's most attractive and well-known mountain valleys** and is popular with visitors during winter due to its pleasant high-altitude climate and the reliable supply of snow. The municipality includes four sections (Riezlern, Hirschegg, Mittelberg and Baad) and has a population of approximately 5000. The inhabitants' forefathers emigrated from the Swiss canton of Valais around the year 1300 – and were welcomed as specialists for the development of rough, high-lying mountain valleys. The medieval territorial lords rewarded the efforts of the settlers with a wide range of freedoms, including self-government, inheritable feudal property, and low rents. The territorial lords eventually changed, but certain freedoms, like the »Schwizer« (Swiss) dialect, remained, as well as the Valais customs and traditional costume.

✱ Landscape and settlements

The initial starting point for a visit to the Kleinwalsertal is Oberstdorf in the Allgäu Alps. 6km/3.7mi outside the town, the Gasthof Walserschanz marks the German-Austrian border. The road then continues further up the valley, with a nice view of the Hoher Ifen and the Gottesackerwände mountains.

Setting out from Oberstdorf

Near the border next to the Walserschanz (991m/3250ft) is the upper entrance to the ruggedly picturesque Breitach Gorge. A steep road featuring countless bridges and viewing points leads downhill past escarpments up to 100m/328ft high and continues past a waterfall to the end of the gorge, which is on German territory.

✱ Breitachklamm

Riezlern

Riezlern (1100m/3608ft), the largest town in the Kleinwalsertal, lies at the mouth of the Schwarzwassertal valley. In addition to the local Walsermuseum, with collections on the history and the traditions of the valley (opening times: Christmas–Easter and late May–late October, Mon–Sat 2pm–5pm), the Skimuseum in the Walserhaus, (opening times: Mon–Sat 2pm–5pm), and a casino, Riezlern offers several leisure facilities (indoor swimming pool, open-air swimming pool, tennis courts).

Kanzelwand-bahn, Fellhorn

South of Riezlern, the Kanzelwandbahn cable car takes travellers to heights of up to 2000m/6560ft, where they can find an extensive hiking and skiing area. The Fellhorn mountain (2039m/6688ft) rises up to the north of the town; cable cars make the ascent up the mountain on the German side of the border.

Hirschegg

Hirschegg (1124m/3687ft) is a popular base for hikers and skiers alike. The parish church is located on a bank where a stag is said to have fought with a bear. The »Walserhaus«, rustic in style, is an events centre and meeting place for guests. The tourist information office is also located here and a country theatre also puts on performances.

Baad, Widderstein

Baad (1251m/4103ft), a group of houses at the end of the Walsertal that belongs to Mittelberg, is located near the 2533m/8308ft-high Widderstein mountain which rises up to the south. In the summer, the Hochalp Pass (1938m/6357ft) provides access to Bregenzerwald-strasse near the Hochtannberg Pass.

✹ ✹ Klosterneuburg

Q 3

Province: Lower Austria	**Elevation:** 192m/630ft
Population: 25,000	

Separated from the Danube by a wide belt of water meadow, the wine-growing town of Klosterneuburg is situated on the northeast edge of the Wienerwald. It entices visitors with the sacral art of Stift Klosterneuburg, the famous Augustinian abbey, and the modern variety in the Essl collection.

✹ Abbey of Augustinian Canons

Abbey building

The extensive grounds of the abbey, located high above the Danube, were founded by the Babenberg Duke Leopold III (also known as St Leopold) in the 12th century. According to the legend, Leopold had the abbey built on exactly the spot where he had found his wife's wedding veil, which she had lost at their wedding ceremony nine years before. The buildings of the abbey, which can only be seen on a guided tour, include the abbey church, the Leopoldskapelle (chapel of St Leopold), a Romanesque-Gothic cloister, the Leopoldihof, and the Stiftskeller (abbey cellar).

Stiftskirche

The Romanesque abbey church was built in 1114–36 and then comprehensively renovated in the Baroque style in the 17th–18th centuries. Both of its steeples received neo-Gothic spires toward the end of the 19th century. Composer and organist Anton Bruckner praised the tonal quality of the famous organ (1642) – the largest preserved monumental organ in the world, whose tone is exactly as it was in 1642.

Leopoldskapelle
✷ ✷
◄ Verdun Altar

A stairway leads up to the Leopoldskapelle (12th century; formerly the chapter house), the burial chapel of Leopold III, which also contains the famous Verdun Altar behind a wrought-iron grille. This **magnificent example of medieval enamel work** consists of 51 plates featuring biblical scenes, depicted using the champlevé technique with gilded copper. Nicholas of Verdun – who had also worked on the Shrine of the Three Kings at Cologne Cathedral – created the enamel plates as an encasement for the ambo (pulpit) in the Romanesque church in 1181. Following a fire in 1330, the panels were put together to form the current Gothic winged altar. The mortal remains of the founder, St Leopold, rest in the gilded casket. The lovely stained glass windows from 14th and 15th centuries are also worth a closer look.

The Verdun Altar is a beautiful example of medieval enamel art

▶ KLOSTERNEUBURG

INFORMATION

Tourismusverein Klosterneuburg
Bahnhof Kierling, Niedermarkt 4
A-3400 Klosterneuburg
Tel. 0 22 43/3 20 38, fax 2 67 73,
www.klosterneuburg.net

In 1730, Emperor Karl VI, Maria Theresia's father, began building a large-scale extension. New religious and secular buildings were to increase the site to four times its original size. Yet ten years after the emperor's death, the construction was halted, and the building work was finally completed in 1834–42 on a significantly smaller scale. The Residenztrakt (residence wing) nevertheless represents an excellent example of Baroque design; both domes are capped with the German imperial crown and the Austrian archducal hat. Above the Baroque entrance hall is Austria's largest private academic library, the contents of which are only available to students.

✳ Residenztrakt, library

Stiftsmuseum The abbey museum is well worth seeing. It features a Habsburg family tree and exhibits four panels from the back of the Verdun Altar (opening times: May–Nov, Tue-Sun 9am–6pm). The **guided tour of the abbey** takes in the Kuchlhof, the emperor's rooms with a marble and a tapestry halls (featuring sumptuous tapestries from Brussels), the cloister, and the chapel of St Leopold (daily 10am–5pm).

Klosterneuberg *Site of the Abbey of Augustinian Canons*

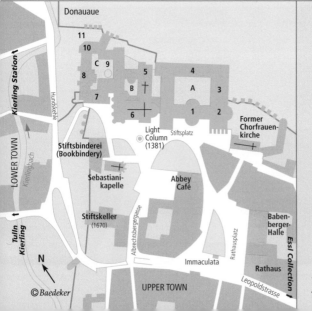

A Kaiserhof in restored chapel buildings (Abbey Museum on 2nd floor)
B Cloister (Freisinger Chapel, Lapidarium)
C Leopoldihof
1 Entrance (library above)
2 Marble Hall
3 Imperial Apartments
4 Prelate's Quarters
5 St Leopold's Chapel (Verdun Altar)
6 Collegiate Church
7 Former Tower
8 Archive Room
9 Fountain (1592)
10 Mosmuller Wing (1620)
11 Orangery

Map labels: Donauaue · Kierling Station · Hundskehle · LOWER TOWN · Kierlingbach · Stiftsbinderei (Bookbindery) · Sebastiani-kapelle · Stiftskeller (1670) · Tulln Kierling · N · © Baedeker · Light Column (1381) · Stiftsplatz · Abbey Café · Albrechtsbergergasse · Immaculata · UPPER TOWN · Former Chorfrauen-kirche · Stiftsplatz · Rathausplatz · Baben-berger-Halle · Rathaus · Leopoldstrasse · Essl Collection

The Stiftsweingut Klosterneuburg, founded in 1114 by Margrave Leopold III, is **the oldest winery in Austria** and creates exquisite wines. 55% of its wines are red and 45% of them white; they are produced on 110ha/272ac of land and can be tasted at the Vinothek (opening times: Mon–Fri 9am–6pm, Sat until 5pm). On a tour of the mighty, four-storey vault with walls up to 7m/23ft thick, visitors can marvel at the **Tausendeimerfass** (»1000-pail-barrel«, capacity 56,000l/14,800 US gal) from 1704.

Vinothek ☉

Other Sights in Klosterneuburg

The Essl Collection is housed in a modern gallery designed and built in the 20th and early 21st century by Austrian architect Heinz Tesar and striking a marked contrast to the quaint little town with its old town houses and its Baroque Rathaus (town hall). The pieces in the collection, which has been internationally oriented since the 1990s, span from Art Informel to Viennese Actionism and the Realist tendencies of the 1970s and on to the »Neue Malerei« of the 1980s and the pluralistic styles and media of the present day. The gallery is an unparalleled collection of postwar Austrian painting and places it within an international context. Several temporary exhibitions are featured alongside the permanent pieces throughout the year (An der Donau-Au 1; opening times: Tue–Sun 10am–6pm, Wed until 9pm).

★ **Sammlung Essl**

> **? DID YOU KNOW …?**
>
> ■ … that Stift Klosterneuburg is heated with environmentally friendly biomass energy? The abbey and the Happyland amusement park began their technically elaborate, forward-looking project with a wood chip system. The carbon dioxide-neutral biomass heating system also supplies the hospital, the Babenbergerhalle, and the Rathaus.

Located to the west in the district of Kierling is the former Sanatorium Hoffmann. The room in which Franz Kafka spent the last days of his life – he died on 3 June 1924 of laryngeal tuberculosis – has been made into a memorial to the writer.

Kafka Memorial

Around Klosterneuburg

Tulln (170m/558ft; pop. 15,000), **one of Austria's oldest towns**, lies on the right bank of the Danube, 25km/15mi west of Klosterneuburg. In Roman times, it was the location of the Comagena military base; the epic poem the Nibelungenlied tells of »Tulne«, where King Etzel receives Kriemhild. The town's most precious historical treasure is the late Romanesque Karner (Charnel House; 13th century), an eleven-sided structure with a very unique vaulted doorway. The buildings of the Minorite monastery, which was founded in the 13th century, originate from the 18th century and are used for art exhibitions as well as being home to the Austrian Sugar Museum (Minoritenplatz 1; guided tours by arrangement, tel. 022 72 / 69 01 22).

Tulln

◄ Zuckermuseum

Römermuseum ► The Roman Museum documents life at Fort Comagena with original artefacts, dioramas and models. One of its rooms is reserved for the »Kaiserliches Frauenstift«, or Imperial Convent, which was founded by Rudolf I (Marc-Aurel-Park 1 b; opening times: April–Oct, Tue–Sun 10am–noon and 1pm–5pm).

Egon Schiele Museum ► The birthplace of the painter Egon Schiele has created a museum for its famous son, which is housed in the former district prison. Visitors can watch a documentary on Schiele's life and work as well as seeing over 100 of his original works (Donaulände 28; opening times: April–Oct Tue–Sun 10am–noon and 1pm–5pm).

★ Krems an der Donau

P 3

| **Province:** Lower Austria | **Elevation:** 221m/725 feet |
| **Population:** 24,000 | |

A stroll through the picturesque alleyways of Krems is like a journey back in time. Well-maintained historical buildings dominate the townscape, which together with the Wachau region has been a UNESCO World Cultural Heritage site since 2000.

Gateway to the Wachau — Surrounded by the terraces of vineyard-lined hills, Krems, one of the oldest towns in Lower Austria, is located on the eastern side of the ►Wachau at the point where the Danube trade route intersects the north-south connection between the Waldviertel and Weinviertel and the alpine foreland. Along with tourism, viniculture continues to play an important economic role here.

History — First mentioned in documents in 995, Krems was granted its municipal charter in the 12th century and developed into the site of a mint (»Kremser Pfennig«). The foundation of monasteries during and after the Carolingian period greatly increased the importance of the vineyards. Until the 19th century, Krems was a prominent trade hub. Its most famous local hero is the Baroque painter Martin Johann Schmidt (1718–1801), also known as **Kremser Schmidt** .

What to See in Krems

★
Old Town
Steiner Tor ► — The Steiner Tor (1480), an emblem of the town, is the last of four medieval city gates still in existence today. It forms the western end of the Old Town's main axis formed by the Obere and Untere Landstrasse. It is topped by a tall Baroque cap (1754) and flanked by two round towers that terminate in points.

WEINSTADT-museum — The former Dominican church (13th century) stands on Dominikanerplatz with its adjoining monastery, which was closed in 1786. To-

Krems *Map*

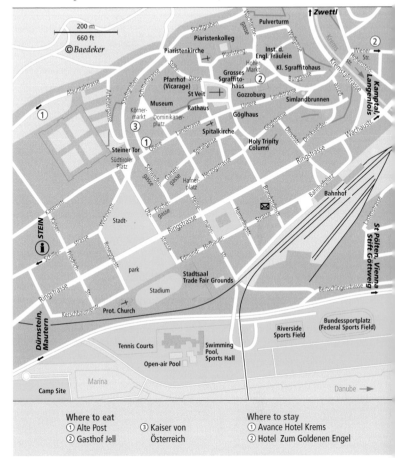

Where to eat		Where to stay
① Alte Post	③ Kaiser von	① Avance Hotel Krems
② Gasthof Jell	Österreich	② Hotel Zum Goldenen Engel

day, the former rooms of the monastery are home to the WEIN-STADTmuseum. Here, visitors can not only have a glimpse into the life of winemakers over 100 years ago, but also see selected artistic treasures, including a copy of a small statue of the **Venus of Galgenberg**, the original of which was discovered not far from Krems. It is 32,000 years old, making it the oldest known statue of a human being to be in existence today (Körnermarkt 14; opening times: March–Nov Tue–Sun 10am–6pm). ⏲

The parish church, Pfarrkirche St Veit, stands on Pfarrplatz opposite the Rathaus (town hall). Originally a Romanesque church, it was **St Veit**

▶ VISITING KREMS AN DER DONAU

INFORMATION

Krems Tourismus
Undstrasse 6 (Kloster Und)
A-3504 Krems
Tel. 0 27 32/8 26 76, fax 7 00 11
www.krems.info

WHERE TO EAT

▶ Moderate

① Alte Post
Obere Landstr. 32, A-3500 Krems
Tel. 0 27 32/822 76
In this comfortable inn with a Baroque summerhouse and a romantic arcaded courtyard diners enjoy homemade Austria specialities and wines from the Wachau.

② Gasthaus Jell
Hoher Markt 8–9
A-3500 Krems
Tel. 0 27 32/8 23 45
Classic Austrian dishes and other delicacies are served here, following recipes by Hildegard von Bingen.

The Wachau is an excellent region for gourmets: the »Alte Post« inn in Krems

③ Kaiser von Österreich
Körnermarkt 9, A-3500 Krems
Tel. 0 27 32/8 60 01
Delightful restaurant in the Old Town, serving Austrian cuisine with a touch of the Mediterranean. Extensive wine list.

WHERE TO STAY

▶ Luxury

① Avance Hotel Krems
Am Goldberg 2, A-3500 Krems
Tel. 0 27 32/7 10 10, fax 7 10 10 50
www.steigenberger.com
This dignified Steigenberger Avance Hotel, offering wellness and therapeutic treatments, is located on the Goldberg in the midst of vineyards.

▶ Budget

② Hotel »Zum goldenen Engel«
Wienerstrasse 41, A-3500 Krems
Tel. 0 27 32/8 20 67, fax 7 72 61
www.hotel-ehrenreich-krems.at
The history of this building in the Old Town dates back to 1658; the hotel has been owned and operated by the Ehrenreich family since 1795.

renovated first in Gothic style and then, in 1616, in Baroque style by Italian master builder C. Biasino. The ceiling frescoes are works by Kremser Schmidt; the high altar, pulpit, and choir were created by J.M. Götz in 1733–35.

Piaristengasse climbs up to the high-lying, original church of the Piarist Order, a splendid late Gothic structure (choir from c1457, nave from 1511–15) that is apparently a work of the cathedral masonic lodge of Vienna. Most of the altar paintings are works by Kremser Schmidt.

Piaristenkirche

The Gozzoburg on Hoher Markt, the oldest city castle north of the Alps, was built in the mid-13th century by Gozzo, the town magistrate of Krems. The court room, heraldic hall, chapel of St Catherine and fresco room are architectural and art-historical jewels of the High Middle Ages (guide tours: Tue–Fri 11am and 2pm, Sat and Sun hourly 10am–6pm; night-time tour rounded off with an Italian buffet every Fri 7pm).

Gozzoburg

Somewhat further south on Margaretengasse is the Grosses Sgraffitohaus (no. 5; c1560), a building featuring masterpieces of sgraffito art by painter Hans von Pruch.

Grosses Sgraffitohaus

The Simandl Fountain can be found on Untere Landstrasse. »Simandl« (= little Simon) kneels before his wife, pleading with her to give him the key. According to legend, the sheepish men of Krems were scared enough to surrender the town to Bohemian forces without any resistance whatsoever. The resolute women of the town thereupon took over the job of defending Krems – and assumed command of their husbands.

Simandlbrunnen

Here is a riddle that's as old as the hills: what lies between Krems and Stein? The answer is of course »and«, or »und« in German. Sure enough, the road west from the Steiner Tor leads to the district of Und. Its former Capuchin monastery is now home to the town's tourist information office.

Kapuzinerkloster Und

The striking »Kunsthalle Krems« in a former tobacco factory displays Austrian and international art from the 19th and 20th centuries (Franz-Zeller-Platz 3; opening times: daily 10am–6pm).
Another part the »Kremser Kunstmeile«, Krems' artistic district, is the wonderful Karikaturmuseum (Museum of Caricature) with its comical exterior façade. It is dedicated to caricature artist **Manfred Deix**, who is famous for his unerring skill in depicting the Austrians and the rest of the world, and **IRONIMUS** (Gustav Peichl), who made contributions to the world of architecture. In addition, it offers temporary exhibits (Steiner Landstrasse 3a; opening times: daily 10am–6pm).

Kunsthalle Krems

Around Krems

Steiner Altstadt Located along Steiner Landstrasse are the historical buildings of **Stein's Old Town**, beginning with the Kremser Tor from the 15th century and the Göttweigerhof from the 13th–14th centuries. The former Minorite church now serves as a worthy venue for art exhibitions. Beyond the parish church, Pfarrkirche St Nikolaus, whose ceiling frescoes and altar paintings are by Kremser Schmidt, is the Passauerhof, which was named in annals dating as far back as 1263 as the Bishop of Passau's Zehnthof, to which farmers had to deliver their ten percent church tax. Then comes the Mauthaus, a magnificent Renaissance building from 1536, and the Mazzettihaus, a Baroque palace from 1721 in which Mozart-researcher Ludwig von Köchel was born. In front of the Linzer Tor stands the former residence of Kremser Schmidt, who lived here from 1756 until his death in 1801.

Mautern On the south bank of the Danube, across from Krems, lies the ancient Roman town of (named »Mutaren« in the Nibelungenlied), a former toll-collecting point. From the 1st to the 5th centuries, the Danube formed the northern boundary of the Roman Imperial territory, protected at this location by Fort Favianis. Artefacts from the Bronze Age through to the end of the Roman reign in AD 488 can be seen in the Römermuseum (Roman Museum; Schlossgasse 12; opening times: April–Oct, Wed–Sun 10am–noon, Fri and Sat also 4pm–6pm).

★
Stift Göttweig Just a few miles south of Krems, standing majestically on a wooded hilltop that can be seen from quite a distance, is Göttweig Abbey – a UNESCO World Cultural Heritage site since 2000. It was founded in 1083 by Bishop Altmann of Passau and was given to Benedictine monks in 1094. It is also known as the **»Austrian Montecassino«**, a reference to its Benedictine mother-monastery in Italy. After a large part of the monastery was destroyed by a fire in 1718, it was partially rebuilt – yet never completed – in Baroque style, beginning in 1719 and following plans by master builder Johann Lukas von Hildebrandt.

The impressive, architecturally unconventional **abbey church** features two noteworthy towers ending in blunt pyramids. Its loggia is positioned between the towers and features four Tuscan columns. Its

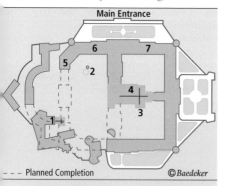

Krems Stift Göttweig

Main Entrance

- - - Planned Completion   ©Baedeker

1 Erentrudis Chapel
2 Obelisk (Fountain)
3 Treasury
  (group guided tours only)
4 Wing of Cloister
5 Imperial Staircase
6 Prince's Apartments
7 Imperial Apartments

pink-coloured exterior is unusual, as are the gold, brown, and blue tones within the richly decorated interior. Particularly noteworthy is its mighty high altar (1639), as well as the glass windows behind it, the choir stalls, the ornate organ front (1703), and the Altmann crypt with the reliquary casket of the abbey's founder.

The west wing of the abbey is home to the three-storey **Kaiserstiege** (1738), one of the most beautiful Baroque staircases, whose ceiling painting (1739) by Paul Troger depicts the apotheosis of Emperor Karl VI. The Fürstenzimmer (Prince's Chamber) and the Kaiserzimmer (Emperor's Chamber) are home to the »Museum im Kaisertrakt«, which has special yearly exhibits of the abbey's own art collection. The permanent exhibit, »Klosterleben« (»Monastery Life«) shows the Göttweiger monks' work and lifestyle both past and present (opening times: abbey site all year round, Museum im Kaisertrakt late March–mid-Nov, daily 10am–6pm, last admission 5pm, Jun–Sept from 9am).

The garden terrace of the abbey's restaurant offers an overwhelming panoramic view of the Danube Valley. It also provides the opportunity to test the wines from the abbey's own winery.

Kremsmünster

M 3

Province: Upper Austria
Population: 6500
Elevation: 345m/1132ft

The main attraction in Kremsmünster is its Benedictine abbey, which can be seen for miles standing majestically atop a bank above the Kremstal valley. This small town is located approx 35km/22mi southwest of Linz.

✱ Benedictine Abbey

According to legend, Gunther, son of the Bavarian Duke Tassilo, was killed while hunting a boar in the surrounding woods in AD 777. His aggrieved father decided to build a monastery on the spot where he lost his son. This makes Stift Kremsmünster the second oldest monastery in Austria after Stift Mondsee, not counting Salzburg as it first became Austrian territory in the 19th century. Gunther's tomb can be seen in the abbey church. In 1680, the original Romanesque-Gothic structure (13th century) was renovated by Baroque master builder Carlo A. Carlone. Lavish stucco work and lovely frescoes adorn the vaulting. The enormous high altar painting of the Transfiguration of Christ is a work of J. A. Wolf; most of the marble cherubs on the side altar were created by Michael Zürn (1682–86).

In the treasury a unique gem of art history is kept: the Tassilo Chalice, which is a good 25cm/10in high and weighs more than 3kg/6.5lbs.

Founding of Stift Kremsmünster

◀ Schatzkammer

This gilded copper vessel was most likely created in AD 768 for the marriage of Duke Tassilo with the Langobard Princess Luitbirg, and numbers among the most beautiful works of early medieval goldsmithery. A tablet-carved cross (1170) and the *Codex millenarius* (an evangelical manuscript from Mondsee; *c*800) are also worth seeing.

Abbey building

What is now the abbey building was constructed in the 17th and 18th centuries. Its magnificent Kaisersaal (Imperial Hall) and the equally impressive library containing approximately 160,000 volumes can be viewed on the guided tour (guided tours: May–Oct daily 10am, 11am, 2pm, 3pm and 4pm, min. 4 persons; www.stift-kremsmuenster.at). The fish ponds by C. Carlone are always accessible. The five water basins in the exterior courtyard are adorned with mythological figures (1691).

The 50m/164ft-high abbey **observatory**, also called the »mathematical tower«, was built in 1748–59 and is **the oldest high-rise building in Europe**. Its collections document scientific developments of the past 250 years, and it has served as a meteorological station since 1762 (guided tours: May–Oct daily 10am and 2pm, min. 5 persons).

The secondary school has been educating young minds since 1549. Adalbert Stifter was a student here.

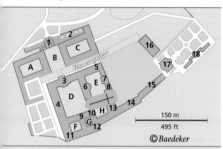

Stift Kremsmünster

A Upper Meierhof
B Outer Abbey Courtyard
C Lower Meierhof
D Prelates' Court
E Seminary Court
F Kitchen Courtyard
G Portnerhof
H Kreuzhof

1 Eichentor (Oak Gate)
2 Fish Ponds
3 Bridge Tower
4 Guest Wing
5 Seminarists' Refectory
6 Seminary Wing
7 Academic Chapel
8 Treasury
9 Art Collections
10 Chapterhouse
11 Imperial Hall
12 Refectory (library above)
13 Lady Chapel
14 Conventual Range
15 Clerical Range
16 School
17 Observatory
18 Garden House

150 m
495 ft
©Baedeker

Around Kremsmünster

Schloss Kremsegg is situated to the east of Kremsmünster. It was once home to a collection of vintage cars, which can now be seen in Hartberg in Styria (Oldtimer Museum Kröpfl).

Yet visitors can still find enough metal and valves here – in the form of a collection of musical instruments boasting such rarities as Tzar Peter's horn or Louis Armstrong's trumpet. Historical pianos are also on display (opening times: daily except Tue 10am–5pm).

Bad Hall

Local doctors got wind of the fact that farmers were using spring water from Bad Hall (388m/1273ft; pop. 5100), a town located 8km/5mi from Kremsmünster, to heal problems with goitres. Indeed, they did make a discovery: the salt springs contained iodine. By the mid-

▶ VISITING KREMSMÜNSTER

INFORMATION

Tourismusverband
Bad Hall – Kremsmünster
Kurpromenade 1
A-4540 Bad Hall
Tel. 072 58/720 00
Fax 72 00 20
www.kremsmuenster.at

WHERE TO EAT

▶ **Inexpensive**
Stiftsschank Kremsmünster
Stift 1
A-4550 Kremsmünster
Tel. 0 75 83/75 55
Trout from the abbey's fish ponds
tastes especially good when it is served
in a monastic atmosphere.

19th century, Bad Hall had risen to become a well-visited spa. Authors Bruckner and Grillparzer visited, and Mahler swung the baton for the spa's orchestra. Today, visitors can relax in the Tassilo thermal baths. Take time to pay a visit to the Handwerk- und Heimatmuseum **»Forum Hall«** to see the displays on arts and crafts and local history (Eduard-Bach-Strasse 4; opening times: April–Oct Thu–Sun 2pm–6pm).

Pfarrkirchen

The village of Pfarrkirchen, located directly south, has a famous church. Originally Gothic, it was then renovated in Baroque style with a delightful Rococo interior. Stucco work, frescoes, and altar paintings are all the work of painter Wolfgang Heindl (1693–1757).

Schlierbach

Schlierbach (407m/1335ft; pop. 2500) is known for its Cistercian abbey, founded in 1355. The church was rebuilt in 1674 by the Carlone family of artists and is adorned with an abundance of stucco work and frescoes. The abbey is also known for two other attractions: its glass painting workshop has already supplied the windows for the Church of the Annunciation in Nazareth, the Memorial Church in Hiroshima, and the Chapel for Europe in Brussels. The abbey's own cheese is delicious; it can age perfectly in the Baroque vaults, and its production is made easy to understand by taking a look in the »Schaukäserei« (guided tours: Palm Sunday–Oct Mon–Sat 10am and 2pm, Sun 10.30am and 2pm, Nov–Palm Sunday Mon–Fri 10am and 2pm, Sat 10am).

Micheldorf

In Micheldorf (448m/1469ft; pop. 5800) there is a rarity worth seeing, the **Sensenschmiedemuseum** (see www.sensenschmiedemuseum.at for more information). It is a little more mystical at the »Klangwelten Phyrn-Eisenwurzen« in the same building, which presents the sounds and music of the region (Gradnstrasse 10; opening times: May–Oct Sat and Sun 10am–1pm and 2pm–5pm and by arrangement; tel. 075 82/517 00).

✳ ✳ **Krimml**

Province: Salzburg **Elevation:** 1067m/3500ft
Population: 900

A chance to see the highest waterfalls in central Europe is more than enough to make stopping off in the small village of Krimml worthwhile.

Wasser-
WunderWelt

Located high above the Salzachtal valley, the village of Krimml is the starting point for a visit to the Krimml Waterfalls. But before heading out, the WasserWunderWelt is well worth a visit. The exhibition colourfully demonstrates the fantastic possibilities that a single drop of water offers and the ways in which water can be used (Haus des Wassers, Aqua-Park; opening times: May–Oct daily 10am–5pm).

✳ ✳ **Krimml Waterfalls**

Spectacular
natural beauty

South of the Gerlos Pass, which connects the Zillertal valley in Tyrol with the Salzachtal valley in the province of Salzburg, the Krimmler Ache flows from a high valley down three cascades to descend a total of 380m/1246ft. In 1961, the Krimml Waterfalls were listed as a nature reserve and number among the most significant attractions in the Eastern Alps. Starting at the waterfalls car park, a hiking trail furnished with numerous viewing points climbs approximately 4km/2.5mi up to the highest cascade, a good 1.5-hour walk.

A visit to the waterfalls can be a pretty wet event, since the plummeting water creates a constant source of spray and mist – the perfect climate for quite a few rare varieties of moss. This includes the fascinating **luminous moss**, a tiny species of moss that possesses cells able to reflect light. It has a golden shimmer, especially when it grows on grey rock between the cliffs, yet as soon as the moss-covered stone is held to the light, the gold disappears immediately – and the fabulous discovery of gold with it.

Around Krimml

Two hours south of the upper end of the waterfalls is the lovely high-lying valley leading to the **Krimmler Tauernhaus** (1631m/5350ft), which offers food and lodging. The mountain dwelling was mentioned in documents dating as far back as 1389. Although it has all of the modern amenities, the old »Gaststube«, or parlour, has remained unchanged throughout the centuries.

Glockenkarkopf

Experienced mountain climbers can then continue for another four hours to the Glockenkarkopf (2913m/9555ft), located on the Italian border. The hike from the Krimmler Tauernhaus to the pass of Krimmler Tauern (2633m/8636ft) takes slightly longer than 3 hours. An ancient mule track then continues to the South Tyrolese Ahrntal valley.

The attractive twists and turns of **Gerlosstrasse** (toll road) wind for approximately 17km/11mi from Krimml over the ridge of the Filzstein Alps and then to the Durlassboden reservoir (1400m/4592ft). The Filzstein (1648m/5405ft; lodge) offers a wonderful view into the valley of the Krimmler Ache.

The Wildgerlostal valley, part of the Hohe Tauern National Park, begins at the Durlassboden reservoir (1376m/4513ft). A hike to the Alpengasthof Finkau, an alpine inn, takes approximately 2 hours. From there, it takes another 3 hours to reach the Zittauer Hütte (2329m/7639ft; lodging) at the splendid top of the valley near the Unterer Gerlossee.

✱ Wildgerlostal

▶ KRIMML

INFORMATION

Tourismusverband Krimml
A-5743 Krimml
Tel. 065 64/72 390, fax 75 39 14
www.krimml.at

✱ Kufstein

H 4

Province: Tyrol
Population: 15,700

Elevation: 503m/1650ft

Kufstein is a well-visited holiday resort in the middle of a delightful lake region. The town, formerly located on the Tyrolese border, is significant for the traffic routes between Bavaria and Tyrol.

A well-known Austrian ballad once named Kufstein the »Pearl of Tyrol«, a town located where the lower Inn river cuts through the Alps between the ► Kaisergebirge in the east and Pendling in the southwest. The striking fortress was built to protect the settlement, which was often subject of disputes between Bavaria and Tyrol in medieval times.

»Pearl of Tyrol«

What to See in Kufstein

The city's emblem, the Feste – or fortress – Kufstein, standing on its rough, rocky bastion far above the banks of the Inn, survived the turbulence of the centuries largely untouched. It is reached via a covered stairway to the right of the

✱ Feste Kufstein

church or in the glass inclined elevator beginning at the Festungs-neuhof, which provides the more comfortable route. First mentioned in documents in 1205, the fortress was snatched away from the Bavarians in 1504 by Emperor Maximilian I (► Famous People): although the fortress was said to have been insurmountable, the Emperor bombarded it with his two enormous cannons »Weckauf« and »Purlepaus« until it could be stormed – he even fired the first shot himself. The defender of the fortress, Hans von Pienzenau, was publicly beheaded because he had dared to mock the besiegers by having the walls of the fortress swept with brushes. After the victory, the fortress was reinforced to become the strongest in the country; a 90m/295ft-tall tower, the Kaiserturm, was erected in 1518–22. Since 1997, the fortress has been part of the **»Via Imperalis«**, Austria's castle route.

Heldenorgel

The famous »Heldenorgel« (Heroes' Organ; 1931) in the Bürgerturm has 4307 pipes and 46 registers. It is played daily at noon (and at 5pm in the summer months) in remembrance of those who fell in the First and Second World Wars. The largest free-standing organ in the world, it can be heard at a distance of 13km/8mi away.

Old Town

A lovely stroll through the city will pass the remains of the former city walls, the Wasserbastei (moated bastion). Several wine taverns can be found on Römerhofgasse. From there, the popular Untere Stadtplatz, with a statue of the Virgin Mary and a fountain, extends over the Inn. Near the Unterer Stadtplatz stands the Rathaus (town hall) and the parish church, Pfarrkirche St Vitus, a late Gothic hall church built in 1400 on the site of an older place of worship. Another worthwhile destination is the **»Tiroler Schauglashütte«**, a glassblowing workshop run by the Riedel company, where visitors can watch objects being created and also visit the adjoining museum (opening times: Mon–Fri 9am–5.30pm, Sat until 5pm).

Ten minutes away from the Obere Stadtplatz is the Kalvarienberg, site of a **memorial** for the most famous Tyrol native of all, **Andreas Hofer** (►Famous People), which was created in 1926 by sculptor Theodor Khuen.

The Kufstein Fortress rises majestically above the city

Kufstein Map

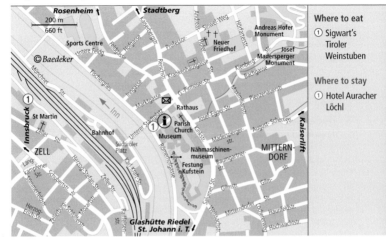

Map labels: Rosenheim, Stadtberg, 200 m, 660 ft, Sports Centre, ©Baedeker, Andreas Hofer Monument, Neuer Friedhof, Josef Madersperger Monument, St Martin, Bahnhof, Rathaus, Parish Church, Museum, Südtiroler Platz, Nähmaschinen-museum, Festung Kufstein, ZELL, MITTERN-DORF, Kaiserlift, Glashütte Riedel, St. Johann i. T., Innsbruck, Inn

Where to eat
① Sigwart's Tiroler Weinstuben

Where to stay
① Hotel Auracher Löchl

Inn cruise
Cruises down the Inn in the vicinity of Kufstein became available again in 1998. The boat departs from the Fischergriess (May–mid-Oct, 2-hour round trip daily from 10.15am and 2.30pm, mid-July–mid-Sept 1-hour round trip daily from1.15pm)

Around Kufstein

Lakes
Kufstein is surrounded by several tiny lakes, which were left behind after the Ice Age. Because the water reaches temperatures high enough for swimming during the summer months, visitors can find bathing beaches and boat hire here. Two especially scenic lakes are the Stimmersee (3km/2mi southwest), surrounded by forest, and the Hechtsee (to the north).

Thiersee
A winding road heads west of Kufstein over the Marblinger Höhe to Thiersee (678m/2224ft; pop. 2700). In this charming town, located in the middle of the deep gorge of the Thierseer Ache, the most famous passion play (with the exception of the play in Oberammergau, Bavaria) within the southern German-speaking region is performed every six years in the Passionspielhaus on the lake.

Wörgl
Approximately 15km/9mi up the Inn river lies the town of Wörgl (511m/1676ft; pop. 11,000), located where the Brixenthaler Ache flows into the Inn from the southeast. The community made the headlines in 1932 when the former Mayor Unterguggenberger created »Schwundgeld«, or depreciative money, as an answer to the high level of unemployment and poverty there: the money was legal tender, but a stamp worth 1% of the original value had to be purchased every

VISITING KUFSTEIN

INFORMATION

Ferienland Kufstein
Unterer Stadtplatz 8, A-6330 Kufstein
Tel. 0 53 72/6 22 07, fax 6 14 55
www.kufstein.com

WHERE TO EAT
▶ **Moderate**
① *Sigwart's Tiroler Weinstuben*
Marktstrasse 40, A-6230 Brixlegg
Tel. 0 53 37/6 33 90
Cosy Tyrolean parlour atmosphere. As
the name indicates, the restaurant
offers a lavish wine list, but the
performance in the kitchen is remarkable as well (closed Mon–Wed).

WHERE TO STAY
▶ **Mid-range**
① *Hotel Auracher Löchl*
Römerhofgasse 2
A-6330 Kufstein
Tel. 0 53 72/6 21 38
Fax 621 38 51
www.auracher-loechl.at
Well furnished rooms in the style of a
Tyrolese country house with a view of
the Inn river and the local Pendling
mountain. Regional specialities are
served in the adjacent wine tavern,
which has been in existence since
1409 and is the oldest in Austria.

month, meaning that the town generated 12% of the circulating capital annually and could fund public projects. Even the former French
Prime Minister Édouard Daladier and US economist Irving Fisher
were impressed by the success of the currency experiment, which was
dubbed the »Miracle of Wörgl«. As an important traffic junction,
Wörgl was heavily bombed during the Second World War, a reason
why few older buildings have been preserved here. The town's few
attractions include the parish church, with Baroque figures and a late
Gothic Madonna statue (»Wörgler Madonna«, *c*1500).

Wildschönau Rich in alpine pasture and a popular ski resort, the high-lying valley
of Wildschönau stretches south of Wörgl, comprised of several
towns belonging to the community of the same name (936m/3070ft;
pop. 4000). According to legend, the Wildschönau was once a lake
that was home to a terrible dragon. A farmer played a trick on the
dragon, which bit through the mountain range all the way to Kundl,
emptying the lake before finally perishing. What remained became
the Wildschönau and the Kundler Klamm.

Rattenberg The small town of Rattenberg (513m/1683ft; pop. 500) offers a
unified **medieval townscape** with its typical Inn town houses, impressive residences with bay windows (15th–16th centuries), Gothic
doorways and atriums, tiny nooks and crannies, and wrought-iron
signs on tavern doors. Of the town walls, once with five gates, the
tower-like Inntor has been preserved. The originally late Gothic parish church, Pfarrkirche St Virgil (15th century) was refurnished in

Baroque style in 1735. The ceiling fresco by Augsburg-born Matthäus Günther in the nave depicts (amongst other things) St Peter and St Catherine over the townscape of Rattenberg. The Augustinermuseum, located in the former Eremite monastery, displays gold and silver pieces of smithery, Gothic statues, and paintings from the 17th and 18th centuries (opening times: May–early Oct daily 10am–5pm). Located on a crag above the town are the ruins of Schloss Rattenberg, which was built by the Bavarians in the 11th century as a stronghold against Tyrol, and later extended by the Tyrolese in the 15th century and made into a powerful fortress with an exterior surrounding wall. In 1651, the castle – then used as a prison – was witness to the beheading of Tyrolese chancellor Dr. Wilhelm Biener, who was executed on false charges. Performances during the castle's theatre festival often pay tribute to the tragedy.

◄ Schloss Rattenberg

Directly opposite Rattenberg on the northern banks of the Inn is the town of Kramsach (519m/1702ft; pop. 500), which is home to Count Taxis's 17th-century castle and a school for glass blowing. The lovely open-air museum »Tiroler Bauernhöfe« enables visitors a look at 14 farms from different parts of the Tyrol region in an area of a good 11ha/27 acres (opening times: late March–late Oct daily 9am–6pm). An interesting sculpture park can be seen in the section of the town known as Mariatal, featuring some 20 works by local artist Alois Schild.

Kramsach

The Alpbachtal valley stretches south of the river Inn and the town of Brixlegg, which is surrounded by seven castles. A 10km/6mi-long mountain road leads to the main town of Alpbach (973m/3191ft). The town, with exclusively wooden houses in the rustic farmhouse style, was once named »**Austria's most beautiful small town**« by a survey. The idyllic town has been a »meeting place for Europe's great

★
Alpbach

! *Baedeker* TIP

»Schmunzelfriedhof«

A curiosity in Kramsach is a small »graveyard without the dead«, with approximately 50 old wrought-iron crosses, which bear original, humorous, but doubtless genuine epitaphs – compiled by Guggenberger, a craftsman specializing in wrought-iron. This is what one widower had to say about his quarrelsome wife: »Here lies my wife, thank God. She liked to fight with me a lot. Oh dear traveller, you'd best leave too, or she'll get up and fight with you.«

thinkers« since 1945, with authors, philosophers, sociologists, psychologists, politicians, economists and artists meeting in the »Europäischen Forum Alpbach«. Arthur Koestler, who, just like Friedrich Dürrenmatt, Max Frisch, Theodor W. Adorno, Herbert Marcuse, Karl Popper, Hermann Josef Abs and Indira Gandhi, was once a guest in the »Forum«, once ironically described the greatly dissonant spectrum of discussion topics in his satirical novel *The Call Girls*. In 1999, the Forum relocated to the newly built, architecturally interesting Congress Centrum Alpbach.

✳ **Lambach**

L 3

Province: Upper Austria   **Elevation:** 366m/1200ft
Population: 3300

Lambach thrived in the protection of the castle, which was changed into a Benedictine monastery by its last lord and master, Count Adalbero (also the Bishop of Würzburg). He had sided with the pope during the Investiture Controversy and on several occasions was forced to seek refuge within the castle walls.

Old trading centre   Lambach lies on the left bank of the Traun, on the old long-distance route from Salzburg to Linz. The town used to be a staple market for the salt from the Salzkammergut, which was reloaded here and then transported to its main destination of the time, Bohemia.

What to See in and around Lambach

Benedictine abbey   The mighty abbey features a magnificently decorated refectory (stucco, frescoes), a library with frescoes by Melchior Seidl, and the only Baroque abbey theatre (1746–70) in existence in Austria today. It opened with a performance for the 15-year-old Marie Antoinette, who was on her way to France for her wedding with Louis XVI.

Abbey church ►   The abbey church was rebuilt in the Baroque style in 1652–56. The only part of the building from the Romanesque and Gothic periods to remain was the west choir, which served as a base for the new towers. Behind the reinforcement of the walls that had now become necessary, the original 11th-century frescoes remained hidden – and protected. The colours are unusually well preserved, and the faces of those depicted are expressive. In terms of style, the paintings were more influenced by East Byzantine sacral art than that of the Western Romans. The central depiction of the Virgin

▶ **LAMBACH**

»Christ in the Synagogue«: Romanesque fresco at Lambach Abbey

Mary with Child and the two midwives is quite interesting. A beautiful scene is that of the Three Kings speaking with Herod – a hidden reference to the Investiture Controversy about secular or religious supremacy? It is correct to assume that the wall paintings had already been finished when the old church was consecrated in 1089 (opening times: Easter Sunday–Oct 9am–noon and 1pm–4pm; guided tours: daily 2pm, groups of min. 15 anytime by arrangement, tel. 072 45/ 21 71 03 34).

★
◀ Romanesque frescoes
⏱

Those who feel happiest on the back of a horse should take a look around the **Austrian horse centre** Stadl-Paura, southwest of Lambach. The location is also known however for its architecturally unconventional pilgrimage church: in 1713 Abbot Maximilian Pagel vowed to build a church if Lambach could be spared from the plague. The beautiful Baroque structure was built from 1714–24 by Johann Michael Prunner as a tribute to the Holy Trinity, with the number three being its key element: the church stands on a three-sided foundation with three spires, three entrances, three altars, and three organs.

Stadl-Paura

Steyrermühl near Laakirchen, around 15km/9mi south of Lambach, has a long tradition in the papermaking industry. Accordingly, the Austrian **Papiermacher-Museum** (Papermaking Museum) was established here in the rooms of the former Steyrermühl paper factory (opening times: late April–Oct daily 9am–6pm).

Steyrermühl
⏱

Vöcklabruck The friendly town of Vöcklabruck (435m/1427ft; pop. 11,000) proudly points to the only towers of arms of Emperor Maximilian I (▶ Famous People) that have survived to this day. Master builder Carlo Antonio Carlone and his brother, stucco-plasterer Giovanni Battista Carlone, created another work of Baroque art here with their Dörflkirche (village church), located in the town's Schöndorf quarter. The Gothic church's highly unusual architecture, however, can be attributed to the turbulence of the Reformation: the gap between the existing tower and the nave, already under construction, was simply filled with a narrower tower.

Landeck

E 5

Province: Tyrol
Population: 8300

Elevation: 816m/2677ft

As early as Roman times, Landeck served as an important traffic hub. During the Middle Ages, builders were in great demand here – passage across the passes had to be safeguarded.

Safe crossing The small town of Landeck lies at the point where the east-west route from Vienna to Zurich crosses the north-south route from Germany to Italy. The powerful walls of Burg Landeck attest to the urgent need to complete the fortification.

The town's current appearance can be strongly attributed to industrialization at the end of the 19th and the beginning of the 20th centuries (chemical and textile industries). The prosperity that was achieved at that time can be seen in the town's commanding homes, particularly in the quarter of Angedair and on Malser Strasse. In addition, Landeck is the centre of a beloved winter sporting region.

▶ VISITING LANDECK

INFORMATION

Touristverband TirolWest
Malser Strasse 10
A-6500 Landeck
Tel. 054 42/656 00, fax 656 00 15
www.tirolwest.at

Tourismusverband Paznauntal/Ischgl
Hnr. 320, A-6561 Ischgl/Tirol
Tel. 0 54 44/52 660, fax 56 36,
www.paznaun.at

WHERE TO STAY

▶ **Mid-range/Budget**
Hotel Auhof
A-6555 Kappl
Tel. 0 54 45/63 11
Fax 63 11 33
www.hotelauhof.at
This well-equipped bike hotel is located directly adjacent to the valley station of the Diasbahn and offers excellent meals.

What to See in and around Landeck

The church of Our Lady was constructed on the site of an older sacral structure in 1471. Its central nave is almost twice as high as its two side aisles. The tympanum of the western entrance shows a relief of the Virgin and Child and two angels. Particularly noteworthy on the inside of the church is a late Gothic winged altar dedicated to St Oswald (16th century), which received later additions. The capstone from the tomb of the knight Oswald of Schrofenstein (15th century) is built into the south wall, on which there are two carved death masks.

Burg Landeck: »defiant« might be a suitable word to describe it

Standing on a high cliff above the Inn is **Burg Landeck** (c1200), which was later altered many times and partially restored in 1949. The most impressive feature of the fortress, which had its heyday when it was occupied by the Knights of Schrofenstein, is the mighty keep from which there is an extensive view. In addition, its Gothic-vaulted hall and chapel with 16th-century frescoes is worth taking a look at. Inside the castle, the **Bezirksmuseum** presents the artistic, cultural, economical, and social history of the region. Besides the peasant living quarters (integrated rooms from the 17th century, smoke room, and sleeping quarters), visitors can see equipment from arable and dairy farming, and the courtroom of the high regional court, which has resided in the fortress since approximately 1300. Several art exhibitions are organized in the Schlossgalerie every year (opening times: mid-March–Oct Tue–Sun 10am–5pm).

Above Landeck to the north – on the north bank of the Sanna – is the old mountain village of Stanz (1035m/3395ft), birthplace of Baroque master builder Jakob Prandtauer (1660–1726). He played a decisive role in the construction of Melk Abbey. The late Gothic church in Stanz numbers among the oldest in the entire region. It also offers a lovely view of the Landeck basin.

The ruins of Burg Schrofenstein, a fortress mentioned in documents from as far back as 1196, stand on a high hill northeast of the town. There are spectacular views from here, though this pleasure was of secondary importance during the Middle Ages, when control of the basin was the top priority.

Approximately 3km/2mi northeast of Landeck on the southern bank of the Inn river lies the community of Zams (775m/2542ft). Its parish church with three Rococo altars is particularly noteworthy. The Kronburg ruins (1380), standing picturesquely on top of a hill, are worth the climb – if only for the view of the surrounding landscape. The »Zammer Loch« gorge and the Lötzer Waterfall are located to the north of the town.

Serfaus

Roughly 25km/15.5mi up the Inn river from Landeck is the resort town of Serfaus (1427m/4681ft; pop. 1200), **one of the oldest sites of pilgrimage in honour of the Virgin Mary** in Tyrol. The old parish church contains a noteworthy miraculous image of the Madonna with Child on her throne (12th century), which is hollowed out in the back as a vessel for relics. Cable cars head up to the Komperdellalm (2000m/6560ft; ski resort), while ski lifts reach elevations of 2475m/8118ft. The Hexenkopf, or Witch's Head, is the highest peak of the Samnaun range (3035m/9955ft).

Nauders

Further up the river Inn from where the borders of Austria, Italy and Switzerland meet, south of the Finstermünz Pass (1006m/3300ft), lies the charming holiday resort of Nauders (1400m/4592ft; pop. 1600). It is often visited as a departure point for hikes and winter sports and still has countless centuries-old Rhaeto-Romanic farmhouses with impressive free-standing stairways, bay windows, and gated passages. The parish church, Pfarrkirche St Valentin, with slim Gothic towers and two carved altars is particularly worth taking a look at. The Roman St Leonhardskapelle is the oldest surviving church in Tyrol, and boasts 12th-century Roman wall paintings that were discovered in 1951 behind late Gothic frescoes.

Towering over the village is the castle of **Naudersberg**, a former judicial fortress (14th–16th centuries), where along with the armoury and picture gallery visitors can see the former dungeons and instruments of torture. The ruins of the former toll stronghold Hoch-Finstermünz, with an imposing bridge tower, stand in the middle of the roaring river Inn.

!

Baedeker TIP

Healthy drink for parched throats

The town of Grins (1006m/3300ft; pop. 1220) west of Landeck at the edge of the Stanzertal valley is well known as one of the most beautiful villages of Tyrol. Grins is also known for its spring: mineral-enriched water with healing powers flows from the well in the middle of the town, and it comes free of charge. Here's to your good health!

Paznauntal

The approximately 35km/22mi-long, narrow Paznauntal valley in western Austria stretches southwest from Landeck to Galtür. It is bordered by the Verwallgruppe mountain range in the north and the Samnaungruppe in the south, and the Trisanna river flows through it. The villages of the valley are the starting point for hikes and tours through the mountains in summer and for a variety of skiing activities during winter. The path through the Paznauntal, which travels from Galtür to Bilerhöhe, provides access to the Silvretta-Hochalpenstrasse (Silvretta High Alpine Road) from the east.

The road crosses the Sanna river behind Pians. It then continues below Schloss Wiesberg (16th century; private property) and the Trisanna viaduct, a bold structure that is part of the Arlberg railway line (scenic car parks), into the Paznauntal valley. The viaduct, constructed in 1884 and renovated in 1923 and 1964, is 86m/282ft high and 230m/754ft long.

◄ Trisanna viaduct

Ischgl (1377m/4517ft; pop. 1250), the main town in the Paznauntal valley, is not only popular as a summer spa resort, but also as a place for winter sporting events (**»Silvretta-Ski-Arena«**). The originally late Gothic parish church, which received its present-day Rococo design in 1757, holds a special relic within its altar: a bone from St Stephen, gilded in silver around 1500, which is said to have originated from the treasury of Charlemagne.

◄ Ischgl

Galtür (1584m/5196ft; pop. 700), is a winter sports village where snow is assured. It was devastated by a disastrous avalanche in February of 1999, but has since been protected by improved avalanche protection dams. Its Baroque church (17th–18th centuries) features a Gothic statue of the Virgin Mary and lovely Rococo altars.

◄ Galtür

✶ Lavanttal

N 6

Province: Carinthia

For travellers who are looking for rest and relaxation in a contemplative atmosphere without the masses of tourists, the Lavanttal is an insider's tip. The valley is characterized by forests and meadows, gentle mountains, and lovely hiking trails.

The Lavanttal valley extends from the Obdacher Sattel on the Styrian-Carinthian border south of ► Judenburg to the Slovenian border. It connects the Murtal valley to the north and the Drautal valley to the south.

What to See in the Lavanttal

In the upper Lavanttal valley, in the **»heart of the Paracelsus district«** (as the advertising campaign has it), lies Bad St Leonhard (721m/2365ft; pop. 4900), a high-lying spa town with a sulphurous spring. The region around Bad St Leonhard has numerous springs, the healing powers of which Paracelsus was

⏵ LAVANTTAL

INFORMATION

Tourismusbüro Wolfsberg
Getreidemarkt 3, A-9400 Wolfsberg
Tel. 043 52/33 40, fax 53 72 77,
www.lavanttal.at

Bad St Leonhard

convinced. The well-marked footpaths in between the springs allow hikers to take a stroll in his footsteps. On a nearby hill stands the mighty pilgrimage church, Wallfahrtskirche St Leonhard (14th–15th centuries), a Gothic basilica with valuable stained glass paintings.

Hüttenberg

A long, but very rewarding side trip begins a good 2km/1mi south of Bad St Leonhard: when the road starts heading west over the Sau Alps, follow it for approximately 25km/15.5mi and then turn right in Hinterberg at the Steierbach toward Hüttenberg. The Heinrich Harrer Museum there is worth a visit. Harrer (▶Famous People), an expeditioner and friend of the Dalai Lama, became known through the film adaptation of his book *Seven Years in Tibet*, featuring Brad Pitt in the leading role. Harrer donated the museum's unique ethnological collection to his home town (opening times: April–Oct daily 10am–5pm).

Heinrich-Harrer Museum ▶

Schaubergwerk Knappenberg ▶

The mines in Hüttenberg were once famous; the Romans prized the Noric swords from the region. In the Middle Ages, Hüttenberg was the central European iron mining capital, and this history is presented at the Knappenberg show mine (opening times: April–Oct daily 10am–5pm, July and Aug till 6pm).

Packstrasse

Back in the Lavanttal valley, the winding Packstrasse begins a few miles south in Twimberg (604m/1981ft) to the east, and is routed through the charming landscape up to the Packsattel (four gates; 1166m/3825ft).

Wolfsberg

Wolfsberg (462m/1515ft; pop. 28,600) is the **main city of the Lavanttal valley and a regional economic hub**. Its delightful Old Town still maintains parts of the former city walls and is overlooked by the towering Schloss Wolfsburg. First mentioned in documents from 1178, the castle has been drastically changed since. Most alterations took place after 1846 when the new owner, Silesian Duke Henckel von Donnersmarck, had it renovated in neo Gothic style.

The Baroque Wallfahrtskirche Maria Loreto of St. Andrä

St Andrä (430m/1410ft; pop. 10,600) was the seat of the Prince-Bishops of Lavant from 1225 to 1859; now the abbey buildings belong to Jesuit monks. The Gothic parish church, whose origins go back to the 9th century, has the remains of 15th-century frescoes and numerous tombs featuring coats of arms. The twin-steepled Jesuit church, Jesuitenkirche Maria Loreto (1697), has a noteworthy Baroque interior. The surrounding region specializes in cultivation of asparagus and fruit. It offers plenty of »Mostwanderwege« (»must« tours) through the countryside – with plenty of chances to stop for a light snack and a drink, naturally!

Standing on a 70m/230ft rocky hill is the Benedictine abbey of St Paul. Founded in 1091, it has been occupied by Benedictines since 1809, who came to the region from St Blasien in the Black Forest. After Gurk Cathedral, the twin-towered abbey church, dedicated in 1264, is **Carinthia's most significant Roman building**. Its particularly impressive features are the choir and the south doorway. The interior features Gothic vaulted ceilings; the Baroque interior has frescoes from 1470. With one of the most comprehensive collections of art in all of Europe, the abbey very aptly dubs its collection the »Schatzhaus Kärntens« (Carinthia's Treasure Chest). It includes handcrafted art, select pieces of sacral art such as the precious Cross of Adelheid from the 11th century, and a valuable collection of paintings. No less important is the library, with approximately 180,000 volumes and precious manuscripts (opening times: May–end Oct, daily 9am–5pm). The abbey's Chinamuseum can only be visited on a guided tour. The abbey also maintains a secondary school, which was attended by composer Hugo Wolf (1860–1903).

★
Stift St Paul

◷
◄ Chinamuseum

Lechtal Alps

D/E 5

Province: Tyrol

Highest elevation: Parseierspitze (3036m/9958ft)

The long chain of the Lechtal Alps stretches from ►Arlberg to the Fernpass, making it one of the mightiest mountain ranges of the Northern Alps. It runs between the Stanzertal and Inntal valleys in the south and the Lechtal valley in the north.

The main peak and highest elevation of the Lechtal Alps is the »Queen of the Northern Limestone Alps«, the Parseierspitze (3036m/8858ft). Other significant peaks include the Wetterspitze (2895m/9496ft), the easily climbed Muttekopf (2777m/9109ft), the several mile-long rocky crest of the Heiterwand, and the proud Valluga (2809m/9214ft).

Parseierspitze

The countless mountain huts in the Lechtal Alps are easy to reach from the Stanzertal and Inntal valleys. A magnificent ridge path (»Höhenweg«) leads from the Ulmer Hütte (2280m/7478ft) near St Anton or from the Stuttgarter Hütte (2303m/7554ft) near Zürs am Arlberg via the Leutkircher Hütte (2250m/7380ft) and the 2300m/

Ridge path from Arlberg to the Fernpass

Cosy mountain huts like the beautifully located Edelweisshaus above Kaisers in the Lechtal Alps offer food and accommodation for hikers

7544ft-high Kaiserjoch-Hütte to the Ansbacher Hütte (2380m/ 7806ft). From here, the demanding Augsburger Höhenweg heads from the Augsburger Hütte (2345m/7692ft) via the Memminger Hütte (2242m/7354ft) located on the Unterer Seewisee, the Württemberger Haus (2200m/7216ft), the Hanauer Hütte (1920m/ 6298ft), and finally the Anhalter Hütte (2040m/6691ft) to the Fernpass (1210m/3969ft).

Fernpass lakes In the area where the foothills of the Eastern Alps drop down into the Fernpass, a number of serene lakes nestle amongst beautiful forests: the Fernsteinsee and the Samaranger See, which are quite popular with divers for their clear water, as well as the Blindsee, the Weissensee, and the Mittersee.

Leoben

Province: Styria
Population: 28,000

Elevation: 540m/1771ft

The mountain village of »Liubina«, located near a loop of the Mur river, was founded by King Ottokar II of Styria in 1263. The ostrich in the town's coat of arms is a reminder of the medieval belief that it was the only animal that could eat and digest iron.

Mining centre Leoben (»Liubina«: slav. »liub« = dear) has been the centre of the iron and heavy industry in the Upper Styrian region since the Middle Ages, and is also home to the Montanuniversität, a university for mining, metallurgy, and materials which is still important today. The town obtained the rights to be a trading port for the Vordernberg iron industry; the Österreichische Alpine Montangesellschaft was founded here for the administration of industrial companies and mines in 1861, and in 1868 it was connected to the rail network.

Leoben Map

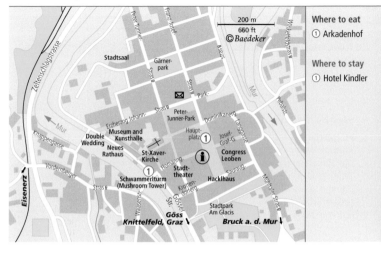

Where to eat
① Arkadenhof

Where to stay
① Hotel Kindler

What to See in and around Leoben

The centre of the Old Town on the Mur loop is the Hauptplatz **Old Town** (main square), redesigned by Boris Podrecca. It is flanked by the Hacklhaus, featuring magnificent Baroque decor (c1660) and the Alte Rathaus (Old Town Hall, 1585), decorated with coats of arms.

On Hohmanngasse stands **one of the oldest civic theatres in Austria**, where performances have been taking place since its foundation in 1790. The Mautturm (toll tower), also known to locals as the »Schwammerlturm« because of its mushroom-shaped dome, was built by P. Carlone. The sculpture *Double Wedding* by Dennis Oppenheim, standing near the Neues Rathaus (New Town Hall) and the docks, is regarded pensively by passers-by.

Leoben's art gallery is connected to the Neues Rathaus. Its remark-**Kunsthalle** able exhibitions focus on the depiction of various exotic ethnic groups and cultures (Kirchgasse 8; opening times: May–Oct Tue–Sun ⊙ 9am– 6pm).

Towering next door is the parish church, Pfarrkirche St Xaver (1660–65), whose interior exhibits the opulent, black-gold decor that is characteristic of the Austrian Jesuit Baroque style.

The 14th–15th-century Kirche Maria am Waasen is located south of the Mur bridge. Beautiful net-ribbed vaulting spans over the four-bayed nave. The stained glass windows of the choir area are also impressive (c1410).

The famous Gösser Brauerei, a brewery in the southern quarter of **Gösser Brauerei** Göss, originated in the **oldest Benedictine convent in Austria** (foun-

▶ VISITING LEOBEN

INFORMATION

Tourismusverband Leoben
Peter-Tunner-Strasse 2
A-8700 Leoben
Tel. 0 38 42/4 81 48, fax 4 83 41
www.leoben.at

WHERE TO EAT

▶ **Inexpensive**

① *Arkadenhof*
Am Hauptplatz 11, A-8700 Leoben
Tel. 0 38 42/4 20 74
The oldest brewery and restaurant in
Leoben (established in 1550) serves six
different beers on tap.

WHERE TO STAY

▶ **Budget**

① *Hotel Kindler*
Straussgasse 7–11
A-8700 Leoben
Tel. 0 38 42/43 20 20
Fax 43 20 26
www.kindler.at
A modern, well-equipped 3-star hotel
with a cosy atmosphere in the centre
of Leoben, very near to the Schwam-
merlturm and the pedestrian zone.

dation in 1020, closed in 1782). The art of brewing has been practised here since 1459. Today, »Gösser« beer is exported to destinations all over the world.

Wild-und
Freizeitpark
Mautern

⊙

Mautern (713m/2339ft; pop. 2,200), to the west of Leoben, is the
main town of the Ennstal valley. Its wildlife and amusement park is
located at an elevation of 1250m/4100ft above the town. Performances featuring birds of prey, a children's amusement park, a petting
zoo, and more than 200 wild animals including bears, wolves, Bar-
bary apes, and chamois attract quite a number of enthusiastic
visitors (opening times: May–Oct daily 9am–5pm, Sat, Sun until
6pm; July and Aug 1 hour longer).

Liechtenstein

B/C 5

Sovereign state
Capital: Vaduz
Population: 35,500

Area: 160 sq km/61 sq mi
Elevation: 460–2124m/1509–6967ft

**Liechtenstein, one of the smallest but richest independent coun-
tries in the world, occasionally hits the headlines as a money laun-
dering paradise.**

Small state
between Rätikon
and Rhine

Approximately 24km/15mi long and 12km/7.5mi wide, the Principality of Liechtenstein is located in the Alps between the Austrian
province of Vorarlberg and Switzerland and extends from the west-

ern camber of the Rätikon mountain range to the river Rhine. The approximately 430m/1410ft-high Rhine plain in the north features occasional hills and low peaks, whereas the foothills of the Rätikon in the south create a more mountainous landscape. The Grauspitze, Liechtenstein's highest mountain, reaches an elevation of 2599m/8525ft. Two thirds of Liechtenstein is mountainous; around 35% of its total area is covered by forest.

A side trip through the tiny country is worthwhile not only for those interested in history, the arts and stamp collecting, but also for hikers, mountain bikers, and fans of winter sports.

Economy

These days only 1% of all employed people work in the agriculture industry, and its contribution to the Gross National Product is a mere 2%, even though 40% of the country's area is set aside for agricultural use (fruit and vegetable farming in the more densely populated Rhine region, dairy and cattle farming in the mountainous regions). Liechtenstein, whose citizens command **one of the highest per capita incomes in the world**, gained its wealth as an industrial location and, above all, as a financial hub of international importance. Because of its confidentiality policies in banking and its advantageous tax laws, so many holding companies have based their businesses here that an estimated 40,000 to 100,000 so-called »post box companies« are registered here.

Population

The official language of the principality is German; the common spoken language is an Alemannic dialect. Approximately 80% of the population are Catholic, while 7% are Protestant. Foreign residents (primarily from Switzerland, Austria and Germany) make up approximately one-third of the total population.

History

15 BC	Liechtenstein belongs to the Roman province Raetia.
5th century	Germanic tribes occupy the territory.
1342	The county of Vaduz is established.
1719	Emperor Karl VI unites various estates to form the Principality of Liechtenstein.
1806	Napoleon incorporates the principality into the Confederation of the Rhine.
1815–66	Liechtenstein is a member of the German Confederation.
1852–1919	Joint customs and tax territory with Austria-Hungary
1923	Customs and currency union with Switzerland
1990	Liechtenstein becomes the 160th member of the UN.
1995	Liechtenstein becomes a member of the World Trade Organization (WTO)
2003	New constitution is enacted

Liechtenstein and Vaduz *Maps*

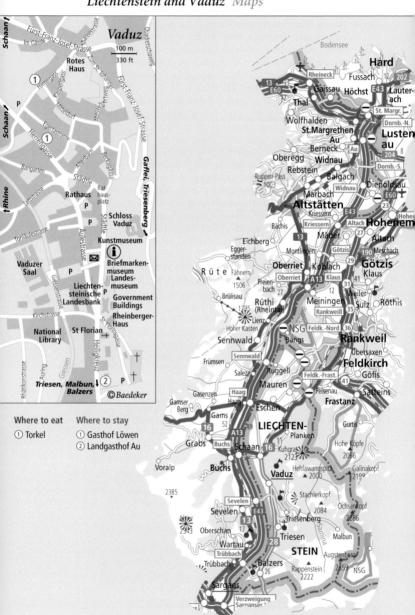

Vaduz

100 m
330 ft

Schaan

Im Gässle
Fürst-Franz-Josef-Strasse
Quaderstrasse

Rotes Haus

Hintergass
Mitteldorf
Äulestrasse
Egertastrasse

Rhine

Bangarten
Städtle

Rathaus
Rathausplatz

Schloss Vaduz

Kunstmuseum

Vaduzer Saal

Liechtensteinische Landesbank

Briefmarkenmuseum
Landesmuseum

Government Buildings

RheinbergerHaus

National Library

St Florian

Kirchstrasse

Tonilaulestrasse

Rheinstrasse

Triesen, Malbun,
Balzers

Gaflei, Triesenberg

©Baedeker

Where to eat
① Torkel

Where to stay
① Gasthof Löwen
② Landgasthof Au

Bodensee
Hard
Rheineck
Fussach
Gaissau
Höchst
Lauterach
St. Margr.
Thal
Wolfhalden
St.Margrethen
Au
Berneck
Lustenau
Oberegg
Widnau
Dornb.-N.
Rebstein
Balgach
Diepoldsau
Rupperi-Pass
1003
Marbach
Widnau
Altstätten
Kriessern
Hohenem
Bächis
Kriessern
Altach
Eichberg
Mäder
Eggerstanden
Montlingen
Götzis
Meschach
Rüte
Fähnern
Oberriet
Koblach
Götzis
1506
Oberriet
Klaus
Klaus
Freienbach
A13
Brülisau
Meiningen
Weiler
Röthis
1795
Rüthi (Rheintal)
Rankweil
Sulz
Lienz
Rankweil
Hoher Kasten
NSG Feldk.-Nord
Sennwald
Bangs
Rankweil
Frümsen
Sennwald
Übersaxen
Salez
Feldkirch
Ruggell
Feldk.-Frast.
Göfis
Gasenzen
Mauren
Felsenau
Satteins
Haag
Gamser Berg
Haag
Eschen
Frastanz
Gams
Gurtis
Grabs
A13
LIECHTEN-
Planken
Hohe Köpfe
2066
Buchs
Schaan
Kuhgrat
2123
Hehlawangspitz
2000
Galinakopf
2199
Voralp
Buchs
Vaduz
2385
Stachlerkopf
Sevelen
Ochsenkopf
2286
Sevelen
E43
Triesenberg
2084
Oberschan
Triesen
Malbun
Wartau
STEIN
Trübbach
Augstenberg
Balzers
2359
Trübbach
Rappenstein
NSG
2222
Sargans
Verzweigung
Sarganser

Schloss Vaduz is Liechtenstein's emblem and the residence of the princely family

The history of the independent Principality of Liechtenstein begins in the 14th century. Prior to that time, the country, whose territory had been settled since the Neolithic Age, had become part of the Roman province of Raetia around 15 BC and then occupied by Germanic tribes in the 5th century. The county of Vaduz was established in 1342, and in 1712 was purchased by Prince Hans Adam of Liechtenstein, of noble Lower Austrian descent, who then united it with the estate of Schellenberg. On 23 January 1719, Holy Roman Emperor Karl VI declared that the two estates be one entity and elevated them to the Imperial Principality of Liechtenstein. After the fall of the Holy Roman Empire, Napoleon claimed Liechtenstein as a member of the Confederation of the Rhine in 1806. It joined the German Confederation in 1815, where it remained as an independent principality until the dissolution of the confederation in 1866. In the meantime, Liechtenstein had strengthened its ties with its neighbour Austria-Hungary with whom it established a joint customs and tax union that lasted from 1852 to 1919. Having lost its most important partner in 1918 with the fall of the Austro-Hungarian empire, the principality entered into a customs and currency union with Switzerland in 1923.

The tiny country, which had dissolved its military in 1868, remained neutral during the Second World War, just as it had in previous conflicts. The sovereign prince, Hans-Adam II (born 1945), who took control of government back in 1984, has been the uncontested head of government since 1990.

The Principality of Liechtenstein has been a **constitutional monarchy** ruled by the male members of the Princely Family of Liechtenstein since 1921. A new constitution, which precisely defines the role of parliament, government

? DID YOU KNOW ...?

■ Following the death of his father, Sovereign Prince Hans-Adam II took over as regent on 13 November 1989 and appointed his son, Hereditary Prince Alois, as his permanent representative on 15 August 2004. He entrusted his son with the sovereign rights that are provided to the prince in the constitution.

and prince, was enacted in 2003. The Landtag (parliament) consists of 25 members elected by secret ballot for a period of four years; the head of government and four councillors form the executive.

▶ VISITING LIECHTENSTEIN

INFORMATION

Liechtenstein Tourismus
Städtle 37, FL-9490 Vaduz
Tel. 0 04 23/2 39 63 00, fax 2 39 63 01
www.tourismus.li

ERLEBNISPASS

A two or six-day pass offers discounted or free admission to many attractions such as museums, baths, and special events.

WHERE TO EAT

▶ Expensive

① **Torkel**
Hintergasse 9, FL-9490 Vaduz
Tel. 0 04 23/2 32 44 10
Splendid view from the terrace. Local dishes (asparagus, milk-fed lamb, lasagne with scampi) – so good that reservations are essential.

WHERE TO STAY

▶ Luxury

① **Gasthof Löwen**
Herrengasse 35, FL-9490 Vaduz
Tel. 0 04 23/2 38 11 44
Fax 0 04 23/2 38 11 45
www.hotel-loewen.li
Oldest hotel in Liechtenstein, with historical rooms and a unique atmosphere. The large outdoor restaurant in the middle of the hotel's own vineyard has a view of the castle.

▶ Budget

② **Landgasthof Au**
Austrasse 2 FL-9490 Vaduz
Tel. 0 04 23/2 32 11 17
Fax 0 04 23/2 32 11 68
Central location with an idyllic, shaded garden terrace. Just a few minutes from the centre of Vaduz.

Since the customs and currency union with Switzerland in 1923, the Swiss franc has been Liechtenstein's **legal tender**. The principality only produces its own postage stamps, which are coveted all over the world and generate large profits for the small country. Liechtenstein is a member of the Council of Europe, the European Free Trade Association (EFTA) and the United Nations (UN). In 1995, it joined the European Economic Area (EEA) and the World Trade Organization (WTO), and in 2008 it signed up to the Schengen Agreement.

✳ Vaduz

Royal residence and seat of government
The town of Vaduz (460m/1509ft; pop. 5100), is royal residence, seat of government, and seat of parliament for the Principality of Liechtenstein – and also a centre for tourism. It is located near the right bank of the Rhine at the foot of the mighty peaks of the Rätikon mountains. Every summer this **lively town**, with its numerous cafés and shops, holds an international open-air pop festival called »Little Big One«. The national holiday on 15 August always ends with a magnificent fireworks display.

Schloss Vaduz
Schloss Vaduz (not accessible), whose origins date back to the 12th century, stands high above the town to the east. The keep and the

buildings on the eastern side make up the oldest part of the complex. After the Swiss set fire to the castle during the Swabian War of 1499, the rounded bastions on the north-eastern and southwestern sides were erected in the 16th century. The west wing gained its present appearance in the 17th century. The castle was restored in the style of the 16th century in 1901–10.

Rathausplatz, home to the Rathaus (town hall), is located in the centre of Vaduz. It is the starting point for the main pedestrian street, **Städtle**, which leads approximately 500m/550yd south to the neo-Gothic parish church (1869–73, royal vault).

The collection of the art museum focuses on international modern and contemporary art

At Städtle 37 stands the Engländer-bau (English Building), home to the **Postage Stamp Museum**, which was established in 1930. The museum documents the world-famous editions of Liechtenstein's postage stamps (opening times: Tue–Sun 10am–5pm, Wed until 8pm). Diagonally opposite is Liechtenstein's Art Museum (Städtle 32). The dark cube was designed by the Swiss architects Morger, Degelo, and Kerez; its façade is of black basalt stone and coloured river pebbles in black cement. ◄ Kunstmuseum Liechtenstein

The ground floor of the museum offers visitors a walk through **art history from the early 19th century into the 1950s**. It particularly focuses on Expressionism, Surrealism, and Concretism. The upper level features an opulent selection of primarily Baroque paintings, sculptures, and artistic treasures from the collections of the Princely Family of Liechtenstein (Rubens, Frans Hals, van Dyck, Brueghel). Modern and contemporary art is represented as well; the emphasis here is on Arte Povera, Rationalism, and Minimalism (opening times: Tue–Sun, 10am–5pm, Thu until 8pm).

The next stop along the Städtle is the historical inn Zum Hirschen (no. 43), which is home to the Liechtenstein National Museum. In over 40 rooms it displays a permanent exhibition on the cultural and natural history of Liechtenstein (opening times: see Postmuseum). ◄ Liechtensteinisches Landesmuseum

The Rotes Haus (Red House) and the Torkel are also worth seeing. The Ski-Museum offers a vivid glimpse of over 100 years of skiing history (Fabrikstrasse 5; opening times: Mon–Fri, 2pm–6pm). The ruins of the Wildschloss castle (840m/2755ft), high above the city, are also a popular destination. **Further attractions**

Other Destinations in the Principality of Liechtenstein

Triesen The town of Triesen (463m/1519ft; pop. 4200) is located approximately 5km/3mi south of Vaduz, with an historic centre in the upper part of the town. The Gothic chapel, the St-Mamertus-Kapelle, has a Romanesque apse and a sumptuous interior comprised of Gothic pietàs and intricately carved altars. The St-Marien-Kapelle (Chapel of St Mary; 17th century) and the Hugentobler wooden ceiling in the parish church, Pfarrkirche St Gallus, are also worth seeing. The town is a starting point for tours in the Lavena, Rappenstein, and Falknis regions.

The steep twists and turns of a mountain road with numerous junctions lead from Vaduz up to the charmingly situated **Triesenberg** (884m/2900ft; pop. 2500), an old Walser settlement. The **Walser-Heimatmuseum** provides a glimpse into the lives of miners who settled along the Triesenberg mountain in the 13th century (opening times: Mon–Fri 7.45am–11.45am and 1.30pm–5.30pm, Sat 7.45am– 11am and 1.30pm–5pm).

Winter holiday in the idyllic Malbuntal valley

Malbun Above Steg (1300), which consists of two ring-shaped settlements surrounding an area of farmland, is the 1600m/5248ft-high Malbun. This is where the high-lying valley and the road ends. In winter, this sleepy little town is Liechtenstein's **main skiing region**. The chairlift, which travels to the 2014m/6606ft-high Sareiser Joch, is also in operation during the summer months.

Balzers Approximately 5km/3mi south of Triesen is Balzers (476m/1561ft; pop. 4100). The fortress of Burg Gutenberg and the Gothic chapel, Kapelle St Peter, in the district of Mäls are worth a visit, as is as the pilgrimage chapel, Wallfahrtskapelle Maria Hilf. Prehistoric artefacts have been found in the region of Balzers during excavations.

Schaan Schaan (pop. 5200), an industrial town, lies 3km/2mi north of Vaduz at the foot of the Drei Schwestern (»Three Sisters«) Massif. The late Gothic chapel, Kapelle St Peter, stands on the foundation walls of a 4th-century Roman fort. The history of Schaan is covered in the Dorfmuseum (Village Museum), with additional temporary exhibitions with artistic works of the region. Idyllically located above the town is a Baroque pilgrimage chapel, Wallfahrtskapelle Maria zum Trost (»Dux«; 18th century), one of the country's few Baroque buildings. A side street leads to a small Walser settlement, **Planken**, whose mountain terrace offers a wide view over the Rhine Valley and the Swiss mountains opposite. It is a starting point for short trips into the Drei Schwestern region.

Approximately 5km/3mi northeast from Schaan on national road 16 lies the village of **Nendeln**, which together with **Eschen**, located further to the west, forms the centre (pop. 3600) of Liechtenstein's lowlands. In both towns some quite noteworthy finds have been unearthed, for example the foundation walls of a Roman villa in Nendeln. Places of interest include the Pfrundhaus, the Heiligkreuzkapelle (chapel of the Holy Cross) on the Rofenberg (former meeting place), and the chapels of St Sebastian and St Roch in Nendeln. The memorial commemorating Pope John Paul II's visit to Liechtenstein on 8 September 1986, located near the Sportpark Eschen-Mauren, is also worthy of mention.

The community of Gamprin-Bendern (pop. 1200) lies in the foothills of the Eschenberg. From here, the »Historische Höhenweg Eschnerberg«, a historical footpath through the mountains, leads to Schellenberg with the ruins of the upper and lower Schellenberg castles. The »Biedermann-Haus« in Schellenberg, a wooden building built in the 16th century, is a branch location of the Landesmuseum and provides a glimpse into rural living around 1900.

Gamprin-Bendern, Schellenberg

> ❗ **Baedeker** TIP
>
> **A recommendable meal**
> Some people consider »Zum Löwen« in Schellenberg to be the nicest restaurant in Liechtenstein. In summer, guests can sit on the lavishly planted terrace, enjoy the view of the valley, and try the homemade »Käsknöpfli« – egg noodles with grated cheese (Winkel 5; opening times: 9am–11pm, Sun from 6pm, closed Wed and Thu).

✴ Lienz

J 6

Province: Tyrol
Elevation: 673m/2207ft

Region: East Tyrol
Population: 12,100

Lienz – known as Tyrol's sunshine city – breaks Austrian records for the number of hours of sunshine per year. People have known of its favourable climatic location in the wide valley basin of the Drave river for years, as attested by traces of human settlement across many eras.

Most likely an early Illyrian settlement, the town was first documented under the name »Luenza« in 1100 and received its municipal charter in 1252. In the 14th and 15th centuries, Lienz was a domicile for the counts of Görz, and later for the counts of Wolkenstein. After that, it lost much of its political importance.

History

Lienz Map

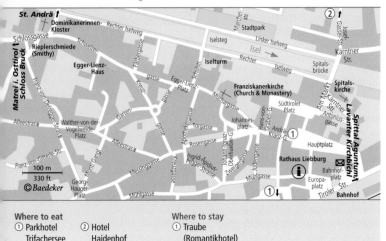

Where to eat
① Parkhotel
　Trifachersee

② Hotel
　Haidenhof

Where to stay
① Traube
　(Romantikhotel)

Sad memories are stirred at the Kosakenfriedhof (Cossack cemetery) in the Lienz district of Peggetz. In the summer of 1945, 25,000 Cossacks who had fought on the German side against the Red Army and Tito's Partisans were encamped in the forests around Lienz. When they were to be handed over to the Soviet Union by the British, many took their own lives.

Townscape This charming town in the Dolomites is characterized by seven old churches, two monasteries, and parts of the town walls (including the Isel tower), yet the townscape's most striking feature is the construction of its buildings. Unlike the towns along the Inn, such as Innsbruck and Hall, where the houses stretch a long way backwards, with narrow façades facing the street and conjoined pitched roofs, the houses in Lienz are one to two storeys shorter, wider, and have eaves facing the street.

What to See in Lienz

Hauptplatz The epicentre of Lienz's Old Town (Altstadt) on the banks of the Isel is the shield-shaped Hauptplatz (main square), on which stands a decorative fountain, the Florianibrunnen. On the square, which is transformed into a pedestrian zone during the summer months, stands Liebburg castle, with its two onion-domed corner towers a reminder of the town's lengthy aristocratic past. It was built as a royal residence by the Count of Wolkenstein during the 17th century. After undergoing renovations, it now serves as the Rathaus (town hall). At the east end of the Hauptplatz is the old Friedhofskapelle (cemetery chapel; orig. 16th century), with a round tower at its front. On Muchargasse, which leads from Johannesplatz to Egger-Lienz-Platz, stands the single-nave Franciscan church with a Gothic pieta and noteworthy medieval frescoes. Schweizergasse heads west from Egger-Lienz-Platz to the Klösterlekirche (partially 13th century), the church of the renovated Dominican convent. Across the way in an old wooden building is the Rieplerschmiede (smithy), which has been an open-air museum since 1966.

Pfarrkirche St Andrä, the parish church located high on the northern bank of the Isel, is **one of East Tyrol's most prominent Gothic structures** (dedicated 1457, choir modified in the 18th century). Tombs of burgraves from the Houses of Görz-Tyrol and Wolkenstein can be found in the organ loft; both are made of red Adnet marble. The well-designed organ front with sculptural work by Adam Baldauf of Brixen and the painted wings originated in 1618. The winged altars are works of Friedrich Pacher, and the wooden crucifix in the right-hand side altar was created around 1500. Frescoed arcades enclose the

Impressions of Lienz: Liebburg on the Hauptplatz

church's courtyard. The war memorial chapel was built in 1925 by Clemens Holzmeister. Four magnificent wall paintings by Albin Egger-Lienz (1868– 1926) adorn the impressive interior. The painter was born in Stribach, near Lienz, and is buried in the chapel.

Schloss Bruck stands on a wooded bank high above the western part of the city. It was built in the 13th century with a mighty keep and extended in the 16th century. The counts of Görz resided here for a number of years; later it was acquired by the Habsburgs. The castle has housed the **Osttiroler Heimatmuseum** (East Tyrol Local Museum) since 1943. Featured are works by the area's local artists, particularly the well-known painter Franz Defregger (1835–1921) and Albin Egger-Lienz (1868–1926).

★
Schloss Bruck

The museum also displays folkloric and scientific collections (opening times: mid-May–mid-Sept daily 10am–6pm, mid-Sept–Oct Tue–Sun until 4pm).

Around Lienz

Aguntum
Approximately 5km/3mi east of Lienz are the exposed remains of the Roman city of Aguntum, the **oldest Roman valley settlement in Austria** (1st and 2nd centuries AD). Extensive excavations of the area, which are by no means finished, have so far uncovered an atrium house, thermal baths, and a town gate. A small museum and an 18m/59ft-tall lookout tower are open to visitors (opening times: May–Sept daily 9am–6pm).

Lavanter Kirchbichl
Around 6km/20mi southwest of Lienz is the »Lavanter Kirchbichl«, which was built on the site of an early mountain settlement and is named after the site of its discovery on the 810m/2657ft-high Kirchbichl mountain. In addition to relief plaques from the period of the Roman Empire, the remains of an Early Christian church, which were uncovered during excavations in 1948, are of particular note. Several phases of the building's construction has been ascertained: after the church was destroyed in the 6th century, Pfarrkirche St Ulrich, a medieval parish church with a peaked Gothic spire, was built in its place. The Kirche St Peter and Paul is located on the peak of the hill. The church was erected on the site of an Early Christian place of worship and its main altar incorporates Romanesque fragments depicting figures and bearing inscriptions.

Lienz Dolomites
South of Lienz, between the Dravetal and Gailtal valleys, lie the Lienz Dolomites, the northwest part of the Gailtal Alps. Their impressive

VISITING LIENZ

INFORMATION

Tourismusverband
Lienzer Dolomiten
Europaplatz 1, A-9900 Lienz
Tel. 0 48 52/6 52 65, fax 65 26 52
www.lienz-tourismus.at

WHERE TO EAT
▶ **Moderate**
① *Parkhotel Tristachersee*
Tristachersee 1, A-9900 Lienz
Tel. 0 48 52/6 76 66
A place for those who enjoy a pleasant atmosphere. Crisp salads and trout from their own stock.

② *Hotel Haidenhof*
A-9900 Lienz

Tel. 0 48 52/6 24 40, fax 62 44 06
Only fresh vegetables, lettuce from local farms, and herbs from the Haidenhof garden are used here. Lienz's own Haidenhof beer is on tap.

WHERE TO STAY
▶ **Mid-range**
① *Romantikhotel Traube*
Hauptplatz 14, A-9900 Lienz
Tel. 0 48 52/6 44 44
Fax 6 41 84
www.hoteltraube.at
A successful combination of modern comfort and tradition. The view from the hotel's panoramic indoor swimming pool is attractive. The manager is also the wine waiter.

Even the Romans and early Christians appreciated nice views, as the location of the Lavanter Kirchbichl shows

peaks, including the Grosse Sandspitze (2772m/9092ft), the highest point of the entire range, and the Hochstadel (2681m/8794ft), with a north face 1500m/4920ft high, are considered to constitute one of the most magnificent ranges of the Austrian Alps. They also offer countless possibilities for mountain climbing and hiking routes at all levels of difficulty.

Located north of Lienz, before the Grossglockner region, is the Scho-**Schobergruppe** bergruppe, a massif over 3200m/10,496ft high between the Iseltal and Mölltal valleys (Petzeck, 3283m/10,768ft; Roter Knopf, 3281m/10,762ft; Hochschober, 3240m/10,627ft). Bizarrely shaped peaks, beautifully formed cirques, tiny lakes, and countless glacial drifts characterize the landscape.

★ Linz

Province: Upper Austria
Population: 190,000

Elevation: 260m/853ft

Linz is the capital of Upper Austria and Austria's third-largest city after Vienna and Graz. The city offers an interesting combination of living history and a future-oriented present.

This traditional commercial and industrial town has become a centre **The past and** for new cultural and economic ideas. Linz offers up a representative **the modern** cross-section of Austrian history: iron and steel, exquisitely performed music and forward-looking technologies such as the virtual worlds in the Ars Electronica Center, but also jovial street theatre, strolls through pleasant alleyways in the Old Town, and cosy inns.

History

799	The Roman settlement of »Lentia« was named »Linz« in a decree issued by Charlemagne.
1490	Elevated to capital city by Emperor Friedrich II
1785	Linz becomes a bishop's see.
19th century	Incipient industrialization away from the city centre during the second half of the century

Because of its strategically advantageous location in a sharp bend in the Danube at the point where the valley, carved into the foothills of the Böhmerwald mountain range, opens out into the Linz basin, Celts and Romans settled here. The Roman settlement of **»Lentia«**, at the intersection of the trade routes to Bohemia, Italy and Vienna, developed into an important trading centre in the Middle Ages. In 1490 Emperor Friedrich III, who resided here from 1485–93, elevated Linz to »Hauptstadt ob der Enns«, the capital on the Enns river. The city was granted the right to construct a bridge over the Danube in 1497 and became a bishop's see in 1785. Alongside trade, transport and industry also play a large role in Linz today, a fact demonstrated by the extensive harbour facilities and the vast industrial area in the eastern part of the city.

Linz has one of the biggest town squares in Austria. In the middle stands the Baroque Trinity Column with its lavish figurative decoration.

Linz Map

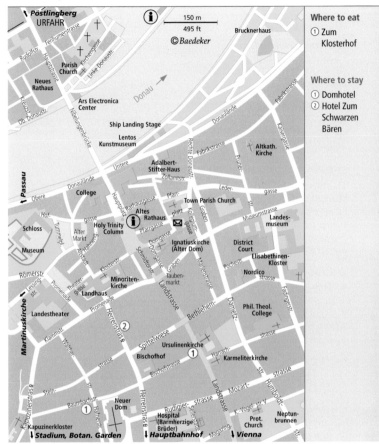

Pöstlingberg
URFAHR

Brucknerhaus

ⓘ 150 m
495 ft
©Baedeker

Fenhumerstrasse
Rudolfstr.
Hauptstrasse
Kirchengasse
Linke Donaustr.

Parish Church
Neues Rathaus

Ars Electronica Center

Donau

Ob. Donaustr.
Kreuzstr.
Nibelungenbrücke

Donaulände
Fabrikstrasse
Kaisergasse

Ship Landing Stage

Lentos Kunstmuseum

Passau

Obere Donaulände

Untere Donaulände

Altkath. Kirche

Rechte Donaustr.
Fabrikstrasse
Pfarrgasse
Plentel

Adalbert-Stifter-Haus

Zollamtstr.

College

Leder-
gasse

Hof-gasse

Hauptplatz

Town Parish Church

Graben
Kollegiumgasse
Museumstrasse

Altes Rathaus
ⓘ ✉

Landes-museum

Schloss

Alter Markt

Holy Trinity Column

Pfarrgasse

Domgasse

Ignatiuskirche (Alter Dom)

District Court

Museum

Römerstr.

Altstadt
Klosterstr.
Schmidtstr.
Graben
Martinsstr.
Pochestr.

Elisabethinen-Kloster

Nordico
strasse

Theatergasse
Promenade

Minoriten-kirche

Tauben-markt

Martinskirche

Landhaus

Promenade

Klammstr.

Landestheater

Herrenstrasse

Bethlehem-strasse

Dametz-strasse

Phil. Theol. College

②

Spittelwiese

strasse

Ursulinenkirche

Landstrasse

strasse

Bischofhof

①

Harrach-strasse

strasse

Karmeliterkirche

Bischofstr.

Kapuzinerstrasse

Steingasse

Baumbachstr.

Hafnerstr.

Neuer Dom

①

Rudigier-strasse

Mozart-strasse

K.-Vogel-str.

Humboldt-strasse

Kapuzinerkloster

Stadium, Botan. Garden

Hospital (Barmherzige Brüder)

Hauptbahnhof

Prot. Church

Magazinstr.

Vienna

Neptun-brunnen

Where to eat
① Zum Klosterhof

Where to stay
① Domhotel
② Hotel Zum Schwarzen Bären

What to See in Linz

The 220m/722ft-long and 60m/197ft-wide Hauptplatz (main square) is the centre of the Old Town and **Austria's largest medieval square**. It features an impressive backdrop of Baroque buildings with beautiful Renaissance courtyards and serves as a stage for weekly open-air concerts every Friday during summer, which are part of the Linz »Kultursommer« programme. The Rathaus (town hall), a 17th-century building, is located on the east side, in which the »Linz Genesis« museum presents a time-lapsed view of the city's history that concentrates on a small number of prominent aspects (Altes Rathaus; opening times: Mon–Fri 9am–1pm and 2pm–6pm, tel. 07 32/70 70 19 20).

★ Hauptplatz

◄ »Linz Genesis«

🕐

⏵ VISITING LINZ

INFORMATION

Touristinformation Linz
Hauptplatz 1, A-4010 Linz
Tel. 07 32/70 70 17 77, fax 77 28 73
www.linz.at

DANUBE CRUISES

Donauschifffahrt Wurm & Köck
Tel. 07 32/78 36 07
www.donauschiffahrt.de

SHOPPING

The Passage Linz, the Arkade Taubenmarkt (both located on the Landstrasse) and the Atrium City Center on Mozartstrasse offer many exclusive shops and restaurants all in one spot.

WHERE TO STAY

▶ Mid-range

① **Domhotel**
Baumbachstrasse 17, A-4020 Linz
Tel. 07 32/65 26 22
www.domhotel.at

The centrally located Domhotel is well equipped with a sauna, solarium, and fitness room.

▶ Budget

② **Hotel Zum Schwarzen Bären**
Herrenstrasse 9–11, A-4020 Linz
Tel. 07 32/77 24 77, fax 77 24 77-47
www.linz-hotel.com
Centrally located, this is a simple hotel in the heart of the pedestrian zone.

WHERE TO EAT

▶ Moderate

① **Zum Klosterhof**
Landstrasse 30, A-4020 Linz
Tel. 07 32/77 33 73
Founded in 1930, this restaurant is located in a listed building and offers one of the most beautiful and largest restaurant gardens in Upper Austria.

Fancy a stroll? The Old Town of Linz at the Landhausportal

The 20m/66ft-high Trinity Column, made of Salzburg marble, was erected in 1723 in gratitude for having averted the danger of the plague, fire, and war. A cheerfully painted yellow miniature train, the **Linz City Express**, departs daily for a tour of the city from the Hauptplatz between 10am and 6pm at least once per hour (for information call tel. 07 32/79 75 55).

Minoritenkirche

Branching off from the Hauptplatz is Klosterstrasse, from which it is just a few steps to the Minorite Church. The Rococo interior features contributions from Kremser Schmidt (side altar paintings) and Bartolomeo Altomonte (high altar paintings).

Landhaus

Next door stands the Landhaus, a spacious Renaissance building with three interior courtyards on the site of the former Minorite monastery, where the Upper Austrian provincial government now holds its sessions. The magnificent entrance portal features the coats of arms of Austria's original provinces. The true highlight of the lovely arcaded courtyard, however, is an octagonal fountain, the Planetenbrunnen from 1582. Astronomer **Johannes Kepler** (1571–1630) taught at the college that was housed in the building from 1612 to 1626.

The alleyway known as »Altstadt«, lines by the city's most beautiful buildings, leads up to the **castle**. Once the residence of Emperor Friedrich III, it was given its current imposing form for Emperor Rudolf II in 1610. Preserved from the original building are the fortification walls, the bastions, and the Friedrichstor, a gate bearing Emperor Friedrich III's coat of arms (1481) and the inscription »AEIOU« – interpreted as »Austria Est Imperare Orbi Universo« (»The whole world is subject to Austria«) or as »Austria Erit In Orbe Ultima« (»Austria will exist for ever«).

Restored and extended during the 1950s, it is now home to the **Schlossmuseum** with collections on Upper Austrian art and cultural history from the Middle Ages to the modern age, as well as folkloristic collections (opening times: Tue–Fri 9am–6pm, Sat and Sun 10am–5pm).

> ! **Baedeker** TIP
>
> **Sweet greeting**
> The original Linzer Torte, that exquisitely tempting confection consisting of dark layers of cake and blackcurrant jam, can be eaten as a tasty pick-me-up during a stroll through the city. But it can also be sent instead of an uninspiring postcard. The Konditorei Leo Jindrak, a cake shop rich in tradition located at Herrenstrasse 22–24, recorded in the Guinness Book of World Records in 1999 for creating the largest Linzer Torte of all time with a diameter of 4m/13ft, also offers a more manageably sized version of the cake small enough to send in the post.

Martinskirche

Before taking Römerstrasse back into the heart of the Old Town, take a detour to the west to the diminutive church of St Martin. Built on a clover-leaf ground plan and first documented in 799, it is **Austria's**

oldest place of worship still in existence. Fragments of Roman gravestones have been used in its construction.

Landestheater From Römerstrasse, the street leads to the promenade with the Landestheater, Upper Austria's provincial theatre, which was built in 1803 and extended by Clemens Holzmeister in 1956 to accommodate chamber music concerts.

Neuer Dom Herrenstrasse leads south to the New Cathedral (1862–1924), constructed in neo-Gothic style according to plans by Statz, the master builder of the famous cathedral in Cologne. It is said that the tower of the three-aisled columned basilica of gold sandstone, featuring an ambulatory surrounded by chapels, was not allowed to exceed a height of 134m/440ft so as not to outdo the Stephansdom in Vienna. The crypt contains the tomb of Linz's most important bishop, Franz Josef Rudigier, who organized and sponsored the construction of the cathedral. Also of note are the beautiful stained glass windows, including the so-called Linz Window that features scenes from the city's history.

The »Linzer Klangwolke« is a fascinating attempt to make music »visible« through modern technology

Karmeliterkirche East of the New Cathedral, Rudigierstrasse proceeds to Landstrasse (pedestrian zone) and then turns north. The Carmelite church (1674–1726; altar paintings by Carlo Carlone and Martin Altomonte) and the Ursuline church (1736–1757) stand on the right hand side. The former Ursuline convent today serves as the »Landeskulturzentrum Ursulinenhof«, a provincial cultural centre.

OK-Zentrum Between the two churches Harrachstrasse leads off to the right to the OK-Zentrum, standing for »Offenes Kulturhaus« (open cultural centre). Contemporary art is on display here (OK Platz 1; opening times: Mon–Thu 4pm–10pm, Fri until midnight, Sat 10am–midnight, Sun until 10pm).

Deutschordens-kirche ► A little further on stands the church of the Teutonic Order, also known as the Seminarkirche. Built in 1718–25 by Johann Michael Prunner according to plans by L. von Hildebrandt, it is one of the **most striking sacred buildings in Linz**.

Stadtmuseum Nordico Located at ethlehemstrasse no. 7, the Stadtmuseum was comprehensively modernized in 2007–08. Here, visitors explore Linz's past in the charming Vorstadtpalais. From 1710 to 1786 the palace served as a Jesuit seminary for young men from northern regions, hence the name »Nordico« (opening times: Mon–Fri 10am–6pm, Thu until 9pm, Sat and Sun 1pm–5pm).

Fadingerstrasse leads to the »Francisco Carolinum«, the headquarters of the Landesmuseum and home of the Landesgalerie, which exhibits mainly art of the 20th century (Museumsr. 14; opening times: Tue– Fri 9am–6pm, Sat and Sun 10am–5pm).

Landesmuseum

Continuing the stroll to the west, take a look inside the parish church, Stadtpfarrkirche Mariä Himmelfahrt, located on Pfarrplatz. The heart of Emperor Friedrich III, who died in Linz in 1493, is entombed to the right of the high altar; the rest of his remains were transferred to the Stephansdom in Vienna.

Stadtpfarrkirche Mariä Himmel- fahrt

Not far away stands the Old Cathedral, built in the Jesuit Baroque style in 1669–78. Its organ was named the **»Brucknerorgel«** after its most brilliant player – the musician and composer was employed as an organist at the church from 1856 to 1868.

Alter Dom

The city's latest attraction is located on the south bank of the Danube: the Lentos Museum of Modern Art Linz is one of Austria's most important museums for modern art. The clear, elongated structure by Zurich architects Weber and Hofer displays German and Austrian paintings from the past century, Anglo-American pop art, and artistic photography (opening times: daily 10am–6pm, Thu until 9pm).

★
Lentos Kunst- museum Linz

Adalbert Stifter lived at Untere Donaulände no. 6 from 1848 his death in 1868. The educator, painter and writer was the school inspector for Upper Austria from 1850 to 1865 in Linz. The house features a memorial, a museum for Upper Austrian literary history, and a gallery with fine arts exhibits (opening times: Tue–Sun 10am–3pm).

Adalbert- Stifter-Haus

Further downstream stands the Brucknerhaus, a concert and conference centre by Finnish architect Heikki Siren that opened in 1974. The international Bruckner festival takes place here every year. The surrounding Donaupark offers an annual special attraction in the form of a classical open-air concert and the **Linzer Klangwolken**, a visualisation of music with the most modern laser technology.

Brucknerhaus

Fans of pretty prickly plants will enjoy the Botanical Gardens west of the Old Town, which feature **one of Europe's most extensive cactus collections** with a total of around 1100 species. It is worth having a good look around the greenhouses, which feature alpine flora, roses, and tropical plants (Roseggerstrasse 20; opening times: Nov–Feb daily 8am–5pm, March and Oct daily until 6pm, April and Sept until 7pm, May–Aug daily 7.30am–7.30pm; greenhouses daily 8am–5pm).

Botanischer Garten

✳
Ars Electronica Center
⊕

The Ars Electronica Center located directly adjacent to the Nibelungen bridge is one of Linz's more unusual museum attractions. At the »museum of the future«, visitors can study and try out the latest technologies and media developments in the areas of education and work, learning and teaching, city planning, and virtual reality. Every year in September the » Ars Electronica Festival« offers concerts, recitals and exhibitions (closed due to renovations until 2009; alternative venue: Graben 15; opening times: Wed–Fri 9am–5pm, Sat and Sun 10am–6pm).

✳
Pöstlingberg

Opened in 1898, the railway on Linz's local mountain, the Pöstlingberg (537m/1761ft) with its Baroque pilgrimage church, is classified as the **steepest adhesion railway in the world**. It covers a height difference of 255m/836ft in just 2.9km/1.8mi. The beautiful view extends over the Mühlviertel and the foothills of the Böhmerwald (Bohemian Forest) mountains in the north, and over the Limestone Alps in the south from the Ötscher region to Traunstein near Gmunden (modernization work until spring 2009).

Märchenwelt
⊕

The **Grottenbahn** cave railway on the grounds of the former fortress takes visitors young and old on a dragon-pulled train through a colourful fairy-tale world. The Märchenwelt also features a scale model of Linz's Old Town (Am Pöstlingberg 16; opening times: March, Sept, Oct daily and Advent Sundays 10am–5pm, June–Aug daily until 6pm).

Linzer Tiergarten
⊕

Around 800 mammals, reptiles, birds and fish have found a home in the Linz Zoological Garden, located at the foot of the Pöstlingberg (Windflachweg 1; opening times: April–Oct, daily 9am–6pm, Nov–March 10am–4pm).

Around Linz

✳
Wilhering

According to many critics, Wilhering is home to **Austria's most beautiful Rococo church**. The church of Wilhering's Cistercian abbey, which was founded in 1146 and rebuilt following a fire in the 18th century, is located a good 8km/5mi up the Danube. Flooded with light, this place of worship captivates visitors with the wonderful atmosphere of its interior. The altar paintings are works by Martin Altomonte; the frescoes were done by his son Bartolomeo.

Schloss Hartheim
⊕

Approximately 15km/9mi west of Linz, in the town of Alkoven, the Renaissance castle of Hartheim is a reminder of one of the most terrible times in Austrian history. Around 30,000 disabled people and prisoners from the Mauthausen concentration camp east of Linz (▶ Danube Valley) were murdered in the gas chamber here. The memorial makes a strong impression (opening times: Mon and Fri 9am–3pm, Tue–Thu until 4pm, Sun 10am–5pm).

Maria Saal

M 6

Province: Carinthia
Population: 4200

Elevation: 505m/1656ft

The pilgrimage church in Maria Saal numbers among the most significant places of worship in all of Carinthia. When Bishop Modestus – who is also known as the Apostle of Carinthia – consecrated a Marian church here around 750, it marked the beginning of the Christianization the country.

Pilgrimage Church

Around 5km/3mi north of ►Klagenfurt, on a hilltop above Zollfeld, stands the pilgrimage church. After Bishop Modestus's first church, a second followed in the 13th century; the late Gothic place of worship, still in existence today, was erected in 1430–60. The church and cemetery are surrounded by fortified walls, which were put to the test in 1480 when Hungarian soldiers with less than friendly intentions stood before the gates. Of particular note amongst the old gravestones on the south wall of the church is the »Keutschach Epitaph« (*c*1510), made of red Adnet marble and depicting the Corona-

Austria's centre of Christianity

Roman wall relief at the pilgrimage church in Maria Saal, possibly depicting a journey into the beyond

The Carinthian ducal throne

tion of the Virgin, as well as two Roman stone reliefs: one of them depicts a Roman mail coach – most likely symbolizing the ride of the deceased into the afterlife – while the other depicts Achilles dragging Hector's corpse around the walls of Troy. The interior of the hall church is multifaceted and harmonious. Beautiful frescoes on the ceiling panels over the nave depict the genealogy of Christ (1490) with both human figures and ornamentation. In the middle of the Baroque high altar (1714) is the venerated portrait of the Virgin with a rapturous expression (1490). Both Gothic winged altars in the choir, the Arndorfer Altar (left) and St George's Altar (right) are also impressive. The second chapel (the Sachsenkapelle) in the left-hand side aisle features a Carolingian altar table from the original church, under which the remains of St Modestus (died in 763) lie entombed in a Roman sarcophagus. The frescoes are also worth taking a look at, particularly the fresco of the Three Magi next to the high altar (15th century). The south wall of the transept is adorned with a large fresco by Herbert Boeckl. A late Gothic lighted column stands in front of the south doorway of the pilgrimage church, and the octagonal Romanesque charnel house, with well-balanced proportions, is surrounded by a leafy frescoed arcade from around 1500.

Around Maria Saal

Kärntner Freilicht Museum

North of the town of Maria Saal, the Carinthian Open-Air Museum (the oldest of its kind in Austria) depicts ways of life and the traditional handicrafts of past centuries in the various valleys of Carinthia. Watermills and lumber mills, charcoal stacks and lime kilns inform visitors about provincial craftsmanship; a nature trail is also included. Visitors should plan a few hours for a visit to this multi-faceted museum (opening times: May–mid-Oct, Tue–Sun 10am–6pm).

Kärntner Herzogstühl

Enclosed by a wrought-iron fence on the side of the highway some 1.5km/.9mi north of Maria Saal is the ancient »Kärntner Herzogstuhl« or Carinthian ducal throne. The double-seated throne is joined by pieces of roman stone and was used by the dukes of Carinthia when granting fiefdoms or giving a verdict.

Virunum

The Zollfeld, a spacious, flat valley with forests, hills, and marshes, stretches north of the ducal throne. It was also the former location of Virunum, the capital of the Roman province of Noricum. Its huge amphitheatre has since been excavated. Artefacts from Virunum can be admired in the Landesmuseum Kärnten (Carinthian State Museum).

From Willersdorf – north of Maria Saal – a road heads a good 6km/4mi eastward to the »Archäologischer Park Magdalensberg« (1060m/3477ft), the well-visited excavation site of a late Celtic/early Roman settlement. The forum, living and working quarters, a temple district, a representation house, and baths are on display here. Inside the restored ancient buildings 22 exhibits have been arranged, featuring ceramics, glass, jewellery, gravestones, wall paintings, and a copy of the bronze statue of the *Jüngling vom Magdalensberg* (*Young Man of Magdalensberg*; opening times: May–mid-Oct, daily 9am–7pm).

 MARIA SAAL

INFORMATION

Gemeindeamt Maria Saal
Am Platzl 7
A-9063 Maria Saal
Tel. 042 23/22 14
Fax 22 14 22
www.maria.saal.at

★ Maria Taferl

O 3

Province: Lower Austria
Population: 850

Elevation: 443m/1453ft

The pilgrimage town of Maria Taferl lies at the spot with most beautiful views in the Nibelungengau (►Danube Valley). Its magnificent early Baroque church is said to stand on the site of an oak tree that had a miraculous picture (Taferl) of the Virgin on its trunk.

What to See in and around Maria Taferl

The twin-towered pilgrimage church was built by Lugaro and Gerstenbrand in 1660–1710; its cupola is the work of Jakob Prandtauer. The interior features Baroque ceiling paintings and other frescoes: scenes with St Joseph in the nave and the legend of the Virgin Mary in the transept. The legend of the church's foundation is depicted under the organ loft. The pulpit, featuring countless figures, and the Rococo organ with gold ornamentation, both from the 18th century, are also noteworthy. On the high altar, also from the 18th century, is the venerated figure of the Virgin Mary, surrounded by rays of light and cherubs. Today's figure is however a copy of the original, which was destroyed by fire along with the legendary oak tree in 1755.

★
Pilgrimage
church

▶ VISITING MARIA TAFERL

INFORMATION

Marktgemeinde Maria Taferl
A-3672 Maria Taferl 35
Tel. 0 74 13/70 40
Fax 70 40 14
www.mariataferl.at

WHERE TO EAT

► **Inexpensive**
Krone
A-3672 Maria Taferl
Tel. 0 74 13/63 55
This restaurant serves delicious meals
to go with the excellent view.

A Celtic stone table stands in front of the church. In fair weather visitors have a wonderful view of the Alps, extending from Vienna's Schneeberg to Traunstein at the Traunsee.

Pöchlarn
Downstream on the south side of the Danube river lies the village of Pöchlarn (213m/699ft; pop. 3800). Settlers first lived here in 4000 BC; the Romans erected a border defence base here. Artefacts from the Roman Danube port of Arelape are displayed in the Heimat-museum (Welserturm; opening times: Mon–Fri 9pm–noon, Sat from 10am; by arrangement only, tel. 027 57/23 100).

»Bechelaren« ►
Pöchlarn is said to be the town of »Bechelaren«, which is mentioned in the Nibelungenlied as the residence of Margrave Rüdiger, who warmly welcomed the Burgundians (Nibelungs) as guests on their way to King Etzel. A modern memorial commemorates this event.

Kokoschka Memorial ►
Painter Oskar Kokoschka was born in Pöchlarn on 1 March 1886. The Oskar-Kokoschka-Documentation (documentation centre) has been established in the house of his birth at Regensburger Strasse 29. Graphics, documents, and temporary exhibitions featuring works by the artist are on display (opening times: May–late Oct daily 9am–5pm).

Schloss Artstetten
Around 5km/3mi north of Kleinpöchlarn, the section of the town on the left side of the Danube, lie the park and castle of Artstetten (16th century), used as the setting for a popular German television series. The castle once belonged to the Austrian heir to the throne, Archduke Franz Ferdinand, murdered along with his wife Sophie in Sarajevo in 1914. The couple is buried here in the castle's chapel in accordance with the wishes of the archduke as the archduchess, born the Countess Chotek and of lower birth rank, was refused burial in the Kapuzinergruft, the tomb of the Habsburg family in Vienna.
The permanent exhibition, »Für Herz und Krone« (»For the Heart and the Crown«) is dedicated to the life of Franz Ferdinand and his family; other thematic exhibitions are displayed for a year at a time (opening times: April–early Nov daily 9am–5.30pm).

Mariazell ★★

04

Province: Styria
Population: 1600

Elevation: 870m/2854ft

The popular alpine health and leisure resort of Mariazell in northern Styria is an appropriate starting point for hiking and mountain tours, especially in the Hochschwab region. Yet Mariazell is first and foremost Austria's best visited and most important place of pilgrimage. The three-towered basilica dominates the townscape and can be seen from quite a distance.

★★ Pilgrimage Church

The legend of the pilgrimage church, which stands slightly above the town of Mariazell, goes back to the following event: Abbot Otker from Stift Lambrecht near Murau sent his monk Magnus into the area to provide pastoral care. Magnus had brought a wooden statue of the Virgin, which he had carved himself, along with him on the arduous trip. Just as he did every night, he was searching for a spot to sleep on the night of 21 December 1157 when he saw that the path on which he was travelling was blocked by a huge boulder. The exhausted monk asked the Virgin Mary for help – and the boulder broke apart, clearing the path. Magnus constructed a tiny cell as a living quarters and a chapel for the statue on the embankment just behind that spot. The location soon became the spiritual centre of the region.

Legend

Mariazell is the most important pilgrimage church in Austria

► MARIAZELL

INFORMATION

Touristverband Mariazeller Land
Hauptplatz 13, A-8630 Mariazell
Tel. 0 38 82/23 66, fax 39 45
www.mariazell.at

Around 1200, the first tiny church was constructed here, in Romanesque style. King Ludwig of Hungary demonstrated his thanks to the Virgin for successful campaigns with by converting it into a Gothic hall church in the 14th century. Emperor Ferdinand III contributed to the financial foundation of the church's Baroque renovation by Domenico Sciassia in the 17th century, who left

Basilica the Gothic tower in place and framed it with two additional Baroque towers. Baroque masters Johann Bernhard Fischer of Erlach the Elder, who created the magnificent high altar around 1700, and Fischer of Erlach the Younger played an authoritative role in the design of the interior. In 1908, the church was elevated to the rank of basilica.

Gnadenkapelle ► The Chapel of Grace, or Gnadenkapelle, serves as the main focal point of the church. The venerated figure, the **»Magna Mater Austriae«**, is no longer the original statue of the Virgin by Magnus but a late Romanesque figure. The silver altar was created by Augsburg masters, and the chapel itself is surrounded by a silver grille by J. Wagner of Vienna, commissioned by Maria Theresia (►Famous People) and her husband in 1750.

Treasury rooms ► The two rooms of the treasury, connected to the domed part of the building, are filled with works of sacred art, including artistic monstrances, pictures, and valuable liturgical vestments. The sheer mass of objects bears witness to the immense meaning the pilgrimage church has had over the centuries (church opening times: daily 6am–8pm).

Around Mariazell

Bürgeralpe An observation tower, the Erzherzog-Johann-Aussichtswarte, offers an incredible panoramic view of the Bürgeralpe (1266m/4153ft). Mariazell's native landmark mountain can be reached via cable car. A visit to the **Erlebniswelt Holzknechtland** offers interesting glimpses into the extremely laborious work of the wood cutters (Holzknechte) in days gone by   (opening times: May–Oct, daily 9am–5pm).

Naturpark Ötscher-Tormäuer Slightly north of Mariazell begins the extensive Ötscher-Tormäuer Nature Park. Its highest peak is the Ötscher (1893m/6209 ft). The steep-sided Ötschergräben gorges are also impressive: the area isn't known as the Austrian Grand Canyon for nothing. A walk through the area is not recommended for vertigo sufferers though – the trail includes hanging bridges several metres from the ground. An underground treat is the 575m/1886ft-long **Ötscher Tropfsteinhöhle**, a dripstone cave (guided tours: May–Oct Sat and Sun 9am–4pm, July and Aug also Wed 11am–4pm).

A special attraction is the **Maria-zellerbahn**, a narrow gauge railway (760mm/30in) that was built in phases starting in 1896 and that was completely electrified in 1911. In the summer months, it travels over 85km/53mi through alpine landscapes, four river valleys, and 21 tunnels to St Pölten (information at tel. 0 27 23/87 90, www.mariazellerbahn.at).

Further to the south, shortly before the Seebergsattel Pass, is the **Brand-hof**, which was purchased by Archduke Johann in 1818 and expanded to create a modest castle with a model farm. In 1829, it was the venue for the Archduke's wedding when he married Anna Plochl, the daughter of the postmaster in Bad Aussee. Today, Brandhof is privately owned.

!   *Baedeker* TIP

Historical tramway

On weekends between July and September, a museum tram runs along the 2.5km/3.8mi-long stretch between the main station in Mariazell and the Erlaufsee. It features the oldest steam tramway locomotive in the world (from 1884). For information call tel. 0 38 82/30 14 or see www.museumstramway.at.

Matrei in Osttirol

Province: Tyrol   **Elevation:** 1000m/3280ft
Population: 4500

At the southern foot of the ►Hohe Tauern lies the market town of Matrei in Osttirol, a popular health, winter sports, and tourist resort located almost exactly at the centre point between Austria's two highest peaks – the Grossglockner (3798m/12,457ft) and the Grossvenediger (3674m/12,050ft).

The town has been accessible from the north via the 5.3km/3.2mi-long Felbertauern tunnel since 1967. This was not always the case: Secluded climatic health resort

 VISITING MATREI IN OSTTIROL

INFORMATION

Tourismusverband
Osttirol
Rauterplatz 1
A-9971 Matrei in Osttirol
Tel. 0 48 75/65 27
Fax 65 27 40
www.matreiinostirol.at

WHERE TO STAY

► **Mid-range**
Hotel Rauter
Rauterplatz 3, A-9971 Matrei
Tel. 0 48 75/66 11, fax 66 13
www.hotel-rauter.at
This alpine hotel organizes trekking tours and offers a swimming pool, tennis courts and a riding hall. In-house cake shop.

the isolated area was previously only accessible from Lienz in the south, which is also why rural culture and traditions have been better preserved here than in other regions.

What to See in Matrei

At the centre of the traditional alpine town is the mighty late Baroque parish church, Pfarrkirche St Alban (c1780), the largest village church in all of East Tyrol, whose Gothic tower originated in the 14th century and still remains today. The interior is adorned with ceiling frescoes (1780). The altars were created around the year 1800.

St-Nikolaus-Kirche
The somewhat remote church of St Nicholas dates back to the Romanesque period. Its façade features 14th-century frescoes. The tower, extended to form a choir, opens out to the nave on two levels. The lower floor features frescoes from the 13th century (depicting the story of Adam and Eve, amongst other things); the upper floor features portrayals of saints and apostles (also 13th century). The medieval wooden figures are also of interest.

Schloss Weissenstein
Standing on a limestone cliff high above the city is **Matrei's city emblem**, Schloss Weissenstein (1029m/3375ft). It was constructed in the 12th century and renovated in the 19th century (privately owned).

✳
Panoramaweg Matrei–Kals
After taking a trip on the Goldried mountain railway, visitors can enjoy a hike along the Matrei–Kals panoramic route. It offers a view of an amazing 63 mountains that are over 3000m/10,000ft in height, including the Grossglockner.

Around Matrei

Kalser Tal
Approximately 9km/6mi south of Matrei, in the town of Huben, the Kalser Tal valley takes a turn toward the east and proceeds 13km/8mi to Kals where it then ends. Its focal point is a small Romanesque church, the Georgskirche, which lies in the middle of a green meadow between Kals-Unterburg and Kals-Grossdorf. A narrow toll road begins beyond Kals and leads to the Luckner Haus at the foot of the Grossglockner, a starting point for beautiful hikes on the southern side of the mountain.

Virgental
The Virgental extends west of Matrei. Its main road heads 17km/10.6mi through gorges and several tunnels to Hinterbichl, offering a lovely view of the head of the valley and the Dreiherrenspitze (3499m/11,477ft).

Zedlacher Paradies ▶
In East Tyrol, valleys are narrow and space is limited. For this reason areas of grazing pasture tend to be at very high elevations, where the sun's rays are intense and the grass is especially rich in minerals. For

View of the Lasörlinggruppe from the Zedlacher Paradies

this very reason, as early as the Middle Ages farmers were already bringing their livestock up to the cleared lynchet – known as the Zedlacher Paradies (Zedlach Paradise; 1500m/4920ft) – above Matrei at the entrance to the Virgental valley. Besides beautiful alpine pasture, the area also features the most splendid stock of larch trees in East Tyrol. With some trees over 500 years old and with trunk circumferences of up to 6m/20ft, this has the feel of primeval forest. A tour through the Zedlacher Paradies lasts approximately 1 hour (rest stop at car park).

The architectural centrepiece of the Virgental valley is a Gothic pilgrimage church, Wallfahrtskirche Unsere Liebe Frau Maria Schnee (Our Lady of the Snows; 1430–56), in Obermauern near Virgen. The excellently preserved frescoes (1484–88) by East Tyrolese painter Simon von Taisten depict the life and death of Jesus Christ. Another fresco cycle filled with rich images is dedicated to the Virgin Mary.

◄ Obermauern

The ascent from Prägraten in the Virgental valley to the Defreggerhaus (2962m/9715ft; restaurant open in summer) takes a good six hours; from there, experienced mountain climbers will need in the order of another 3 hours to reach the peak of the Grossvenediger.

✳
◄ Grossvenediger

✳ ✳ Melk

0 3

Province: Lower Austria
Population: 5300

Elevation: 228m/748ft

Countless visitors from all over the world are enticed by the Benedictine abbey in Melk, which can be seen from miles away. It is one of the most significant and magnificent Baroque monasteries in all of Austria, and was added to the UNESCO World Heritage list in 2000 along with the Wachau, Krems, and Stift Göttweig.

The small town of Melk lies at the point where the Danube enters the ► Wachau. Although it was mentioned in documents as the Roman fort of Namare and is considered by its residents to be the »Medelike« in the Nibelungenlied, it is famous for a different reason. Its well-known Benedictine abbey awaits visitors with a long list of superlatives: an area of 17,500 sq m/4.3ac, a 362m/1187ft-long south façade, 1888 windows, and a 64m/210ft-high dome.

Baroque gateway to the Wachau

STIFT MELK

✳ ✳ **The west-facing narrow side of the abbey complex, which has retained its bright yellow and white colour scheme, is visible from far and wide. The buildings of the Benedictine abbey are grouped around seven courtyards. The abbey stands majestically atop a 60m/200ft-high cliff.**

🕐 Opening times:
Mid-March–April and Oct
daily 9am–4.30, May–Sept until 5.30pm
Guided tours on the hour: May–Sept 10am–4pm,
April and Oct 10am–3pm, March 11am and 2pm,
groups by arrangement; tel. 027 52 / 55 52 32
www.stiftmelk.at

Monks have lived and worked continuously in Stift Melk since 1089. At the time of the so-called »Melk Reform« in the 15th century, the abbey was the starting point of one of the most important medieval monastery reforms.

① **Stiftskirche**
The highlight of the Baroque monastery site is the abbey church, which is considered one of the most beautiful Baroque churches north of the Alps. According to the wishes of the abbot and the monks the church should express the religious basis of the entire site and the orientation to God in clearly visible form – which the special light effects support.

② **Library**
Medieval monasteries were not only of spiritual significance, they also served as strongholds of knowledge. A school was associated with the

abbey from as early as the 12th century. In the library precious manuscripts were collected and prepared.

③ **Marble hall**
The hall, a masterpiece of Baroque interior design, served as a dining hall for the imperial family and was used for receptions and ceremonies. Today it is part of the abbey museum.

④ **Altane**
From the Altane, the connecting balcony between the marble hall and the library, there is a wonderful view across the Danube, the Wachau and the town of Melk.

⑤ **Stiftsmuseum**
The abbey museum provides information about the founders of the abbey and its history, which naturally is closely interwoven with that of the whole of Austria. Some of the monastic treasures are on display; for reasons of conservation, the most precious items such as the late medieval Melker Kreuz (Melk Cross) are only visible as illustrations.

Stift Melk

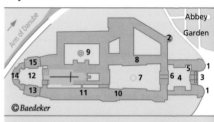

1 Bastions
2 Defensive Tower
3 Entrance Gate: St Koloman
  on the right, St Leopold on the left
4 Forecourt (Torwartlhof)
5 Ticket Office
6 Galleries (statues of
  Peter and Paul, abbey coat
  of arms, Melker Kreuz above)
7 Prelates' Court with Fountain
8 School
9 Konventshof: Mor
  Quarters
10 Imperial Staircase
11 State Apartments
   (exhibition rooms)
12 Kolomanihof
13 Marble Hall
14 Gallery
15 Library

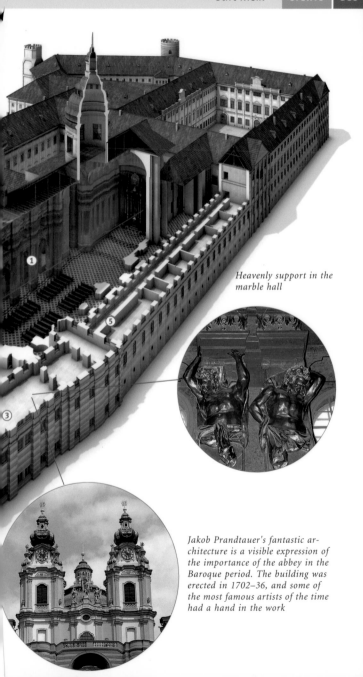

Heavenly support in the marble hall

Jakob Prandtauer's fantastic architecture is a visible expression of the importance of the abbey in the Baroque period. The building was erected in 1702–36, and some of the most famous artists of the time had a hand in the work

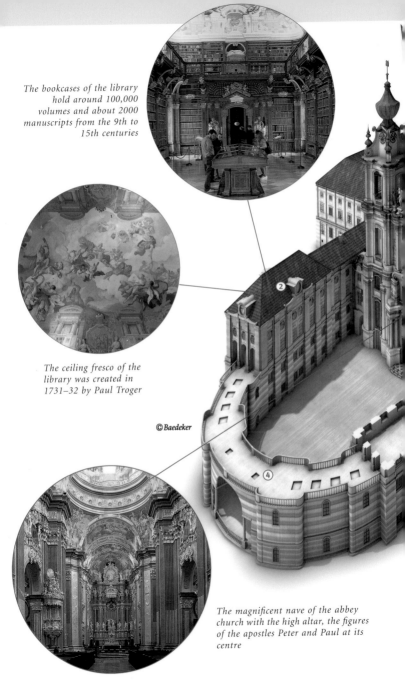

The bookcases of the library hold around 100,000 volumes and about 2000 manuscripts from the 9th to 15th centuries

The ceiling fresco of the library was created in 1731–32 by Paul Troger

© Baedeker

The magnificent nave of the abbey church with the high altar, the figures of the apostles Peter and Paul at its centre

History By the end of the 10th century, a fortress of the Bavarian Baben-berg family had been built on this spot. In 1089, Margrave Leopold II handed the fortress and its church over to the Benedictines. When the remains of St Koloman were transferred here in 1113, the monastery developed into the spiritual and cultural centre of the region. After it had suffered the effects of the Reformation, invasions by the Turks, and several fires, master builders Jakob Prandtauer and Joseph Munggenast built the magnificent Baroque abbey in 1702–38.

✶ ✶ Stift Melk

Abbey buildings The Benedictine abbey, one of the most monumental examples of Austrian Baroque, is located on a steep ridge overlooking the Danube and is only accessible from the east. Nowadays, the monastery is home to 30 monks, and some 800 students visit its renowned secondary school. The former orangery, located next to the abbey's gardens, is now home to the abbey restaurant.

Courtyards The buildings of the abbey complex are grouped around seven courtyards. The octagonal entrance gate is flanked by statues of the abbey's two patron saints, St Koloman (right) and St Leopold (left). Next follows the fore-courtyard (Torwartlhof), which features a view of the palace-like east façade of the abbey with a large replica of the magnificent Melk Cross (Melker Kreuz), the original of which is stored in the abbey treasury. The abbey's coat of arms is mounted above the rounded gateway. Following the Hall of St Benedict – which is dedicated to the order's founder – is the Prälatenhof or Prelates' Court, which is decorated with statues portraying the prophets and the four so-called cardinal virtues of prudence, temperance, fortitude and justice.

Kaisergang and Kaiserzimmer (Museum) Both the entrance to the abbey's secondary school and the entrance to the Kaiserstiege, or Imperial Staircase – whose banisters are adorned with cherubs and stone statues – are located to the right of the Prelates' Court. The staircase leads to the prelature, the Imperial Rooms (Kaiserzimmer) and the 196m/643ft-long Imperial Corridor (Kaisergang), which features portraits of Austrian rulers. The Imperial Rooms, which were once reserved for members of high nobility who were passing though, now serve as a **museum of the abbey's past and present**.

Marmorsaal The Marble Hall, or Marmorsaal, is a festive hall with a fascinating combination of strict structure and beautiful ceiling paintings by Paul Troger: the ruling house of Austria is depicted in the mythological scenes, which extol the family for its ability to direct people away from the forces of evil. The doorframes are of genuine marble, while the walls are of marble stucco.

Connecting the Marble Room and the library is a balcony, the Altane, a mighty terrace offering a wonderful view of the church's west façade and the Kolomanihof (St Koloman's Court) in front of it, as well as the town of Melk and the Danube Valley.

Altane

To the north of the Kolomanihof is the magnificent library, maintained in hues of brown and gold. The library is the second most important building in a Benedictine monastery after the church. The ceiling frescoes by Paul Troger (1731–32) are a symbolic depiction of faith. The library contains 100,000 volumes, including 1888 manuscripts, 750 incunabula (early prints prior to 1500) and other works from the 16th century to the present day.

★ Library

The abbey church numbers among **one of the most beautiful Baroque churches north of the Alps**. The interior of the domed structure captivates with its unity of architecture, sculpture, and painting, and its harmonious red and gold hues. A special effect has been created by positioning the high altar and the cupola into the church's natural light source. The ceiling frescoes of the nave, created by Salzburg's Michael Rottmayr in 1722, depict the Apotheosis of St Benedict. The sarcophagus of St Koloman is located in the transept. The splendid high altar features figures of the apostles Peter and Paul (18th century; Peter Widerin), while the painting in the cupola depicts the Holy Trinity surrounded by numerous saints. A modern altar from 1976 (H. Hütter, F. Fürst) incorporates elements from the Baroque interior.

★ Stiftskirche

> **? DID YOU KNOW …?**
>
> ■ …that Stift Melk has the literary honour of being the birthplace and later residence of the monk Adson, the narrator in Umberto Eco's novel *The Name of the Rose*.

Other Sights in Melk

The town below the abbey is also worth a visit. Its main axes are formed by the Rathausplatz (Town Hall Square), the Hauptstrasse (High Street) the Hauptplatz (Main Square), and Sterngasse – the oldest street in Melk – which runs parallel to the Hauptstrasse. The former Lebzelterhaus (1657; now a pharmacy) and the Rathaus (1575), with an elaborate entrance door of wood and copper, line the Rathausplatz. The shingle roof of the old bakery at the end of the Rathausplatz is around 400 years old, and an ancient grapevine growing on the side of the »Haus am Stein« behind Sterngasse is protected as a nature conservation site. The high water marks on the shipping master's house near the shore show water levels of the Danube at various times of flooding. South of Linzerstrasse stands the late Baroque Alte Post, or Old Post Office, which was commissioned by the postmaster Freiherr von Fürnberg in 1792 (currently an events and convention centre).

Melk (town)

Around Melk

Around 5km/3mi south of Melk is the **Renaissance Schloss Schallaburg**, with its two-storey arcaded courtyard featuring terracotta ornamentation. It is the most celebrated work of Renaissance architecture in Lower Austria, now serving as a cultural centre with annual exhibitions on cultural history and archaeology (opening times: Mon–Fri 9am–5pm, Sat and Sun until 6pm).

✶✶ Millstätter See

L 6

Province: Carinthia   **Elevation:** 588m/1929ft

The Millstätter See is often referred to as Carinthia's sunshine region, a claim confirmed by its average temperatures: the lake itself can reach temperatures of up to 26 °C/79 °F!

Sunshine region on the lake

Countless swimming areas with gorgeous natural beaches have established themselves along the lake, which is 12km/7.5mi long, 1.5km/1mi wide and up to 141m/463ft deep. A wide array of sporting opportunities both in and out of the water make the lake a popular summer

The charm of the turn of the century lives on in the villas of the Millstätter See

⏵ VISITING MILLSTÄTTER SEE

INFORMATION

Tourismusbüro Millstatt
Marktplatz 8, A-9872 Millstatt
Tel. 0 47 66/20 22, fax 34 79
www.millstatt.at

WHERE TO EAT

► Moderate
Forelle
Fischergasse 65, A-9872 Millstatt
Tel. 0 47 66/2 05 00
On summer days a table on the
terrace is recommended.

WHERE TO STAY

► Mid-range
Hotel Römerbad
Straussweg 1
A-9546 Bad Kleinkirchheim
Tel. 0900/35 06 05
Fax 82 34 57
www.roemerbadhotels.at
The south-facing balconies offer a
splendid view of the Nockberge
mountains. Pleasant rooms, various
sporting opportunities and a healthy
menu complete the package.

holiday destination with a charming backdrop: the Nockberge Mountains and the national park to the north and the woody, sparsely populated southern banks, which can be travelled on narrow roads.

What to See around the Millstätter See

The main town, Millstatt (604m/1981ft; pop. 1300), is located on the north shore of the lake and was **a Celtic and a Roman settlement**. The Benedictines also found the city appealing, establishing Millstatt Abbey here in 1070, of which several buildings still remain. These include the courtyard, with its impressive two-storey, arched arcaded gallery. The mighty, 1000-year-old »Gerichtslinde«, a linden tree where assemblies and judicial courts were held, has also been preserved.

✳ **Millstattt**

◄ Stift Millstatt

The magnificent abbey church is also interesting. It is a Romanesque columned building with a nave and two aisles, a doorway with steps (c1170), noteworthy arches with reticulated vaulting, the expressive Last Judgement fresco (1513–19) – a masterpiece of the Austrian Renaissance – and a precious Baroque interior attributed to the last spiritual rulers of the abbey, the Jesuits (1598–1773). During Lent, the high altar is draped with the »**Millstätter Fastentuch**«. This Lenten veil, an art-historical treasure from the year 1593, shows 41 scenes from the Old and the New Testaments on a surface of over 50 sq m/ 538 sq ft. The lovely cloister, built in the early 12th century and later decorated, offers a glimpse into medieval times. The abbey serves as a worthy setting for the Millstätter Musikwochen, a summer musical festival.

The abbey museum documents the history of Millstatt, in particular the abbey, which was a centre of book art under the Benedictines

◄ Stiftsmuseum

(until 1469) and a centre of visual art under the Knights of St George (1469–1598). It also explores the geological formation of the Carinthian uplands by examining minerals and ore discovered there (opening times: June–late Sept daily 10am–noon and 2pm–6pm).

Seeboden In Seeboden (580m/1902ft; pop. 6100), located at the west end of the Millstätter See, the Kärntner Fischereimuseum (Carinthian Fishing Museum) reveals everything that creeps and swims in the Millstätter See (opening times: June–Sept daily 10.30am–6pm).

Burg Burg Sommeregg is a **very special destination**: at weekends, the cas-
Sommeregg ▶ tle restaurant invites guests to dine like a knight, and for several weeks during July and August, visitors can enter the medieval world of the knights, with jousting tournaments, jugglers, swordfights, and fire shows providing entertainment. The more gloomy side – and not just of the Middle Ages – is on display in the **Foltermuseum** (Torture Museum), accompanied by documentation from amnesty international (opening times: April, Sept, Oct daily 11am–5pm, May, June daily 10am–6pm, July, Aug until 8pm).

Döbriach (606m/1988ft) on the east bank of the Millstätter See is an ideal starting point for hikes and climbing tours in the Nockberge National Park. Those who would like to practice a little beforehand can try the climbing wall, which ranges in difficulty from levels 3 to 8.

Around the Millstätter See

Radenthein Just a few miles east of the lake lies Radenthein (588m/1929ft; pop. 6900), whose region holds very special buried treasure: the magnesite mined here is perfectly suited for fireproof clothing. Near the village of Kaning, located to the north in the Rossbachgraben gorge, six of the original 22 mills can be admired along 3.5km/2mi-long trails, the Kneippwanderweg and Mühlenwanderweg.

Bad Further to the east lies the village of Bad Kleinkirchheim (1100m/
Kleinkirchheim 3608ft; pop. 1900), known for its excellent skiing area in the Nock-

berge mountains, which is attractive for beginners and experts alike. Visitors can, for example, meet 1976 Olympic champion Franz Klammer here at the carving buffet. In the Roman thermal baths, guests go straight from the slopes into steamy water, surrounded by antique Romanesque architecture. The Therme St Kathrein offers fun and relaxation in the water for the whole family.

Mittersill

H/J 5

Province: Salzburg　　　　**Elevation:** 789m/2588ft
Population: 5600

Mittersill is the principal city of the upper Pinzgau valley and is located on the Salzach river at the northern edge of the ► Hohe Tauern National Park. To the north, the Thun Pass leads to Kitzbühel and St Johann in Tirol. To the south, the Felbertauernstrasse – a toll road constructed in the 1960s – leads to the 5.3km/3.2mi-long Felbertauern tunnel, the safest route between East Tyrol and Carinthia in the winter.

Mittersill offers a wide variety of sporting activities, including golf, marathons, hiking and mountain climbing – in the beautiful mountain landscape of the Hohe Tauern National Park – or cycling on the lovely **Tauernradweg**. The 330km/205mi-long cycle way begins in Krimml, a little way from Wald, and continues via Salzburg to Passau. Despite the initially high alpine terrain, the route is fairly flat – the low number of small inclines make it ideal even for families with small children. It can be slightly difficult for those on racing

Sports

● VISITING MITTERSILL

INFORMATION

Tourismusverband Mittersill
Stadtplatz 1, A-5730 Mittersill
Tel. 0 65 62/42 92, fax 50 07,
www.mittersill-tourismus.at

WHERE TO EAT

► Moderate
Meilinger Taverne
Stadtplatz 10, A-5730 Mittersill
Tel. 0 65 62/42 26
A small, pleasant restaurant with delicious food – children welcome.

WHERE TO STAY

► Mid-range
Hotel Jagdschloss Graf Recke
A-5742 Wald im Oberpinzgau
Tel. 0 65 65/64 17
Fax 69 20
www.ila-chateau.com/jagdschl
This hotel in a manor house is located at the foot of the Grossvenediger in the foothills of the Hohe Tauern National Park. Comfortable rooms and a good restaurant (closed Oct–mid Dec, mid-March–mid-May).

bikes, however, as a quarter of the cycle way has a fine sandy surface. The route gets even better as it turns west in Salzburg and continues up the Saalach river – it joins the Salzach again near Zell am See.

What to See in Mittersill

Felberturm
The museum in the Felberturm, or Felber Tower, is certainly worth a look. This old, 12th-century watchtower, which was also used to store grain during part of its history, now houses minerals and exhibits on the area's mining history, sacred works of art, and old manual tools (opening times: May and Oct Sat and Sun 1pm–5pm, June–Sept Tue–Fri 10am–5pm, Sat and Sun from 1pm).

Schloss Mittersill ▶
Enthroned high above the town is Schloss Mittersill – constructed in 1180 and extended and renovated several times over the years, it now serves as a Christian conference centre.

Around Mittersill

Bramberg
Some 12km/7.5mi up the Salzach river to the west lies the town of Bramberg (819m/2686ft; pop. 3900), whose museum houses a valuable collection of alpine minerals, including emeralds from the Habachtal valley – **the only emerald stones to be found in Europe** (opening times: May–mid-June and Oct Mon–Fri 3pm–5pm, Sun 10am–noon, mid-June–Sept daily 10am–6pm). The museum also offers mineral-hunting excursions; those who want to strike it lucky can move on to the gold-washing station.

A good 6km/3.5mi up the valley is **Neukirchen am Grossvenediger** (856m/2808ft; pop. 2600), which, along with Mittersill, is Oberpinzgau's holiday resort. The town is a starting point for beautiful hikes through the mountains. A gondola leads up to the Wildkogel rising majestically in the north (2225m/7298ft; upper station 2093m/6865ft) in the Kitzbüheler Alps, an outstanding and popular ski resort with an excellent view of the Tyrolean Alps and the Hohe Tauern.

Wald im Pinzgau
Wald im Pinzgau (885m/2903ft; pop. 1200) is part of a commune with Almdorf Königsleiten at an elevation of approximately 1600m/5248ft. Those wishing to get considerably closer to the sky have come to the right place at **Europe's highest-altitude planetarium** and observatory at Königsleiten (presentations: June, July, Sept and Oct Wed–Sun 2.30pm and 8.30pm; guided tours: Aug Tue–Sun 10.30am, 1.30pm, 3.30pm and 8.30pm).

The Vorderkrimml district awaits visitors with a mineral cave (especially fluorite crystals) that has been made into a show mine (guided tours: mid-June–mid-Sept Wed 6pm; museum: June–Sept Mon–Fri 2pm–5pm).

Vorderkrimml

At Uttendorf (804m/2637ft; pop. 2800) around 6km/4mi east of Mittersill, the charming landscape of the **Stubachtal valley** stretches to the south. At the end of the 18km/11mi-long valley is the Enzingerboden (1468m/4815ft), where there is also a power station of the same name. The rounded dam at Tauernmoossee is one of the longest retaining walls in Austria (1100m/3608ft). The gondola, which travels over the Grünsee to the Weisssee (2323m/7619ft), leads to the Alpine Centre Rudolfshütte mountain station (2315m/7593ft), a lovely way of entering the beautiful alpine world of the Hohe Tauern. Two glacier nature trails at the Sonnblick and Ödenwinkel glaciers explain everything there is to know about these powerful natural phenomena.

▶Krimml

Krimml

✳ Mölltal

J 5/6 K 6

Province: Carinthia

The pretty Möll Valley, which takes its name from the river whose source is on the Grossglockner mountain, runs south from Heiligenblut, stopping shortly before Lienz where it then turns to the east. Mölltal has had strategic importance as a transport route since Roman times.

What to See in Mölltal

Grosskirchheim (1024m/3359ft; pop. 1600) is the main borough of the upper Mölltal valley, an area particularly well-loved by hikers, with its main town of Döllach, located 10km/6.2mi southeast of Heiligenblut. In the 15th and 16th centuries, it was the centre of silver and gold mining in the Tauern region – the museum in the castle at Grosskirchheim is a reminder of that period.

Grosskirchheim

Lying at the foot of the Iselberg mountain, which separates Carinthia from East Tyrol at this point, is the market village of Winklern (967m/3172ft; pop. 1200), located where the river and the valley bend toward the northeast. The Mautturm, or toll tower, at Winklern is worth a visit; it serves as a memorial to the for-

▶ MÖLLTAL

INFORMATION
Urlaubsinformation Mölltal
A-9822 Mallnitz 11
Tel. 0 47 84/290, fax 635
www.mallnitz.at

Rafting, like here on the Möll, is one of the most popular and thrilling sports

mer strategic importance of this traffic hub. Though probably constructed in the 14th century, its foundation is most likely to be of Roman origin. The placement of the tower's windows leaves reason to believe that messages were sent and received using light signals.

Lainach   Lainach is home to a rather bizarre museum – the **»Zeitfabrik«**, or »time factory«, in Rangersdorf-Lainach. The museum demonstrates the evolution of man from the very beginnings of civilization all the way to the era of genetic engineering (opening times: April–Oct daily 11am–5pm).

Obervellach   Obervellach (676m/2217ft; pop. 2500) is known for its favourable climate and high prevalence of sunny days. Gold was discovered in the vicinity of the town in the Middle Ages; countless tunnels in the region still bear witness to that fact. Burg Groppenstein and Burg Falkenstein (both castles are privately owned) tower high above.

The late Gothic parish church, Pfarrkirche St Martin, contains an art-historical treasure: a triptych of the Holy Family by Dutch painter Jan van Scorel. The artist created this piece on commission when he stopped at Burg Falkenstein on his way to Rome in 1520. Towering to the southwest of Obervellach is the **Polinik** (2784m/9132ft), the highest peak of the Kreuzeckgruppe mountain range. This ostensibly uninhabited massif is used for forestry and alpine farming.

Between the villages of Penk and Kolbnitz, rising slightly unexpectedly up from the floor of the Mölltal valley, is the **Danielsberg**,

---

! **Baedeker TIP**

Interactive nature

The Bios-Erlebniswelt Mallnitz is a special kind of visitor centre: the 600 sq m/6500 sq ft laboratory invites guests to playfully discover biological connections and the laws of physics under the theme »Water, Air, Rock, Sun« – an exciting experience for both children and parents! (Mallnitz 36; www.bios-hohentauern.at; opening times: April–Oct daily 10am–6pm)

where there is evidence of human settlement from as early as 6000 years ago. The Celts built a temple here, the Romans added a Hercules temple to it, and the first Christian chapel, dedicated to St Daniel (the Christian equivalent of Hercules), was built around 313. The Georgskirche (St George's Church), which stands there today, originated in the 16th century.

✶ Mondsee

K 4

Province: Upper Austria   **Elevation:** 481m/1578ft

The sickle-shaped Mondsee, a 11km/6.8mi-long, over 2km/1.2mi-wide lake with a backdrop formed by the steep cliffs of the Drachenwand and the Schafberg, is, with water temperatures reaching 26 °C/79 °F, the warmest lake of the Salzkammergut and a paradise for water sports enthusiasts. Along with the market town of Mondsee, other small villages, idyllic hotels and country houses line its partially wooded banks.

What to See around the Mondsee

The town of Mondsee lies at the northwestern end of the lake. A Bavarian duke founded Upper Austria's oldest monastery here in 748. Some of its Benedictine monks were talented illuminators: the *Montpellier Psalter* from 788 is considered the oldest work to have been written in Austria; the *Mondseer Matthäus* or *Mondseer Matthew* (*c*800) is referred to as the oldest German translation of the Bible. The monks' love of art was also demonstrated by the fact that the heads of the monastery requested that **Baroque sculptor Meinrad**

✶
Mondsee (town)

▶ VISITING MONDSEE

INFORMATION
Tourismusverband MondSeeLand
Dr.-Franz-Müller-Strasse 3
A-5310 Mondsee
Tel. 0 62 32/22 70, fax 22 70 22
www.mondsee.org

WHERE TO EAT
▶ **Expensive**
Schloss Mondsee
Schlosshof 1 A, A-5310 Mondsee
Tel. 0 62 32/50 01

These days the former monastery has a kitchen that uses only the very finest ingredients.

▶ **Moderate**
Café-Restaurant Fisherman's
Robert-Baum-Promenade 1
A-5310 Mondsee
Tel./fax 062 32/364 79
Delicious fish specialities and a lovely view of the lake.

Guggenbichler (1649–1723) come to Mondsee, where he was to work for 44 years until his death. The monastery was dissolved in 1791; today, a hotel is found within its restored walls. The parish church, Pfarrkirche St Michael is also noteworthy: a Baroque twin-towered façade was added to the original Gothic structure. Inside, Guggenbichler's main works include the Corpus Christi altar in the left side aisle, decorated with cherubs holding grapevines.

»Mondsee Culture« As old as the monastery may be, there are much older artefacts around the Mondsee in the form of **traces of Early Stone Age settlements** (*c*1900 BC). Due to the abundance of lake dwellings with stilt construction in the Eastern Alpine regions, they were given the name »Mondsee culture«. Some of the rooms of the former monastery were used to establish a museum for the structures; the former monastery library is home to the Heimatmuseum, featuring numerous sacred and everyday artefacts such as the Mondseer Einbaum, a log boat (opening times: May–early Sept 10am–6pm, until early Oct until 5pm).

Southeast of the church is the »Mondseer Rauchhaus«, or smoke house, an old furnished farmhouse that now serves as an open-air museum. In this prime example of a Bavarian »Einhaus«, quite literally an »all-in-one house«, the smoke of the oven's fire did not exit

through a vent, but rather drifted from room to room – warming both the occupants and the animals, drying the grain, and smoking the sausage and the ham (opening times: May–Aug Tue–Sun 10am–6pm, Sept until 5pm, Oct Sat and Sun 10am–5pm).

Towering upwards on the southwest shore of the Mondsee is the 1000m/3280ft-tall **Drachenwand**. Its legend goes as follows: the dragon that lived on the Drachenwand once fell in love with the cook at the Mondsee parish church, but she spurned him as she had a soft spot for the church's minister. Boiling with rage, the dragon flew down from the mountain to kidnap her. Unfortunately, his beloved was considerably heavier than he had expected. As a consequence the pair crashed straight into the rock face – and left a hole that can still be seen today.

A house without a chimney: smoke house in Mondsee

Montafon

Province: Vorarlberg

Montafon is a 40km/25mi-long high mountain valley, with the Ill river flowing through it and eleven towns (600–1450m/1968–4756ft), which is bordered by mountains up to 3312m/10,863ft high. Hydroelectric power has brought economic momentum to the valley.

The valley starts south of ►Bludenz and extends between the mountain masses of the Rätikon mountains in the west and the Verwallgruppe range in the east. It continues southeast all the way to the Bielerhöhe (2032m/6665ft), which is now traversed by the ►Silvretta High Alpine Road. The lower Montafon valley lies in the shadow of the 2600m/8528ft-high Zimba mountain to the west, the so-called **»Austrian Matterhorn«**, named for its peaked pyramid shape. The ascent is a challenge even for experienced mountain climbers. The upper part of the valley is dominated by the alpine lakes and glaciers of the Silvretta mountains (Piz Buin, 3312m/10,863ft). Montafon's first settlers were Rhaeto-Romanic, as many local place names and surnames suggest. The pleasant valley and the series of smaller valleys surrounding it constitute a **sought-after holiday destination**: in summer, hikers and climbers can easily find challenging climbing tours in this beautiful, sometimes bizarre mountain landscape; during winter, skiers can enjoy the deep snow on the glacial slopes and the sunny ski runs.

Rhaeto-Romanic roots

> ## ! *Baedeker* TIP
>
> ### Skis or tyres?
>
> Montafon is not only perfect for getting around on two thin skis (or one wide one), but also provides the perfect conditions for travel on two sturdy wheels. More than 20 mountain bike tours of varying lengths and levels of difficulty are available (more information at www.montafon.com).

Montafon also enjoys its international popularity thanks to the American author and winner of the Nobel Prize in Literature Ernest Hemingway (1899–1961), who stayed at the Hotel »Taube« (room 22) in Schruns as he travelled across Europe over two winters (1924–25 and 1925–26) with his first wife Hadley, his son John and his writer friend John Dos Passos. Hemingway thoroughly enjoyed his time in Montafon, where in those days it was still possible to reside much more inexpensively than in the world-famous winter resorts of Switzerland and France. Reading the memoirs of the 60-year-old writer, you would think that he and his wife had spent the entire time on skis. Several of their day trips led them to the Madlenerhaus, located on what is now the ►Silvretta High Alpine Road

Ernest Hemingway

Winter evening in Gargellen

next to the Silvretta reservoir. But Hemingway worked here as well: he completed his first major novel (*The Sun Also Rises*), which later became an international success. »Schruns was a great place to work,« he wrote in one of his letters. In his narrative *The Snows of Kilimanjaro* he recalled his winter in Vorarlberg, the narrative *An Alpine Idyll* takes place on the Tyrolese side of the Silvretta, and in the last chapter of his posthumous work from 1964, *A Moveable Feast*, he declared his love for Montafon: »We loved Vorarlberg and we loved Schruns.«

What to See in Montafon

Vandans   Located at the valley entrance, where the Rellstal and the Illtal valleys meet, is the borough of Vandans (650m/2132ft; pop. 1500), an old Rhaeto-Romanic settlement whose name is derived from the Rhaeto-Romanic word »fantauns« (body of water). The town, where each year more than half a million flowers are planted for the summer, is a provincial winner many times over at the competition for Vorarlberg's best community for flowers. It has even been named »Europe's best flower town«.

Schruns   Schruns (690m/2263ft; pop. 3500), the valley's main town, is situated on the right bank of the Ill river near the mouth of the Litzbach, where the valley widens. Together with Tschagguns (686m/2250ft; pop. 2400) on the left bank of the Ill, it forms the touristic centre of the valley.

Montafoner   The bucking bull on Schruns's coat of arms indicates that the loca-
Braunvieh ▶   tion had a reputation as a market for livestock up until the First

World War: every year up to 2000 cattle of the famous Montafoner Braunvieh breed were sold to Southern Germany, Hungary, Italy and the Balkan States. An over 500-year-old Rhaeto-Romanic house, the former seat of the so-called »Bergrichter« (a judge who had jurisdiction in the mountains), is home to the interesting and worthwhile Heimatmuseum, which exhibits cultural artefacts from the entire valley and provides information on the Montafon way of life (opening times: May, June, Sept and Oct Tue–Sat 2pm–5pm, July and Aug Tue–Sat 10am–5pm, Sun from 2pm; guided tours by arrangement, tel. 055 56 / 747 23).

Tschagguns

There are various hypotheses as to the origin of the name »Tschagguns«. The most likely is that the word stems from the Celtic word »iaccana«, meaning bath or fountain. The great significance of water for the valley is made clear on a walk along the **Aqua-Wanderweg**. The trail along the Latschau, a compensating reservoir for the Ill power plants, and continues past both tame and wild brooks, a water-powered lumber mill, a sulphurous spring, and the Lederquelle, one of Europe's largest and most water-rich springs, which stays at a cool temperature of 4 °C/39 °F in both summer and winter.

◄ Wallfahrtskirche Tschagguns

The pilgrimage church at Tschagguns, standing amongst the rocks, dates back to 1339. After additions and renovations this place of worship now contains Gothic, Renaissance, and Baroque elements.

Silbertal

A road begins in Schruns and leads northeast 5km/3mi through the Litzbachtal valley, ending in the town of Silbertal (889m/2916ft). The almost 20km/13mi-long valley of the same name has a picturesque wild brook; intensive silver and copper mining also took place here between the 9th and the 17th centuries. The area's mining history is documented in the **Bergbaumuseum** housed in the Silbertal community hall; the museum also presents the history of the Vorarl-

▶ VISITING MONTAFON

INFORMATION

Montafon Tourismus
Montafoner Strasse 21
A-6780 Schruns
Tel. 055 56/72 25 30, fax 748 56
www.montafon.at

WHERE TO STAY

► **Budget**
Gasthof Stern
Dorfstrasse 37, A-6773 Vandans
Tel. 0 55 56/7 27 45, fax 72 74 57

A family-friendly inn in a countryside setting. In winter, a ski bus takes guests to the nearby skiing areas.

Hotel Zimba
Veltlinerweg 2, A-6780 Schruns
Tel. 0 55 56/7 26 30, fax 7 26 30 45
www.hotel-zimba.at
Comfortable rooms, a playground for children, and dance music in the evenings in the Zimba-Keller.

berg Ill power plants and the production of hydroelectricity. A cable car leads to the Kristberg (1442m/4730ft) with the oldest originally preserved place of worship in Montafon – the Bergknappenkapelle, or miner's chapel, which miners donated in 1507 after they were rescued after an accident.

Bartholomäberg   The town of Bartholomäberg (1085m/3559ft; pop. 2300), which is most likely Montafon's oldest settlement, is located to the north of Schruns. On a ride through the mineshaft at the historical mine, visitors are informed of the arduous and almost inhumane methods used to extract ore in days gone by.

Gargellental   The Gargellental valley turns southwest approximately 7km/4.3mi southeast of Schruns and separates the Rätikon mountains from the Silvrettagruppe range. At the end of the valley, past the town of Gargellen, travellers can proceed on foot over the Schlappiner Joch (2203m/7226ft) to reach Switzerland. This is an ancient crossing that was heavily used in medieval times: Klosters lies at the end of the route.

Gaschurn   Gaschurn (1000m/3280ft; pop. 1100) is the starting point for the »Silvretta Nova« winter sports region, which has several ski lifts. The Tourismus-Museum in Gaschurn demonstrates the development of ski tourism in Montafon with old posters and documents surrounding Ernest Hemingway. With a total of 27,000 sq m/6.7ac, the »Mountain Beach« water park is **Austria's largest nature park**. The two swimming areas, with 7000 sq m/1.7ac of water, include a pool and a pond; their biological ability to cleanse themselves provides perfect water quality without using aggressive chemicals. Highlights include a rafting route that can be negotiated on an air-mattress, a climbing wall, a miniature cable car and Kneipp facilities.

Partenen   Partenen (1027m/3369ft; pop. 650) is located at the top of the Illtal valley. The town serves as a base for mountain and ski tours into the Silvretta and the Verwallgruppe ranges. The magnificent ▶ Silvretta High Alpine Road begins here. A funicular travels from Partenen to Trominier (1730m/5674ft), from where it is another 45-minute walk (part of which passes through a tunnel) to reach the Vermunt reservoir. Those with a good level of fitness can also climb Europe's longest straight stairway up to the Trominier. The 4000 steps were used as access for maintenance of the former hillside elevator to the Ill power plants. At slopes between 20% and 86%, the steps cover a 700m/22,960ft height difference. It is possible to electronically record your best time for the ascent.

? DID YOU KNOW …?

■ … that the film adaptation of the bestselling novel *Brother of Sleep* was filmed in the beautiful natural landscape of the Silbertal valley?

✳ Mühlviertel

Province: Upper Austria

The scent of resin and pine needles, bright green glades, babbling brooks, silent lakes, ancient rocks, quiet moors – and every kind of forest: this is the image of the Mühlviertel, both past and present.

»As far as the eye could see, it received no other image than that of the fusion of the forests, spread over hills and valleys,« as poet Adalbert Stifter once wrote of the Mühlviertel region. Forests do play a significant role here: as a supplier of wood for everything from firewood to violin production, as a refuge for those taking a break from the stresses and strains of everyday life, and as a nature reserve for the preservation of flora and fauna. Fortresses and palaces standing high on the hills await visitors in a region that borders Germany in the west, the Czech Republic in the north, the Danube in the south and the Waldviertel in the east. The cultural richness and traditions of this border region are conveyed to visitors in several ways: the Gothic, Museum, and Weber routes through the Mühlviertler region, idyllic hiking, riding, and biking trails, the resurrection of a small portion of the horse-drawn railway, which once extended from Gmunden on the Traunsee all the way to the southern Bohemian town of Budweis, beer culture tours, and the »Klingende Gaststube«, a folk music event, one of a whole range of musical events in the area. In the Mühlviertel, a relaxing holiday without the slightest hint of boredom is the order of the day.

Forests, forests, forests ...

◄ *Peaceful recuperation*

From the Bärenstein, you can see across the treetops of the Nordwald all the way to the Bohemian Vltava lakes

What to See in the Mühlviertel

Aigen-Schlägl The conjoined borough of Aigen-Schlägl (596m/1955ft; pop. 3300) in the northwest part of the Mühlviertel is popular with hikers and visitors to the abbey, Stift Schlägl. Scenic paths lead to the Schwarzenberg-Schwemmkanal, once a rafting route from the Bohemian Forest to the Danube, and continue further to the Hochficht (1337m/4385ft), the Bärenstein (1076m/3529ft), or the Moldaublick observation tower.

Stift Schlägl ▶ Founded in 1218 and rebuilt in the 17th century, the Premonstratensian abbey, Stift Schlägl, features an originally neo-Gothic abbey church that was later renovated in the Baroque style. The artistic choir screen (1684), the pulpit (1646–47), and the richly carved choir stalls (1735) are particularly worthy of note. The abbey is known for its **active involvement in musical activities** which range from concert series to organ competitions. Tours include the cloister, the Romanesque crypt, the painting and portrait gallery, the library, the former chapter house and the prelate's sacristy with old liturgical articles (opening times: May–late Oct Tue–Sun 10am–noon and 1pm–5pm and by arrangement, tel. 072 81/880 10).

Haslach Haslach (531m/1742ft; pop. 2600), located 10km/6mi southeast of Schlägl on the southern edge of the dark green Bohemian Forest and formerly situated amongst blue fields of flax, has been and continues to be a centre of Mühlviertel weaving. Accordingly, a trip to the **Webereimuseum** on Kirchenplatz (opening times: April–Oct Mon–Fri 9am–noon) and to the Haslach textiles workshop (Stahlmühle 3; opening times: Mon–Fri 8am–noon and 2pm–5pm) is worthwhile, as is a visit to the **Handels- und Kaufmannsmuseum** (Museum of Trade and Sales), which presents a charmingly nostalgic old-fashioned retail store (Windgasse 17; opening times: May–Oct Tue–Sun 9am–noon).

> **! *Baedeker* TIP**
>
> **Old weaving traditions**
> Fans of textiles are sure to enjoy the annual weavers' market (Webermarkt), which takes place in the Old Town of Haslach on one of the weekends in July. It offers all that the heart desires: clothing, rugs, shawls, tablecloths, and much more.

A detour to the south leads to the **Wildpark Altenfelden**, home to diverse animal species including llamas, raccoons, zebras, monkeys, and birds of prey. Children will especially enjoy the petting zoo and the pony rides (opening times: summer half-year 9am–5pm, winter half-year 10am–4pm).

Bad Leonfelden A good 30km/18.6mi east of Haslach lies the town of Bad Leonfelden (749m/2457ft; pop. 3700), a popular resort for mud bath and Kneipp treatments. The pilgrimage church, Wallfahrtskirche »Maria Schutz am Bründl«, was built in 1762–91, partly in Baroque and partly in

▶ VISITING MÜHLVIERTEL

INFORMATION

Oberösterreich Tourismus
Freistädter Str. 119, A-4041 Linz
Tel. 07 32/72 77 100, fax 72 77 130
www.muehlviertel.at

WHERE TO STAY

► Mid-range
Sporthotel Almesberger
Marktplatz 4
A-4160 Aigen-Schlägl
Tel. 0 72 81/87 13
www.almesberger.at
A fitness studio, indoor swimming pool, sauna, and indoor and outdoor tennis courts make it possible to enjoy a sporting break at this hotel on the market square.

Watchtower at the Tanner Moor in the eastern Mühlviertel

Rococo style. Rising up to the north of Bad Leonfelden is the Mühlviertel's highest peak, the Sternstein (1125m/3656ft; chairlift), which is popular with visitors thanks to its pleasant hiking trails and the diverse opportunities to enjoy winter sports.

Freistadt

Freistadt (560m/1837ft; pop. 7500), located a good 30km/18.6mi northeast of Linz, lies on the old commercial route to Bohemia and features a **well-preserved medieval Old Town** at the foot of the mighty castle keep and the almost completely preserved fortifications. Visitors can stroll through idyllic narrow side streets, past handsome façades, and through countless beautiful courtyards. At the northeast corner of the spacious Hauptplatz, featuring a Baroque fountain of the Virgin Mary, is a gate leading to Schloss Freistadt Castle (14th century). The Mühlviertel **Heimatmuseum** is spread over nine (!) storeys in the castle's keep. The exhibits cover the themes of ethnology, handicrafts, town history, and »verre églomisé« (a form of painting on glass; opening times: Mon–Fri 9am–noon ⏲ and 2pm–5pm, Sat and Sun pm only).

Rainbach

The nostalgic horse-drawn railway, beginning 7km/4.3mi north of Freistadt in the town of Rainbach, is an invitation to visitors to travel back in time. In the 19th century, the railway was used to transport salt (Kerschbaum 61; operating times: May–Oct Sat and Sun ⏲ 1pm–5pm, Aug daily 2pm–4pm).

Fans of nostalgia

Nostalgic motorcycle fans get their money's worth in Königswiesen: the inner courtyard of the Heimathaus is home to the Zündapp-Motorradmuseum (Motorcycle Museum; visits by arrangement, tel. 079 55 / 62 55).

Kefermarkt (512m/1679ft; pop. 2100) lies 10km/6.2mi south of Freistadt and features a special attraction: the parish church, Pfarrkirche St Wolfgang, contains a 13.5m/44ft-high, magnificent Gothic carved limewood altar, crafted in 1409–97 and partially adorned with life-size figures. The name of its artist is unknown; the piece was commissioned by the lords of Schloss

★
Winged altar ► Weinberg, whose seat is one of the Mühlviertel's most impressive buildings. St Wolfgang, clothed in his bishop's garments, stands at the centre of the shrine flanked by St Christopher and St Peter (opening times: daily 9am–6pm).

Grein ►Danube Valley

★ # Murau

Province: Styria
Population: 2300

Elevation: 832m/2729ft

What town could possibly claim that it owes its existence to a minnesinger? Murau, situated at the foot of the over 1800m/5904ft-high Stolzalpe, certainly can: the town was founded by minnesinger and Styrian governor Ulrich von Liechtenstein in the 13th century.

What to See in Murau

St Matthäus Standing over the Old Town centre on the bank of the Mur is the town parish church, Stadtpfarrkirche St Matthäus (13th century), an early Gothic building with lovely frescoes, created primarily during the 14th century, and a masterful Baroque high altar.

Schloss Murau Schloss Murau (1628–43), in turn, towers over the church. It was built on the foundations of the town's former fortress. Ulrich von Liechtenstein and his descendents lived here for some 300 years; they were followed by the royal Schwarzenberg family, whose descendants still live in the castle today. Renovation work in the 17th century made Schloss Murau into a Renaissance building with four wings and a lovely arcaded courtyard (guided tours: mid-June–mid-Sept Wed and Fri 3pm).

 ► MURAU

INFORMATION

Informationsbüro Murau
Bundesstr. 13 a, A-8850 Murau
Tel. 035 32/27 200, fax 27 204
www.murau.at

Around Murau

Surrounded by extensive forests and beautiful mountain pastures, Murau is a popular holiday destination in both summer and winter. The **Murtal valley** stretches to the east and to the west, framed by largely unspoiled mountains and ideal for extended hikes. The Mur river originates at Murtörl, located east of Bad Gastein in the province of Salzburg, flows through the Lungau, and reaches Styrian territory at Predlitz. | **Murtal**

The Mur valley railway is mainly serviced by modern locomotives. Yet fans of nostalgic rail travel still find what they are looking for in the form of slow-moving steam locomotives with vintage carriages that journey between Murau and Tamsweg in Salzburg and between Murau and Teufenbach on a regular basis from late June to early September. | **Murtalbahn**

During amateur locomotive rides, the truly adventurous are allowed to drive the locomotive themselves – under the supervision of an experienced engine driver of course (for more precise information call tel. 0 35 32/22 31-0; www.stlb.at).

Styria's unusual **Holzmuseum** (Wood Museum), located 12km/7.5mi up the Mur river in St Ruprecht ob Mur, demonstrates everything that can be made of and with wood (www.holzmuseum.at; opening times: April, May and Oct 10am–4pm, June–Sept 9am–5pm). | **St Ruprecht**

> ## ! Baedeker TIP
>
> ### The art of beer brewing
> The tiny Braumuseum (Brewing Museum) in the arched cellar of Murau's brewery informs its visitors on the art of beer brewing. Beer tastings are naturally part of the process (tel. 035 32 / 326 60; opening times: Fri 3pm–5pm).

The market town of **St Lambrecht**, located at the edge of the Naturpark Grebenzen, is home to a large Benedictine monastery, founded in the 11th century. The first monks most likely came from St Blasien in the Black Forest. The monastery church, with two bulbous spires, originated as early as the 14th–15th centuries, while the other buildings were renovated in the 17th–18th centuries. During the Second World War, there was a sub-camp of the Mauthausen concentration camp here.

The abbey possesses an impressive art collection as well as a bird museum; both of which are included on the guided tour (guided tours: Mon–Sat 10.45am and 2.30pm, Sun after Mass and 2.30pm).

Oberwölz, the smallest town in Styria with a population of only 1000, lies around 30km/19mi northeast of Murau and is home to the **Österreichische Blasmusikmuseum**, a museum of brass band music in Austria. It boasts a particularly large collection of instruments (opening times: May–Oct daily 10am–3pm). | **Oberwölz**

The solitary reed bays offer some peace and quiet

★ ★ Neusiedler See

Province: Burgenland   **Elevation:** 115m/377ft

Shimmering light, rustling reeds, the twittering and chattering of thousands of birds in the spring and the autumn – it is almost impossible to escape the singular enchantment of Lake Neusiedl. In December of 2001, this cross-border region was declared a UNESCO World Cultural Heritage site.

Unique steppe lake

Four fifths of the **only steppe lake in central Europe** are on Austrian soil; the southern part belongs to Hungary. At approximately 35km/22mi length and 5km/3mi–15km/10mi width, it is only 1.0m/3.28ft–1.80m/6ft deep. That helps its saline water rise in temperature unusually quickly in the summer, easily reaching temperatures of up to 30 °C/86 °F. The only tributary of note is the Wulka, which contributes a maximum of a quarter of the water lost through evaporation alone; otherwise the lake acquires its water from precipitation. The Neusiedler See has no outflow. Depending on the rate of evaporation, the water level can vary dramatically: the lake has (almost) completely dried out several times during its history. According to old almanacs, that occurred in 1773, 1811–13, and 1864–70.

The lake is almost completely surrounded by a reed belt, 5km/3mi wide at times, which makes it almost impossible to see the lake from the shore. Approximately 10–15% of the reeds are cut and used for basketry or as raw material for stucco work. The only relatively accessible shoreline is the east bank near Podersdorf. Surfers and sailors will find perfect conditions here due to excellent wind conditions – motorboats are, however, prohibited under nature preservation regulations.

Lake Neusiedl is a true El Dorado for nature lovers, with its reed belt providing the perfect shelter for rare animals such as the aesculapian snake or the scarab beetle, but also for an approximate 300 bird species, especially wading birds and waterfowl. Its scenery is especially impressive in the spring and the autumn, when migrating birds rest here. Botanists enjoy the countless rare (water) plants. To protect this unique fauna and flora, Austria and Hungary established the Lake Neusiedl-Seewinkel National Park in 1993, which also includes the southern part of the lake as well as the »Lacken« area, smaller saltwater lakes in the puszta east of the Neusiedler See. The information centre and biological station are located in Illmitz (opening times: April–Oct Mon–Fri 8am–5pm, Sat and Sun from 10am, Nov–March Mon–Fri 8am–4pm).

★★
Nationalpark
Neusiedler See-
Seewinkel

The Pannonian climate in Burgenland is characterized by low precipitation, cold winters, and hot summers. The climatic conditions are perfectly suited for wine-growing. Today Burgenland produces **top-class European red wines**. However, to maintain the high level of quality only particular breeds of grape may be cultivated. Two scenic wine routes extend to the east and west along the shores of the Neusiedler See. Tourism on the lake is especially popular during the grape harvest.

Viniculture

Around the Neusiedler See

Mörbisch (115m/377ft; pop. 2300), located on the southwest bank near the Hungarian border, is a small, charming town with characteristic arcaded homes and long alleyways with courtyards. A 1.7km/1mi-long causeway leads to the beach, with an island just offshore. The area also provides opportunities to surf or sail. Every July and

Mörbisch

 VISITING NEUSIEDLER SEE

INFORMATION

Neusiedler See Tourismus
Obere Hauptstr. 24, A-7100 Neusiedl
Tel. 021 67/86 00, fax 86 00 20
www.neusiedlersee.com

WHERE TO EAT

► Moderate
Mooselechners Rusterhof
Rathausplatz 18, A-7071 Rust
Tel. 026 85/61 62
Delicious fish dishes are served in the lovely garden.

WHERE TO STAY

► Mid-range
Weinlaubengasthof
Rathausstüberl
Kirchengasse 2
A-7100 Neusiedl am See
Tel. 0 21 67/28 83, fax 2 88 37
www.rathaussteuberl.at
Central, quiet location. From affordable overnight stays to deluxe accommodation, this hotel offers the right atmosphere for everyone. The marvellous hotel garden has an ancient vine-covered arbour.

Here, the stork has made a delivery to his own home: a storks' nest in Rust

August, the »Mörbischer See-bühne« floating stage hosts performances at the »Seefestspiele«, an operetta festival with a closing fireworks display.

Rust (123m/403ft; pop. 1700), a tourist resort that is well-known for its viniculture (»Ruster Ausbruch«) and the most attractive town on the lake, is home to the Austrian Wine Academy, which offers wine seminars and tastings. In 1681 Rust paid 30,000l/7925gal of wine and 60,000 guilders to become a royal Hungarian free city. Numerous well-preserved Renaissance and Baroque town houses are found in Rust; its Old Town

✱ Rust

✱ Fischerkirche ►

centre is the subject of a protection order. The large number of storks' nests, and their clattering occupants, makes a charming eyecatcher. A 1km/1100yd-long causeway leads to a swimming area and a lakeside restaurant through the reed belt (car park). The unusual Fishermen's Church is surrounded by old defence walls and features an irregular floor plan and noteworthy frescoes (14th–15th century). According to legend, its name originated from Rust's fishermen, who saved a queen from drowning at sea and received a respectable sum of money in order to build the church.

St Margarethen

Near the street leading from Rust to St Margarethen is a quarry that has been in operation since Roman times. Its Leitha limestone was used in the construction of the Stephansdom, the National Theatre and other Viennese buildings. The large sculptures here, created by contemporary artists, give the entire setting its own unique appearance. The rocky environs also serve as a backdrop for Passion plays, which are performed here every five years during summer. An opera festival is also held in the quarry. The Märchen- und Freizeitpark in St Margarethen enchants visitors with a fairy tale world, petting zoo, circus, and other attractions (Märchenparkweg 1; opening times: March–Sept daily 9am–6pm, Oct daily 10am–5pm).

Purbach (124m/407ft; pop. 2600) is both a wine and holiday resort with a well-maintained protective wall system and four massive gates still remaining from the times of the Turkish invasions.

The town's emblem, the »Purbacher Türke« or Purbach Turk, is on the chimney of a house in the vicinity of the »Türkentor«.

Neusiedl

Neusiedl (131m/430ft; pop. 6000), at the northern end of the lake, one of the local **centres for water sports**: the 1.5km/1mi-long causeway leads through the reed belt to the swimming facilities on the open water, with a beach and schools for sailing, surfing, and yachting. The ruins of Burg Tabor are – contrary to rumours that they are Romanesque – from the Middle Ages.

Halbturn

A short detour to the southeast leads to the market town of Halbturn (128m/420ft; pop. 1900). The imperial hunting palace, built by Lukas von Hildebrandt in 1711, is considered one of Austria's most beautiful Baroque castles. Maria Theresia (►Famous People) had the ceilings in the large hall painted by artist Anton Maulpertsch. Today, it is often used as a pretty setting for art exhibitions and concerts (information at www.schlosshalbturn.at)

Some 6km/3.7mi south of Halbturn lies **Frauenkirchen** (124m/407ft; pop. 2900), named after its Baroque pilgrimage church that was built by Italian master

> ! **Baedeker TIP**
>
> ### Wildly good
>
> Brown bears aren't exactly native to the steppe. Yet some of the species receive board and lodging in the zoo, the Steppen-Tierpark Pamhagen, along with storks, Mangalitza pigs, steppe horses, wolves, lynx, and many other animals (southeast of Apetlon, opening times: March–Oct daily 9am–6pm).

builders from 1695 until 1702. The Gothic miraculous image on the high altar was originally from the medieval church, which was destroyed during the Turkish wars. It is said that the original miraculous image was the Maria Lactans in the side altar. Next to the church stands a unique Calvary hill with a Way of the Cross ascending in a spiral.

Podersdorf

Podersdorf (121m/397ft; pop. 2100), 15km/9mi south of Neusiedl, has the lake's **only reed-free beach**. They really take sports seriously here: cycling, horseback riding, sailing, surfing, skating, swimming and hiking. A visit to the local windmill is recommendable for non-sports fans (opening times: mid-May–end of Sept daily guided tour at 7pm). Alternatively take a look at the Mangalitza pigs, one of Europe's oldest pig breeds, in the enclosure on the road leading to Illmitz.

Seewinkel

Stretching between Lake Neusiedl and the Hungarian border south of Podersdorf is the so-called Seewinkel, a steppe area of tiny saltwater lakes that is home to interesting plant and animal species. In the spring and autumn, the lakes serve as a rest-stop for countless migrant birds.

Puszta villages such as Illmitz (117m/384ft; pop. 2600) and Apetlon (121m/397ft; pop.1900), with their characteristic farmhouses with reeded roofs, are quite typical for the Seewinkel and could just as well be located a good 100km/62mi further to the east in the Hungarian lowlands. The Seewinkel is a perfect starting point for wonderful cycling and hiking routes through the saltwater steppe and to Lake Neusiedl. East of the Zicksee lies St Andrä, which is located in the middle of the Seewinkel and is a popular surfing destination despite the shallow waters of only 1m/3ft. The broad village green, surrounded by a series of typical Burgenland farmhouses, gives St Andrä its unique character.

★ Niedere Tauern

L/M/N 5

Provinces: Salzburg and Styria

Highest elevation: Hochgolling (2863m/9391ft)

Dense forest and sparsely populated valleys, dreamy alpine landscapes, majestic peaks, bubbling brooks and clear lakes – wide stretches of this idyllic setting are still common for the Niedere Tauern.

Idyllic mountain range

The Niedere Tauern range extends from Murtörl in the west, where the Mur river originates, to the Secker Alps in the east. It is bordered by the Ennstal, Paltental, and Liesingtal valleys in the north and by the Murtal valley in the south. Numerous north-south valleys cut through the range, yet only a small number of passes truly lead through it – making it perfect for those seeking solitude and relaxation closer to nature. The higher peaks of the main range present some difficult ascents even for experienced mountain climbers. The outlying areas of the Niedere Tauern, however, provide outstanding conditions for hikers and winter sports enthusiasts.

Radstädter Tauern ►

The westernmost section of the Niedere Tauern is formed by the **Radstädter Tauern**, which extend from Murtörl to the Radstädter Tauern Pass. Dramatic rock formations characterize the highest peaks; the Hohes Weisseck (2712m/8895ft) and the Mosermandl (2680m/8790ft) offer beautiful views. The Radstädter Tauern enjoy wide popularity as a ski resort, especially the slopes north of the main range. The best ski runs are located in Wagrain's winter sporting paradise, with the Wagrainer Haus and the wide open spaces at the

▶ NIEDERE TAUERN

INFORMATION

Tourismusverband Schladming
Rohrmoosstr. 234
A-8970 Schladming
Tel. 036 87/227 77, fax 227 77 52
www.schladming.com

Trappenkar See – located in the largest high-lying cirque of the Salzburger Alps – and the area around the Radstädter Tauern Pass (1738m/5701ft).

The Schladminger Tauern begin east of the Radstädter Tauern Pass and probably constitute the most interesting group that the Niedere Tauern can offer mountain hikers.

◄ Schladminger Tauern

Their highest peak, the Hochgolling (2863m/9391ft), with its massive north face, and the wide, pyramid-shaped Hochwildstelle (2747m/9010ft), are easy to reach from Schladming in the Ennstal valley by way of the mountain huts the Golling-Hütte (1630m/5346ft) or the Preintaler Hütte (1656m/5432ft); they are therefore well-frequented. The northern outlying hills such as the Planai (1894m/6212ft) with the Schladminger Hütte or the Hauser Kaibling (2015m/6609ft) with the Krummholz-Hütte are especially favourable ski runs. Characteristic for this high-altitude area are **beautifully situated mountain lakes**: the Giglach lakes near the Ignaz-Mattis-Hütte, the Riesach lake on the way to the Preintaler Hütte, the area around the Klafferkessel, or the sparsely inhabited Sölktäler Nature Park in the eastern part of the Schladminger Tauern, accessible from the north by way of Grosssölk and the Erzherzog-Johann-Strasse (road closed in winter).

! **Baedeker TIP**

Hofmann's faith ...

... used to be the term for Protestantism in Styria many centuries ago. Hofmann of Grünpichl, to be exact, resident of the Burg Strechau near Rottenmann in the Palten valley, was able to obtain the freedom of religion for Styria in 1579 and established a Protestant chapel in his own castle. The castle can only be visited on a guided tour (information at www.burg-strechau.at; guided tours: May–Oct daily 10am–4pm).

The main ridge of the Wölzer Tauern is far removed from any larger settlements. Its mountains have lush vegetation all the way to the highest peaks, including the Greim (2474m/8115ft), the Oberwölzer Schoberspitze (2423m/7947ft) and the Hohenwart (2361m/7744ft), and do not pose too difficult a challenge for mountain climbers. The northern side ridges number among some of the easier ski areas of the Austrian Alps; the Planneralm, a lovely 1600m/5248ft-high mountain, is particularly popular.

Wölzer Tauern

The central chain of the Niedere Tauern ends with the expansive Rottenmanner and Seckauer Tauern. Beginning in Trieben, a climb to the sharp-edged Grossen Bösenstein (2449m/8033ft) is certainly worthwhile; it can be reached by way of the Edelraute-Hütte (1725m/5658ft) at the Kleiner Scheiblsee, then by continuing on the mountain path to the Hochschwung and the Seitner Zinken to the Breiteckkoppe. The highest peak of the Seckauer Tauern, the Hochreichhart (2416m/7925ft), is accessible from Kalwang in the northeast or by way of the ridge path from the Seckauer Zinken (2398m/7865ft) in the south.

Rottenmanner and Seckauer Tauern

✳ Ossiacher See

Province: Carinthia   **Elevation:** 501m/1643ft

The long, narrow Ossiacher See, slightly off the beaten track of mass tourism, is located northeast of the bustling town of ▶Villach. Carinthia's third-largest lake attracts visitors with its beautiful location and pleasant water temperatures of up to 26 °C/79 °F.

Popular holiday destination

Not only water sports fans enjoy the 11km/7mi-long, 1km/0.6mi-wide and up to 47m/154ft-deep Lake Ossiach. The area offers a wide variety of other sporting opportunities as well. Those wishing to explore are best served by a boat ride on the lake: from the spring to the autumn; the boats zigzag between almost all of the towns on the shores several times a day.

What to See on the Ossiacher See

Burg Landskron

It is impossible to miss the magnificent ruins of Burg Landskron (676m/2217ft) on the way from Villach to the Ossiacher See. The former Renaissance castle, a long-time property of the Khevenhüller family estate, not only offers a wonderful view of the lake and the surrounding countryside, but also boasts a unique animal attraction: a **zoo for birds of prey**, in which eagles, owls, falcons and vultures show off their flying skills (opening times: May, June, Sept, Oct, Mon–Sat 10.30am–4pm, Sun until 5.30pm, July and Aug daily until 6.30pm; flying demonstrations: 2–3 times weekly)

From Bodensdorf, roads and a cable car lead up to the Gerlitzen (1909m/), a mountain for paragliding

From Seebad Bodensdorf, a toll road on the northern bank leads 12km/7.5mi through countless twists and turns to a car park located at 1764m/5786ft, from which visitors can proceed either on foot or via chairlift to the **Gerlitzen** (1909m/6261ft). The well-maintained ski and hiking area is also an El Dorado for paragliders. The panoramic view is overwhelming: the Karawanken rise up in the south, the Nockberge in the northwest, and peaks of the Hohe Tauern can be seen far to the west.

The Gerlitzen is more easily accessible via the gondola beginning at Annenheim am See and leading over the Kanzel.

Around 1000 years ago, Benedictine monks made their home on the southeastern bank of the lake in what is now known as **Ossiach** (505m/1656ft; pop. 750). One of the abbots at the then-famous Benedictine abbey, which was dissolved by Emperor Joseph II in 1783, even owned a small fleet of Venetian galleys that were used to escort Emperor Charles V over the water in 1552. The **abbey church**, an originally Romanesque columned basilica that was renovated in the Baroque style in the 18th century, is worth a visit. It features elaborate stucco décor by a Wessobrunner master. The ceiling frescoes were partially the work of the most well-known Carinthian Baroque painter, Joseph F. Fromiller, around 1750. The late Gothic winged altar in the northwest chapel is also noteworthy; the central shrine depicts a Madonna with Child between St Catherine and St Margaret. Ossiach is a destination for countless music lovers every year in July and August. Opera performances, concerts, and recitals can be enjoyed as part of the famous »Carinthian Summer« music festival. Some performances take place in Villach.

◄ Carinthischer Sommer

Doll lovers will be attracted to the **Puppenmuseum** (Doll Museum) in Einöde-Winklern on the road to Radenthein. Doll-maker Elli Riehl (1902–77), a Villach native who moved to Winklern in 1950, created absolutely matchless doll »portraits«, first of children and later of adults going about their everyday business. A small piece of Carinthian culture and its way of life has thus been preserved in a very unique way (opening times: April and May daily 9am–noon 2pm–6pm, June–Sept daily 9am–6pm, Oct from 2pm).

Einöde-Winklern

⊙

▶ VISITING OSSIACHER SEE

INFORMATION

Tourismusinformation Ossiach
Ossiach Nr. 8
A-9570 Ossiach See
Tel. 0 42 43/497
Fax 87 63
www.ossiach.com

WHERE TO EAT

▶ **Expensive**

Stiftsschmiede
Ossiach Nr. 4
A-9570 Ossiach
Tel. 0 42 43/4 55 54
Freshly caught fish specialities in the former smithy next to the abbey.

✷ Ötztal

Province: Tyrol

The name Ötztal is famous thanks to a 5300-year-old mummy that was discovered here; for disco fans, DJ Ötzi, born in Ötz, might be the reason the name rings a bell. The valley has become especially popular amongst mountain tourists who can find an excellent local infrastructure here.

A way out of poverty

Of the three Tyrolese high mountain valleys (Kaunertal, Pitztal, and Ötztal), the latter is not only the longest (at 55km/34mi), but has also gained the most experience with tourists. The reason for this is that mountain tourism was »invented« at the southern end of the valley in Vent, so to speak: the presiding minister **Franz Senn** (1831–84), an enthusiastic mountain-climber himself, mused about relief for the poverty of the mountain farmers there and found the solution in tourism. Hence in 1860, partially using his own funds, he had the first paths built, trained locals as mountain-climbers, and offered tourists a place to stay and eat in the rectory. It goes without saying that the resolute minister was also one of the founders of the Austrian Alpine Club in Vienna in 1862 and of the German Alpine Club (DAV) in Munich in 1869.

The mouth of the Ötztal valley is wide and fertile; the central part narrows into a series of gorges and alternating expanses of extensive pastureland. The road increases in altitude toward the south, running past several waterfalls and offering a tremendous view of the peaks and glaciers of the Ötztal Alps. The ► Timmelsjochstrasse, open for passage only a few months out of the year, leads from the end of the valley to South Tyrol.

Ötzi

On 19 September 1991, a German couple found **a mummified corpse** on their way down from the Fineilspitze in the southern Ötztaler Alps. The body of a hunter or warrior – experts are still unsure – was soon named Ötzi. He had been preserved in ice for approximately 5300 years, since the New Stone Age. In view of the importance of the discovery, the site was precisely identified and it was revealed that Ötzi had actually been found a good 90m/295ft from the Austrian border on Italian soil. As a consequence he can now be visited in the South Tyrolean Museum of Archaeology in Bolzano, where he is stored in an air-conditioned display case and kept at a steady –6 °C/21 °F.

What to See in the Ötztal

Ötz

Ötz (820m/2690ft; pop. 2200) is located around 5km/3mi south of the point where the Ötztaler Ache meets the Inn river, and is a popular tourist destination due to its pleasantly mild climate. Its buildings, with Gothic entryways, bay windows, and painted façades from Renaissance times, include the Gasthof Stern lodge. The parish church (14th century; extended in the 17th–18th centuries), on a high elevation, has a Gothic tower and a pretty altar. The Gothic chapel, the St-Michaels-Kapelle, is located underneath the choir; it features the so-called »Höllenrachenrelief« (»the vengeance of hell relief«): a three-horned devil with gaping eyes sticks out two tongues while St Michael stands upon the devil's chest in a victorious pose. A gallery

Traditional flat bread is still baked at the open-air museum in Ötztal

highlighting the Ötztal valley's past is now located in an old farmhouse on Piburgerstrasse; it displays a collection of historical illustrations of the Ötztal as well as contemporary art. Sculptures are also on display in the garden.

◄ Piburger See

Some 3km/2mi southwest of Ötz, located on a wooded terrace above the valley, lies the 800m/2624ft-long and 30m/99ft-deep Piburger See (915m/3001ft; nature reserve), one of Tyrol's warmest lakes. Due to nature conservancy regulations, however, swimming is only allowed on the south side.

Umhausen

The oldest settlement of the valley is located south of Ötz: Umhausen (1036m/3398ft; pop. 2800) is a friendly holiday resort town on the alluvial fan of the Hairlachbach. Both the Gothic parish church (15th century; numerous renovations), with a Renaissance cross (1580), and the Gasthaus Krone, featuring façade paintings and a Renaissance bay window with stucco décor (1684), are worth a closer look.

★
◄ Stuibenfall

Approximately 3km/1.8mi southeast of Umhausen (road and 15-minute walk), is the Stuibenfall, Tyrol's highest waterfall. It plummets 160m/525ft downwards under a natural rocky bridge.

Längenfeld

10km/6.2mi up the valley from Umhausen is the health resort town of Längenfeld (1179m/3867ft; pop. 4000). The townscape is dominated by the parish church, Pfarrkirche St Katharina (originally late Gothic), with its 74m/243ft-high tower. Tourists will like the newly constructed **Aqua Dome** swimming and wellness facility, which was designed based on the principles of feng shui.

Sölden and Hochsölden

After Huben, the Ötztal valley narrows to a wild gorge and does not widen again until Sölden (1377m/4517; pop. 3300), a scattered settle-

⏵ VISITING ÖTZTAL

INFORMATION

Ötztal Tourismus
Hauptstrasse 66, A-6433 Ötz
Tel. 0 52 52/66 69
www.oetz.com

WHERE TO STAY

► Luxury
Central Spa Hotel
Auweg 3, A-6450 Sölden
Tel. 0 52 54/2 26 00, fax 2 26 05 11
www.central-soelden.at
Equipped with a spa, a steam bath, and a hot whirlpool, this resort hotel takes sports and fitness very seriously. A good restaurant provides sustenance.

► Mid-range
Posthotel Kassl
Hauptstrasse 70, A-6433 Ötz
Tel. 0 52 52/63 03, fax 21 76
www.posthotel-kassl.at
The venerable Posthotel, which has been a family-owned lodge since the 17th century, offers generous swimming and sauna facilities and a well-run restaurant.

---

ment that is internationally known as both a winter sporting area and a summer retreat. The parish church, an originally late Gothic structure that was renovated in the Baroque style in 1752 and features noteworthy ceiling frescoes and a Gothic baptismal font (1522), is worth seeing.

✳
◄ Wildspitze

The Ötztal Alps reach their greatest elevation along the ridge toward the north, with the steep, gleaming snow-covered peak of the Wildspitze (3774m/12,379ft). Several routes lead there: the shortest begins at the Breslauer Hütte (2840m/9315ft) near Vent; probably the most beautiful leads from Mittelberg in the Pitztal valley below the spectacular Mittagskogl (3162m/10,376ft); or from Sölden via the Braunschweiger Hütte (2759m/9050ft) and the magnificent Mittelbergferner. Mountain climbers love this alpine range, but it is especially popular amongst skiers because of the marvellous view that the numerous peaks – often navigable all the way up to the cornice – and the spacious, relatively easy slopes provide. With a difference in elevation of 2400m/7872ft, the descent from the Wildspitze over Hochsölden to Sölden numbers among the longest and most beautiful downhill ski runs in the entire Alps.

Vent

From Zwieselstein (1472m/4828ft), where the Ötztal valley branches out into the Gurglertal (left) and the Ventertal (right), a 13km/8mi-long road leads southwest up the Ventertal valley to the scenic mountain town of Vent (1896m/6219ft). A sign-posted footpath (902) runs alongside it from Obergurgl to the Inntal valley. The highest Austrian settlement that is inhabited all year round, the Rofenhöfe (2014m/6606ft), is accessible via an extremely steep mountain road (slopes of up to 30%) to the west.

Pitztal

E 5

Province: Tyrol

Between the Ötztal valley in the east and the Kaunertal valley in the west lies the Pitztal valley. Lying somewhat removed from the major traffic routes, it provides access to the mountain scenery of the Ötztal Alps and the region's numerous waterfalls.

A 39km/24mi-long road runs through the valley along the Pitzbach stream. South of Imst, the road takes a turn and ends at the magnificent head of the valley at the foot of the Mittelbergferner. The Pitztal valley is popular as both a quiet summer retreat and as a destination for winter sports, and is a starting point for countless mountain hikes. The first town coming from the direction of Imst is Arzl, the »gateway to the Pitztal«. Here, **Europe's highest footbridge** extends over the Pitzenklamm gorge at a height of 94m/308ft (137.5m/451ft long). Brave souls can also risk a bungee jump from here.

Pitztalstrasse

The charming town of Wenns (979m/3211ft; pop. 2000) is located on a fertile valley terrace. Above Wenns, some 5km/3mi to the southwest, lies the village of **Piller** (1349m/4425ft); just 4km/2.5mi further uphill is the Pillerhöhe (1558m/5110ft), which offers a wonderful view.

Wenns

Further up the valley – below the towering Rofele-Wand (3352m/10,995ft) in the southwest – is **St Leonhard** (1371m/4497ft; pop. 1500). The main town of the Pitztal and the fourth largest borough in Tyrol extends 34km/21mi through the valley.

 PITZTAL

INFORMATION

Tourismusverband Pitztal
Unterdorf 18, A-6473 Wenns
Tel. 054 14/869 99, fax 869 99 88
www.pitztal.com

★ Radstadt

K 5

Province: Salzburg   **Elevation:** 856m/2808ft
Population: 4600

The lively, friendly town of Radstadt at the start of the Radstädter Tauern Road lies between the Radstädter Tauern to the south and the Dachstein Massif to the north.

Radstadt is a centrally located starting point for skiing and hiking routes in the surrounding mountain massifs; it also belongs to the Ski Amadé region (►St Johann im Pongau).

An old mountain town

VISITING RADSTADT

INFORMATION

Tourismusverband Radstadt
Stadtplatz 17
A-5550 Radstadt
Tel. 064 52/747 20
Fax 67 02
www.radstadt.com

WHERE TO EAT

► **Expensive**
Hubertusstube
Am Dorfplatz 1
A-5532 Filzmoos
Tel. 064 53/82 04
Head chef Johanna Maier is one of
Austria's top cooks.

History Already settled as early as the Hallstatt period, the town was an important station along the Roman road from Venice to Salzburg in Roman times and was significant for Salzburg's archbishops in their desire to expand their territory southward during the Middle Ages. Much to the pleasure of the archbishop, the town was able to withstand a siege by 5000 farmers during the Peasants' War in 1525–26. One of the archbishop's successors banished 3000 Protestants from the entire Radstädt region in 1731–32 in return. Radstadt – along with Salzburg – became Austrian territory in 1861.

What to See in Radstadt

Historical townscape The pleasant, narrow streets, lined with lovely old town houses, certainly provide a nice setting for a good long stroll. The remnants of the town walls, including three massive round towers from the 16th century, surround the long, narrow town centre. A local committee ensures that the historical townscape remains intact despite any new building work.

The **Kapuzinerturm** (Capuchin tower) still possesses its original roof truss from 1534 and is home to a section of the **Heimatmuseum**. The larger section – exhibits from Roman times, sacred art, old craftwork and a portrait of the composer Paul Hofhaimer (1459–1537) – can be seen at **Schloss Lerchen** (opening times: in summer daily 10am–noon and 2.30pm–5pm; in winter daily 10am–11.30am and 2.30pm–5pm).

Milleniumpfad ► The Millenium Path starts near the town's pond, the last remnants of the former town moat. On the path the town's history is explained on 33 panels. It was created in 1996 for Austria's 1000-year anniversary and is 1000 paces long – one step for each year.

Around Radstadt

Rossbrand Radstadt's prominent local mountain, the Rossbrandgipfel (1770m/5806ft; Radstädter Hütte, food and drink available), is located north of the town. During clear weather it offers a panoramic view of approximately 150 alpine peaks.

From Eben im Pongau, a road leads west around the Rossbrand to Filzmoos(1055m/3460ft; pop. 1200), the southern starting point for mountain treks in the Dachstein Massif (►Dachstein). A 5km/3mi-long toll road leads to the Hof-Alm (1268m/4159ft).

◄ Filzmoos

Altenmarkt im Pongau (850m/2788ft; pop. 3400), west of Radstadt, originated in Roman times and is considered the **oldest town of the Ennstal valley**. 12km/7.5mi south lies the charmingly located Zauchensee (1350m/4428ft); there are a wide variety of hiking trails around the lake.

Altenmarkt im Pongau

Flachau (927m/3040ft; pop. 2600), located some 10km/6mi southwest of Radstadt in the Ennstal valley, offers a comprehensive variety of ski and après-ski activities and is the eastern starting point for the winter sports area around the Griessenkareck (1991m/6531ft). A cable railway to the south leads to the pretty Durchachalm above the Zauchensee.

Flachau

The 22km/14mi-long Radstädter Tauern Road begins near Radstadt and heads south by way of Obertauern and the Tauernpasshöhe (1738m/5701ft). The road has lost its importance as the main thoroughfare toward Styria and Carinthia since the completion of the west-bound highway with the Tauerntunnel, but it continues to serve as the northern access road to the holiday resort area around the Tauernhöhe, which is popular for winter sports.

Radstädter Tauernstrasse

◄ Tauernstrasse

Obertauern (1650m/5412ft) has developed into a well-visited area for both summer holidays and winter sports, and is wonderfully

Traditional houses in Altenmarkt

A little help from their friends

Although their music is not normally associated with the area, it is Obertauern snow on the Beatles' ski boots on the cover of their LP *Help*. The stars arrived on 13 March 1965 to shoot some scenes for the film of the same name on the slopes here – with the help of stunt doubles, of course. On 21 March the clapperboard snapped shut for the last time in Austria, and in the evening of the same day the Beatles and their 66-person film crew bought a ticket to ride out of the famous winter sports resort.

equipped with drag lifts, chairlifts, and gondolas, such as those leading to the Seekarspitze (2350m/8298ft) or the Gamsleitenspitze (2357m/7731ft). Experienced hikers have a choice between several mountains over 2000m/6560ft, which can be climbed in 2–4 hours.

18km/11mi east of Radstadt, old mining houses in **Schladming** (750m/2460ft; pop. 5000) are a reminder of the former economic foundation of the population here. The only remaining part of the old fortification walls of the town is the 17th-century Salzburger Gate. The impressive Catholic parish church has a Baroque interior; the Lutheran church (1862) is the largest Protestant place of worship in Styria and features a winged altar from the Reformation. The **Stadtmuseum**, located in the so-called Bruderladenhaus (1681), provides reminders of the turbulence of the Reformation but is mainly dedicated to mining and to the cultural and natural history of the region (opening times: Tue–Fri 10am–1pm and 4pm–7pm, Sun 11am–2pm).

★ Rätikon

Province: Vorarlberg

Highest elevation: Schesaplana (2965m/9725ft)

With deep side valleys, jagged cliffs and bizarre peaks, the Rätikon mountain range is located between the Illtal valley (Montafon), the Rhine Valley and the Swiss Prättigau on the southern border of Vorarlberg. Its main ridge forms the Swiss border.

Schesaplana

Vorarlberg's most impressive mountains include the huge rocky massif of the Schesaplana (2965m/9725ft), the long Vandanser Steinwand with the dramatic horn of the Zimbaspitze (2645m/8676ft), the staggering Drusenfluh (2835m/9299ft) with the Drei Türme (Three Towers) at the end of the magnificent Gauertal valley, the Sulzfluh (2824m/9263ft) with its small glaciers, and the splendid horn of the Madrisa (2774m/9099ft), the emblem of the Gargellenal valley.

 RÄTIKON

INFORMATION

Tourismus Nenzing-Gurtis
Landstrasse 25, A-6710 Nenzing
Tel. 055 25/630 31
www.nenzing-gurtis.at

A multitude of mountain huts make it easier to visit this wonderful region. The principal huts are connected by a lovely high-elevation trail, the **Rätikon-Höhenweg**, which leads from the Gamperdonatal valley up to the Schesaplana and then down to the Lüner See (1970m/6462ft; ► Bludenz), continuing further to the small Tilisuna-See (2102m/6895ft) and down into the Gargellental valley. Various peaks of the Rätikon feature trails that are easy enough even for inexperienced climbers, but some of the more difficult ascents can only be mastered by advanced climbers.

Skiers find an ideal range of possibilities in the Rätikon. Besides the mountains in the Gargellental valley, the slopes of the Golmerjoch near Schruns-Tschagguns and the northern foothills of the Schesaplana, which line the Brandnertal valley near Bludenz, are also very popular. One of the most beautiful alpine downhill runs is on the Sulzfluh, with a difference in elevation of over 2100m/6888ft.

Snowboarders create their own snowstorm in the Rätikon mountains

Reutte

E 5

Province: Tyrol
Population: 5500

Elevation: 854m/2801ft

Reutte, located in a broad valley basin of the Lech river, is the principal town of the northern Tyrolese district of Ausserfern. It serves as an important traffic hub between Füssen, Pfronten, the Fern Pass, the upper Lechtal valley, and the ►Tannheimer Tal.

The Ausserfern is a mountainous region possessing a raw beauty. Only accessible from Tyrol via the Fern Pass (1216m/3988ft), linguistically it belongs to the Alemannic culture. It receives a great deal of precipitation, has a somewhat cool climate, and boasts lush green vegetation due to its location, as a result of which it functions as a topographical weather barrier of the Northern Limestone Alps.

Almost 2000 years ago the Via Claudia Augusta, the only imperial Roman road through the Alps, led through the Ausserfern. From AD

Alemannic meteorological divide

▶ REUTTE

INFORMATION

Tourismusverband Reutte
Untermarkt 34
A-6600 Reutte/Tirol
Tel. 056 72/623 36, fax 623 36 40
www.reutte.com

WHERE TO STAY

▶ **Mid-range**
Wellness- & Familienhotel Alpenrose
A-6652 Elbigenalp/Lechtal
Tel. 0 56 34/66 51, fax 66 52 87
www.alpenrose.net
This hotel's highlights include sauna facilities and a swimming pond, cosmetic treatments and massages, childcare, and a wide range of entertainment.

50 to approximately AD 200, it ran from Altinum near Venice over the Reschen Pass and the Fern Pass to the Danube, forming the most important connection between the Roman motherland and the rich provinces of the north.

What to See in Reutte

The town of Reutte, which has always been the commercial and economic centre of the region, is dominated by 18th-century town houses. The paintings on the buildings' façades are special feature of the Ausserfern artistic landscape. Created by the same painters who also designed the frescoes in the region's churches, the paintings document the specific lifestyle of Reutte's middle class and the trades people of the Oberlechtal who had returned home after earning their riches abroad.

Zeillerhaus ▶ A lovely example of buildings adorned with **Lüftlmalerei**, or tromp l'oeil painted façades, is the Zeillerhaus on Untermarkt, the residence of Reutte's wealthiest family of artists. The depictions of animals above the painted cornice on the north wall are especially noteworthy: Franz Anton Zeiller (1716–94) decided to take revenge on his neighbours, two older ladies who had insulted his paintings, by immortalizing them here as a pair of monkeys with a shopping basket.

Heimatmuseum ▶ With its green façade and lavish fresco paintings (1779) by Johann Jakob Zeiller (1710–83), the »Grünes Haus« (»Green House«; 16th century) on Untermarkt immediately catches the eye of passers-by. It is home to the Heimatmuseum, in which exhibits on the history of the Ausserfern region are on display (opening times: May–Oct Tue–Sun 10am–4pm; in winter by arrangement, tel. 056 72 / 723 04, fax 72 305).

Around Reutte

Lakes The area's lakes, such as the Urisee, which is popular as a diving lake, and the Frauensee, good for swimming, liven up the landscape. Approximately 6km/4mi east of Reutte, located between two wooded hills, lies Tyrol's second largest lake, the over 6km/4mi-long, 1km/0.6mi-wide, dark green Plansee (976m/3201ft). It is connected to the 3km/1.8mi-long Heiterwanger See by a short river.

The road to Lermoos (►Zugspitze) and to the Fern Pass enters into the narrow passage of the Ehrenberger Klause (946m/3103ft) after passing Reutte. As part of the 150m/492ft-high castle and boundary fortifications (c1290), located on a steep cliff and only accessible on foot, it once secured the pass. Today, only ruins of the castle that was so violently fought over in the 16th and 17th centuries remain; all of its fortified grounds were auctioned off without much ado in the 18th century.

Ruins of Burg Ehrenberg

Some 10km/6mi to the east lies Bichlbach (1079m/3539ft; pop. 900), with a sacred building that is unique to Austria: a **guild church**. It once served as the place of worship for the guild fraternity of the Aussenfern's masons and carpenters and was constructed toward the end of the 17th century. The church's exterior is quite modest; the early Baroque, lavish interior is attuned to the iconography of the fraternity. The high altar (c1710) numbers among the most beautiful and decorative in the Ausserfern.

Bichlbach

Between the Allgäu Alps in the north and the Lechtal Alps in the south, the Lechtal valley runs southwest from Reutte to Arlberg and then on to Warth (62km/38.5mi). According to Bavarian travel writer Ludwig Steub (1812–88), it is **»Europe's most beautiful high-lying valley«**. The bottom of the valley is home to numerous towns, well-visited in both summer and winter. Several canyon-like side valleys lead to serene mountain towns, which also act as good starting points for worthwhile treks in the high mountains.

Lechtal

In Elbigenalp (1040m/3411ft; pop. 750), a beautifully situated resort, visitors should take the time to see the woodcarving school. The interior of the parish church, Pfarrkirche St Nikolaus, which was al-

◄ Elbigenalp

The Plansee, Tyrol's »fjord«, near Reutte is a popular destination for day trips

most entirely renovated in the 17th century, was painted by Johann Jakob Zeiller. The cemetery chapel, Friedhofskapelle St Martin, located above the town to the west and originating in the 11th–12th centuries, features a depiction of the Dance of Death by Anton Falger (1791–1876). The Heimatmuseum presents objects from the life of this painter and lithographer, who was born in Elbigenalp.

Saalfelden am Steinernen Meer

J 5

Province: Salzburg
Population: 15,100

Elevation: 744m/2440ft

The old Salzburg market town of Saalfelden is located at the foot of the so-called Steinernes Meer, a high-lying karst plateau. Saalfelden serves as the centre of a series of smaller holiday and winter sports resorts in the central Pinzgau region.

What to See in and around Saalfelden

Pfarrkirche
At the centre of this modern small town stands the neo-Romanesque parish church (19th century) with a nave and two side aisles, and a Gothic crypt. The late Gothic winged altar (1539) in the baptismal chapel is particularly noteworthy.

Pinzgauer
Heimatmuseum ▶
Schloss Ritzen, located on the shore of the Ritzen See in the southern part of the town, is now home to the Pinzgauer Heimatmuseum. It features the **largest collection of nativity scenes in Austria**, a considerable collection of minerals, and Celtic and Roman artefacts found in archaeological excavations (opening times: Jan, Feb, May, June Wed, Sat and Sun 2pm–5pm; July–Sept Tue–Sun from 11am).

⏵ SAALFELDEN

INFORMATION

Saalfelden Leogang Touristik
Bahnhofstr. 10, A-5760 Saalfelden
Tel. 065 82/706 60, fax 753 98
www.leogang-saalfelden.at

WHERE TO EAT

▶ **Inexpensive**
Schatzbichl
Ramseiden 82, A-5760 Saalfelden
Tel./fax 065 82/732 81
The Schatzbichl serves delicious traditional dishes from the Pinzgau region.

A chairlift climbs up onto the Huggenbergalm on the Biberg (1115m/3657ft; food and drink served), where you can experience the wind in your face on a 1600m/5248ft-long **summer toboggan run** (operates depending on the weather between May and Sept usually 9am–5pm; tel. 065 82/7 21 73).

Rather resembling swallows' nests clinging onto the rugged rocky face of the Palfen, a **hermitage** (1664) and a chapel, the St-Georgs-Kapelle, are approximately one hour away from Saalfelden.

The **Steinernes Meer** (»Sea of Stone«) north of Saalfelden is a massive, heavily karstified high-lying plateau of the Salzburger Limestone Alps with rugged limestone rocks, caves, and striking peaks. Taken as a whole, it truly does resemble the ocean of rock and stone that the name suggests. It forms the boundary between the Salzburger Land and Bavaria. Together with the Reiteralpe to the northwest, the southeast range of the ▶ Hochkönig, and the Hagengebirge further to the east, it encases the triangular piece of German ter-

Situated beyond the Loferer Steinbergen, the broad and sunny Saalachtal valley

ritory, the Berchtesgadener Land and the Königssee, which juts far southward into Salzburg. The Steinernes Meer is connected to the Hagen mountains in the northeast by the Teufelshörner. From either Saalfelden or Maria Alm at the western edge of this **popular hiking and climbing region**, it takes four hours to reach the Riemannhaus (2177m/7141ft; food and drink, lodging). It also serves as a starting point for trips to the peaks of the Sommerstein (2306m/7564ft), the Breithorn (2504m/8213ft), the Schönfeldspitze (2651m/8695ft), and the Selbhorn (2643m/8669ft). Although challenging, the hiking paths leading west to the Ingoldstädter Haus (2132m/6993ft) or east to the Hochkönig (2941m/9646ft) are very impressive.

Some 5km/3mi west of Saalfelden lies Leogang, located in a beautiful valley at the foot of a mountain of the same name. Visitors are treated to a highly sensory experience at the mid-way station of the Leogang mountain rail route: during operating hours, they can stroll through the **»Sinne-Erlebnispark«** (»Sensory Experience Park«) to feel (barefoot trail), taste (bakery station), hear (listening island), smell (herb garden) and see (distorting mirror). The **Bergbaumuseum** (Mining Museum) and the demonstration mine in Leogang display the tradition of ore and mineral mining in the region (opening times and guided tours: May–Oct daily 11am–5pm).

Leogang

Northwest of Saalfelden, the Saalach river forces itself through a narrow valley between the Steinernes Meer, the Hochkalter range, and the Reiteralpe in the north and between the Leogang and Loferer mountains in the south. The ruggedly picturesque Seisenbergklamm gorge near Weissbach is around 600m/1968ft long. It was formed approximately 12,000 years ago when the alpine ice melted during the last Ice Age. The gorge is accessible from May to October. A visit takes approximately one hour and is recommended only for those who are not afraid of heights.

Saalach valley

✱
◀ Seisenberg-
klamm

✳
Lamprechts-
ofenloch ►

Approximately 1km/0.6mi after Weissbach on the left side of the road to Lofer is the entrance to the Lamprechtsofenloch, the start of the gigantic cave system several hundred metres of which has been designated a **show cave with an underground waterfall** (opening times: mid-May–mid-Oct, Tue–Sun 11am–5pm). According to legend, the greedy daughter of the knight Lamprecht, who resided in nearby Burg Saalecker, pilfered her father's fortune little by little and hid it in the cave. Treasure hunters have been drawn into the caves again and again – some of them never to return.

The Lamprechtshöhle **numbers among the longest and deepest traversable caves on earth**. In 1992, the Lamprechtsofen was crossed in its entire length for the first time; the total difference in elevation recorded by the cave's researchers totalled 1632m/5353ft.

! **Baedeker TIP**

A mountain for bikers

Between mid-May and the end of September, bold souls on two wheels and those who are just willing to have a go are attracted to Bikeworld in Leogang. Downhill, freeriding, biker cross, dual or dirt jumps are par for the course here. The Leogang mountain railway helps in getting to the top. Further information available at www.bike-world.at or by calling tel. 065 42/80 48 00.

✴ ✴ Salzburg

J/K 4

Province: Salzburg	**Elevation:** 425m/1394ft
Population: 150,000	

Where and how does a visit to Salzburg begin? With Mozart? In 2006 the city held a large-scale celebration on the occasion of the 250th birthday of the musical genius. Or with a play perhaps: _Jedermann_ attracts thousands of festival-goers to the Domplatz every year. Maybe bite to eat is the best way to start: but should you sit down to some »Nockerln«, or nibble on a few »Mozartkugeln«? Welcome to Salzburg!

Jedermann and
Mozartkugeln

»The whole city is a stage ...«, as Max Reinhardt (► Famous People), co-founder of the world-famous Festspiele, said of Salzburg. It is the city of Mozart and of the archbishops, of Baroque and the coffee house, of Georg Trakl the expressionist and Stefan Zweig (► Famous People) the intellectual. This metropolis for conferences and conventions has been a World Cultural Heritage site since 1997. It is the setting and subject of many works of literature and makes its mark on anyone with a sweet tooth with its tempting Salzburger Nockerln and Mozartkugeln.

✴ ✴
Cityscape

The capital city of the province of the same name, located on both sides of the Salzach river, Salzburg is known as **one of Europe's most**

Always full of visitors – Getreidegasse

beautiful cities. It welcomes several million visitors every year, and gets extremely crowded during the festival months. The compact Old Town is located between the left bank of the Salzach and the two hills, Mönchsberg and Festungsberg. The city quarter on the river is more romantic, with narrow alleyways and slender houses, whereas the district between the Neutor and the Neugebäude offers splendid buildings and the magnificent sight of a Baroque royal residence. The newer city districts lie on the right hand side of the bank, and the Kapuzinerberg rises above them in the east.

Salzburg is best explored on foot. Those who only have one day to spend here should first see **Hohensalzburg Fortress**, which offers a magnificent panoramic view and an impression of the cityscape. A **stroll through the Old Town**, starting at Residenzplatz, is a must. Those who are really in a hurry should try a taxi ride through the romantic city centre. Schloss Mirabell, located on the other side of the Salzach, is also worth a visit. From May to September, visitors can enjoy a lovely panoramic view of the city from the water. And those who want to combine the city with winter sports can take the Snow Shuttle from Salzburg up to the nearby ski regions from mid-December until the end of March.

Exploring Salzburg

Artefacts found on the Rainberg reveal that human settlement of Salzburg goes back to Neolithic times. The Illyrians gave it the name Juvavum, or »**Seat of the Sky God**«, which was later kept by the Celts and the Romans. The Roman city of Salzburg emerged in the middle of the 1st century AD in the area that is now the Old Town. Juvavum underwent a dramatic decline during the Migration Period. New and significant episodes in Salzburg's history came with the annexation by the heathen Bavarians (6th century) and the foundation

Antiquity, Roman times and Christianization

AD 1–5	Roman settlement of Juvavum
739	Bistum founded
16th–17th C.	Baroque period, redesigning of the city
from 1620	Fortification of the city by Archbishop Paris Count Lodron
1803	Salzburg loses its sovereignty.
1816	Salzburg belongs conclusively to Austria.
1920	Salzburg Festival opens
after 1945	Rebuilding work proceeds with caution after heavy damage during the war.
1997	Salzburg Old Town becomes a World Cultural Heritage site.
2006	Salzburg celebrates the 250th birthday of Wolfgang Amadeus Mozart.
2007	Reopening of the Neue Residenz as the »Salzburg Museum«

of the Benedictine abbey, Stift St Peter, and the nunnery, Stift Nonnberg, by St Rupert (c696). Under Bishop Virgil (745–784) and his successor Arno, both Irishmen, the diocese that had been founded in 739 became the starting point for the Christianization of the alpine countries and the central Danube region.

Romanesque and Gothic During the period in which Romanesque art dominated (c1000 to 1250), many solidly built churches arose in addition to Hohensalzburg Fortress. Germany's King Konrad III said he had never encountered churches built better than those in the Salzburg region. During Gothic times (1250–1530), the secular power of the archbishops suffered severe setbacks, partly due to the Hungarian wars. Art, however, was thriving. The bourgeoisie established itself as a new **social class** in the city, which had prospered through trade relations with Nuremberg, Augsburg, Vienna, and Venice. Archbishop Leonhard von Keutschach (1495–1519) became responsible for the new appearance of Hohensalzburg Fortress, which still remains today.

Influential Baroque period Archbishop Wolf Dietrich von Raitenau (1587–1612) initiated the Baroque age, the third major period in Salzburg's art history. Raised as a grandchild of the Medici on his mother's side in Rome, the church dignitary introduced extensive changes to the city, although the majority of the plans could first be implemented only by his successors. Markus Sittikus von Hohenems (1612–19) began with the construction of the cathedral in its current form, and Archbishop Paris Count Lodron (1619–53) completed it and assisted the city in creating its strong fortifications as of 1620, saving Salzburg from the horrors of the Thirty Years' War. A sense of Baroque harmony emerged under Archbishop Johann Ernst von Thun (1687–1709) and through the work of master builder Johann Bernhard Fischer von Erlach, which resulted in worldwide fame for the city. Franz Anton Fürst Harrach (1709–27) replaced Fischer von Erlach with his rival Lukas von Hildebrandt, the builder of Vienna's Schloss Belvedere. Salzburg owes the redesigning of the Residenz and Schloss Mirabell to him.

Salzburg's political relevance in modern times remained limited. Archbishop Leopold Anton Freiherr von Firmian expelled around 30,000 Protestants from the country in 1731. The city lost its sovereignty in 1803, yet still remained the seat of the archbishop. After changing hands between the French and the Bavarians, it **finally became Austrian territory in 1816**, experiencing an economic upsurge in the 19th century and becoming connected to the modern transport network through the railway. The city experienced its second Renaissance in the 20th century, largely attributable to the Festspiele, which began in 1920 with Max Reinhardt's production of Hugo von Hofmannsthal's *Jedermann* (*Everyman*). Bombings in the Second World War caused profound damage to the city's unique architecture, but cautious reconstruction after the war restored the city to its original form as a cultural metropolis.

Development after 1800

Highlights Salzburg

Residenz
A visit to the Residenz is an absolute must for fans of art and antiques.
▶ page 432

Neue Residenz
Since its reopening in 2006, several museums and exhibitions have been united under one roof.
▶ page 433

Dom
The cathedral is a true highlight – and not only when beautifully illuminated at night!
▶ page 433

Stiftskirche St Peter
The church of the Benedictine abbey is home to many interesting tombs and artistic objects.
▶ page 437

Franziskanerkirche
Its former status as a parish church gives the Franciscan church special importance, a fact displayed in its interior.
▶ page 438

Grosses Festspielhaus
The magnificent 1950s Large Festival Hall is worth a visit even without tickets for a performance.
▶ page 438

Mozart's birthplace
The birthplace of Wolfgang Amadeus Mozart, the child prodigy who became a legendary musician, is almost a place of pilgrimage.
▶ page 441

Hohensalzburg Fortress
Salzburg's emblem has been enthroned above the beautiful Old Town and the Salzach river since the 11th century.
▶ page 443

Many monuments commemorate the virtuoso artist – like this one in Vienna

Street café in front of the house in which Mozart was born at Universitätsplatz

AMADEUS SUPERSTAR

He was extremely productive, yet Mozart's genius is disputed. Despite his high earnings he became impoverished, and after his early death speculation about a possible murder was rife. The rumours contributed to the musician's growing popularity, unrivalled by any other classical composer.

Serenades, divertimentos, chamber music, symphonies, instrumental concerts, church music, operas – Wolfgang Amadeus Mozart (1756–91) felt comfortable in **all musical genres**, from dance music to Masses. He composed several hundred works, including more than 50 symphonies and 24 operas. He set **standards** in all musical styles.

The greatest musical genius of all time?

Yet his genius is disputed by music experts and enthusiasts. His contemporary Joseph Haydn, also a representative of the **First Viennese School**, called Mozart the greatest composer known to him in name or person. In commemoration of the 100th anniversary of Mozart's death, Felix Mottl wrote in 1891: »In a sense it was he who first discovered music.« Even today many consider him the greatest musical genius of all time, while others see his creations as shallow and banal and ridicule his success as that of a »**classical pop star**«. Glenn Gould, the ingenious and eccentric

piano virtuoso who played Mozart's sonatas perfectly, considered him »by far the most overrated composer« whose peak was in his teenage years.

In dire straits

Though Mozart's diligently produced pieces turned into veritable hits, his contemporary audience did not always react positively, not least due to his **unreliability**: despite the tickets sold in advance he often cancelled concerts, and even the Prussian king, Frederick the Great, waited for commissioned pianos sonatas and string quartets in vain. The grand master probably had only himself to blame for his financial crisis, for he was a big earner. After disagreements, he dared to quit his service for his patron, the Archbishop of Salzburg, to try his luck in Vienna, and still he earned the equivalent of a quarter of a million euros per year as a freelance artist. Nevertheless, he would persistently ask a merchant friend of his for cash. Mozart was bad with money: he was a **fashion victim, a bon vivant**, and liked to gamble.

The rumour of his murder

On 5 December 1791 Mozart died at the **young age of 35**. To this day, it is speculated whether he was actually assassinated. Among the possible culprits are the Italian composer and court music director in Vienna, **Antonio Salieri**, whose envy of Mozart's musical genius was well documented. The Hollywood film *Amadeus* from 1984 pinned the murder on him. Even Mozart's freemason friend, **Franz Hofdemel**, was suspected of having committed the murder out of jealousy, for the composer was a notorious womanizer and gave piano lessons to Hofdemel's young wife.

Another erroneous rumour had it that Mozart had allegedly revealed secrets kept by his fellow masons about the **rites and theories of Freemasonry** in *The Magic Flute*, performed shortly before his death. However, a murder by any one of them was never proven. Most likely, Mozart died of an infection.

Classical money-spinner

It was only after his death that Mozart became a megastar and his widow **Constanze** played a major role in his growing popularity. Having inherited her late husband's enormous debts, she exhibited great business acumen in the way she managed his musical heritage. She sold Mozart's compositions and letters to the highest-bidding publishers and private collectors. But her **greatest coup** of all: the *Requiem*, commissioned by the Duke of Walsegg-Stuppach, which her husband never completed was finished by one of his pupils and sold highly profitably as Mozart's »final« work.

Even today, many still believe the story of Mozart finishing his requiem on his deathbed and picture the composer's hearse with no-one following – but that all is pure fantasy. The circumstances of Mozart's death shall forever occupy his devotees and he will surely remain **classical music's most enduring money-spinner** of all time.

For eminences and excellencies: the Audience Hall at the Alte Residenz

Old Town

Residenzplatz The focal point of the Old Town (Altstadt) on the left bank of the Salzach is the spacious Residenzplatz. The Residenzbrunnen, a work of Untersberg marble known as the **largest and most beautiful Baroque fountain this side of the Alps**, is attributed to Tommaso di Garona and contains snorting steeds, Atlas figures, dolphins, and a Triton figure with an upraised shell.

✳
Residenz The west side of the Residenzplatz is the location of the former prince-archbishops' living quarters, the Residenz, which was built in 1596–1619 on the site of the medieval bishop's seat. It surrounds three courtyards. Its main front received a marble entrance in 1710; the series of buildings in the northwest was added in 1792 but is of little architectural importance. Painter Hans Makart was born in the Residenz in 1840.

State rooms ▶ The state rooms on the second floor are used for state ceremonial purposes; they can, however, be viewed in conjunction with a tour if no special events are taking place (opening times: daily 10am–5pm). The interior of the rooms is defined by late Baroque style and early Classicism; the second floor features wall and ceiling frescoes by Johann Michael Rottmayr and Martin Altomonte as well as lavish stucco work and lovely fireplaces. The huge Carabinieri Hall still remains from the 17th century; concerts take place in the Knights' Hall (Rittersaal). The magnificent Audience Hall contains Flemish tapestries (c1600) with scenes from Roman history and priceless Parisian furniture. Portraits of holy Roman emperors and kings of the Habsburg dynasty are featured in the Imperial Hall (1273–1740).

Residenzgalerie ▶ The Residenz Gallery displays European paintings from the 16th to the 19th centuries; the most prominent are works by Dutch masters of the 17th century and Austrian masters of the 19th century (opening times: Tue–Sun 10am–5pm, mid-July–mid-Aug also Mon).

The **Neue Residenz** on the east side of Residenzplatz was created in 1588–1602 as a residence for guests of the archbishops. After a long period of renovation and rebuilding (and the closure of the Museum Carolino Augusteum), the Neue Residenz finally became the home of the »Salzburg Museum« in summer 2007. The museum contains the extensive and valuable **art historical and cultural** collections of the city and the province of Salzburg. In particular, the permanent exhibitions »Mythos Salzburg« and »Salzburg persönlich« offer interesting insights into the history of the city and the former principality (opening times: Tue–Sun 9am–5pm, Thu until 8pm).

Salzburg Museum

Also housed in the Neue Residenz, the **Panorama Museum** was opened back in autumn 2005. Its exhibits include the large and famous painting of the **Salzburg panorama** (1824–28) by Johann Michael Sattler. The glockenspiel in the tower of the Neue Residenz, equipped with 35 different bells, has been in use now for almost 300 years. It plays three times a day, at 7am, 11am, and 6pm, mostly melodies by Michael Haydn, Wolfgang Amadeus Mozart and Leopold Mozart. It is »answered« by the Salzburger Stier, a barrel organ at Hohensalzburg Fortress.

The south side of Residenzplatz is dominated by the cathedral, built by Santino Solari in 1614–28 using dark grey »Nagelfluh«, a conglomerate of pebbles, sand and sediments from the Mönchberg. It is the **first early Baroque church north of the Alps**. Both of its 79m/ 259ft towers were completed in 1657. The first structure, built by Abbot-Bishop Virgil, was dedicated in 774; it was replaced at the end of the 12th century by a Romanesque basilica with a nave and four aisles, which was later destroyed in a fire in 1598. The present building, the third to occupy the site, was severely damaged by bombing raids in 1944 but restored to its original form by 1959. The front doorway features four colossal light marble statues facing the Domplatz. On the outside stand patron saints Rupert and Virgil, one holding a salt barrel and the other a church model, while the inner statues are of saints Peter and Paul, holding a key and a sword. Three mighty

** Dom

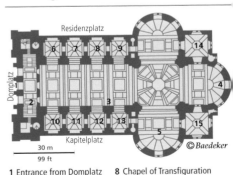

Salzburg Dom

1 Entrance from Domplatz (three bronze doors)
2 Entrance to Museum
3 Pulpit
4 High Altar
5 Entrance to Crypt
6 Baptistery
7 St Anne's Chapel
8 Chapel of Transfiguration
9 Chapel of the Cross
10 St Sebastian's Chapel
11 Chapel of St Charles Borromeo
12 St Martin's Chapel
13 Chapel of Holy Ghost
14 St Rupert's Oratory
15 St Virgil's Oratory

30 m
99 ft

© Baedeker

Illuminated glory: the Salzburg Dom at night

bronze doors were added in 1957–58, containing the symbols of faith (left), love (centre), and hope (right) by Toni Schneider-Manzell, Giacomo Manzù, and Ewald Mataré. The two crests on the pediment are reminders of the two founders of the cathedral, Markus Sittikus and Paris Lodron. The **interior of the cathedral** is overwhelming in its cool magnificence. The baptismal fonts, taken from the old Romanesque cathedral (1321), were once used to baptize the future cathedral organist, Wolfgang Amadeus Mozart. Arsenio Mascagni is responsible for the 1628 depiction of the Resurrection of Christ on the high altar. The frescoes between the stucco work in the vaulting were also painted by Mascagni and his students. In 1959, Toni Schneider-Manzell created the bronze pulpit on the third column on the left. The organ in Salzburg Cathedral is known for its beautiful tone.

Crypt ► Underneath the crossing, amongst the foundations of the former structures, a new multi-roomed **crypt** was built in 1957–59 as a new resting place for the archbishops. In the central room, the Kryptkapelle (Crypt Chapel), the altar stands on a fragment of wall still remaining from the Carolingian cathedral. The Romanesque crucifix is from the beginning of the 13th century. The northern room was once part of the lower church of the Romanesque cathedral, of which the central piers, pilasters, and column bases still remain. The room continues on to the east, stretching beyond the cathedral walls above, and is accessible as a separate museum for cathedral artefacts, the **Domgrabungsmuseum** (opening times: July and Aug daily 9am–5pm; otherwise by arrangement, tel. 06 62 / 620 80 81 31).

The **Dommuseum** (Cathedral Museum) exhibits valuable sacred objects such as the Carolingian Rupertuskreuz (St Rupert's Cross), as well as unusual pieces from the archbishops' collection of art and curiosities (entrance in the foyer; opening times: May–Oct, Mon–Sat 10am–5pm, Sun 11am–6pm).

Domplatz West of the cathedral, the Domplatz is connected to the Residenz and Stift St Peter by archways. Standing at the centre is the Mariensäule (Marian column), which was created around 1770. Since 1920 the square has been used for the performance of Hugo von Hofmannsthal's *Jedermann* (*Everyman*), a play about the death of a wealthy man, during the Salzburg Festival.

Kapitelplatz

Horses were once given water to drink and washed at the white marble Pferdeschwemme (horse trough) on the Kapitelplatz. The palace

Salzburg Map

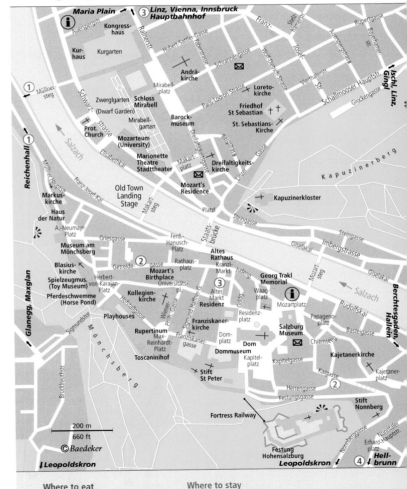

200 m
660 ft

© *Baedeker*

► VISITING SALZBURG

INFORMATION

Salzburg Information
Auerspergstrasse 6, A-5020 Salzburg
Tel. 06 62/8 89 87-0, fax 8 89 87-32
www.salzburg.info
Further information centres include
those in the main station and on
Mozartplatz.

SALZBURG CARD

With the Salzburg Card, valid for a
period of one, two, or three days and
available at information centres and
hotels, visitors have free admission to
numerous sights and museums, as
well as free use of public transport.
Card holders also receive discounts
for a variety of events.

SHOPPING

The Old Town (Altstadt) offers the
best places to shop with its variety of
diverse stores, located on the Getreidegasse, Linzer Gasse, Judengasse and
the Pferdeschwemme. A farmer's
market is held daily on Universitätsplatz.

TRANSPORT

Salzburg's city centre is an almost
pedestrian-only zone. Those who do
not want to park their cars in one of
the city's expensive car parks should
use one of the large car parks on the
outskirts of the city and then take the
bus into town.

SALZBURG FESTIVAL

A bit of luck is necessary in obtaining
the sought-after tickets for the Salzburg Festival. Orders must be sent in
writing at the beginning of the year (!)
to: Kartenbüro der Salzburger Festspiele, Hofstallgasse 1 or Postfach 140,
A-5010 Salzburg; tel. +43 (0) 6 62/
80 45-5 00, www.salzburgfestival.at

WHERE TO EAT

► Expensive

② Mozart
Getreidegasse 22, A-5020 Salzburg
Tel. 06 62/84 37 46
Perfect table culture and flawless
service are the trademarks of this
small oasis for gourmets.

► Moderate

① Augustiner Bräu Kloster Mülln
Lindhofstr. 7, A-5020 Salzburg
Tel. 06 62/43 12 46
Rich in tradition, this »Bräustübl« has
its own brewery and the largest beer
garden in Austria.

③ Café Tomaselli
Alter Markt 9, A-5020 Salzburg
Tel. 06 62/8 44 48 80
The famous Café Tomaselli has been
on the Alter Markt since 1705 – even
Mozart stopped in for an occasional
meal.

④ Purzelbaum
Zugallistr. 7, A-5020 Salzburg
Tel. 06 62/84 88 43
Outstanding light creative cuisine that
is sure to please.

WHERE TO STAY

► Luxury

① *Hotel Schloss Mönchstein*

Mönchsberg Park 26
A-5020 Salzburg
Tel. 06 62/8 48 55 50, fax 84 85 59
www.monchstein.at
The exclusive, top-class »Paris Lo-dron« restaurant, named after the archbishop who founded the university, is found here in the »most enchanting city centre hotel in the world«.

► Mid-range

② *Altstadthotel Kasererbräu*

Kaigasse 33
A-5010 Salzburg
Tel. 06 62/84 24 45, fax 84 24 45 51
www.kasererbraeu.at
With its location in the centre of the Old Town, all of the city's sights can be easily reached on foot from this charming hotel. The restaurant on the first floor offers Ayurveda-Indian specialities.

③ *Hotel Hohenstauffen*

Elisabethstrasse 19
A-5020 Salzburg
Tel. 06 62/87 76 69, fax 87 21 93 51
www.hotel-hohenstauffen.at
With well-equipped rooms and a location near the main railway station, this city centre hotel has been family-owned for three generations.

---

on the east side of the square has served as the seat of Salzburg's archbishops since 1864.

The Benedictine abbey of St Peter was founded around 690 by St Rupert on the west side of the Kapitelplatz and was the residence of the archbishops until 1110. Most of the buildings still standing were built in the 17th and 18th centuries. The expansive monastery grounds are grouped around three inner courtyards; the easternmost courtyard, attached to the church to the north, is a section of the cloister and therefore not accessible to visitors. The centre of the abbey is its outer courtyard, which features a hexagonal Petrusbrunnen, or Fountain of St Peter, from 1673. The entrance to the Stiftskeller St Peter, probably Salzburg's oldest restaurant, is located on the south side. The western corridor leads to the third courtyard, on which the Benedictine academy stands. Built in 1925–26 by Peter Behrens, it features façade frescoes by Anton Faistauer. A wooden crucifix by Jakob Adlhart (1925) stands in the northwest corner. The rooms between the accessible courtyards harbour a memorial for Johann Michael Haydn, the brother of Joseph Haydn, who moved to Salzburg in 1763 and became Mozart's successor in 1781 as the organist of the court and the cathedral (opening times: July–Sept, Thu–Tue 10am–4pm).

Stift St Peter

◄ Monastery grounds

⏱

The steep, rocky face of the Mönchsberg is simultaneously the back wall of the venerable St Peter's cemetery in the south, surrounded on three sides by arcades (1627) containing family burial sites. The catacombs have been cut into the rock face and are only accessible via a steep flight of steps. It still remains unclear when exactly these **early**

◄ Friedhof St Peter

◄ Catacombs

Christian shrines originated (possibly in the 3rd century AD). The guided tour first enters the communal crypt with the tombs of Michael Haydn and Nannerl, Mozart's sister. It then proceeds downstairs to the chapels of St Gertrude and St Maximus (guided tours: April–Sept daily 6.30am–7pm, Oct–March daily 6.30–6pm; information at tel. 06 62 / 84 45 76 89).

Stiftskirche St Peter ►

The abbey church was built in 1130–43, renovated in 1605–25, and given a Rococo interior in 1770–77. The tower cupolas also originated during this time. The tower's foyer features a Romanesque western doorway (c1240) with sculptures in the archway; the Rococo door originated in 1768.

The church's interior is still reminiscent of the former Romanesque basilica and contains numerous interesting tombs. The third chapel behind the altar houses the rock tomb of St Rupert, with a gravestone from 1444. Nearly all the paintings on the 16 marble altars were created by Kremser Schmidt (1718–1801). The Marienkapelle (Chapel of St Mary), located on the north side of the church, was created in 1319. The statue of the Virgin from the same period is particularly noteworthy, as are the early Gothic and modern frescoes (1955).

Franziskaner-kirche

Towering to the north of Stift St Peter is the Franciscan church, which as the Marienkirche served as the city's parish church until 1635. Its plain exterior provides an extreme contrast to its gripping interior: a dark, late Romanesque nave (13th century) is connected to the bright, High Gothic choir, a masterful artistic work by Hans von Stethaimer (15th century). The reticulated vaulting was created by Stephan Krumenauer. The high altar, most likely built by J.B. Fischer von Erlach and featuring a carved Madonna by Michael Pacher (1498), stands before the Baroque ring of chapels (1606–1704).

Salzburger Festspiele

Salzburg's renowned festival, featuring performances by world-famous artists, was established in 1920, Hugo von Hofmannsthal, Max Reinhardt, and Richard Strauss each playing a part. Opening with a performance of *Jedermann* (*Everyman*) on the Domplatz, the festival draws international audiences to Salzburg every year from the end of June to the end of August.

Festspielbezirk

West of the Franciscan church and Stift St Peter, between Max-Reinhardt-Platz with Hofstallgasse and the Mönchsberg, lies the so-called festival district. The **225m/738ft-long building** is comprised of the »House for Mozart« (formerly the Small Festival Hall or Kleines Festspielhaus) and the Large Festival Hall (Grosses Festspielhaus). In between are the newly designed foyer, offices, workshops, and the Karl Böhm Hall (guided tours: Oct–May daily 2pm, June and Sept daily 2pm and 3.30pm, July and Aug daily 9.30am, 2pm and 3.30pm).

Haus für Mozart ►

The history of the former Small Festival Hall has been shaped by numerous renovations over the years: in 1924–25 it was converted from the large Winter Riding School to the Small Festival Hall, then reno-

»Everyman« is performed every year at the Salzburg Festival on the Domplatz

vated in 1926, 1937–38 and 1963. Based on plans by architects Wilhelm Holzbauer and Francois Valentiny, alterations to the Small Festival Hall were completed punctually to coincide with the Mozart Year 2006, and the new building was renamed the »House for Mozart«. Today, the hall offers 1495 seats and standing room for 85 people. Its three entrances were designed by the Salzburg sculptor Josef Zenzmaier, and the *Goldene Wand* (*Golden Wall*) in the foyer is by the German artist and designer Michael Hammers.

The Large Festival Hall was built in 1956–60 by Clemens Holzmeister. His 40m/131ft-high, magnificent playhouse is built deep into the Mönchsberg: over 55,000 cubic m/1,942,307 cubic ft of rock had to be removed for construction, some of which was then used to cover the reinforced concrete columns. The floor in the foyer consists of Adnet marble, while the Pausensaal (Intermission Hall) features green serpentine flooring with embedded horse mosaics by Kurt Fischer. The steel relief *Homage to Anton von Webern* is by Rudolf Hoflehner. Two sculptures by Wander Bertoni, *Musik* and *Theater*, stand in the entrance hall, while the four large, free-standing paintings in blue, red, gold, and black were created by Robert Longo. The almost square theatre has 2179 seats and is famous for its wonderful acoustics.

✳
◀ Large Festival Hall

The Rock Riding School, otherwise known as the Summer Riding School, was founded in a former quarry on the Mönchsberg in 1693 (renovated in 1968–69 by Clemens Holzmeister). Three rows of audience galleries have been hewn from the rock and offer seating for 1549 spectators. Originally, tournaments and riding demonstrations took place here, whereas the space is now used for theatre and opera – also during the Salzburg Festival.

Rock Riding School

Opposite the House for Mozart stands a unique narrow, tall structure, the Rupertinum. For centuries, it was used as a seminary; in

Rupertinum

Happy horses – the Marstallschwemme

1983, it became the home of the **Museum der Moderne Rupertinum** (Rupertinum Museum of Modern Art). Its focus is on works from around 1900 (Toulouse-Lautrec, Klimt, Klinger), Expressionism (Kokoschka, Kollwitz, Barlach), and the Austrian avant-garde (Rainer, Brus). The Rupertinum also contains the **Österreichische Fotogalerie** (Austrian Gallery of Photography) and is known for its large number of special exhibitions (opening times: Tue–Sun 10am–6pm, Wed until 8pm). The Rupertinium is complemented by the Museum der Moderne on the Mönchsberg.

Max-Reinhardt-Platz is home to the Baroque-style **Kollegienkirche** (collegiate church), built in 1696–1707 by J. B. Fischer von Erlach for the former **university**. West of the Kollegienkirche and the Wilhelm Furtwängler Garden, the former Botanical Garden, is the newly opened Paris Lodron University. It was founded in 1622 by Archbishop Paris Count Lodron and was dissolved in 1810 due to the annexation to Bavaria.

Marstall-schwemme
West of the university building lies Herbert-von-Karajan-Platz, on which stands the Marstallschwemme, a well-like structure built in 1695 for the purpose of washing horses. The sculptural group of the horse tamers is by Michael Bernhard Mandl. The Neutor (or Sigmundstor) gate between the Festival Hall and the Marstallschwemme leads into the city districts of Riedenburg and Maxglan. The gate's façades were decorated by the Hagenauer brothers. The 123m/403ft-long road tunnel was cut out of the Mönchsberg in 1764–67.

Spielzeug-museum
It is a short walk to the former public hospital to the northwest. Today, it not only houses a toy museum that interests children and adults alike (the Folk Collection) but also exhibits a lovely collection of historical musical instruments (opening times: Tue–Sun, 9am–5pm, July, Aug and Dec also Mon).

Mönchsberg
The Mönchsberg lift near Anton-Neumayr-Platz has been in operation since 1890. It awaits visitors wishing to enjoy the splendid panoramic view of the city from the Mönchsberg plateau (operating times: daily 8am–7pm, Wed until 10pm, July and Aug until 1am).

MdM ►
As a supplement to the Rupertinum, the **Museum der Moderne Mönschberg (MdM)** was opened on the plateau. Since 1945 it has been exhibiting a significant collection of classical modern and international art (opening times: Tue–Sun 10am–6pm, Wed until 9pm, also Mon during Salzburg Festival).

On Museumsplatz, the northern extension of Neumayr-Platz, the ★
Haus der Natur (House of Nature) is housed in a former Ursuline **Haus der Natur**
convent. This fascinating museum of natural history, whose attractions include an aquarium, a reptile zoo and a space hall, enthrals
children and adults alike (Museumsplatz 5; opening times: daily ⊙
9am–5pm).

Getreidegasse (corn alley) is an old alley with beautiful town houses, **Getreidegasse**
wrought-iron signs for businesses and pubs, and pretty shops. A memorial plate on house no. 3 commemorates **August Bebel**, who
worked here as a turner's assistant in 1859–60. To the south, passage-
ways through the houses (so-called »Durchhäuser«) lead to Universitätsplatz.

A popular tourist destination is Getreidegasse no. 9: Wolfgang Ama- ★
deus Mozart (►Baedeker Special p.430) was born here on 27 January ◄ Mozart's
1756; the Mozart family lived on the third floor from 1747 to 1773. **birthplace**
The rooms now house a **museum**, displaying items and objects from
the composer's life and work including the young Mozart's violin,
pictures, a clavichord from 1760, a pianoforte from 1780 and original scores. The exhibition on the
second floor is dedicated to the
theme »Mozart and Theatre«,
whilst the first floor features special
exhibitions. The rear building
shows the exhibition »Salzburg's
Town Houses in Mozart's Time«
(opening times: daily 9am–6pm,
July and Aug until 7pm).

At the eastern end of Getreidegasse
the Baroque **Rathaus** (town hall;
1616–18), with pretty shell orna-
ments from the Rococo period, is surrounded by old Salzburg town
houses. Even in the Middle Ages they were built up to four or five
storeys high due to a lack of space.

> **!** *Baedeker* TIP
>
> **Mr Punch's Austrian relation**
> The toy museum's monthly programme reveals
> on which days at 3pm the museum's Kasperl
> marionette, cut from the same cloth as Mr
> Punch, comes out to ask children his famous
> question: »Seid ihr alle da?« (»Is everybody
> here?«). Oh yes, we are.

Further southeast is the Alter Markt, one of the most atmospheric **Alter Markt**
and oldest (13th century) squares in Salzburg. The traditional Tomaselli Café is a great place for a coffee break – Mozart himself would
drop in. Opposite, the »fürst-erzbischöfliche Hofapotheke«, the
prince-archbishop's court pharmacy, opened in 1591, is beautifully
furnished in Rococo style. The Marktbrunnen or Florianibrunnen
(1698) at the centre of Alter Markt features an even older beautiful
Renaissance-style spiral grid (1583).

Following the Judengasse east leads to Waagplatz, where poet Georg **Trakl**
Trakl was born in house no. 1 in 1887. Today it houses a research in- **memorial**
stitution and memorial (guided tours: Mon–Fri 11am and 2pm).

! *Baedeker* TIP

Mozartkugeln

An irresistible destination for fans of chocolates and sweets is Brodgasse no. 13: it was here in the ancestral home of the Fürst family that in 1890 the Salzburg confectioner Paul Fürst invented the Mozartkugel (Mozart ball), which is still manufactured to the original recipe today!

The **Mozart memorial** by Ludwig Schwanthaler (1842) stands on the adjacent Mozartplatz. In 1525 **Paracelsus** lived on Pfeifergasse (no. 11) branching off to the east. In 1540 the physician returned to Salzburg, where he died on 24 September 1541 at Kaigasse 8. Paracelsus is buried at the Sebastianfriedhof (St Sebastian's cemetery).

At Kajetanerplatz stands the **Kajetanerkirche**, a towerless church with a wide palace façade, which Caspar Zuccalli built from 1685–1700. Viewed from the outside, the sacral character of the building is emphasized only by the oval-shaped dome. The furnishings of the Baroque church date back to 1730, and the dome fresco was created by Paul Troger.

Stift Nonnberg

South across Kajetanerplatz, Stift Nonnberg (455m/1492ft) can be reached directly via the steps of the Nonnbergstiege. The nunnery was founded by St Rupert around 700 who appointed his niece Erentrudis abbess. The **oldest existing nunnery in the German-speaking region**, it is not accessible to visitors. Stift Nonnberg owes its fame to Maria Kutschera, better known under her later name of Baroness von Trapp. She was about to enter a novitiate at Nonnberg when in 1926 the nunnery sent her to the widower Baron von Trapp to become the governess of his children. One year later, she married the baron and soon founded the choir of the **Trapp family**, which was hugely successful in Austria even before their emigration to the US in 1938.

Abbey church

The late Gothic Nonnberg abbey church was built from 1464 on the site of a Romanesque basilica that had burnt down in 1423. Only the doorway and frescoes underneath the nun's choir depicting *Paradise* still remain. The glass painting in the central window of the main apse, donated in 1480, was created by the Strasbourg glass painter Peter Hemmel von Andlau. The late Gothic high altar was built around 1515, with statues of St Rupert and St Virgil. The three side chapels were all constructed during the mid-18th century in Baroque. Two of them are on the site where the nuns and abbesses were buried earlier. The rock tomb of St Erentrudis is honoured down in the crypt, which also features a marvellous reticulated vault. In order to visit the *Paradise* fresco and the Johanneskapelle (Chapel of St John), with a precious late Gothic winged altar (a gift from Archbishop Wolf Dietrich), ask for the key at the abbey gateway.

✳ ✳   Hohensalzburg Fortress

To reach the southeastern summit of the Mönchsberg and its fortress, 120m/394ft above the Salzach river, take a two-minute ride on the funicular (Festungsgasse) or a 30-minute walk – from Kapitelplatz and then Festungsgasse or from Mönchsberg through the Schartentor. The ascent alone provides plenty of fantastic views. Mönchsberg, 60m/197ft above the Old Town, is an almost 2km/1.2mi-long mountain ridge covered with deciduous trees that stretches west and northwest of the Hohensalzburg Fortress. Its shady parkland footpaths offer a number of beautiful vantage points.

History

Archbishop Gebhard had the fortress built in 1077, during the Investiture Controversy, to strengthen the power of the church. It owes its present appearance (since 1500) largely to Archbishop Leonhard von Keutschach, whose coat of arms – the turnip – is ubiquitous. The Thirty Years' War induced Archbishop Paris Count Lodron to undertake further fortification and refurbishment. The extension work was finished with the completion of the Kuenburg Bastion in 1681. Hohensalzburg was occupied only once in its history: in 1525 revolting farmers stood before the fortress, but were unable to take it. The fortress was abandoned in 1861 and temporarily served as a prison and barracks until 1938. In 1953 Oskar Kokoschka and the Salzburg gallery-owner Friedrich Welz established the »School of Seeing«, now the International Summer Academy, in the fortress. To this day art lovers from all over the world gather here every summer.

Salzburg's emblem rises high above the Old Town – the fortress of Hohensalzburg

HOHENSALZBURG FORTRESS

✳ ✴ **High above Salzburg's Old Town, the emblem of the city proudly stands. From this vantage point, visitors can take in the view across the Salzach river to the Kapuzinerberg. The huge fortress of Hohensalzburg (542m/1778ft), with its medieval and Baroque defensive fortifications, is one of the best preserved castles in Europe.**

🕐 Opening hours:
Jan—April and Oct daily 9.30am—5pm, May, June and Sept daily 9am—6pm, July and Aug daily 9am—7pm.
The Burghof, St George's church and the museums can be viewed without a guided tour. The representational rooms of the Salzburg bishops can only be seen as part of a guided tour (duration: c40 min).
Tel. 0662/84243011
www.hohensalzburg.com

① Burghof
The main courtyard is the centre of the castle. Along with the well, dug in 1539, and St George's church, this is the heart of Hohensalzburg.

② Salzburg Stier
The »bull« barrel organ from 1502 plays daily at 7am, 11am and 6pm after the glockenspiel in the new building of the Residenz. The organ's horn mechanism with 200 tin pipes was drawn up under Archbishop Leonhard von Keutschach.

③ Princes' Apartments
The Goldene Stube (Golden Room) boasts marble portals whose doors are artfully adorned with wrought-iron tendrils. The adjacent Goldene Saal (Gold Hall; also the Grosse Saal or Large Hall) is resplendent with its blue and red painted wood panelling and its columns of red marble from the quarries near Adnet.

④ Georgskirche
On the outer wall of the church of St George, built in 1501–02, is Hans Valkenauer's magnificent high relief of Leonhard von Keutschach from 1515, completed during the lifetime of the archbishop. In the interior, 13 reliefs, carved from red marble from the Adnet quarries, depict Christ and the twelve apostles.

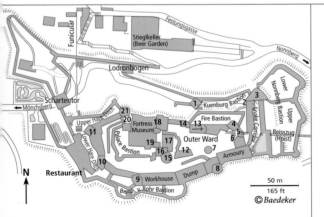

1 Keutschach Gate
2 Bridge
3 Mayor's Tower
4 Trumpeter's Tower
5 Reissturm
6 Hell Gate
7 Cistern
8 Smith's Tower
9 Vulture's Tower
10 Hare Tower
11 Rack Tower
12 Chaplain's Quarters
13 St George's Chapel
14 Krautturm
15 Kuchelturm
16 Bakery
17 Sergeant's Quarters
18 Prison
19 Fire Towers
20 Keutschach Well
21 Bell Tower

50 m
165 ft
©Baedeker

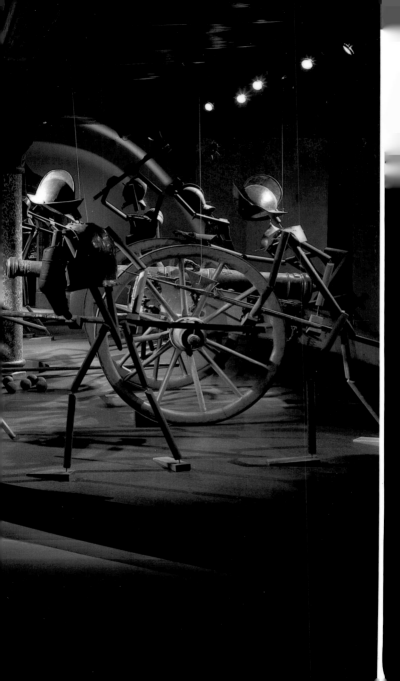

The cable car takes visitors up to the fortress in a mere two minutes.

In the permanent exhibition at the prize-winning fortress museum medieval machines and the history of the fortress are vividly illustrated and a comprehensive insight into the everyday life of former times is given.

In the Golden Room stands the famous tiled oven, a fine specimen of the art of pottery in Salzburg from 1501.

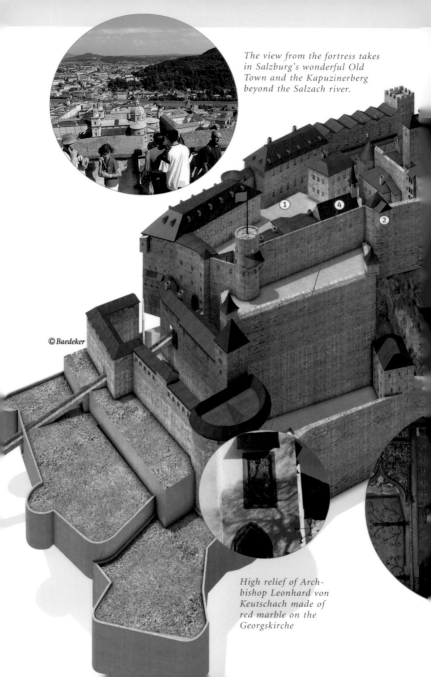

The view from the fortress takes in Salzburg's wonderful Old Town and the Kapuzinerberg beyond the Salzach river.

© Baedeker

High relief of Archbishop Leonhard von Keutschach made of red marble on the Georgskirche

Burghof The steep driveway (no private traffic!) leads through three arched gateways past the massive wall of the Feuerbastei (Fire Bastion) from 1681 to a hoist for supplies from 1504, which was once operated by horses and is still in use today. The road then continues through the Rosspforte (Horse Gate) into the **Haupthof** (Outer Courtyard) with ancient linden trees and a cistern from 1539.

Interior rooms The guided tour starts in the former court of justice (Gerichtsstube) in the Reckturm (Rack Tower) or Gerichtsturm (Court Tower). Its platform (170m/558ft above the city) also offers an excellent view. The tour continues pass the defensive corridor (Wehrgang) to the **»Salzburger Stier«** (Salzburg Bull), an organ from 1502 with 200 pipes, which is played daily in answer to the glockenspiel in the Neue Residenz. A spiral staircase leads to the third floor to the late Gothic Prince's Apartments.

Fortress museums In 2001, the Festungsmuseum in the »Hohe Stock« (high storey), which is part of Salzburg's Museum Carolino Augusteum, received the **Austrian Museum Award** for its display of the fortress's history, medieval jurisdiction and medieval living conditions. Also housed in the fortress, the so-called Rainermuseum deals with the history of the Salzburg household regiment known as Archduke Rainer's 59th Infantry Regiment, which was stationed here from 1871 to 1928 (closed during winter).

Neustadt

Right bank of the Salzach The main crossing from the Old Town to the Neustadt is the wide Staatsbrücke bridge from the »Rathausbogen« to the **Platzl**, around which a bridgehead-like suburb arose as early as the 12th century. From the Platzl, Dreifaltigkeitsgasse leads to Makartplatz – the former Hannibalplatz that was later renamed after the Salzburg painter Hans Makart (1840–84) – past Lederergasse and the narrow Königsgässchen, which both mark the progression of the first city wall of the 13th century.

Dreifaltigkeitskirche Towering over the square is the Dreifaltigkeitskirche (church of the Holy Trinity), a Baroque dome structure with a half-oval shaped façade that was erected by J. B. Fischer von Erlach in 1694–1702. After a fire in 1818 the top storeys of the tower were raised markedly, which considerably changed the appearance of the church.

✳ Mozart House Mozart's house can be found at Makartplatz no. 8, where Leopold Mozart and his family lived from 1773 until his death in 1787. By moving into this eight-room flat the Mozart family fled the cramped medieval conditions on Getreidegasse. Here there was enough room for social entertainment, playing music or enjoying the garden. Leopold Mozart's wife Anna Maria died in 1778, Wolfgang Amadeus left Salzburg in 1780 and his sister Nannerl married in 1784, after which Leopold lived alone in the spacious apartment. During the Second World War the building was severely damaged. The Mozarteum Foundation bought it in 1989 and had it restored to its original condition (opening times: daily 9am–6pm, July and Aug ☉ until 7pm).

The building now also houses the **»Mozart Ton- und Filmsammlung«** (Mozart sound and film collection), with archives of all Mozart-related audio and video recordings (opening times: Mon, Tue and Fri ☉ 9am–1pm, Wed and Thu 1pm–5pm, admission free).

At the southern end of Makartplatz stands the Landestheater (Provincial Theatre). It was built in 1892–93 and modified in 1939 and 1977–78. The side wing houses the Marionette Theatre, which founded in 1913 (entrance Schwarzstrasse 24). Performances not only include simple puppet shows, but also ballet, operettas and in particular the five main operas by Mozart.

Landestheater Marionetten-theater

The building at Schwarzstrasse no. 26 was designed by the Munich architect Richard Berndl in 1910–14 for the International Mozarteum Foundation, whose objective and responsibility it is to **preserve Mozart's legacy**. It houses teaching and administration rooms of the »Academy of Music and Performing Arts Mozarteum«, a library, and two concert halls. In the Basteigarten, pay a visit to the so-called Zauberflötenhäuschen (Magic Flute House), a garden house of the former Freihaustheater at Naschmarkt in Vienna, where Mozart was said to have composed *The Magic Flute* in 1791. In 1873 it was given to Salzburg, and has stood at its present location since 1950.

Mozarteum

Where could a Mozart concert be nicer than in the Marble Hall of Schloss Mirabell?

The Mirabellgarten (main entrance on Makartplatz), with terraces, marble statues and fountains, is an excellent example of **Baroque landscape gardening**. It was designed around 1690 by J. B. Fischer von Erlach. The fontanella in the middle of the garden is surrounded by groups of mythological figures, allegories for the elements earth, water, air and fire. In the southwestern corner of the garden stands the French-style Heckentheater, which was created in 1717.

★ **Mirabellgarten**

Around 1715, Archbishop Franz Anton Harrach had 28 grotesque-looking dwarfs set up in the Zwerglgarten (dwarfs' garden). Crown Prince Ludwig of Bavaria found them so despicable that he had them

★ **Zwerglgarten**

removed in 1812. Unfortunately only some of the figures were found again and returned to their original place. The stone figures, ranging between 1.20m/4ft and 1.40m/4.5ft in height, vaguely represent various characters or professions, including a farmer's wife, a ball player, a limping man and a hunchbacked woman.

Schloss Mirabell Archbishop Wolf Dietrich von Raitenau had Schloss Mirabell built in 1606 for his mistress and mother of his 15 children, the merchant's daughter Salome Alt. When Wolf Dietrich was overthrown in 1612 she was forced to leave the palace, which then served as an archiepiscopal summer residence. Between 1721 and 1727 it was redesigned by Lukas von Hildebrandt and converted into a late Baroque palace. After the great fire of Salzburg in 1818, the palace was reconstructed by Peter von Nobile in the classicist style of his time. Since 1947 Schloss Mirabell has been the **mayoral residence** and the seat of the city administration. Of Hildebrandt's palace, the magnificent staircase (Engelsstiege or angel's staircase) has been preserved, with a marble balustrade, stucco ornaments and lovely cherubs by Georg Raphael Donner. The staircase leads to the fantastic Marmorsaal (Marble Hall) on the first floor, which is now often used as a concert venue or for wedding ceremonies.

Engelsstiege ►

> ## ? DID YOU KNOW ...?
>
> ■ ... that the parish vicar Joseph Mohr, who penned the famous Christmas carol *Silent Night*, was born at Steingasse no. 9 in 1792?

Barockmuseum One section of the former Orangery of Schloss Mirabell now belongs to the Salzburg Baroque Museum, in which mainly European art from the 17th and 18th centuries is displayed including oil sketches, models and drafts by Rubens, Rottmayr, Veronese, Tiepolo and others (opening times: Wed–Sun 10am–5pm, July and Aug, Christmas and Easter also Tue).

Friedhof St Sebastian Instead of turning left after the Staatsbrücke to Makartplatz, heading straight on leads directly to Linzer Gasse. A few hundred yards down the road is the church and cemetery of St Sebastian. The church was originally built in the 16th century, then reconstructed in Rococo style in 1749–53. Left on the wall in the passageway is the tomb of physician and natural scientist **Theophrastus Paracelsus** who died in Salzburg in 1541. The cemetery of St Sebastian was laid out under the aegis of archbishop Wolf Dietrich in the style of an Italian Campo Santo and offers a good overview of the funerary art of the 17th to the 19th centuries. At the centre stands the artfully designed mausoleum for Archbishop Wolf Dietrich (†1617), the Gabrielskapelle (Chapel of St Gabriel). On the way to the chapel are the tombs of Mozart's father Leopold (†1787), Mozart's sister Constanze von Nissen (who had remarried, †1842) and Genoveva von Weber (†1798), mother of composer Carl Maria von Weber and aunt of Constanze Mozart.

South of the Sebastianskirche at Linzer Gasse no. 14, Stefan-Zweig-Weg leads past 18th-century chapels of the Way of the Cross and the Capuchin monastery up to the Kapuzinerberg (638m/2093ft). There is a magnificent panoramic view from the so-called »Kanzel« (pulpit) below the monastery. The mountain is covered by thin forest and offers several vantage points including the »Aussicht nach Bayern« (view to Bavaria). It takes 30 minutes to reach the summit on foot, where the Franziskischlössl (with a garden restaurant) from 1629 awaits visitors. From the Capuchin monastery there is also a path that leads via the Imbergstiege and the medieval-looking Steingasse back into town.

Kapuzinerberg

Around Salzburg

In Bergheim, at the northern edge of Salzburg, Wallfahrtskirche Maria Plain (1671–74), a Baroque pilgrimage church, stands on the Plainberg (530m/1738ft). It is visible from great distances. The **miraculous image** inside, created by an anonymous master, has been revered since 1633 when it survived a fire in Regen in Lower Bavaria. In 1652 it was put on display in a small wooden chapel on the Plainberg, and as pilgrims surged to see the image a new and bigger church was built. The miraculous image was solemnly crowned in 1752. The magnificent interior decoration of the hall, maintained in blue and gold, is also well worth taking a look at.

✳
Wallfahrtskirche Maria Plain

Gold and blue altars from the time when the pilgrimage church was first built around 1674

Markt Oberndorf Some 15km/9mi northwest of the Wallfahrtskirche Maria Plain lies Markt Oberndorf (394m/1292ft) on the river Salzach. The **Stille-Nacht-Gedächtniskapelle** (Silent Night Memorial Chapel) was erected in 1937 on the site of the Kirche St Nikolai, which was heavily damaged by a flood in 1899. It was in this chapel that the famous Christmas carol *Silent Night* was first played on the Christmas Eve of 1818.

Salzburg lake flats The Salzburg lake flats lie about 15km/9mi northeast of Salzburg. The largest and warmest lake, only 23m/75ft deep, is the 6km/3.7mi-long Wallersee. While anglers associate the lake with its rich population of fish, literature enthusiasts are reminded of Carl Zuckmayer and his time in Henndorf. Zuckmayer bought the »Wiesmühl« house in 1926; when the Nazis forced the German writer of Jewish descent to leave Germany, he made the house his sole residence from 1933 to 1938. But beer fans are drawn to Henndorf, too, and many a toast is made at the traditional Caspar-Moser-Bräu inn. Fancy a tipple, Zuckmayer-style?

Henndorf ►

✴
Gaisberg The Gaisberg (1288m/4225ft), one of Salzburg's local mountains, is easy to recognize by its tall radio tower. It can be reached either on foot via a charming hiking trail from Glasenbach past the Glasenbachklamm or by car coming from the north. During the rush hour, traffic is limited in favour of public transport. Up on top, the fantastic panoramic view extends from Dachstein to the Chiemsee. Northeast lies the **Salzburgring**, where national and international motorbike and car races are held.

The approximately 4km/2.5ft-long tree-lined Hellbrunner Allee leads up to Schloss Hellbrunn. From 1613 to 1616 Archbishop Markus Sittikus had the castle, the park and the trick fountains designed in Romanesque style by master mason Solari. The **Mannerist early Baroque ensemble** survived the centuries almost without alteration.

✴
Schloss Hellbrunn The hand-painted Chinese wallpaper in the bedroom, the marvellous tiled stove in the dining-hall, and the banqueting hall are all extraordinary. The palace and the trick fountains are only accessible as part of a guided tour (opening times: March, April, Oct 9am–4.30pm, May, June, Sept until 5.30pm, July and Aug until 6pm, fountains until 10pm).

✴
Trick fountains, mechanical theatre ► The ornamental garden is decorated by numerous statues, fountains and grottoes including water-powered gimmicks and jokes – made at

The park at Schloss Hellbrunn

the expense of others, of course. The most original installation is the »mechanical theatre«, representing everyday life in a Baroque small town, with 256 figures and an organ mechanism.

Above the central pond on the Hellbrunner Berg stands the Monatsschlössl (»month castle«), built in 1615, which was in use for only one month of the year during the hunting season. Since 1924 it has housed Salzburg's **Volkskundemuseum** (Folklore Museum), a department of the Carolino Augusteum Museum (opening times: April–Oct daily 10am–5.30pm). Situated behind the palace, the Steinernes Theater (Stone Theatre) is a natural but artificially expanded gorge where in 1617 one of the first opera performances in a German-speaking country took place.

◀ Monatsschlössl

🕐
◀ Steinernes Theater

Adjacent to the Schlosspark to the south is Zoo Salzburg, known until 2003 as Tiergarten Hellbrunn. Developed from a game park in 1961, the zoo is especially striking for its success in housing its animals in largely natural enclosures (opening times: Nov–March daily 9am–4pm, April–June, Sept and Oct until 5pm, July and Aug until 6.30pm; »night zoo«: Aug Fri and Sat until 11pm).

◀ Zoo Salzburg

Some 6km/3.7mi southwest of Hellbrunn, in St Leonhard, is the valley station of the over 2800m/9184ft-long cable railway leading up to the **Salzburger Hochthron** (1856m/6088ft), the highest Austrian peak of the Untersberg. The **only massif rising directly from ground level** of the Northern Limestone Alps, it is by far the most noticeable mountain near Salzburg.

Untersberg

The former archiepiscopal Schloss Leopoldskron, built in 1736 in Rococo style, is situated on the Leopoldskroner Weiher lake in the south of Salzburg. From 1918 to 1956 it belonged to Max Reinhardt and his heirs; today it serves as a venue for the »Salzburg Seminar in American Studies« (not open to the public).

Schloss Leopoldskron

The Salzburg open-air museum was opened in 1984 near Grossgmain, just a few miles southwest of Salzburg. On 50ha/124ac, some 60 farmhouses from the Salzburg region from several eras (16th to the 20th centuries) have been built true to the original and displayed

✳
Salzburger Freilichtmuseum

in a beautiful setting. At weekends it is possible to watch traditional artisans at work (opening times: late March–early Nov, Tue–Sun 9am–6pm)

Schloss Klessheim

The Baroque castle of Klessheim is located some 3km/2mi northwest of Salzburg's Maxglan district. Designed by J. B. Fischer von Erlach, it was built between 1700 and 1709 for the Prince-Archbishop Johann Ernst Graf von Thun. Today it is owned by Salzburg's regional government and provides a grand setting for the city's casino.

★ ★ Salzkammergut

K/L 4

Provinces: Upper Austria, Salzburg and Styria

The Salzkammergut region is the epitome of Austrian holiday destinations and its praises are sung in the famous operetta *Im Weissen Rössl* (*The White Horse Inn*). Germany's former chancellor Helmut Kohl used to regularly spend his summer holidays here.

Holiday region

Nature and culture are beautifully united in this enchanting lake district in the Alps and alpine foreland, making it **one of the most visited tourist regions in Austria**. Guests can choose from a wide range of sporting activities – from leisurely to extreme. While the magnificent countryside is sure to fascinate all visitors to this lovely region, many towns also offer pleasant summer cultural programmes featuring concerts, readings and exhibitions.

The vast contrast between the shimmering surfaces of the more than 40 lakes, both large and small, and the impressive peaks and cliffs of the surrounding mountains is absolutely stunning. The Schafberg is the place to go for a marvellous view of the scenery.

Geographical location

Geographically, the Salzkammergut region is composed of the ►Attersee, Ausseer Land (►Bad Aussee), ►Bad Ischl and the ►Wolfgangsee, the holiday region of ►Traunsee, the Fuschlsee (►Wolfgangsee), the Inner Salzkammergut with the ►Hallstätter See, ►Dachstein, and the holiday region of ► Mondsee. Hence, the Salzkammergut is mainly a part of Upper Austria, with the exception of the Wolfgangsee and the Fuschlsee, which extend to Salzburg, and the Ausseer Land reaching into the Styria region. In early modern times the Salzkammergut centre was the area around Ischl. As a baronial property and »Kammergut« (crown es-

 SALZKAMMERGUT

INFORMATION

Salzkammergut Tourismus
Salinenplatz 1, A-4820 Bad Ischl
Tel. 061 32/269 09, fax 269 09 14
www.salzkammergut.at

tate) with special rights, it was an enormously lucrative »state within a state«. The once political-economic term now only refers to the geographical and tourist region.

★ ★ St Florian

M 3

Province: Upper Austria
Population: 5500

Elevation: 296m/971ft

Art lovers of all kinds will appreciate this town: architecture, music and the old library with its many treasures attract numerous visitors to St Florian every year.

When it comes to the most splendid examples of Baroque architecture in Austria, the market town of St Florian, some 15km/9.5mi southeast of the state capital of ► Linz, is particularly noteworthy. Music lovers will associate the famous Augustinian abbey with the brilliant composer **Anton Bruckner**, who was born in the near vicinity. During his childhood he lent his voice and musical talent to the St Florian Boys' Choir and later became the abbey's cathedral organist.

Baroque and music

★ Augustinian Abbey of Augustinian Canons

St Florian, a chief administrative officer in the Roman province of Noricum, was drowned in the Enns river when he converted to Christianity in the early 4th century. Legend has it that, although his body was tied to a heavy stone, it rose to the surface. His remains were buried at the Augustinian abbey. Honoured as the patron saint of fire fighters and rescue workers, he is also commemorated with the ironic saying *Oh heiliger Sankt Florian, verschon' mein Haus, zünds andere an!*, which translates as »O holy St Florian, spare my house, kindle others«.

Legendary monastery

The oldest sections of the abbey wall date back to the 4th century. A Romanesque church (burned down in 1235) and a Gothic church followed. After defeating the Turks in 1683, the emperor made a pilgrimage to St Florian's grave as a display of gratitude, and the abbey administration decided

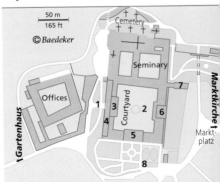

Stift St Florian

50 m
165 ft

© Baedeker

Cemetery

Seminary

Offices

Gartenhaus

Courtyard

Marktkirche

Markt-platz

1 Gateway and Bläserturm
2 Fountain
3 Grand Staircase
4 Imperial Apartments
5 Marble Hall
6 Library
7 Summer Refectory
8 Statue of
   St John Nepomuk

ST FLORIAN

INFORMATION

Tourismusverband St Florian
Marktplatz 2, A-4490 St Florian
Tel. 0 72 24/56 90, fax 57 88
www.tiscover.com/st.florian

on a Baroque reconstruction based on the design by Carlo Carlone. Following Carlone's death in 1708, Jakob Prandtauer led the building work until 1751 (guided tours: Easter to 1 Nov daily at 10am, 11am, noon, 2pm, 3pm and 4pm; group visits outside tour hours by arrangement, tel. 072 24 / 890 20).

★★
Abbey basilica
The mighty abbey basilica, with its two 80m/262ft-high towers, is located at the northern end of the west wing. The monumental impact of the interior is achieved through the huge semicircular columns on tall bases, the high windows, the 36m/188ft-high dome, lavish stucco decoration and frescoes covering the entire ceiling. The choir stalls and organ loft are richly carved and adorned with putti; the pulpit is made of black marble from Lilienfeld.

Anton Bruckner ►
Anton Bruckner began his musical career with the St Florian Boys' Choir. Under the provost's patronage he became the abbey's organist in 1848, before moving to Linz in 1854. The sarcophagus of »**God's musician**« can be found in the crypt beneath the large church organ, which bears his name. From mid-May to mid-October, visitors have a chance to hear this wonderful instrument in a 20-minute organ recital daily at 2.30pm (except Tue and Sat).

Abbey buildings
Prandtauer's masterpiece is the grand staircase on the courtyard side of the west wing, with two levels of arcades, arches and pilasters. Magnificently designed according to Carlone's drafts, it provides access to the imperial chambers in the west wing, which once accommodated important guests. The Gothic gallery features 14 gloriously colourful tableaux of the Sebastian Altar by Albrecht Altdorfer (1480–1538), the most significant painter of the Danube School. A symbol of secular power, the Marble Hall, also designed by Prandtauer, is situated in the abbey's south wing. Today it provides a festive setting for summer concerts. Directly opposite stands the basilica, which represents the power of the clergy.

★
Library
The east wing of the abbey houses a splendid library with a ceiling painting by Bartolomeo Altomonte depicting the union of virtue and science. With some 150,000 volumes, 950 incunabula and 800 valuable manuscripts, the library possesses a vast wealth of bibliophile treasures.

St Florian
Boys' Choir
The St Florian Boys' Choir looks back on nearly **1000 years of history**: it was first mentioned in a document dating from 1071, when Augustinian monks took over the abbey. Today the choir not only sings at church services, but also undertakes lengthy concert tours. Anton Bruckner was a member of the choir as a boy.

Around St Florian

Schloss Hohenbrunn lies on the Ipf river, 2km/1.2mi south of St Florian. Designed as a hunting castle, it was built between 1725 and 1729 by Jakob Prandtauer. Since 1966 the castle has been home to the **Oberösterreichische Jagd- und Fischereimuseum** (Upper Austrian Hunting and Fishing Museum (open April–Oct Tue–Sun 10am–noon, 1pm–5pm).

Schloss Hohenbrunn

⊙

The Sumerauerhof Open-air Museum, some 2km/1.2mi east of St Florian in the district of Samesleiten, is a large »Vierkanthof« (a farmhouse arranged around a square) dating back to the 13th century. The building has not changed since 1856 and was in operation until 1970. The exhibition of painted farmhouse furniture spanning four centuries is well worth seeing (opening times: late April–Oct Tue–Sun 10am–noon and 1pm–5pm).

Freilichtmuseum Sumerauerhof

⊙

Anton Bruckner was born on 4 September 1824 in Ansfelden, 4km/2.5mi west of St Florian. Today the house in which he was born is home to the Anton Bruckner Museum, dedicated to the life and work of the composer (Augustinerstrasse 3; opening times: April–Oct Wed 2pm–5pm, Sun 10am–noon and 2pm–5pm).

Ansfelden

⊙

★ St Johann im Pongau

K 5

Province: Salzburg
Population: 10,300

Elevation: 650m/2133ft

St Johann im Pongau, the district capital and modern centre of Pongau in the middle of the Salzachtal, offers a customized winter holiday geared mainly to younger people.

 VISITING ST JOHANN IM PONGAU

INFORMATION

Tourismusverband
St Johann–Alpendorf
Ing.-Ludwig-Pech-Str. 1
A-5600 St Johann
Tel. 0 64 12/60 36
Fax 60 36-74
www.sanktjohann.com

WHERE TO EAT

► **Inexpensive**
Silbergasser
Hauptstrasse 49
A-5600 St Johann
Tel. 0 64 12/84 21
The regional cuisine includes »gebackenes Allerlei« (mixed roast) and »Jägerpfandl« (pork with mushrooms).

Ski and après-ski: Sportwelt Amadé

The town has united with Altenmarkt, Flachau, Radstadt, Wagrain and others to form Sportwelt Amadé, a **local tourism association**. Winter sports in particular are promoted, and the ski-pass for numerous ski lifts, ski slopes of all levels of difficulty, and an extensive programme of further activities and après-ski offers appeal especially to a younger target group. In summer, too, the emphasis is on sports, with a broad variety of opportunities for rafting, climbing and hiking.

What to See in St Johann im Pongau

Pongauer Dom

St Johann im Pongau lies on a sunny terrace above the right bank of the Salzach. Dominating the townscape is the neo-Gothic, twin-spired parish church of St John, which is also called the »Pongauer Dom« due to its great architectural impact. First documented in 924, the church was rebuilt in 1855–61 after it was destroyed in a big town fire.

✳ **Liechtenstein-klamm**

About 5km/3.1mi south of the town centre, the roaring waters of the Grossarlbach flow down one of the most splendid gorges in the Alps in a stunning natural spectacle. The gorge owes its name to the Prince of Liechtenstein, who made development of the area possible through a donation in 1876. The almost 300m/985ft-deep gorge is best viewed from the secured paths during the morning, when the light is at its best. The waterfall is almost 60m/187ft high (accessible: May–Sept daily 8am–6pm, Oct 9am–4pm).

Around St Johann im Pongau

Bischofshofen

About 8km/5mi north of St Johann, where the Mühlbach valley meets the Salzach valley, lies the town Bischofshofen (550m/1804ft; 10,100 inhabitants). Every year on 6 January, the **ski-jumping final of the international Vier-Schanzen-Tournee** (Four Hills Tournament) takes place here, which is the main highlight in a wealth of winter sporting activities in Bischofshofen.

In the church of St Maximilian, frescoes and the marble tomb of bishop Sylvester von Chiemsee († 1453) are notable. The precious Rupertus Cross (around 700), the original of which can be marvelled at in the Salzburger Dommuseum (it is a copy here in the vicarage), is reminiscent of an Irish High Cross and of the fact that it was Irish monks who first brought Christianity to the province of Salzburg.

Pfarrwerfen

Another 8km/5mi north lies Pfarrwerfen (553–1500m/1814–4921ft; pop. 2200), set before the backdrop of the Tennen mountains and the Hochkönig. The emblem of the village is the outdoor mill museum »7 Mühlen«. Six of the mills are still in good condition (opening times: May–Oct daily 8am–7pm; milling demonstration: Fri 3pm–6pm).

Dramatic natural sight – the Liechtensteinklamm

In Werfenweng (901m/2956ft; pop. 800), a few miles above Pfarr-werfen, the excellent Salzburger Landesskimuseum is a must-see for ski enthusiasts (opening times: Mon–Fri 9am–noon and 1pm–5pm, Sat 2pm–5pm, Sun from 10am).

Werfenweng

🕐

About 8km/5mi east of St Johann lies the popular winter sport location of Wagrain (838m/2749ft; pop. 2600), situated within the beautiful Wagrainer Tal valley. In Wagrain's cemetery are the graves of the author Heinrich Waggerl (1897–1973), a controversial figure due to his affinity for National Socialism, and the Reverend Joseph Mohr, who wrote the Christmas carol *Silent Night*.

Wagrain

Back in the Salzachtal valley, around 10km/6mi southwest of St Jo-hann lies the railway-junction town of Schwarzach (591m/1939ft;

Schwarzach

pop. 3600). On display at the Rathaus (town hall) is the table top of the Salzleckertisch, at which Protestant farmers met in 1731. The Archbishop of Salzburg gave them the choice between conversion and emigration. As a result, as many as 30,000 Protestants left the province of Salzburg.

Goldegg

Goldegg (850m/2789ft; pop. 2100), on the shores of an idyllic lake, boasts 70km/43mi of cross-country ski runs. The romantic Schloss Goldegg features an impressive Knight's Hall with a beautiful wooden ceiling. A number of the rooms are used by the **Pongauer Heimatmuseum** (opening times: mid-June–mid-Sept daily (except Wed) 10am–noon and 3pm–5pm, Sun pm only; castle tours: mid-June–mid-Sept daily (except Wed) 2pm, mid-Sept–mid-June Thu 2pm; for information tel. 064 15 / 82 13).

✳ St Pölten

P 3

Province: Lower Austria	**Elevation:** 267m/867ft
Population: 51,000	

The large town of St Pölten has been the capital of Lower Austria since 1986. Up until then, the province was governed from Vienna. In 1159, St Pölten was the first place in Austria to obtain its municipal charter.

New provincial capital

The commercial and industrial town is situated 40km/25mi west of Vienna, on the banks of the Traisen river. Famous Baroque artists such as Jakob Prandtauer lived here and gave the town its rich Baroque character. The town is where Paula von Preradovic, composer of the Austrian national anthem (»Land der Berge, ...«), went to school.

What to See in St Pölten

Rathausplatz

At the heart of the Old Town is Rathausplatz (town hall square). Once a market square, it was redesigned by Boris Podrecca in 1995. In the middle of the square stands an impressive trinity column (1782). On the northern side of Rathausplatz stands the Franciscan church (18th century), which can be classified as Rococo. The magnificent pulpit and four altarpieces were built by Kremser Schmidt. South of the Rathaus (14th century), many building styles can be recognized, from Renaissance portals to Baroque façades (Josef Munggenast, 1727). During the renovation of the western façade in 1984, a fresco painting from the 16th century was discovered and restored. The Rathaus spire is the emblem of St Pölten. Beside it is the Schubert House, where the first Schubertiade was held in 1821, featuring the composer himself.

The organ dominates the nave of the cathedral

Domplatz

Heading along Marktgasse and Kremser Gasse, past the Stöhr-Haus (no. 41), a remarkable art nouveau building by the Viennese architect Maria Olbrich (1867–1908), eventually Domgasse leads to the Domplatz. This was once the **central point of the Roman settlement Aelium Cetium**. Today it is a setting for summertime open-air events. The Bischofshof, a Baroque monastic building, was built in the 17th century. Today it houses the Diözesanmuseum (Diocesan Museum), displaying sacral art (opening times: Tue–Fri 10am–noon and 2pm– 5pm, Sat and Sun 10am–1pm).

Dom

The originally Romanesque cathedral (12th–13th century), with its plain exterior, was refurbished in Baroque style according to designs by Jakob Prandtauer in 1722. Take a look at the frescoes and paintings by Daniel Gran and Bartolomeo Altomonte, as well as the finely carved and gilded choir stalls designed by Mathias Steinl. A Romanesque chapel, the Rosenkranzkapelle (12th century), was incorporated into the monastery church, but remained largely unmodified.

Riemerplatz

Riemerplatz, in the heart of the Old Town, was designed at the end of the 11th century as the centre of the episcopal settlement. Beautiful palaces with Baroque façades and wrought-iron balcony grilles frame the square.

Stadtmuseum

Rathausgasse leads to Prandtauerstrasse and the former Carmelite convent, founded by the Princess Montecuccoli and designed by Jakob Prandtauer. Today it accommodates the Lower Austrian Dokumentationszentrum für Moderne Kunst (Documentation Centre for Modern Art) and the Stadtmuseum St Pölten: alongside an elaborate presentation of the town's history are important works by St Pölten's art nouveau artists (opening times: Wed–Sun 10am–5pm).

Former synagogue

Along the Dr-Karl-Renner-Promenade in the southeast of the Old Town stands the former synagogue, the only **art nouveau synagogue** in Lower Austria (restored). Today it hosts cultural events and houses the Institute of Jewish History in Austria.

Governmental quarter and cultural district

In 1992 the governmental district with its elegantly curved parliament building, the »Landtagsschiff« (architect: Ernst Hoffmann), and administration buildings for the Lower Austrian provincial government were built southeast of the Old Town. Included is a cultural district with the new building of Lower Austria's provincial museum,

St Pölten *Map*

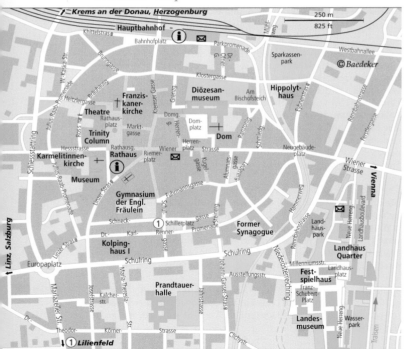

Where to eat
① Alt Wien

Where to stay
① Austria Trend Hotel Metropol

▶ VISITING ST PÖLTEN

INFORMATION

Tourismusinformation St Pölten
Rathausplatz 1
A-3100 St Pölten
Tel. 027 42/35 33 54
Fax 333 28 19
www.st-poelten.gv.at

WHERE TO EAT

▶ Moderate
① *Alt Wien*
Mariazeller Str. 42
A-3100 St Pölten
Tel. 027 42/733 17

The Alt Wien offers an ethnic Heuriger cellar and a well-stocked wine shop.

WHERE TO STAY

▶ Mid-range
① *Austria Trend Hotel Metropol*
Schillerplatz 1
A-3100 St Pölten
Tel. 0 27 42/7 07 00, fax 70 70 01 33
www.austria-trend.at
This elegant hotel offers comfortable accommodation and modern conference facilities.

the **Niederösterreichisches Landesmuseum**, which was designed by Hans Hollein and presents the nature, art and history of Lower Austria in a rather unusual way.(opening times: Tue–Sun 10am–6pm). ⊕ The modern concept of the museum is particularly evident in the field of history where previous ways of life are represented in context under such topics as communication, rulership, borders, settlement, communal living and the world of work.

The provincial library and the Festival Hall (architect: Klaus Kada) are also part of the cultural district. The architectural hallmark of the new part of the town is the 62m/203ft-high »**Klangturm**« (sound tower) by Ernst Hoffmann.

Around St Pölten

Herzogenburg Abbey, 12km/7.5mi north of St Pölten, was established in the 12th century. Jakob Prandtauer, Joseph Munggenast and J. B. Fischer von Erlach are responsible for the Baroque abbey buildings (from 1724), Franz Munggenast for the richly furnished abbey church (1743–50). The 70m/230ft-high tower (1767) is crowned with the duke's hat. The abbey holds an **important collection of sacral artworks**, including late Gothic works of the Danube School (guided tours: April–Oct daily 9.30am, 11am, 1.30pm, 3pm and 4.30pm, Nov–March by arrangement, tel. 027 82/831 12 11).

Herzogenburg

★

◀ Augustiner-Chorherrenstift

⊕

In the community Inzersdorf-Getzersdorf, further north at the western end of the Traisen valley, the first Lower Austrian »Bildstockweg« was created. The 10km/6.2mi-long hiking trail leads past 21 shrines and crucifixes – and some wine taverns.

Bildstockweg

✳
Lilienfeld

South of St Pölten lies Lilienfeld, whose **Cistercian abbey**, founded in 1202, is well worth seeing. During the Middle Ages it was the largest monastery in Austria, equipped with a very beautiful abbey library and a remarkable Gothic fountain house. The Romanesque-Gothic columned basilica originated in the 13th century, its Baroque interior is from the 18th century. Alongside exhibits on local history, the **Lilienfeld Museum** contains items that recall skiing pioneer Mathias Zdarsky, who invented the first solid binding thus making a controlled descent on two skis possible (historic gate tower; opening times: Thu, Sat and Sun 4pm–6pm).

! **Baedeker TIP**

Impressive prehistoric creatures

North of Traismauer, a primeval attraction awaits visitors to the Danube-Traisen water meadows: Along 3km/1.9mi of hiking trails stand more than 45 replicas of dinosaurs, often enormous in size. A petting zoo and playground complete the scene (opening times: late March–Oct daily 10am–6pm).

Mostviertel

»Where the pear feels comfortable, people also like to live« is the motto of the Mostviertel (Must Quarter). It stretches eastwards to the Wienerwald, in the south it borders on Styria, in the west with Upper Austria, and the Danube forms its northern border. This alpine foreland with its rolling hills, charming villages and splendid square barnyards is an eminently suitable place for a relaxing holiday. Hundreds of thousands of blossoming pear trees offer an enchanting sight during spring and, from late summer on, provide the main ingredient for the region's down-to-earth pear beverage, called Most.

✳ St Veit an der Glan

M 6

Province: Carinthia
Population: 13,800

Elevation: 476m/1530ft

From 1170–1518, until Klagenfurt took on this function, St Veit an der Glan was the residence of the dukes of Carinthia and the capital of the province. In addition to a charming and well-visited Old Town centre with 15th-century fortification walls, this lively industrial town also offers interesting modern architecture.

Ducal seat and »city of flowers«

Situated about 20km/12mi north of ▸Klagenfurt, the former ducal seat of St Veit an der Glan, a town full of flowers and a popular holiday destination and cultural centre, hardly leaves tour operators at a loss for words when it comes to appealing attributes. The town has received a number of national and international awards for its floral displays.

What to See in St Veit an der Glan

The elongated Hauptplatz (main square) is surrounded by splendid, **Hauptplatz** mostly three-storey buildings. Three monuments decorate the Hauptplatz: the marble **plague column** in the middle, built by Angelo de Putti in 1715; alongside numerous figures is St Rosalia Sanibaldi of Palermo, who was worshipped as the plague saint. North of the plague column stands the Schlüsselbrunnen (Key Fountain), with a Roman marble bowl originating from Zollfeld. The large **bronze figure of a miner** in the middle of the bowl (1566) is a remarkable work of art. The southwest half of the square features a fountain decorated with a bronze figure of Walther von der Vogelweide (built in 1676, renovated in 1960), who lived in St Veit for some time.

The late Gothic town hall received its grand Baroque façade in 1754, **Rathaus** and the three-floored Renaissance arcaded courtyard is wonderfully painted using the sgraffito technique. The conference hall owes its notable filigree stucco work to the artist Joseph Pittner, who is also responsible for the outer façade.

Railway enthusiasts will be irresistibly drawn to the Transport Museum. More than 100 exhibits offer insight into the development of transportation – from the stagecoach to the steam engine. The huge model railway is a real highlight (Hauptplatz 29; opening times: April–Oct daily 9am–noon and 2pm–6pm, July and Aug all day on weekdays). **Verkehrsmuseum**

Strolling amongst the colourful floral display on St Veit's Hauptplatz

Stadtpfarrkirche

The town parish church, Stadtpfarrkirche St Veit, is a late Roman columned basilica with a Gothic choir and frescoes dating from the early 15th century. The antlers over the west doorway are suggestive of a Celtic symbol.

Modern architecture

A stark contrast to the historic atmosphere is provided by **the longest glass shopping gallery in Austria** at Herzog-Bernhard-Platz, east of the town's parish church and the **first art hotel in Carinthia** (Prof.-Ernst-Fuchs-Platz 1), with its colourful Tiffany outer façade and imaginative interior decoration based on the signs of the zodiac, by the artist Ernst Fuchs. The Zodiac restaurant and the »Mondscheinbar« (moonshine bar) are designed in the same style.

Around St Veit

★ ★
Burg Hochosterwitz

Hochosterwitz is by no means the only castle in the area surrounding St Veit, but it is by far the most remarkable. About 10km/6mi east of St Veit, it stands impressively on a conical chalk cliff, which rises from the valley floor by a good 150m/492ft. It was officially documented as early as 860. In 1571, following a turbulent history, the castle went to the house of Khevenhüller. Due to the threat of Turkish invasions, Georg Freiherr von Khevenhüller (1534–87), governor and imperial counsellor, had it converted into a fortress. Indeed, 14 fortified gates and a well equipped armoury for about 700 men made sure that Hochosterwitz Castle was never captured. By the way, the proud building is to this day a possession of the Khevenhüller nobility. There is a lift for those who are not so fleet of foot or who wish to avoid the **steep climb**. The ascent is rather exhausting: in around 30 minutes the steep, 620m/2034ft-long castle path leads through the 14 gate buildings – the family crest of white marble is displayed on the Khevenhüller-Tor – and over five drawbridges, up to the inner castle courtyard surrounded by arcades (opening times April–Oct 9am– 5pm, high season 8am–6pm; regular guided tours). The lift only takes two minutes and then there's always the walk down! The castle restaurant offers refreshments for weary climbers.

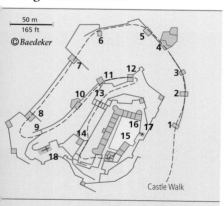

Burg Hochosterwitz

50 m
165 ft
©Baedeker

Castle Walk

Sergeant's Gate	10 Arms Gate
Watchman's Gate	11 Wall Gate
Nau Gate	12 Bridge Gate
Angel's Gate	13 Church Gate
Lion's Gate	14 Kulmer Gate
Man's Gate	15 Inner Ward
Khevenhüller Gate	16 Restaurant
Land Gate	17 Chapel
Reiser Gate	18 Church

⏵ VISITING ST VEIT AN DER GLAN

INFORMATION

Stadtgemeinde St Veit
Hauptplatz 1
A-9300 St Veit an der Glan
Tel. 0 42 12/55 55
Fax 55 55 112
www.stveit.carinthia.at

WHERE TO STAY

▶ **Mid-range**
Hotel St Veit – Fuchspalast
Prof.-Ernst-Fuchs-Platz 1
A-9300 St Veit an der Glan
Tel. 0 42 12/4 66 00, fax 4 66 06 60
www.fuchspalast.com
At this centrally located hotel, de-
signed inside and out by the painter
Ernst Fuchs, all rooms are decorated
according to the signs of the zodiac.

✳ Seefeld in Tirol

F 5

Province: Tyrol
Population: 3050

Elevation: 1185m/3888ft

**The climatic spa of Seefeld, where the Nordic ski competitions
were held during the Winter Olympics in Innsbruck (1964 and
1976), offers an extensive winter sports area and is one of the
most visited towns in Tyrol.**

Seefeld is situated between Mittenwald and ►Innsbruck, in the broad
pastures of the Seefelder Sattel. The old mountain farming village
has been a destination for pilgrimages ever since the **communion wafer miracle in the Late Middle Ages**: during holy communion on
Maundy Thursday in 1384, the autocratic knight Oswald Milser
threateningly demanded that, instead of the small consecrated wafer
(»for the normal people«), he receive the big one, which was originally reserved for the priest. As the bread touched the lips of the less
than god-fearing man, he sunk into the ground up to his knees. The
floor only became solid again when the sinner was relieved of the
wafer, which showed traces of blood. Converted, the knight retreated
to a monastery.

**Pilgrimage and
winter sports**

What to See in Seefeld

In the centre of the town, which stretches far across the valley, stands
the parish church (15th century). The communion wafer miracle is
portrayed on the late Gothic southern doorway. The inside is decorated with frescoes and sculptures. The Gothic baptismal font with a

Pfarrkirche

▶ VISITING SEEFELD IN TIROL

INFORMATION

Informationsbüro Seefeld
Klosterstrasse 43
A-6100 Seefeld in Tirol
Tel. 052 12/50 88 00, fax 508 80 51
www.seefeld.com

WHERE TO EAT

▶ Moderate

Tiroler Weinstube
Dorfplatz 130
A-6100 Seefeld in Tyrol
Tel. 052 12/222 08
Diners enjoy delicious Tyrolese delicacies and good wines in comfortably furnished surroundings.

WHERE TO STAY

▶ Luxury

Klosterbräu
A-6100 Seefeld in Tirol
Tel. 052 12/2 62 10
Fax 38 85
www.klosterbraeu.com
The »Klosterbräu« is a five-star hotel in Seefeld's pedestrian area. People meet here during the day for some winter sports fun on the Olympic ski-runs and later on at the disco.

▶ Mid-range

Hotel Inntalerhof
A-6100 Seefeld-Mösern
Tel. 0 52 12/47 47
Fax 47 47 47
www.inntalerhof.com
Situated high above the Inntal valley, this hotel offers a magnificent view and excellent wellness facilities. Nearby is an Olympic ski-run network and a golf course.

Renaissance wooden cover, the relief of the Pentecost miracle and the pulpit also deserve attention. Further southwest stands the emblem of Seefeld, the wonderfully situated Baroque Seekirchl (»lake church«), a round building from 1628. At the southern end of the small town lies the small, wild lake with a very nice lido (two heatable basins).

Around Seefeld

Mösern About 4km/2.5mi southwest of Seefeld by way of a very pleasant footpath lies the quiet hamlet of Mösern (1250m/4101ft; pop. 100), situated in a prime location high above the Inntal valley with an extensive view of the mountains. Surrounded by flowery pastureland and larch trees, the village holds the distinction of having the most sunshine in Tyrol, and is well-suited for those seeking rest and recuperation or hiking holidays.

Leutaschtal The Leutaschtal valley extends northwest from Seefeld, reaching between the Wetterstein range and the Mieminger range northeastwards to the border with Germany, and is one of the most beautiful mountain valleys of Northern Tyrol.

Seefeld's emblem is the Baroque Seekirchl

✶ Semmering

Provinces: Lower Austria and Styria
Population: 620

Elevation: 985–1291m/3231–4236ft

Rugged cliffs, broad ridges and wide valleys characterize this romantic landscape with numerous passes, which was considered wild and inaccessible during the Early Middle Ages.

The first bridleway was established over the pass dividing the Viennese Basin and the Mürztal valley only in 1160. From 1854 on, with the construction of the Semmeringbahn railway, the first summer holidaymakers made their way up to Semmering, which boomed as a **summer retreat for the Viennese**. For a while it was somewhat forgotten, but today, with the enlargement of the Hirschenkogel ski area, extensive hiking trails and a variety of cultural events, Semmering has regained its reputation as a worthwhile holiday destination.

Settlement and pass

 Baedeker TIP

Railway trail

A hiking trail runs alongside the railway. The starting point of the 23km/14mi-long tour, which requires a good level of fitness, is the station at Semmering. The highlight is the marvellous panoramic view from the observation tower at the Doppelreiterkogel.

The 41km/25mi-long Semmeringbahn between Gloggnitz and Mürzzuschlag was designed by the railway engineer Carl Ritter von Ghega (1802–60). Following six years of construction, it was opened in 1854 as the first mountain railway in Europe. At the time, at an elevation of 895m/2936ft, the station in Semmering was the highest

✶✶
World Cultural Heritage: the Semmeringbahn

That's how it all started: the nostalgic skiing group Traisen

SKI COUNTRY

Although skis were not invented in Austria, the country's ingenious technicians and tinkerers provided the prerequisites for alpine skiing. With its stars, tragedies, scandals and medals the alpine republic proves to the world time and again that it is a »ski country«.

4500 to 5000-year-old petrographs of a skier discovered in the north of Norway and a ski found in a bog near Hoting in Sweden suggest that skis probably came into existence at the same time as the first Egyptian pyramids. Whether this faster means of transportation was first used for snow or bogs is unknown. In any case, skiing as a sport developed in Norway: the first ever documented race was held in Tromsö in 1843, and in 1877 Norwegians founded the world's first skiing club.

Ingenious skiing pioneers

The first impetus came from Austria and was given by Toni Schruf and Max Kleinoschegg from Mürzzuschlag: the two Styrians had skis delivered from Norway and organized the first central European skiing competition in the region around Semmering in 1893. Competitive skiing quickly spread all over Austria. Franz Reisch became Tyrol's »skiing pioneer« when in 1893 he was the first to climb a mountain on skis, and laid the foundation for Kitzbühel to become a world-famous skiing resort. But it is ►Lilienfeld's **Mathias Zdarsky** from Moravia who is the ultimate father of skiing. He considered the almost 3m/10ft long skis unsuitable for skiing in steep alpine terrain and shortened them to 1.80m/5.9ft. He also invented the fixed metal binding for better support on the sides, and wrote a book, *Techniques for Alpine Skiing*. He is the one who laid the foundations for the sport of alpine skiing. He planted flags for the first slalom course in Lilienfeld in 1905, at a time when slalom was still judged in terms of style rather than time. There is a museum dedicated to him in Lilienfeld.

The cradle of skiing

Zdarsky's stem-turn technique was further refined by Georg Bilgeri, who introduced the use of ski sticks. Later, Viktor Sohm from Bregenz organized the first skiing courses in Stuben and Zürs (Arlberg); **Hannes Schneider** from Stuben, founder of the St Anton Skiing School, invented the world-famous »Arlberg Technique« and triggered a skiing boom in Japan in particular. Sepp Bildstein invented the first ski binding and played a part in building the first Austrian ski lift in Zürs.

In 1928, the first international **Arlberg-Kandahar race** (named after cup sponsor Frederick Leigh Earl Robert of Kandahar) took place on the Arlberg, involving the two disciplines of slalom and downhill. The downhill race, regarded by many as the actual moment that alpine ski racing was born, was won by Benno Leubner of Austria. He had learnt alpine skiing when he played in the first major skiing film, 1927's *The Great Leap* by Arnold Franck.

Stars, scandals and tragedies

Toni Sailer from Kitzbühel caused a major sensation at the Winter Olympics of 1956 in Cortina d'Ampezzo in Italy: at the age of 20 he was the first person to ever win gold in all three alpine contests (giant slalom, slalom and downhill). His gold medals may have been even more significant for Austria in creating a national post-war identity than the 1954 World Cup victory in Bern was for Germany. »We found new courage,« said the »Blitz from Kitz« 45 years later. However,

What would the snow-rich alpine republic be without skis?

the Winter Games of 1972 in Sapporo in Japan were disastrous for Austria: downhill champion Karl Schranz was banned from the games after being accused of self-marketing and violating amateur rules; and the clear favourite **Annemarie Pröll** was beaten by newcomer Marie-Theres Nadig from Switzerland in the downhill

The numerous skiing resorts offer countless pistes for beginners and advanced skiers

and giant slalom competitions. Annemarie Pröll later became the most successful skier of all time – though she still hadn't won Olympic gold. This all changed in Lake Placid in 1980 when Pröll finally beat Nadig and won gold in the downhill race. Millions of TV viewers witnessed Austria's worst skiing tragedy when on 29 January 1994 26-year Ulrike Maier (Super G world champion in 1989) was killed in an accident at a downhill race in Garmisch. Her death on the piste is not the only one, but of skiing's 16 victims she was the first woman to die. Another »woman« caused a very different stir: Erika Schinegger from Carinthia surprised the world when she became world champion in the women's downhill race in Portillo in Bolivia in 1966. From the moment of her victory, however, rumours about her gender would not be silenced. Finally, in 1968 she had to undergo a gender test – it turned out that Erika was a man and she didn't even know herself! Her, or rather his sexual organs had grown into his stomach. After lengthy operations Erika became Erik, and his world championship title was disallowed. He now runs a skiing school in Carinthia.

Tu felix Austria

Many Austrians define their home country above all as a land of skiing. And the country's success confirms this: having won 78 alpine World Championship titles in 70 years, Austrian ski aces were frequently seen on the **winner's rostrum** at the World Ski Championships in Åre in Sweden in 2007. With a total of 9 medals (including 3 golds), the Austrian skiers left the others far behind.

point in the world accessible by rail. The train goes over the pass through 14 tunnels and across 16 sometimes two-storey arched viaducts above deep chasms. This masterful feat of technology afforded Austria a fast connection from Vienna to Italy and access to the harbour of Trieste, which was welcomed by military strategists. In 1998, UNESCO declared the Semmeringbahn and the surrounding landscape a World Cultural Heritage site.

Chairlifts lead from Semmering Pass up to the Hirschenkogel (1324m/4343ft), the site of a world cup ski run, and from Maria Schutz to the Sonnwendstein (1523m/4996ft; mountain station 1481m/4859ft). From here there is a great circular view of the Rax and the Schneeberg, the alpine foreland and the low-lying Semmeringbahn.

Hirschenkogel
◄ **Sonnwendstein**

Gloggnitz (442m/1450ft; pop. 6300), the northern starting point of the Semmeringbahn and the Passstrasse, is a convenient base for tours into the area around the Raxalpe and the Wechsel, a timbered mountain range on the border between Lower Austria and the Styria. Schloss Gloggnitz, once a Benedictine abbey, has made a name for itself as a **wedding castle**.

Gloggnitz

Two famous citizens of Gloggnitz also helped shape the later history of Austria: Dr. Michael Hainisch, the first Federal President of the first Federal Republic (1920–28), and Dr. Karl Renner, the first chancellor and federal president of the second republic of Austria (1945–50), were both born here. From 1910 on, the latter owned a villa in the village, which nowadays houses a **museum** commemorating him, as well as the history of the past century (Rennergasse 2; opening times: early March– late Nov Fri–Sun 9am–5pm).

SEMMERING

INFORMATION
Tourismusbüro Semmering
Passhöhe 248, A-2680 Semmering
Tel. 026 64/200 25, fax 200 29
www.semmering.or.at

Southeast of Gloggnitz, shortly before Kirchberg am Wechsel, is the Hermannshöhle, a more than 4km/2.5mi-long dripstone cave with wonderful rock formations (opening times: Easter and May–Sept daily, April and Oct Sat and Sun 9am–5pm; guided tours 9.30am, 11am, 1.30pm, 3pm and 4.30pm).

Hermannshöhle

Mürzzuschlag (672m/2204ft; pop. 10,000) is the lively principal town of the Mürztal valley and a popular holiday destination both in summer and winter. As early as 1884 and 1885, Johannes Brahms stayed here during summer and composed his 4th symphony. The Brahms Museum offers interesting insights into his life and work (Wiener Strasse 4; opening times: May–Sept daily 10am–noon and 2pm–5pm, Oct–April Thu–Sun 10am–noon and 2pm–4pm).

Mürzzuschlag

It is worth paying a visit to the Wintersportmuseum, featuring the **world's most extensive documentation of winter sports**, particularly of alpine skiing – as it happens the first ever official ski race was held in Mürzzuschlag in 1893 (Wiener Strasse 79; opening times: Wed–Sun 9am–noon and 2pm–5pm).

Neuberg About 10km/6mi higher up the Mürztal valley – at the foot of the Schneealpe (1904m/6246ft) – lies the town of Neuberg (732m/2401ft). Of interest here is the former Cistercian abbey, whose 14th–15th century church holds the famous Neuberg Madonna (14th century).

Krieglach Krieglach (612 m/2007ft; pop. 5200), situated southwest of Mürzzuschlag, is where the socio-critical popular poet **Peter Rosegger** (1843–1918) lived from 1877 on. He is buried at the southwest corner of the old graveyard, and the country house now functions as a museum (Roseggerstrasse 44; opening times: April–Oct Tue–Sun 10am–noon and 2pm–4pm).

Alpl ► Alpl (1100m/3608ft), Rosegger's »forest retreat« southeast of Krieglach, is well worth a visit. The »Waldschule«, a hedge-school founded by Rosegger in 1902 with the intention of providing an education for local children and discouraging migration, is also here (Erinnerungsraum and Österreichisches Wandermuseum (Austrian Hiking Museum); Alpl 2; opening times: April–Oct Tue–Sun 9am–5pm). From there it takes 30 minutes – on foot only – to Unteren Kluppeneggerhof, **Rosegger's place of birth** (Alpl 14; opening times: April–Oct Tue–Sun 9am–5pm, otherwise Tue–Sun 11am–4pm).

★ Silvretta Road

C/D 6

Provinces: Vorarlberg and Tyrol

Until tourists discovered the Silvretta Road, its original purpose was to provide access to the construction sites of dams and power stations. It was completed in 1953.

Winding alpine road The Silvretta-Hochalpenstrasse is a toll road that consists of a total of 32 hairpin bends over 23km/14mi. It is considered to be a great challenge by professional cyclists and can be used only in summertime. It leads from Partenen to Galtür, so connecting ► Montafon with the Paznauntal valley.

The pass is the border between the provinces of Vorarlberg and Tyrol. From various vista points, which have large car parks, the glaciated peaks of the Silvretta range on the Swiss border seem tangibly close.

Route of the Silvretta Road

9km/5.6mi past Partenen along the Silvretta High Alpine Road lies **Vermunt reservoir** the Vermunt reservoir (1743m/5718ft; power station) with its 50m/164ft-high and 273m/895ft-long dam. About 5km/3.1mi beyond the reservoir, beneath the huge dam of the Silvrettasee, is the access road to the Madlenerhaus (1986m/6515ft; accommodation) on the right. It is an ideal starting point for mountain treks into the Silvretta mountains – advisable only for expert mountaineers or with a guide. From here, it takes six hours to reach the Grosslitzner (3111m/10,206ft), the most dramatic and difficult peak of the Silvretta range.

> **? DID YOU KNOW ...?**
>
> ■ The roadway from the Bielerhöhe to Galtür was more or less developed by accident after the Second World War: a large excavator was left standing as a relic from the time when the big dam was built. Rather than disassembling it for removal, it was decided that the excavator should dig its way along the future Silvretta Road to Galtür.

The Bielerhöhe, at 2032m/6666ft, is the highest point along the route and functions as the watershed between the Rhine and the Danube. It lies on the border separating the provinces of Vorarlberg and Tyrol. The Silvrettasee at the foot of the Piz Buin (3312m/10,866ft) contains 38.6 million cubic m/8490 million gal of water, is 2.5km/1.5mi long and 0.75km/0.4mi wide. The dam wall is 80m/262ft high, 52m/170ft wide and 430m/1410ft long. A motorboat trip around **Europe's highest-lying reservoir** is a unique experience. The walk around the lake takes about two hours.

★ **Bielerhöhe and Silvretta reservoir**

Now the road leads to the Klein-Vermunttal valley, which is surrounded by good skiing areas, before heading steadily downwards into the Paznauntal valley toward Galtür.

◄ Klein-Vermunttal

★ Spittal an der Drau

K 6

Province: Carinthia
Population: 16,000

Elevation: 556m/1824ft

Spittal (pronounced with a long »a«) was always of great strategic importance: located at the intersection of the Tauern route from north to south and the Drautal route from west to east, the town has evolved into the economic and intellectual centre of upper Carinthia over the last centuries.

The town is situated west of the ►Millstätter See at the opening of the Liesertal valley into the Drautal valley. In 1191, the counts of Ortenburg founded a chapel and a hospice or »Spitel« here, a respite for pilgrims and travellers – hence the name of the town. Spittal was

★ **The intersection of two trade routes**

Spittal Map

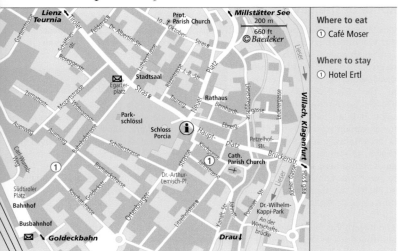

Where to eat
① Café Moser

Where to stay
① Hotel Ertl

burned down by the Turks in 1478, an act which did not succeed in discouraging its robust citizens.

What to See in Spittal an der Drau

Hauptplatz and Neuer Platz

Old town houses stand on the elongated Hauptplatz (main square), among them the Fuggerhaus, with a beautiful arcaded courtyard, the Burgstaller Erkerhaus and the Apothekerhaus (apothecary's house) with an Empire façade. Today the former palace of the Khevenhüllers functions as the Rathaus (town hall).

★ Schloss Porcia

Schloss Porcia (or Schloss Salamanca), in art-historical terms the most interesting building in Spittal, is found at Burgplatz. The palace was built in the Florentine style by the Spanish Count Gabriel Salamanca beginning in 1527, and is considered to be **Austria's most beautiful Italian Renaissance-style building**. However, its name comes from the Friulian noble family who resided here from 1662 until 1918. The doorway, framed by columns, has a Baroque attachment displaying the emblem of Porcia – gold lilies on a blue background – surrounded by foliage and allegorical figures. The three-storey arcaded courtyard, decorated with fantastic figures and medallion reliefs, is especially magnificent; during summer it is an ideal venue for »Komödienspiele«, or comical plays. The arcaded courtyard and palace gardens are accessible free of charge.

Museum für Volkskultur ►

The extraordinarily elaborate Museum für Volkskultur on the upper floors offers a detailed view of the history of everyday life in Carin-

▶ VISITING SPITTAL AN DER DRAU

INFORMATION

Stadtgemeinde Spittal an der Drau
Burgplatz 5
A-9800 Spittal an der Drau
Tel. 047 62/565 00
Fax 56 50 156
www.spittal-drau.at

WHERE TO EAT

▶ **Inexpensive**
① *Café Moser*
Jahnstr. 7
A-9800 Spittal an der Drau
Tel. 047 62/257 90

A large, beautiful garden for guests, 40 different cakes and gateaux and 30 daily and weekly newspapers.

WHERE TO STAY

▶ **Budget**
① *Hotel Ertl*
Bahnhofstrasse 26
A-9800 Spittal an der Drau
Tel. 047 62/204 80, fax 204 85
www.hotel-ertl.at
Good food and welcoming, newly designed rooms with all modern amenities.

thia (open early May–Oct daily 9am–6pm, otherwise Mon–Thu 1pm–4pm).
The Porcia gallery is housed it the Salamanca or West Cellar (open Mon–Fri 10am–1pm and 4pm–6pm, Sat, Sun and holidays 10am– noon).

◀ Galerie Porcia

Around Spittal an der Drau

On a wooded hill about 4km/2.4mi northwest of Spittal, on the road to the Mölltal, lies the village of St Peter in Holz (590m/1935ft). Hallstatt-period excavations attest to the settlement of the hill as early as the 6th century BC. The Celts followed in the 3rd century BC, naming their settlement »Teurnia«, which the Romans adapted to »Tiburnia«. Around 600, the settlement was destroyed by the Slavs. Teurnia was built on the southeastern side of the hill, on terraces of different levels (Obere Wohnterrasse and Untere Wohnterrasse). Excavations have revealed the forum and remains of the town walls and housing foundations. At the end of the forum stood the thermal baths. Teurnia was also the seat of a bishop: at the western offshoot of the plateau of the Holzer Berg a bishop's church and a guest house (hospitium) was found. Higher up, a large house (4th century) was excavated, which now functions as an **open-air museum**. The remains of the floor heating are also interesting.
The **Museum Teurnia** at the foot of the hill documents excavation discoveries, including Roman stones with reliefs and inscriptions, the remains of a pedestal painting (2nd century) with lance ornaments and rosettes, as well as coins (opening times: May–mid-Oct Tue–Sun 9am–5pm).

St Peter in Holz (Teurnia)

Cemetery church ▶ Very close to the museum, an early Christian cemetery church (Friedhofskirche) was discovered. The chapel its southern side holds an **especially beautiful, well-preserved floor mosaic** (c500): Christian symbols originating from the animal symbols of antiquity are portrayed in round or square fields, e.g. a rabbit, a bull and a deer, as well as a cup showing a pigeon and a snake, and birds in a tree.

✳ Steirisches Thermenland

Q 5

Province: Styria

The Styrian thermal region is composed of idyllic wine-growing country and river landscapes, with gently rolling hills and a mild climate. With a chain of thermal springs lined up like pearls on a string for about 60km/37mi, it reaches from Bad Waltersdorf in the north of East Styria to Bad Radkersburg at the border with Slovenia.

»Styrian Tuscany« This wine-growing region, also referred to as the »Styrian Tuscany«, boasts five well-known thermal spas that offer warm springs, numerous wellness and sport programmes, and distinctive cultural variety in the surrounding areas. Known only to insiders until a few years ago, the rising number of visitors shows that increasingly more people are taking pleasure in the healthy relaxation to be found within this beautiful landscape.

Bad Waltersdorf Bad Waltersdorf (290m/951ft; pop. 2000), about 65km/40mi east of Graz, is the northernmost of the **five thermal spas**. The healing

▶ VISITING STEIRISCHES THERMENLAND

INFORMATION
Steirisches Thermenland
Radersdorf 75
A-8263 Grosswilfersdorf
Tel. 033 85/660 40, fax 66 04 20
www.thermenland.at

WHERE TO EAT
▶ Expensive
Gasthof Fink
A-8333 Riegersburg 27/29
Tel. 031 53/82 160
The award-winning restaurant at the foot of Riegersburg castle serves exquisite Styrian and international delicacies. The Riegersburger Turmschinken is highly recommended.

WHERE TO STAY
▶ Luxury
Rogner-Bad Blumau Hotel
A-8283 Blumau 100
Tel. 0 33 83/51 000, fax 51 00 808
www.blumau.com
Those wishing not merely to see Hundertwasser architecture, but to actually live in it, should reserve a room here.

waters here include several thermal baths, with temperatures ranging between 30–36 °C/86–97 °F, sauna facilities and a diversity of therapeutic possibilities, e.g. a Native American medicine wheel. A stay provides suitable treatment for complaints of the musculoskeletal system and respiratory ailments, as well as offering general recuperation. Of course, there is plenty of opportunity to take part in wellness and beauty treatments, health education and sporting activities.

Just a few miles southeast of Bad Waltersdorf, a very special thermal bath attracts guests from near and far: close to the town of Bad Blumau lies a unique spa and leisure landscape with hotel, facilities for sports and special offers for children. The cheerful and colourful design is by Friedensreich Hundertwasser (► Baedeker Special p.535) – and therefore the Blumau Therme is deservedly called **the largest inhabitable work of art**. »Free forms, fluid contours and all the colours of the rainbow« reads an apt description of the construction, which is also open for day visitors, and is particularly recommended for those with skin conditions, back problems and rheumatic pains.

★ **Rogner-Bad Blumau**

Continuing southwest from Bad Blumau via Fürstenfeld, about 10km/6mi down the road lies the thermal spa of **Bad Loipersdorf** (250–350m/820–1148ft; pop. 1300), with fun pool facilities and a modern congress centre. Aimed at both the entrepreneur and the enterprising family, it's all here – for a day trip or a longer stay. Alongside multimedia water-slides, underwater music, a baby beach and other amusements, there is a selection of beauty and wellness offers. The thermal waters help relieve joint and spinal pains, circulatory disorders and exhaustion.

Only a steep and rocky footpath leads up to the Riegersburg

Those who need a break from the water can head 20km/12mi west of Bad Loipersdorf to the friendly town of Riegersburg, which is mainly known for its mighty castle complex.
Enthroned upon high basalt cliffs above the town Riegersburg is what has often been called the **mightiest castle of Christianity**. First mentioned in the 12th century, two defensive fortifications were built beginning in the 13th century. In the 16th and 17th centuries, the main castle was expanded as a fortification against the Turks. Since 1822, the largest castle complex in Styria has been owned by the

Riegersburg

★
◄ Castle complex

! *Baedeker* TIP

The chocolate factory

During the »ChocoMania« tour through Josef Zotter's chocolate factory in Riegersburg, visitors can immerse themselves in the sweet realm of the food of the gods and learn a few interesting facts about chocolate making in the process (Bergl 56; guided tours: Mon–Sat 8am–5pm; www.zotter.at).

princes of Liechtenstein, who arranged for its reconstruction.

It is a 15-minute climb from the south along a very steep cliff path, defended by seven gates and numerous bastions, up to the castle – no other access exists. The Wenzelstor gate is part of the outer bailey with a trench and drawbridge, stack and powder tower. The steep donkey track, carved into the stone, begins here, the means by which the castle was supplied with food in time of need. The actual castle encloses two courtyards surrounded by arcades. Lovely doorways, paintings and a wooden ceiling decorate the Rittersaal (Knights' Hall). The Fürstenzimmer (Prince's Room) and the Baroque Weisse Saal (White Hall) are also worth seeing (opening times: April–Oct daily 9am–5pm).

Hexenmuseum ▶ The Witchcraft Museum in the castle documents one of the darkest chapters of European history, with special emphasis on Styria, where 300 people accused of witchcraft, mostly women, were executed between 1546 and 1746 (opening times: May–Sept daily 9am–5pm, March, April and Oct daily from 10am).

Bird of prey station ▶ The Riegersburg's bird of prey station features eagles, vultures, hawks, red kites and eagle owls (flight demonstrations Mon–Sat 11am and 3pm, Sun and holidays 11am, 2pm and 4pm).

Gsellmanns Weltmaschine A sense for the abstruse is helpful when making a trip to Edelsbach, slightly southwest of Riegersburg, home of »Gsellmanns Weltmaschine«. The »world machine«, put together by the farmer Franz Gsellmann, is quite indescribable. Inspired by the Brussels Atomium (!), it is made of gears, blowers, tubes, food processors, holy figures, flashing blue lights, music boxes and many other things. It took about 20 years to create this fascinating, utterly useless, and delightful object (opening times: Wed–Mon 9am–6pm).

Bad Gleichenberg The oldest of Styria's thermal spa communities, Bad Gleichenberg (300m/984ft; pop. 2200), located 20km/12mi south of Riegersburg, promotes itself and its thermal springs with the sonorous sobriquet **»Oasis of Calm«**. There is a good reason why many renowned training schools for the tourist sector can be found here. The thermal waters, with a high mineral content, are taken both internally and externally by those with skin, heart and circulation diseases, respiratory problems and illnesses of the muscoloskeletal system and bones.

Styrassic Park ▶ In prehistoric times our planet was populated by huge animals. Life-size reproductions await the visitor to the Dinoplatz: Styrassic Park – home to more than 70 dinosaur figures (opening times: daily 9am–5pm).

Bad Radkersburg (210m/689ft; pop. 1900), situated in the outermost southeast of Styria, did an exemplary job renovating its town centre in recent years. The delightful Old Town possesses an almost **Mediterranean flair**. The spring water is suitable for the relief of joint and spinal diseases, intervertebral disk problems or rheumatism. The small border town has a lot to offer, too: it is an ideal base for a day-trip to Slovenia on foot – a simple walk across the bridge over the Mur river is all it takes.

✳ **Bad Radkersburg**

✳ Steyr

M 3

Province: Upper Austria
Population: 39,500

Elevation: 311m/1020ft

Steyr was already a famous iron working metropolis during the Middle Ages, and to this day is the seat of important industrial firms such as BMW, MAN, SKF or Steyr-Mannlicher. In the meantime Steyr, with its picturesque Old Town centre, has made itself known as the »Christkindlstadt« with its Christmas market.

At the place where the Steyr flows into the Enns river, the Otakars, margraves and later dukes of Styria built the Styraburg castle in 980, on the site of the today's Schloss Lamberg. In the period that fol-

History

Journey to medieval times: the Old Town of Steyr between the Steyr and Ems rivers

lowed, a settlement was formed in the surroundings of the castle and the parish church. In 1287, it was granted its municipal charter. The Enns was used to transport iron made from Styrian ore here; the water power of the Steyr was use for machining. Since the 14th century, Steyr has been a centre of the arms industry. When a certain Josef Werndl (1831–89) constructed the breech-loader gun, its serial production led to Steyr becoming the **armoury of Europe**. Steyr-Daimler-Puch AG (drive and automotive engineering) and Steyr-Mannlicher are descendents of Werndl's company, the Steyr-Werke.
Flood waters are not unusual in Steyr, but are rarely so extreme as in August 2002, when the entire Old Town was submersed. The damage cost millions.

What to See in Steyr

The beautiful Old Town, situated on a spit of land between the Enns and the Steyr, testifies to the wealth of the town. Especially worth noting are the noble town houses from the Gothic, Renaissance, Baroque and Rococo periods around the Stadtplatz (town square). The Rathaus (town hall; 1765–78) features a beautiful Rococo façade; the Bummerlhaus opposite (the oldest parts date from the 13th century) was even home to Maximilian I (► Famous People). The Baroque Sieben-Sterne-Haus, the splendid Meditzhaus and other similarly richly decorated buildings form an impressive ensemble.

 VISITING STEYR

INFORMATION
Tourismusverband Steyr
Stadtplatz 27, A-4400 Steyr
Tel. 0 72 52/53 22 90, fax 5 32 29 15
www.steyr.info

WHERE TO EAT
► **Moderate**
① **Bräuhof**
Stadtplatz 35, A-4400 Steyr
Tel. 072 52/42 000
Visitors sit just as comfortably in the 300-year-old vaulted cellar as they do in the »Schanigarten« (restaurant garden); rich choice of fish.

WHERE TO STAY
► **Mid-range**
① **Stadthotel Styria**
Stadtplatz 40–42, A-4400 Steyr
Tel. 0 72 52/5 15 51, Fax 5 15 51 51
www.styriahotel.at
This hotel in a historical building is located in the centre of Steyr's Old Town. It offers comfortable rooms, empire suites, a VIP-guesthouse, a hotel bar, a Gothic conference room and restaurants in the hotel passage.

► **Budget**
② **Gasthof Mayr**
Pfarrplatz 3, A-4400 Steyr
Tel. 0 72 52/5 20 91, fax 5 20 91 53
The long-established guesthouse has been in the family since 1409. The rooms are equipped with a telephone and a TV. A spacious event hall and a shady garden are available to guests.

Pfarrgasse leads to Brucknerplatz and the Gothic town parish church, the **Stadtpfarrkirche** (15th–17th century), built by the cathedral masonic lodge of Vienna. Anton Bruckner was often a guest at the Mesnerhaus.

After a town fire, the castle at the northern end of the Old Town was reconverted in 1727–31 into an imposing **palace**, according to plans by the master builder Johann Michael Prunner from Linz. The castle's moat can be crossed via a pretty arcade bridge.

North of the Steyr stands the parish church, Pfarrkirche St Michael (1635–77), built by the Jesuits as a sign of the Counter-Reformation, with mighty towers and a remarkable gable fresco. Opposite, there is a special surprise: the **Christkindlwelt** with the **Weihnachtsmuseum**. On display are Christmas decorations and an »Engerl-Werkstatt« (»angel workshop«). Board the »Erlebnisbahn« (»experience railway«) to be taken on a journey through Christmas traditions from all over the world (opening times: late Nov to 6 Jan daily 10am–5pm).

Take a stroll through the streets and alleys to the west, too: on Kirchengasse (no. 16), the picturesque Dunklhof (16th century) with its beautiful arcaded aisle is remarkable (summer concerts); on Sierninger Strasse (no. 1) stands the Lebzelterhaus, today a bakery and café (façade from 1567). The Schnallentor gate on Gleinker Gasse features rich sgraffito decoration.

Steyr Map

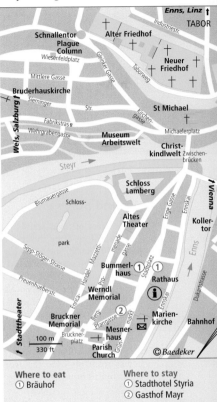

Where to eat
① Bräuhof

Where to stay
① Stadthotel Styria
② Gasthof Mayr

Don't miss a visit to the Museum Arbeitswelt (Wehrgrabengasse 7), housed in a former knife factory in the historic fortification trench. Changing exhibits show developments since the beginning of industrialization and their consequences on the life, work and culture of the population, from robotics to Catholic social teachings (opening times: early March to mid-Dec Tue–Sun 9am–5pm).

Museum Arbeitswelt

Christmas cards from Christkindl

Around Steyr

Wallfahrtskirche Christkindl

✳ To the west of Steyr stands the pilgrimage church, Wallfahrtskirche Christkindl, built by the Baroque architects Carlone and Prandtauer from 1702. It has the following history: the 17th-century tower keeper and bandmaster Ferdinand Sertl, who suffered from epilepsy, exhibited a little figure of Christ made out of wax in a spruce concavity and prayed before it daily – and recovered from his illness. This wax figure is still on view at the high altar today.

At Christmas time, an antique shuttle bus runs between the Christmas post office in Christkindl and town square in Steyr. The Christmas post office is open each year from the beginning of advent until Epiphany (6 January), and meanwhile adorns more than two million letters from all over the world with a special postmark and the Christmas stamp.

Seitenstetten

Founded in 1112, the **Benedictine abbey** of Seitenstetten, about 16km/10mi east of Steyr, can take pride in a unique collection of about 80 works by Kremser Schmidt. The abbey church, which has been adorned with Baroque stylings and stucco work, is nearly overshadowed by the marvellous abbey staircase with its ceiling fresco by Altomonte. The ceiling fresco by Troger in the marble hall also exhibits a fascinating lightness (guided tours of the abbey: Easter Monday–Oct daily 10am and 3pm, groups by arrangement, tel. 074 77 / 42 30 02 33; www.stift-seitenstetten.at).

Waidhofen a. d. Ybbs

Further southeast, in the picturesque Ybbs valley lies Waidhofen (469m/1538ft; pop. 12,000), the **»town of towers in the heart of the iron road«**. There are various exhibitions in the Stadtturm, Ybbsturm and Schlossturm towers, such as »Stadt und Recht« (»Town and Law«), as well as those in the »5-Elemente-Museum« (opening times: Tue–Sun 10am–6pm).

Stodertal

Province: Upper Austria

The seclusion of the Stodertal lends this high-lying valley its down-to-earth character. Nevertheless, tourism is well-developed here and, with eleven peaks of 2000m/6560ft or more contributing to the scenery, there are plenty of opportunities for sport enthusiasts.

The Stodertal valley, east of the Toten moutains, is the westernmost part of the Pyhrn-Eisenwurzen region, which includes the Ennstal valley, the Steyrtal valley and the Pyhrn region. The Warscheneckgruppe range (up to 2389m/7837ft) in the southeast and the Hutterer Höss (1831m/6007ft) offer good conditions for hikers and skiing enthusiasts, and since 1986 world cup ski runs have been organized at the Bärenalm. It takes seven hours to climb the 2515m/8251ft-high Grossen Priel of the Toten mountains from Hinterstoder.

Hiking and skiing area

STODERTAL

INFORMATION
Pyhrn-Priel Tourismus
Hauptstr. 28, A-4580 Windischgarsten
Tel. 075 62/526 60, fax 52 66 10
www.pyhrn-priel.net

What to See in and around the Stodertal

Hinterstoder (585m/1919ft; pop. 1100), the principal town of the valley, is the **centre of the Pyhrn-Priel holiday region** . With its modern exhibitions, the Alpineum imparts information about the development of winter sports and the settling of the Alps under the motto »Flötzer, Firn und steiler Fels« (roughly translated as rafts, snow and steep cliff) (Hinterstoder 38; opening times: May–Oct Tue–Sun 9am–5pm, between Christmas and Easter Tue–Fri 2pm–5pm). A beautiful hike on the Flötzersteig leads to the Strumboding waterfall, the mountain cave Kreidelucke and the beautifully situated Schiederweiher lake.

Hinterstoder

From **Windischgarsten** (600m/1968ft; pop. 2300), a climatic spa and winter sports centre south of the Sengsengebirge, the climb up to Warscheneck (2389m/7837ft) takes about five hours. A chairlift leads up to the Wurbauerkogl (859m/2818ft).

Baedeker TIP

A-hunting we will go...
St Pankraz, at the foot of the Sengsengebirge mountains, is home to a curious museum: the only museum in Europe dedicated to poaching. Visitors here learn about poaching and its background, and the marksmen among them get a chance to test their accuracy at the shooting stand (opening times: March and April Tue–Sun 10am–4pm, May–Oct daily 9am–6pm).

In 1997 the area around the Sengsengebirge and the Reichraminger Hintergebirge to the north and east of Windischgarsten was declared a national park. The highest peak in the Nationalpark Kalkalpen is the Hohe Nock (1963m/6440ft). With the motto »experience, explore, understand and protect nature«, the idea of attracting guests seeking relaxation while preserving the diversity of flora and fauna has proved rather successful. North of the park, in Molln, the national park centre offers information about the species that live here, as well as covering the theme of water and its essential importance to the Limestone Alps (opening times: April–Oct daily 9am–5pm, Nov–March Mon–Thu 7.30am–5pm, Fri from 1pm).

Nationalpark Kalkalpen

✳ Stubaital · Stubai Alps

F 5

Province: Tyrol

The Ruetzbach flows through the scenic Stubaital valley, bordered by steep hillsides and rocky mountain tops. Near Schönberg it branches off, leaving Brennerstrasse and heading southwest into the highly glaciated Stubai Alps.

Popular destination

»The area is well-suited for summer breaks, hikes and half-day trips, as well as for tourists for whom the earth's surface only becomes interesting at 3000m above sea level,« said Erich Kästner, who lived here for a while in 1945. The towns of the Stubai valley are also popular with those keen on winter sports. The Stubaier glacier offers **skiing all year round**.

What to See in and around the Stubaital

Mieders

The principal town of the Stubaital valley is Mieders (982m/3221ft; pop. 1500), a picturesque village that became a popular resort town in the 19th century thanks to its mineral baths. The wooden swimming pool from 1927 is, along with the baths of Telfs and St Johann, the oldest still in existence in all of Tyrol.

! *Baedeker* TIP

A different kind of tram

Between Fulpmes and the Wilten Basilica in Innsbruck, rolling through the impressive mountain scenery of the glaciated Stubai Alps, is the Stubaitalbahn narrow-gauge railway (total length: 18km/11mi). In addition to the »normal« alpine tram, a nostalgic tram operates during the summer months.

Fulpmes (960m/3149ft; pop. 3900), a famous climatic spa and ski resort as well as the main town of the valley, is found amidst high mountain chains, and is the final station of the Stubaital narrow-gauge railway. It is home to an important small-scale iron industry, which developed from mining in the Middle Ages. Its ice picks and climbing irons, as well as tools such as knives and especially the herb plane for the kitchen, were known far beyond the borders of the valley.

With machines and tools from the 19th century, the Schmiedemuseum (Blacksmith Museum) in the Riedlhaus on Fachschulgasse informs its visitors about the blacksmithing industry of the Stubaital valley (opening times: in summer Wed 2pm–5pm). The parish church, from 1747, is decorated with charming Rococo plastering.

Telfes

About 2km/1.2mi above the small town lies Telfes (1002m/3287ft), which was documented as early as 1344 and is the oldest parish village of the Stubaital valley. The Baroque church (1754) features beautiful ceiling frescoes. On a trip to the Telfes Greifvogelpark, visitors can watch birds of prey at close quarters.

Neustift

Neustift (993m/3257ft; pop. 4200), the **touristic centre of the valley**, is a climatic spa, winter sports area and good base for tours. Rebuilt in 1768–74, the splendid parish church impresses with the width of its inner hall, and the lavish ceiling paintings are well worth seeing. The cemetery, with only wrought-iron grave crosses, holds the grave of Franz Senn (1831–84), co-founder of the Austrian and German Alpine Association (►Ötztal).

A trip to the impressive Grawa waterfall, which is located near the Grawa Alm (car park) about 13km/8mi from Neustift in the direction of the glacier, is recommended.

Stubaier Gletscherbahn

About 18km/11mi beyond Neustift, reached via the Stubaier glacier road, lies the Mutterbergalm (1728m/5669ft). Here too is the valley station of the Stubai glacier railway, the **highest funicular in Austria**.

VISITING STUBAITAL

INFORMATION

Tourismusverband Stubai
Stubaitalhaus, Dorf 3, A-6167 Neustift
Tel. 050 18/810, fax 811 99
www.stubaital.at

WHERE TO EAT

► **Inexpensive**
Gasthof Leitgeb
Haus Nr. 9, A-6165 Telfes im Stubai
Tel. 052 25/6 23 04
The service is friendly and the dishes are excellent at this well-attended old farmhouse parlour.

WHERE TO STAY

► **Mid-range**
Hotel Bergcristall
Volderau 5, A-6167 Neustift
Tel. 0 52 26/3 00 99, fax 3 00 99-90
www.bergcristall.at
This relaxing hotel with a unique view of the Stubai glacier is decorated with lots of wood and light colours. A swimming pool, sauna, massage and fitness room as well as various activities, also for children, complete the offer.

The first stop is the middle station Fernau (2300m/7545ft), followed by the mountain station Eisgrat (2900m/9514ft). From here the Stubain glacier trail leads in about an hour to the Eisjoch, where the **highest ski hut in Austria** stands (3150m/10,334ft), offering visitors a breathtaking view of the Stubai Alps, the Dolomites and the Ötztal Alps. During summer, depending on wind and weather conditions, free daily guided tours of the glacier are offered from the mountain station to the Eisjoch.

Stubaier Alpen

The Stubai Alps are one of many ranges adjoining the Ötztal Alps to the northeast in a complicated arrangement divided by numerous valleys. The main ridge, which extends between the Timmelsjoch and the wide Brennersenke, forms the Austrian-Italian border with Southern Tyrol. The mighty glaciers do not quite reach the dimensions of the Ferner mountains in the neighbouring massif, but nevertheless rival them for sheer savagery. Their average ridge height and the steepness of their inclines beat all of the other mountains in the central Alps hands down.

The range, which extends between the Ötztal, Inntal and Wipptal valleys can be easily reached from the provincial capital of Tyrol, ▶ Innsbruck, via the Stubaitalbahn and the Brennerbahn, which leads through the Wipptal valley, as well as on good roads. The Stubai Alps are the best in this high-lying region for accommodation and paths: nearly every high-lying valley has its refuge, and numerous climbing and connecting paths offer many possible combinations for hiking in summer and ski-tours during winter.

The Stubai Alps reach their highest elevation and strongest glaciation at the main ridge, the **Pfaffengruppe**. Here stand the sharp-coned Zuckerhütl (3507m/11,505ft), the snow-cap of the Wilden Freiger (3418m/11,213ft) and the proud peak of the 3333m/10,935ft-high Schaufelspitze. From

The Kalkkögel dominates the view of Telfes near Fulpmes

Neustift in the Stubaital, the most travelled paths lead into the snow-covered world of the Pfaffengruppe via the Dresdner Hütte (2302m/7552ft) and the Nürnberger Hütte (2280m/7480ft). From the ►Ötztal valley, the high region can be reached by way of the Hildesheimer Hütte (2899m/9511ft) and via the Siegerlandhütte (2710m/8891ft) near Sölden.

The **Schrankogel** (3426m/11,240ft) is accessible from the Amberger Hütte. It forms the splendid main peak of the second largest glacier area of Stubai Alps, the rocky Alpeiner Gruppe. Northeast of the Alpeiner mountains rises the bizarre chain of the Kalkkögel. ◄ Alpeiner Gruppe

North of Gleirschjöchl the glaciation decreases and expands into **one of the most popular ski areas of Tyrol**. The alpine hotel Jagdschloss Kühtai and the nearby Dortmunder Hütte (1948m/6391ft), reachable from the Sellraintal and the Ötztal valleys, constitute the popular headquarters of this winter paradise. It is dominated by the Sulzkogel (3016m/9895ft), at the foot of which is the Finstertaler reservoir, and the Zwieselbacher Rosskogel (3060m/10,039ft), from which the only larger glacier of the area leads down to the small Kraspessee. ◄ Kühtaier Berge

A second ridge, which leads off northeastwards from the Pfaffengruppe, is home to the massive Habicht (3277m/10,751ft), accessible from Fulpmes and Neustift in the Stubaital valley or Gschnitz in the Gschnitztal valley via the Innsbrucker Hütte (2369m/7772ft). ◄ Habicht

Eastward in the direction of Brenner lies the Tribulaungruppe range, a fantastic multi-peaked bastion of the Dolomites. The brown-white »Matterhorn of the Stubaier Alps«, the Pflerscher Tribulaun (3096m/10,157ft), looms majestically and presents a difficult climb from the Tribulaun-Hütte (3096m/10,157ft) at the border South Tyrolese border. ◄ Tribulaungruppe

◄ Pflerscher Tribulaun

✱ Tamsweg

Province: Salzburg
Population: 6,000

Elevation: 1021m/3349ft

Even though the Lungau opens topographically only eastwards in the direction of Styria, politically it originally belonged to Carinthia and, since the Middle Ages, to Salzburg. The area remained very isolated for a long time, in spite of the fact that the ancient trade route from Italy to Salzburg passed through it.

Tamsweg is the main town of the Lungau, a densely wooded high-lying valley basin (1000–1200m/3280–3937ft) between the Niedere Tauern and the Gurktal Alps. The Lungau was first opened up to tourism in the 1970s with the construction of the Tauern toll highway, including the Tauern and Katschberg tunnels, and has since become a popular holiday destination. The locals like to point out that the ratio of cows to hotel beds still favours the cows. **Remote idyll**

What to See in and around Tamsweg

Wallfahrtskirche St Leonhard

Tamsweg's well known late Gothic pilgrimage church, Wallfahrtskirche St Leonhard (1430–33), which lies somewhat to the southwest of the town, is one of Austria's most important pilgrimage churches. Its **marvellous glass windows**, especially the »Goldfenster«, made predominantly of blue and gold-yellow plates, are famous. The Gothic panel paintings of the altars (c1460) and the frescoes in the choir (1433) are also worth seeing.

Heimatmuseum ►

Alongside items to do with the church and farming, and Roman finds, the museum of local history accommodates an approximately 6m/19ft-high and 98kg/216lbs Samson. The figure of Samson seems to have been adopted from Slavic mythology, and according to tradition represents the great god who reawakens nature in springtime. During processions the Samson is ceremonially carried through the streets by strong men (the Heimatmuseum can only be visited as part of a guided tour: June–mid-Sept Tue–Fri 10am, 2pm and 3.30pm).

Prebersee

Situated 10km/6mi northeast of Tamsweg, the Prebersee is an inviting lake for hikers. On the last weekend of August an unusual competition called »Wasserscheibenschiessens« is held: the target stands on one side of the shore, the marksman on the other – and aims at the reflection in the water! Beginning from the Prebersee, the towering Preber (2741m/8992ft) to the north can be climbed in about three hours.

Mariapfarr

Located 5km/3mi west of Tamsweg, Mariapfarr is Austria's self-proclaimed sunniest town and – like nearly all of the places in Lungau – has a Samson, as well as a lovely pilgrimage church with very old

► VISITING TAMSWEG

INFORMATION

Tourismusverband Tamsweg
Kirchengasse 8, A-5580 Tamsweg
Tel. 0 64 74/21 45, www.tamsweg.at

KULTURWANDERWEG

The Lungauer Kulturwanderweg (signposted) crisscrosses nearly every place in the Lungau, with interesting facts about the country and its people, history and tradition written on plaques. The local tourist offices offer information about distances and routes.

WHERE TO STAY

► **Budget**
Hotel Grössingbräu
Gartengasse 402
A-5580 Tamsweg
Tel. 0 64 74/22 41
Fax 22 41 14
www.groessingbraeu.at
This central yet quietly situated hotel offers comfortably furnished rooms and holiday apartments, sauna and solarium facilities, a sun terrace and a mountain hut at an elevation of 2000m/6560ft.

The colourful, up to 6m/20ft-tall Samson figures are carried through the streets in festive parades, heralding spring

frescoes. In 1816, at the rectory of the small town, the assistant pastor Joseph Mohr wrote the lyrics of the famous Christmas song *Stille Nacht, Heilige Nacht* (*Silent Night*), which was set to music by Franz X. Gruber (▶ Hallein) two years later. From Mariapfarr, a varied day's hike leads through the Göriachtal valley north to the Hochgolling (2863m/9393ft), the highest peak of the Schladming Tauern.

Situated another 5km/3mi to the west, Mauterndorf was **the site of a toll gate in Roman times**. During the Middle Ages it developed into the most important transport hub of the Lungau, as the splendid town houses around the market square attest. Burg Mauterndorf, built beginning in 1253 on the foundation walls of a Roman fort, is today a cultural centre and houses the Lungauer Landschaftsmuseum (Lungau Landscape Museum) (opening times: mid-May–mid-Oct daily 10am–6pm). The Taurachbahn, a narrow-gauge historic railway (760mm/30in) and once part of the Murtalbahn (▶ Murau), nowadays operates between Mauterndorf and St Andrä with a steam and diesel engine at weekends in summer (information tel. 06472/79 49).

Mauterndorf

🕐

◀ Taurachbahn

Some 6km/3.7mi south of Mauterndorf stands the impressive Schloss Moosham. It holds folkloristic collections, a courtroom and a torture chamber (guided tours only by arrangement, tel. 0 64 76/3 05).

◀ Schloss Moosham

St Michael lies a good 6km/3.7mi south of Mauterndorf. Its numerous lifts make it a popular centre for winter sports enthusiasts and hikers. The Gothic parish church contains frescoes from the 13th and 14th centuries; in addition, the octagonal Wolfgang chapel, a former charnel house, is also worthy of attention.

St Michael

Muhr Heading west up the Murtal valley for 15km/9.3mi leads to the village of Muhr, the site of the processions with so-called »Prangstangen«. Legend has it that farmers once decorated sticks a few metres high with flowers in thanks after the end of a plague of locusts, then carried the glorious blossoms through the town to the church. For the pleasure of the tourists, this colourful tradition is practised to this day in Muhr and also in Zederhaus, slightly to the north.

Rotgüldental At the end of the Murtal valley lies Rotgülden, from where it is possible to climb up to the Grossen Hafner (3076m/10,091ft) in about four to five hours, passing the Untere and Obere Rotgüldensee. From the High Middle Ages on, gold and silver were mined close to Rotgülden. But of even more significance was the rich **supply of arsenate ore**, which led to Rotgülden becoming the world's biggest arsenic supplier. The mines were finally closed only in 1924.

✶ Tannheimer Tal

D/E 5

Province: Tyrol

Picture book villages, idyllically situated lakes, expansive pasture sometimes covered with crocuses during springtime, wooded hillsides, and behind them craggy, towering cliffs – the attractive scenery makes the Tannheimer valley a popular summer and winter holiday destination.

Sunny hiking destination In the west, the Tannheimer Tal valley borders on the German Allgäu, which can be reached via Sonthofen and Oberjoch (border). To the east, the road over the Gaichtpass opens out to the Lechtal valley, 10km/6mi southwest of Reutte. The highest elevation is the Gaishorn, at 2247m/7372ft, close to the Vilsalpsee south of Tannheim.

▶ VISITING TANNHEIMER TAL

INFORMATION

Tourismusverband Tannheimer Tal
Oberhöfen 110
A-6675 Tannheim
Tel. 056 75/622 00
Fax 62 20 60
www.tannheimertal.com

WHERE TO STAY

► **Mid-range**
Bogner Hof
Bogen 9, A-6675 Tannheim
Tel. 0 56 75/62 97
Fax 62 97 50
www.bognerhof.at
A familial alpine hotel with a rustic atmosphere, situated on the outskirts of town in the direction of the Vilsalpsee nature reserve.

A salt route once led through the broad Tannheimer Tal – rich in mountain pasture and, in the eyes of the locals, the most beautiful high-lying valley in Europe – from Tyrol over the Gaichtpass and Oberjoch to Lake Constance. With its excellent and elaborate road and path network the area is an El Dorado for those who enjoy hiking, climbing, mountain biking or paragliding. The **balloon festival in early January** attracts numerous visitors every year. In all five villages there are pistes and ski schools, plus 80km/49mi of cross-country ski runs. A ski bus transports fans of winter sports throughout the entire valley for free.

Tannheim

Tannheim (1097m/3599ft; pop. 1000), the valley's principal village, lies at the point where the Vilstal valley opens out into the Tannheimer Tal. Sporting offers include a skating rink, tennis courts and a climbing wall. From the Neunerköpfle, reachable with the Gondelbahn Vogelhorn lifts, skiers can descend down into the valley.

◀ Vilsalpsee

Situated in midst of a nature reserve, the Vilsalpsee, 4km/2.4mi south of Tannheim, is among the most beautiful of tour destinations. The road leading to the lake is closed during the day. Instead, take the Alpenexpress from car park P1 (east entrance), or the shuttle bus or a horse-drawn carriage from car park P2 (west entrance). Alternatively, go on foot or by bicycle. There is a restaurant at the Vilsalpsee and a convenient hiking track (1 hour) leads around the lake. More energetic visitors can climb up to the Obere Traualpe, with the Traualpsee, and continue further (1 hour) to the Landsberger Hütte.

Grän-Haldensee

The pleasant village of Grän-Haldensee (1134m/3720ft; pop. 600), about 2km/1.2mi east of Tannheim, offers a variety of possibilities

Worth a trip: the Haldensee at Tannheimer Tal

for swimming and sunbathing in a mountain setting: the large outdoor pool lies directly beside the Haldensee and is heated with environmentally friendly solar energy. Those wishing to bathe in the Haldensee itself will find cooler temperatures, but excellent water quality. Boats can be rented at the beach café.

✴ Timmelsjoch Road

F 6

Province: Tyrol

A toll road connecting the ►Ötztal valley in Tyrol with the Passeiertal valley in South Tyrol runs along the ridge of the nearly 2500m/8202ft-high Timmelsjoch. The border between Austria and Italy also follows the pass.

The Route of the Timmelsjoch Road

Untergurgl From about the middle of June until the middle of October the road over the Timmelsjoch is open during the day, though on the Italian side only passenger cars are allowed (closed for caravans). The Timmelsjochstrasse begins at Untergurgl (1793m/5882ft), from where it takes about 11km/7mi to reach the summit of the pass (max. slope 11%). There is a chairlift from Untergurgl to Hochgurgl. First, the road runs four loops up to Angerer Alm (2175m/7135ft), where the hotel colony of Hochgurgl (2150m/7053ft) is situated. From here, a chairlift leads up to the Grosser Kar (2410m/7906ft) and continues further to the Wurmkogl (3082m/10,111ft).

✴ Timmelsjoch The Timmelsjoch Road now leads through the Timmelsbach valley upwards and, in seven loops, reaches the Timmelsjoch (2497m/8192ft; Ital. Passo di Rombo) and the Austrian-Italian border. On the Italian side the road proceeds downwards into the Passeiertal valley via Moos (1007m/3303ft) to St Leonhard (683m/2240ft), where many reminders of **Andreas Hofer** (1767– 1810; ►Famous People), the keeper of the Sandwirt inn, can be found. From here it is another 20km/12.4mi to Meran.

 TIMMELSJOCH ROAD

INFORMATION
Öztal Tourismus Informationsbüro Obergurgl-Hochgurgl
A-6456 Obergurgl
Tel. 05 72 00 100
www.obergurgl.com

At the end of the Gurgltal, east of the Ötztal valley, a little south of Untergurgl and the Timmelsjoch Road, lies the small town of **Obergurgl** (1927m/6322ft), **Tyrol's highest church village**. Today it is a modern tourist centre with an excellent ski area where snow is virtually assured.

To the south rises the Grosse Gurgler Ferner, where Auguste Piccard landed with his stratosphere balloon in 1931, having become the first human being to reach the height of 15,781m/51,774ft. By first taking the chairlift south of the Gaisberg (2071m/6794ft), then afterwards the glacier-lift to the Hohe Mut (2659m/8723ft), marvellous views of the Gaisbergferner and its surroundings with 20 glaciers can be enjoyed.

Glacial area

✳ Traunsee

L 4

Province: Upper Austria   **Elevation:** 422m/1384ft

The picturesque lake, which in the east nestles between the prominent peaks of the Traunstein (1691m/5547ft), the Hochkogel (1486m/4875ft) and the Erlakogel (1575m/5167ft) – also called the »schlafende Griechin« (sleeping Greek woman) – and between the Gmundner Berg (830m/2723ft) and the Höllengebirge in the west, is well worth a thorough visit.

»Der Traunsee – ein Traumsee«, proclaims the advertisement for this lakeland region, where pretty small towns line the shores. 12km/7.4mi in length, up to 3km/1.8mi wide and 191m/118.6mi deep, the Traunsee is one of the largest lakes in the Salzkammergut, which is apparent from the range of sports on offer here, from angling to diving to water skiing.

»A dream lake«

The picturesquely located Johanneskirchlein (built in 1632) of Traunkirchen rises high above the Traunsee

What to See at the Traunsee

Gmunden

The principal town is Gmunden (pop. 15,000), once a salt-trading hub, today a spa town, which is situated around the northern point of the lake. A walk from the pretty Rathaus (town hall) with ceramic glockenspiel via the Esplanade along the banks offers a view out to the Toscana peninsula and a castle, the **Landschloss Ort**, which is connected with the Seeschloss Ort by a boardwalk. The latter serves as a picturesque location of an early evening TV series.

»Nautilus« model (1904): exclusive lavatory from Gmunden

For over a hundred years the name **Gmundner Töpferware** has been known to those who appreciate fine ceramics. Those who are not able to visit the widely renowned pottery market on the last weekend in August – ideally arriving in one of the Gmund historic railcars – can catch a glimpse of the production of these beautiful objects of both practical and aesthetic use at two pottery manufacturers.

The town parish church, Stadtpfarrkirche **Mariä Himmelfahrt**, was originally Gothic, then redesigned in Baroque style in the 18th century. It houses a carved group of the Three Magi by Thomas Schwanthaler (1678); the high altar contains a ceramic Virgin of Mercy (1947).

In an exhibition area of 2000sq m/21,500sq ft, the **Stadtmuseum** in the former Kammerhof (15th century) documents the development of the Traunsee region and Gmunden's past as a salt distribution hub. It also displays fossils and minerals and recalls famous guests in the »Brahmszimmer« (opening times: late April–early Nov daily 9am–6pm). The **»Gmundner Jahrtausendweg«** (»Gmund Millenium Path«) shows the geographical and cultural historical development of the Traunsee area over the past 20,000 years.

Traunstein

From Gmunden's district of Weyer, a cable railway leads to the Grünberg (1004m/3294ft), where in addition to beautiful hiking trails a mountain bike path is also signposted. The Traunstein (1691m/5547ft) rising up in the south can be reached by experienced climbers in more or less three hours.

On the west bank of the Traunsee, Altmünster (pop. 9500) awaits with a special museum: the Radmuseum documents the development of the bicycle, from the »Laufmaschine« or »walking bike« to the »Waffenrad« or »weapon bicycle« (www.radmuseum.at; Maria-Theresia-Strasse 3 a; opening times: early May–late Oct daily 10am–noon and 2pm–5pm).

Altmünster

Alpine ibexes, sika deer, red deer, yaks and wild horses can all be seen at the Hochkreut game reserve, located southwest of Altmünster on a mountain ridge (960m/3149ft) between the Traunsee and the Attersee. For young guests, the birdsong path and mushroom path, as well as the frog pool, are of interest. An explanation of the surrounding mountain peaks can be found at the Panoramamuseum (opening times: daily 9am–6pm).

Wildpark Hochkreut

The holiday destination of Traunkirchen (pop. 1800) is picturesquely situated on a peninsula in the Traunsee and is home to a particular rarity: the original **»Fischerkanzel«** (Fisherman's Pulpit) in the parish church is in the form of a boat. Fish floundering in a net and an illustration of Peter as »Fisher of Men« (1753) complete the picture. Above the town on a wooded rock stands the Johanneskirchlein (church of St John; 1609). A strong magnet for tourists here is the gorgeous Corpus Christi boat procession, held since 1632.

✶
Traunkirchen

> **!** *Baedeker* TIP
>
> ### A boat trip – always a treat!
> The Traunsee was the first Austrian lake to make use of the steamboat. The paddle steamer Gisela (built in 1871), named after a daughter of Emperor Franz Joseph I and Empress Elisabeth, still casts off from Gmunden for a grand tour of the lake (early July–early Sept, every Sun).

Ebensee (pop. 8700), situated at the southern end of the Traunsee, is today mainly characterized by industry. The »Zeitgeschichte Museum« next to the Catholic parish church in the centre of town shows in detail the political history of the country from 1918–55 (opening times: Tue–Sun 10am–5pm; tel. 0 61 33/56 01; www.ebensee.org).

The Concentration Camp Memorial is also part of the museum. From November 1943 until liberation by US-troops in May 1945, one of the many **subsidiaries of the Mauthausen concentration camp** near Linz (► Danube Valley) was based here. About 27,000 prisoners from 20 different nations were forced to build tunnels, which were originally intended for the Nazi rocket testing facilities in Peenemünde on the Baltic Sea island of Usedom. Instead, they housed an oil refinery and facilities for the production of tank parts by Steyr-Daimler-Puch AG. A third of the prisoners died as a result of inhumane working conditions. Signs in the town direct visitors to the former site of the concentration camp, of which only one gate remains. As early as 1948, the wife of a prisoner had a memorial put on one of the mass graves. Today there are memorials from various

◄ Concentration Camp Memorial

VISITING TRAUNSEE

INFORMATION

Traunsee Touristik
Toscanapark 6, A-4810 Gmunden
Tel. 0 76 12/64 01 40, fax 6 68 43
www.traunsee-touristik.at

WHERE TO EAT

► Expensive
Seeschloss Orth
Orth 1
A-4810 Gmunden
Tel. 076 12/624 99, fax 637 24
At the Orther Stub'n, with its centuries-old wooden ceiling, the emphasis is on fresh regional products, whereby fresh fish is the speciality of the house, best accompanied with a good bottle of wine from the diverse and well-stocked wine cellar.

► Inexpensive
Seegasthof Hois'n Wirt
Traunsteinstrasse 277
A-4810 Gmunden
Tel. 0 76 12/7 73 33, fax 7 73 33 95
Freshly caught fish from the lake and other meals typical of the region are served here.

WHERE TO STAY

► Mid-range
Hotel Annerlhof
Mitterndorf 23 A-4801 Traunkirchen
Tel. 0 76 17/22 19, www.annerlhof.at
Cosy family business in the centre of town, with a swimming area 200m/656ft away and a bike rental outlet in the hotel. The restaurant offers good plain Austrian fare.

countries here. The tunnels can be visited – due to the constant temperature of 8°C/46°F during both summer and winter, warm clothing is recommended (opening times: May, June and Oct Sat and Sun as well as July–Sept Wed–Sun 10am–5pm).

Höllengebirge   West of Ebensee, between the Traunsee and the Attersee, extends the Höllengebirge range, a drawn-out limestone massif with steep flanks, a good skiing and hiking area. The funicular leads west of Ebensee up to the Feuerkogel (1594m/5229ft), where during summer the Riederhütte (1765m/5790ft) and the Hochleckenhaus (1572m/5157ft) provide food and drink.

Langbathseen   About 10km/6.2mi northwest of Ebensee, the idyllic Langbathseen (664m/2178ft and 753m/2470ft) are worth a visit, as is the Offensee, about 15km/9.3mi to the southeast, at the foot of the Tote Gebirge (651m/2135ft).

Scharnstein   About 15km/9mi east of Gmunden begins the beautiful Almtal valley. In the palace of the borough of Scharnstein is the **Österreichische Kriminalmuseum**, which opened its doors in 1973. Here, Austria's criminal history and penal system are explained, from the Middle Ages until the abolition of the death penalty – not an exhibition for the faint of heart (opening times: May to mid-Oct Tue–Sun

9am–5pm). The **Museum für Zeit-geschichte** (Museum of Contemporary History) in the palace is also worth seeing.

In the idyllic village of **Grünau** (527m/1729ft), the play-paradise and the fairy-tale forest at Kinderland Schindelbach are sure to make children's eyes light up (opening times: May, June and mid-Sept–late Oct Sat and Sun, July and Aug daily 10am–6pm).

! **Baedeker** TIP

Wildlife in Grünau

South of Grünau, Cumberland-Wildpark invites visitors to survey around 500 animals from about 70 species, including elks, European bisons and moufflons (opening times: April–Oct daily 9am–6pm, Nov–March Mon–Fri 11am–4pm, Sat and Sun from 9am). Greylag geese and ravens can also be seen – the Konrad-Lorenz research centre is just next door.

Turracher Höhe

L 6

Provinces: Styria and Carinthia

Thanks to the reliable supply of snow the Turracher Höhe – a popular skiing area, with a hotel colony at its base – has been made accessible with many ski lifts.

Hikers also appreciate the wooded areas around the Turrachersee, Schwarzsee and Grünsee. The peaks in the Nockgebiet can be discovered during rewarding mountain tours. The Turracher Höhe (1763m/5784ft) lies at the westernmost point of Styria, east of the Nockberge National Park at the border pass over the Gurktal Alps to Carinthia. **Paradise for hikers and skiers**

In previous centuries there were several iron mines here, and anthracite was also extracted. Around 1900, it was actually the site of Europe's most modern furnace. These traces of the past can be followed at the Montanmuseum in Turrach (visits by arrangement, tel. 035 33 / 214, 230 or 255). **Montanmuseum**

The »Nocky Flitzer«, **Austria's highest summer toboggan run**, on the Turracher Höhe offers a lot of downhill fun (in operation: June–Oct daily 10am–5pm, July and Aug until 7pm, otherwise until 4pm). The **alpin+art+gallery**, a museum of minerals located at Berghotel Zirbenhof, will delight lovers of beautiful stones (opening times: Mon–Sat 9am–5pm).

 TURRACHER HÖHE

INFORMATION

Tourismusverband Turracher Höhe
A-9565 Turracher Höhe 218
Tel. 0 42 75/83 920
Fax 83 92 10
www.turracherhoehe.at

★★ **Vienna**

Q 3

Province: Vienna
Population: 1,680,000

Elevation: 170m/557ft

Vienna, the town »on the beautiful blue Danube«, is a place of contradictions: its flair appears at the same time cosmopolitan and nostalgic, extravagant and provincial. And there is no getting away from the renowned charm of its inhabitants.

»Vienna, city of my dreams...«

Merry waltzes and coffee house culture, the Prater and Heuriger wine, the Dual Monarchy and the UN, Sachertorte and New Year's Concerts, the Secession and Hundertwasser, Fiaker and the Stephansdom, Maria Theresia and Sisi, Ludwig van Beethoven and Sigmund Freud, Hans Moser and Helmut Qualtinger, Karl Kraus and Alfred Polgar – the list of associations with this beautiful metropolis appears endless.

Austrian capital

The municipality of Vienna is the **capital of the Republic of Austria**, but also has the status of a federal province. With an area of 415 sq km/160 sq mi and a circumference of 133km/83mi, Vienna is a medium-sized European metropolis divided into 23 districts.

Wall fountain with fallen giants and sea monsters decorating the Michaeler Wing of the Hofburg

Highlights Vienna

Stephansdom
Vienna's emblem in the Old Town, St Stephen's Cathedral, represents the art history of eight centuries!
▶ page 517

Hofburg
The richly historical imperial castle where Austria's rulers wrote more than six centuries of European history
▶ page 534

Imperial Apartments
Alongside the chambers of the unhappy fairy-tale princess Sisi, the Emperor's living and working apartments can also be visited.
▶ page 535

Silberkammer
In the so-called »Silver Chamber« visitors see how tables were set for the court.
▶ page 535

Spanish Riding School
Fans of horses can marvel at the high art of horse-riding at one of the gala performances.
▶ page 536

Schatzkammer
The Imperial Treasury contains a collection of treasures of inestimable artistic, historical and monetary value – beginning from the 16th century.
▶ page 536

Österreichische Nationalbibliothek
The Austrian National Library not only impresses with its architecture, but also with the content of its old stock.
▶ page 536

Naturhistorisches Muaseum
Founded in the 18th century, the Natural History Museum is a highlight for both young and old.
▶ page 539

Kunsthistorisches Museum
It is easy to spend an entire day at the Museum of Art History – the world's most significant art collections are on display.
▶ page 540

Museum District
It is a duty for lovers of modern and contemporary art to pay a visit to the Museum District!
▶ page 540

Belvedere Castles
Prince Eugene of Savoy had these two castles built as a summer residence – they number among the most beautiful Baroque creations in Vienna.
▶ page 551

Schloss Schönbrunn
The most frequently visited sight in Austria and former summer residence of the Habsburg dynasty has played host to many a royal guest and other luminaries.
▶ page 554

Every district has its distinct features. The first district equates to the Old Town, the second to the ninth are considered as inner districts, 10 to 20 as outer districts and 21 to 23 as outlying districts. **Districts of Vienna**

A part of the third district (Landstrasse) is considered the diplomatic quarter, the fourth district (Wieden) along with the first (city centre) the most elegant; in the 5th (Margareten), 6th (Mariahilf) and 7th (Neubau) there is evidence of trading and business, and upper-class buildings stand next to workers' flats. The 8th (Josefstadt) has always been favoured by executives, the 9th (Alsergrund) is Vienna's aca-

Vienna Map

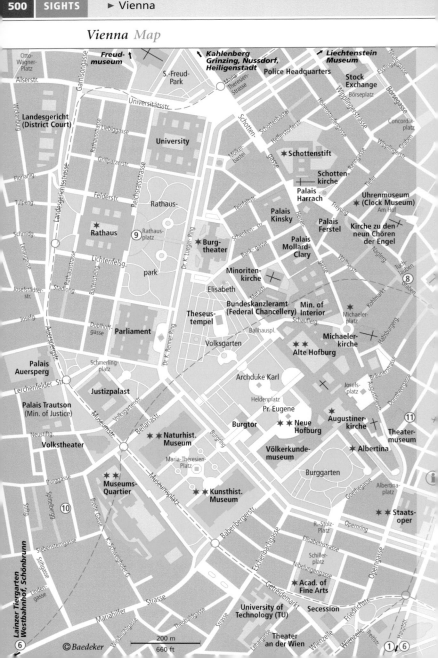

Otto-Wagner-Platz · Alserstr. · Florianig. · Tulpeng. · Schmidg. · Lerangasse · Josefstädterstr. · Josefg. · Neustiftg. · Stiftg. · Spitelberg.

Freud-museum · S.-Freud-Park

Kahlenberg Grinzing, Nussdorf, Heiligenstadt · Police Headquarters

Liechtenstein Museum

Stock Exchange · Börseplatz · Concordia-platz

Garnisongasse · Universitätsstr. · Maria-Theresien-Strasse

Landesgericht (District Court) · Liebiggasse · Rathausstrasse · Grillparzerstr. · Reichsratsstrasse

University

Schottenbastei · Schottenring · Helferstorferstr. · Hohenstaufengasse · Wipplingerstrasse · Renngasse

★ **Schottenstift**

Schotten-kirche

Mölkerbastei · Schottengasse · Teinfaltstr. · Schenken-str. · Herreng.

Palais Harrach · Freyung · Strauchg.

Palais Kinsky

Uhrenmuseum (Clock Museum) · Am Hof

★ **Rathaus** · Rathaus-platz ⑨

Felderstr. · Rathausstrasse · Lichtenfelsg. · Stadiong. · Bartensteing. · Doblhoffgasse · Schmerling-platz

Rathaus-park

★ **Burgtheater**

Dr. K. Lueger-Ring

Palais Ferstel

Kirche zu den neun Chören der Engel

Palais Mollard-Clary

Bankgasse · Herreng. · Wallnerstr. · Naglerg. · Tuchlauben · Graben ⑧

Minoriten-kirche

Elisabeth

Bundeskanzleramt (Federal Chancellery)

Theseus-tempel

Min. of Interior · Schauflerg. · Michaelerplatz

Parliament

Dr. K. Renner-Ring · Ballhauspl. · Löwelstr. · Metastr.

Michaeler-kirche

Habsburgerg.

Volksgarten

★★ **Alte Hofburg**

Palais Auersperg

Lerchenfelder Str. · Schmerling-platz · Volksgartenstr. · Bellariastr.

Archduke Karl

Justizpalast

Palais Trautson (Min. of Justice)

Heldenplatz · Josefs-platz

Pr. Eugene

★ **Augustiner-kirche**

Bräunerstrasse · Augustinerstr. · Dorotheerg.

⑪ **Theatermuseum**

Volkstheater

Museumstr. · Burgring

Burgtor

★★ **Neue Hofburg**

★ **Naturhist. Museum**

Maria-Theresien-Platz

Völkerkunde-museum

★ **Albertina** · Albertina-platz

Burggarten

Goethegasse

Burggasse · Siebensterngasse · Breite Gasse · Mariahilfer

⑩ ★★ **Museums-Quartier**

Museumsplatz

★★ **Kunsthist. Museum**

Babenbergerstrasse · Getreidemarkt

R.-Stolz-Platz · Operning · Elisabethstrasse

★★ **Staatsoper**

Eschenbachgasse · Nibelungengasse · Schiller-platz

Theobaldgasse · Windmühlgasse · Gumpendorfer · Lehargasse · Millöckerg.

★ **Acad. of Fine Arts**

Secession

University of Technology (TU)

Wienzeile · Friedrichstr. · Operngasse

⑥ **Lainzer Tiergarten Westbahnhof, Schönbrunn**

Mariahilfer Strasse

Theater an der Wien

① ⑥

© *Baedeker*

200 m
660 ft

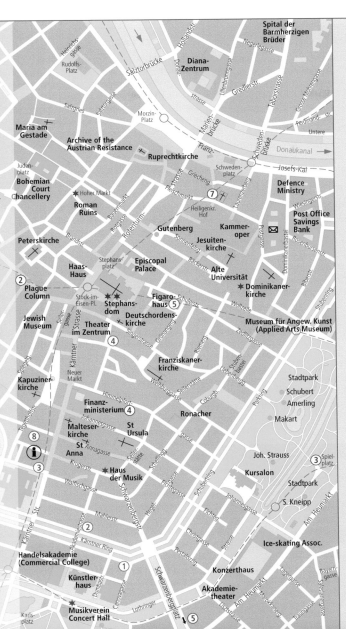

Where to eat
① Artner
② Meinl am Graben
③ Steirereck
④ Zum Kuckuck
⑤ Fasanlwirt
⑥ Hauswirth
⑦ Fleischmarkt 16
⑧ Zum Weisshappel
⑨ Wiener Rathauskeller
⑩ Witwe Bolte
⑪ Reinthaler

Where to stay
① Imperial
② Grand Hotel
③ Sacher
④ Kaiserin Elisabeth
⑤ König von Ungarn
⑥ Hotel Papageno

▶ VISITING VIENNA

INFORMATION

Tourist-Info Wien
1st district, Maysedergasse
(Albertinaplatz)
A-1010 Wien
Tel. 01/245 55, fax 24 55 56 66
www.wien.info

A further tourist information office is to be found in the Arrivals Hall at Vienna's airport.

WIEN-KARTE

It is recommended that you buy a Vienna ticket or Wien-Karte. An ideal »ticket to the city«, it is available at the tourist office, at the airport, in hotels and at ticket booths of the tram lines in Vienna. It contains a 72-hour pass for the U-Bahn (underground), buses and trams, and holders receive discounts in many museums, shops, theatres and restaurants as well as reduced prices for guided tours of the city.

SHOPPING

Vienna's most popular shopping promenades are Kärntner Strasse, Graben and Kohlmarkt. Mariahilfer Strasse also offers many possibilities for shoppers.

WHERE TO EAT

▶ Expensive

① Artner
4th district, Floragasse 6
A-1040 Vienna, tel. 01/5 03 50 33
Excellent local restaurant with traditional food; only serves wine from its own vineyard.

② Meinl am Graben
1st district, Graben 19
A-1010 Vienna
Tel. 01/5 32 33 34
First rate culinary institution on the first floor of the gourmet department store.

Baedeker recommendation

③ Steirereck
3rd district, Am Heumarkt 2 a
A-1030 Wien
Tel. 01/7 13 31 68
A veritable temple for gourmets, with unusual creations and well-stocked wine cellar, located in the Meierei (dairy farm) in the Stadtpark.

④ Zum Kuckuck
1st district, Himmelpfortgasse 15
A-1010 Vienna, tel. 01/5 12 84 70
Small but exquisite gourmet restaurant that has plenty to offer its guests.

▶ Moderate

⑤ Fasanlwirt
3rd district, Rennweg 24
A-1030 Wien, tel. 01/7 98 45 51
Named after the many pheasants that used to live here, this restaurant serves hearty home cooking.

Fine textiles are sold on Graben

⑥ Hauswirth
6th district, Otto-Bauer-Gasse 20
A-1060 Wien, tel. 01/5 87 12 61
Traditional Viennese cuisine and good wine from the cellar are served in a Biedermeier setting.

⑦ Fleischmarkt 16
1st district, Fleischmarkt 16, A-1010 Wien
Tel. 01/513 23 18
The excellent staff in the Fleischmarkt bring Austrian delicacies and exotic specialities to the table.

⑧ Zum Weisshappel
1st district, Petersplatz 1
A-1010 Wien
Tel. 01/5 33 90 96
Nice view of the Petersplatz. Specialities include fresh fish, meat from the house butcher and typical Viennese deserts.

⑨ Wiener Rathauskeller
1st district, Rathausplatz 1
A-1010 Wien
Tel. 01/4 05 12 10
Restaurant in the vaulted cellar of Vienna's city hall; modern Viennese cuisine.

⑩ Witwe Bolte
7th district, Gutenberggasse 13
A-1070 Wien, tel. 01/5 23 14 50
Emperor Joseph II is said to have visited this eatery once, disguised as a local citizen. In summer, guests can sit out in the garden.

► Inexpensive
⑪ Reinthaler
1st district, Gluckgasse 5
A-1010 Wien
Tel. 01/5 12 33 66
Traditional Vienna tavern with great service and hearty food.

WHERE TO STAY
► Luxury
① Imperial
Kärntner Ring 16, A-1015 Wien
Tel. 01/50 11 03 13, fax 50 11 03 55
www.luxurycollection.com/imperial
Built for the Duke of Württemberg in 1869, the house became a hotel in 1873 for the occasion of the World Exhibition. Today it is clearly one of Vienna's best luxury hotels. Numerous state visitors and their entourages have stayed here.

Baedeker recommendation

② Grand Hotel
Kärntner Ring 9, A-1010 Wien
Tel. 01/51 58 00, fax 515 13 10
www.grandhotelwien.com
In this high-class hotel, opened in 1870, the rooms and suites promise a perfect ambience, as do the large ballroom and the two top restaurants »Le Ciel« and »Unkai«.

③ Sacher
Philharmonikerstrasse 4
A-1010 Wien
Tel. 01/51 45 60, fax 51 45 68 10
www.sacher.com
Queen Elizabeth II, Pandit Nehru, John F. Kennedy and Maria Callas are among the luminaries to have spent a night at the Hotel Sacher. The house, founded in 1876 by the general dealer Eduard Sacher, is today in every sense a modern hotel with restaurants, bar and the world-famous Café Sacher.

④ **Kaiserin Elisabeth**
Weihburggasse 3, A-1010 Wien
Tel. 01/5 15 26, fax 51 52 67
www.kaiserinelisabeth.at
The classy palace of the nobility in
Vienna's first district offers elegant,
comfortable rooms and suites. Much
attention is paid to service.

⑤ **König von Ungarn**
Schulerstrasse 10, A-1010 Wien
Tel. 01/51 58 40, fax 51 58 48
www.kvu.at
This hotel, founded in 1815, receives
its guests with a certain Austrian-
Hungarian flair, which is also pleasantly noticeable in the restaurant
menu.

► **Mid-range**
⑥ **Hotel Papageno**
Wiedner Hauptstrasse 23–25
A-1040 Wien
Tel. 01/5 04 67 44
Fax 5 04 67 44 22
www.hotelpapageno.at
Many of Vienna's sights can be
reached on foot from this familial,
well-equipped hotel.

demic district. Workers, pensioners and residents of tower blocks live
in the 10th (Favoriten), 11th (Simmering), 12th (Meidling) and 15th
(Rudolfsheim-Fünfhaus) districts, where Vienna is most densely
populated. The outskirts in the west and northwest (13th–19th districts), with village-like centres, extend up to the vineyards and the
heights of the Wienerwald. Beyond the Danube Canal (Donaukanal)
lies the 2nd district (Leopoldstadt) with the Prater, the convention
centre, the stadium and high-rise office buildings. The 22nd district
(Donaustadt) is a modern urban cityscape, dominated by the UN
and Donau-City.

Exploring Vienna The Old Town, which is to a large extent pedestrianized, is best explored by U-Bahn, S-Bahn, tram or bus. Those wishing for a roman-
tic way to travel should take a Fiaker, the famous horse-drawn carriages, which stand on Stephans-
platz or Heldenplatz or on
Augustinerstrasse in front of the
Albertina. The fare depends on the
route, time of day, carriage and
harness – it is best to negotiate the
price with the coachman before
starting the journey.

! **Baedeker TIP**

»Vorortelinie«
The old »Vorortelinie« (suburban line, now S 45)
between Hütteldorf and Döbling was reopened
in 1987. Its bridges, tunnels and stations were
designed in pure art nouveau style by the
architect Otto Wagner.

Vienna is not just a historical and
cultural metropolis, it also has
much to offer when it comes to
lifestyle and indulging yourself. This includes not only the many restaurants, cafés, »Beisln« and bars, but also countless **possibilities for
shoppers**. Designer boutiques and trendy shops alternate with high-
class stores, which were already an attraction during imperial times.

While a well-filled purse can be quite advantageous here, it is also fun to just stroll along the window displays, which range from simply elegant to positively aristocratic.

History of Vienna

AD 50	Romans construct the fortified military camp of Vindobona.
1137	First documented reference of Vienna as a town
1683	The Turks are fought off and retreat.
1740–90	Vienna becomes a centre of commerce and finance.
1806	Franz II, Holy Roman Emperor, is crowned Franz I of Austria.
1814–15	Congress of Vienna
1848–1916	Emperor Franz Joseph I
1918	First Republic declared, with Vienna as capital
1955	The Allies depart, Austrian independence
1978	First U-Bahn line is opened.
1979	Opening of the UN building on the north bank of the Danube
2001	The city centre is declared a World Cultural Heritage site.
2006	The Theater an der Wien becomes the new opera house.

Early history

The settlement of the Viennese Basin can be traced back to the Late Stone Age. The Illyrian population of the Early Iron Age (from around 800 BC) was displaced by the Celts around 400 – the Leopoldsberg was probably the location of a Celtic castle.

Roman settlement

Around AD 50 the Romans constructed the fortified military camp of Vindobona (from the Celtic word vedunia = wild stream) on the Danube to provide protection from the local Germanic people who lived in the north. From the 2nd century AD a Roman civil town was established in the surrounding area; the Romans withdrew from the Danube region around 487.

From the Franks to the Babenbergs

No less a figure than **Charlemagne** is reported to have founded the Peterskirche (St Peter's church) in 792. In 955, after Otto I prevailed over Hungary, the Ostmark (Ostarrichi) was constructed as a borderland of the empire. The Babenbergs, presumably Frank-based, were given the title of margraves in 976. Because of its river harbour, Vienna developed into a **fortified merchants' settlement**. Vienna was first documented as a town (civitas) in 1137. The Babenbergs, who were promoted to dukes, moved their residence from Kloster-

She led the way: Maria Theresia

neuburg to Vienna. Vienna's fortifications were expanded with part of the ransom collected for the release of the imprisoned English king, Richard the Lionheart, in 1192. Under Leopold VI the Glorious (1198–1204) the town experienced a tremendous boom: the Order of Teutonic Knights came to Vienna, and minnesingers such as Walther von der Vogelweide were guests at court. In 1246 the last of the Babenbergs died out.

Rise of the House of Habsburg

With the election of Rudolf I from the House of Habsburg as German king in 1273 began the 650-year rule of this dynasty, so inseparable from Vienna. The **rise of Vienna to a metropolis** was underlined by the formation of a university in 1365. During the Middle Ages, Vienna's population definitely participated in guiding the history of the town: the »Bürgermeister- und Ratswahlordnung« from 1396 allowed trades and craftsmen to sit on the Stadtrat, or town council. Under Duke Friedrich V (1440–93), the later Holy Roman Emperor Friedrich III, Vienna became an imperial residence, which led to a gradual displacement of citizens from the Old Town by imperial officials from the nobility.

Turkish threat

In 1529 the recently built outskirts of Vienna were razed by the Turks. The threat of further attacks led to the installation of mighty fortification facilities by Emperor Ferdinand I. In 1683 the Turks, again, stood in front of the town gates, though after a month-long siege it was possible, with the help of Jan Sobieski and Pope Innocence XI, who initiated the **Holy League**, to fight them back in the Battle of Kahlenberg on 12 September. It was the first time that

Prince Eugene of Savoy (►Famous People) proved his military savvy, and his legend lives on in folk songs as the »edle Ritter« (noble knight).

Absolutism

After fighting back the Turks, the Habsburg Empire began to expand broadly to the southeast. Vienna rose to become a glamorous centre of a European empire. The town was now divided into the »city« (inside the fortification walls), which was reserved for the court, the nobility and the clergy, and the middle-class outskirts between Glacis and the Linienwall – the second fortification of the town – and the rural periphery, where also the summer residencies of the nobility developed. The vast demand for goods and capital made Vienna a **trade and finance centre**, and splendid Baroque buildings underlined its significance. Among them was Schloss Schönbrunn, which Maria Theresia had built in 1740–80. Her son Joseph II (1780–90) acknowledged an independent Vienna municipal authority in 1783.

From Napoleon I to the revolution

At the end of the 18th century Austria's separation from the German Empire had come so far that the Holy Roman Emperor Franz II abdicated his title in 1806 and governed as Emperor Franz I of Austria. After two short occupations of Vienna by Napoleon – which ruined the city's finances – Europe's statesmen deliberated on the realignment of Europe at the Congress of Vienna in 1814–15. After this the old absolutist glory of the dukes in Vienna was restored. This did not hold up cultural and technical progress: in 1842 the **Vienna Philharmonic Orchestra** was founded; in 1843 gas lighting was launched. Big railway terminals were constructed, and the textile industry and mechanical engineering attracted more and more workers. In the face of the February Revolution in Paris the Viennese claimed civil liberties and options for participation, which led to the March Revolution against the regime of Duke Metternich (►Famous People) in 1848. Although the revolution was put down, Metternich was forced into exile. Emperor Ferdinand I, who had governed since 1835, also resigned.

Franz Joseph I (1848–1916)

At just 18, the strongly militaristic Franz Joseph I ascended the throne in 1848 and managed the political balancing act between conservative-national inertia and economic-industrial vision. With the construction of huge apartment buildings for cheap accommodation, much of the city's Baroque substance was lost, but with regard to the population explosion it was a true necessity: between 1880 and 1905 the population increased from 592,000 people to two million! To achieve better organization of the city council, the outskirts were incorporated from 1850, the periphery from 1890 on. Instead of the city wall (sanded in 1856) and the glacis, the slope running down from the fortification, a generously proportioned circular road was built around the medieval city centre. In 1873 Vienna presented itself to an international public at the **World Exhibition**. Due to the regulation of the navigation of the Danube from 1870 to 1874 the town was now able to expand on the left bank of the river as well.

First Republic and fascism After the First World War, the abdication of Karl I and the decline of the Danube monarchy, the First Republic was proclaimed on 12 November 1918, with Vienna as its capital. Overnight, the centre of an empire with 50 million inhabitants and twelve nationalities was reduced to a role as capital of a small state with only 6.6 million inhabitants, 2.3 million thereof in Vienna itself. The polarization of the political life between the Social Democrats and the clerical Conservatives seriously complicated the development of a functional democratic commonwealth in Vienna as well. The Dollfuss austrofascist regime started in 1933 and was followed by the **annexation of Austria** into the German Reich in 1938, with Vienna as the capital of the province of »Ostmark«. The National Socialists banished or systematically murdered their political opponents and the Jewish citizens of Vienna. During the Second World War more than 200,000 Viennese lost their lives. The Red Army captured Vienna in the middle of 1945.

Second Republic The Allied forces – USSR, USA, Great Britain and France – divided Vienna into four zones of occupation. With financial help from the Marshall Plan, reconstruction was accelerated from 1947 on, and the city took on an increasingly higher national and international profile. With the ratification of the Austrian State Treaty in 1955, the Allies withdrew their troops and the city and nation became independent again. In 1956 the International Atomic Energy Agency moved to Vienna, and the United Nations Industrial Development Organization (UNIDO) followed in 1967. With the opening of the UNO-City in 1979 Vienna became the third headquarters of the UN. In 1990 the city once again became the focus of central Europe with the fall of the Iron Curtain, as political, economic and cultural contacts with eastern European states were re-established. In 1994 the construction in the Donau-City, the second modern city centre in Vienna, began. The city's symbol for the dawning of the 21st century is the 202m/662ft-high **Millenium Tower** on the right bank of the Danube.

Tour of Vienna's City Centre

Starting at Stephansplatz At least half a day is needed for a round trip through the city centre of Vienna. Stephansplatz in front of the Stephansdom (St Stephen's Cathedral) is the **centre of the city of Vienna** and a popular pedestrian area, surrounded by shops, cafés and interesting buildings like the house »Zur Weltkugel« (no. 2), the Churhaus (no. 3), the Domherrenhof (no. 5) or the archiepiscopal palace (no. 7). The Haas-Haus is situated on Stock-im-Eisen-Platz (no. 4–6). The square's curious name comes from a tree trunk studded by many nails – see it at house no. 3/4, at the corner of Grabenstrasse and Kärntner Strasse – which was first documented in 1533.

The large open space of Stephansplatz was remodelled after the removal of war debris and the construction of the U-Bahn station. In the process the foundations of the chapel of Mary Magdalene were opened up, which today is marked with coloured stones next to St Stephen's Cathedral. Beneath the chapel crypt, which is used as a charnel house, is the chapel of St Virgil. On the basis of the ornamentation the origins of this sacral building, where a collection of historical ceramics from Vienna is also on display, dates back to the 13th century (closed at present for conservation work).

✴
◄ Virgilkapelle

Vienna's most famous landmark and **Austria's most important Gothic building** is the mighty cathedral and metropolitan church of St Stephen. Generations of architects have contributed to this 107m/351ft-long and 39m/128ft-wide sacral building since the 12th century; it therefore represents the art history of eight centuries. The Stephansdom was badly damaged in the last days of the Second World War. Austria's provinces cooperated to carry out the reconstruction and restoration work: Upper Austria sponsored the new bell, Lower Austria the floor, Vorarlberg the benches, Tyrol the windows, Carinthia the chandeliers, Burgenland the communion bench, Salzburg the tabernacle, Vienna the roof and Styria the portal. On Stephansplatz close to the Singertor gate, whose iron coil on the left pillar is interpreted as a medieval »asylum handle« (anyone holding it was protected by the church), stands a bronze model of the cathedral to a scale of 1:100 for the blind and visually impaired.

✴ ✴
Stephansdom

Portrait of Master Pilgram at the foot of the late Gothic organ

At the Riesentor (Giant Gate), built in 1230, justice was dispensed during the rule of the Babenbergs. Left of the porch two iron scales are immured representing units of measure: the longer one represents the Wiener Normalelle, the shorter one the Wiener Leinenelle. The name of the 66m/216ft-high Heidentürme (Heathen Towers) dates back to a heathen sanctuary that allegedly stood here before. From the northern tower, also called the Adlerturm, hangs the 21-ton »Pummerin« bell, which was cast in 1951 partly from debris of the earlier bell, which was destroyed in 1945. It is only rung on special occasions. An express lift takes visitors to the top (opening times: daily 8.30am–5pm, July and Aug until 6pm).

◄ Exterior

🕐

The southern tower, which was first constructed in 1365, commonly known as »Steffl«, is 137m/449ft-high and, along with Freiburg's Munster tower, the most beautiful tower of German Gothic architecture.

◄ »Steffl«

Clustered piers carry the nave and two side aisles with a reticulated and stellar vault. The most valuable figure is that of St Christopher at the left choir column (1470), probably a donation by Emperor Friedrich III. The most important work of art is the late Gothic pul-

✴
◄ Interior

STEPHANSDOM

✳ ✳ **The story of the creation of St Stephen's Cathedral reaches as far back as the 12th century; the Riesentor (Giant's Gate) and the Heidentürme (Towers of the Heathens) date from the 13th century. Duke Rudolf IV of Habsburg, the cathedral's founder, initiated the conversion into a Gothic church with stellar and cross-ribbed vaulting as well as the 137m/450ft South Tower. The North Tower remained incomplete and received a Renaissance-style helm roof in 1557.**

🕐 Guided tours:
Mon–Sat 9am–11.30am, 1pm–4.30pm,
Sun 1pm–4.30pm
Tel. 01 / 515 52 35 26, www.stephanskirche.at

① South Tower
After the towers of the cathedrals in Cologne and Ulm, the South Tower is the third highest church tower in central Europe. It stands on a square ground plan and then turns into an octagon, tapering continuously as it does so. A bronze ball with double-headed eagle is fixed to the finial at the top. The effort of the ascent is rewarded with a splendid panoramic view (access daily 9am–5.30pm).

② Pulpit
The most dazzling work of art in the cathedral's nave is the pulpit, a masterpiece of late Gothic sculpture made from sandstone. The sculptor is unknown, but it was possibly Master Pilgram who created this pulpit with the busts of the four Fathers of the Church.

③ High Altar
Tobias and Johann Jakob Pock made the High Altar from black marble in 1640–60. The statues next to the altarpiece depict St Leopold and St Florian, Austria's patron saints, as well as St Roch and St Sebastian, the plague saints. To the right and left behind the high altar Gothic glass paintings have been preserved.

④ Dienstbotenmadonna
The most valuable statue in the cathedral is the Madonna of the Servants from around 1340. The legend tells of a count's maid who turned to the Virgin for help when suspected of stealing. The true culprit was found and the maid is said to have donated the figure to the cathedral.

⑤ Raised Sarcophagus of Friedrich III
In the South Choir stands the mighty raised sarcophagus of Emperor Friedrich III. It is made of red marble. Work on the sarcophagus lasted two generations. The overall design and the covering slab are by Gerhaert Niclas van Leyden (1467–1513).

⑥ Catacombs
The catacombs are the final resting place for the mortal remains of 15 Habsburgs and the innards of the 56 Habsburgs that are buried in the Kaisergruft (Imperial Crypt).

View from the South Tower

pit (1510–15; sandstone) possibly by Master Pilgram, who presented himself as a figure at the bottom of the pulpit in the form of a »Fenstergucker« (»window gazer«). At the late Gothic organ foot (1513), clearly made by Pilgram, the artist also immortalized himself – with a compass and a set square. Tobias and Johann Jakob Pock built the high altar out of black marble in 1640–60. In the southern choir stands the mighty raised sarcophagus of Emperor Friedrich III who donated the wing altar for the choir opposite. The statues in the Eligiuskapelle (Eligius chapel) number among the most important sculptures of the 14th century; the »Hausmuttergottes« (the Protective Mother of God) was revered by the Empress Maria Theresia. The Tirnakapelle is the burial chapel of Prince Eugene (died in 1736). The altar crucifix dates back to the 15th century: Jesus has a beard made of natural hair, which according to legend grows constantly.

The **catacombs** on several floors, inaccessible to the public, contain the bones of thousands of Viennese. The dead were mostly buried carelessly at the church cemetery and exhumed soon afterwards to make space for the next resident, and a foul odour spread accordingly. Therefore it was decided to build the catacombs. In

Vienna Stephansdom

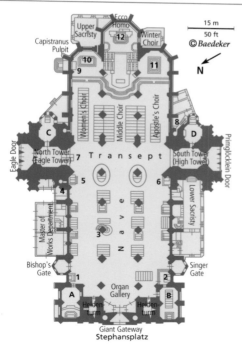

A Tirna Chapel (Holy Cross Chapel; burial place of Prince Eugene † 1736; Treasury Chapel above it)
B Eligius Chapel
C Barbara Chapel
D Catherine Chapel

1 H. Prachatitz's Altar Canopy
2 Canopy with Pötscher Madonna
3 A. Pilgram's Pulpit (with »Peeping Tom« on the plinth)
4 Lift to Pummerin Bell
5 A. Pilgram's Organ Case (with his self-portrait)
6 H. Puchsbaum's Canopy
7 Entrance to Catacombs
8 Tower Stairs (313 steps)
9 Donor's Gravestone
10 Wiener-Neustadt Altar (»Friedrich's reredos«)
11 Emperor Friedrich III's († 1493) Raised Sarcophagus
12 T. and J. J. Pock's High Altar

Friedrich III donated the winged altar from 1447, which was brought to Vienna from the Neukloster in Wiener Neustadt in 1884. In the lower section of the middle reliquary there are carved statues of the Holy Virgin and St Catherine.

At the foot of the pulpit the portrait of the self-confident artist – possibly Anton Pilgram – looking out of the window in the pose of the »Fenstergucker«

The pulpit is one of the most beautiful works of art in the cathedral.

The Singertor was the entrance for the male visitors. The figures of the founders, the nine apostles and the legend of St Paul in the tympanum were created around 1378.

The nave has a four-bay reticulated vault. The figures on the compound pillars do not follow a unified iconographical scheme.

© Baedeker

1783 Emperor Joseph II prohibited further burials here. The centre point is formed by the **Herzogsgruft** (Ducal Crypt), which was built for the House of Habsburg in 1363. After the construction of the Kaisergruft (Imperial Burial Vault) at the Capuchin church only the copper urns with the intestines were kept here, while the bodies are entombed in the Kaisergruft of the church of St Augustine, and the hearts in the Herzgruft (Heart Crypt) in the same church (guided tours: daily 10am–11.30am, 1.30pm–4.30pm, Sun pm only).

★ Dom- und Diözesanmuseum

Zwettlerhof (Stephansplatz no. 6) next to the Archbishop's Palace houses the Cathedral and Diocesan Museum. Its treasure chamber contains the **most valuable pieces from the church treasury** of St Stephen's Cathedral, including two Syrian glass bottles (13th–14th century), cross reliquaries, the shroud of Duke Rudolf IV, enamel panels (12th century) with scenes from the Old Testament, a Carolingian Book of Gospels (9th century), Gothic panel paintings and a large collection of sculptures (opening times: Tue–Sat 10am–5pm).

★ Mozarthaus Vienna

Fans of classical music absolutely must visit the Mozarthaus on Domgasse, which extends eastwards from Stephansplatz. House no. 8 is where Mozart lived with his wife and child in 1784–87 and composed his opera *The Marriage of Figaro*. Today the apartment serves as a memorial (www.mozarthausvienna.at; opening times: daily 9am–7pm).

Old university quarter

From Schulerstrasse left over the Wollzeile comes the Bäckerstrasse, with a number of beautiful old town palaces (nos. 7, 8, 12 and 16). To the east follows the Dr.-Ignatz-Seipel-Platz, one of the most beautiful enclosed squares in Vienna. Here stands the Alte Üniversität (Old University), which was built in 1425 and altered in 1725. **Franz Schubert** visited the Academic College from 1808 to 1823. Inside the former university church, today the Jesuit church (1703–05), the moving impression of the room created by the illusionist perspective painting in the barrel vault is fascinating. The best standing position for viewers is marked by a light-coloured plate at the middle entrance. The Neue Aula at the university, Vienna's most important secular Rococo building, has been the headquarters of the Austrian Academy of Sciences since 1857 (not accessible).

Hoher Markt

Directly to the west follows the historically significant Hohe Markt, the oldest square of the Danube metropolis on the edge of the textile quarter, also known by the Viennese as the »Fetzenviertel«. This is where Emperor Marc Aurel allegedly died. The scaffold site, the fish market and the trading square of the »Gewandkrämer« were situated here during the Middle Ages. At the centre stands the Vermählingsbrunnen (Wedding Fountain), whose figural decoration depicts the wedding of Mary and Joseph. The striking clock of the Anker insurance company on the candle arch (Schwibbogen) spanning Rotgasse is on the eastern side. Every hour this musical clock made in 1914 shows a parade of historical figures, including Aurel, Charlemagne, Theodora von Byzanz, Walther von der Vogelweide, Prince Eugene, Maria Theresia and Joseph Haydn. At house no. 3, at the southern side of Hohe Markt, it is possible to descend into the underground excavations and to enter the Roman Museum with video guide and 3D animation (opening times: Tue–Sun 9am–6pm).

Römermuseum ▸

🕑

Ruprechtskirche

The **oldest church in Vienna**, St Ruprecht, is reached via Judengasse, branching off to the north. Bishop Virgil of Salzburg is said to have built the church in the 8th century on the site of an underground meeting house of the two apostles of the faith, Cunard and Gisalrich. It was altered many times. Its treasures include the oldest glass windows in Vienna (13th century) in the middle window of the choir (opening times: Mon–Fri 10am–noon, Tue and Thu 2pm–4pm).

🕑

Documentation archive of the Austrian resistance

At Wipplingerstrasse, which runs to the west Hohe Markt, stands the Altes Rathaus (old town hall) with a documentation archive of the Austrian resistance. It shows exhibits on the history of the active rebellion against the Austrofascism of 1934–38 and on the resistance against National Socialism (opening times: Mon–Fri 9am–5pm, Thu until 7pm). Five minutes walk northwards, at Salztorgasse 6 is a memorial to Austrian freedom fighters and the victims of the Nazi regime (opening times: Mon 2pm–5pm, Thu and Fri 9am–noon and 2pm–5pm).

🕑

🕑

Judenplatz

After the Bohemian Staatskanzlei (State Chancellery), on the left hand side comes Judenplatz, which has been the centre of Vienna's medieval Jewish quarter since the end of 13th century. In 1421 hatred and envy led to »Wiener Geserah«, the banishment and murder of Jews. This is pointed out at the house no. 2 »Zum grossen Jordan« (15th century) by a relief of the baptism of Christ with anti-Semitic inscriptions. The **Holocaust memorial** by Rachel Whiteread recalls the murder of 65,000 Austrian Jews by the Nazis. Beneath the memorial are the foundations of the medieval synagogue and a small **museum** (opening times: Sun–Thu 10am–6pm, Fri until 2pm).

🕑

✴

Uhrenmuseum

From the southern side of the Bohemian Hofkanzlei (Court Chancellery) a little alley runs to the »Harfenhaus« (»Harp House«), one of the oldest houses in Vienna. Since 1921 it has been home to the Clock Museum, where the development of chronometers from the 15th century to the present and a large variety of different clocks are presented on three floors (opening times: Tue–Sun 10am–6pm,

🕑

guided tours: every 1st and 3rd Sunday of the month 10am and 11am).

Directly to the west follows the largest square of the city centre, **»Am Hof«**, a place with a great history. The Romans settled here, and the Babenbergs built their first palace here in 1135. The square was also the site of glorious parties, which inspired Walther von der Vogelweide to the laudatory verse claiming »Das ist der wunnigliche Hof ze Vienne« (»This is the most wonderful courtyard in Vienna«). In 1806 Emperor Franz II declared the end of the Holy Roman Empire of the German Nation from the balcony of the former Jesuit church of the Nine Choirs of Angels.

Peterskirche

Further southeast, on Petersplatz, stands the church of St Peter. According to legend it was built on the site of a church founded by Charlemagne, of which nothing remains today. Started by Gabriel Montani and probably finished by Lukas von Hildebrandt, the building on a central oval ground plan stems from 18th century. Numer-

> ! **Baedeker TIP**
>
> ### Art nouveau toilets
> A quaint sight on Graben are the underground art nouveau toilets (1905) by Adolf Loos. They offer a stylish setting for answering calls of nature.

The »Hof« is the largest square in the city centre

ous famous artists including Rottmayr, Altomonte and Kupelwieser participated in creating the glorious interior decoration.

Graben
Now comes Graben, the former fortification trench of a Roman camp, later a flour and vegetable market and today a popular shopping area. Turn right into Dorotheergasse, where at no. 6 one of the most beautiful artist and writer cafés in Vienna, **Café Hawelka**, can be found (opening times: daily except Tue 8am–2pm, Sun from 10am).

✳
Jüdisches Museum
🕑
Dorotheergasse no. 11 is home to the Jewish Museum. It thematizes the relationship between Jewish and non-Jewish citizens in Austria and Europe. Changing exhibitions deal with Jewish Vienna, the East-European Jews and Viennese Salon Culture. The remarkable permanent exhibition is based on three collections: the collection of Max Berger on the art of Ashkenazi Judaism, the collection of the Israeli cultural community of Vienna and the collection of Martin Schlaff, which with its approx. 5000 objects documenting anti-Semitism is unique (opening times: Sun–Fri 10am–6pm, guided tours: Thu 7pm, Sun 11am and 3pm).

Neuer Markt
Between the Jewish Museum and the Dorotheum is Plankenstrasse, which leads eastwards to Neuer Markt. Since 1220 this square has served as a flour and herb market, for jousting and sleighing. The four graceful putti at the Providentia or Donner Fountain (1737–39) by Georg R. Donner symbolize the Enns, Traun, Ybbs and March rivers.

! **Baedeker TIP**

»Tante Dorothee«
One of the world's largest auction houses is the Dorotheum at Dorotheerstrasse 17, known to the Viennese as »Tante Dorothee« (Aunt Dorothy) or simply »Pfandl«. A visit is worthwhile for the stylish atmosphere alone (viewing: Mon–Fri 10am–6pm, Sat 9am–5pm; auctions: Mon–Fri at 2pm, Sat at 10am).

The plain **Capuchin church** (built 1622–32) on the western side of Neuer Markt, including the monastery, was founded by Anna († 1618), wife of the Emperor Matthias. The entrance to the left of the church leads down to the Capuchin or Imperial Burial Vault,

✳
Kaisergruft ►
🕑
the **Habsburg family crypt since 1633**. Here lie the embalmed bodies of 138 members of the House of Habsburg. The last burial took place in 1989, when the former Empress Zita von Habsburg found her final resting place here. The nine vaults are in chronological order, which makes it easy to follow the change of different artistic styles from individual epochs (opening times: daily 10am–6pm).

Kärntner Strasse
Those with some money left over after a stroll along the Kärntner Strasse shopping area can try to top it up again at the casino (no. 41), housed in Palais Esterházy, which was constructed in 1648. To the north, the route heads back to Stephansplatz.

Hofburg and Surroundings

The monastery and church received their name due to the Irish monks who were called from Regensburg to Vienna in the 12th century: they were called Scotsmen as Ireland was known as New Scotland at the time. In the crypt of the Baroque Schottenkirche (»Scottish church«; originally 12th century; reconstructed in 1638–48) rest Duke Rüdiger of Starhemberg, who defended Vienna against the Turks in 1683, Duke Heinrich II Jasomir († 1177), the founder of the abbey, and the painter Paul Troger († 1762). The Schottenstift (full name: Benedictine Abbey of Our Dear Lady to the Scots) supports a renowned grammar school, which the former **Federal Chancellor Schüssel** once attended, and an important picture gallery with works of religious subjects from the 16th to the 19th century, as well as portrait and landscape paintings (opening times: Thu–Sat 11am–5pm). **Schottenstift**

The Schottenkirche is situated at the Freyung (»free place«), a triangular square, whose name is reminiscent of the right of the abbey as well as the Stephansdom to grant church asylum to the persecuted. Where »Wurstelprater« (sausage friers) and »Küchelbäcker« (bakermen), jugglers and carnival barkers used to stand, the place today is mainly known for its Easter market and a magical pre-yuletide advent atmosphere. The **Austriabrunnen** (Austria Fountain) by Ludwig von Schwanthaler was cast in Munich in 1846 and all its allegorical figures represent Austria and the former main rivers of the monarchy: the Po, Elbe, Weichsel and Danube. The story goes that Schwanthaler filled the Austria figure with cigarettes in Munich to bring them to Vienna without having to pay duty, but never got a chance to retrieve his contraband – so the tobacco is still inside to this day. **Freyung**

Around Freyung, pretty town palaces were created during the 17th and 18th centuries: Palais Harrach (no. 3), since 1995 one of the exhibition spaces of the Museum of Art History, Palais Kinsky (no. 4) and Palais Ferstel (no. 2). The last was built for the National Bank in 1856–60, which had already moved again by 1878. The Café Central is still here though, and significantly more famous. It was once said of the café: »On every other stool is either an emerging poetry genius, an Austro-Marxist or nobleman, a twelve-tone musician or at least a psychoanalyst...«. Regular guests have included Peter Altenberg, Egon Friedell, Franz Werfel, Stefan Zweig (► Famous People), Karl Kraus and Leon Trotsky – and Alfred Polgar, who wrote: »Café Central is not an ordinary coffee house, but a world view whose essence it is not to view the world« (opening times: daily 7.30am–10pm, Sun from 10am). ◄ Café Central

Beethoven admirers head along Teinfaltstrasse and Schreyvogelgasse for the Pasqualatihaus, Mölkerbastei 8, where the composer with a **Pasqualatihaus**

Less a coffee house, more a life philosophy: Café Central

rather complicated personality lived on and off from 1804 onwards. When **Beethoven** wanted to move out yet again, it is said that the owner, Pasqualati, Beethoven's friend and supporter, said: »The lodging will not be rented; Beethoven will be back.« The exhibit includes pictures, furniture, notes and personal belongings (opening times: Tue–Sun 10am–1pm and 2pm–6pm).

Michaelerplatz Continue along Herrengasse to the elegant Michaelerplatz, with buildings from various epochs. The southwestern side of the square is dominated by the round façade of the Michaeler Wing of the Old Palace, followed by the Winter Riding School. Furthermore, **a »scandalous« piece of Vienna's architectural history**, today headquarters of the Raiffeisenbank, stands here: the Adolf-Loos-Haus. In 1910 the architect planned the plain functional building for the tailors Goldmann & Salatsch to contrast sharply with the pomp of the Ringstrasse style of the Hofburg – and attracted the disapproval of Emperor Franz Joseph I, who found this »house without eyebrows« (Loos dispensed with window frames) simply abominable. In the meantime, the reconstructed rooms of the tailor's shop are used as an exhibition space.

The **Salvatorianerkirche St Michael**, the former court parish church of the Imperial family, was built in the first half of the 13th century at the same time as the old castle and the Romanesque re-modelling of the Stephansdom. Later revamped in Gothic style, a Baroque front hall was added, and in 1792 came the west doorway with the *Fall of the Angels* sculpture by Lorenzo Mattielli as well as the Classical façade.

Café Griensteidl on Michaelerplatz (no. 2) also numbers among the legendary symbols of old Viennese coffee house culture. From 1847 to 1897 the former apothecary Griensteidl ran a coffee house that was frequented by artists and writers, including such luminaries as Hugo von Hofmannsthal, Arthur Schnitzler, Hugo Wolf and Arnold Schönberg (► Famous People). After Griensteidl's death the coffee house had to give way to the Palais Herbertstein, whereupon Karl Kraus ensured its place in literary history with his satirical pamphlet *Die demolirte Litteratur* (*Demolished Literature*).

Café Griensteidl

For those with a sweet tooth, the finest – and most expensive – confectioner in Vienna is **Demel, purveyor of fine pastries to the court**, at Kohlmarkt (no. 14), branching off from Michaelerplatz to the northeast. The well over 200-year old establishment provided Empress Sisi with violet sorbet and Emperor Franz Joseph I and his mistress with doughnuts. After an eventful history it was recently acquired by the businessman Attila Dogudan who is well known in Viennese society circles and, ironically, from the very country that provided Vienna's legendary coffeehouses with their main ingredient during the Turkish siege. The »Demelinerinnen«, as the waitresses at Café Demel are known, will continue to put their time-honoured question, »Have you already decided?« (»Haben schon gewählt?«), on Kohlmarkt in the future. A chocolate and marzipan museum has been set up in the Demel's cellar.

Demel

Further southeast from Michaelerplatz is Josefsplatz, offering a beautiful view with its late Baroque to neo-classical image. It is framed by the Winter Riding School, the Austrian National Library and the Pallavicini and Pálffy palaces. The latter, the **»Österrreichhaus«** also hosts cultural events. In the middle of the square stands a memorial to Joseph II, created by Franz Anton Zauner in 1795–1806.

Josefsplatz

The church of St Augustine was built in 1330–39 and is part of a former monastery (1327–1838), where the popular preacher Abraham a Santa Clara lived from 1689–1709. It served repeatedly as the setting for important weddings, including the one between Franz Joseph I and Princess Elisabeth of Bavaria in 1854. At the Loreto Chapel on the right side of the choir lies the Herzgruft, or Heart Crypt. Through a window, it is possible to see 54 urns containing the hearts of members of the Habsburg dynasty and of archbishops. The large heart urn contains the hearts of Maria Theresia and her husband Franz I (guided tours: Mon–Fri 11am and 3pm). Antonio Canova's

★ Augustiner-kirche

monumental marble grave for Maria Christina, Duchess of Teschen (died in 1798), a daughter of Maria Theresia, is a highlight of neo-classical tomb art. The marble sarcophagus for Emperor Leopold II, a neo-classical work by Franz A. Zauner, is empty.

Theatermuseum Palais Lobkowitz at Lobkowitzplatz 2, where Beethoven conducted the debut performance of his third symphony in 1804, and in 1807 that of his fourth, has been home to the Austrian Theatre Museum since 1991. The permanent exhibition shows stage models, costumes and props while changing exhibitions document different theatrical epochs. The associated theatre museum for children offers doll ex-
⊕ hibits and puppet theatre (opening times: Tue–Sun 10am–5pm, Wed until 8pm; guided tours by arrangement, tel. 01/525 24 34 60). An extension of the museum is located in the nearby Hanuschgasse 3.

✱
Albertina The Albertina ranks among the **most famous and comprehensive graphical collections in the world**. Founded in 1768 by Maria Theresia's son-in-law, Albert Duke of Teschen (1738–1822), it contains about 65,000 drawings of the German (Dürer, Holbein d. Ä., Menzel, Liebermann), Austrian (Rottmayr, Troger, Makart, Klimt, Kubin), Italian (Fra Angelico, Mantegna, da Vinci, Raphael, Canaletto, Tiepolo), Old Dutch-Flemish (van Leyden, Brueghel d. Ä., van Dyck, Rubens), Dutch (Both, van Goyen, Ruisdael, Rembrandt), French (Poussin, Watteau, Matisse, Chagall) and English (Reynolds, Gainsborough, Romney) schools. In addition, there are nearly one million print graphics from the late Gothic to the modern era, an architectural collection including some 25,000 plans, sketches and models as well as the collection of historical and contemporary photography
⊕ founded in 1999 (opening times: daily 10am–6pm, Wed until 9pm).
Filmmuseum ► The Austrian Film Museum is also situated here. It has no exhibitions, but shows classic and avant-garde films. The current programme is announced in daily newspapers and what's-on guides (shows from October to May).

Memorial against war and fascism (see ill. p.70) Albertinaplatz is dominated by a memorial against war and fascism (Mahnmal gegen Krieg und Faschismus) designed by the Austrian sculptor Alfred Hrdlicka (1988–91). It was built to commemorate the victims of the Nazi regime and the victims of the Second World War, who rest beneath the Albertinaplatz in air raid shelters buried during the bombing. The bronze sculpture recalls 12 March 1938, when the Nazis forced Jewish citizens to scrub away pro-Austrian slogans painted onto the street.

✱
Vienna State Opera The famous musical theatre, constructed from 1861 to 1869 in historicized forms of the French early Renaissance and known as the Hofoper until 1918, was officially opened with a performance of Mozart's *Don Giovanni*. In 1955, the reconstruction of the building, which was destroyed during the Second World, was opened with

The Vienna Opera Ball was once used as the setting for a thriller

Beethoven's *Fidelio*. The Viennese enthusiasm for music is rooted in the history of the Habsburg dynasty – practically all the monarchs were music lovers. The theatre has room for 2211 guests and offers space for the 110 musicians of the Vienna Philharmonic Orchestra – the house orchestra since 1842. The curtain rises on 300 evenings every year. The last Thursday of the carnival season is a very special performance night: the occasion is the most famous of the nearly 150 balls in Vienna, the **Vienna Opera Ball** (www.wiener-staatsoper.-at; guided tours: tel. 01/5 14 44-26 06).

Behind the Oper, at Philharmonikerstrasse 4, stands the Hotel Sacher, arguably Vienna's most popular traditional accommodation. Even today it is furnished with precious silk wall paper, exquisite Biedermeier furniture and valuable paintings, and its nostalgic marble hall offers an elegant setting for important official receptions. An ancestor of hotel founder Eduard Sacher is said to have created the legendary Sachertorte on the occasion of the Congress of Vienna (►Baedeker Special p.105). **Hotel Sacher**

Hofburg

The Imperial Palace served as the residence of Austrian monarchs for more than six centuries: here the Habsburg dynasty governed their multi-ethnic state until 1918 and made European history. Today the **Austrian Federal President** officiates at the Hofburg. The huge complex, including squares and gardens, covers an area of approx. 240,000 sq m/59ac and looks back over 700 years of construction. Sections of the building are from the Gothic, Renaissance, Baroque, Rococo, Classical and Wilhelminian periods. The »city within a city«

Hofburg Plan

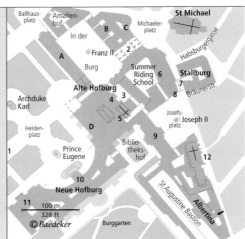

A Leopoldine Range
B Imperial Chancellery Range
C Michaeler Range
D Ceremonial Apartments Range

1 Burg Gate, with
  Monument to Heroes
2 State Apartments,
  Sissi Museum and Silberkammer
3 Schweizerhof
  (Entrance to Treasury)
4 Secular and
  Ecclesiastical Treasuries
5 Hofburg Chapel and
  Imperial Music Chapel
6 Winter Riding School
7 Entrance to Lippizaner Stables
8 Entrance to
  Spanish Riding School
9 National Library
10 Ephesos Museum,
  Arms Collection
11 Museum of Ethnology
12 Augustinian Church

includes about 18 wings, 54 staircases, 19 courtyards, 2600 rooms and employs approx. 5000 people.

Tour ▶ Only the Kaiserappartements (Imperial Apartments) and the Silberkammer (Silver Collection) at the Alte Hofburg have the same entrance and can be visited with a combined ticket. For everything else – whether the sights at the Alte Hofburg, the National Library or the museums at the Neue Hofburg – it is necessary to buy an extra ticket at each entrance.

✶ ✶
**Imperial
Apartments**

Lukas von Hildebrandt began his construction of the Imperial Apartments in 1723. Joseph Emanuel Fischer von Erlach completed the connecting wings between the Schweizerhof and the Amalienburg in 1739. The apartments of Franz Joseph include the waiting and audience chambers, the conference hall of the privy councillors and ministers, the emperor's study and private bedroom, the small salon and the large salon with the famous painting of Empress Elisabeth in her fine gown and gem-encrusted pins, called »stars«, that she wore in her hair.

The so-called Alexander's apartments were placed at the disposal of Tsar Alexander I during the Congress of Vienna (opening times: daily 9am–5pm, July and Aug until 5.30pm).

Sisi-Museum ▶ The Amalienburg offers six chambers in which visitors can retrace the steps of the famous empress: here it is possible to visit Sisi's living and sleeping chambers, the dressing room where she kept her gymnastics equipment, her bathroom, as well as the preciously decorated large and small salons containing mementoes of their beautiful resident.

Tickets for a gala performance of the Lipizzaner horses are in great demand

The Silberkammer contains an impressive display of the valuable festive and daily tableware of the imperial court (opening times: as Imperial Apartments).

✱ ✱
Silberkammer
🕐

Mainly during the Congress of Vienna, the Baroque Winter Riding School, built from 1729 until 1735 by Joseph Emanuel Fischer von Erlach, served as an illustrious location for glamorous parties. Today it is used by the Spanish Riding School for presentations. Due to great demand, especially for gala events on Sunday mornings, tickets should be reserved well in advance (fax: 01/5 33 90 32-40; tickets@srs.at). The beautiful **Lipizzaner** horses are kept at the attached Stallburg. The Lipizzaner Museum, opened in 1997 at the Hofapotheke, a listed building, is worth visiting – and not only for horse enthusiasts (opening times: daily 9am–6pm).

✱ ✱
**Spanish
Riding School**

In 21 rooms, the treasuries contain the imperial regalia and relics of the Holy Roman Empire, coronation and chivalric insignia, badges of rank, secular and sacred treasures, and ornaments and mementoes formerly owned by the Habsburg dynasty. The pieces, collected since the 16th century, are of inestimable artistic, historic and material value (opening times: daily except Tue 10am–6pm).

✱ ✱
Schatzkammern

🕐
◀ Burgkapelle

The castle chapel was built by order of Emperor Friedrich III in 1447–49 and is now a popular venue for weddings. Some may say that the 500-year old wooden statues of the 13 »Nothelfer« (helpers in time of need) – the 14th was removed to make room for the pulpit – are in the right place in a church used for bethrothals (opening

🕐

times: Jan–June and mid-Sept–mid-Dec Mon–Thu 11am–3pm, Fri until 1pm). The court music orchestra associated with the Burgkapelle founded the imperial court chap choir, which then brought about the world famous Vienna Boys' Choir (Wiener Sängerknaben).

! *Baedeker* TIP

Vienna Boys' Choir
The performances of the Vienna Boys' Choir during the Sunday concerts at the Burgkapelle are very popular (9.15am, except July and Aug). Reservations required (tel. 01/5 33 99 27).

The Baroque building of the **National Library** on Josephsplatz was constructed according to plans by Fischer von Erlach the Elder and the Younger in 1723–26, and is linked with the Hofburg by means of the reconstructed Redoutensaal. The extensive collections date back to the 14th century and today contain some 3 million documents, 43,000 hand-written texts some dating back to the 6th century, 8000 incunables, 240,000 autographs, a similar number of map sheets, valuable globes, a portrait collection and a picture archive. Extending over two floors, the **ceremonial room**, which features a mighty cupola, wonderful ceiling frescoes and 15,000 books from the former library of Prince Eugene, is impressive. The contents of the library are spread over several buildings (opening times: Tue–Sun 10am–6pm, Thu until 9pm). The international **Esperantomuseum** at Herrengasse 9 is also part of the library (opening times: July–Sept Mon–Fri 9am–1pm, otherwise Mon–Wed 9am–4pm, Thu noon–7pm, Fri 9am–1pm).

Neue Hofburg Southwest of the Alte Hofburg stands the Neue Hofburg (New Palace), built in the new Baroque »Ringstrasse style« by Carl von Hasenauer, Gottfried Semper and others. It is the site of exceptional museums (opening times: Mon, Wed–Sun 10am–6pm.)

Ephesos Museum ► At the turn of the 19th to the 20th century, during excavations at the ancient trading town of Ephesos on the coast of Asia Minor, Austrian archaeologists found valuable statues, reliefs and bronzes, which came to Vienna as a gift to the Emperor from the sultan. Today they are shown at the Ephesos Museum.

Musikinstrumentensammlung ► The collection of musical instruments, exhibited in the middle section of the Neue Hofburg, contains **unique objects from the Renaissance era** as well as a large collection of pianos, including instruments owned by Joseph Haydn, Gustav Mahler, Richard Strauss and Hugo Wolf.

Waffensammlung ► The weapons collection of the Neue Hofburg became one of the most important collections of its kind when all of the Habsburg's weapons collections were put together in 1889. The objects on display here are more for use in a sporting or ceremonial context.

Museum für Völkerkunde ► The Museum of Ethnology was developed from the Ethnographical Department of the Museum of Natural History, and contains more than 150,000 cultural documents of peoples without a written lan-

Ceremonial room of the National Library

guage, among them bronzes from Benin (15th century), Aztec feather jewellery and craftwork from Polynesia.

Burggarten

At the Burggarten, southeast of the Neue Hofburg, stand memorials of famous figures such as Mozart, Goethe or Franz Joseph I. A special attraction is the **Palm House**, a glassy jewel from the art nouveau era, which includes a **Butterfly House** (opening times: April–Oct Mon–Fri 10am–4.45pm, Sat and Sun until 6.15pm, Nov–March daily 10am–3.45pm).

Heldenplatz

The Burgtor (castle gate), built in 1821–24 and transformed into a heroes' monument in 1934, forms the southwestern end of Heroes' Square. The two statues represent Prince Eugene and Archduke Karl. The place became infamous on 15 March 1938, when Adolf Hitler announced the annexation of Austria from the balcony of the Neue Hofburg and was cheered by huge crowds on Heldenplatz.

Ballhausplatz

Continue northwest to Ballhausplatz, from which in house no. 2 **Austrian politics have been run for 250 years**. The dukes of Kaunitz and Metternich operated at the former »Geheime Hofkanzlei« (Secret Court Chancellery), and in 1934 Chancellor Dollfuss was murdered here in the Marmorecksalon. Since 1945 it has been the seat of the federal chancellor and the foreign ministry.

Along the Ring Boulevard

Vienna's boulevard

The Ring Boulevard (Ringstrasse) was constructed on the medieval fortifications from 1859 on. Counter-clockwise, beginning in the northwest, it consists of the Schottenring, Dr.-Karl-Lueger-Ring, Dr.-Karl-Renner-Ring, Burgring, Opernring, Kärntner Ring, Schubertring, Parkring and Stubenring. It surrounds the city centre on three sides over a distance of 4km/2.5mi, the fourth side being made up of Franz-Josefs-Kai along the Danube Canal. A walk along the Ring Boulevard that covers all the sights but does not include any lengthy visits to the museums will require a whole day.

✱

Burgtheater

»Die Burg«, as this temple of the Muses is known to the Viennese, was built according to plans by Hasenauer and Semper. Of **German-language theatres**, it is one of the **richest in tradition** (Dr.-Karl-Lueger-Ring no. 2). Here, theatre-goers could and still can experience famous German-speaking performers such as Hedwig Bleibtreu, Werner Kraus, Käthe Gold, Attila Hörbiger, Paula Wessely, Hilde Krahl, Klaus Maria Brandauer, Erika Pluhar, Ulrich Tukur or Eva Mattes. Frescoes by Gustav and Ernst Klimt, as well as Franz Matsch, adorn the staircases, and the beautiful interior of the building is decorated in French Baroque style (guided tours: daily 3pm, July and Aug additionally Fri and Sat 4pm, Sun 11am and 4pm; tickets: tel. 01/514 44 41 40).

Fischer von Erlach's Hofstallbau in the Museum Quarter

The neo-Gothic Rathaus (city hall) opposite (built 1872–83) is the seat of Vienna's city or provincial assembly and the administrative centre of the city. The iron figure of the **»Eiserne Rathausmann«** on the nearly 98m/321ft-high tower is the town hall's emblem. The Vienna summer concerts take place in the Arkadenhof (arcaded courtyard), at 81 x 35m/265 x 114ft the largest of seven courtyards (guided tours in groups of five or more Mon, Wed and Fri (except during city hall meetings) 1pm; tel. 01/5 25 50).

✳ Rathaus

The design of the ceremonial parliament building (Dr.-Karl-Renner-Ring 3), built in 1873–83, alludes to the origins of democracy in Greek antiquity, with Corinthian columns and rich decoration of attics and gables. The Nationalrat and Bundesrat have held their sessions here since 1918 (to visit sessions of the Nationalrat or Bundesrat call 01/4 01 10-23 33; for guided tours call 01/4 01 10-20 03).

✳ Parliament

Continuing along the Burgring, the route reaches the Museum of Natural History. Displayed in 39 exhibition rooms and one domed hall, the collection numbers among the most important natural science collections in Europe today. It was founded by Franz I as a collection of natural history specimens, and his wife Maria Theresia opened it to the public in 1765. It offers fantastic mineral and gemstone finds from all over the world, fossils, world-famous prehistoric finds such as the 27,000-year-old »Venus of Willendorf«, and the oldest sculpture of the human form in the world – the 32,000-year-old »Venus of Galgenberg« – as well a great botanical and zoological department. Younger visitors can discover nature for themselves with the help of microscopes and video cameras at the children's hall (Hall 18; museum opening times: Thu–Mon 9am–6.30pm, Wed until 9pm; www.nhm-wien.ac.at).

✳✳ Natur-historisches Museum

Opposite stands the Museum of Natural History's twin building, the Museum of Art History, which contains **one of the most famous art collections in the world**. The main building contains the Egyptian and Near-Eastern collection, the antiquities collection, the Kunstkammer with sculpture and decorative arts, the picture gallery and the coin collection. You can easily spend a whole day perusing the treasures in this comprehensive museum (opening times: Tue–Sun 10am–6pm, Thu until 9pm; tel. 01/52 52 40; www.khm.at).

✳✳ Kunsthistorisches Museum

Gemma Augustea (antiquities collection)

Beyond the Ring Boulevard a kind of second Ring continues, along which further famous sights of Vienna can be found. Southwest of Maria-Theresien-Platz is the MuseumsQuartier Wien. The former

✳✳ Museums-Quartier

imperial Hofstallungen (Royal Mews), a 360m/394yd-long building complex, was constructed in 1723–25 according to plans by J. B. Fischer von Erlach. Behind its listed façades, in 1997 the architects Ortner & Ortner designed theMuseum Quarter for contemporary **interdisciplinary art and cultural activities** . It consists of various cultural segments: from the modern creative centre for children to the classical art museum, from departments of dance, film, architecture and theatre to forums for new media and art theory. The whole complex is complemented by shops and restaurants. The area is free to enter, and information about tickets and combined tickets are available at the visitor centre at the main entrance (Museumsplatz; open daily 10am–7pm; www.mqw.at).

MUMOK ▶ »MUMOK« is the nickname for the Museum of Modern Art, Ludwig Collection, Vienna. It owns **one of the largest European collections of modern and contemporary art**. Its focal points are classical modernity, the 1960s and 1970s, Fluxus objects, recent installations and object art as well as contemporary media art (opening times: daily 10am–6pm, Thu until 9pm).

Leopold Museum ▶ In 1994 the Austrian state acquired the collection of the art enthusiast and Viennese ophthalmologist Rudolf Leopold. He collected Austrian art from the 19th and early 20th century, especially works of Egon Schiele, and above all craftwork from the turn of the 19th to the 20th century (opening times: daily 10am–6pm, Thu until 9pm).

More museums ▶ The KUNSTHALLE Wien presents changing exhibitions about the tendencies and trends of contemporary art (opening times: daily 10am–7pm, Thu until 10pm). International developments in architecture, a permanent exhibition on 20th-century Austrian architecture and changing shows can be seen at the **Architekturzentrum Wien** (opening times: daily 10am–7pm). The **Art Cult Center** – Tabakmuseum features concerts, theatre, musicals, readings and art; the collection displays the cultural history of tobacco with 2500 exhibits (opening times: Tue–Fri 10am–5pm, Thu until 7pm, Sat, Sun 10am–2pm). Interactive exhibits for children can be found at the **ZOOM Kindermuseum**, where children can also work with the artists in their workshop. Another hands-on attraction is the multimedia lab (opening times: Mon–Fri 8.30am–5pm, Sat and Sun 10am–5.30pm).

Other facilities ▶ Also under the umbrella of the Museum Quarter is the »basis wien«, a unique information archive on the subject of recent art; the Depot offers a theoretical debate about art in lectures, workshops and panels; the quartier 21 focuses on the production, intervention and presentation of contemporary cultural offerings and modern art; in addition there is the Tanzquartier Wien, the wienXtra-kinderinfo (leisure facilities for children in Vienna), and the Theaterhaus for children. Halls E + G are at the disposal of the Tanztheater Wien, the ImPuls Tanz Festival, the **Wiener Festwochen** (May/June) and many other cultural events.

Kunsthistorisches Museum *Plan*

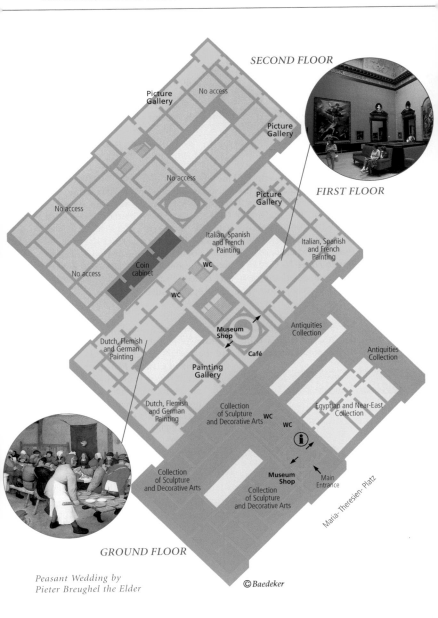

SECOND FLOOR

Picture Gallery

No access

Picture Gallery

No access

No access

Picture Gallery

No access

Italian, Spanish and French Painting

WC

Coin cabinet

WC

FIRST FLOOR

Italian, Spanish and French Painting

Dutch, Flemish and German Painting

Museum Shop

Café

Antiquities Collection

Antiquities Collection

Painting Gallery

Dutch, Flemish and German Painting

Collection of Sculpture and Decorative Arts

WC

WC

Egyptian and Near-East Collection

(i)

Collection of Sculpture and Decorative Arts

Museum Shop

Main Entrance

Collection of Sculpture and Decorative Arts

Maria- Theresien- Platz

GROUND FLOOR

Peasant Wedding by
Pieter Breughel the Elder

© Baedeker

The Viennese lovingly call it »Krauthappl«

East of the Museum Quarter lies Schillerplatz with the **Akademie der Bildenden Künste** (Academy Of Fine Arts). The internationally renowned school for painters, sculptors, graphic artists, stage designers, conservators and architects also includes an important collection of etchings and a valuable painting gallery with works from the 15th to the 20th centuries (opening times: Tue–Sun 10am–6pm).

Secession

South of the Academy of Fine Arts stands the famous Secession, the exhibition building of the artists' association of the same name. The first and epoch-defining building of Vienna's art nouveau style, designed by the student of Otto Wagner, Josef Maria Olbrich, and opened in 1898, is recognizable by its dome: a laurel tree made of gold-plated bronze, colloquially known as the »goldenes Krauthappl« (golden cabbage head). The most popular exhibit is the mighty **Beethoven Frieze** by Gustav Klimt (►Famous People). Up to 20 exhibitions are organized each year (Friedrichstrasse 12; opening times: Tue–Sun 10am–6pm, Thu until 8pm; guided tours: Sat 3pm, Sun 11am).

Theater an der Wien

At Linke Wienzeile (Left Vienna Row) no. 6 stands the Theater an der Wien, Vienna's third well-known suburban theatre along with the Leopoldstädter Theater and the Theater in der Josefstadt. In 1791 Mozart's *Magic Flute* and in 1805 Beethoven's *Fidelio* had their debut performances here. This long-time popular stage for music has been Vienna's »Neues Opernhaus« since 2006.

The Karlskirche stands to the east of Friedrichstrasse. The church, built by Fischer von Erlach the Elder and the Younger, is the **most important Baroque sacred building in Vienna**. Emperor Karl VI had promised to build a church after the end of the plague in 1713, which claimed the lives of 8000 inhabitants. It is consecrated to the plague saint Charles Borromeo. All of the so-called crownlands, component territories of the Austrian half of Austria-Hungary, had to contribute to the construction – even the city of Hamburg

Karlskirche

! **Baedeker TIP**

Culinary expedition

A visit on weekdays to Naschmarkt, between the Linke Wienzeile and the Rechte Wienzeile, is a special experience. At this, the biggest and most interesting of Vienna's food markets, a whole range of culinary treats can be enjoyed (Mon–Fri 6am–7.30pm, Sat until 5pm). On Saturdays the picturesque flea market at the southern end of Naschmarkt is worth a visit (6.30am–6pm).

contributed reparation money for the destruction of the Austrian legation church in the Hanseatic city. The spiralled relief strips on the 33m/108ft-high triumphal columns show scenes of the life of St Borromeo. The inner space is dominated by Rottmayr's dome and organ fresco and the magnificent high altar.

On the northern side of Karlsplatz stand the Handelsakademie (Academy of Commerce), the Künstlerhaus (Artists' House) and – a mecca for music lovers – the building of the Society of Friends of Music, the Musikverein, with the Golden Hall. Gustav Mahler and Hugo Wolf taught here; it was here that Furtwängler, Böhm, Karajan, Bernstein and Abbado enthused their public. The Golden Hall holds an audience of about 2000, offers room for 400 musicians and numbers among the concert halls with the best acoustics worldwide. The **Vienna Philharmonic Orchestra's legendary New Year's Concert** is broadcast from here (opening times: Mon–Fri 9am–8pm, Sat until 1pm).

★ **Musikverein**

Fans of art and architecture will find another charming attraction on Karlsplatz: the Pavillons, built in 1901 by art nouveau architect Otto Wagner, decorated with marble and gold. One of them serves as a U-Bahn entrance and for smaller temporary exhibitions of the Vienna History Museum, the other as a café and popular meeting point during the summer months.

★ **Otto Wagner Pavillons**

The City of Vienna Historical Museum on the eastern side of Karlsplatz vividly presents the history and development of the Danube metropolis from the Stone Age to the middle of the past century (opening times: Tue–Sun 9am–6pm).

Historisches Museum der Stadt Wien

East of Karlsplatz lies the long Schwarzenbergplatz, from which Schwarzenbergstrasse runs toward the city centre. At the end of Schwarzenbergstrasse (Seilerstätte 30) stands the Haus der Musik (House of Music). Opened in 2000, it has an interesting concept: visitors are invited to listen, watch and feel music. Anyone can conduct virtually, compose and play their own music thanks to many interactive facilities. Viennese musicians such as Haydn, Mozart, Beethoven, Schubert, Strauss (► Famous People), Mahler and Schönberg are portrayed in their own living environment with documents, costumes and theatre notes. The house is also home to the **Museum der Wiener Philharmoniker** (Museum of the Vienna Philharmonic Orchestra). Their founder, the composer Otto Nicolai, once lived here (opening times: daily 10am–10pm).

★ **Haus der Musik**

The Museum of Applied Arts (MAK) is situated at the northern end of the Stadtpark. The commercial, industrial and artistic development of Austria have taken essential impulses from this museum. Founded in 1864, it was inspired by London's South Kensington Mu-

★ **Museum für Angewandte Kunst (MAK)**

Installation at the MAK

seum (today's Victoria & Albert Museum), with the idea of supporting the development of current decorative art by studying old craftworks, at the same time documenting them. In 1868, a school for decorative arts was added – now the independent Academy for Applied Arts – which, for the first time, offered systematic education in handicrafts. In eleven rooms the exhibition presents single objects from various epochs from the museum's extensive collection, while every study room downstairs is devoted to a particular type of material. The redesigning of the rooms was conceived by international artists in close collaboration with the curators, with the intention of placing the exhibits in a contemporary context. In addition there is the contemporary art collection, the Sammlung der Gegenwartskunst, founded in 1986 (opening times: Tue 10am–midnight, Wed–Sun 10am–6pm).

Around Vienna's City Centre

The following description of sights outside of Vienna's city centre begins in the north of Vienna and runs clockwise around the city.

Augarten
Vienna's oldest park, the 52ha/128ac Augarten (2nd district, Leopoldstadt), stretches between the Danube Canal and the Nordwestbahnhof (northwest railway station). The garden was established in the middle of the 17th century as an imperial pleasure garden, but at the behest of Emperor Joseph II it was opened to the public in 1775 as »a place of amusement dedicated to all people«.

Augarten Palais ▶
Since 1948 the Augarten Palais has been the boarding school of the Vienna Boys' Choir. The neighbouring Baroque Gartensaal houses the showrooms and shop of the **second oldest porcelain manufacturer in Europe**, founded in 1718 – only Meissen is ten years older (guided tours: Mon–Fri 9.30am).

Karl-Marx-Hof
Those interested in the history of social housing should take a trip to Heiligenstadt and visit the Karl-Marx-Hof (19th district, Döbling; Heiligenstädter Strasse 82–92). To counter the unimaginable shortage of housing, the city of Vienna, governed by Social Democrats, built nearly 400 community buildings from 1919–34, for which the over 1km/1094yd-long building stands as a symbol. The Karl-Marx-Hof was built in 1927–30 according to plans by Karl Ehn. It includes various green inner courtyards and originally consisted of 1382 flats. After extensive renovation there were 1252 flats left. It is said that some residents have lived here ever since the building's completion in 1930.

Striking views: the lighthouse on the Danube Island and the Millenium Tower

Vienna's popular leisure area, the Donauinsel or Danube Island, owes its existence to the second round of legislation on the Danube, the Donauregulierung, which took place in the 1970s. The long, narrow island was created between the Danube and the New Danube, a man-made flood-relief channel, and offers a recreation area close the city with 700ha/1730ac of water, forest and meadow areas as well as 42km/26mi of beach.

Countless bays at the northern end of the island are a paradise for sailors and surfers, and the many cafés and restaurants here provide sustenance. Sports enthusiasts are mainly attracted to the middle section for its sports grounds, a 800m/2624ft-long water ski lift as well as a diving, sailing and canoeing school. Nudists are provided for in the southern section and the 1500m/4921ft-long Cyclodrom offers possibilities for cycle and wheelchair racing. Barbecue areas are ideal for summer parties. There are some excellent angling spots away from the crowds, as well as the »Toter Grund« nature preserve.

The Donaupark between the New and the Old Danube (22nd district, Donaustadt) is the second largest park in Vienna, planned in 1964 for the International Flower Show. A mini train runs around the grounds; the Seetheater with seats for 4000 is situated on the Iris-See, an artificial lake. At the **Donauturm** (1964), at 252m/826ft Vienna's highest building, two high-speed elevators lead to a viewing platform at 150m/492ft, as well as to two revolving restaurants at heights of 160m/524ft and 170m/557ft respectively.

After New York and Geneva, Vienna is the third official headquarters of the United Nations. UNO-City is the name of the district south of the Donaupark (22nd district, Donaustadt), where since the late 1970s and early 1980s various architecturally unique office buildings have been springing up on the exterritorial area. Based here are the International Atomic Energy Association (IAEA), to which not all UN members belong, the United Nations Industrial Development Organization (UNIDO) and the United Nations High Commission for Refugees (UNHCR). In 1987 the international conference centre, the Austria Center Vienna, was opened (visitors' information: www.acv.at and tel. 01 / 26 06 90).

Donau-City
Neighbouring the UNO-City, on the grounds of the planned World Exhibition (which was rejected by the Viennese in 1991 by popular vote), the new Donau-City is now being developed. It will not only offer space for offices and shops, but also include cultural facilities and flats (22nd district, Donaustadt). Architecturally, it presents a vast contrast to the Old Town. In 1998 the Andromeda Tower (113m/370ft) was ready for occupancy, and today many foreign companies have their offices there. Completed in the summer of 2000 the Mischek Tower (110m/360ft) is currently the highest residential building in Austria. In 2001 the Ares Tower (100m/328ft), a modern office complex, and the Tech Gate Vienna Science and Technology Park were added. Part of this is the 202m/662ft-high Millenium Tower (20th district, Brigittenau), which was completed in 1999.

KunstHausWien
East of the city centre, at Untere Weissgerberstrasse 13 (3rd district, Landstrasse), the (redesigned) KunstHausWien opened its gates in 1991. Friedensreich Hundertwasser has constructed a double monument to himself: the museum building, itself a work of art, serves as an exhibition location for the many endeavours of the rebellious architect (opening times: daily 10am–7pm). From 1892 on, the Thonet brothers used the original building as a production facility for their world famous furniture – at the museum café it is possible to test about 100 different Thonet chairs.

Hundertwasser-haus
A few junctions further south, on the corner of Löwengasse/Kegelgasse (3rd district, Landstrasse), the »nature and human-friendly« house with 50 flats was constructed after a design by Hundertwasser in 1983–85. Colourfully painted façades, golden onion towers, round corners and windows of various sizes characterize the complex. Its concept, »Tolerance of Irregularities«, was a source of much controversy.

Prater
The huge nature park between the Danube and the right Danube Canal (2nd district, Leopoldstadt) is virtually a world of its own: the 1287ha/3180ac park expands southeast of the Praterstern nearly 10km/6mi to the Praterspitz. The section near the city centre is the Wurstelprater or Volksprater with Beisln bistros and pubs, carousels, a rollercoaster, and a ghost train. In addition there are typical old Vienna style attractions such as autodromes, hippodromes, swings,

THE »ARCHITECTURE DOCTOR«

His trademarks were colourful picture-book façades, golden onion domes, and crooked floors: Friedensreich Hundertwasser was one of the greatest representatives of Austrian post-war art. The »enfant terrible« of the Austrian art scene and a committed peace and nature activist, he was also someone who quite enjoyed wealth.

Friedrich Stowasser (his birth name) was born to a Jewish family in Vienna in 1928. As a pupil he already had an »extraordinary sense for shapes and colours«. In 1948, the adolescent enrolled in an art school, though bored by the purely academic education he dropped out only three months later. Instead he drew inspiration from **personal encounters** with artists in France or Italy.

Nomen est omen

In 1949, the artist germanized his half-Slavic surname from Stowasser (sto = hundred) to Hundertwasser – and chose a more poetic-sounding first name. Besides »Friedensreich«, the painter, graphic designer and architect also adopted the **first names** »Dunkelbunt« (darkly coloured) and »Regentag« (rainy day), »for rain brightens the colours«. His new name finally turned into a trademark within the international art scene.

»Straightness won't get us anywhere,« he preached, and he only accepted straight lines (»devil's tools«) and right angles in the picture format. The self-made man reacted to the »cold« architectural style of the post-war period and to the tonal asceticism of the then upcoming art movements, abstraction and concept art, with **playful elements**, ornamental art-nouveau-style motifs, bright colours, variety and individuality. Even nine years after the Nazi regime he called contemporary art »degenerate«. He compared reconstructing architects using concrete and glass to the »mafia« and to »Nazi war criminals«. With his art, he wanted to better the world, to promote a **lifestyle closer to**

nature, to open windows to a paradisiacal »parallel world«. From 1953 he was fascinated with spirals, which to him represented the cycle of life. The »architecture doctor« (as he

Hundertwasser's waste incineration plant in Vienna

called himself) primped and grassed roofs, façades and windows. Later he decorated buildings, such as the **Hundertwasserhaus** (1983–86) in Vienna, with onion domes, irregular colonnades, uneven floors and rooftops covered in grass.

His art was also financially successful. He soon he won bids for **government contracts**, not only in Austria but also in Germany and from the United Nations. The idiosyncratic artist designed churches, day-care centres for children, residential homes, factories, stations, public toilets, a spa village (Bad Blumau in Styria), and even a waste incineration plant. Hundertwasser considered himself a loner and an extreme individualist. To him, the idea of not having any kitsch in his life was »unbearable«.

»Kitschist« with a head for business

Sometimes the extremely opinionated artist would publicly convey his artistic beliefs in the nude. In front of ecological and environmental parties he preached against wasting water and for ecologically-friendly mould

Asymmetrical, colourful, overgrown: the KunstHausWien art centre

toilets and purification plants. Needless to say, he had his critics. He was belittled and condescended as a »kitschist« and a **»façade primper«**. Many complained that besides his basic leitmotif, the »spiral of life«, he only modified and never actually created anything new; the interior design of his houses was usually very similar to ordinary buildings, his constructions mere »façade« – despite his commitment to humane architecture close to nature.

His **business skills** were equally controversial: he earned money mainly from selling reprints of his original works of art. So many of his posters and postcards decorated in art nouveau style were sold at museum shops that for a long time up until his death he was the richest artist in Austria. He was particularly criticized by those who considered the poor genius who is dedicated only to art as the true artist, and condemned everyone who actually made money from it. To them, art could never become a commercial proposition – and Hundertwasser was the antithesis of this notion.

Retreat

In the 1990s the enigmatic artist withdrew from the public gaze, after he had become rich from his buildings and paintings at a time of environmental, peace and anti-nuclear movements. For at least six months per year he retreated to his own peaceful sanctuary in **New Zealand** to paint and plant trees, and no longer seemed interested in the political events back home. He wasn't there when a large number of artists protested against the former rightwing populist from Carinthia, the late Jörg Haider. He chose his country estate in New Zealand, a spacious jungle landscape, as his final resting place. On 19 February 2000, on the Pacific Ocean on his way to his home country, Friedensreich Hundertwasser died of heart failure on board the cruise ship the *Queen Mary II*. According to his wishes, he was buried on his New Zealand estate in the **»Garden of the Happy Dead«**, which he himself had created.

shooting galleries, sword swallowers, roundabouts, ventriloquists, barrel organists (Werkelmänner) and fairground dummies (Watschenmänner), sightseeing trains and mini trains (opening times: high season 15 March to 31 Oct 10am–1pm, otherwise individual attractions open depending on the weather).

Ferris wheel ► A highlight and one of Vienna's most popular emblems is the Ferris wheel. The monumental iron construction designed by Englishman Walter Basset was built in a record time of eight months and has been operating since 1897. Destroyed during the war and rebuilt afterwards, the wheel has been spinning continuously since 1946. It was repainted for its 100th anniversary, requiring five tons of paint. It has 15 wagons (originally 30), the diameter is 61m/200ft, and the rotation speed is 0.75m/s (2.4ft/s) (opening times: Jan, Feb, Nov and Dec 10am–7.45pm, March, April and Oct until 9.45pm, May–Sept 9am–11.45pm).

! *Baedeker* TIP

In search of Harry Lime
Passionate cineasts will naturally wish to go out in search of the original film locations of The Third Man, particularly the Ferris wheel and Vienna's sewer system. On guided tours, fans can see where Rollo Martins and Harry Lime alias Joseph Cotten and Orson Welles fought their bitter battles (e.g. Vienna Walks & Talks, tel. 01/7 74 89 01).

Planetarium The Planetarium, situated close to the Ferris wheel and donated by the company Zeiss from Jena in 1927, is one of the oldest in Europe (programme information Mon–Fri 9am–2pm; tel. 01/7 29 54 94). In an entertaining exhibition that will also interest children, the **Pratermuseum** shows the development of the Prater from an imperial hunting ground to today's pleasure park (opening times: Thu 10am–1pm, Fri, Sat and Sun 2pm–6pm).

Gasometer In the district of Simmering at the Guglgasse stands **one of the most interesting residential building projects in Vienna**: the four huge gas tanks of the Vienna gasworks. Opened in 1899 they were appropriately altered by renowned architects and now, a hundred years later, offer space for 600 flats, 70 shops and pubs as well as some 11,000 sq m/118,403 sq ft of office space.

Zentralfriedhof »Death must be Viennese, just as love is French,« wrote and sang Georg Kreisler. The dimensions of Vienna's Central Cemetery (11th district, Simmering), 2.5 sq km/0.9 sq mi, the largest in all of Austria, make such suggestions seem plausible. Various memorials symbolize the cult of the dead, piety, melancholy and, despite all the mourning, also an indestructible love for life.

The monumental gate construction of the main entrance was built according to the plans of the art nouveau architect Max Hegele in 1905, who also planned the Karl Lueger Church (1907–10) in the

The Prater wouldn't be half as nice without its Ferris wheel

middle of the cemetery. At the main entrance is a detailed map of the cemetery, where many popular composers (Gluck, Beethoven, Schubert, Brahms, Johann Strauss Sohn, Millöcker, Wolf, Lanner), painters (Makart), actors (Hörbiger, Lingen), writers (Nestroy, Anzengruber) and other famous people have found their final resting place. Opposite the main gate, on the other side of the Simmeringer Hauptstrasse, is the urn cemetery with the idiosyncratic crematorium by Clemens Holzmeister (1922).

Prince Eugene of Savoy (1663–1736; ▶Famous People) had the palace at Versailles in mind when he had his summer residence built south of Schwarzenbergplatz by Lukas von Hildebrandt from 1700. In 1716 the prince's domicile, the Lower Belvedere, was finished, followed by the Upper Belvedere in 1722, which was meant for ceremonial functions (3rd district, Landstrasse). The palaces are connected by a beautiful terraced garden. The unique ensemble of buildings and landscapes make Schloss Belvedere one of Vienna's most beautiful Baroque creations. From the terrace of the Upper Belvedere there is a wonderful view of the towers of Vienna and the mountain ridges of the Wienerwald.

★ ★
Belvedere palaces

Since 1923 the collection of painting and sculpture from the heyday of Austrian Baroque (from 1683 to about 1780) has been displayed in the Lower Belvedere. The magnificent Marmorsaal (Marble Hall), the ceremonial Marmorgalerie (Marble Gallery) and the elaborately decorated Goldkabinett with Balthasar Permoser's *Apotheosis of Prince Eugene* are well worth seeing (opening times: daily 10am–6pm, Wed until 9pm).

Unteres Belvedere
◀ Austrian Baroque Museum

🕐

Basing it on the Palace of Versailles, Prince Eugene built the Upper Belvedere Palace for ceremonial purposes

Museum mittel-alterlicher Kunst ▶ The collection of the Museum of Medieval Art in the Orangery at Lower Belvedere shows sculptures and panel paintings from the 12th to the 16th century. The oldest exhibit – the »Crucifix of Stummerberg« – dates back to the mid-12th century (opening times: daily 10am–6pm).

Oberes Belvedere Until 1914 the heir apparent Archduke Franz Ferdinand lived at Upper Belvedere, and in 1955 the Austrian State Contract returning the country's sovereignty was signed in the domed hall here. Today the palace is home to the **Galerie des 19. und 20. Jahrhunderts**. The collection offers a good overview of Austrian art from Biedermeier, to art nouveau, to contemporary art. Changing exhibitions on the ground floor are dedicated to art after 1918. The first floor is reserved for Historicism, Realism, Impressionism, Symbolism and the Vienna Secession, with works by international artists such as Menzel, Renoir and Munch alongside Austrian artists. Furthermore, Austrian art from around 1900 is presented in the context of international development. In particular, works by Schiele and Klimt as well as Kokoschka, Hanak, Gerstl, Van Gogh and Khnopff are shown. On the second floor works of Classicism, Romanticism and Biedermeier are on display, represented by Caspar David Frederick, von Schwind, Angelika Kauffmann, Spitzweg, Amerling and Waldmüller (opening times: daily 10am–6pm).

Botanischer Garten The cultivated garden area east of Belvedere developed from the growing of medicinal herbs, which Maria Theresia planted on the advice of her doctor Gerard van Swieten in 1754. Expanded to become the botanical gardens soon afterwards, she donated this green sanctuary to the university. Particularly worth seeing are the succulent plants, orchid nursery and the Alpinum brought here from Schloss Schönbrunn (opening times: mid-March–Oct 9.30am–4.30pm, Sat and Sun until 5pm, closed in bad weather conditions).

Heeresgeschicht-liches Museum

Built in 1850–56 following plans by Ludwig Foerster and Theophil Hansen, the Museum of Military History, situated southeast of Belvedere and the southern train station (3rd district, Landstrasse), is **the oldest museum building in Vienna**. Moorish, Byzantine and neo-Gothic are the dominant styles in this, the most magnificent historicist construction in Vienna. It contains comprehensive collections about the military history of Austria from the late 16th century until 1945. The world's largest weapons collection can be seen in the Artillery Halls (Arsenalstrasse; open Sat–Thu 9am–5pm).

Haydn Memorial

Enthusiasts of classical music will feel the aura of the composer: Joseph Haydn acquired the little house in the former Steingasse – today Haydngasse 19 (6th district, Mariahilf) – in 1793 and lived here until his death in 1809. Here he composed his great oratorios *The Creation and The Seasons*. In 1899 a museum opened on the first floor, exhibiting letters, manuscripts, personal affects and pianos belonging to the composer. Furthermore a there is a Johannes Brahms memorial room with furniture and utensils from Brahms' last apartment (opening times: Tue–Sun 10am–6pm).

✷ ✷ Schönbrunn

From the city centre, take the Linke Wienzeile in a southwesterly direction to reach a Baroque Gesamtkunstwerk (»total work of art«), Schloss Schönbrunn and its park (13th district, Hietzing; U-Bahn stations: Schönbrunn, Hietzing, line U4).

Baroque »total work of art«

After the defeat of the Turks in 1683, J. B. Fischer von Erlach was commissioned by Emperor Leopold I to design a palace on the Gloriettehügel. It was to be even bigger and more impressive than the one at Versailles. The Baroque Schloss Schönbrunn, completed in 1696, with 1441 rooms and halls, could be considered rather moderate in comparison to the original idea. Napoleon stayed here in 1805 and 1809, in the favourite chambers of Maria Theresia; the Congress of Vienna was held here in 1814–15; Karl I ab-

DON'T MISS

- The Million Room: the height of Rococo splendour
- Great Gallery and Small Gallery: glorious ceremonial hall in white gold
- A leisurely walk through the palace gardens up to the Gloriette
- Vienna Zoo: the oldest existing zoo in the world

SCHLOSS SCHÖNBRUNN AND ITS PARK

✳ ✳ Under the rule of Maria Theresia, Schloss Schönbrunn became the glorious centrepiece of the imperial court. Nikolaus Pacassi redesigned the summer residence for her in Baroque and Rococo style. Schönbrunn Park, one of the most significant and best preserved Baroque gardens in the French style, has an area of almost 2 sq km/500ac and is open to the public during the day.

⏲ Schloss opening times:
April–June, Sept, Oct daily 8.30am–5pm, July, August until 6.30pm, Nov–March until 4.30pm
www.schoenbrunn.at

Rooms of Schönbrunn were furnished by Maria Theresia with a great feeling for art

① Neptunbrunnen

The Neptune Fountain, designed by Hetzendorf, forms the southern border of the parterre garden. Around 1780 Zauner designed the lovely decorative water features for which he delivered stone sculptures based on motifs from Greek mythology, including »Thetis begs for Neptune's help on the sea voyage of his son Achilles«.

② Maze

In 1998 a site for a 49m/54yd x 35m/38yd maze, based on historical models, was laid out next to the Neptunbrunnen. The original maze, created in 1678–1740, was finally cleared in 1892. In the centre of the site there is a viewing platform (opening times: mid-March–Oct 9am–5pm, April–June and Sept until 6pm, July and Aug until 7pm).

③ Schöner Brunnen

The old artesian well, the »Kaiserbrünnl«, gave the palace its name, and legend has it that whoever drinks from it will become beautiful (hence the name »beautiful well«). Emperor Matthias (1557–1619) discovered it during a hunt, and Emperor Joseph I had his drinking water brought from it. In 1799 the well received a grotto-like pavilion, in which the nymph Egeria by Johann Christian Beyer offers the water.

④ Gloriette

Serpentine paths lead behind the Neptunbrunnen up the hill to the classical columned hall of the Gloriette, built by Hetzendorf in 1775 as the crowning glory of the park grounds. Between 1993 and 1997 the body of the building was restored true to the original, and the middle section received its former glazing once more. The former summer dining room of the emperor is crowned by a magnificent domed ceiling. Today a café is housed in the Gloriette.

Maria Theresia depicted in a painting by Martin von Meyten (around 1743)

Pacassi relocated the Great Gallery onto the courtyard side above the five gates that form the entrance into the garden. The ceiling fresco is by Gregorio Guglielmo and depicts the income and riches of the Habsburg territories.

The Palm House in the Schönbrunn Park is Europe's largest greenhouse.

...unnen is ...otif from ...gy.

A magnificent coach from the Wagenburg collection

There is a fantastic view of the Schloss from the café in the Gloriette.

In the Vieux-Laque Room lacquer pictures are set into the dark wood panelling. Maria Theresia was a passionate collector of these panels.

The Neptun
based on a
Greek myth

© Baedeker

stained from his regency here in 1918 and the English high commissioner made the palace his headquarters in 1945. In 1996 the former summer residence of the Habsburg dynasty became a UNESCO World Cultural Heritage site. Today Schönbrunn is the most visited sight in Austria.

Peculiar rental agreement ▶ This Habsburg legacy features a curiosity, namely about 190 tenants who live permanently inside the palace. But they are not really to be envied, as in spite of the more or less normal rent those who move in must either pay a lot of money to renovate the flat or accept rather poor living standards compared to the distinguished surroundings. The public authorities only take care of the renovation of the state apartments.

Those who wish to see it all are best advised to buy a Schönbrunn Pass Gold, as this ticket includes all admission to the palace, Wagenburg museum, the zoo and the Palm House (more detailed information available at tel. 01/8 11 13-0; www.schoenbrunn.at). Of the 1441 rooms, either 22 (Imperial Tour; approx. 30 min.) or 40 ceremonial rooms (Grand Tour; approx. 50 min.) can be viewed.

State Apartments Because of its simple decoration, Franz Joseph's Study (room 4) contrasts with the rich décor of the Audience Chamber. It displays numerous pictures and photographs of the private life of the emperor, including many of Empress Elisabeth. Franz Joseph I died on 21 November 1916 at the age of 86 after a reign of nearly 68 years, in the simple soldier's bed in the bedroom (room 5). The Stairs Cabinet (room 7) served Empress Elisabeth as a writing chamber, and her bathroom was equipped for beauty care and fitness. The Marie Antoinette Room (room 11) served as a dining room in the time of Franz Joseph I; dining here was a hasty affair, for the minute the emperor, who was a very fast eater, had finished his meal, everyone else had to finish as well.

The wood-panelled Children's Room (room 12) is decorated with portraits of Maria Theresia's 14 children. The monarch held the swearing-in ceremony of her ministers in the Mirror Room (room 16); the six year old Mozart also played here for Maria Theresia in 1762. The Great Gallery (room 21), a festival room in Rococo style with marvellous crystal mirrors, rich stucco decoration and ceiling frescoes, provided a glorious setting for gala dinners, receptions and court balls. Hand-painted Far Eastern wallpaper, blue-white Japanese vases and light blue silk were stylish forms of decoration at the end of the monarchy: in the Blue Chinese Salon (room 28) Emperor Karl I signed the declaration renouncing his regency in 1918. Room 29, the luxurious Vieux-Laque Room, combines Asian art and Viennese Rococo. Maria Theresia's private salon is panelled with precious rosewood – hence the apt name the »Million Room« (room 32). 260 Indian and Persian miniatures set under glass, which the empress had brought to Vienna from Constantinople, are embedded in the panels. Room 37 accommodates the state bed

Schloss Schönbrunn Plan

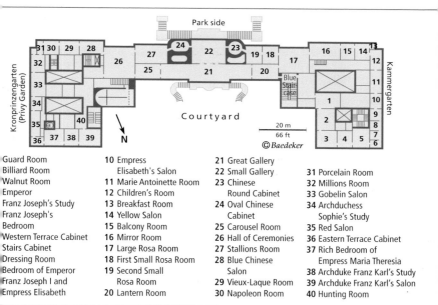

Park side

Kronprinzengarten (Privy Garden)

Courtyard

Kammergarten

Blue Staircase

20 m
66 ft
© Baedeker

N

Guard Room
Billiard Room
Walnut Room
Emperor
Franz Joseph's Study
Franz Joseph's
Bedroom
Western Terrace Cabinet
Stairs Cabinet
Dressing Room
Bedroom of Emperor
Franz Joseph I and
Empress Elisabeth

10 Empress
 Elisabeth's Salon
11 Marie Antoinette Room
12 Children's Room
13 Breakfast Room
14 Yellow Salon
15 Balcony Room
16 Mirror Room
17 Large Rosa Room
18 First Small Rosa Room
19 Second Small
 Rosa Room
20 Lantern Room

21 Great Gallery
22 Small Gallery
23 Chinese
 Round Cabinet
24 Oval Chinese
 Cabinet
25 Carousel Room
26 Hall of Ceremonies
27 Stallions Room
28 Blue Chinese
 Salon
29 Vieux-Laque Room
30 Napoleon Room

31 Porcelain Room
32 Millions Room
33 Gobelin Salon
34 Archduchess
 Sophie's Study
35 Red Salon
36 Eastern Terrace Cabinet
37 Rich Bedroom of
 Empress Maria Theresia
38 Archduke Franz Karl's Study
39 Archduke Franz Karl's Salon
40 Hunting Room

made of red velvet and valuable gold and silver embroidery, which formerly stood in Maria Theresia's rooms at the Hofburg.

Schlosstheater

Vienna's **only existing Baroque theatre** was built by the monarch's favourite architect, Nicolaus Pacassi, in 1747 and was later redecorated in Rococo style. At the »Habsburgs' private theatre«, the regent took part in the performance herself. Today the stage is used by the Max-Reinhardt-Seminar (tours: mid-July–mid-Sept daily 10am–4pm on the hour).

Wagenburg

Some 60 historical state carriages, sleighs and travel litters exhibited at the Wagenburg show how the imperial family travelled at that time, sometimes inconspicuously, sometimes with pomp and ceremony (opening times: Jan–mid-March daily 10am–4pm, April–Oct daily 9am–6pm, Nov/Dec Tue–Sun 10am–4pm).

★
Schönbrunn Park

Planned in 1706 by Jean Trehet, the park received its present form between 1765 and 1780 thanks to Ferdinand von Hohenberg and Adrian van Steckhoven. They combined natural elements, geometrical flower beds, numerous marble sculptures and architectural details such as the Neptune Fountain or the Roman ruins. The Japanese garden between the Palm House and the zoo was restored according to old plans. Southwest of the Neptune Fountain stands – eponymous for the castle – the Beautiful Fountain.

Gloriette ► The neo-classical columned hall of the Gloriette was built to commemorate the battle of Kolin (1757), where Maria Theresia's troops triumphed over the army of Frederick the Great. Today the imperial summer dining room, crowned by a magnificent dome, serves as a coffee house.

Tiergarten On the western side of Schönbrunn Park lies Vienna Zoo, which dates back to the menagerie of Franz I from 1752 and therefore counts as the **oldest zoo in the world**. The approximately 750 animal species are kept in indoor or outdoor enclosures, which are adapted to mimic the natural surroundings of the animals (opening times: daily Feb 9am–5pm, March and Oct until 5.30pm, April–Sept until 6.30pm, Nov–Jan until 4pm).

Palm House North of the zoo stands **Europe's largest glass house**. The fantastic iron-glass construction was built by Franz Segenschmid in 1883 and shows exotic flora in three differently air-conditioned sections (opening times: May–Sept daily 9.30am–6pm, Oct–April until 5pm).

Further Sights in Vienna

Technisches Museum Wien North of Schönbrunn, at the end of Mariahilfer Strasse (14th district, Penzing), is a veritable El Dorado for technical enthusiasts. Vienna's Technical Museum delivers a fascinating cross section of the entire development of technology, commerce and industry. The exhibits range from Prick's steam engine to robots, from the depiction of heavy industry to the design of luxury goods (opening times: Mon–Fri 9am–6pm, Sat and Sun from 10am). The Technical Museum has come up with a special attraction for children: at the **Mini TMW**, three to six year olds can playfully learn about technical phenomena. Parents who wish to visit the museum in peace can do so on Wednesdays, Thursdays and Sundays between 1pm and 6pm, leaving their curious offspring in the care of the staff at the Mini-TMW.

Sigmund-Freud-Museum For nearly half a century, from 1891 until he went into exile in 1938, Sigmund Freud (►Famous People) lived at Berggasse 19 (9th district, Alsergrund). It was here that the **founder of psychoanalysis** compiled his basic writings about the Oedipus complex and his interpretation of dreams and developed the theory of the »ego, id and super-ego«. In 1971 the Sigmund Freud Society reconstructed the foyer, waiting room, treatment room and working room of the 15-room apartment of the father of psychoanalysis and turned it into a museum – partly with original pieces (opening times: daily 9am–5pm).

»Zum roten Krebsen« One of Vienna's most famous figures, **Franz Schubert**, was born in 1797 a few streets further north on Nussdorfer Strasse 54 (9th dis-

Music to go with the Heuriger wine

trict, Alsergrund), at the house »Zum roten Krebsen« (»the red crab«). The city of Vienna has kept the house nearly unchanged since the 18th century. Today scores, manuscripts, pictures and personal belongings of the composer are shown (opening times: Tue–Fri 10am–4pm, Sat 2pm–6pm, Sun 9am–1pm).

The traditional Heuriger district of Grinzing (19th district, Döbling), perhaps one of the most beautiful, still inspires the classic image of Viennese »Heuriger« wine bars, with its old houses and alleys amidst gardens and vineyards. The wine from the latest grape harvest, the so-called Heuriger, is drunk in local wine taverns of the same name as soon as they display a bunch of pine twigs (= Föhrenbusch) above the entrance. Grinzing Heuriger wine taverns, which only serve their own wine, are open for only three weeks to a maximum of six months a year, whereas the Heuriger restaurants are open all year round, and often also serve wine from other regions.

✳ Grinzing

 The best known peaks of the Wienerwald on the northwestern edge of Vienna are the »brothers«, Kahlenberg and Leopoldsberg (19th district, Döbling). In good weather the 484m/1587ft-high Kahlenberg with a Heuriger restaurant and a panoramic terrace offers a great view of the Vienna Basin, the Wienerwald hills, the Schneeberg region and the Danube Valley all the way to the Marchfeld. A television tower and the Stephanie watchtower – named after the donor of the television tower, Crown Princess Stephanie – mark the peak.

✳ Kahlenberg, Leopoldsberg

★ Villach

L 6

Province: Carinthia
Population: 58,300

Elevation: 500m/1640ft

Villach owes its reputation as a charming spa town to its generous sparkling thermal springs in Warmbad Villach. But the town also has a good reputation as a carnival stronghold!

Austria's gateway to the south

Villach, the second largest town in Carinthia and the »gateway to the south«, lies close to the point where the borders of Austria, Italy and Slovenia meet, in the wide valley basin of the Drau river. The Gail, flowing from south, joins the Drau here. The Villach Alps in the west and the Karawanken range in front of the jagged Julian Alps in the south make for a beautiful mountain panorama.

History

As early as the **Hallstatt period**, the area was valued as the crossing point of two important trade routes. The Romans built a bridge here and constructed the settlement of Bilachinum. In 1007, Emperor Heinrich II donated the town of Villach to the Diocese of Bamberg, which he himself had founded. Maria Theresia (▶ Famous People) acquired the town in 1759 and affiliated it with Austria. Today Villach is the undisputed transport hub of Carinthia.

 VISITING VILLACH

INFORMATION

Tourismusinformation Villach
Rathausplatz 1
A-9500 Villach
Tel. 0 42 42/2 05 29 00, fax 2 05 29 99
www.villach.at

WHERE TO EAT

▶ Moderate

① *Stadtrestaurant*
Hauptplatz 26
A-9500 Villach
Tel. 042 42/26 10 10
This very well-kept restaurant has been awarded a »Haube«, an award for Austria's best cooking. There is a garden for guests in the Renaissance courtyard. Try the Postbräu beer, only available here!

WHERE TO STAY

▶ Mid-range

① *Romantikhotel Post*
Hauptplatz 26, A-9500 Villach
Tel. 0 42 42/26 10 10, fax 26 10 14 20
www.romantik-hotel.com
This well-established hotel has already seen royal visitors: in 1552 Emperor Charles V stayed here, and King Henry III of France resided here in 1574.

② *Bleibergerhof*
Drei Lärchen 150
A-9530 Bad Bleiberg ob Villach
Tel. 0 42 44/22 05, fax 22 05 70
www.bleibergerhof.at
The enchantingly situated wellness centre also has a deservedly popular restaurant.

What to See in Villach

Due to its strategic importance, Villach was heavily bombarded during the Second World War, and not much of its historic Old Town was left intact. A few of the houses along the elongated Hauptplatz (main square) do still originate from the High Middle Ages: Theophrastus von Hohenheim, better known as Paracelsus (1493–1541), spent many years of his life at Hauptplatz 18. House no. 26 (early 16th century) belonged once to the Khevenhüllers; it has been the Hotel Post since 1748.

Hauptplatz

The parish church, Stadtpfarrkirche St Jakob, stands on a terrace at the end of the Hauptplatz. The arches of this Gothic hall church are very beautiful. The huge St Christopher fresco in the choir and the great Baroque baldachin altar were built around 1740, the large Gothic crucifix stems from 1502, the stone pulpit from 1555. At the baptistery stands a Gothic baptismal font and choir stalls from 1464. Also remarkable are the numerous excellently worked gravestones (16th century) for members of old noble families, including the Khevenhüllers. The elegant high spire is connected to the nave only by an archway.

Stadtpfarrkirche St Jakob

Villach Map

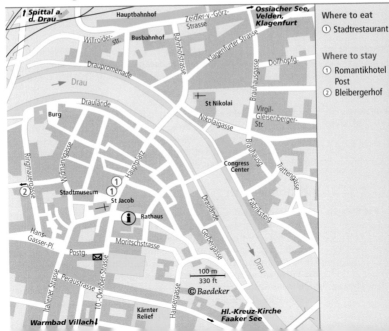

Where to eat
① Stadtrestaurant

Where to stay
① Romantikhotel Post
② Bleibergerhof

© Baedeker

Alpine plants and flowers all in one garden

Stadtmuseum Widmanngasse features beautiful buildings, including no. 30 with its gorgeous arcaded courtyard. The Stadtmuseum at no. 38 is remarkable, with collections from ancient and early history, works of art and craftwork (opening times: May–Oct Mon–Sat 10am–4.30pm; tel. 02 42 / 205 35 00).

Kärntner Relief With an area of 182 sq m/1959 sq ft, the Kärntner Relief at the Schillerpark is **one of the biggest landscape models in Europe**: it shows Carinthia and its neighbouring areas at a scale of 1:10,000 (see Stadtmuseum for opening times).

Wallfahrtskirche Hl. Kreuz Not far south of the Schillerpark stands the richly decorated pilgrimage church of the Holy Cross, with its remarkable three-floored twin-spired façade and interesting architecture: the cross-formed ground plan seems almost compressed; the central crossing of the late-Baroque composition is overarched by a beautiful cupola.

Around Villach

Bad Bleiberg The name already suggests where the wealth of this community comes from – a »lead mountain«. The area around Bleiberg (920m/3018ft; pop. 3100), about 10km/6.2mi west of Villach, was the site of lead and zinc mines for centuries. Today a family thermal bath, the Heilklimastollen Friedrich, as well as the minerals and gemstones in the Europamuseum are of interest to numerous visitors.

Terra Mystica ▶ First a 68m/223ft-long slide leads down into the mountain, then further on with the mining railway to a multimedia spectacle »Geology in Fast-motion« (at a constant 9 °C/48 °F!). The **Bergbaumuseum** (Mining Museum) proudly displays the oldest miners' flag in the world (opening times: May, June, Sept and Oct daily 10am–3pm, July and Aug from 9.30am).

Southwest of Villach, the extensive hiking and skiing area of the Villacher Alpe soars above the Gailtal valley, accessible via a nearly 17km/10mi-long, panoramic toll road. Plenty of car parks guarantee great views. In 1973, the **Villacher Alpengarten** was opened at car park no. 6, an El Dorado for botanists. At the end of the road, a cable car waits to lift visitors up to nearly 2000m/6561ft before the trip continues on foot for about an hour, up to the highest peak, the Dobratsch (2167m/7109ft), from which the nature park takes its name.

Villacher Alpe

Some 3km/2mi south of Villach's town centre lies the Warmbad Villach spa. Here around 40 million litres of warm (29 °C/84.2 °F) radon-enriched water flow every day. The spring waters were much appreciated by the Romans, and are still recommended as a treatment for rheumatism, as well as circulatory disturbances and neuropathy. Paracelsus was not convinced of the water's healing power, but Napoleon considered building extensive spas. However, his time as an emperor did not allow for anything more than the levelling of the Napoleon lawn. Today the well-kept thermal baths and numerous leisure facilities are very popular.

Warmbad Villach

The showpiece of the old parish church, Pfarrkirche Maria Gail, in the eponymous town southeast of Villach is the precious winged altar (c1520) with the Coronation of the Virgin carved by a carving workshop in Villach. The depiction of Judgment Day (13th century) on the southern outer wall is also worth seeing.

Maria Gail

Völkermarkt

N 6

Province: Carinthia
Population: 11,500

Elevation: 461m/1512ft

Völkermarkt owes its affiliation to Austria to a popular vote held in 1920 when, despite having many ethnically Slovenian citizens, the area decisively chose to remain part of Austria.

The town was founded in 1105 by a Rhenish-Franconian merchant named Volko. Due to its location close to the border, it was often disputed, but ever since the popular vote decided for Austria the small town has been able to develop in peace. Today Völkermarkt is the economic centre of the Carinthian lowlands.

»A civic decision«

What to See in and around Völkermarkt

Hauptplatz To the west, the long Hauptplatz (main square) is lined with pretty little Biedermeier houses. At the northern end stands the neo-classical Rathaus (town hall) – presumably at the former site of the ducal castle from the 13th century. The plague column recalls the outbreak of the horrible epidemic in 1715. At the other end of the square, the beautiful arcaded building from 1499 is today the seat of the **Stadtmuseum**. Here the popular vote of 1920 is documented, along with the culture and traditions of the region (Faschinggasse 1; opening times: May–Oct Tue–Fri 10am–1pm and 2pm–4pm, Sat 9am–noon).

VÖLKERMARKT

INFORMATION

Stadtgemeinde Völkermarkt
Hauptplatz 1, A-9100 Völkermarkt
Tel. 0 42 32/25 71
www.voelkermarkt.at

WHERE TO STAY

▶ **Mid-range**
Strandhotel Amerika-Holzer
Am See XI, A-9122 St Kanzian
Tel. 042 39/22 12
www.amerika-holzer.at
This comfortable hotel, located right on the lake, offers a wellness area, a heated beach swimming pool, golfing grounds and child care.

In the 15th century the Romanesque town parish church **Stadtpfarrkirche** St Magdalena, was converted into a Gothic-style building. Only the twin-towered Romanesque westwork remained. Inside, take a look at the Gothic wall paintings from the 15th century. The light column in front of the church dates from 1477.

About 8km/5mi northeast of Völkermarkt lies the market of **Griffen** (484m/1587ft; 3700 inhabitants), the **birthplace of the writer Peter Handke** and the site of the only Premonstratensian abbey in Carinthia, founded in 1236 and closed in 1786. The fortified construction includes two churches: the old **Premonstratensian abbey ▶** Romanesque parish church and the gorgeous abbey church, which is late-Romanesque with a rather idiosyncratic Baroque façade.

Schlossberg, dripstone cave ▶ A pretty trail leads up to the 130m/426ft-high Schlossberg, the ruins of which mostly stem from the 16th century. The Schlossberg tavern is in contrast much newer, with a wonderful view of the surroundings. The dripstone cave (temperature: 8 °C/46 °F) below the Schlossberg is considered to be the most **colourful show cave in Austria** and served as a shelter for man and beast as many as 10,000 years ago, as animal bone findings and a fireplace attest (hourly guided tours: Oct 10am–11am and 1pm–4pm, May, June and Sept 9am–noon and 1pm–5pm, July and Aug 9am–5pm).

Klopeiner See Head southwest from Völkermarkt over the Drau, which here accumulates to create a 21km/13mi-long lake. After a few miles the road comes to the pleasant Klopeiner See. With temperatures of up to

Who wouldn't want to spend a few hours here?
Relaxing at the Klopeiner See

28 °C/82 °F, it lays claim to being the warmest lake in Carinthia. There are no motor boats on the 1.9km/1.2mi-long, 800m/2624ft-wide lake, but during the summer holidays it gets very crowded here nonetheless. St Kanzian am Klopeiner See (448m/1469ft; pop. 4300) boasts the largest number of overnight stays in all of Carinthia. The Kleinsee, directly to the west, and the Turnersee, 2km/1.2mi south of the Klopeiner See are also both very popular holiday destinations.

A good 8km/4.9mi south of Völkermarkt lies Eberndorf (477m/ **Eberndorf**
1564ft; pop. 6000). The abbey in the ►Lavanttal, founded by Augustinian monks in around 1150 and fortified during the Turkish wars in the 15th century, has belonged to the Benedictines of St Paul since 1809. The Romanesque monastery church with the second largest crypt in Carinthia and an enchanting arcaded courtyard are worth taking a look at.

During the time of the Roman Empire, on the site of the village of **Globasnitz**
Globasnitz (541m/1774ft; pop. 1600) about 10km/6.2mi southeast of Eberndorf, stood the settlement Iuenna, where the remains of building foundations and a floor heating system have been excavated. Findings from Iuenna and from the nearby Hemmaberg are exhibited in the highly interesting **Archäologisches Pilgermuseum Hemmaberg** (opening times: May–Oct to Tue–Fri 10am–noon and ⏲
2pm–5pm, Sat and Sun 9am–noon and 1pm–5pm).

From Globasnitz, a 4km/2.4mi-long road leads westwards up to the ✱
Hemmaberg (841m/2759ft). The mountain ridge was settled as early ◄ Hemmaberg
as the 2nd millenium BC and is considered the biggest Christian pilgrimage centre in central Europe during the 5th and 6th centuries.

! *Baedeker* TIP

Bright plumage

Cockatoos and parakeets, macaws and pheasants, owls and parrots, toucans and ducks – just about everything with feathers and a beak feels at home here. Around 1000 animals of 340 species can be seen at the Turnersee Bird Park near St Primus (opening times: April–Sept daily 9am–6pm).

Foundation walls of early Christian churches were found, which have been excavated and preserved in an open-air museum. The wall that surrounded the former settlement is still partly visible.

South of Eberndorf lies **Bad Eisenkappel** (558m/1830ft; pop. 3000), the main town of the Vellachtal valley, just before the Seebergsattel (1218m/3996ft) and the Austrian-Slovenian border. Shuttle buses take interested visitors from Bad Eisenkappel to the Obir dripstone caves, which are constantly at a cool 8 °C/46 °F. The beautiful stone chambers were discovered in 1870, during the construction of tunnels for lead mining. They are situated on the northern side of the Hochobir, west of Eisenkappel. A tour of the caves takes about 90 minutes (guided tours: Easter–late Oct; registration: Obir-Tropfsteinhöhlen GmbH, Hauptplatz 7, Bad Eisenkappel; tel. 042 38/82 39 13; www.hoehlen.at).

◄ Obir dripstone caves

🕐

✱✱ Wachau

O/P 3

Province: Lower Austria

Every year hoards of tourists are attracted to the Wachau region with its mild climate, the gorgeous spring bloom, cheerful Baroque architecture and, last but not least, excellent white wine and some gourmet restaurants. The region was declared a World Cultural and Natural Heritage site by UNESCO in 2000.

Culture and nature in harmony

This unique Danube region, about **30km/19mi long, between Melk and Krems**, where the river between the Bohemian Massif in the northwest and the Dunkelstein Forest southeast forms a narrow rocky valley, was occupied in prehistoric times. Old towns set the scene, surmounted by legendary castles and ruins, and surrounded by steep, terraced vineyards. Those wishing to cross from one bank of the Danube to the other must use the **ferry** – in the Wachau there are no bridges crossing the Danube. The tremendous flood of August 2002 showed that the current can turn into a torrential flow and flood the bordering cultivated land;

? DID YOU KNOW ...?

■ The famous »Venus of Willendorf«, an approx. 27,000-year-old figure, was discovered in Willendorf on the left bank of the Danube. Today it can be seen at the Museum of Natural History in Vienna (ill. p.61).

for this reason, by 2009 flood barriers should have been erected near Wösendorf and Weissenkirchen, among other places.

Wine-growing in the Wachau dates back to Celtic times, but only with the Romans did simple wine growing become a cultural phenomenon. During the Renaissance, 31 monasteries owned vineyards in the Wachau. In 1784 Emperor Joseph II allowed the serving of wines at wineries – and the tradition of the **»Buschenschank«** developed. Today, wines from the Wachau, essentially Riesling, Grüner Veltliner, Neuburger and Müller-Thurgau, are world famous.

★
Viniculture

Down the Danube from Melk to Krems

About 5km/3mi down the Danube from ► Melk the impressive Schloss Schönbühel stands 40m/131ft-high on the right bank of the river above the town of the same name. Originally from the 12th century, it achieved its current form in the 19th century, with the inclusion of the old walls. The outer walls feature a relief of the Last Supper. The small Servite monastery, built not far from the castle in 1666, holds a beautiful sculpture of the Burial of Christ.

Schloss
Schönbühel

Another 5km/3mi downstream, the road branches off at Aggsbach Markt, which boasts the self-proclaimed most beautiful embankment of the Wachau, to the pilgrimage site of **Maria Laach** (580m/1902ft). The late Gothic pilgrimage church is richly decorated.

The winemaker from Spitz surely knows the way to the next snack bar

North of Maria Laach stands the 959m/3146ft-high Jauerling, **the highest mountain in the Wachau**. It is home to a broadcasting station with a 139.5m/458ft-high pylon and an observation tower. Besides pretty hiking trails and unspoiled nature, the **Naturpark Jauerling-Wachau** also offers a mushroom and medicinal herb museum with a nature trail (further information is available at the Tourismusverein in Maria Laach, tel. 027 12 / 82 22, www.marialaach.at).

Further down the Danube, on a high, steep cliff, stand the castle ruins of Burg Aggstein, 300m/984ft above the river, with a marvellous view over the Danube Valley. Founded in 1231 and destroyed and reconstructed several times, the enormous dimensions of the castle ruins are impressive. Parts of the towers, the kitchen and eat-

Aggstein ruins

! Baedeker TIP

The wonderful world of Hubhof

Over 200 3D holograms, a historical hall of mirrors, collections of fossils and minerals and much more is all on offer at the Hubhof near Aggsbach Markt. The »Wonderful World of Optical Illusions and Phenomena« and a hands-on exhibition are part of the programme (information tel. 027 12 / 241; opening times: June–Aug Tue–Sun 1pm–7pm, Sept and Oct only Fri–Sun).

ing house, the chapel and some mighty walls have been preserved. The Kuenringer robber knights once lived here as the ships passing through the valley and merchants' carriages offered good prey.

Spitz is an old market town with beautiful Renaissance and Baroque buildings. It is famous for its **apricot bloom** and celebrates the fruity result on »Marillenkirtag«. During the post-war years a number of Austrian films with regional backgrounds were made here. The Gothic parish church is worth visiting for its impressive Apostle sculpture (1380) and the high altar picture by Kremser Schmidt. Spitz's emblem, the Tausendeimerberg, produces a thousand buckets or »Eimer« of wine (one bucket is the equivalent of 53l/11.6gal!).

▶ VISITING WACHAU

INFORMATION
Donau Niederösterreich Tourismus
Schlossgasse 3, A-3620 Spitz
Tel. 027 13/300 60 60, fax 300 60 30
www.wachau.at

WHERE TO EAT
► Moderate
Loibnerhof
Unterloiben 7, A-3601 Dürnstein
Tel. 0 27 32/8 28 90
The most colourful time of year here is when the apricots are in bloom, though delicious food and excellent wines are always available in the romantic Danube Valley.

► Inexpensive
Sänger Blondel
Dürnstein 64, A-3601 Dürnstein
Tel. 0 27 11/253
This restaurant is known to be cyclist-friendly and serves typical specialities from the Wachau.

WHERE TO STAY
► Luxury
Hotel Schloss Dürnstein
A-3601 Dürnstein
Tel. 0 27 11/21 20, fax 2 12-30
www.schloss.at
Schloss Dürnstein greets visitors from a cliff high above the Danube. The hotel terrace is considered one of the most beautiful in Austria, while gourmets are attracted to the restaurant.

Baedeker recommendation

Romantik Hotel Richard Löwenherz
A-3601 Dürnstein 8
Tel. 0 27 11/2 22, fax 2 22-18
www.richardloewenherz.at
Besides the neat rooms and the dining hall, the restaurant garden is particularly impressive, offering a wonderful view across the Danube.

»In Dürnstein the Danube is especially wonderful,« as Austrian cabarettist
Georg Kreisler once sang

The **Schiffahrtsmuseum** at the Baroque Schloss Erlahof documents
the navigation on the Danube with rowing boats and rafts (opening
times: April–late Oct daily 10am–noon and 2pm–4pm, Sun
10am–4pm).

In the town of Oberarndorf opposite there is a beautiful monument
to the Neuburg vine – a statue of St Urban, the patron saint of wine,
and a chapel. A fresco depicts the legend: in 1860, two vintners from
Oberarndorf collected a vine from the Danube, planted it and named
it after the Bavarian town of Neuburg, situated upstream.

Oberarndorf

Pass the fortified church of St Michael, crowned with battlements on
the left bank of the Danube, and continue to Weissenkirchen, **possibly the prettiest wine village in the Wachau**. Its picturesque setting
is characterized by the mighty fortified church, old houses and
courtyards from the 16th century, and winding alleys. The Teisenhofer Hof, with a perron, arcade balconies and towers, is especially beautiful. The **Wachaumuseum** shows regional art (Wachau
painters, Kremser Schmidt) and folk cultural exhibits (opening
times: April–Oct Tue–Sun 10am–5pm).

★
Weissenkirchen

Surrounded by old, fortified walls, Dürnstein (220m/721ft; pop.
1100) is the most frequently visited town in the Wachau. However,
its most famous visitor stayed here unwillingly and paid a tidy sum
for his release: at the towering Kuenringerburg, a freely accessible,
mighty ruin, the English king **Richard the Lionheart** was imprisoned
in 1193. According to legend, the singer Blondel was strolling
through the country in search of his king, and found him because
the king knew the fitting answer to his serenade.

★
Dürnstein

Parish church ▶ Alongside the former Augustinian monastery (1410–1788), the parish church is another **highlight of Baroque architecture**. Some consider its blue tower to be the most beautiful Baroque church tower in Austria. The former monastery church, built in 1721–25, is the work of the Baroque architects Josef Munggenast, Jakob Prandtauer and others, who worked according to the plans of Matthias Steinl. Inside are beautiful stucco reliefs; in the middle side chapels are altar paintings by Kremser Schmidt (1762), a pulpit carved by his father, Johann Schmidt, as well as pretty choir stalls. The Baroque cloister contains a large crib also made by Johann Schmidt (c1730).

✳ Waldviertel

O/P 2/3

Province: Lower Austria

Some visitors come to the Waldviertel in search of rest and relaxation amongst the wide variety of animal and plant species here, while others take to the numerous cycle ways, hiking tracks or golf courses for an active, healthy holiday.

Rugged solitude »In the Waldviertel, it is winter for eight months and cold for four,« goes an old saying about the region situated between the Danube in the south and the Czech border to the north, the Mühlviertel in the west and the Weinviertel in the east. An unsuitable place for a holiday? Closer inspection shows that the raw climate and the isolation in the shade of the Iron Curtain has largely contributed to the preservation of the beauty of this thoroughly diverse countryside with its species-rich biota. In the west, towering granite mountains reach heights of more than 1000m/3280ft, and coniferous forest, ponds, small lakes, moors (especially around Heidenreichstein) and sparse soils set the scene. Landscape and climate become increasingly friendly moving in an eastward direction.

Land of myths The Waldviertel is also known as the country of myths and cult sites of prehistoric people. Its remote beauty has attracted a variety of visitors in search of spiritual experience in recent years. The many heavy boulders, most of which weigh tons and were polished by ice-age glaciers, scattered about the Waldviertel contribute to the attractiveness of the region. The Skorpionfelsen near Kautzen in the north of the Waldviertel are said to be an exact image of the constellation of Scorpio. Dowsing tends to be more popular here than elsewhere.

▶ WALDVIERTEL

INFORMATION
Waldviertel Tourismus
Sparkassenplatz 4
A-3910 Zwettl
Tel. 0 28 22/541 09
www.waldviertel.or.at

Tour through the Waldviertel

The tour leads from Zwettl (►Zwettl), in the centre of the Waldviertel to the northwest via Weitra, the oldest brewery town in Austria (since 1321) with the smallest guesthouse brewery in the country, to **Gmünd**. The small border town has a glass and stone museum, which besides conveying information about the centuries-old art of stone masonry, also gives visitors an impression of the art of glass making, which also has a long tradition here in the Austrian-Bohemian border region (Stadtplatz 34; opening times: May–Sept Mon–Fri 10am–noon and 2pm–4.30pm, Sat and Sun 9am–noon).

The two sgraffito houses (nos. 31 and 32) on the Stadtplatz in Gmünd are especially worth seeing. They display motifs from Roman and Greek mythology.

These rocks near Gmünd are called the »Teufels Brotlaib« (»devil's loaf«)

Sgraffito painting was a popular technique for wall surfaces, in the 16th century in particular.

From May to October every Wednesday, Saturday and Sunday the diesel and steam trains of the **Waldviertel narrow gauge railway** clatter and chuff their way from the Bahnhofsplatz in Gmünd in the direction of Gross-Gerungs (43km/27mi) and to Litschau (25km/16mi). The line runs through two tunnels, over two viaducts and covers a height difference of approx. 300m/1000ft (information tel. 02 52 /52 50 61 00).

Northeast of Gmünd lies the Naturpark Blockheide-Eibenstein – which happens to lie exactly on the 15th meridian east of Greenwich, as indicated by the sun dial. Imposing examples of granite boulders found in this region are the »Pilzstein«, »Teufels Brotlaib« and several »Wackelsteine« or »rocking stones«. The granite processing path (Granitbearbeitungspfad) shows how to work with the hard material. The information centre at the lookout tower explains the history and origins of the Blockheide. **Naturpark Blockheide-Eibenstein**

Heidenreichstein (560m/1837ft; pop. 4500), northeast of Gmünd, is known for its mighty castle on the water, whose oldest sections stem from the 12th century. It looks like a classical example of a knights' castle, appropriately accessible via two bridges and furnished with original pieces from various epochs (opening times: mid-April–mid-Oct, visits only in a guided tour with a minimum group of five, daily except Mon, 9am, 10am, 11am, 2pm, 3pm and 4pm). **Heidenreichstein** ⏲

»Heidenreichsteiner Moor« ▶ In the nature park »Heidenreichsteiner Moor« the forest and moor path reveals interesting facts about natural phenomena, as well as about the development of the mysterious fen fires or the life of carnivorous moorland plants. The internationally known Torf- und Moormuseum (Turf and Moor Museum) is unique in Austria: the economic utilization of the moors and their biota, not forgetting the myths entwined with the moor, are documented.

! **Baedeker TIP**

Presidential dining

The former Czech presidential plane, a Iljuschin Il 62 M, made its last flight quite some time ago and is now used at Heidenreichstein – as Austria's most original pub, which bears the pretty name Magic Jet (Industriestrasse 8; opening times for Flugzeugrestaurant and Towerstüberl: daily 10am–midnight, tel. 028 62/535 83).

From Heidenreichstein the tour leads via Waidhofen an der Thaya, Gross-Siegharts, Raabs and Drosendorf to Geras (460m/1509ft, pop. 1400). The abbey of Premonstratensian canons in Geras was founded in 1153. Its originally Romanesque-Gothic abbey church

✳ Geras
Nature park ▶
was later remodelled in Baroque style. The abbey offers diverse courses in fine arts and music (guided tours: Tue–Sun 9am–6pm). The beautiful Naturpark Geras awaits visitors old and young with a game reserve and petting zoo (opening times: Easter–Oct).

✳ Riegersburg
One of the most beautiful Baroque palaces in Austria is situated some 12km/7.5mi northeast: Schloss Riegersburg in the town of the same name. The still functioning palace kitchen and the completely furnished show rooms are presented under the motto »noble country life in Baroque times«.
⊘ The 19th-century dog cemetery in the palace garden is a curious addition (opening times: Easter–mid-Nov daily 9am–5pm, July and Aug until 7pm).

Felling
On the way from Riegersburg to Hardegg, a stop at the small town of Felling is worthwhile. Visitors can take a look at the activities of
⊘ Austria's one and only mother-of-pearl processing facility (opening times: Mon–Thu 8am–noon and 1pm–5pm, Fri 8am–noon, April–Sept also Sat 9am–noon).

Hardegg
Hardegg is **Austria's smallest town** (308m/1010ft; pop. 250). On a rocky cliff above the border river, the Thaya, the mighty castle complex (11th century) overlooks the town. The Maximilian-von-Mexiko-Museum – one of the former lords of the castle accompanied the younger brother of Emperor Franz Joseph I on his adventure to Central America that ended in his death – and the gun collection of the dukes of Khevenhüller-Metsch are interesting. The museum can only
⊘ be visited in groups of 20 or more by prior arrangement (opening times: April to 15 Nov daily 9am–5pm, July and Aug until 6pm).

Hardegg is the starting point for a short trip to the Thayatal National Park, largely situated on Czech soil (passport required!). The Thayatal is among the most beautiful natural valleys in Europe. A special feature of this unspoiled wilderness is the Umlaufberg, which is almost entirely circumflowed by the Thaya river. Very rare animal species such as the green lizard, the praying mantis and the black stork can be found here.

✱
◄ Nationalpark Thayatal

Via Retz (► Weinviertel) the road leads further west to Horn (► Altenburg, Surroundings) to the perhaps most scenically beautiful part of the Kamptal valley: the winding road south of Horn. In the Naturpark Kamptal, along the lower reaches of the Kamp river, are three worthwhile nature trails on the themes river, forest and wine, as well as the wine-growing community of **Langenlois**, the largest in Austria. Eleven boroughs have joined together with the Kulturpark Kamptal and present the geological development of the country in different museums (www.kulturpark-kamptal.at).

Kamptal

✱ Weinviertel

Q/R 2/3

Province: Lower Austria

Rolling hills with green vineyards and spreading corn fields, which are sometimes interrupted by forests or prehistoric burial mounds, characterize this landscape.

Between Vienna in the south, the Czech and Slovak border in the north and east, and the Waldviertel in the west, several island-like uplands reach heights of almost 500m/1640ft (Leiser Berge, 492m/1614ft). In the Weinviertel, Austria's biggest wine-growing area, are some 800 »Kellergassen«, »wine alleys« where wine cellars line up in a row. Grüner Veltliner, Riesling, Müller-Thurgau, Weissburgunder and Chardonnay as well as Blauer Portugieser and Zweigelt are made here.

Wine country par excellence

Round Trip through the Weinviertel

The starting point is **Korneuburg** (167m/547ft; 11,000 inhabitants), about 15km/9mi northwest of Vienna on the left bank of the

Mailberg with Malteserschloss

Danube. At the main square stand late Gothic burghers' houses, a Baroque plague column and the pretty neo-Gothic town hall with its old tower. The 18th-century Augustinian Church features a neo-classical high altar and a Rococo organ case. The **ruin of the oldest synagogue in Austria** (*c*1308) is also remarkable. South of Korneuburg lies Empress Sisi's beloved holiday destination of Bisamberg (360m/ 1181ft), which is why the summit is now called Elisabethhöhe.

Burg Kreuzenstein

Northwest of the town, visible from afar, rises the castle of Kreuzenstein (266m/872ft). Based on the original medieval castle, which was destroyed by the Swedish in 1645, it was reconstructed between 1874 and 1915 – a real treat for fans of romantic castles (guided tours only, starting on the hour: mid-March to Oct daily 10am–4pm, Sun until 5pm). The Adlerwarte puts on shows of **eagles in flight** (April– Oct daily except Mon 11am and 3pm, Sun and holidays 11am, 2pm and 4pm).

Stockerau

Stockerau (175m/574ft; pop. 15,700) lies at the edge of the Tullner Basin. The poet Nikolaus Lenau was once inspired by the meadows to write his lyric poems, the *Schilflieder* (*Reed Songs*).

Retz: the Verderberhaus on the Hauptplatz was built in 1580

Near Niederhollabrunn and Grossmugl are two **Celtic burial mounds**. The unmistakable forms of these testimonies to a long-vanished past loom abruptly over the landscape.

Hollabrunn (227m/744ft; pop. 13,400) is not only endowed with three Kellergassen, 300 wine cellars and several »Heuriger« wine taverns, but also has pretty decorated burghers' and art nouveau houses on the main square that attract many visitors. The fountain (Florianibrunnen, 1862) with a statue of St Florian is a reminder of the many fires in the town, while the plague column (1681) commemorates the end of a plague epidemic. The Alte Hofmühle museum is an interesting portrayal of the settlement and cultural history of the region (opening times: Sat 2.30pm–5.30pm, Sun and holidays also 10am–11.30am).

Hollabrunn

A small detour leads southwest to Kleinwetzdorf to a special kind of Valhalla: in the spacious palace gardens of Heldenberg, which is full of memorials and monuments to heroism, the former owner, boot maker and supplier of the imperial army, Pargfrieder, is buried next to field marshals Radetzky and von Wimpffen. A vernacular saying goes like this: »Hier liegen drei Helden in seliger Ruh, zwei lieferten Schlachten, der dritte die Schuh« (»Here three heroes rest in peace; two distinguished in warfare, the third in footwear«).

Heldenberg

▶ WEINVIERTEL

INFORMATION

Weinviertel Tourismus GmbH
Kolpingstrasse 7
A-2170 Poysdorf
Tel. 0 25 52/35 15
www.weinviertel.at

Go northwest from here to **Eggenburg** (314m/1030ft; pop. 3600). This nice little town has medieval walls some 2km/1.2mi long which support the screen for summer »Mondscheinkino« (moonlight cinema) and offer beautiful views of the historic market place. The Krahuletz Museum – the name refers to the geologist Krahuletz whose collection forms the basis of the holdings – displays fossils, minerals, archaeological and folklore exhibits and an interesting clock collection (Krahuletzplatz 1; open April–Dec Mon-Fri 9am–5pm, Sat and Sun 10am–5pm). The **Österreichisches Motorradmuseum** allows motorbike fans to stroll through approx. 80 years of motorbike and scooter history, from Puch to BMW, from Vespa to Ducati (Museumsgasse 6; open 6 Jan to 20 Dec daily 8am–4pm, Sat and Sun until 5pm).

◀ Krahuletz Museum

◀ Motorcycle Museum

The ancient charm of the border town of Retz (264m/866ft, pop. 6400) is evident at the main square, where 16th-century burghers' houses catch the eye, including the Verderberhaus and the Sgraffitohaus (1576) with illustrations of famous tales and biblical themes.

Retz

The other sights worth seeing are the Baroque Ratssaal – the city hall is actually built over a Rococo chapel of blue and gold; the Dominican church, remodelled in Baroque style; and the town fortifications, partly well-preserved with corner towers and two gateways.

The emblem of Retz is the historic **grain mill** from 1722, picturesquely situated above the town (tours daily 11am–5pm).

Wine growing in Retz has been documented since 1150, and the town gained privileges in the wine trade in the 15th century. The town has about 25km/16mi of cellars: Austria's largest historic **wine cellar** was dug two or three levels deep, like mole tunnels through firm, sandy soil (tours: May to October daily 10.30am, 2pm and 4pm, Nov and Dec, March and April daily 2pm).

Mailberg

Continuing the tour eastwards, the town of Mailberg (217m/711ft) on the right-hand side possesses an impressive castle, the oldest property of the **Order of Knights of Malta** in Austria. The castle has a **vinotheque**, where wines from Mailberg and its surroundings can be tasted and purchased (opening times: April–Dec Fri 1pm–6pm, Sat and Sun 10am–6pm).

Laa an der Thaya

Directly on the border the charming small town of Laa lies on the river Thaya (186m/610ft; pop. 6100). Remains of the fortification from the Middle Ages and the strong 13th-century moated castle are evidence of an eventful history. Unusually in the Weinviertel, beer brewing was first documented here in 1436. For those wishing to learn more, a visit to the beer museum in the castle is recommended (opening times: May–Oct Sat and Sun 2pm–4pm).

Poysdorf

Poysdorf (205m/672ft; pop. 7400) lies near the Czech border on the little river of the same name. The informative and entertaining town museum (Weinstadtmuseum Poysdorf) is worth a visit and offers special activities for children (Brünner Strasse 9; open Easter–Oct Wed 1pm–6pm, Sat and Sun 9am–noon and 1pm–6pm).

Herrenbaumgarten

Those who love the bizarre and can make sense of nonsense will enjoy a visit to Herrenbaumgarten, the »nonsense village«. It contains at least 26 Flaschenpostämter (post offices for bottled mail) and the so-called Nonseum, founded in 1994 by the Association for the Exploitation of Surplus Thoughts. Here, things are presented that nobody ever thought to be useful (Poysbrunnenstrasse 9; open Palm Sunday to 1 Nov Sat, Sun and holidays 1pm–6pm; www.nonseum.de).

Asparn an der Zaya

In the nature reserve of the Leiser Mountains, west of Mistelbach, the imposing manor in Asparn an der Zaya houses the Niederösterreichisches Museum für Urgeschichte, which is dedicated to the **ancient history of Lower Austria**. The **open-air museum in the palace garden** is also part of it (opening times: April–Nov Tue–Fri 9am–5pm, Sat–Sun 10am–6pm).

The Weinland museum at the Minorite monastery is devoted to the history, art and folk culture of the country (April–Oct Sat 1pm–5pm, Sun from 9am).

The Österreichisches Schulmuseum (Austrian School Museum) in Michelstetten provides information ranging from the educational system in classical antiquity to the development of the school book (opening times: April to mid-Nov daily 9am–5pm).

The museum village near Niedersulz (southeast of Mistelbach) contains about 70 buildings from the Weinviertel which were removed from their original locations and rebuilt here in authentic style. They document the unique breadth of the local folk and working culture (opening times: mid-March to early Nov, Mon–Fri 10am–4pm; Sat, Sun and holidays until 6pm).

Niedersulz Museum village

It is little known that in the early 20th century the Dual Monarchy of Austria-Hungary was the third-largest oil-producing country in the world. The existing fields in the Viennese Basin are very small by today's standards, but their oil production still covers approx. 10%

Prottes

The Weinviertel offers many quiet corners and romantic spots, such as here in front of the city wall of Eggenburg

of Austrian oil and 15% of its gas requirements. The community of Prottes, northeast of Vienna, has established a museum and a 4.2km/2.5mi-long **educational trail about oil and gas** with about 150 exhibits, including a 30m/100ft-high drilling rig and a museum (opening times: Easter to 1 Nov, Sun 9.30am–11.30am and 2pm–4pm, or by appointment, tel. 022 82/21 82; the educational trail is accessible all year).

★ ★ Weissensee

K 6

Province: Carinthia   **Elevation:** 930m/3051ft

The fjord-like Weissensee, unlike the other large Carinthian lakes, lies a little off the beaten track and is therefore visited as an idyllic place of recreation in summer.

Pure relaxation
Somewhat hidden in the Gailtal Alps southwest of ▶ Spittal an der Drau, the Weissensee (930m/3051ft) is the highest Carinthian lake and the highest of all bathing lakes in the Alps. Despite its size – it is about 11.5km/7mi long, some 500m/550yd wide and up to 99m/324ft deep – its water reaches temperatures 25 °C/77 °F and has the quality of drinking water. Only a third of the approximately 23km/14mi-long shore is built up, and then sparsely. Practically every hotel has its own beach. Visitors can enjoy untouched nature above all at the eastern shore of the lake, where the woods reach down to the water.

Motor boats are not allowed, while everything else is possible, from swimming to canoeing, surfing and sailing. The Weissensee is not only the starting point for long hiking and mountain tours, but with its well kept ski runs is also an inviting place for a winter holiday. Furthermore, during winter the lake is **one of the largest surfaces of natural ice in Europe**, a thrill for skaters and ice-hockey enthusiasts, as well as many other winter sport fans. In recognition of its ecologically friendly use of nature, the region received a European award for tourism and environmental awareness from the European Union.

? DID YOU KNOW ...?

- The Weissensee had its moment of cinematic glory in 1987, when 007, alias Timothy Dalton, sped across the frozen lake in an Aston Martin during the shooting of *The Living Daylights*. The scene where 007 slides downhill in a cello case featuring co-star Kara Milovy alias Maryam d'Abo was filmed near the Naggler Alm.

Boat trips
Between May and October there is a boat service from Techendorf to the eastern end of the lake with several stops on the northern bank and two on the southern bank.

What to See at the Weissensee

Houses in the old Carinthian rural style and beautiful promenades characterize Techendorf, the main town of the valley on the north-western bank of the Weissensee (946m/3103ft; pop. 750).

Techendorf

A bridge leads from Techendorf to the south bank and to the valley terminus of the chairlift up to the Naggler Alm (1350m/4429ft), the starting point for ridge hiking tours between the Weissensee and ►Gailtal as well as downhill ski routes to the lake.

◄ Naggler Alm

About 2.5km/1.5mi east on the south bank of the bridge lies the residential area of Naggl. From there a circular hike leads around the lake – over the peak of the Laka (1851m/6072ft) to the fjord-like eastern part and back to Neusach on the north bank, at varying heights via steep wooded cliffs.

Circular route

 VISITING WEISSENSEE

INFORMATION

Weissensee Information
Techendorf 78
A-9762 Weissensee
Tel. 0 47 13/2 22 00
Fax 22 20 44
www.weissensee.com

On the idyllic Weissensee floating stage concerts are held in July and August

WHERE TO STAY

► **Budget**
Hotel Alte Post
Techendorf 13, A-9762 Weissensee
Tel. 0 47 13/2 22 80, fax 22 28 40
www.altepost-weissensee.at
All rooms have a lake view; Finnish sauna and steam bath, conservatory and sun deck as well as a large lawn for sunbathing.

✳ Wels

M 3

Province: Upper Austria
Population: 61,000

Elevation: 317m/1040ft

The town's attractions are the horse and piglet markets at the trade fair centre and the beautiful town centre.

Lively centre of commerce Wels lies around 20km/12mi southwest of Linz in the Alpenvorland on the left bank of the Traun. During Roman times, Ovilava (as it was called then) was the administrative centre of a region, and during the Middle Ages the town became an **important trade centre**. Emperor Maximilian I (► Famous People), too, enjoyed coming to this town. He died here on his way from Innsbruck to Vienna in 1519. Today the lively place is still commercially important.

What to See in and around Wels

✳ City square The historic town square, impressive in its coherence, is surrounded by 64 fine townhouses from very different epochs. At the west end stands the Ledererturm, built in the 13th century and altered in the 17th century. It is the emblem of Wels. Like the Wasserturm (1577) it is part of the medieval town wall. Diagonally opposite the town hall (Stadtplatz no. 34), the Haas-Hof has one of the most beautiful arcaded courtyards in Wels.

Lebensspuren. Museum An unusual museum opened its doors south of the Ledererturm: the Lebensspuren.Museum (Traces of Life Museum), which is devoted to seals and stamps, with a collection ranging from the first imprints of

 VISITING WELS

Wels *Map*

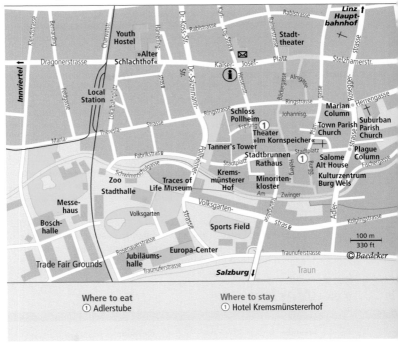

Where to eat	Where to stay
① Adlerstube	① Hotel Kremsmünstererhof

human life to the latest high-tech stamps (Pollheimer Strasse 4; open
Tue–Fri 10am–4pm, Sat and Sun noon–6pm).

An impressive sight on the south side of the town square is the
stately Kremsmünsterer Hof, former town house of the monastery of
the same name, as well as the beautiful town hall (1748) built in the
Rococo style. A little alley leads south to the former Minorite monastery with the **archaeological museum**. The focus is on Roman Wels
(Minoritengasse 5; opening times: Tue–Fri 10am–5pm, Sat 2pm–
5pm, Sun 10am–4pm).

Archäologische Sammlung

In 1622 Salome Alt von Altenau, the long-term mistress of Wolf Die-
trich von Raitenau, Archbishop of Salzburg, bought the house at
Stadtplatz no. 24 opposite the parish church – a beautiful example of
Renaissance fresco painting.

Salome-Alt-Haus

Burggasse leads to the castle at the southeastern corner of the Old
Town, where Emperor Maximilian I died on 12 January 1519. Today
the castle is used as a cultural centre, and summer concerts and thea-

Castle

tre performances take place in the courtyard. The building also houses collections about town history, the Österreichisches Gebäckmuseum (**Austrian Museum of Bakery and Confectionery**) and a museum devoted to agriculture (opening times: Tue–Fri 10am–5pm, Sat 2pm–5pm, Sun 10am–4pm).

Welser Tierpark

The animal park in Wels, west of the Old Town, at the northern edge of the trade fair centre, is an attraction for animal lovers young and old. Some 650 animals, predominantly local species, along with exotic birds and various primates, can be seen (opening times: April and Oct 7am–7pm, May–Sept 7am–7.45pm, Nov–March 7am–5pm).

Zoologischer Garten Schmiding

Northwest of the town, some 7km/4.5mi away, another animal attraction beckons: the Schmiding Zoological Gardens in Krenglbach emerged from a bird park with more than one thousand bird species from all continents. They are joined by other species from the African savannah and the tropical forest (opening times: daily 7am–7pm, last admission 5pm).

The Museum Begegnung der Kulturen (Museum for Cultural Encounters) at the edge of the zoo highlights traditions and customs of »primitive« peoples of the earth on an area of about 1600 sq m/ 17,000 sq ft (closed for renovation at present).

★ ★ Werfen

K 5

Province: Salzburg
Population: 3000

Elevation: 524m/1719ft

The old market town Werfen offers two attractions: the impressive castle of Hohenwerfen and the fantastic ice cave Eisriesenwelt. They are embedded between the Hochkönig, Hagen and Tennen mountains along the main road from Salzburg to the south in the direction of eastern Tyrol and Carinthia.

★ **Hohenwerfen Castle**

North of Werfen, Hohenwerfen Castle stands majestically on a wooded cliff (680m/2230ft). The fortress, built in 1077 by Archbishop Gebhard and used for hundreds of years as a prison, was thoroughly renovated in 1931 after a fire and acquired by the state of Salzburg in 1938. The interior including the castle chapel, the prison and a weapons collection, can be visited as part of a guided tour. The Österreichisches Falknereimuseum (Austrian Falconry Museum) here demonstrates the magnificent feats of flight of its birds of prey. (opening times: April and Oct daily except Mondays 9.30am–4.30pm, May, June, Sept 9am–5pm, July–Aug 9am–6pm).

✳ ✳ Eisriesenwelt

With an area of about 30,000 sq m/322,917 sq ft of ice, the Eisriesenwelt (»world of ice giants«) at the western edge of the Tennen range **is the world's largest glacial cave** and one of the most fantastic sights of the Eastern Alps. The nature and animal filmmaker David Attenborough regards it as one of the 30 greatest miracles of nature in the world. The cave, created by a river during the Tertiary period, was discovered in 1879 and opened in 1912. Around 1km/1100yd of the cave's 40km/25mi is covered by ice. This section is publicly accessible as a show cave.

During the one-hour guided tour, 134 metres (440ft) have to be climbed, and despite this exercise warm clothing is a must, in addition to sturdy footwear. Even dur-

Defiant walls protecting Hohenwerfen Castle

ing summer, temperatures remain at an average of 0 °C/32 °F! The cave is lit only with hand-carried carbide lamps and magnesium light.

An entire **round trip through Eisriesenwelt** takes about four hours. It is accessible either by car from Werfen or in small shuttle buses via the 5km/3mi-long Bergstrasse to the parking lot, which is not far from the lower station of the funicular. A gently ascending footpath leads to the station within 15 minutes. The funicular ride takes 3 minutes (approx. 90 minutes on foot). It takes a further 15 minutes to walk from the mountain inn, Dr.-Frederick-Oedl-Haus, to the impressive cave entrance at 1664m/5459ft in the steep rock wall of the Tennen Mountains. Through the Posselthalle and the Great Ice Wall visitors reach the massive Hymirhalle – named after the ice giant in the prose Edda. Hymir's Castle is the largest ice figure in the cave;

 WERFEN

INFORMATION

Tourismusverband Werfen
Markt 24, A-5450 Werfen
Tel. 0 64 68/53 88, fax 75 62,
www.werfen.at

Medieval feasts

Burgschenke Hohenwerfen
Burgstrasse 2, A-5450 Werfen
Tel. 0 64 68/52 03
www.ritterschmaus.at
Minimum 30 people, prior reservation
»Hold up the jugs filled with wine, to your health, that'll be fine.«

the Ice Organ at the Niflheim, also called Frigga's Veil, is a dome-like formation of rare beauty. Through Mörkdom – named after cave explorer Alexander Mörk – the path continues to the great Ice Palace, some 1km/1100yd inside the mountain, and back again into daylight (opening times: cable car and **cave tour** are run by the same operator: May to late Oct 9am–3.30pm, July/Aug until 4.30pm;www.eisriesenwelt.at; tel. 0 64 68/52 48 or 52 91).

✴ Wiener Neustadt

Q 4

Province: Lower Austria
Population: 37,600

Elevation: 265m/869ft

The lively industrial town of Wiener Neustadt, situated 30km/20mi south of Vienna, features a few worthwhile architectural monuments, although much was destroyed during the Second World War.

Old border fortress

Wiener Neustadt was founded as a border fortress against Hungary by Leopold the Virtuous in 1194 – with part of the grand ransom which England had to pay for the release of King Richard the Lionheart. It was the seat of royal power under Friedrich III from 1440 to 1493. His son, Maximilian I (► Famous People), the »last knight«, was born here in 1459 and buried beneath the high altar of St George's Cathedral.

What to See in Wiener Neustadt

Castle

The castle is strategically situated in the southeast of the town, close to the river Leitha. Heavily damaged by earthquakes on several occasions, it was rebuilt and enlarged each time. Maria Theresia (► Famous People) founded the Kaiserliche Militärakademie (Imperial Military Academy) here in 1751. With interruptions, the **oldest military academy in the world** has existed to this day.

Only one of four corner towers of the castle still remains. The front and courtyard are dominated by St George's Church, one of the most beautiful late Gothic churches in Austria. On the courtyard side of the church is the famous Wappenwand (Heraldic Wall, 1453): 14

✴
Wappenwand ►

Habsburg and 93 fantasy crests are arranged above a statue of Friedrich III and his slogan AEIOU, variously interpreted as »Austria Est Imperare Orbi Universo« (»the earth shall be ruled by Austria«) or »Austria Erit In Orbe Ultima« (»Austria will last for eternity«). The church, which has an almost square plan, is decorated with numerous unidentifiable crests, with the crest of the Habsburgs' inherited lands displayed on the ceiling. Three wonderful glass windows from the 15th and 16th centuries glow above the altar.

Wiener Neustadt Map

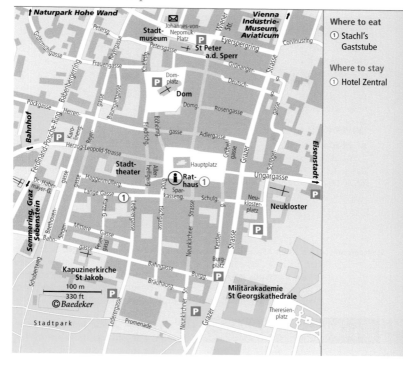

Where to eat
① Stachl's
   Gaststube

Where to stay
① Hotel Zentral

The old quarter north of the castle was constructed as a regular rectangle with sides measuring 600m/2000ft and 700m/2300ft. At the main square surrounded by attractive balconied houses stands a Baroque column dedicated to the Virgin (1678), and to the southwest the 16th-century town hall with its neo-classical façade.

Old quarter

East of the main square the Gothic Neuklosterkirche holds marvellous Baroque altars and the tomb of Eleanor of Portugal (died 1467), wife of Emperor Friedrich III and mother of Maximilian I. Niclas Van Leyden made the tomb slab in 1467.

The westwork and nave of the massive cathedral are Romanesque (13th century), the transept and choir Gothic (mid-14th century). At the south side is the »Brauttor« (Bride's Gate) with a Romanesque portal (c1238). Inside, on the columns by Lorenz Luchsperger, note the remarkable life-sized statues of the apostles (c1500). The mural of the Last Judgment above the chancel arch from 1300, and the high altar and choir stalls in cheerful Rococo style (1760–77) are also worthy of note.

◄ **Cathedral**

● VISITING WIENER NEUSTADT

INFORMATION

Tourist office
Hauptplatz 1–3
A-2700 Wiener Neustadt
Tel. 0 26 22/37 33 11
Fax 37 33 14
www.wiener-neustadt.at

WHERE TO EAT

▶ **Moderate**

① *Stachl's Gaststube*
Lange Gasse 20
Tel. 0 26 22/2 52 21
Stachl's Gewölbekeller is a cultivated

palce to satisfy an appetite. Wine list
with Austrian emphasis.

WHERE TO STAY

▶ **Budget**

① *Hotel Zentral*
Hauptplatz 27
A-2700 Wiener Neustadt
Tel. 0 26 22/2 31 69, fax 23 79 35
www.hotelzentral.at
The hotel lies at the centre of Wiener
Neustadt, directly on the picturesque
main square.

Stadtmuseum The Town Museum is housed in the former monastery of St Peter an der Sperr at Petersgasse 2a. It owns a replica of the finely crafted, gilded Corvinus goblet (1487), a gift of the Hungarian king Matthias Corvinus »to the brave citizens« (opening times: Tue and Wed 10am–5pm, Thu until 8pm, Fri until noon, Sun until 4pm).

❗ *Baedeker* TIP

Young wine from apples and pears

The word »Heuriger« is normally used to designate a young wine. The rustic exception to this rule is best tasted at the eastern branches of the Alps south of Wiener Neustadt, the area known as »Bucklige Welt«: Its orchards supply excellent wine made from apples and pears.

The heart of the **industrial museum** is an old locksmith's workshop and a utility room; changing exhibitions are held (Anna-Rieger-Gasse 4; open Mon–Fri 9am–4pm).

The excellent flight museum, **Aviaticum**, is dedicated to the early history of flying and is worth a visit not just for aviation enthusiasts and experts. Among diverse historic aircraft, the world's oldest licensed gas balloon is exhibited, as well as a still flight-worthy Lohner-Etrich Taube, constructed in 1912 (Graf von Zeppelinstrasse 1; open Tue–Sun 10am–8pm). The first aircraft to be made in Austria was built in Wiener Neustadt.

Around Wiener Neustadt

At the Hohe Wand nature reserve (altitude: 800–1000m/2600–3300ft), west of Wiener Neustadt, numerous guest houses and huts await hungry and thirsty hikers. There is an information centre and an Alpine Museum; young ones can enjoy the playgrounds, a petting zoo and a park with ibex and cute marmots.

Some 15km/9mi south of Wiener Neustadt lies Seebenstein (348m/ **Seebenstein** 1141ft), at the edge of the nature reserve of the same name. The stately castle from the 11th and 17th centuries contains valuable furniture and collections including a Madonna statue by Riemenschneider (opening times: Easter–Oct; tours Sat and Sun at 10.30am, ⏲ 2pm and 3pm).

✴ Wienerwald

Q 3

Province: Lower Austria

The Wienerwald, or Vienna Woods, at the gates of the capital, was not only a source of inspiration for artists, but today is a Sunday excursion for the Viennese with a 6000km/3750mi network of paths for hiking, and countless Heuriger taverns.

The mere mention of the name »Vienna Woods« conjures up music! **Sounds** Think of Beethoven's Sixth Symphony, the Pastorale, or the immor- **like music** tal waltz *Tales from the Vienna Woods* by Johann Strauss (►Famous People). The Wienerwald is the northeastern extension of the Alps, which here descend into wooded and finally vine-covered hills.

The Wienerwald and the Viennese owe the appearance of the area, its unabated beauty and luxuriant cloak of green, to a man from Mödling, **Josef Schöffel**: some 130 years ago speculators hoped for huge profits from reckless tree felling. Schöffel actively opposed this, for which he was initially vilified. Finally he was able to convince the citizens of Mödling with his arguments for sustained development of the Wienerwald and thereby prevented major deforestation. Today Schöffel is an honorary citizen of more than a hundred communities at the Wienerwald – how times ·hange!

View from the foothills of the Wienerwald

Round Trip through the Southern Wienerwald

Mödling
Leaving Vienna in a southerly direction, the town of Mödling (240m/787ft; pop. 24,000) a few miles further was a popular summer destination for three famous composers: Ludwig van Beethoven, Arnold Schönberg (▶Famous People) and Anton von Webern. Mödling has a Renaissance town hall dating from 1548, the late Gothic church of St Othmar, whose vaulted ceiling rests on twelve columns – symbolizing the twelve apostles – and a late Romanesque charnel house with old frescoes.

The Hussar Temple, Austria's oldest war memorial, and romantic ruins are popular hiking destinations at the Föhrenberge nature reserve to the west, with its characteristic umbrella pines.

Laxenburg
Due to its proximity to the capital and its location by the game-rich Schwechat meadows, Laxenburg (177m/580ft; pop. 2700), some 10km/6mi east, was a preferred spring residence of the Habsburg dynasty from the 14th century. The extensive castle park (entry fee) with its castles and ponds (boat rental), old trees, monuments and bridges **is one of the most important landscape gardens in Austria**. History was made at the Old Castle: Here Emperor Charles VI enacted the Pragmatic Sanction, which enabled his daughter, Maria Theresia (▶Famous People), to govern as his successor. Today the Austrian Film Archive is based here.

The neo-Gothic Franzensburg, built on a lake from 1798 to 1836, seems like a medieval knight's castle and now serves as a summer location for comedy dramas. The state rooms, some of them richly decorated, are accessible as part of a guided tour (Easter to early Nov, daily 11am, 2pm and 3pm).

▶ **WIENERWALD**

INFORMATION

Tourismusverband Wienerwald
Hauptplatz 11, A-3002 Purkersdorf
Tel. 0 22 31/6 21 76
www. wienerwald.info

Gumpoldskirchen
Gumpoldskirchen (260m/853ft; pop. 3300) is famous for its excellent white wines. The atmospheric little town on the Weinwanderweg (wine hiking route) with a strong castle of the Teutonic Knights, St Michael's Church and a pretty Renaissance town hall is a pleasant place for a stroll, while the Heuriger bars and two big wine festivals in June and August guarantee good entertainment.

Baden bei Wien
▶Baden bei Wien

Helenental
Helenental, a romantic valley west of Baden, was already appreciated by hikers in the 19th century. To the left and right rise the ruins of the robber-knight castles of Rauheneck and Rauhenstein. In 1830–31 cholera raged in Vienna and Baden, so in gratitude for the end of th...

Schlosspark Laxenburg *Map*

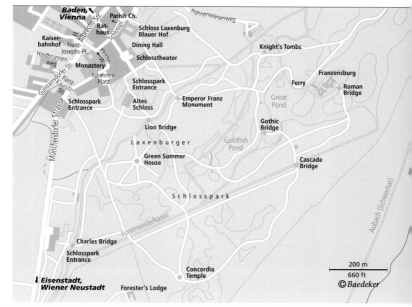

epidemic the Viennese citizens donated the Cholera Chapel a few miles upstream. A popular destination is the Krainerhütte, founded by lumberjacks who once settled here from Krain.

With a little bit of luck dippers or even kingfishers can be spotted on the banks of the Schwechat. Sadly, the Aesculapian snake has become quite rare, but wild boar, deer and a variety of butterflies constitute a varied local fauna.

The former hunting palace of Mayerling, 19km/12mi northeast of **Mayerling** Baden, **is where Crown Prince Rudolf of Austria** shot his eighteen-year-old lover, **Baroness Mary Vetsera**, and himself on 30 January 1889. The circumstances remain a mystery to this day. The crown prince was buried in the Imperial Crypt in Vienna, Mary Vetsera at the village cemetery in Heiligenkreuz. At the behest of Emperor Franz Joseph I the castle was turned into a Carmelite convent. The bedroom of the crown prince, the location of the presumed double suicide, is today the convent's chapel for the dead (opening times of the memorial chapel: daily 9am–12.30pm and 1pm–6pm, in winter until 5pm).

few miles northeast, in Heiligenkreuz, stands the **second-oldest** **Heiligenkreuz** rcian abbey in Austria**, founded in 1133 by Margrave Leopold

The last Babenberg was laid to rest in the chapter house of Heiligenkreuz in 1246

III, who wanted to establish a burial place here for the Babenberg monarchs. The abbey is named after a relic of the True Cross which Duke Leopold V donated to the monastery. The son of the founder, Otto von Freising, joined the Cistercians and ensured that the fraternity settled here. It is the only Cistercian monastery to have been used continuously by the order since its foundation.

Monastery church ▶ The western façade of the abbey church has the three windows that are typical for Cistercian churches. The impressive Romanesque nave creates a strong contrast to the Gothic hall choir with its precious glass windows (*c*1300). In the Romanesque and Gothic cloister (1220–50) stand two sculpture groups by Giuliani and a remarkable well-house. The beautiful chapter house accommodates a few graves, among them that of Friedrich II. His death in 1246, during a battle against the Hungarians, also ended the rule of the Babenberg dynasty in Austria. The hall where the monks worked still has parts of its 13th-century wall paintings. The monastery is only accessible as part ⊙ of a guided tour (Mon–Sat 10am, 11am, 2pm, 3pm, 4pm, Sun from 11am).

Sparbach Nature Park The beautiful hiking circuit (9km/5.5mi) at the **oldest nature reserve in Austria** leads past the idyllic Lenau Pond and romantic ruins. Starting point for the tour is Sparbach, 7km/4.5mi northeast of Heiligenkreuz.

Perchtoldsdorf (265m/869ft; pop. 14,200) is situated on the way back to Vienna. The **medieval town centre** with its impressive castle-church complex and the strong freestanding defensive tower, where Hugo Wolf wrote a few of his most beautiful songs (Museum at the Brunnengasse 26), has attracted visitors since the 19th century.

Perchtoldsdorf

✶ ✶ Wolfgangsee

K 4

Provinces: Salzburg, Upper Austria

It was not only Ralph Benatzky's waltzy operetta *Im Weissen Rössl* that drew visitors to what is probably the best-known lake in the Salzkammergut region. The pilgrimage church of St Wolfgang already attracted streams of pilgrims during the Middle Ages.

The Wolfgangsee, 10km/6mi long, 2km/1.2mi wide and up to 114m/374ft deep, is beautifully located: to the north the Schafberg rises above the steep Falkensteinwand, near St Gilgen looms the Zwölferhorn. Not only spiritually-minded pilgrims, but also sport enthusiasts find what they are looking for here: the activities on offer range from swimming, surfing, sailing and angling to water-skiing, parasailing and tube-riding.

Operetta and pilgrimage

What to See at the Wolfgangsee

At the west end of the lake lies the idyllic summer resort of St. Gilgen, with villas from the late 19th century. At Ischler Strasse 15, today home to the district court, Mozart's mother Anna Maria Pertl (1720–78) was born. Her father worked here as a judicial officer, and Mozart's sister Maria Anna (Nannerl), also gifted, married one of her grandfather's successors in the post and in 1784 became the landlady of the house where her mother had been born (open June–Sept 10am–noon and 2pm–6pm). The fountain with a statue of Mozart commemorates her famous brother.

✶
St Gilgen

The **local museum in the Wetzhäusl**, which was built in 1655, covers local history and has 4700 exhibits from the animal collection of Karl von Frisch, who studied the communication methods of bees and received a Nobel Prize (Pichlerplatz 6; open June–Sept Tue–Sun 10am–noon and 3pm–6pm).

> ! *Baedeker* TIP
>
> **Floating nostalgia**
>
> On 20 May 1873 passenger shipping on the lake was officially opened with the paddle-wheel steamer *Franz Joseph I*. It still ploughs through the waves today, though no longer fired with coal but with diesel (during the high season in July and August between Gschwendt, St Wolfgang and St Gilgen).

▶ VISITING WOLFGANGSEE

INFORMATION

Tourismusinformation St Gilgen
Bundesstrasse 1 a, A-5340 St Gilgen
Tel. 0 62 27/23 480, fax 23 489
www.gemgilgen.at

WHERE TO EAT

▶ Expensive
Timbale
Salzburger Strasse 2
A-5340 St. Gilgen
Tel. 0 62 27/75 87
Eating is an unforgettable experience
at this small but excellent restaurant.

▶ Moderate
Brunnwirt
Wolfgangseestr. 11
A-5330 Fusch
Tel. 06 64/280 71 92
The gate to this cosy restaurant is only
open in the evening. The excellent
cuisine attracts many guests.

WHERE TO STAY

▶ Luxury
Ebner's Waldhof
Seestrasse 30, A-5330 Fuschl am See
Tel. 0 62 26/82 64, fax 86 44
www.ebners-waldhof.at
The hotel complex at the end of
Fuschl has its own beach, an indoor
swimming pool and a sauna.

▶ Mid-range
Im Weissen Rössl
Markt 74, A-5360 St Wolfgang
Tel. 0 61 38/2 30 60, fax 23 06 41
www.weissesroessl.at
Often celebrated in songs, this romantic hotel on the Wolfgangsee
offers first-class and stylishly furnished rooms with a view of the lake.
The house became famous through
the operetta *Im Weissen Rössl* by the
Austrian composer Ralph Benatzky
(1930).

St Wolfgang on the Wolfgangsee: water skiing with a famous skyline –
the parish church and the White Horse Inn

From St Gilgen there is a chair lift to the Zwölferhorn (1522m/ 4993ft). During summer it is an attractive hiking area, during winter a challenging ski terrain.

◄ Zwölferhorn

The bathing resort of St Wolfgang, celebrated in many songs, is among the most popular destinations in the Salzkammergut region. Situated on the sunny northeastern bank of the lake at the foot of the Schafberg, it is actually part of the Salzburger Land. St Wolfgang and the hotel Weisses Rössl, run by one family for five generations, became world famous through **Ralph Benatzky's operetta** of the same name. The restaurant has a marvellous view of the Wolfgangsee and the surrounding mountains.

★ St Wolfgang

★ ◄ Weisses Rössl

Directly next to the Weisses Rössl stands the late Gothic pilgrimage church, rebuilt after a fire from 1429 to 1477 and painted in Baroque style between 1683 and 1697. The richly decorated late Gothic winged altar by Michael Pacher (completed in 1481) at the high altar is a unique work of art. On the magnificent middle shrine the Virgin Mary kneels in intercession before Christ, at her side St Wolfgang and St Benedict. The upper part of the altar consists of many slender pinnacles. The glorious Baroque double altar for St Wolfgang and St John the Baptist, one of Thomas Schwanthaler's main works (1675–76) is also very fine. In the left half of the altar stands a 15th-century statue of St Wolfgang from the church that burnt down in 1429. Three other altars, a moving depiction of the suffering of Christ, and the pulpit were made by Meinrad Guggenbichler, the master artist from the monastery at Mondsee (18th century). In 1713 the Wolfgang Chapel at the western part of the church was built in Rococo style in order to integrate the cell of St Wolfgang, which formerly stood outside, into the church. North of the church, at the well-house, stands a bronze pilgrimage fountain (1515) with allegorical figures. Its superstructure is the first Austrian work in Renaissance style.

★ ★ ◄ Pilgrimage church

St Wolfgang *Church*

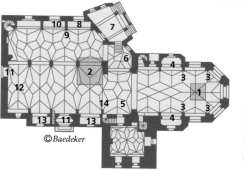

1 Pacher Altar
2 Double Altar by Schwanthaler
3 Guild Posts
4 Marble Altars
5 Sacristy Doorway
6 Rosary Altar
7 St Wolfgang's Chapel
8 All Souls' Altar
9 Ecce Homo
10 Antonius Altar
11 Doorway with Relief
12 Organ
13 Josef and Anna Altars
14 Pulpit

©Baedeker

Schafberg ✳

Old-fashioned means of travel are not only to be found on water, but also on land in the mountains: the Schafberg (1783m/5849ft) can be tackled with the Schafbergbahn between May and October. Sometimes an old steam cog train is used for the rides. In total, seven lakes of the Salzkammergut region can be seen from the summit of the Schafberg, which lies centrally between the Wolfgangsee, Mondsee and Attersee lakes with **a wonderful view of the Eastern Alps**. It takes about 4 hours to walk from St Wolfgang.

Fuschlsee

The bank of the idyllic, 4km/2.5mi-long and 1km/0.6mi-wide Fuschlsee, northwest of the Wolfgangsee, is a nature reserve and has a nice **small nudist beach**. The pleasant path around the lake is about 12km/7.5mi long. The Frauenkopf (»woman's head«, 1287m/4222ft), also known among climbers as Schober Südgrat, offers beautiful and safe climbing even for less experienced mountaineers.

Frauenkopf ▶

✳ ✳ Wörther See

Province: Carinthia

The tourist centre of Carinthia has everything a top holiday destination should have: besides good transport connections, numerous places on the banks of the lake cater to all tastes, from simple to glamorous, sporting and cultural.

Picturesque Alpensee

The somewhat distant mountain world to the south, west and north allows many sunny days by keeping away cold winds and clouds. With a length of 16km/10mi, a width of 1–1.5km/0.6–1mi and a depth of up to 84m/275ft, the Wörther See is **the largest of the Carinthian alpine lakes**. The livelier north bank has more passing traffic, while the south bank is a little quieter. The places on the shore are clearly focussed on tourism: the rich, the aristocracy and celebrities meet in Velden, while Pörtschach is known for its vibrant nightlife; Krumpendorf promotes itself as a paradise for skating and cycling, and the picturesque Maria Wörth is an ideal place for a gentle stroll. During July and August water temperatures rise to 26 °C/79 °F, sometimes even higher – ideal conditions for angling, paddling, waterskiing, surfing and sailing.

! **Baedeker TIP**

Where Mahler worked

In a lightly wooded area directly west of the beach at Maiernigg and close to Klagenfurt stands the small house where Gustav Mahler composed. From 1900 until the death of his older daughter Maria in 1907 he lived in a villa on the lake, which is now private property, then retreated to his little refuge for composing (opening times: May–Oct daily 10am–4pm). His symphonies 5 to 8 and the *Kindertotenlieder* (*Songs on the Death of Children*) were written here.

The lake is named after the former church and abbey of Maria Wörth

What to See at the Wörther See

The biggest and most visited place on the lake is the **elegant health resort** Velden (440m/1441ft; pop. 8500). After the opening of the Vienna–Trieste railroad in 1864, Viennese nobility discovered the beauty of the region and chose the Wörther See, especially Velden, as their summer health resort – visible in the many villas in Wilhelmine or Art Nouveau style (Wörther See Architecture). Crowned and un-crowned heads, the jet-set and those wanting to catch a glimpse of them still come here. The pleasant Schubertpark, the elegant lake promenade and the exclusive casino are the places to see and be seen. **Velden**

South of Velden, in a loop of the Drau, lies the small town of Rosegg (483m/1584ft). The visitor attraction here is the castle, in possession of the dukes of Liechtenstein since 1831, with the Figurencabinett Madame Lucrezia, Austria's first wax works, and a deer park. **Rosegg**

The second-biggest place at the north shore of the lake is the resort of Pörtschach (446m/1463ft; pop. 2600), part of which is charmingly situated on a peninsula with a magical view of the lake, the town of Maria Wörth opposite and the Karawanke range rising in the far **Pörtschach**

● VISITING WÖRTHER SEE

INFORMATION

Wörther See Tourismus
Villacher Strasse 19, A-9220 Velden
Tel. 0 42 74/38 28 80, fax 382 88 19,
www.woerthersee.com

WHERE TO EAT

► **Expensive**
Rainer's
Monte-Carlo-Platz 1
A-9210 Pörtschach
Tel. 0 42 72/30 46
Friendly staff serve tasty dishes and
good wine. During summer the bar is
lively.

► **Moderate**
Hubertushof
Europaplatz 1
A-9220 Velden
Tel. 0 42 74/2 67 60
The chef uses fresh regional produce
to prepare light meals known as
»Carinthian Summer Cuisine«.

WHERE TO STAY

► **Luxury**
Hotel Carinthia
Karawankenplatz 3
A-9220 Velden
Tel. 0 42 74/21 71, fax 2 17 11
www.carinthia-hotel.com
This jewel of Wörther See architec-
ture, only a few metres away from the

Kurpark and lake, treats guests to an
excellent imperial breakfast and
modern spa and beauty treatments.

Hotel Schloss Leonstain
Leonstainerstrasse 1
A-9210 Pörtschach
Tel. 0 42 72/28 16, fax 28 23
www.leonstain.at
The castle was first mentioned in
records in 1166. The most prominent
guest was Johannes Brahms who
composed his second symphony here
in summer 1877 and 1878.

► **Mid-range**
Strandhotel Harrich
Wörtherseesüduferstrasse 182
A-9082 Maria Wörth
Tel. 0 42 74/5 12 33, fax 5 12 30
Situated on the idyllic and quiet south
bank. All rooms are furnished very
comfortably with balconies facing the
lake; wonderful lakeside terrace and
beach.

► **Budget**
Strandhotel Kärntnerhof
Hauptstrasse 217–219
A-9210 Pörtschach
Tel. 0 42 72/23 47
www.strandhotel-kaerntnerhof.at
A small hotel with a marvellous view
of the lake and its own beach.

south. From 1877 till 1879 Johannes Brahms came to spend the
summer and wrote his second symphony here. Pörtschach entertains
its guests with diverse sporting events and concerts, and gets very
busy during summer.

✳
Maria Wörth
One the most photographed motifs on the lake is the Old Town
centre of Maria Wörth (450m/1476ft; pop. 1500) on a **peninsula on
the south bank** that extends into the Wörther See. Already docu-

mented in 875, Maria Wörth was one of the spiritual centres of the alpine region during the Middle Ages, partly because it possessed the relics of St Primus and St Felician. The late Gothic parish church, an emblem of the Wörther See, is now a popular church for weddings. The Baroque decoration inside, the Romanesque crypt and the high altar (15th–16th century) with a late Gothic Madonna are noteworthy. The round charnel house in the cemetery dates from 1278. It is only a few steps from the parish to the small 12th-century Rosenkranzkirche (Church of the Rosary, also known as the Winter Church), featuring well-preserved Romanesque frescoes with depictions of the apostles.

Southwest of Maria Wörth towers the Pyramidenkogel (851m/ 2791ft), accessible from Maria Wörth via Keutschach on an 8km/ 5mi-long mountain road (on foot it is a good 90-minute walk). At the top a lift transports visitors a further 54m/177ft up to the **viewing platform** (opening times: daily April and Oct 10am–6pm, May and Sept 9am–7pm, June until 8pm, July–Aug until 9pm).

✱ Pyramidenkogel

✱✱ Zeller See

Province: Salzburg   **Elevation:** 750m/2460ft

Embedded in a beautiful valley, the Zeller See has a most stunning location between the snow-covered peaks of Grossglockner and Kitzsteinhorn in the south and the grey giants of the Steinernes Meer (Stone Ocean) in the north.

Formed by the Saalach glacier, but not fed by either the Saalach or the Salzach due to halted end moraines, the lake is filled only with melt water. The lake, which is 4km/2.5mi long, 1.5km/1mi wide and up to 69m/226ft deep, sometimes warms up to 23 °C/74 °F during summer. During winter, however, it freezes over regularly, to the delight of guests.

Between a glacier and the beach

The Zeller See and places situated farther up the valley are noted as an excellent sports venue. Not for nothing does the tourist joint venture of Zell am See and ▶ Kaprun call itself a **European sports region**. Water and winter sports of all kinds are available, and those interested in riding, golfing, tennis or mountain biking are well catered for. The school for alpine gliding (flights over the Alps) and skiing schools rounds it all off. The range of »après sports« entertainment is also good.

❓ DID YOU KNOW …?

■ … that Zell became important as a distributor of ice blocks in the 19th century? They were cut out off the Zeller See, which fairly reliably froze over. Breweries in southern Germany got their ice for cooling beer from here.

What to See at the Zeller See

Zell am See

Zell am See (757m/2483ft; pop. 9700), the lively regional capital of the Pinzgau, has an exposed location between the lake and Schmittenhöhe. First documented in 749 as »Celle am Bisontio«, it developed quickly from a modest settlement into an important market town on a significant north-south connection across the Tauern.

The interesting sights in the town are the originally Romanesque parish church of St Hippolyt, with two apostle frescoes (*c*1200), the 1000-year-old tower (Vogtturm) on the town square with the **museum of local history** (opening times: mid-May to mid-Oct Mon, Wed, Fri 1.30pm–5.30pm, July and Aug also Tue and Thu; from Christmas to Easter Wed–Fri 1.30pm–5.30pm), and the 16th-century Renaissance-style Rosenberg Palace, now the town hall. On Sundays in the summer months the **narrow-gauge railway** (760mm) of Pinzgau puffs along a stretch of nearly 53km/33mi from Zell via the Salzach westwards to Krimml – something for lovers of railway nostalgia.

Schmittenhöhe

West of Zell a cable car goes up to the Schmittenhöhe (1965m/6446ft). Hikers can expect a good three-hour tour. The Schmittenhöhe belongs to the Kitzbüheler Alps. The Grossglockner (in front the catchment basins of the Kapruner Tal) and the Grossvenediger are visible to the south, the Limestone Alps of the Kaisergebirge as far as the Dachstein to the north. At the upper terminus, the Elisabeth Chapel commemorates Empress Sisi, who came here a few times during summer. A beautiful ridge walk leads to the Sonnkogel (1856m/6989ft) within 45 minutes, where a chair lift goes up to the Sonnenalm (1382m/4534ft), and back down to Zell.

Pinzgauer Spaziergang ►

The Schmittenhöhe is the start of **one of the best-known alpine trails of Austria**, the so called Pinzgauer Walk. The six- to seven-hour walk at a consistent height of about 2000m/6600ft provides a plethora of fantastic views of the surrounding mountain crests. The path ends at the mountain station of the Schattbergbahn, which rides down to Saalbach (combined ticket including the Schmittenhöhe train available). Exhausted hikers can take the bus back to Zell.

Saalbach

North of the Zeller See the Glemmtal valley turns west, with the popular ski resorts of Saalbach (1003m/3290ft) and Hinterglemm (1074m/3523ft). The **huge skiing area** is very well equipped with about 60 lifts and many huts. A ski swing connects Saalbach with Leogang in the north. Everything the ski lover's heart desires is to be found here, including numerous offers for lively après ski such as the big annual »**Rave on Snow**«, an alpine techno party.

Thumersbach

Diagonally opposite Zell on the eastern bank of the lake, also reachable by ship, lies the district of Thumersbach, popular amongst visitors who prefer a quieter place with a beach and spa. There is a charming view of Zell and the mountains behind it. Beautiful lake promenades lead from Thumersbach around the lake to Zell within two to three hours. In the east Thumersbach is crowned by the Hundstein (2117m/6945ft; food and accommodation at Statzer Haus). The ascent takes about four hours.

◄ Hundstein

Some 12km/7.5mi east of Bruck, the Rauriser Valley turns southward. Shortly before the Rauriser Ache opens out into the Salzach, it forms the great Kitzlochklamm, a gorge with a dripstone cave and the Kitzloch waterfall (opening times: mid-May to mid-Oct daily 8am–6pm).

Kitzlochklamm

Rauris, the main town of the Rauriser Tal valley (948m/3110ft; pop. 3100) and once wealthy through gold mining, is now a popular holiday and winter sports destination. The **Rauristal Museum** presents the history and development of gold mining, the fauna of the Hohe

Rauris

 VISITING ZELLER SEE

INFORMATION
Europa Sportregion Marketing
Brucker Bundesstrasse 1 a
A-5700 Zell am See
Tel. 0 65 42/7 70-0, fax 7 20 32
www.zellamsee-kaprun.com

WHERE TO EAT
► **Moderate**
Zum Hirschen
Dreifaltigkeitsgasse 1
A-5700 Zell am See
Tel. 0 65 42/77 40
A family-run specialty restaurant that offers Austrian *Gemütlichkeit* in a rustic atmosphere.

► **Inexpensive**
Troadkast'n (Hotel Sonnleiten)
Hinterhagweg 361, A-5753 Saalbach
Tel. 0 65 41/64 04 20
The chef is a master of hearty traditional fare.

WHERE TO STAY
► **Luxury**
Salzburger Hof
Auerspergstrasse 11
A-5700 Zell am See
Tel. 0 65 42/7 65, fax 7 65 66
www.salzburgerhof.at
The top hotel locally provides old-style hospitality. Antiques and an open fire make for a pleasant atmosphere. Guests relax with sauna, pool and beauty facilities.

► **Mid-range**
Sporthotel Ellmau
Haidweg 357
A-5754 Saalbach-Hinterglemm
Tel. 0 65 41/7 22 60, fax 72 26 56
www.sporthotel-ellmau.at
This pleasantly situated house has cosy rooms, a wide-ranging beauty and sports programme and excellent cooking.

► **Budget**
Gasthof Tauernstüberl
Salzachtalbundesstrasse 54
A-5700 Zell am See
Tel. 0 65 42/5 71 74, fax 5 64 32
www.tauernstueberl.at
A friendly inn with cosy, rustic rooms, only a five-iron shot away from a nice golf course.

Long-distance views over the Rauristal valley

🕐 Tauern and the rural working world (Marktstrasse 59; open late Dec–Easter, June, Sept, Oct Mon–Wed and Fri 4pm–6pm, July and Aug daily 10am–noon and 4pm–6pm).

Kolm-Saigurn In Kolm-Saigurn (1598m/5242ft) at the end of the valley or at the foot of the Goldberg group the old conveying systems at the former gold mine are of particular interest. Teenagers on summer work camps cleared the 7km/4.5mi-long Tauerngold path, which starts at Neubau, a house for nature lovers. A 2km/1.2mi-long educational nature trail named Rauriser Urwald, which includes a Waldmuseum (**Forest Museum**) begins at the Ammererhof.

Hoher Sonnblick The ascent to the Hohe Sonnblick (3105m/10,187ft) in the south-west, with the Zittelhaus and a meteorological station established in 1886, takes about 5 hours.

✱ Zillertal

G 5

Province: Tyrol

One of the most visited areas of the Tyrol region is the famous Zillertal, a picturesque valley that has the Zillertal Alps with their numerous glaciers as a panoramic backdrop.

Popular holiday area This is where holiday dreams of guests from the lowlands come true: lush green meadows on the wide valley floor, picturesque villages with old guest houses and traditional meals as well as ice-cold mountain streams. A narrow-gauge railway, the Zillertalbahn, leads through the valley, and mountain railways ascend the surrounding heights.

What to See in Zillertal

In Fügen (544m/1784ft; pop. 2300), a climatic spa and winter sports area, the castle (15th century; Baroque additions around 1700) is worth seeing. The Gothic parish church (1497) is decorated with 14th-century murals, reliefs and statues. The Christmas carol **Silent Night, Holy Night** became widely known in the 19th century through the Rainer family from Fügen, who called themselves »Nationalsänger« (national singers). When the Russian tsar heard the Rainers sing at Fügen Castle, he was so full of enthusiasm that he invited them to St Petersburg. The **Zillertaler Nationalsänger** performed very successfully throughout Europe, and besides the famous Christmas carol also made the name of their homeland internationally known.

Fügen

Kaltenbach is the starting point for the Hochzillertal ski centre to the west: a cabin lift leads up to the Forstgartenhöhe (1730m/5675ft), a chair lift even further up to 2200m/7200ft. From the Zillertaler Höhenstrasse (toll road) on, which is accessible from Kaltenbach or Stumm, a marvellous view can be enjoyed.

Hochzillertal ski centre

Zell am Ziller (575m/1886ft; pop. 1900), the main community of the lower Zillertal and known as a summer and winter resort, was previ-

Zell am Ziller

▶ VISITING ZILLERTAL

INFORMATION
Zillertal Tourismus
Bundesstrasse 27 d, A-6262 Schlitters
Tel. 0 52 88/8 71 87, fax 87 18 71
www.zillertal.at

HÖHENSTRASSE
For real mountain bikers only!
From 550m/1800ft to 2020m/6625ft height, with a gradient of up to 15%, and 25km/15.5mi long – the Zillertaler Höhenstrasse is a real challenge for mountain bikers (and some car drivers too!). Effort, sweat and a racing heart are rewarded with a grand view.

WHERE TO EAT
▶ **Moderate**
Bräu
Dorfplatz 1

A-6280 Zell am Ziller
Tel. 0 52 82/ 23 13
Bräu serves its own beer and regional dishes to match.

WHERE TO STAY
▶ **Luxury**
Sporthotel Stock
A-6292 Finkenberg 142
Tel. 0 52 85/67 75
Fax 6 77 54 21
www.sporthotel-stock.com
During winter Sporthotel Stock near Mayrhofen is an oasis for ski and snowboard fans. This place is all about wellness: herbal steam grotto, panoramic indoor swimming pool, hay and stone oil baths.

ously a gold-mining area. Tradition and customs are still widely practiced. The Gauderfest on the first Sunday in May is the oldest and largest folk festivity in Tyrol. For this occasion the Zillertaler brewery, founded in 1500, brews Gauder beer containing 20% alcohol.

Mayrhofen

The well-known holiday resort Mayrhofen (630m/2066ft; pop. 3700) is situated in the wide part of the valley, framed by a circle of mountains. At the Europahaus, which is used for conferences and other events, there is a relief of the Zillertal Alps. Mayrhofen is an excellent base for mountain and ski tours in the Zillertal Alps.

Tuxer Tal

The Tux Valley branches off to the west of Mayrhofen (take the road until Hintertux 20km/12mi, not recommended for caravans). It is a climatic spa and winter sports area. The word **»Tuxer«** refers less to the inhabitants of the valley than it does to a piece of clothing: a grey loden jacket with red-checked lining. Going »tux-style« used to mean something like showing up properly in leather trousers. Tuxers are also a short-legged breed of cattle.

Hintertux ►

Hintertux (1494m/4901ft) is a much-visited hotel village with a thermal spring (22.5 °C/72.5 °F) in a great location near the end of the valley. About one hour to the south, the Tux waterfalls rush into a deep rock bowl.

Gauderfest in Zell with the unique »Widderstoßen«, a trial of strength between rams

✳ Zillertal Alps

G/H 5

Provinces: Tyrol and Salzburg

Since 1991 the Zillertal Alps have been a protected area, called »Ruhegebiet Zillertaler Hauptkamm«. Since 2001 the region has been a nature reserve.

The massif of the Zillertaler Alps, a group of the central Alps consisting of granite gneiss and mica schist, extends between Birnlücke (Birluckn) and ► Brenner. The Austrian-Italian border runs along the main ridge. The Zillertal Alps have all the characteristics of high mountains, with their clear forms, glaciers, ridges dotted with many summits and steep peaks.

Group of the Central Alps

The high-altitude path Höhenweg no. 102 leads from St Jodok on the Brenner through the nature reserve around the Hohe Kirche (2634m/8641ft) to the Schlegeis reservoir and, below the whole of the main ridge of the Zillertal Alps, down into the Zillergrund (► Zillertal).

▶ ZILLERTAL ALPS

INFORMATION

Hochgebirgs-Naturpark
Zillertaler Alpen
Sportplatzstr. 307
A-6290 Mayrhofen
Tel. and fax 0 52 85/6 36 01

The sharp **main ridge** of the Zillertal Alps rises between glacier basins. The melting waters gush into the deeply cut hollows and reservoirs which spread fan-like from the Zillertal to the south, west and east. A few of the peaks that are suitable for climbing have ridges with a northwestern orientation – the prominent Feldkopf (3087m/ 10,127ft), for example. From the Berliner Hütte to the Feldkopf the path leads along the Schwarzensee (2470m/8104ft), where the ice falls of the Waxeck glacier are reflected in the water.

Almost parallel to the main crest of the Zillertal Alps, divided by the Zamser Grund, the Tuxer Kamm (Tux Ridge) runs north. It has many extensive glaciers and proud peaks. The Olperer (3476m/ 11,404ft), connected with the steep Schrammacher (3410m/11,187ft) by a long ridge, is an imposing mountain.

Tux Ridge

◄ Olperer

Tuxer Tal, Tuxer Joch (Pass) and Schmirntal divide the Tuxer Kamm from the Tuxer Voralpen, an upland area between Wipptal, Unterinntal and Zillertal that reaches heights of over 2800m/9186ft and is suitable for winter sports. However, the section between the Lizumer Reckner (2886m/9468ft) and the 2479m/8133ft-high Mölser Berg is a closed area.

Tuxer Voralpen

The Zillertal Alps – a climbing paradise

The northwestern branch of the Tuxer Voralpen, called **Patscherkofel** (2247m/ 7372ft; cable car from Igls), is known as a »weekend mountain« for trippers from Innsbruck. Its neighbour in the east, the 2677m/8782ft high Glungezer, which can be reached most quickly from the mountain station of the Patscherkofelbahn (1945m/6281ft), is known for its long descent: the difference in altitude is about 2100m/6900ft.

East of the Zillergrund, off the main crest of the Zillertal Alps, the **Reichenspitzgruppe** runs northwards over the border between the federal states of Tyrol and Salzburg. In an extremely confined space is a group of **especially wild high peaks, flanked by jagged glaciers**, among them the towering horn of the Reichenspitze (3303m/ 10,836ft) and the double-peaked Wildgerlosspitze (3282m/10,767ft). The massif of the Reichenspitzgruppe can be reached either from Mayrhofen in the Zillertal via the Plauener Hütte (2373m/7785ft) or from Krimml at the end of the Salzachtal valley via the Richterhütte (2374m/7788ft).

Zugspitze

E 5

Province: Tyrol

The 2963m/9721ft summit of the Zugspitze, marked with a gilded cross, lies on the German side of the border. A short flights of steps connects the Austrian with the German summit building and its big sun terraces.

Border peak

The views – in clear weather 150km/95mi including 400 summits – attract a multitude of visitors every year. The border between Tyrol and Bavaria runs over the Zugspitze massif, which is part of the Wettersteingebirge.

Zugspitzbahn

The Zugspitzbahn (Zugspitze train) ascends from Ehrwald on the Austrian side to the peak, where a small museum recounts its history since 1926. On the German side the electric rack railway runs from Garmisch-Partenkirchen, Grainau and Eibsee through a 4.5km/ 2.8mi-long tunnel to Zugspitzplatt station; from there the Gletscherbahn (glacier train) goes up to the Zugspitze summit. Another option is **one of the biggest cable cars in Europe**, from Eibsee straight to the summit in 10 minutes.

Ehrwald (996m/3267ft; pop. 2500) previously lived from the lucrative salt trade and is today a popular climatic spa and winter sports area. It is situated at the eastern edge of the meadows of the Ehrwald Basin. Its church holds a modern Via Crucis by H. D. Alberti (born 1938), which is well worth seeing.

Ehrwald

Wettersteingebirge

At the Wettersteinkamm, running east from the Zugspitze, several high peaks provide opportunities for climbing tours: for example the Hochwanner (2746m/9009ft), whose 1400m/4593ft north face is one of the longest rock tours of the Limestone Alps, and the magnificent Dreitorspitzen trio (2674m/8772ft, 2633m/8638ft and 2606m/8549ft).

Hochwanner Dreitorspitzen

South of the Wettersteingebirge, separated by the gentle pastures of the Ehrwalder Alm (1493m/4898ft), are the less frequented Mieminger range. The best-known mountain here is the Hohe Munde (2661m/8730ft), which dominates the Inn Valley, but the most beautiful is the Sonnenspitze (2414m/7919ft), which looks down onto the Fernpass lakes; the highest is the eastern Griesspitze at 2759m/9051ft.

Mieminger range

Austrian view of the Zugspitze behind the Blindsee

▶ VISITING ZUGSPITZE

INFORMATION

Tourismusverband
Ehrwald-Zugspitze
Kirchplatz 1
A-6632 Ehrwald
Tel. 0 56 73/20 00 02 08
www.ehrwald.com

WHERE TO STAY

▶ **Mid-range**
Spielmann
Wettersteinstrasse 24
A-6632 Ehrwald
Tel. 0 56 73/2 22 50, fax 2 22 55
www.hotel-spielmann.com
This holiday hotel offers luxury:
guests can enjoy a large sauna and
relaxation area as well as eight suites
and a heated open-air pool.

Lermoos   In a basin about 3km/2mi west of Ehrwald lies the holiday resort of
Lermoos (995m/3264ft; pop. 1100). The Baroque parish church
(*c*1750) with an octagonal floor plan and Rococo decoration is worth
viewing. Beneath the choir is a crypt-like lower church with a sculpture group of approx. 1760 depicting the Passion of Christ.

✶ **Zwettl**

`O 2`

Province: Lower Austria   **Elevation:** 520m/1706ft
Population: 11,500

In 2000 the brewing town of Zwettl celebrated its 800th anniversary. The transport and administrative centre of the ▶Waldviertel is mainly known for the nearby Cistercian monastery founded in 1138 by Hadmar von Kuenring.

What to See in Zwettl

Stadtplatz   Some parts of the medieval town wall have remained, including a few towers. The elongated town square is surrounded by townhouses from the 16th and 17th centuries, all with charming façades. Here also stand a plague column of 1727and the old town hall, built in 1307 and later often altered, with exterior frescoes that date back to the 15th century. The fountain by Friedensreich Hundertwasser is an attractive contrast.

Probsteikirche ▶   The elevated Provost's Church (12th century) was once part of Kuenring castle, and along with the cemetery, the round 13th-century charnel house and the Romanesque St Michael's Chapel it forms an interesting architectural ensemble.

✴ Zwettl Cistercian Abbey

Some 3km/2mi northeast of the town on a loop of the river Kamp stands a Cistercian abbey, Zisterzienserstift Zwettl, according to legend on the site where green leaves sprouted on an oak tree during winter (tours at groups of ten or more Mon–Fri 10am, 11am, 2pm and 3pm, Sun from 11am, July–Sept also 4pm). ⊙

The choir of the abbey church is **one of the most important works of the Austrian late Gothic period**. Originally Romanesque, the choir was altered to a large hall with a ring of chapels (1343–83). The 90m/295ft Baroque west tower of granite ashlar, a masterly design of 1722–1727 by Josef Munggenast, is decorated by figures, vases and obelisks. A gilded figure of Christ crowns the cupola. The Baroque decoration of the church is impressive. It includes a wooden carving at the high altar (1733) depicting the Assumption of the Virgin, and a Return of the Prodigal Son that crowns a confessional.

Monastery church

The impressive cloister can be reached through the prelature building. It was built between 1204 and 1240, which makes it the **oldest**

✴ **Cloister**

Hunderwasser Fountain on the market square in Zwettl

completely preserved cloister in all of Austria The capitals of the 330 columns are decorated with leaves and buds, the windows of the reading passage with late Gothic tracery.

Chapter house
The eastern wing of the cloister is bordered by the even earlier chapter house (1159–80) whose ribbed vault rests on a middle column of granite. The refectory, remodelled in Baroque style, and the dormitory along with an old latrine complex have also survived from the early Middle Ages.

The **library**, situated on the eastern courtyard (Konventshof), was reconstructed from 1703 to 1732 by Josef Munggenast and painted by Paul Troger. It contains over 400 manuscripts, more than 300 valuable incunabula and some 50,000 volumes. Recently, previously unknown fragments of the Song of the Nibelungen, probably dating back to the 12th century, were discovered at Zwettl. Over the next few years these fragments will be analysed and examined.

The courtyard named Dürnhof accommodates the unique **Museum for Medicine and Meteorology**. Its theme is the **influence of the weather and climate on the human organism**. The museum has a test path for divining rods, an educational medicinal herbs garden and a display of meadow and cultivated plants (opening times: May–Oct Tue–Sun 10am–5pm).

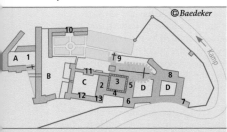

Stift Zwettl

©Baedeker

A Binder Court
B Linden Court
C Abbey Court
D Convent Courts

1 Hospital Church
2 Doorway, with Prelate's House above
3 Cloister
4 Refectory
5 Chapter House
6 Dormitory
7 Convent
8 Library
9 Chapel of the Saint's Tomb
10 Garden Pavilion
11 Choir School
12 School House
13 Banqueting Hall

Museum for Medicine and Meteorology

Around Zwettl

Waldviertler Lakes
Follow the Kamp from Zwettl eastwards to one of the most popular leisure destinations of the Waldviertel, surrounded by picturesque castles and ruins: the 12km/7.5mi-long Ottensteinsee and the Dobrastausee. Both were created by damming the Kamp. It is a sporting paradise: swimming, surfing, sailing, boating and fishing, as well as horse-riding, golfing, biking and hiking are on offer.

★ Schloss Rosenau
West of Zwettl on a small hill lies Schloss Rosenau (620m/2034ft; hotel), built in its recent form from 1730 to 1748 in Rococo style and decorated by Daniel Gran and other artists. It includes a museum of freemasonry with the only 18th-century ritual chambers that

► VISITING ZWETTL

INFORMATION

Tourismusinformation Zwettl
Sparkassenplatz 4
A-3910 Zwettl
Tel. 0 28 22/50 31 29
Fax 515 08
www.zwettl.info/tourismus

WHERE TO EAT

► **Moderate**
Gasthof zum goldenen Hirschen
Landstrasse 49
A-3910 Zwettl
Tel. 0 28 22/20 20 236
Regional specialties such as the tasty
Zwettler Bierknödel (beer dumplings)
are served here.

are preserved in their original condition and open to the public (opening times: April–Oct daily 9am–5pm; tours on request, tel. 0 28 22/58 22 15).

Southwest of Zwettl, on a tree-covered rock above the Kamp, stands the strong castle of Rappottenstein. The keep and the pentagonal tower at the southern tip date back to the foundation of the castle in the 12th century. Five courtyards surround the castle complex. The brewing house can be seen in the first courtyard (1548–49), a three-storey Renaissance loggia in the innermost court. Some windows bear sgraffito paintings (tours 11am, 2pm, 3pm and 4pm; in second half of April and Oct Sat, Sun; May–Sept daily except Mon; July and Aug also 10am, 5pm).

Burg Rappottenstein

The museum in the small village of Roiten, only a few miles east of Rappottenstein, was built by **Friedensreich Hundertwasser** and exhibits old craftsmanship, for example wooden school bags and old ice skates.

Roiten

Situated some 20km/12mi south of Zwettl is the village of Armschlag, which has devoted itself to a special agricultural product: Graumohn or the grey poppy. Until 1933 Waldviertler Graumohn was even quoted at the London stock exchange. About 25 years ago the cultivation of poppy seed and its various uses were rediscovered. The seeds of the plant, which blooms red, purple and white and bears the trademark name **»Waldviertler Graumohn«**, have various culinary uses and are also processed for cosmetic use.
A 1km/0.6mi poppy seed nature trail leads through the village and tells more about the cultivation and processing of the poppies. The poppy seed farmers sell their products from their farmyards, and from May to October at weekends (in July and August daily) from 11am to 3pm at the farmers' shop.

Armschlag poppy village

INDEX

PHOTO CREDITS

Archiv für Kunst und Geschichte: p. 73, 74, 78, 79, 81, 85, 301, 542 (below)
Bergisel BetriebsgesmbH: p. 292, 293, 294
Bohnacker: p. 205
Borowski: p. 15 (centre), 258, 307, 325, 367, 376, 463, 477, 540, 550, 553
CMA: p. 7 (below)
Werner Dieterich: p. 107, 510
dpa: p. 82, 197
dpa fotoreport: p. 77
Friedrichsmeier (PhotoPress/Rauh): p. 425
Friedrichsmeier (PhotoPress/Seve): p. 442
Friedrichsmeier (Siepmann): p. 170 (above), inside front cover
Friedrichsmeier (Stankiewicz): p. 588
Graz Tourismus: p. 246
Graz Tourismus (Harry Schiffer): p. 251
Graz Tourismus (Hans Wiesenhofer): p. 5 (above), 253
Hackenberg: p. 16 (below), 47, 126, 179, 223, 379, 498, 542 (above), back cover
Haile: p. 102
Hautzinger: p. 511 (above left, above right, below left), 517
HB-Verlag/Böttcher/Tiensch: p. 4, 10, 67, 225, 227, 406, 408, 536
HB-Verlag/Dorfstetter: p. 267
HB-Verlag / Heimbach: p. 25, 327
HB-Verlag/Holz: p. 7 (above), 8 (above), 9 (above), 16 (centre), 18, 24, 35, 37, 45, 63, 101, 142, 150, 161 (below, above right), 166, 172 (above, below left), 182, 219, 229, 235, 240, 261, 321, 323, 329, 334, 352, 375, 384, 385 (below right), 385 (below left, above left, centre right, centre left), 386, 388, 390, 394, 412, 459, 469, 547, 555, 557, 559, 561, 562, 565, 567, 578, 583, 595
HB-Verlag/Krause: p. 16 (above), 45, 56, 70, 72, 86/87, 98, 105, 110, 259, 436, 502, 506, 511 (centre left), 515, 518, 521, 523, 525, 526, 532, 533, 537, 539, 543 (above right, below right, below left), 575
HB-Verlag/Krüger: p. 6
HB-Verlag/Spitta: p. 14, 17, 21, 42, 52, 134, 160, 164 (above), 176, 177, 276, 279, 281, 282, 289, 290, 296, 313, 315, 345, 349, 354, 365, 383, 415, 423, 466, 486, 491, 590, 593, back cover inside

HB-Verlag/Trummer: p. 3 (below), 5 (below), 8 (below), 11 (above), 13, 15 (above, below), 65, 87, 100, 158/159, 170 (below left), 174/175, 240, 242, 256, 268, 269, 274, 302, 303, 312, 419, 427, 431, 432, 434, 440, 445 (above left), 447, 449, 451, 489, 517, 580
HB-Verlag/Widmann: p. 3 (above), 11 (below), 12/13, 60, 129, 130, 131, 137, 161 (above left), 163, 168 (above right), 170 (below right), 186, 211, 213, 271, 272, 299, 305, 347, 370, 372, 396, 401, 403, 470, 479, 482, 493, 494
HB-Verlag/Wiener Festwochen/Wartha: p. 430
Historia-Photo: p. 74
Huber: p. 445 (above right), 520
Huber/Gräfenhain: p. 189
Laif: p. 69, 529 (above)
Laif/Caputo: p. 439, 457
Liechtenstein Tourismus: p. 359, 361, 362
Look/Endler: p. 421
Look/Fieger: p. 165 (above)
Look/Pompe: p. 317
Look/Wiesmeier: p. 592
Look/Wothe: p. 1, 164 (below), 175
Madej/Bilderberg: p. 2
Mauritius/Pigneter: p. 168 (above left), 220
Naturhistorisches Museum: p. 61
Österreich Werbung/Trumler: p. 543 (centre)
pa/akg-images: p. 53
pa/akg-images/Lessing: p. 527
Porschemuseum Gmünd: p. 233
Dr. Reincke/Cabos: p. 511 (below right), 530
Salzburger Burgen und Schlösser: p. 443, 444, 445 (below left, below right, below centre), 446
Schloss Schönbrunn: p. 543 (above left)
Stankiewicz: p. 40, 75, 154, 165 (below), 168 (below), 172 (below right), 255, 285, 342, 398
Storto: p. 22, 88
Strüber: p. 529 (below)
M. Thomas: p. 543 (above centre), 544
Verein dt. Salzindustrie: p. 46
Wandmacher (Archiv Wais + Partner): p. 48, 128
WMF: p. 503

Cover photo: Mauritius/Weimann

LIST OF MAPS AND ILLUSTRATIONS

PUBLISHER'S INFORMATION

Illustrations etc: 299 illustrations, 67 maps
and diagrams, one large map
Text: Rosemarie Arnold, Walter R. Arnold, Isolde
Bacher, Achim Bourmer, Prof. Dr. Wolfgang
Hassenpflug, Dr. Peter Jordan, Rolf Lohberg,
Christine Wessely
Editing: Baedeker editorial team
(Robert Taylor)
Translation: Robert Taylor, Margit Sander
Cartography: Franz Huber, München;
MAIRDUMONT/Falk Verlag, Ostfildern (map)
3D illustrations: jangled nerves, Stuttgart
Design: independent Medien-Design, Munich;
Kathrin Schemel

Editor-in-chief: Rainer Eisenschmid,
Baedeker Ostfildern

1st edition 2009

Based on Baedeker Allianz Reiseführer
»Österreich«, 12. Auflage 2009

Copyright: Karl Baedeker Verlag, Ostfildern
Publication rights: MAIRDUMONT GmbH & Co;
Ostfildern

Printed in China